anu

to accompany

Management
Control Systems

Ninth Edition

Robert N. Anthony
Emeritus, Harvard University

Vijay Govindarajan
Dartmouth College

Boston   Burr Ridge, IL   Dubuque, IA   Madison, WI   New York   San Francisco   St. Louis
Bangkok   Bogotá   Caracas   Lisbon   London   Madrid
Mexico City   Milan   New Delhi   Seoul   Singapore   Sydney   Taipei   Toronto

Irwin/McGraw-Hill

A Division of The McGraw·Hill Companies

Instructor's Manual to accompany
MANAGEMENT CONTROL SYSTEMS, NINTH EDITION

1 2 3 4 5 6 7 8 9 0 BKM/BKM 9 0 9 8 7

ISBN 0-256-16879-2

http://www.mhhe.com

INTRODUCTION

The Management Control Systems course, which was relatively new when the First Edition of this book was published, is now well established, both here in the U. S. as well as in other countries. In this revision of the *Instructor's Manual*, therefore, we have not dwelt at length on the rationale and content of such a course.

The chapters are arranged essentially in the order in which we currently take up the topics. We hold no particularly strong belief for this arrangement, and indeed probably will change it as time goes on. We do believe that the first seven chapters belong at the beginning of the course and that Part III should follow Part II. Within Part II, the chapters have a natural teaching order. In other respects, particularly the sequences of chapters in Part III, other outlines are undoubtedly as good as the ones we have indicated.

One of our goals in these teaching notes is to attempt to serve as colleagues in "absentia" for our counterparts at other schools. Thus, these notes are intentionally chatty, sometimes philosophical, first-person accounts of the ways we have tried to reach a difficult, occasionally frustrating, but nevertheless fascinating subject. Our classroom experience with these cases, recounted here, are not offered as examples to be duplicated; no two discussions of such broad cases as these are even identical. But, we hope that these experiences will illustrate some of the ways that these cases may be used successfully.

The other primary purpose of these notes is to provide the instructors with some sort of map on which they may base their own expectations of how the course will unfold and develop during the term. Our own experience has been that, because the topic is a completely new one for the students (and because of its administrative rather than quantitative orientation), their early reaction is one of frustration. In particular, Chapters 1 – 3, in which we explore some of the "givens" that must be recognized and dealt with in the design of a control system, frequently do not make the impact on the students (at the time) that the instructor would desire. Fortunately, this gap between student achievement and instructor expectation closes rapidly in Chapters 4 and 5 when the students begin to fit the earlier pieces together in specific case contexts. Typically, the light dawns on one group of students with New Jersey Insurance Company and on the balance of the class with North Country Auto. After that, the classes are increasingly exciting and fruitful for the students.

This delayed student appreciation of the intellectual content and administrative importance of the course is, in our experience, unavoidable. An Alternative—teaching two or three of the cases in Chapters 4 – 7 first—is even more frustrating for the students because they lack an analytical framework that permits them to deal with these cases. The advantage of the sequence we suggest is that it does permit a rapid snowballing of understanding. The instructor can facilitate this process, and insure that it occurs by repeated references to earlier cases and readings as the course progresses, and we have attempted in these notes to point out some of the opportunities for such reinforcement and consolidation of earlier gains.

Prior to presenting the teaching notes for the individual cases, we have provided model outlines for a one-quarter (20 sessions) and one-semester (30 sessions) course on Management Control Systems.

An excellent reference on teach by the case method is: C. Roland Christensen, David A. Garvin, and Ann Sweet. *Education for Judgement: The Artistry of Discussion Leadership*. Boston: Harvard Business School Press, 1991.

We would welcome comments and constructive criticisms from instructors who would like to join our efforts to develop an effective pedagogy for teaching management control. Please forward your comments and suggestions to: Vijay Govindarajan, Earl C. Daum 1924 Professor of International Business, The Amos Tuck School of Business Administration, Dartmouth College, Hanover, NH 03755; Phone (603) 646-2156; Fax (603) 646-1308.

RNA & VG

February 1997

Overall Table of Contents

Videotapes accompany several of the cases. We have pointed them out in the Instructor's Manual. Please note that the videotapes are not available from Irwin. Most of the videotapes should be purchased directly from Harvard Business School (Phone: (617) 495-6117).

PART I

Model Syllabi

PART I

Contents

Management Control Systems

Model Syllabus for One-Quarter (20 Sessions)

Model Syllabus for One-Semester (30 Sessions)

The Amos Tuck School of Business Administration

Dartmouth College

Hanover, New Hampshire

MANAGEMENT CONTROL SYSTEMS

Spring Term 1997
Second-Year Program

Professor Vijay Govindarajan ("VG")
Office 311 Tuck
Secretary: Susan Schwarz, 310 Tuck
Phone: (603) 646-2156
Fax: (603) 646-1308

MANAGEMENT CONTROL SYSTEMS

Course Overview

This course is designed to help you think through how you would manage the strategy implementation dilemmas in which operating managers find themselves. In particular, the course is designed to allow you to gain knowledge, insights, and analytical skills related to how a corporation's senior executives go about designing and implementing those ongoing formal systems used to plan and control the firm's performance. The key ideas underlying this course are: (i) different organizations typically have different strategies, and (ii) different control systems are needed to effectively implement different strategies.

The importance of the subject matter covered in this course is captured well in the widely accepted "truism" among management consultants that over 90% of businesses (as well as nonprofit organizations) keep foundering on the rocks of implementation—either the strategies never come into being, or get distorted, or the implementation is much more costly and time consuming than anticipated. However laudable strategic intentions may be—to change the product mix, to improve the quality of products, to become the lowest cost producer, to build market share, or to maximize short-term earnings and cash flow—if they do not get converted into reality, they are usually not worth the paper they are written on.

Most of you will soon be in positions where you will be directly responsible for getting strategy implemented. As such, I view the materials covered in this course to be of high relevance in your immediate job situations.

The conceptual materials for the course are primarily provided in the textbook. Though I have called it a "textbook," it is a misnomer. Unlike a textbook, which presumably is designed for a specific point of view or perspective on a given subject, the book for this course should be viewed as a ledge from which you spring into a dialectical discussion of ideas. The intent of every class session is to move from a given starting point in the history of ideas and through diverse perspectives of students to achieve a better understanding of other world views. We will accomplish this by discussing a case study for each session.

I will use a case study each day to:

(1) introduce and discuss the key issues for several of the most important control systems in use in businesses.

(2) illustrate and emphasize the need for a good "fit" between a particular control system and the strategy chosen by the organization.

(3) emphasize the necessity for overall compatibility within the set of control systems in use.

The course is appropriate for any prospective general manager, as well as for those contemplating careers in management consultancy, and controllership. The perspective of the course usually is that of general management, rather than that of the corporate controller or chief accountant.

Course Requirements

Course Materials

Text: *Management Control Systems* by Anthony and Govindarajan (Richard D. Irwin, 1997). To be referred to as MCS in the Course Outline.

Class Preparation

Catch a fish for a man and he is fed for a day. Teach a man to fish and he can afford a good wine to go with it.

—Arthur Anderson

The most important requirement for this course is a thorough preparation and analysis of the assigned case and reading material and active participation in the classroom. The course is built almost exclusively around the case method. As is captured in the quote above, the learning in the class focuses more on the thought process in analyzing business situations, not just on the solutions per se. In order to derive maximum benefit from the cases, it is essential that you mentally "get inside" the case situation. Do not approach a case as you would a chapter in a book or an article in a magazine. You are not an observer but a participant. If a case centers on a decision that needs to be made, put yourself in the shoes of the decision maker. Feel the frustration he or she feels with respect to data limitations. Feel the pressures he or she feels with respect to difficult tradeoffs, limited resources, political conflicts, or whatever. Once in class, share your ideas with others as we work jointly to resolve the issues.

The cases included in this course represent broad organizational situations and encompass many facets of a company's control systems. In some instances, the case may represent a good system and you are expected to learn what makes the system work well. Other cases may present a system which has failed and the purpose here is to learn from the failures. Most cases seldom present examples of absolutely perfect or totally flawed systems. There are always some weaknesses in the best of control systems. However, the evaluation of these weaknesses is always relative to the resources—monetary, manpower, etc.—available to a company. Thus, it may be costly to remove flaws. Any recommendation for changes when analyzing cases should carefully weigh the organizational costs involved. In preparing the cases, the following simple rules may be helpful:

1. Do not automatically assume that a case represents a good or bad stem. Adopt a framework which will provide you the criteria for evaluating each case on its merits.

2. Adopt a management posture in analyzing cases. Use the assignment questions as a guide only. Your answer should highlight what you, as a manager, see as the strengths or weaknesses in a given situations.

3. Familiarize yourself with the facts of a case. Outline the industry and competitive context and the core strategic tasks that the firm should excel at. You'll have to evaluate the control systems of the firm in the context of its strategy.

4. Support your analysis with facts from the case. Most cases will not contain all the data that your might like to have. Nevertheless, you'll be surprised at how easily you can make accurate inferences and useful assumptions if you simply give the current management the benefit of the doubt; i.e., if you assume (in the absence of contrary data) that they are running the business the way you would run it—smartly! If there are contrary data, it's wise to think again. Maybe, they're right, and your task then is to understand why the company does what it does.

5. You are encouraged to test your ideas on others prior to the class meeting. Students tend to find study groups to be very beneficial in this course. For the sake of preparation, you should assume that every class will begin with your being called upon to lead off.

In the Classroom

My expectation is that you will come to the class having already thought through and analyzed the cases. This way, we can devote the bulk of the class to thinking about and responding to each other's analyses to the cases and only the necessary minimum to getting the facts out.

I encourage active student participation in class. I should point out that most students typically tend to underestimate—rather than overestimate—the worth of what they have to say. Thus, if you are ever in doubt, we would encourage you to speak up instead of staying quiet.

Each class session will begin with one student being asked to provide an analysis of the case. An effective lead-off can do a great deal to enhance a class discussion. It sets a tone and quality level and encourages the class to probe more deeply into the issues of the case. After the individual lead-off presentation, the discussion will be opened to the remainder of the group. Others may choose to build on the lead-off discussion, may choose to present a significantly different alternative, or may focus sharply on one or more issues which seem to have been developed inadequately or perhaps overlooked. If you are inadequately prepared to lead off the discussion of the particular case you may:

(1) ask before class not to be called on,

(2) pass when your are called, or

(3) "wing it."

These actions are listed in increasing order of negative evaluation.

My role in the class is to help facilitate discussion. In part, I serve as a recording secretary, clarifier, and intensive questioner in order to help you present and develop your ideas. My primary role is to manage the class process and to assure that the class achieves an understanding of the case situation. Clearly, there is no single correct solution to any of these problems. There are, however, a lot of wrong solution. There are also solutions which are inadequately supported with analysis, and there are solutions and analyses which are ineffective because they are not presented in an orderly and persuasive fashion. We should work together to see to it that each class session is a lively, stimulating, and intellectually rewarding venture in group learning. We are individually and collectively responsible for achieving that end.

Each case has its own integrity and, thus, it stand on its own. You may draw on personal experiences if you believe they are substantive, insightful, and generalizable. Generally, I am not concerned with what was the actual outcome of the case. Such an approach would imply that there was a "right answer." The outcome of a situation may or may not reflect a good solution. In those instances where there was a particularly interesting outcome, it will be shared with the class.

Evaluation of Class Participation

The vast majority of managers' interactions with others are oral. They generally spend very little time reading and even less time writing reports. For this reason, the development of oral skills is given a high priority in this course. The classroom should be considered a laboratory in which you can test your ability to convince your peers of the correctness of your approach. Some of the characteristics of effective class participation are as follows:

1. Are the points that are made relevant to the discussion in terms of increasing everyone's understanding, or are they merely regurgitation of case facts?

2. Do the comments take into consideration the ideas offered by others earlier in the class, or are the points isolated and disjointed? The best contributions following the lead off tend to be those which reflect not only excellent preparation, but good listening, and interpretative and integrative skills as well.

3. Do the comments show evidence of a thorough reading and analysis of the case?

4. Does the participant distinguish among different kinds of data; that is, facts, opinions, assumptions, and inferences?

5. Is there a willingness to test new ideas or are all comments cautious/"safe"?

6. Is the participant willing to interact with other class members by asking questions or challenging conclusions?

Clearly, you must participate in class if you are going to share your ideas with others. There is no need to contribute in every class. Some of the best contributors in the past have been those who participated in only three or four sessions. Their contributions, however, were truly insightful and persuasive. The issue is one of quality not quantity or frequency.

Given below is a description of how I propose to "calibrate" your class contributions:

Outstanding Contributors: Contributions in class reflect thorough preparation. Ideas offered are usually substantive, provide one or more major insights as well as direction for the class. Arguments, when offered, are well substantiated and persuasively presented. If this person were not a member of the class, the quality of the discussions would be diminished significantly.

Good Contributor: Contributions in class reflect thorough preparation. Ideas offered are usually substantive, provide good insights and sometimes direction for the class. Arguments, when presented, are generally well-substantiated and are often persuasive. If this person were not a member of the class, the quality of the discussion would be diminished considerably.

Adequate Contributor: Contributions in class reflect satisfactory preparation. Ideas offered are sometimes substantive, provide generally useful insights, but seldom offer a major new direction for the discussion. Arguments are sometimes presented, and are fairly well substantiated and sometimes persuasive. If this person were not a member of the class, the quality of the discussions would be diminished somewhat.

Non-participant: This person has said little or nothing in this class to date. Hence, there is not adequate basis for evaluation. If this person were not a member of the class, the quality of the discussions would not be changed.

Unsatisfactory Contributor: Contribution in class reflects inadequate preparation. Ideas offered are seldom substantive; provide few, if any, insights; and never a constructive direction for the class. Integrative comments and effective arguments are absent. Class contributions are, the best, "cherry-picking" efforts making isolated, obvious, or confusing points. If this person were not a member of the class, valuable air time would be saved.

Written Work

Two *individual* written assignments will be required during the quarter, and these assignments will be an analysis and recommendations for any of the cases used in the course. The report should be no more than three pages of text (typed, double spaced, proper margins) plus exhibits. Your written assignments should be submitted at the start of class on the date that case will be discussed.

Please bear in mind that the reports should illustrate your reasoning, defend it with proof and back-up material, and present and support your conclusions and recommendations. You should assume that the reader is familiar with the facts in the case, It may be helpful to think of an executive who is very busy and is not likely to spend a lot of time trying to decipher your report. Use of visual cues and format to emphasize your main points will increase your impact.

Please use the sign-up sheet posted on my office door to indicate the cases you plan to write up.

Videotapes

Please note that a number of class sessions involves viewing videotapes of executives discussing various issues and problems. You might note that these tapes require much more attention and alertness than one typically brings to televiewing. In short, the complexities and subleties of these tapes are considerably more profound than, say, the reruns of "Leave it to Beaver."

Grading

Grading for the course will be based on class participation, the two written case assignments and the final examination (a case). I do not use fixed percentages across these three categories. The final exam is cumulative and is designed to be a fair test of your comprehension of the ideas discussed in the classes. The best way to prepare for the final is to prepare carefully for each of the classes which precede it.

Additional Guidelines

1. Attendance is obviously important, and other activities, including job interviews, ought to be scheduled so as not to conflict with class meetings.

2. Classes will begin and end on time. I will appreciate it if you are in the classroom before the class starts.

3. Since I frequently call on students who do not have their hands raised, if you are not prepared for class, please notify me in advance.

With the possible exception of the "wrap-up" period at the end of each class, note-taking is unnecessary and even undesirable. You should be following and reacting to the class discussion instead of writing. I usually have handouts summarizing the key issues raised in each case.

Personal integrity is crucial. While it is desirable for you to work together for purposes of general case preparation, the written assignment must be solely your own work.

Model Syllabus for a One-Quarter (20 Sessions) Course on Management Control Systems

Session No.	Case	Reading
1	Stewart Box Company (1-3)	Chapter 1
2	Rendell Company (3-1)	Chapter 3
3	New Jersey Insurance Company (4-1)	Chapter 4
4	North Country Auto (5-2)	Chapter 5
5	Birch Paper Company (6-2)	Chapter 6
6	Quality Metal Service Center (7-3)	Chapter 7
7	T&J's (2-1)	Chapter 2
8	Codman & Shurtleff, Inc. (8-1)	Chapter 8
9	Pasy Company (9-2)	Chapter 9
10	Galvor Company (10-3)	Chapter 10
11	Analog Devices (11-1)	Chapter 11
12	Enager Industries (11-4)	Chapter 11
13	Lincoln Electric Company (A) (12-1) and (B) (12-2)	Chapter 12
14	United Instruments (13-1)	Chapter 13
15	Nucor Corporation (13-2)	Chapter 13
16	Cookie, Inc. (15-1)	Chapter 15
17	AB Thorsten (17-1)	Chapter 17
18	Vick International (17-2)	Chapter 17
19 and 20	General Electric Company (1-1)	Chapter 1

Model Syllabus for a One-Quarter (30 Sessions) Course on Management Control Systems

Session No.	Case	Reading
1	Stewart Box Company (1-3)	Chapter 1
2	Rendell Company (3-1)	Chapter 3
3	New Jersey Insurance Company (4-1)	Chapter 4
4	North Country Auto (5-2)	Chapter 5
5	Pasy Company (9-2)	Chapter 5
6	Transfer Pricing Problem (6-1)	Chapter 6
7	Birch Paper Company (6-2)	Chapter 6
8	General Appliance Company (6-3)	Chapter 6
9	Investment Center Problems (7-1)	Chapter 7
10	Enager Industries (11-4)	Chapter 11
11	T&J's (2-1)	Chapter 2
12	Codman & Shurtleff, Inc. (8-1)	Chapter 8
13	Sound Dynamics (9-1)	Chapter 9
14 and 15	Boston Creamery (9-3)	Chapter 9
16	Galvor Company (10-3)	Chapter 10
17	Analog Devices (11-1)	Chapter 11
18	Warren Insurance Company (11-2)	Chapter 11
19	Quality Metal Service Center (7-3)	Chapter 7
20	Lincoln Electric Company (A) (12-1) and (B) (12-2)	Chapter 12
21	United Instruments (13-1)	Chapter 13
22	Nucor Corporation (13-2)	Chapter 13
23	Texas Instruments and Hewlett-Packard (13-3)	Chapter 13
	and Texas Instruments (13-4)	Chapter 13
24	Motorola (14-2)	Chapter 14
25	Cookie, Inc. (15-1)	Chapter 15
26	Chemical Bank (A) (16-1) and Metropolitan Bank (16-2)	Chapter 16
27	Vick International (17-2)	Chapter 17
28	AB Thorsten (17-1)	Chapter 17
29 and 30	General Electric Company (1-1)	Chapter 1

PART II

Teaching Notes for Cases
In The Ninth Edition

PART II

Management Control Systems: Teaching Notes

9th Edition

Table of Contents

Chapter 6: Transfer Pricing

Chapter 7: Measuring and Controlling Assets Employed

PART 2   THE MANAGEMENT CONTROL PROCESS

Chapter 8: Strategic Planning

Chapter 9: Budget Preparation

Chapter 10: Analyzing Financial Performance Reports

Chapter 11: Performance Measurement

Chapter 12: Management Compensation

Case 12-1: Lincoln Electric Co. (A)
Case 12-2: Lincoln Electric Co. (B)
Case 12-3: Anita's Apparel
Case 12-4: Wayside Inns, Inc.
Case 12-5: May Kay Cosmetics

PART 3   VARIATIONS IN MANAGEMENT CONTROL

Chapter 13: Control for Differentiated Strategies

Case 13-1: United Instruments
Case 13-2: NuCor Corporation
Case 13-3: Texas Instruments and Hewlett Packard
Case 13-4: Texas Instruments
Case 13-5: 3M Company

Chapter 14: Modern Control Methods

Case 14-1: Iron River Paper Mill
Case 14-2: Motorola
Case 14-3: Responsibility Accounting versus JIT

Chapter 15: Service Organizations

Case 15-1: Cookie, Inc.
Case 15-2: Williamson and Oliver
Case 15-3: Harlan Foundation
Case 15-4: Piedmont University
Case 15-5: Riverview

Chapter 16: Financial Service Organizations

Case 16-1: Chemical Bank
Case 16-2: Metropolitan Bank
Case 16-3: Citibank Indonesia

Chapter 17: Multinational Organizations

Case 17-1: AB Thorsten
Case 17-2: Vick International
Case 17-3: Nestle
Case 17-4: Xerox Corp. (B)

Chapter 18: Management Control of Projects

Case 18-1: Northeast Research Laboratory
Case 18-2: Modern Aircraft Co.

CHAPTER 1
THE NATURE OF
MANAGEMENT CONTROL SYSTEMS

Changes from the Eighth Edition

The principal changes are in the last section, "Overview," to reflect changes in the structure of the book.

Approach

On the first day, the usual objective is to create interest in the subject, to set the scene, and to give an overview of the course. The chapter does this. It pays special attention to the meaning of "control," and to the differences among the three distinct types of planning and control processes. If students have had an earlier course, they may have become accustomed to a different way of organizing the material and different definitions than those used here. The material that is included in our definition of "management control systems" therefore may need to be emphasized (pointing out, however, that the ideas will be greatly amplified in later chapters). For example, others may include material on what we call "task control" as a part of management control rather than as a separate subject. Moreover, terms such as goals, strategies, objectives, and control are used consistently throughout this book as defined in this chapter, which may be different than others define them. Confusion that occurs later on in the course will be lessened if the definitions used here are made clear at the outset.

Case 1-1

General Electric Company

Prologue

My preference is to use this case as a two-day case at the end of the Management Control Systems course. Used this way, the case does an excellent job of pulling together the various ideas in the book.

I usually divide the class discussion as follows:

Day One

1. Discuss the key elements of General Electric's control systems that support its strategy implementation process (45 minutes). This discussion will bring students up-to-date on the systems used by Reginald Jones to manage GE as of 1980.

2. Then show the following two videotapes:

    > Reginald Jones, former chairman and CEO on "Management Development, Strategic Planning, and Personal Style" (15 minutes)

    > John F. Welch, Jr., Chairman and CEO on "Corporate Culture, Managerial Philosophy, and Personal Style" (27 minutes)

    These are available in a videotape No. 9-882-003 from Harvard Business School (Phone (617) 495-6117). I strongly recommend that instructors show the two CEOs "in action."

3. Give the following assignment question for day two: "Given the differences in management style between Jones and Welch, how is Welch likely to change the management systems inherited from Jones?"

Day Two

1. Compare and contrast the management styles of Jones and Welch, based on the case plus the videotapes. (20 minutes)

2. Ask: "How and why was Jack Welch chosen as the CEO?" (10 minutes)

This case was prepared by Paul Browne (under the direction of Richard F. Vancil).

3. Then show the following videotape where Jones explains how the company picked the next CEO:

>   Videotape No. 9-882-054: Reginald Jones on "Management Succession." (12 minutes)

4. Then ask: "Now that we understand the differences in management style between Jones and Welch, how would this affect the controls within GE in the 80s?" (25 minutes)

5. Then show the following videotape where Jack Welch explains what changes he brought about *within the first three weeks* of taking over as CEO.

>   Videotape No. 9-882-004: Jack Welch on "The First Three Weeks." (12 minutes)

6. Wrap-up. (10 minutes) You can use any number of recent articles from *Fortune, Business Week* to update students on GE under Jack Welch.

Again, I strongly recommend the videotapes; they can be purchased from HBS Case Services (Phone (617) 495-6117).

I have had a great deal of success with this case with both MBA and executive audiences. Please call me at (603) 646-2156, if you need to discuss aspects of this case.

For more updated information on GE, the instructors can refer to an interview with Jack Welch published in *Harvard Business Review*, September – October 1989.

Reproduced below is the detailed teaching note prepared by the author of the case, Richard F. Vancil (HBS No. 5-182-232), Copyright © Harvard University.

>   VG

Classroom Pedagogy

Day One

With no action question, and no controversy or people in the case, you run the risk of a pretty dull class. I try to pep it up at the start by asserting that GE is probably the best managed corporation in the world, even though I can't document that. It is true, however, that Reginald Jones was selected as the best chief executive officer for the last two years of his tenure (1979 and 1980) in a *Fortune* magazine survey. The broad question for us today is to figure out how GE does it. In order to do that, we need to inspect each of the piece parts in GE's management systems, and the relationships among those parts. Such an approach is particularly useful in studying a company as large and diverse as GE; the problems of implementing strategy in a smaller, single-business firm are multiplied dozens of times over in GE.

Decentralization

GE did write the modern-day textbook on decentralization. Its massive reorganization in the early 1950s was not triggered by any crisis such as that faced by Alfred P. Sloan at General Motors in the 1920s as he attempted to gain control over the barons in his empire. Instead, GE's move was a calculated risk that the gains from the *adaptability* of new profit center managers would more than offset the reduction in the *efficiency* of its old functional organization (Sloan's terms for the trade-off). GE's size, and its overt pride in the new structure,[1] made the reorganization highly visible on the U. S. corporate scene, and it served as a model for the widespread adoption of profit centers in U. S. manufacturing firms during the next two decades. You may want to lecture briefly on the history and theory of decentralization.

The first assignment question is intended simply to get the students to examine the data on GE's structure and its financial performance; the data are too thin to prove any relationship. GE's rationale for each structural change is explained, believably, in the case, and the pendulum analogy is a useful one. Still, it may be useful to let the students walk through each of the major changes by asking them to explain why GE broke up its "finely honed" organization in the early 1950s, and what the effect of establishing SBUs was on the autonomy of the profit center managers.

Creating Sector executives in 1977 really was fine-tuning, in the broader sweep of things. I believe GE's original reorganization had only two levels of general managers below the CEO: department managers at the lowest level grouped under division managers reporting to the CEO. The Group level was added sometime during the 1960s, and by 1977 the span of direct reports to the top had simply grown too large, and another layer was inserted.

Finally, to close off this section of the discussion, you might ask the students to comment on the new feature of GE's 1981 corporate plan—the definition of *Arenas* with explicit assignments for specific organizational units in several SBUs. One of the costs of decentralization is that each profit center manager tends to take a single-minded focus on the performance of his or her unit, and cooperation among such units is difficult to achieve. Efforts to cope with this problem at the corporate level tend to be resisted because they are contrary to GE's fundamental philosophy of decentralization.

Infrastructure

I use this term to refer to the two primary management systems in business corporations: the organization design and the financial performance measurement system. The analogy to the infrastructure of a country is pretty good: an underdeveloped country, lacking networks for transportation, communication, and other public utilities cannot operate as efficiently as a country that had made the necessary investment in those systems. GE has an extremely well-developed infrastructure, while at Cummins Engine we see that it had almost nothing in 1974.

The important point about infrastructure is that it changes very slowly and usually incrementally. GE's basic organizational building block—the deportment headed by a general manager—was established in 1953. There are more of them now, and the superstructure above them keeps evolving, but the basic concept of the organization, in terms of where the work gets done, has not changed for nearly 30 years. *How* that work gets done, in terms of the role of the department manager and his freedom to take action, changes more frequently as people come and go and the pendulum swings. I label those changes as changes in the management *process*. The top corporate managers design and incrementally evolve the infrastructure of the organization, and

---

[1] GE's president at the time was Ralph J. Cordiner, and his series of lectures at Columbia University was published as *New Frontiers for Professional Managers* (New York: McGraw Hill, 1956). Cordiner and Sloan are quoted extensively in chapter 2 of my book, *Decentralization.*

then, working within that structure, they interact with their subordinates in a more or less formal set of management processes such as planning, budgeting, and monitoring performance.

In a firm with a well-designed infrastructure, the organization design and the routine financial reporting system are as integrated as the two sides of a coin. The basic structure of GE's financial measurement system was also put into place in the 1950s, and two points about it deserve comment. First, the way that GE has structured its operating statement (as shown in *Table A* near the end of the case) is instructive. GE operates in many businesses, but its managers share a common profit model. How does a unit of GE make a profit? By having capacity available (readiness-to-serve costs) and then selling enough volume with sufficient contribution margin to provide funds that will pay for the development of new products (programmed expenses), cover the corporate overhead, and still leave a profit. This profit model is not unique to GE—it can't be, given its diversity—but it does lay out clearly the primary variables that managers at all levels need to focus on.

The other point about GE's measurement system is that it reflects the company's managerial philosophy that a department manager should be responsible for the bottom line, and this means that each manager is assigned his or her share of corporate overhead, corporate interest expense, and income taxes. This definition of the financial responsibility of a profit center manager is not unique to GE either, but neither is it pervasive among U. S. manufacturing firms. The primary reason that GE had adopted this practice, I believe, is that GE's managers feel that the primary constraint on growth is their ability to develop enough good general managers. Somewhere among those 181 department general managers are the future corporate leaders of GE, and it's not too soon for those managers to start thinking about the whole ball of wax rather than just their directly controllable revenues and costs.

This discussion of infrastructure does not relate directly to any of the assigned questions, and you may not want to use the term at all. Some of the comments on organization design can be brought up during the discussion of *Exhibit 1*, if you choose, and the resource allocation example given in the next section can be used to permit a broader discussion of the financial measurement system, if that seems appropriate.

The Resource Allocation Process

GE's resource allocation process is not difficult to understand, but the discussion of it leading to that understanding is greatly enhanced if the students are aware of the process used by Texas Instruments. If the students have not previously studied that case, I think it is worth taking three or four minutes to describe the process, using a simple example. That example can then be recast, as shown below, first to convert it to the GE system of measurement, and subsequently to illustrate the role of sector executives in allocating resources to SBUs.

TI uses its "two-hat" concept to achieve a clear separation between current operating activities and activities focused on the future growth and profitability of the firm. GE's creative solution to the same problem was to develop the dual organization shown schematically in *Exhibit 1* of the case. By 1970, GE's new decentralized operating structure was more than 15 years old, was working well, and not to be tampered with lightly. But "profitless growth" could not be mindlessly continued; choices needed to be made, and the new strategic technology called portfolio management arrived on the scene in the nick of time. Applying those concepts to GE's diverse operations required that GE define the businesses about which strategic decisions could be made, and the concept of the SBU was born.

Many other diversified companies were wrestling with the same set of problems at the same time, and the conventional solution was to use the existing organization design and require each division (or whatever the profit centers were called) to prepare strategic plans for submission to corporate headquarters. GE really couldn't follow that approach, at least not at the department level, because there were too many operating units. A rather obvious alternative would have been for GE to require strategic planning to be done at the division level, or perhaps only at the group level. This would have reduced the number of units requiring corporate review and, perhaps more important, added symmetry in the sense that all organizational units at the chosen level would be treated the same. (More on symmetry below.) The creative aspect of GE's solution was that it chose to define its SBUs in terms of: (1) the external competitive marketplace, and (2) the relative operating independence of each SBU from other SBUs in the company. The result was that SBUs fell where they may, ending up at three different hierarchical levels in the operating structure. It might not be very neat, but it was certainly pragmatic, and a clear signal to the entire organization that GE was serious about strategic planning and strategic choice.

Mechanically, GE's resource allocation process is very similar to that used by TI. What TI calls OST funds, GE calls programmed expenses. Simple numerical examples are shown in *Tables A* and *B*.

Table A

Resource Allocation at TI ($)

		PCC #1	PCC #2	PCC #3	Corp. Total
1.	Sales	200	200	200	600
2.	Operating expenses	100	100	100	300
3.	Operating profit	100	100	100	300
4.	OST allocation	40	40	60	140
5.	Profit before tax (PBT)	60	60	40	160
6.	Total expense (2 + 4)	140	140	160	440

Table B

Resource Allocation at GE ($)

		SBU #1	SBU #2	SBU #3	Corp. Total
1.	Sales	200	200	200	600
2.	Expenses	150	150	150	450
3.	PBT (proposed)	50	50	50	150
4.	PBT (assigned)	60	60	40	160
5.	Total expense (1 – 4)	140	140	160	440

At TI, corporate management decides how many expense dollars can be devoted to strategic activities ($140 in the example) and then allocates those funds across its Objectives and, through the Objectives' managers, down into the OST organization. At GE, each SBU submits a proposed budget to corporate headquarters, and a visible part of that budget (not shown explicitly in *Table B*) is the proposal for programmed expenses. GE's managers first decide that the total corporate profit needs to be higher than the $150 proposed by the SBUs collectively, and establishes a target of $160. Then, they assign a portion of that target to each SBU based on the strategic category for each business. In a purely mechanical sense, the net result of either approach could be identical, as shown by the last line in each of the two tables.

Philosophically, GE's resource allocation process is radically different from that used at TI. GE's corporate managers do not attempt to make choices among the vast array of development proposals that could be funded. They know that they are implicitly making those choices when they assign a profit target for an SBU, but they choose to make that decision in strategic terms, based on the relative attractiveness of each business, rather than in terms of specific projects. This simple example is a beautiful illustration of the difference between centralized and decentralized management. In either company, top management must make the ultimate decision about the profit target for the coming year, but how that target is achieved, and which approach is right, given its circumstances, and GE's approach in particular is totally consistent with its desire to develop a strong cadre of general managers at low levels.

With the establishment of the Sector executive positions, it was almost inevitable that the resource allocation process at GE would change. The sector executives were intended to be super-SBU managers, adding value strategically, and in order to fill that role they needed to have clout where it counted. Again, I think GE's top management dealt with this problem creatively. At one extreme they could have simply allocated resources (profit requirements) to each sector and let the sector executives do the allocations to their SBUs. At the other extreme, corporate could have continued to make allocations to the SBU level, using the sector executives as chief operating officers to implement the corporate decisions. The middle ground is one which keeps corporate informed at the SBU level of detail; that information does constrain the range of reallocations that a sector executive is likely to make, but it allows some elbow room.

A second reason why a revision in the resource allocation process was needed is that in order to add value, a sector executive needed to be able to undertake some initiatives on his own that were not a part of any existing SBU. By being allowed to reallocate resources to the SBUs, the sector executive could create some slack resources at his level, as illustrated in *Table C*.

Table C

Resource Allocation at GE ($)

	SBU #1	SBU #2	SBU #3	Sector Executive	Sector Total
1. Sales	200	200	200		600
2. Expenses	150	150	150		450
3. PBT (proposed)	50	50	50		150
4. PBT (assigned)					160
5. Sector assignments	60	65	45	(10)	160

Assuming that the corporate allocation to SBUs was determined as is shown on line 4 of *Table B*, under the new process the entire $160 requirement would be assigned to the sector level. The sector executive might then make assignments to individual SBUs, as shown on line 5 of

Table C, leaving himself with a kitty of $10 that could be used either to fund additional development proposals in exiting SBUs, or to establish new ventures or other forms of business development.

Symmetrical Systems and Differentiated Strategies

A theoretical problem that has caught the attention of a few academics in recent years is the following: portfolio management defines the strategic position of each business unit and establishes radically different objectives for units with different positions. Implementing strategy for one of those units requires that unit to use a set of management systems consistent with its objectives. Diversified companies, however, tend to have a single corporate set of management systems which are applied uniformly to all business units. In order to deal with this conflict of symmetrical systems and differentiated strategies, diversified corporations must revise their management systems. At the extreme, a tailored set of management systems should be designed for each SBU, or at least for each major portfolio category of SBUs.

This problem, in my view, is mainly a theoretical one. It may have caused a little trouble for a little while in some diversified corporations, particularly when the idea of portfolio management and differentiated strategies was being introduced to the organization. But the basic problem is a generic one that top managers have always dealt with, long before portfolio management appeared on the scene; each subordinate manager has a unique set of responsibilities, problems and opportunities and objectives. The subordinate and his boss are both aware of the primary items on the subordinate's agenda, and most such managers use a more or less formal management-by-objectives system for validating that agenda. GE's way of coping with this problem is more comprehensive and more formal than that found in most companies, because of its size and great diversity.

Symmetry ("the hobgoblin of little minds," according to Ralph Waldo Emerson) is a powerful force in large corporations. The responsibilities of the top managers at GE are awesome. One way to optimize the use of their time is to institutionalize the formal processes (primarily meetings) in which they engage, and to use standardized forms for the paper flow which feeds those processes. Because the forms and procedures are the same for each SBU, a casual observer might assume that they are bureaucratically treating each SBU in an identical fashion. That's nonsense, of course, as we can see in GE. Each SBU may have to fill in the same number of boxes on the same number of forms, but top management then focuses on the relevant set of boxes for each SBU and, more important, on the content of those particular boxes.

The third assignment question asks the students to articulate how GE's management systems aid its top management in this task. The four primary elements are enumerated below.

1. **Selection.** GE has a highly organized executive manpower management system that has been in place a long time. This works to the great benefit of GE because, no matter how unique the strategy of a particular SBU, there's probably a manager somewhere in the GE system with the right combination of skills, personal orientation, and ambition to match that job—and GE can find that manager. This large cadre, and the policy of relatively frequent job changes, at least for fast-track managers, makes it easier to replace an SBU manager with someone better suited for that job as the strategy of the SBU evolves over time.

2. **Budgeting.** This old and powerful management tool has long been used to deal with the generic problem referred to above. The numerical example given in *Table B* above illustrates how GE uses its resource allocation process to clarify the strategic mission of each SBU manager. It should also be noted, perhaps as more than a footnote, that the strategic plan prepared by each SBU can be highly differentiated; the contents of each strategic plan are mandated, but there are no standardized forms to be filled except for the long-range forecast appended to the plan.

3. **Performance Reporting.** *Exhibit 7* of the case reproduced the primary standard form used for GE's monthly internal financial reports. Most of the boxes are applicable to all SBU's, but it is important to remember that the variances are calculated against each SBU's budget, which is a reflection of its strategic objectives. Further, each reporting component can define a half-dozen "key measures" that are appropriate for its particular situation.

4. **Performance Screens.** This is GE's term for its MBO system; here the distinction between financial and non-financial objectives is really a distinction between current operating performance and strategic activities that will affect the future positioning of the SBU. The scheme by which a weight is assigned to each objective of either sort is simple, but the relative weights assigned to the major types of activities must be consistent with the strategic mission of the SBU. This final element of tailoring GE's management systems to individual SBU strategies close the loop as far as the SBU manager is concerned. Performance screens are clearly important in determining incentive compensation. A manger's bonus is not determined simply by a formula, but the bonus ranges are wide even at the department manager level, and documented performance against predetermined objectives must count for something.

My closing comments for this class are brief. I refer back to the objective stated at the beginning of this note, and may comment additionally that it is useful to take a careful look at General Electric because its management systems have been consciously evolved over a long period of time. In particular, GE has paid careful attention to the balance between centralization and decentralization, a fundamental management problem. GE may also be credited with several important managerial inventions and innovations, such as profit centers, SBUs, "value added by management," resource planning as a specific task for staff officers, and most recently, current cost accounting as a workable managerial tool during a period of high inflation. In sum, GE's management systems probably represent the best of current goods practice, and we will use our knowledge of these systems as a reference point in discussing the other cases in this module.

Tape for Day One

General Electric Company

> Videotape 9-882-003
> Reginald Jones, former chairman and CEO
> John F. Welch, Jr., chairman and CEO
> "Corporate Culture, Managerial Philosophy, and Personal Style"

1. Jones on management development, strategic planning, and person style (15 minutes)

2. Welch on corporate culture, managerial philosophy, and personal style (27 minutes)

Classroom Pedagogy

Day Two

I can't give you much advice on how to conduct this class, but I'm pretty sure that the foolproof opening question is: What do you think of Jack Welch? Alternatively, you might solicit dichotomized adjectives contrasting Welch and Jones.

The comments below are a melange of my own analyses and conclusions, enriched by students' comments in class discussions. I've attempted to organize these thoughts into broad topics, but do not mean to suggest by this that the discussion may flow in the sequence shown below. In particular, my attempt here to distinguish between energy, leadership, and style seems useful to me at this moment, but I don't believe that I would try to organize student comments around that framework.

Energy

Students attempting to describe Jack Welch will use a lot of adjectives and, playing secretary, I record them all. I let the game continue for as long as there are hands in the air. Then, I try to facilitate the discussion by focusing the students on the single word *energy*. That term is likely to have been offered by one of the students, or if not, I synthesize it from several of the comments that are recorded. To me, Welch's energy level is an independent variable that I can separate from other topics such as leadership and style.

Welch is a personal dynamo. The edited videotapes really don't capture the atmosphere that existed in the MBA classroom when Welch was videotaped in late April 1981. Fourth-semester students at Harvard Business School are a pretty savvy and self-assured lot, but Welch literally took their breath away. He would listen to a question, and then, assuming that they knew most of the answers that they were expecting him to give, would skip right through that and go way beyond their expectations. He treated them as if they were just as intelligent and impatient as he is, but he left them gasping in an attempt to find a question that would allow them to test the mettle of the man.

The effect of Welch's energy on regular General Electric managers is hard to imagine. As a brief "war story," I disclose that when Welch took over the new and undefined job of sector executive in 1977, his first move was to go to the headquarters of each of his SBUs and spend two 12- or 14-hour days in a prolonged meeting with a handful of the top managers of that unit. Welch refused to sit still for canned presentations in those meetings, wanting to "get behind the presentations" to the substance of the business and perform his own analysis of each situation. I also admit that on the two occasions when I've had scheduled 30-minute meetings with Welch in his office I have been hard put to keep up with him, although I did not find him "intimidating." I really can't imagine spending 12 hours with such a man. I think the characteristic is more than just intelligence; he's fast.

At some point, one of the questions to ask the students to address is, What effect can a single individual have on the management of a company as large and diverse as GE? The answer may be, "Not much," but the students will also agree that Welch will have a bigger impact than a mere mortal. Pursuing that question, I suggest that Welch knows that one man can't do very much, and ask them to speculate on what Welch personally (and privately) would say that he is trying to do. I let that run for a minute or two, and then return to the question of energy. In one sense, Welch is trying to use his tremendous energy to energize the whole corporation, to get it moving faster. The ambience in GE's gracious corporate headquarters is quiet and relaxed, but it won't be long before people start walking faster down its carpeted corridors.

Leadership

Welch has stepped quickly into his role as GE's corporate leader. He's quoted in the press as saying, "We're not a disparate holding company sort of thing. . . . It really is one culture here." When a student questions him about that, he makes clear what the culture is—and describes it very effectively. GE is professional: "Winging it doesn't make it." GE people are competitive, not among themselves but with their external competitors. My label for GE's corporate culture is *meritocracy*, and I think that GE people do there the values implied in that term, but it's a long way from the culture that we saw in IBM or Cummins.

When the same student pursues Welch on the corporate loyalty dimension that we have seen in prior cases, Welch is candid in admitting that there is more loyalty among IBM employees, but he disdains the result. GE ends up with better people because their people are able to "do their own thing." Here, I think, Welch is talking about the same basic issue regarding culture that is discussed in my Culture lecturette—the dichotomy between paternalism and performance. There's no doubt where Welch stands on this issue.

Welch's cryptic response to the student that "the last three years are not typical," deserves some elaboration in class, based on Jones's comment on the "Management Succession" tape. There were several candidates in the semifinals for the chairman's job, and when the three vice chairmen were selected, three other candidates left GE for high-level positions in other companies within three or four months. Such departures are not unusual at GE; it is practically a finishing school for CEOs of U. S. corporations. By contrast, I tell the story about Corning Glass in 1970 when its president reached retirement age. There were three or four candidates for that job, and MacAvoy got it, but the other candidates did not leave the company—and nobody there was surprised at that, either.

Welch himself epitomizes GE's culture. During the 18 months of the semifinals, our conversations when he came to the campus were casual enough that I was able to probe discreetly about the race then in progress. In April of 1979, Welch told me that he had decided to stay in the race, even though he had recently been offered a very attractive position. A month or two later, Allied Chemical announced that it had hired a new CEO from outside, and it would have been an ideal spot for Welch's credentials. I realized at that point that Jack Welch should not be described as a competitor—he's a *winner*. He was willing to win at GE, but if he couldn't win there, he was going to win some place.

All this is consistent with Welch's closing statement on the homework tape about his vision for GE. "Better than the best!" will be his rallying cry as he attempts to lead GE's army of managers to greater achievements.

Welch's Mandate

There are two topics that could be discussed regarding Welch's selection as the new chairman; one is Why? (the second assignment question for this class), and the other is How? (the process used by Jones and his board of directors). Those are easily separable questions, and if you want to address the second one you should use the Jones tape on the third cassette. That tape, I believe, will become a classic for use with executive groups. Weren't you surprised at what Jones did?

As to why Welch, we don't know anything about the other two candidates, but the board chose the maverick, and it is tempting to infer that his selection carries an implicit mandate for Welch. The alternative hypothesis seems more likely: the board chose a man who was young and energetic, a technologist, and a proven developer of new businesses for GE. In effect, the board chose a new chairman to serve as a model for GE's managers. If there is a mandate there for Welch, it is: don't change what you've been doing, just do more of it. And, of course, that's what we see Welch doing, at least in the first three weeks.

Style and Its Implications

It is important to discuss the third assignment question (or some variation of it) before showing the in-class tape. How will Welch begin to put his stamp on the organization? Specifically, what actions will he take? How fast should he move?

Answers to these questions can only be drawn inferentially from an analysis of Welch's personal style as a manager. Some descriptors of his style will have been suggested earlier in student responses to Question 1, and with these as a starting point, that list might now be enriched because we do have an action question to deal with. A checklist for your own use, as you help the students crystallize their thinking, is more easily found from some of Welch's comments on the in-class tape. Here are some of the words he uses: candor, conflict; small meetings, small rooms; no ceremonies, informal, coats off; real-time stuff, compressed time; staff must belly-up. Welch uses these terms, of course, as he describes and explains what he has done during the first three weeks, but even before the students see the tape they know that they can expect some action from Welch.

Another way to cast this set of questions for the students is to use the pendulum analogy. I put the simple diagram, shown in Figure A, on the blackboard, leaving enough space below the dates to write in student comments as they talked about the pendulum.

There are really two questions to be dealt with here: In which direction will/should Welch attempt to move the pendulum in 1981? What are the alternative actions that he might take and how will each such action affect the pendulum? The latter question is easier to deal with, and is more instructive for the students at this point. Once the two lists have been created, it should then be easier for the students to predict what Welch will do, given their understanding of him as an individual. I'm not sure that there's anything he *should do*, unless I'm wrong about his implicit mandate.

Figure A

The Pendulum of Decentralization at General Electric

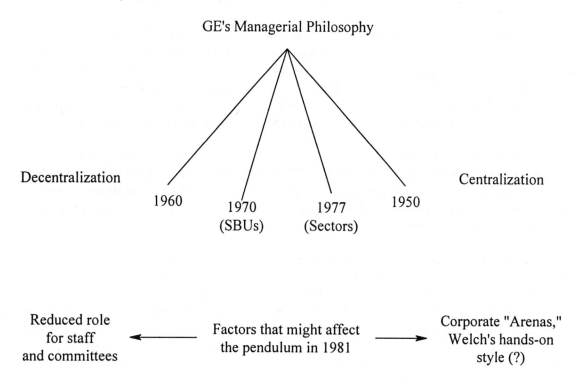

The in-class tapes then tell us what Welch did do in his first three weeks, and his first year. The students will have easily predicted that Welch will change the role of corporate staff at GE, but they may be surprised at how dramatically he has done that. He has simply disbanded the Corporate Policy Board (CPB). To take up the slack, he talks about a "three-man committee doing most of the work," where that committee consists of himself and the two vice chairmen.

Several times on the two tapes, Welch refers to his three-man team, and this deserves a brief comment. The role of that team is best illustrated in the bonus incident that he discusses on the homework tape. Welch knows his own foibles; he's aggressive, impatient, and hard driving. In that incident, his two colleagues "wouldn't let me do what I wanted to do," and he's clearly proud of that. Both of the vice chairmen are older than Welch; he needs and values their counsel; and he's aware of the tradition that might lead them to leave GE. One way to keep them is to give them a clear share of the action, and if power is a zero-sum game, then the corporate staff must lose in order to expand the scope of the Corporate Executive Office.

In his first three weeks, Welch is already continuing his previous practice as a sector executive of visiting the headquarters of each SBU for marathon discussions. The meetings are kept small and substantive by bringing no more than three people from corporate: Welch, the vice chairman with oversight for that sector, and the sector executive in charge of the host SBU. We really don't have to speculate much about who asks most of the questions in those meetings.

What is the effect of such a meeting on the SBU manager? How would you like to spend 12 hours responding to Welch's questions? If there was some honorable way, without marring your record, to avoid such a meeting, would you rather have it or not? When I tried that last question, it really seemed to have bite. The students gulped, and then did a pretty good job of laying out the costs and benefits of such a meeting from the point of view of an SBU manager. A softer question, What is the effect of such a meeting on your autonomy as an SBU manager?, didn't work quite as well but it does get us back to the pendulum issue. On the diagram shown above, I put a question mark on the effect of Welch's hands-on style. I'm really not sure what effect that will have on the autonomy of an SBU manager. Welch obviously can't make all the operating decisions that have to be made in GE, but in 12 hours of conversation it's almost inevitable that an SBU manager will make some implicit promise to Welch and then live to rue the day.

Another effect of Welch's meetings is that it makes the sector executives' role somewhat ambiguous. They clearly are not staff, but the CEO and the CXO are much better informed than before by having developed a direct channel of communication with the subordinates of the sector executives. This aspect of Welch's meetings will clearly have the effect of nudging the pendulum towards more centralized management at GE.

Let me make one last comment about Welch's style, which you can insert into the discussion at some point. In the fall of 1981, I learned that Welch had arranged to have the two edited videotapes of his class on April 27 shown to the top 50,000 people in GE. I was surprised, pleased, and then curious. He certainly was not trying to save GE the cost of making a first-class videotape of himself for that audience. Why did he use my tapes? That answer is easy: he could act out the real Jack Welch in my classroom far better than in a forum of, say, a group of GE employees or a group of security analysts. A lot of people in GE didn't know him, and these tapes were a vivid calling card.

Disclosing that, I then ask the students: What were the explicit messages in the tapes that Welch was sending to his people? There were many, of course, including the "better than the best" battle cry. But my hypothesis was that Welch was also trying to send a subtle but important message of another sort. He knows he is a maverick and has a reputation as a tough, impulsive manager. He knew that many people in GE might be worried about that, and his message is in the role of the vice chairmen in the bonus incident where "they wouldn't let me do what I wanted to do." He's proud of that, and he wants the GE organization to take comfort from it.

Lessons from Welch

I personally have learned a great deal from my exposure to Jack Welch, probably more than I realize, and certainly more than I can articulate. The brief comments below represent my current best effort to crystallize my thoughts.

One man *can* make a difference—at least this man can—even in a very large organization. I think Welch sees *his* job as one of providing dynamic leadership for GE rather than personally making a series of substantive decisions that will change the company. I believe him when he says that selecting people is his most important job, but he is not going to choose passively from some slate of candidates for promotion. He is actively trying to develop the capabilities of GE's managers. His leadership is not that of a showman, but of an analyst. He's interested in the substance of GE's business and, by matching wits with each SBU manager, he gains the knowledge that will permit him both to cull out the losers and to raise the performance standards for the ones with greater potential. I think he can pull it off.

There is a substantive lesson from Welch which does have broader relevance—intellectual content, if you will. There is a clear relationship between the personal style of an executive and the management processes that he uses to do his job. The point is dramatically illustrated by Welch and is executed by simple changes such as the use of committees, the size and role of staff, and the conduct of meetings (the number of people involved, the length of the meetings, and the formality of them). Welch has quickly put his stamp on GE; he has not changed GE's infrastructure much at all, but the management processes are extremely malleable. In my view, they can and should be changed by an executive so that they are consistent with his style of management.

Finally, I think it is fair to say that under Welch, GE will be more of a line manager's organization. I find this refreshing and also instructive in terms of the way that he has achieved it. There are winners and losers, of course, and I'm glad that I wasn't a staff person at GE headquarters during that transition. But the change seems healthy to me, at least with Jack Welch in charge, and it will be fun to watch how the story plays out over the next few years.

Tapes for Day Two

General Electric Company

> Videotape 9-882-004 (19 minutes)
> Jack Welch, chairman and CEO
> Videotape 9-882-054 (2 segments, 17 minutes)
> Reginald Jones,
> "Management Succession"

Richard F. Vancil

IMPLEMENTING STRATEGY: THE MULTIBUSINESS CONTEXT

General Electric Company

Vijay Govindaraian

The Amos Tuck School of Business Administration

Dartmouth College

Hanover, NH 03755

General Electric Case Series
Learning Objectives

- Strategy Implementation in the Multi-Business Firm

- Chief Executive Leadership Style and Strategy Execution

- Challenge of Corporate Transformation and Renewal

- Dynamics of Strategy Implementation

- Usefulness of Careful Historical Analysis in Understanding Company's Current Strategic Problems

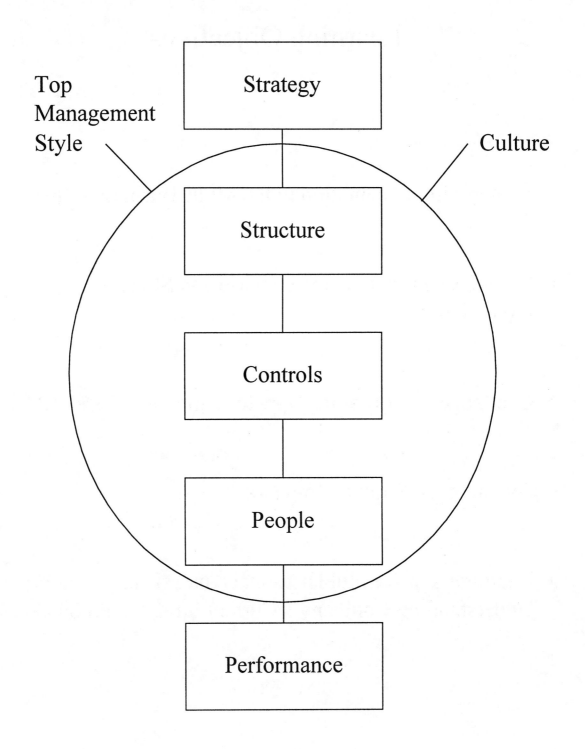

CEOs of General Electric

I.   Birth

1892 – 1922   *Charles Coffin.* Started GE by purchasing Thomas Edison's patents on electric light bulbs.

1922 – 1939   *Gerald Swope.* Strategy rooted in the notion of "benign cycle."

II.   Growth

1940 – 1952   *Charles Wilson.*

1953 – 1962   *Ralph Cordiner.* Championed diversification and decentralization.

III.   Consolidation

1963 – 1971   *Fred Borch.* Created SBUs.

1972 – 1980   *Reginald Jones.* Implemented formal strategic planning; create sectors.

IV.   Renewal

1981 –   *Jack Welch.* Corporate transformation without crisis.

General Electric
Management Systems

I.   Organizational Structure

- Decentralization

- Profit Centers

- SBU

- Sectors

- Arenas

- "Value Added" Concept

II.   Strategic Planning System

- SBU Mission

- SBU Competitive Strategy

III.   Budgeting

IV.   Internal Reporting

- Multiple Measures of Performance

- Replacement Costing

V.   Incentive Compensation System

- Link incentives to strategies

VI.   Strategic Human Resource Management

Cost and Benefits of Decentralization

I. Economic

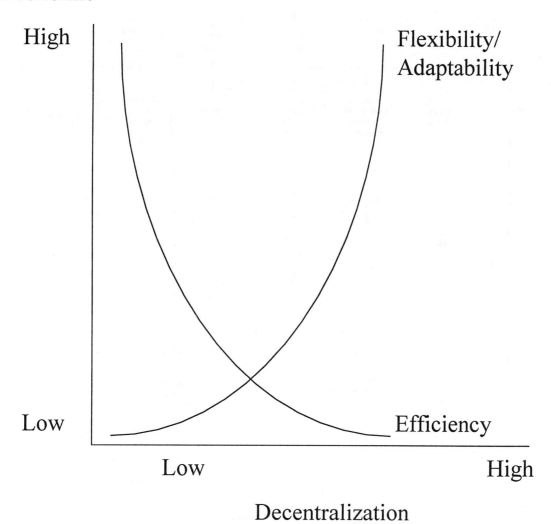

II. Social

- Best developer of people

- Professionalization of management

Exhibit 1

Partial Representation of Organizational Structure

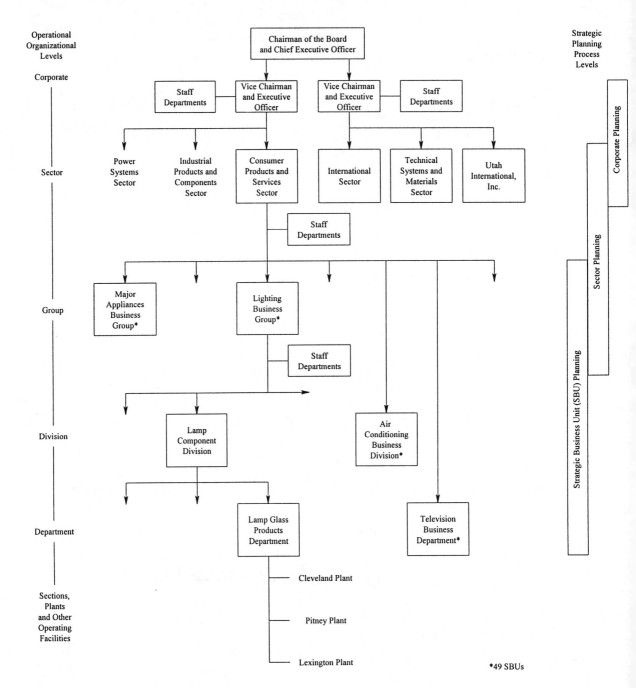

Development of Financial Control Systems

Phase I   General Motors/DuPont

- Divisionalization

- ROI-Based Control System

Phase II General Electric

- Residual Income Instead of ROI

- Multiple Performance Measures

  Profitability

  Market Development

  Product Development

  People Development

  Public Responsibility

- Subjective Performance Appraisal

Phase III General Electric

- Link Performance Measures to SBU Strategies

Current Performance

Profit	$ 3 million	ROI — 30%
Investment	$ 10 million	GE
		A 40%
		B 20%
		C 5%

New Project

Profit	$ 1 million	ROI — 20%
Investment	$ 5 million	K — 15%

"ROI"-Based Control System

	Before New Project	After New Project
Profit	$ 3 million	$ 4 million
Investment	$ 10 million	$ 15 million
ROI	30%	26%

"Residual Income"-Based Control System

	Before New Project	After New Project
Profit	$3 million	$4 million
Less		
Capital Charge 15% on Investment		
	$1.5 million	$2.25 million
"Residual Income"	$15 million	$1.75 million

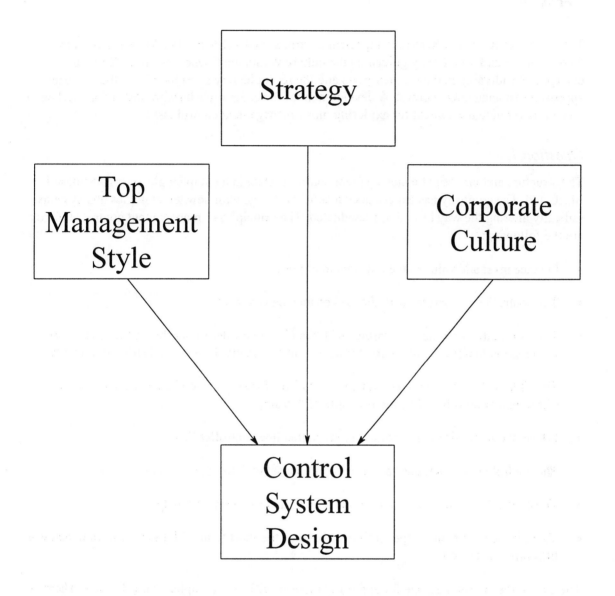

Case 1-2

Xerox (A)

This case focuses on the Xerox management control systems (MCS). The MCS is part of the Xerox culture and specifically guided by the culture within the finance function. Xerox has changed considerably in the past ten years and the recent history strongly affects the company's approach to management control. A development of the company's background and an outline of its culture provide the context for exploring many management control issues.

Question 1.

The structure and process of a management control system in a complex global organization is illustrated. The company has experienced a cultural change with new technologies and systems radically altering the way business is conducted. The principles of management control at Xerox are the following:

- Finance must add value to the management process.

- The controller is a partner with the GM or line management.

- The Corporate controller is a partner with the Unit controller rather than a "checker." Trust in the individual (personal control) is important in effectively communicating unit results.

- The FEC will develop and recommend candidates for key financial executive positions. Communication is based on the principle of "no surprises."

- Informal communication is critical in the dotted line controller link.

- The controller is a facilitator and source of counsel to their business units.

- The controller is the officer of ethics and takes this role very seriously.

- There is the continuing responsibility to balance the short term with the long term to achieve the corporate targets.

The case serves to set the stage for exploring more specific and complex control issues. There is a significant amount of material, both books and articles, about the company. The Leadership Through Quality culture at Xerox is the subject of many studies which offer different vantage points and make for very interesting reading. Understanding the background, history and culture of the organization is critical to solving management control issues.

Question 2.

The evolution toward operational measures and away from the traditional financial measures is central to the management control system at Xerox. The FEC had the insight to see the need for change. The change in metrics links very nicely with the TQL and Benchmarking activities which form the core of the new Xerox operating culture.

The key to a total quality management program is good and reliable measures of the operations. The traditional financial measures do not serve this purpose very well. Xerox's use of operational measures and their embracing of competitive benchmarking work to support the quality culture. This evolution should be thoroughly explored in the class discussion.

Question 3.

The Xerox culture is directly linked to the control process. Note the changes in culture taking place in harmony with changes in the control process. It is clear the principles of TQL link to the management control process.

This question can be used to discuss the types of control. K.A. Merchant (1985), *Control In Business Organizations* provides an excellent vehicle to discuss the role of personal controls. The FEC and the personality of the Corporate Controller, Sach, support the portfolio theory of types of control. Both culture and personality are key to making the system work. Xerox maintains the control system would not change with a change in the key financial players. Interviews and field visits suggest the opposite. There is, however, truth in the fact that the culture molds the personality. This issue can make for a very lively class discussion.

I introduce the case at the start of the Management Control Course, distribute the 10K and Annual Report, and encourage the students to read more about the company. As we progress through the course the series of cases are introduced to support the topics as follows:

- The effect of organizational change on the control process.

- The control of foreign operations with an emphasis on currency trading, transfer pricing and measurement systems.

- The role of management incentives and performance measurement on the control system.

- The future needs and programs for management control.

- The impact of employee empowerment on management control.

- The use of technology to gain efficiency and enhance control.

- The maintaining of ethical standards.

— Larry Carr

Case 1-3

Stewart Box Company

Approach

This is an introductory case that covers many of the topics that will be discussed in the course. Students should be able to deal with it satisfactorily on the basis of a first course in management accounting, but they are not expected to get into all the fine points. Primarily, it provides a view of "where are we going" that is often useful on the first day.

Students who have not had a first course cannot deal with Questions 1 and 2, but they can nevertheless benefit from discussing the more general questions. The case is unchanged from the seventh edition, except that the case has been updated to 1993.

Comments on Questions

1. a. There must be a transfer price in order to obtain the item "transfers to carton factory," which is a revenue item for the Board Mill. The same amount appears in standard cost of goods sold, as materials cost, for the Carton Factory.

   b. If inventory remains unchanged, the actual cost of goods manufactured in December is the difference between standard cost of goods sold $787,000 and the favorable manufacturing variance of $26,000 or $813,000.

   c. If inventory levels changed, we have no way of knowing how much of the cost of goods manufactured appears in cost of goods sold and how much is lodged in inventory (or, if sales exceeded production, how much of cost of goods sold came from the current production and how much came from inventory). We would have to know both the inventory amounts and the company's policy with respect to the disposition of variances in order to obtain the results if inventory levels changed.

   d. The actual corporate expense was $83,000 and there was a favorable variance of $3,000 so the budgeted amount must have been $86,000.

   e. Since there was a favorable volume variance (of $24,000), actual volume must have exceeded standard volume.

2. a. The actual labor cost of labor-pressmen was $9,416.

   b. The budgeted amount of total controllable cost was the actual of $16,847 minus the unfavorable variance of $830, equals $16,017. Actual cost exceeded the budgeted amount at the actual volume level.

   c. The amount of total controllable cost applied to products was the standard cost. This is the budgeted cost of $16,017 (as above) minus the unfavorable volume variance of $544 equals $15,473.

d. The departmental fixed costs and allocated costs are noncontrollable; therefore, no variance is shown. If the system were such that a variance was generated for these items, it would imply that the Department 14 supervisor was responsible for them, which is not the case.

3. To: Mr. Stewart
   Re: Income Statement Analysis - 1993

Board Mill Operations

Board Mill profit was $16,000 more than budgeted for December, and $44,000 more than budgeted for the year 1993. The main reason for this is that both external sales and transfers to the Carton Factory were higher than budgeted. The volume variance was $54,000 for the year. About half of this occurred in December, which indicates that December was a month of operating above standard volume. The cost of goods sold and other variances were unfavorable, indicating that the costs of direct materials and direct labor increased. More was spent for selling and administrative expense than budgeted. The company seems to be competing well in the market for paper board, since there is a total yearly favorable sales variance of $61,000 more than 30 percent of which occurred in December.

Carton Factory

Carton Factory profit was $245,000 more than budgeted for the year, and $26,000 more than budgeted for the month of December, indicating that the company is meeting competition with favorable results. The standard cost of goods sold and selling expenses show unfavorable variances for both December and the year 1993. Carton production and sales were both higher than budgeted for the month of December and the year, resulting in favorable volume variances. Forty percent of the $64,000 favorable manufacturing variance occurred in December.

If the trend toward higher cost of goods sold continues, it would be well to review standard cost estimates for possible revisions.

Company

Net income was $217,000 more than budgeted for the year, and $31,000 more than budgeted for December. The biggest reason for this was the greater than expected profits of both the Board Mill and the Carton Factory. Another reason for the increased net income was the reduction of $29,000 in corporate expenses from what was budgeted for the year. The unfavorable variance of $104,000 for the income tax for the year 1993 is of course due to the increased income before tax.

4. To: Mr. Stewart
   Re: Spending Report - Department 14

The favorable volume variance of $1,619 indicates a higher production volume than budgeted in Department 14. Labor showed unfavorable spending variances, probably necessitated by the higher production volume for the year as well as for December. Press supplies showed a favorable spending variance of $234 of which $192 was for the month of December. Power and other overhead showed favorable variances also, but repairs, while showing a favorable variance of $192 for the year, showed a large unfavorable variance of $996 for December, indicating unexpected breakdowns.

The total spending variance of $1,887 for the year was favorable, indicating that spending in Department 14 was less than expected.

5. This case was selected to illustrate a good system. Thus, the student should find it easier to identify strong points than weak points. Some of them are: the company has a standard cost system and the standard costs seem current (which often is not the case.) These costs are useful without much adjustment in arriving at selling prices. The company has a five-year plan. (Some may question the need for a five-year plan in a company of this size and simplicity, but it was not very time consuming.) In preparing this plan, the company made correct calculations of equipment acquisition proposals (many companies still do not use present values or handle the depreciation tax shield properly).

6. The budget is a flexible budget. Managers participate in its preparation. Actual performance is checked against budget. The two profit centers seem to facilitate management understanding of what is going on (although it can be argued that since the paperboard mill sells almost exclusively to the carton factory the profit centers are artificial).

Some students may assert that the list of reports is too long. If asked which ones should be discontinued, however, it turns out that each contains information. Note also that management only skims the reports and puts them aside if nothing significant is observed. For possible weak points, it could be pointed out that there is no objective way of determining which variances are significant. In a company like this, however, management probably has an excellent intuitive feel for significance. The validity of the profit center profit depends on how the transfer price was calculated, and it may not be feasible to arrive at a sound price. The volume variance in Exhibit 5 is difficult for us to understand, but perhaps is understood by those involved.

Note: A few very perceptive students may ask about Exhibit 4: How as the $(26,000) variance in cost of goods sold for the Board Mill in December arrived at? Also, for the carton factory. The frank answer is that I don't know. One possibility is that the inventory records were maintained at both actual cost and standard cost, and this variance developed as specific goods were sold (or transferred) in December that had a variance between actual and standard cost. However, this is not the way the usual standard cost system works. Another possibility is that the amount represents inventory losses after completion of the manufacturing process (e.g. damages in finished goods inventory), although such losses often are excluded in cost of goods sold. Another possibility is that orders were filled with more expensive goods than those that were ordered. You can blame this ignorance on the author. I was unable to go back to the company.

CHAPTER 2
UNDERSTANDING STRATEGIES

Changes from the Eighth Edition

The basic thrust of this chapter is unchanged from the eighth edition. This chapter describes the generic strategic options at the overall firm level and at the business unit level. This chapter provides the background for the rest of the book since management controls are designed to implement strategies. Management control implications of different strategies are explicitly considered in Chapter 13.

This chapter gives a more detailed description of the core competency concept and its central role in corporate diversification.

Cases

T&J's is designed to discuss the fit between responsibility structure and competitive strategies. This case appeared under the title, Smith Company, in the eighth edition.

General Motors Corporation focuses on the problem of relating the control system to the objectives of the organization.

DairyPak is new to this edition. This case focuses on the construction of the value chain and its use in developing strategies.

Case 2-1

T&J's

Purpose of Case

Note: This case is a rewrite and update of an earlier case titled South American Coffee Company. More coffee industry data are added. The issues remain unchanged.

Smith Company sold its own brands of coffee throughout the Midwest. Stock of the company was closely held by members of the family of the founder. The president and secretary-treasurer were members of the stock-owning family; other management personnel had no stock interest.

Sales policies and direction of the company were handled from the home office in Cincinnati. All salespersons reported to the sales manager through two assistants. The sales manager and the president were responsible for the marketing functions including advertising and promotion work.

The company operated three roasting plants in the Midwest. Roasting, grinding, and packaging of coffee were under the direction of the vice president of manufacturing, whose office was in Cincinnati. Each plant had profit and loss responsibility and the plant manager was paid a bonus on the basis of a percent of his plant's gross margin. For the past several years, plant managers had expressed some dissatisfaction with the method of computing gross margin subject to bonuses which led to a study on the whole method of reporting on results of plant operations and the purchasing operation.

The purchasing department was responsible for the procurement of green coffee for the roasting operations. The unit was located in the section of New York City where the green coffee business was concentrated, but reported to the secretary-treasurer in Cincinnati. The purchasing unit operated on an autonomous basis, keeping all records and handling all financial transactions pertaining to purchasing, sales to outsiders, and transfer to three company-operated roasting plants.

Smith is a very "rich" management control system case which raises the following key issues:

1. What is the strategy of the company? Doing an analysis of the coffee industry will help determine the company's strategy.

2. Is the company organized and controlled in line with its chosen strategy?

3. What are the key success factors by function (i.e., purchasing, manufacturing, and marketing)?

4. What are the behaviors you desire, by function (i.e., purchasing, manufacturing, and marketing)?

5. Are the current controls inducing those behaviors?

Assignment Questions

1. Evaluate Smith's current control system in the manufacturing, marketing, and purchasing departments. Are these controls good ones?

2. Explain in detail, using specific examples, why you think the current system is or is not effective, in each department.

3. What changes, if any, would you propose in the present reporting and control system? (Hint: Be sure to consider Smith's competitive strategy when making suggestions.)

Exhibit 1, A Note On Coffee, is attached to this teaching note and is provided to the students with the case, to help gain an understanding of the coffee business.

Case Analysis

Strategy

A good starting point for class discussion is to use Exhibit 2 to this note as an overhead to set up the framework with which to tackle the case. Students must be aware that the effectiveness or otherwise of management control systems should be evaluated in the context of the company's chosen strategy. Performance evaluation—which is a critical component of the management control process—needs to be tailored to the strategy being followed by a company. The following set of arguments supports this position: (1) Different strategies imply different tasks and require different behaviors for effective performance; (2) Different control systems induce different behaviors; (3) Thus, superior performance can best be achieved by tailoring control systems to the requirements of particular strategies.

The first logical step in the class discussion is to consider the coffee industry and identify the strategy and objectives of Smith. The case facts do not explicitly state Smith's strategy.

Therefore, some discussion should be devoted to what implicitly is the strategy for a small regional coffee company like Smith. In terms of competitive strategy, Porter has proposed the following two generic ways in which *any* business can develop a sustainable competitive advantage:

Low Cost. The primary focus of this strategy is to achieve low cost relative to competitors. Cost leadership can be achieved through approaches such as economies of scale in production, learning curve effects, tight cost control, and cost minimization in areas such as service, sales force, or advertising. Examples of firms following this strategy include: Texas Instruments in consumer electronics, Emerson Electric in electric motors, Hyundai in automobiles, Briggs and Stratton in gasoline engines, Black and Decker in machine tools, and Dell in computers.

Differentiation. The primary focus of this strategy is to differentiate the product offering of the company, creating something that is perceived by customers as being unique. Approaches to product differentiation include: brand loyalty (Coca-Cola in soft drinks), superior customer service (IBM in computers), dealer network (Caterpillar Tractors in construction equipment), product design and product features (Hewlett-Packard in electronics), and/or product technology (Coleman in camping equipment).

The discussion should now turn to whether Smith is striving to be a low cost producer or a differentiated company. Although some students may argue for one or the other, the company does not seem to have any "sustainable" competitive advantages as evidenced by the following problems with each strategy.

Low Cost:

- It is unlikely that a small regional company ($8.5 million) like Smith can be a low cost player since it lacks the size to realize scale economies.

- In terms of purchasing efficiency, they probably cannot match a large producer like General Foods or Nestle.

- In terms of manufacturing, marketing, and distribution, they lack the size vis-a-vis General Foods or Nestle to drive down costs to a point where they can effectively compete.

- Smith is really not a price leader in this business.

Differentiation:

- Smith's low margins of approximately 16 to 19 percent (482,640/2,233,860 = 19%, and 1,369.410/8,569,200 = 16%) do not leave enough margin for marketing expenses, administrative expenses, and profit. Considering the fact that Procter and Gamble spends about 30% of its sales on marketing, Smith does not appear to be a typical differentiated company. Because of these low margins, it will be difficult for Smith to match national brands.

- It may not be possible for Smith to build regional brand loyalty for their coffee as large players like Nestle and General Foods will most probably challenge any attempts that Smith makes to create a niche for itself in a regional market.

The overall conclusion so far is that Smith, given its current situation, cannot successfully compete as a low cost player or as a value player. If we had more detailed information on Smith's competitors, suppliers, buyers, etc., it would be possible to recommend ways by which Smith could develop a competitive advantage. The instructor can close off this part of the discussion by noting that we will consider the implications for control system design for Smith under both a low cost scenario as well as a differentiation scenario.

Teaching Note: Exhibit 3 shows the organization structure for the company. The company seems to be organized appropriately.

The next step is to look at the current control system and the problems associated with it. It will be helpful, however, to first recognize the key factors for success in this business if Smith's strategy is to be a low cost producer or a differentiated producer. The key success factors by function, assuming they choose to be a low cost producer, are as follows:

1. **Manufacturing**—Costs of manufacturing must be controlled and kept as low as possible. In addition a consistent, acceptable quality of coffee must be maintained.

2. **Marketing**—Sales volume and prices must be kept as high as possible in light of the low cost strategy. In addition, marketing must provide accurate forecasts for purchasing and manufacturing so that maximum efficiencies in purchasing and manufacturing are realized.

3. **Purchasing**—Competent traders must be employed so that coffee beans are purchased on time and at the lowest possible market prices.

The question now arises as to whether or not the key factors for success would be different should Smith choose to pursue a strategy of differentiation. The key success factors by function for a differentiated strategy are as follows:

1. **Manufacturing**—Producing a differentiated coffee will result in less emphasis on cost for both the producer as well as the buyer. However, the quality of coffee must be maintained at very high standards at all times since the quality of output directly affects sales.

2. **Marketing**—Prices must be kept as high as possible for a differentiated product. Sales volume will not be as important as long as Smith can carve out a niche for itself in the market. The marketing department must provide accurate forecasts for purchasing and manufacturing so that there is an adequate supply of coffee to meet consumer demand.

3. **Purchasing**—The purchasing department must procure a wide variety of consistently high quality coffee beans in order to produce a high quality differentiated coffee. Also, competent traders must be employed so that coffee beans are purchased on time and at the lowest possible market prices.

We can now look at the problems in the current control system and the behaviors we wish to induce in each of the three departments in order to devise a better control system.

Controls over Manufacturing

Each of the three plants are currently run as profit centers. One of the principal problems in operating a profit center system is to devise a satisfactory method of accounting for the transfer of goods and services when there are interdependencies across profit centers. The profit center idea does not make sense for Smith since each of the plant managers are paid a bonus on the basis of their plant's gross margin when many of the components of gross margin are out of their control. This is especially true if the actual costs at which green coffee is transferred from the purchase department to plants. Students will identify the following among the chief problems with the profit center idea for plants.

a. Plant managers have no control over green coffee costs which make up about 60% of manufacturing costs.

b. Plant managers have no influence over sales volume, price, or mix.

Since manufacturing has no control over these areas, the current system is leaving them frustrated and dissatisfied. The next step in the analysis is to provide recommendations for controls if Smith chooses a low cost strategy or a differentiation strategy.

Low Cost

We must first address how the problem of green coffee costs can by solved. One solution might be to eliminate this cost from the plant managers' performance reports. Yet this could potentially lead to unfavorable usage variances if the plant manager is not accountable at all! A better solution is to transfer green coffee at a standard price and hold the plant manager accountable for usage. Monthly reports would help ensure that usage is at acceptable levels.

We must next address the issue of inducing cost minimizing behavior in the plants. The best way to do this would be to set up a standard cost center using a flexible budget with variances on controllable costs. The plant manager could be evaluated by comparing actual manufacturing costs with standard costs. It would make sense to evaluate the manager tightly against cost budgets. That is to say, meeting the cost targets will be greatly emphasized in the monthly performance evaluation of plant managers. The positive aspects of this system are that tight financial controls will motivate the plant managers to control costs which is the key in a low cost strategy.

There is a potential problem with this expense center concept: the plant manager may not make the appropriate investment decisions if that decision making authority is given to him/her. A plant manager may forego an investment that is good for the company if it increases manufacturing costs and thus decreases his/her bonus. However, this is not an issue at this time because those decisions are most likely made by the vice-president of manufacturing. Management, however, must be aware of the potential conflict if plant managers are ever given that authority. This issue is analyzed more thoroughly in the Quality Metal Service Center (B) case.

Differentiation

If Smith differentiates itself on the basis of product quality (i.e., a "gourmet" coffee), then plant managers will have a profound influence on sales via their direct control over product quality. Under these conditions, a profit center concept is appropriate for evaluating plant managers.

Unlike the low cost scenario, plant managers should not be evaluated tightly against profit targets. For instance, with a strategy of differentiation, some usage variance is expected in order to produce a coffee of very high standards (e.g., if a batch of coffee does not meet quality levels, it is better to waste it than sell it to a customer whose expectations are for higher quality). Evaluating green coffee usage every six months or every year (as opposed to every day) will ensure that the plant manager's usage variance is not excessive and is not habitual. It will also help quality control as the plant manager will realize the emphasis is on producing that "gourmet" coffee.

Inn summary, plant managers under the differentiation scenario will be profit centers with more flexible financial controls. That is to say, meeting the budgeted targets will not be emphasized month by month but rather at longer time intervals.

Controls over Marketing

The current system provides no formal controls in the marketing department. The president, a major shareholder, is in charge of this function. One can question if the controls over the marketing function are adequate or if they need more formal controls. The president's personal involvement in marketing may suggest that this is all the "control system" that is needed. This reminds students that the absence of *formal* controls does not necessarily mean that an operation in *uncontrolled*. Although the case does not specify how the marketing people are evaluated, it is likely that the president evaluated them on some basis of sales volume. Recommendations for controls if Smith chooses a low cost strategy or a differentiation strategy are as follows.

Low Cost

We want to motive the marketing department to maximize sales volume and sales prices and provide accurate sales forecasts to purchasing and manufacturing if the company chooses a low cost strategy. Marketing could be operated as a revenue center with the marketing people evaluated on the basis of the revenue they generate. This would provide motivation for them to maximize revenue through aggressive marketing, advertising, and selling. Although this would establish some control over sales volume and sales price, it is not clear that formal controls are needed in this department (especially given the president's personal involvement).

In addition, the marketing department should be evaluated on the accuracy of their sales forecasts. Sales forecasts will depend in part on accurate forecasts of Smith's market share; as such, the marketing department is also responsible for accurately predicting market share. These forecasts are critical in realizing efficiencies in purchasing and manufacturing operations. One way to evaluate the marketing department would be to compare their forecasted sales to actual sales on a monthly basis. This will motivate them to provide good forecasts which in turn will allow the company to maximize revenue by purchasing, manufacturing, and selling the amount of coffee demanded by consumers.

Differentiation

If Smith plans to pursue a strategy of differentiation, the marketing department will have to establish a niche for their "gourmet" coffee. It will be more important for the marketing department to emphasize price and product image rather than sales volume since a differentiated product is viewed by consumers as worth the higher price. Again, marketing could be operated as a revenue center with particular attention given to price and margins.

Here again, it is critical for the marketing department to provide accurate sales forecasts (again, based on accurate forecasts of market share) to the purchasing and manufacturing departments. In this case it will also be necessary to evaluate the marketing people by comparing forecasted sales to actual sales on a monthly basis. Like the low cast strategy, this will motivate them to provide good forecasts which in turn will allow the company to maximize revenue by purchasing, manufacturing, and selling the amount of coffee demanded by consumers.

Controls over Purchasing

The current system provides no formal controls in the purchasing department, yet this is the key function! The secretary-treasurer, another major shareholder, is in charge of this function. However, he is in Cincinnati and the purchasing office is in New York City; hence there is a need for formal controls. That need is reinforced if students realize that the caliber of the purchasing function is probably the greatest profit-determining factor in this company.

One can assume that the purchasing department is evaluated on the trading profit they produce and their ability to have green coffee at the plants when needed. Coffee purchase costs are recorded by the purchasing department on a contract-by-contract basis. When green coffee is shipped to a plant, a charge is make for the cost represented by the contracts which covers that particular shipment of coffee, with no element of profit or loss. When green coffee is sold to outsiders, the sales are likewise costed on a specific contract basis with a resulting profit or loss on these transactions. This current system induces dysfunctional behavior on the part of the purchasing manager. Because the manager decides which lots to transfer to the plants, it will most likely be the most costly ones that are transferred. The result of this is that the purchasing people can make additional trading profits at the expense of the plants; they can transfer higher-priced lots to the plant and sell the lower-price lots on the open market. For example, say four lots of coffee have been purchased at four different prices. The plants only need two lots, so two will be traded. It is in the purchasing department's best interest to sell the two lowest-cost lots on the open market (thus showing higher trading profits) and stick the plants with the higher cost lots. In addition, the purchasing manager may also speculate excessively and buy surplus lots when they are low-price and sell them on the open market when prices increase, thus using company funds to increase their personal wealth via higher bonuses because of higher trading profits. The fact that the purchasing unit is located in New York City while the remainder of the company operations are in the Midwest makes this behavior all the more likely.

The net conclusion is that the current controls on the purchasing department's efficiency are highly inadequate. A starting point in designing a better control system would be to look at the benchmarks (or standards) for purchasing. In this context, we should consider what the company can do *without* a purchasing department. There are two alternatives if the company does not have a purchasing department.

1. Buy on the "spot" in the market at the time coffee beans are actually needed.

or

2. Buy "forward" based on sale forecasts provided by the marketing department.

    Students will argue that without a purchasing department, the company will buy "spot" and not "forward." If they buy "forward," they have two risks—quantity and price. By buying "forward," Smith is speculating on the quantity the company will need at a later date as well as the price of green coffee at that time. If they buy "forward," it is possible that the price of green coffee will decrease and/or that the company does not need all the green coffee purchased. In that worse case situation, the company will have a surplus of green coffee that will either be wasted or sold to an outside party at a loss. If they buy "spot," they only have one risk—price.

    Some students will recommend the following standard to evaluate the purchasing efficiency:

3. Use as "standard" the *minimum* forward price between the time of the sales forecast and the time of delivery. In other words, the purchasing department should know the coffee bean market so well that they are able to pay the lowest price possible for green coffee beans. For

example, say the marketing department forecasts on September 1 that the company will need one lot of green coffee beans on October 1. There will be 31 different forward prices for one lot of green coffee beans from September 1 (the time of the forecast) and October 1 (the time delivery is required), one for every day of the month. In addition, there will be the on the "spot" price on October 1 for one lot of green coffee beans. Students will argue that the purchasing department should be able to obtain the lowest price possible of all the different prices (both "spot and "forward") during the month. This would mean evaluating the purchasing department by comparing actual price paid with the lowest price available during the time the forecast is made and the time delivery is required. A "zero" variance will indicate the *best* possible performance by the purchasing department. At this time, the instructor must point out that this "standard" represents the *best* job that a purchasing department can do. This standard should be compared to alternatives #1 and #2 noted above, which represent what the company would do *without* a purchasing department. Further, the students will realize that alternative #3 is not an effective standard by which to motivate the purchasing department since they will never be able to show a positive variance under this benchmark.

The net conclusion of this discussion is that the appropriate standard to evaluate the purchase department is the "spot" price at the time of delivery. The instructor can now move the discussion to the topic of how to organize the activities of the purchasing department. There are three alternatives:

1. The purchase department should buy exactly in accordance with the sales forecast. When the marketing department provides a monthly sales forecast, the purchasing department will buy *only* the quantity of green coffee beans needed as indicated by the forecast.

or

2. They can buy a larger volume of green coffee beans by committing to purchase in future months when the "forward" price is better than the "spot" price. This will mean that the purchasing department is buying a larger quantity than forecasted by the marketing department since they think they can get a better price by making forward commitments now. (The company will have to set limits on forward commitments to prevent "overexposure" from speculation.)

or

3. They can speculate completely.

How one sees the best method of organizing the purchasing department depends on whether purchasing is viewed as a separate business or not.

At this time, the instructor should move the discussion to recommendations for controls in the purchasing department if Smith chooses to follow a strategy of low cost or differentiation.

Low Cost

In looking at the alternatives of how the purchasing department should operate, we can conclude that the key task for a low cost company is to pay the lowest price possible for green coffee beans, with sufficient margin to cover their overhead plus a reasonable return on the inventory investment that is tied up in the department. The following metrics can be used to measure the performance of the purchasing department depending on what one thinks is the best method to purchase green coffee beans (alternatives 1, 2, and 3 considered separately).

Alternative #1

If one believes that the purchasing department should buy green coffee beans as described above in alternative #1, then the profit center concept will be a good measure of performance. Exhibit 4 shows how profit will be calculated if the purchasing department is evaluated on a profit center concept. Here, since the purchasing manager has *no* discretion to buy green coffee beans over and above the quantities given by the marketing department, investment center idea is not relevant for alternative #1.

Alternative #2

If one believes that the purchasing department should buy green coffee beans as described above in alternative #2, then the investment center concept using the residual income metric is appropriate. Exhibit 5 shows how this would be calculated. Here, the purchasing manager has discretion in affecting the inventory of green coffee beans; hence the need for investment center concept.

Alternative #3

If one believes that the purchasing department should buy green coffee beans as described above in alternative #3, the best way to measure their performance is with the investment center concept using the residual income metric. In addition, since purchasing manager can speculate on the coffee market, outstanding purchase commitments at the end of each month should be reported. A comparison of committed price and spot price at the end of each month will deter someone from entering into an unreasonable future commitment which could eventually cause the company to go out of business. Exhibit 6 gives an example of how residual income would be calculated under this alternative. Future purchase commitments are shown on a separate line. This report should be generated monthly so the company always has up to date information.

This new system will produce the following benefits:

1. It will motivate the purchasing department to watch the market closely and pay the lowest possible price; in fact, it must be lower than "spot" price at the time of delivery in order for them to have sufficient margin to cover overhead and return on investment.

2. It will keep their inventory investment at a minimum. Without this system, the purchasing department could be tempted to buy surplus green coffee beans in large lots and wait for the "spot" price to increase before selling it on the open market at a profit.

3. The plants will be properly supplied on a continual basis.

4. The purchasing department will maximize trading revenue without their accomplishments being at the expense of the manufacturing department.

Differentiation

In looking at the alternatives of how the purchasing department should operate, we can conclude that the key task for a differentiated company is similar to a low cost company in many respects. They want to pay the lowest price possible for green coffee beans and still have sufficient margin to cover their overhead plus a reasonable return on the inventory tied up in the department. Thus the performance metrics will be the same as described for a low cost strategy under the three alternative scenarios in which purchase department can be organized.

However, unlike the low cost strategy, one additional area needs to be monitored. The purchasing department under a differentiated strategy must procure a wide variety of consistently high quality coffee beans in order to produce a "gourmet" coffee. It will be difficult to evaluate the purchasing department on the basis of the quality of raw coffee purchased until the coffee has been through the roasting and grinding process and is ready for consumption. At that point, if the coffee is not of "gourmet" standards, it needs to be investigated as to whether that is the fault of purchasing or manufacturing. Certain nonfinancial performance measures (example: percentage yields) could be reported to track the purchasing department's effectiveness in procuring high quality beans.

To summarize the recommendations for management control systems for Smith Company under a low cost scenario and under a differentiation scenario, the instructor can use Teaching Note Exhibit 7 as an overhead.

Teaching Strategy

This case can be used as a summary case to review the basic control concepts such as cost centers, profit centers, and investment centers. We have successfully used this case both in the MBA in the required Managerial Accounting course as well as in the second-year elective on Management Control Systems. This case can be covered in one class period.

In teaching this case, we recommend the classic case approach. Start by asking someone "what would you recommend and why?" During the discussion, we give the students free rein to see what changes they think are appropriate. Most of the ideas and insights in this teaching note can be developed based on student-to-student exchanges. The instructor's role should be one of pacing the discussion instead of over-controlling it.

V.G.

Exhibit 1

*Note on Coffee**

The Commodity

Prior to reaching its final form in grocery stores as ground (percolator) or soluble (instant), coffee is referred to by buyers and sellers as "green coffee." This refers to the green beans which are picked from the coffee trees. The coffee leaves the grower countries in this raw state packaged in 60 kilogram bags. It is then roasted and processed in the consuming countries. There are two types of coffee beans, arabica and robusta. Arabica is the coffee favored by American consumers and is grown primarily in South America. Its flavor is not as strong as that of the robusta variety. Robusta coffee's major grower is the Ivory Coast. Not only is its flavor stronger than arabica's but it is also favored by processors (General Foods, Nestle) in the production of instant coffee. Thus, with the growing demand for instant coffee there has been a concomitant growth in the demand for robusta beans.

The Suppliers

Coffee is generally grown in tropical regions. Brazil is the largest producer and supplies between 20 and 30 percent of the world's green coffee. Other large exporting countries include Colombia, Indonesia, the Ivory Coast, and Mexico. Coffee is harvested somewhere in the world during almost every month of the year. For example, Brazil's main harvesting season is April – September; Colombia's is October – March; and the Ivory Coast harvests from November – April.

The Buyers

The United States is the world's largest single importer of coffee. It buys most of its coffee from Brazil and Colombia. Europe is second, purchasing a little less than half of all coffee exported.

Buyers fall into two categories: roasters and brokers. Roasters include the large food processing companies such as General Foods and Nestle as well as regional and local coffee companies. The General Foods and Nestles of the world usually purchase their coffee supplies direct from the growers. Their financial strength allows them to generally negotiate favorable terms with the buyers and they are also able to inventory coffee stock in order to protect themselves against future price increases. The smaller coffee processors normally buy their coffee from brokers. This second category of buyers consists of both trade firms and "pure" brokers. Trade firms actually purchase the coffee from the country of origin and then sell it to the processors. "Pure" brokers never actually take title to the coffee, they merely match buyer and seller in the marketplace. Trade firms generally finance their transactions via secured loans from commercial banks. Banks generally allow a creditworthy company to borrow between 80 and 90 percent of the market value (based on the spot price) of the coffee purchased. The loan is secured with the title to the coffee given to the bank until the trade firm sells the coffee to an end-user. The trade firm then pays down its loan and takes the remainder of the sale as profit.

---

* This note was prepared by Scott Barrett for use in conjunction with the case study, South American Coffee Company. All rights reserved. The Amos Tuck School of Business Administration, 1989.

It is important to note that the coffee business is a relationship driven business for buyers whether they are large or small. The development of strong relationships with the growers is important in maintaining a steady supply of coffee. While it is true that coffee is a commodity product and the supply and demand of coffee depends on price, one simply cannot fly down to Colombia and expect to easily be able to buy a million bags of coffee. Growers want to deal with buyers they can trust and vice versa. The buyer may be from General Foods or a small New York City brokerage but one can be sure that he/she has spent a great deal of time cultivating a relationship. A strong relationship provides two things: information about the coffee market; and hopefully an inside track on a grower's crop. This is especially important if a roaster needs a certain type of coffee (i.e., Colombian mild) to maintain a standard blend of ground coffee which deeps the consumer drinking "to the last drop."

Factors Affecting Price

Weather, specifically frost and drought, is the most important factor affecting production and hence price for Western Hemisphere coffees. The commodity sections in most major newspapers will often print stories concerning the effect of frost or drought on the future harvests. Eastern Hemisphere coffee producing countries' crops are most often damaged by insects. Inventory levels of green coffee in major producing and consuming countries is another important market consideration. Furthermore, actual and threatened dock strikes may cause a buildup of coffee stocks at the port of exit. This is a very real possibility especially in African countries. Marketing policies of various exporting countries can also play a role in the price of coffee. On the consumer side, high retail prices or health concerns can result in lower consumption which in turn may exert downward pressure on prices. Finally, most producing countries belong to the International Coffee Organization (ICO). The objective of this organization is to support coffee prices through the use of export quotas.

The Futures Market

Futures markets for coffee exist in New York, London, and Paris. In New York, coffee futures are traded on the Coffee, Sugar, and Cocoa Exchange. The normal use of the coffee futures market is to set up a hedge to protect one's inventory position against price fluctuations. A hedge is commonly defined as the establishment of a position in the futures market approximately equal to but opposite in direction to a commitment in the cash market (also known as the physical or actual commodity). For example, one who owns a certain amount of coffee hedges by selling an equivalent amount of coffee short in the futures. This protects the value of his inventory against a price decline. If the price of coffee does in fact fall the owner will sell the actual coffee at a loss. However, since the price has fallen in the actual market it normally follows that prices in the futures market for coffee have also fallen. By selling short in the futures market when prices are high and covering the sale when prices decline, the individual earns a profit which hopefully will offset his loss on the physical side. It is virtually impossible to set up a perfect hedge position due to imperfections between the physical and futures markets but it does provide some protection due to imperfections between the physical and futures markets but it does provide some protection to one's inventory. (Note: although it is possible for the liquidation of futures contracts to result in actual delivery of the commodity, less than 2 percent of all contracts are settled in this manner. Most contracts are liquidated through offset against a similar contract in the opposite direction.) Hedging also allows the coffee merchant to obtain credit from banks. Banks will seldom lend money to the holder of a commodity who has not attempted to properly hedge his/her inventory position.

Exhibit 2

Framework for
Management Control System Design

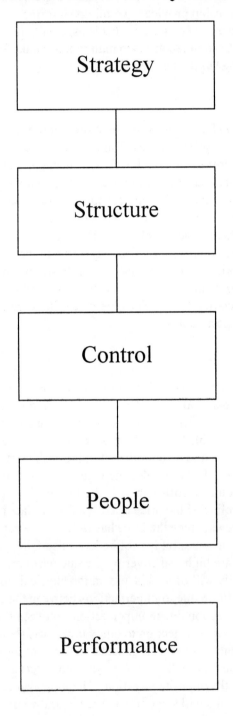

Strategy

Structure

Control

People

Performance

Exhibit 3

Organizational Chart

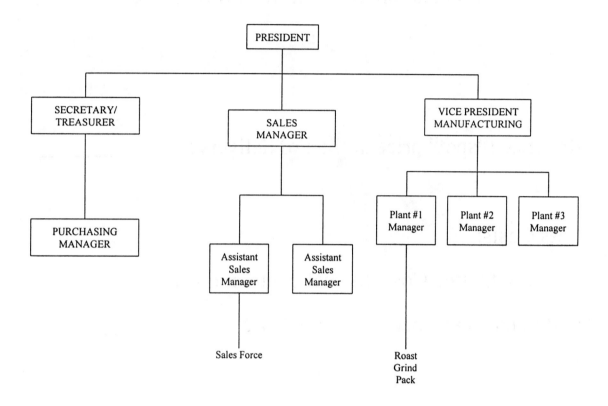

Exhibit 4

Purchasing Department

Calculation of Profit in a Profit Center

Revenue ("spot" price at time of delivery)   _____

Less Costs:

    Green Coffee Costs (actual contract cost)   _____

    Purchasing Department Overhead   _____

PROFIT   _____

Exhibit 5

Purchasing Department

Calculation of Residual Income in an Investment Center

Revenue ("spot" price at time of delivery) _____

Less Costs:

    Green Coffee Costs (actual contract cost) _____

    Purchasing Department Overhead _____

Less:

    Capital Charge on the Inventory Investment _____

RESIDUAL INCOME _____

Exhibit 6

Purchasing Department

Calculation of Residual Income in an Investment Center with Forward Commitments

Revenue ("spot" price at time of delivery)   _____

Less Costs:

    Green Coffee Costs (actual contract cost)   _____

    Purchasing Department Overhead   _____

Less:

    Capital Charge on the Inventory Investment   _____

RESIDUAL INCOME   =========

Forward Commitments
(Quality and Price)   =========

Exhibit 7

Recommendations for Control Systems

	Possible Strategies	
Department	Low Cost	Differentiation
Manufacturing	Expense center with tight financial controls.	Profit center with more flexible financial controls.
Marketing	Revenue center with emphasis on sales volume.	Revenue center with emphasis on sales price and margins.
Purchasing:		
Alternative #1	Profit center.	Profit center.
Alternative #2	Investment center concept without information on forward commitments.	Investment center concept without information on forward commitments.
Alternative #3	Investment center concept with information on forward commitments.	Investment center concept with information on forward commitments, with additional non-financial performance measures.

T&J's

Vijay Govindaraian

Earl C. Daum 1924 Professor of International Business

The Amos Tuck School of Business

Dartmouth College

Hanover, NH 03755

Phone: 603/646-2156

KEY ISSUES

1. Do industry analysis. What is the strategy of the firm?

2. Is the firm organized and controlled in line with its chosen strategy?

3. What are the key success factors, by functions?

4. What are the behaviors you desire, by functions?

5. Are the controls inducing those behaviors?

Responsibility Center

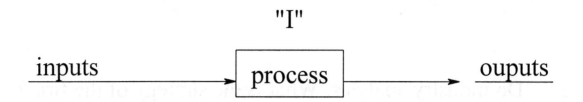

"I"

inputs ————————→ | process | ————————→ ouputs

- Cost Center   Only measure inputs

- Profit Center   Measure inputs and outputs

- Investment Center   Measure inputs and outputs in relation to investment

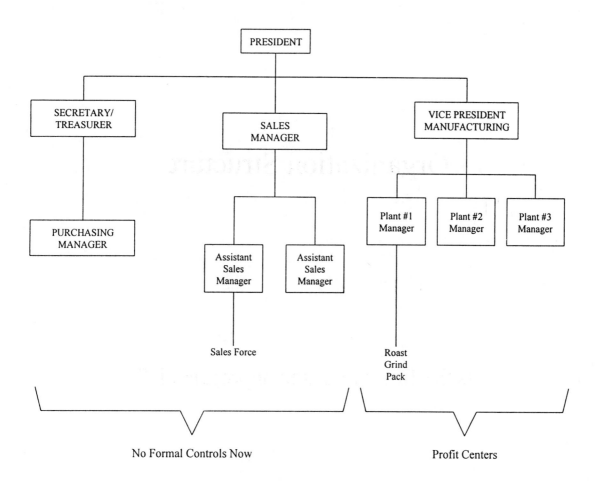

Organization Structure

Is the firm organized appropriately?

Seems okay; problem is the *controls*

Manufacturing

- Cannot control enough variables to use profit center idea

- Cost center

- Flexible budget with variances on controllable costs

- Control "quality" issue as well

- Use standard price for green coffee (held accountable only for coffee usage)

Marketing

- President is in charge of this function

- Is the controls over the marketing function "adequate"?
  Do we need formal controls?

- Absence of *formal* control does not mean an operation is
  uncontrolled

- Could be a revenue center

- Key is aggressive selling

- Also, need good sales forecasting to help the purchasing
  department

Purchasing

- *No* controls now! Yet, the key function!!

- What is the alternative to having a purchase department? Buy in "spot."

- So, the key task is to beat spot prices by sufficient margin to cover purchase department overhead plus a return on the inventory investment required.

- Investment center; residual income idea.

What is the role of the purchasing department? Three alternatives:

1. Should buy only in accordance with sales forecast

   or

2. Can buy larger volume when the "forward" is better than "spot"

   or

3. Can speculate

The answer to this question depends on "whether purchasing is viewed as a separate business or not."

Benchmarks for Purchasing

1. "Spot" at the time of delivery

2. "Forward" at the time of placing the order

$$\Downarrow$$

Standard says "What can I do without a purchasing department?"

OR

3. Minimum forward price between the time order is placed and the time of delivery ("zero" variance indicates best performance)

$$\Downarrow$$

Standard says "What is the *best* job purchasing department should do?"

Three Different Job Definitions

1. Should buy only in accordance with sales forecast

OR

Investment Center idea

2. Can buy larger volume when the "forward" is better than "spot" (but cannot exceed some limits)

OR

3. Can speculate

Is Purchasing a "Business" or not?

Purchase Department

Investment Center

Revenue ("spot price at the time of delivery")

Less Costs:

    Green Coffee—actual contract cost

    Overhead costs to run the department

Less capital charge on the inventory investment

                                  _____

    Residual Income   =======

T&J's
Strategic Options

1. Low Cost

- Can a $100 million sales firm be a low cost player?

- Can they match the "biggies" on purchasing and manufacturing efficiencies and R&D and Marketing scale?

DEBATABLE

2.   Broad differentiation

- Can they outspend on R&D and Marketing to gain differentiation?

	Nestle	P&G	Phillip Morris	T&J's
Gross Margin	55%	36%	32%	16%
Marketing & R&D as % of Sales	37%	32%	23%	?

DEBATABLE

3. Focused Differentiation

A La Starbuck and GMCR

- Will our 16% Gross Margin allow us to be competitive on the R&D and Marketing front?

- Do we have financial resources to forward integrate into retail chains?

- Will the "biggies" allow us to enter this area?

DEBATABLE

4. Regional Private Label Supplier

    • Would our current cost structure allow us to be competitive as a private label supplier?

DEBATABLE

One Inference

We do not have a sustainable competitive advantage!

Design of Management Control System

Objectives of the Company

|

Organization of the Company

|

Key Success Factors at each
Organizational Level

|

Design Responsibility Structure
(Profit Centers, Cost Centers)

|

Tie incentive compensation to
carrying out the responsibility

Acid Test: "Does the system induce intended behavior?"

General Motors Corporation

Objectives

This case focuses on the problem of relating the control system to the objectives of the organization. The general line of approach, therefore, is to deduce what the objectives of General Motors Corporation are from the information given in the case, to see whether the system described is consistent with these objectives, to see whether some other system would be better, and, if time permits, to examine the social implications of General Motors' objectives. The following discussion will be organized in terms of the above questions, which are a little different from those given at the end of the case.

Discussion

I. The case makes clear that General Motors' objective is , in some sense, to earn a specified return on its investment. The first problem is to make this statement as specific as possible, that is, to define "investment and return." By "investment," we are not certain what General Motors means, and various alternatives can be discussed to the extent the instructor wishes. With respect to the working capital component, the use of the word "gross" implies that the formula includes current assets, without a deduction for current liabilities. The advantages and disadvantages of using net working capital can be discussed, but this is probably getting in deeper than one needs to. With respect to fixed assets, the alternatives are gross book value, net book value, or some form of current value such as replacement cost. Probably the company actually uses one of the accounting figures, (gross book value or net book value), rather than replacement cost; again, it may be getting too far afield to discuss the alternatives in much depth here.

With respect to the word "return," the principal question implicit in the General Motors treatment is whether depreciation should be included in figuring the profit. Is the inclusion of depreciation double counting? The answer is no, for the depreciation charge recovers the cost while the return represents the profit over and above the cost.

It is also important for the students to understand that the GM goal is a specified *average* return over a period of years, rather than the same return each year. The average is an average related to volume. That is, it is assumed that volume will fluctuate up and down around an average which in the example is 1,000,000 units, whereas all other cost estimates are made currently for the specific year under consideration. If the objective was to earn a return of 20 percent each and every year, the system would require that prices be high in years of low volume, which is just the time when it is probably most difficult to increase prices. This is the reason why the goal is an average return.

II. Turning to the question of whether the system is consistent with the objective, the best way to discuss this is to work through the figures called for by Question 1. Calculations are shown in Exhibit A. Note that if the student blindly follows the formula given in Exhibit 1 of the case, he will not come out with the right answer. This is because the facts given do not fit directly into the formula. In particular, if the $250 commercial cost is added as a straight element of cost, then the formula does not provide for any return on the investment that is associated with this cost. The investment is the working capital, cash and receivables, which is assumed to vary with the selling price, which is, in turn, affected by the commercial cost. Therefore, the student should modify the formula to take this fact into account. Perhaps he will set up a simple equation, such as that in Exhibit A, which is more informative than the formula shown in the case, since it shows how the standard selling price is computed.

Testing the $1,913 selling price (and it must be recognized that students might come out to a slightly different figure depending on how they round), we can see that it does in fact produce a 30 percent return on the investment. Thus, the system is consistent with the objective.

Exhibit B is the calculation called for by Question 2 and shows how the return would vary as volume varies. This also produces a return of 30 percent on the average if one works with the dollar amounts. A simple average of the three return percentages does not come out to 30, but this is because such an average is unweighted; an average computed by weighting each return will come out to the 30 percent.

Question 3 is asked in order to show the relevance to the current situation of the material described in the case, which goes back to the 1920s. We do not have information on General Motors pricing policy that is more recent than that discussed in the case, but we have reason to believe that the description given in the case is still reasonably valid. The specific wording of Question 3 relates to a situation that existed in 1975. The instructor perhaps can substitute a more recent incident that he happens to hear about (e.g., competition with foreign cars; cost of pollution control equipment) in order to make the question up to the minute.

Those who believe in marginal cost pricing can argue that the rebates granted in 1975 when demand declined demonstrates the classical interaction between demand and price. Another explanation is equally plausible: General Motors set its prices initially on the basis of its long-run pricing policy as described in the case. It knew that such prices were probably too high in view of current economic conditions, but it wanted to establish the legitimacy of such prices in the event that price controls were reimposed. If, instead of a rebate, GM had set list prices lower, it could not have justified its normal price if price controls were reimposed. Further, varying the amount of the rebate for different models and time periods permitted GM to experiment with the effect of various tactics, and thus arrive at an optimum price under the unusual conditions of 1975. In this interpretation, the list price was the normal price, perfectly consistent with the policy described in the case, and the rebates were short-run tactical devices.

There is quoted below the press release issued by General Motors on August 13, 1975, explaining prices of the 1976 model year. It may be used in connection with Question 3.

DETROIT—General Motors announced today that the Manufacturer's Suggested Retail Prices, or sticker prices, on its 1976 base cars will increase by an average of $206, or 4.4%, over current prices.

In a statement on the pricing action, Chairman Thomas A. Murphy said: "With the beginning of production of our 1976 cars, we have established introductory prices with two principal considerations in mind. On the one hand, there are the pressures of the extremely large increases in costs which we have experienced in the past year. On the other hand, there are the continuing intense competitive pressures coupled with our determination to maintain the recent momentum of recovery in the automobile sales and to continue to contribute to the achievement of price stability in our country.

"The Suggested Retail Prices of our 1975 models have not been increased since their introduction a year ago. Actually, they were reduced by $13 to reflect the removal, last December, of the seat-belt ignition interlock. But our costs, in that same period, have increased dramatically. The cost increases which we have already experienced, or for which we are so far committed, have added about $375 to the cost of the average GM base car. For example, payroll costs are up about 11%, and the cost of materials, including the steel increases announced last week, has increased over 12%. However, to increase prices to our customers by the full amount of these cost increases would, in our judgment, tend to dampen the returning demand in the marketplace, a demand which has been strengthened by an increase in used-car prices. For example, the value of the average two-year-old used car has increased by more than 13% during the past year.

"For these reasons, we are increasing our wholesale prices to our dealers on a 1976 base car with comparable standard equipment by an average of $216, or 5.9%--only a little more than half of our cost increases. At the same time, we are adjusting our suggested dealer markups so that retail sticker prices will increase an average of only $206, or 4.4%. This increase is well below the recent increases in the Consumer Price Index and testifies to our commitment to compete aggressively for an expanding market in 1976.

"Adjustments, principally downward, have also been made in some of our base-car prices to reflect changes in the level of standard equipment. On many models, equipment has been made optional in order to achieve the lowest possible retail price on the base model and to give the customer wider latitude in equipping car. Some examples of equipment changed from standard to optional are steel-belted radial tires on most compact models, and power brakes on selected sub-compact models. In some instances, equipment has been added, but the net effect has been to minimize the increases in base-car prices and give the customer even greater flexibility in ordering a car suited to the individual's taste and pocketbook.

"The price adjustments in the 1976 model lineup, including the addition and deletion of equipment and dealer-markup changes, range from a decrease of $211 on the Chevrolet Monza Towne Coupe to an increase of $808 on the Chevrolet Corvette. Taking into account the net equipment adjustments, together with $13 reduction of last December when the seat-belt interlock was removed, a 1976 base-car retail prices will average $187, or 4.0%, over the 1975-model introductory retail prices. The suggested retail prices of optional equipment will increase an average of 6%, and the wholesale prices will increase an average of 5%.

"GM has long been committed to the proposition that its success depends upon offering its customers outstanding product values. The success of this effort is seen in the fact that industry car prices, as measured by the Bureau of Labor Statistics (which recognizes quality changes), have increased only 14% in the past three years, while consumer prices generally have increased 26%. The new cars we will offer in 1976 are fully in this tradition.

"Equally important, GM is expanding its 1976 product line with the introduction of the small Chevette, the prices of which will be announced later. This will enlarge the customer's choice of new cars at the lower end of the price range, and assure fully competitive low-cost transportation for our buyers.

"While we have no illusions that the competitive efforts of one company or, in fact, one industry can reverse national economic forces, we are convinced that our responsible pricing action will contribute to the nation's goals of economic expansion and price stability. We hope that our example of holding price increases below the level of cost increases, which anticipates our ability to improve our efficiency and productivity, and thereby remain competitive, will encourage a similar dedication to restraint on the part of all upon whom we depend for the purchase of the materials and services we need."

At this point, alternative pricing formulas can be discussed. The most common alternative pricing practice in industry, is to add a mark-on to the cost. Except in the unusual case where investment is completely stable, such a formula will not be consistent with the goal of earning a specified percentage return on investment. Another alternative is to adopt the approach of the economists and try to figure the optimum point on a demand curve. This is consistent with the profit maximization objective, but such an objective is to be rather sharply distinguished from the specified return that General Motors seeks. Furthermore, it seems highly unlikely that General Motors can construct the demand curve and, without this, it is in no position to estimate what the optimum point is.

As another way of showing how the formula is consistent with the objective, we might consider how Ford or Chrysler would approach its pricing problem. Presumably, General Motors is the price leader, and therefore, there is no point in either Ford or Chrysler arriving at an independent price, since they must follow the General Motors price. What they can do, however, is to estimate what price General Motors is going to charge by using the General Motors formula and, insofar as feasible, General Motors' figures. Having arrived at this price, they can then work backwards to decide what cost they can incur in order to earn their own desired return on investment. They can modify their own costs to the extent necessary by changing the design of their automobiles. Thus, Ford or Chrysler can use an approach that has a formula, but the formula is used differently from the way the price leader would use it. This general question can be gotten at in various other ways. For example, other questions are: Will the system correctly signal the need for a price change or other action such as cutting cost, when there is a change in the underlying cost factors? (The answer is yes.) Will the system properly take account of changes in manufacturing such as increased automation which adds to investment and decreases labor costs? (The answer is yes.)

Finally, it can be pointed out that the pricing system that we are examining is but a part of the total management control system. The remainder of the system essentially seeks to insure that the cost estimates that we have been studying are, in fact, turned into actual costs as operations proceed.

III. The last question opens up broad economic and social policy issues if one wants to get into it. The answer, of course, is highly debatable. Personally, I think that the approach given in the case is much better both for General Motors and for the country than the alternative suggested in classical economics. It is better for General Motors simply because I doubt that the economic approach is feasible. It is better for the country because, I believe, it leads to more stability and counter-cyclical forces than the alternative of gearing price closely to the demand situation in a given year. Of course, whether the 20 percent return is too much for a company such as General Motors to earn is a matter that can be debated without limit, but there is no very firm way of resolving this question.

RNA

<h1>Exhibit A</h1>

<h1>Calculation of Question 1</h1>

	(a) Ratio to Sales	(b) Ratio to Factory Cost
Gross working capital	0.150	0.250
Fixed investment[2]	_____	.4615
Total investment	0.150	0.7115
Required return at 30%	0.045	0.21345

Gross margin:

First approximation: $1 + b/1 - a = 1.21345/(1. - .045) = 1.271$

$1.271 \times 1,300 = \$1,652$

$+$ Commercial $250/\$1,902$

But this does not include return on Commercial

So either add $\$250 \times .045 = \$11 + \$1,902 = \$1,913$
or let $x =$ selling price and $y =$ cost. Then
$x = y + ax + by + \$250 = 1,300 + .045x + (.21345)1,300 + 250$
$.955x = 1,827 \qquad x = 1,913$

---

[2] Fixed investment:

Investment in plant	$600,000,000
Practical annual capacity	1,250,000 units
Standard Volume Equivalent (80%)	1,000,000 units
Factory cost per unit	$1,300
Annual Factory Cost	$1,300,000,000
Standard Factor (600,000/1,300,000)	.4615

Exhibit B

Calculation of Question 2
(000 omitted from dollar amounts)

	60%	80%	100%
Volume, units	$ 750,000	$1,000,000	$1,250,000
× P/V margin (1,913 – 1,200) = $713	713	713	713
Contribution	$ 534,750	$ 713,000	$ 891,250
Less nonvariable	350,000	350,000	350,000
Profit	$ 184,750	$ 363,000	$ 541,250
Change, for 25% change in volume	–49%		+49%
Investment			
1. Variable with sales 1,913 × .15 = $286.95	$ 215,250	$ 286,950	$ 358,700
2. Variable cost 1,300 × .25 = 325	243,750	325,000	406,250
3. Plant	600,000	600,000	600,000
Total Investment	$1,059,000	$1,212,000	$1,365,000
Return	17%	30%	40%

Note: We have tried unsuccessfully to obtain more recent data on General Motors pricing policy. So far as we can tell, however, the policy is substantially the same as that described in the case. If you have more current information, we would appreciate your sharing it with us.

Case 2-3

DairyPak

Overview

This case is a fairly simple, straightforward exercise in creating a value chain (for the paper milk carton industry) and in using it to facilitate managerial decision making (product emphasis, customer emphasis, capital expenditure analysis, make/buy analysis).

The value chain concept has been discussed in the strategy literature since at least 1980. As a generic concept for organizing our thinking about strategic positioning, its significance is widely accepted. But empirical examples of the power of the concept for shaping cost analysis are not plentiful. This case reports a field study in which a value chain is constructed. The insights for cost management which emerge are contrasted with those which are suggested by two traditional analysis techniques—a 2×2 growth/share matrix and conventional cost analysis. The objective of the case is to extend our knowledge about how to construct and use value chains in managerial accounting. I believe the concept is powerful and deserves far more empirical study as a way to make the strategic perspective more explicit in managerial cost analysis.

Answers to Assignment Questions

Question 1

Calculational Difficulties

I do not wish to imply that constructing a value chain for a firm is easy. There are several thorny problems to confront: calculating a value for intermediate products, isolating key cost drivers, identifying linkages across activities, and computing supplier and customer margins.

The analysis starts by segmenting the chain into those components for which some firm somewhere does make a market, even if other firms do not. This will catch the segments outlined in Exhibit 6 for the milk carton industry, for example. One could start the process by identifying every point in the chain at which an external market exists. This gives a good first cut at identifying the value chain segments. One can always find some narrow enough stage such that an external market does not exist. An example would be the progress of a roll of paper from the last press section of a paper machine to the first dryer section on the same machine. There is obviously no external market for paper halfway through a continuous flow paper machine! Thus, seeing the press section and the dryer section of the paper machine as separate stages in the value chain is probably not operational.

Part of the "art" of strategic analysis is deciding which stages in the value chain can meaningfully be decoupled, conceptually, and which cannot. Unless some firm somewhere has decoupled a stage by making a market at that stage, one cannot independently assess the economic profit earned at that stage. But the opportunities for meaningful analysis across a set of firms that have defined differently what they make versus what they buy and what they sell are

---

This teaching commentary was prepared by Professor John Shank of the Amos Tuck School.

often very significant. The fact that this is not always possible does not, in my view, negate the significance when it is possible.

Despite the calculational problems, I contend that every firm should attempt to estimate its value chain. Even the process of performing the value chain analysis, in and by itself, can be quite instructive. In my experience, I have found this exercise invaluable to managers by forcing them to carefully evaluate how their activities add value to the chain of customers who use their product (service).

A suggested solution is as follows:

A Process Flow Value Chain

	Regional Dairy		Branded OJ	
	Milk	OJ	MM/CH	Tropicana
Consumer Pays	$1.16	$1.50	$1.89	$2.26
Store Margin	.12	.30	.47	.47
Store Pays	1.04	1.20	1.42	1.79
Dairy/Juicer Margin	.09	.20	.25	?
Processor Cost	.87	.92	1.11	
Carton Cost	.08	.08	.06	

	Per Ton	Per Ton
Price to Processor	$1,152	$864
Converter Margin	318	30
Freight to Processor	10	10
Converter Cost 231	231	
Price to Converter*	593	593
Extruder Margin	(22)	(22)
Freight to Converter	35	35
Extruder Cost 94	94	
Price to Extruder*	486	486
Mill Margin 59	59	
Freight to Extruder	3	3
Mill Cost: Pulp	319	319
Other	105	105

*Estimated Market Value Transfer Prices. The converting operations have a "true" market price for sales to the processors. But how can we approximate "value" for intermediate products? Uncoated board in transferred internally from the mill to the extruder and coated board is transferred internally from the extruder to the converter. Sine uncoated and coated paperboard are also traded in external markets, we used the competitive market prices for the intermediate products. Calculating profit per ton for each value activity based on the competitive market price, as opposed to arbitrary accounting transfer prices, helps to identify the fundamental sources of economic value and allows each stage to be evaluated independently as show below.

Estimating a Market Price for Coated Board
(Extruder to Converter)

We exported 32,000 tons of Coated Board in 1987.

			Per Ton
Selling Price (Exhibit 5)			$577
Cost:	Mill Cost	$424	
	Freight to Extruder	3	
	Extruder Cost	94	
	Freight (plug)	19	
			540
	Margin		$ 37

Approximated market price between Extruder and Converter for Coated Board:

	Per Ton
Mill Cost	$424
Freight to Extruder	3
Extruder Cost	94
Freight to Converter	35
Margin (as above)	37
Approximated Market Price	$593

Estimating a Market Price for Uncoated Board
(Mill to Extruder)

In 1987, we sold 10,000 tons of uncoated board domestically and exported 12,000 tons.

		Per Ton
Selling Price (Exhibit 5)		$530
Cost: Mill Cost ($319 + $105)	$424	
Freight (plug)	47	
		471
Margin		$ 59

Approximated market price between Mill and Extruder for Uncoated Board

	Per Ton
Mill Cost ($319 + $105)	$424
Freight to Extruder	3
Margin (as above)	59
Approximated Market Price	$486

Question 2

A suggested solution is as follows:

Margins Per Ton of Board

	Regional Dairy				Branded OJ	
	Milk		OJ			
Store	$ 1,728		$ 4,320		$ 6,768	
Dairy/Juicer	1,296		2,880		3,600	
Converter	318		318		30	
Extruder	(22)	$355	(22)	$355	(22)	$67
Mill	59		59		59	
Total	$ 3,379		$ 7,555		$10,435	
CHAMPION %	11%		5%		0.6%	

New Insights? Does the information based on value chain analysis lead to new insights? We believe it does. Dramatically different strategic insights emerge when one considers the value chain analysis summarized above.

Of the total profit of $3,379 per ton of paperboard created in the commodity processor segment, DairyPak realized $355 (11 percent of the total value). In sharp contrast, in the differentiated processor segment, DairyPak's share of the total profit in the chain is only .6 percent! The buyer power in the differentiated segment is extremely strong! The average customer in the differentiated segment is much larger than the average commodity segment customer. Even though the carton is of higher quality and is much more a marketing tool in the differentiated segment, volume discounts and overall buyer power hold unit prices below those for the commodity carton. Thus, DairyPak actually does more work here with more assets for a lower sales price, on a per unit basis.

There is no particular reason, *ex ante*, to believe that 11 percent of the overall profit in the commodity segment is a "reasonable" or "unreasonable" share for the carton manufacturer versus the processor or the retailer. But, whatever the share is for the carton manufacturer in the commodity segment, the share *should be higher* in the differentiated segment where the carton is more expensive to make and is much more important as a point-of-sale marketing tool. Although DairyPak does not separate commodity end-use carton stock from differentiated end-use carton stock as it is produced, the differentiated end-use product must run slower to produce smoothness, thus yielding fewer tons per hour and higher cost per ton. For the share of overall profit to drop from 11 percent to .6 percent is dramatic evidence of the lack of seller power in the higher value segment. The $.06 carton price in the differentiated segment presumes a product which meets quality standards. That is, there is no way to charge more than $.06 (the prevailing price in this segment once the quality improvements are achieved.

Question 3

Estimated Asset Investment. Assets per ton of board at each value activity, are estimated using current replacement costs and assuming full utilization of capacity. Current replacement costs were estimated from discussions with plant engineers and equipment vendors. Tons of production at full capacity were estimated from discussions with manufacturing management and equipment vendors. With profit and assets, Return on Assets for each value stage is calculated as summarized below.

DairyPak's Return on Assets (ROA) in the commodity segment is 2 percent at the mill, negative at the extruder, and 38 percent at the converter. On the other hand, in the differentiated segment, the ROAs are 2 percent, negative, and 4 percent for the mill, extruder, and converter, respectively. This further reinforces the unattractiveness of the differentiated segment.

Return on Assets Per Ton of Board

| | Regional Dairy | | | | | | Branded OJ | | |
| | Milk | | | OJ | | | | | |
	Margin	*Assets*	*ROA*	*Margin*	*Assets*	*ROA*	*Margin*	*Assets*	*ROA*
Store*	$ 1,728	$ 1,800	96%	$ 4,320	$ 1,800	240%	$ 6,768	$ 1,800	376%
Dairy/Juicer	1,296	5,400	24%	2,880	2,890	100%	3,600	2,890	125%
Converter	318	830	38%	318	830	38%	30	830	4%
Extruder	(22)	190	negative	(22)	190	negative	(22)	190	negative
Mill	59	2,800	2%	59	2,800	2%	59	2,800	2%
Total	$ 3,379	$11,020	31%	$ 7,555	$ 8,510	89%	$10,435	$ 8,510	123%

*Gross margin level before store operating expenses.

From a conventional BCG-grid (Exhibit A, here), the differentiated processor segment would look extremely attractive. But, based on the value chain analysis, this market looks much less attractive. The differentiated processors have enormous leverage (buyer power). Why invest over $60 million to build market share in the differentiated segment where we are currently able to extract less than 1 percent of the total value created in the chain? This insight is neither apparent in the BCG-type strategic analysis nor in a conventional management accounting approach relying on DCF-based project returns from the capital investments (Exhibit C here). Further, conventional management accounting is of little help in quantifying buyer power since it ignores the total value created in the chain. It is highly unlikely that DiaryPak will be able to extract any more of the total value in the differentiated segment even after it matches it's leading competitor's investment, due to the buyers' tremendous bargaining power (unless the differentiated processors are willing to share some of their profit in order to entice an investment by a new competing supplier).

Question 4

On the choice or market segments, DairyPak considered three specific alternatives (see Exhibit B here). First, the company could continue to emphasize the commodity processors whose total market had been declining 3 percent a year but who had always been their main customers. Second, they could try to aggressively build market share with differentiated processors whose market was growing at 10 percent or more and who would pay top dollar for board (holding quantity discounts constant), but who demanded a consistent high quality.

Exhibit A

Boston Consulting Group Grid

	Low ← Relative Market Share → High	
High	Question Mark BUILD Branded OJ Export	Star HOLD
Market Growth		
	Dog DIVEST	Cash Cow Milk vs. OJ HARVEST
Low	Low	High

Relative Market Share

Where is DairyPak on this grid as of 1987?

- Regional Dairy Segment?

- Branded OJ Segment?

- Export Market?

Exhibit B

1. Commodity Dairies

Overall Size of the Market	375,000 Tons
Our Market Share	40%
New Volume in 1988	Nil. Stable Market

Opportunities?

- Uncertain supply of plastics. This is a by-product for the oil companies.

- Environmental indignation over plastics.

- Nutritionally, paper is better than plastics.

- Potential to realize price premium for cartons by working with dairies to create *differentiated* milk, just like the branded OJ?

2. Branded OJ Segment

	Size of the Market 1987	Annual Growth in "Base" Business (10%)	New Growth in OJ Consumption (5% of Base Business)	Total Growth in Volume
Tropicana	15,000 tons	1,500 tons	750 tons	2,250 tons
Minute Maid	10,000 tons	1,000 tons	500 tons	1,500 tons
Citrus Hill	7,000 tons	700 tons	350 tons	1,050 tons
	32,000 tons	3,200 tons	1,600 tons	4,800 tons

Champion's Potential Volume:

Growth in Volume in M/M + C-H	2,550 tons
25% of Volume from Tropicana as second viable supplier	
25% of (15,000 + 2,250)	4,300 tons
	6,850 tons

Is it worth the $62 million investment to chase this volume?

3. Export

Overall Size of the Market	1,112,000 Tons
Annual Growth	16%
New Volume in 1988	180,000 Tons

How about spending $1.75 million to participate in 180,000 tons of new potential business?

Exhibit C

Capital Investment Analysis for DairyPak Projects
(Per Internal Documents)

All Numbers Disguised

Differentiated Segment

Capital investments needed in year 0:

Primary manufacturing	$43	million
Third extruder	17	million
Rotogravure printing	1.5	million
Total	$61.5	million

Annual Cash Flows: Per Ton

Revenue (assumes a 30% price increase
due to a better quality board 7.7¢ × 14,400) $1,109   (Per carton price almost matches "standard" price of $.08)

Costs (per Exhibit 2)
$(319 + 105 + 3 + 91 + 35 + 234 + 10)$ (797)

Plus additional printing costs
(due to rotogravure printing)   (10)

Profit per ton   302

Total market (differentiated segment)	= 400,000 tons
Projected market growth	= 14%
Additional volume next year (400,000 × 14%)	= 56,000
Assume we can capture 50% of this additional volume	= 28,000
Plus a 5% increase in our share of the existing market	
(400,000 × 5%)	= 20,000
Additional Volume	48,000 tons*

*(We ignore additional growth beyond 1 year, to be conservative.)

Annual Cash Profits (48,000 × $302)	= $ 14.5 million
After-tax profits (40% tax rate)	= $ 8.7 million
Plus depreciation tax shield (straight-line depreciation for 10 years) $6.15 million × 40%	= $ 2.46 million
Total annual after-tax cash flows	$ 11.16 million

Time horizon for the project	= 10 years
Salvage value of the plant and equipment in year 10 (after tax)	= $ 3 million

All cash flows are in "real" dollars; inflation is not incorporated

Internal Rate of Return = approximately 13% (after tax, "real" return)

DairyPak recognized its weaknesses vis-a-vis the differentiated segment:

- Technologically obsolescent manufacturing. Most of the plant and equipment had been bought in the 1960's.

- Nagging problems with the quality of the board, caused by lack of up-to-date machinery.

- Limited extrusion capacity.

- Lack of rotogravure printing in the conversion plants.

Their low market share in the differentiated segment reflected their status as largely a "backup" supplier. Major capital investments (a total of $61.5 million) had to be made if DairyPak was serious about rebuilding market share in this fast growing segment. Three specific new investments would be:

- About $43 million to upgrade its primary manufacturing facility to improve board strength, printability, and smoothness.

- About $17 million to add a new extruder to compete in multilayered polymer coating applications. Differentiated processors required multiple coatings to extend the shelf life of products and to hold difficult products (liquids, for example).

- About $1.5 million to purchase a rotogravure printing press. Currently DairyPak printed the cartons with flexographic presses which use rubber printing rolls. This method is inexpensive but produces lower quality images. After the initial capital investment, the rubber plates cost about $150 each, with six needed for a standard six color process. Although the quality was not as good as with rotogravure printing, high quality printing had never been required by the commodity processors. Rotogravure printing uses etched metal printing rolls and gives an extremely precise and high quality finish—but it is expensive. After the initial capital expense, each etched metal printing plate costs $2,500. With a six color process, $15,000 must be spent for only one run. Once that run is complete, those etched cylinders will probably never be used again.

Third, DairyPak could push for a larger position in the Export market.

Conventional Analysis of the Strategic Options

How should DairyPak's senior executives evaluate the marketing and investment options open to them? Conventional capital expenditure requests, using discounted cash flow analyses had been prepared to "justify" the proposed investments (Exhibit C, here). These focused solely on projected "value added." Using assumptions recommended by the marketing group, these DCF analyses showed acceptable returns for investing $61.5 million to build market share in the differentiated segment.

Another way to address these options would be through the simple 2×2 growth/share matrix as originally introduced by the Boston Consulting Group (Exhibit A, here). Even though volume had been shrinking at 3 percent per year over the past five years, the firm had maintained market share at 40 percent in this large segment (375,000 tons per year). This segment appears to be the classic "cash cow" in the BCG terminology—"high market share with low-growth." The strategic inference from the BCG grid would be that Dairy Pak should "harvest" this commodity segment.

The firm, on the other hand, had a relatively modest 15% of the market in the differentiated package segment. The overall market in this segment was growing at 10% per year with projection to grow even faster in the future. DairyPak has a low market share in this high growth segment. The strategic inference from the BCG-grid would be to aggressively "build" market share in this segment by making the $61.5 million in new investments. This was, in fact, the prevailing sentiment within DairyPak at the time of the case. This point of view was supported by formal financial analysis using DCF techniques (Exhibit C, here), as indicated above. A 13 percent "real" return certainly argues for investing $61.5 million to build share in the differentiated segment.

An alternative way of viewing the problem, using different input assumptions, might yield different analytic inferences. For instance, value chain analysis, as we will show later, casts severe doubt on the assumption in Exhibit C that the differentiated segment will give DairyPak a 30% price increase.

Strategic Analysis—A Value Chain Perspective

Organizing the information in the value chain framework provides a *fundamentally different* view of the marketing and investment options. Question 2 and 3 above summarize the inferences from the value chain framework.

As noted:

- There are very few buyers in the differentiated segment—fewer than ten versus more than 1,000 in the commodity segment.

- Buyers are very large.

- The average order size tends to be quite large.

- Differentiators typically keep two or more sources of supply. Poor service, quality, or uncompetitive prices are punished by cuts in order size.

- Plastic has several attractive features as a packaging material—break resistance, design versatility, eye appeal, printability. Plastic poses a more significant threat to coated board in the differentiated segment since this segment values more highly the marketing appeal of the package. This substitution threat sets a cap on paperboard carton prices and a corresponding cap on investment returns, once the overwhelming buyer power is factored into the analysis.

Buyer power can be summarized as in Exhibit D here.

Overall, the value chain perspective yields a much different picture of this industry. It appears to be an industry where the closer one gets to the end-use customer and the more one creates product differentiation, the more money will be make. DairyPak seems to lose on both counts. They lack the ability to forward integrate into the processor and supermarket segments. Further, we have already argued that they lack the product quality to successfully compete as a supplier to the differentiated processor segment. What should they do? Their position is similar to having failed to improve your hand in the draw in a poker game. Do you put more money in the pot, even if you know you have a bad hand? Do you fold? Or do you stay in as long as possible without adding much to the pot?

- Instead of de-emphasizing the commodity segment as would be recommended by the BCG-type analysis, they need to find ways to effectively compete in the commodity segment by being the low cost producer. Here again, the value chain framework can provide important insights. They need to understand the structural and executional drivers of cost behavior for the major cost items in the mill, extruder, and converter operations. They then need to manage these drivers better than the competitors. Staying in the commodity segment is the only logical choice. The attractiveness of this option is further enhanced by possible significant growth in commodity carton demand in export markets. Their manufacturing system is geared to this market, and their reputation has been made in this market. Also, they have a low investment base to support this business, since most of the plant and equipment were bought before 1970. Major new investments are not required to compete here.

- Looking at the economics of the mill, extruder, and converting operations, DairyPak is currently destroying value (rather than creating value) by selling in the differentiated segment. Also, the profitability at the mill is well below satisfactory levels. A cost driver analysis at the mill and extruder stages might go a long way in identifying profit improvement opportunities. Such analysis is beyond the scope of this case.

The SCM-value chain perspective thus extends our ability to achieve meaningful managerial cost analysis. A summary of the key differences between value chain and traditional management accounting perspectives is shown in Exhibit E here.

Since virtually no two companies compete in exactly the same set of value activities, value chain analysis is a critical first step in understanding how a firm is positioned in its industry. Building sustainable competitive advantage requires a knowledge of the full linked set of value activities of which the firm and its competitors are a part.

Once the value chain is fully articulated, critical strategic decisions regarding make/buy and forward/backward integration become clearer. Investment decisions can be viewed from the perspective of their impact on the overall chain and the firm's position within it. For strategic decision making, cost analysis today cannot afford to ignore this critical dimension.

Teaching Strategy

I use this case to introduce the value chain analysis in the required course on managerial accounting. I assign it with the value chain technical note as background for the students.

The case can be covered in one class period. In class I go through the assignment questions in order, using the suggested analysis from this commentary.

Exhibit C
Buyer Power Analysis

	Commodity Dairies	Branded OJ Products
Number of Buyers (buyer concentration)	1,000	3
Size of Buyer, as a Corporation	Relatively Small	Same size as the paperboard manufacturers
Average Customer Volume	375 Tons (375,000 tons/1,000)	Tropicana 15,000 tons M/M 10,000 tons C-0H 7,000 tons
Buyer Switching Costs	Low. Buy commodity board	High. Buy differentiated board
Ability to backward integrate into paperboard	Nil. Do not buy in volume for a scale efficient plant	Nil. Do not buy in volume for a scale efficient plant
Substitutes products relative to paperboard	Plastic, others?	Plastic, glass, others?
Cost of Carton/Total Cost	8.5% (8¢/95¢)	5% (6¢/117¢)
Buyers' Margin	8.6% (9¢/104¢)	17.6% (25¢/142¢)
Value Extracted by Segments		
Champion's share of margins as % of Total Margins	11%	0.6%
Champion's ROA	9%	2%

Exhibit E

	Traditional Management Accounting	**Value Chain Analysis in the SCM Framework**
Focus	Internal	External
Perspective	Value-added raw material suppliers to ultimate	Entire set of linked activities from end use customers

Cost Driver Concept	• A single fundamental cost driver pervades the literature—Cost is a function of volume	• Multiple cost drivers
		  • Structural drivers (examples: scale, scope, experience, technology, complexity)
		  • Executional drivers (examples: participative management, total quality management, plant layout)

	• Applied too often, only at the overall firm level	• Each value activity has a set of unique cost drivers
Cost Containment Philosophy	• Cost reduction approached via responsibility centers or via product cost issues	• Cost containment is a function of the cost driver(s) regulating each value activity
		• Exploit linkages with suppliers
		• Exploit linkages with customers
		• "spend to save"
Insights for Strategic Decisions	None are readily apparent. This is a major reason why the strategic consulting firms typically throw away the conventional reports as they begin their cost analyses	• Identify cost drivers at the individual activity level; develop cost/differentiation advantage either by controlling those drivers better than competitors or by reconfiguring the value chain (examples: Federal Express in mail delivery, MCI in long distance telephone)

		• For each value activity, ask strategic questions pertaining to:
		  • make versus buy
		  • forward/backward integration

		• Quantify and assess "supplier power" and "buyer power"; exploit linkages with suppliers and buyers

CHAPTER 3
BEHAVIOR IN ORGANIZATIONS

Changes from the Eighth Edition

This chapter retains the basic thrust of the eighth edition.

Cases

Rendell Company focuses on the responsibility of the division controller.

National Tractor and Equipment Company is a vehicle to discuss the proper limits on the function of the controller.

Rendell Company

Objectives and Approach

Rendell focuses primarily on the divisional controller and his relationship to the corporate controller. However, Rendell also describes conflicting views about the function of the corporate controller, so it can be used to discuss this issue also.

The proper role of the division controller is one that is debated heatedly and repeatedly. The principal arguments used on both sides of this debate are contained in this case. In part, of course, the solution in a particular company depends on the personalities of the executives in that company. In discussing the problem, we should like, if feasible, to exclude the influence of personalities, and see if we can find general principles that are, at least to a certain extent, independent of the particular personalities involved.

Comments on Questions

1. There can be considerable difference of opinion as to what the organizational philosophy of the Martex Co. actually is. If we accept the literal reading of the controller's responsibility as set forth in Exhibit 1, then we must conclude that the controller is actually acting as an administrator, because a function of administration is certainly to "question the failure and recommend changes to accomplish the desired results" of the work done by the division managers. If the controller really does this, then he is acting in the way that an executive vice president normally would act. This is made even more specific by the statement in the next paragraph that disputes between the controller and the division managers are referred to the president for resolution. Personally, I don't believe the controller, in fact, acts the way the position description says. I would believe this only if the controller were, in fact, an executive vice president, which I doubt that he is. He is not the division manager's "boss," and without this superior-subordinate relationship, I doubt that he actually is performing the function specified. More likely, he is raising pointed questions on a good many items that affect profit, but I think that his authority stops at the point of raising these questions. It is unlikely that he answers these questions, either in the sense of deciding the action that should be taken or in the sense of formulating new policies for the division. However, others may argue that the controller can and does perform the functions just as they are stated in Exhibit 1.

   I certainly would not advocate this policy for the Rendell Company. I believe that the controller at all levels should be an adviser to management, but that he should never exercise

This case was prepared by Robert N. Anthony.

Copyright © 1964 by the President and Fellows of Harvard College. Harvard Business School case 109-033.

authority over managers. Again, there is a difference of opinion on this point, and particularly there is room for advocacy of some difficult-to-define role that lies between the extremes of purely advisory work and of purely line authority.

2. In order to decide the person to whom the divisional controller should report, it may be useful to consider first what his function should be. I think his function should be to collect actual accounting and other data on performance, following prescribed rules; to *assist* in preparing the budget; and to analyze results so as to inform the division general manager of trouble spots and possibilities for improvement. In connection with both the second and the third of these functions, it should be emphasized that the division controller is *assisting* the general manager. It is the general manager who makes the crucial decisions that shape the budget, not the controller. It is the general manager who takes action on the trouble spots that are located, not the controller.

   If this is a valid statement of the divisional controller's functions, then it seems reasonable that the division controller should report to the division general manager.

   Other arguments on both sides of this question are presented in Mr. Bevins' comments in the first part of the case and Mr. Harrigan's comments toward the end of the text. I think these arguments boil down to the essential question of whether the divisional controller is to be regarded as an adviser to the general manager or whether he is to be regarded as a headquarters representative, which is a polite way of saying "front-office spy."

   Various specific instances might be posed in getting at this question. For example, suppose that the personnel department wants to add one man, making a total of six. Who should decide whether this man can be added, the controller or the division manager? If the former, what is the general manager's responsibility for running the division? Another example would be deciding on the size of the research budget, or the advertising budget.

3. In line with my answer to the above question, I would suggest that the corporate controller should exercise what is called "functional control" over the division controllers. This means that the corporate controller should prescribe the details of systems, definitions, and rules for the collection of figures and other information that affect more than one division, including financial accounting, budgeting, capital budgeting, and the like. The corporate controller should decide questions of information handling that affect more than one division, such as the acquisition of a computer to do the work of several divisions. He should study and at least suggest the use of new procedures and techniques for the better performance of the controller's work in the divisions. Very importantly, the corporate controller should educate the division controllers in better ways to perform their jobs. This education process may involve formal courses, informal meetings for an exchange of views, or even an analysis and constructive criticisms of work that flows up to the corporate office from the divisions. In the Rendell situation, there is no evidence that much attention is given to this education process, I expect that this is an explanation of the difficulties that apparently exist.

4. In line with the above comment, I personally think no basic change in responsibility is needed. Arguments can be made for detailed shifts, and these will generally be in the direction of shift of responsibility up to the corporate controller, but the dangers of going too far with this have been suggested above.

Summary

We have here a corporation that once was highly profitable but which has become less profitable in recent years. A new, aggressive management has come aboard and is attempting to turn the company around. The new management wants to move fast and make important changes. As a part of this effort, it wishes to introduce modern control concepts in a situation in which the control has been fairly backward.

The division controllers, brought up in the old-fashioned way of doing things are less responsive to change than the management wishes. Two of these have already been replaced with younger men who presumably, have the new outlook. Five are still there. The division managers, also, have not been used to the new way of doing things.

The controller sees an opportunity to speed up the process of change, both change in the attitude of the controller and in the division managers. He proposes to have the division managers report to him, and then he will have a freer hand in training them, exhorting them, influencing them in the new techniques, and through them, influencing their managers.

I personally believe this effort won't work. Ultimately, the controllers will be useful only as they assist their division managers. The managers run the divisions. If the controllers are not viewed by the managers as useful advisers, the managers will not rely on the division controllers for advice. They will be viewed as spies, as irritants, rather than as helpers. Therefore, I would counsel the corporate controller to restrain his impatience, to be willing to work a little more slowly, to achieve his aims by a process of education, by attempting to change the organization's relationships.

RNA

Case 3-2

National Tractor and Equipment Company

Approach

This case can be used for either or both of two purposes: (1) to discuss methods of analyzing performance, particularly techniques for decomposing the difference between actual performance and a standard into the elements that account for the difference; and (2) to discuss the proper limits on the function of the controller. The following discussion deals with each of these points in turn.

Discussion

It is noteworthy that the company recognized that it has a problem even though the return on investment for Type X tractors is the highest it has been in recent years. The whole market has expanded, thus producing good profits for everyone, but the problem is that National has for the first time dropped behind Competitor A. Hence, the analysis described in the case.

The question arises: Why is this analysis being made? Its purpose is to quantify, insofar as possible, the reasons for the difference in volume between National and Competitor A. In order to analyze National's performance, we must compare it with some standard, and here Competitor A is being used as the standard. Quantification of the reasons for the difference is helpful for essentially two purposes: (1) so that attention can be focused on the most important reasons, and thus avoid frittering away time, effort, and discussion on causes which although present are of minor consequence, and (2) to have a basis of judging the significance of explanations offered by the parties at interest. For example, accepting the figures at face value, if the sales department says that the explanation has to do with the larger owner body of Competitor A, we see from the analysis that this explains at the most only 700 units out of the 3,093 difference. Such an alibi is, therefore, by no means a complete explanation. (There is a tendency, which the "owner body" matter illustrates, to blame poor performance on some noncontrollable outside factor.)

Having established the above, I then proceed to the analysis, going through Exhibit 1, line by line. First of all, we see that the purpose of this exhibit is solely to explain the 3,093 difference between National and Competitor A. The analysis does not compare National with itself in the past or National with a budgeted standard, which are the other two possibilities. (In the following discussion, I shall restrict myself mostly to 1975, but the same analysis, of course, can be made for the earlier years.)

This case was prepared by Robert N. Anthony.

The first cause is the fire. It is important to note that the 1,500 figure has a specific narrow meaning; namely, that 1,500 customers who would have bought Competitor A's tractors in 1974, in fact, waited until 1975. It does not indicate the total effect of the fire on Competitor A since another consequence, the shift of Competitor A's customers to some other brand because they were unwilling to wait, is in no way taken into account.

The sales to government agencies item is exactly what is said, and raises no problem.

The owner body item is a fascinating one to discuss. The analysis is described in considerable detail, both in the exhibit and in the text of the case. It sounds like a very ingenious and plausible analysis. However, careful study shows that the difference in owner body between National and Competitor A is, in fact, not reflected in the slightest in the figures; that is, although the arithmetic leading to the 700 difference is impeccable, the logic behind this arithmetic is something that I have never been able to work out despite a good deal of effort. I believe that what we have here is the multiplication of one number with another without any underlying rationale for doing so.

The product differences figure we must accept on faith. It is significant that the figure is getting worse from year to year.

CHAPTER 4
RESPONSIBILITY CENTERS:
REVENUE AND EXPENSE CENTERS

Changes from the Eighth Edition

This chapter retains the basic thrust of the eighth edition. The discussion on discretionary centers (Administrative Centers, R&D Centers, and Marketing Centers) is tightened.

Cases

New Jersey Insurance Company introduces the problem of controlling discretionary costs in the context of a legal department of a life insurance company.

Whiz Calculator Company continues the emphasis on discretionary costs with a focus on control over the marketing function.

Westport Electric Company examines the control issues over legal and training staffs.

Grand Jean Company is new to this edition and is an excellent mid-term exam case on responsibility center structure and control.

Case 4-1

New Jersey Insurance Company

Approach

This case introduces the problem of controlling discretionary costs. The situation, the legal department of a life insurance company, is a particularly striking one since it should be obvious that relatively little can be done to established the "correct" level of cost and relatively little emphasis should be placed on cost control and relatively much emphasis on assuring a good quality of legal work.

Comments on Questions

1. Mr. Somersby probably depends largely on personal observation to control the operations of the sections of his division; that is, he observes what is going on and discusses the situation with his section leaders, and this is the main basis he has for judgments as to how well things are going. In addition, and as probably a relatively minor part of his work, he pays some attention to the comparison of actual cost versus budgeted cost and to the preparation of the budget underlying this. The process of sitting down and agreeing on the budget for a year is a means of exercising control, and an important one.

   Top management is exercising a similar kind of control with Mr. Somersby. In addition, top management has various other devices that relate to the control of the law division. For example, there are company policies regarding salaries, steady employment, practices of various kinds, all of which tend to restrict and hence to control operations. The basic decisions governing what the law department is to do (for example, the decision that it is to do relatively little work on corporate loans) helps control operations of the division.

2. Although students can and will suggest many additional statistics that might be gathered or control devices instituted, I personally doubt whether any of them are worth the effort in this situation. Some of these suggestions relate to a better means of measuring the work load in the law department, such as the number of contracts processed in the individual sections. Suggestions of this type are more palatable to me than others, but even here I am not sure how useful the information would be if one had it. Suggestions for a stricter control over the individual loan contracts are, I think, not practicable.

3. Probably, the individual loan section's overrun on its budget reflects additional work load. I would first want to assure myself that this is so. The figures raise the possibility of adding an additional person to this section and hence reducing the overtime by a more than an

This case was prepared by J. Hekimian (under the direction of Robert N. Anthony).

offsetting amount. Of course, this would be done only if the additional work load, in fact, existed, and if it were expected to continue to exist; otherwise, no permanent addition should be made because of the company's policy of level employment.

In the corporate loan section, the problem is somewhat the opposite. Here the section is apparently undermanned, and one wonders why this is so and what, if anything, should be done about it. In effect, the questions relate to why the section is not spending enough rather than why it is spending too much. It may be desirable to raise questions about some of the individual overruns just to indicate to Mr. Somersby that Mr. Montgomery is aware of the importance of keeping control over costs.

The basic question that this case raises is whether the whole attempt to exercise control through the budget is worth the effort involved. The effort is clearly not great, but neither is it possible to do much about assuring efficiency in a situation like the law department. Personally, I think the budget and the attempt to compare budget and actual is worthwhile. In the first place, the budget of the law department is one figure which must be worked in with others to see whether the projected profit of the whole company is satisfactory. If the overall profit is not satisfactory, some action must be taken somewhere, and the law department provides one such place to look at. In the second place, the mere act of preparing the budget and occasionally comparing actual cost with budget tends to make people be more concerned about waste than would otherwise be the case. In this sense, the budget is a device for dampening the influence of Parkinson's first law.

RNA

Case 4-2

Whiz Calculator Company

Approach

This case deals with budgeting the cost of getting business (more accurately, the cost of *trying* to get business) and controlling the sales organization. These costs should be contrasted with production costs and the costs of handling and filling orders (packing, warehousing, billing, shipping, etc.); the latter are jobs for which standards can be set with about the same degree of certainty as standards for factory costs.

There may well be some discussion on the technique of setting the proposed standards. The chart in Exhibit 2 shows how this was done; the slope of the line was determined by one method, and one point on the line was decided upon by another method; from these data the formula for the line could be easily computed. The procedure is open to criticism because the variable rate was determined by one means and the total expense as of 65 percent of capacity was determined by another. The fixed allowance has no significance other than as part of the formula. Moreover, since regression is based on historical data, and the calculator industry has been dynamic, the appropriateness of regression for budget setting is questionable.

It may be well to spend considerable time comparing the figures of Exhibit 1 with the figures in Exhibit 3. The differences between performance measured against the fixed budget and performance measured against the variable budget have reasonable explanations which can be deduced, and the deductions show something about the nature of the items. Exhibit 1 was the budget under which the Branch Manager actually worked; s/he of course had no knowledge of the budget allowances of Exhibit 3. This will illustrate the difference between engineered, discretionary, and committed costs.

Although the comments below are made item by item, my experience in class on an item-by-item basis has been unsatisfactory. I have better luck when I ask Question 1 as given, and permit students to classify the items in any order they choose. Usually they start with sales force compensation which is perhaps the easiest. Advertising is a good item to take up next if students do not select one.

The contrast between an imposed budget and a self-imposed budget, which is one of the differences between the present and the proposed procedure, may well be alluded to:

This case was prepared by James S. Reece.

Comments on Questions

Question 1

My deductions are as follows:

Executive Salaries: Entirely fixed by executive decision. Budget is the same amount on both reports.

Office Salaries: Actual is practically the same as the fixed budget; over on variable budget. Deduction: Varies according to Branch Manager's decision; s/he made it equal the budget allowance. If s/he had been operating on a variable budget, s/he probably could have made actual equal that allowance. The theory of variable allowance would be to *permit* more office help when sales were better; but this increment would not necessarily be needed.

Sales Force Compensation: Under on fixed budget because sales are under; no variance on variable budget. Deduction: Varies directly with sales, is caused by sales; salespersons are paid straight commission of 5 percent.

Travel Expense: Under on fixed budget; over on variable. Can't deduce for sure, but looks as if the variance may indicate either 1) not enough traveling done (by $293) to produce budgeted sales volume, in which case this is bad performance, or 2) too much traveling done (by $288) for the sales that were obtained, which is also bad performance.

Stationery, Office Supplies, and Postage: Probably partly variable with sales volume.

Light and Heat: Seasonable influence probably accounts for favorable variance on both budgets.

Subscriptions and Dues: Same as Office Salaries.

Donations: Same as Office Salaries; note how close Branch Manager was keeping to the permitted expenditure in the year-to-date column.

Advertising: Same as Office Salaries.

Social Security Taxes: Allowances on both forms determined mathematically from salary items.

Rental Depreciation: Clearly fixed expense; same allowance on both budgets.

Other Branch Expense: Under on fixed; over on variable. Shows expenses were not high against a standard based on $310,000 sales, but were too high against a standard based on $261,000 sales. (The unfavorable variation on the variable budget would have disappeared if sales had been over $310,000.)

Question 2

From the above analysis, we may conclude:

1. Some selling expenses, principally commissions (often *only* commissions), vary directly and automatically with sales volume. these are "engineered costs."

2. Some are fixed without regard to sales volume or short-run Branch Manager decisions. These include executive costs, rent, depreciation, and probably heat and light. These are either "discretionary" or "committed" costs.

3. Many expenses vary, but the variation is not *caused* by sales volume; it is the direct result of the Branch Manager's decision. The apparent tendency for it to vary with volume often reflects only *permission* to spend more when sales are high. Items in this category include office salaries, travel expense, subscriptions and dues, donations, advertising, supplies, postage, and other. These are also "discretionary" costs.

4. Neither budget is a real standard for measuring the job done. They show how dollars were spent compared with permitted expenditures (like a child accounting to his parent) but not the results accomplished. To emphasize this, I ask a student, "How did Branch A do in October?" Better students will answer that we cannot tell, because there are no data on *sales* results versus plans. (The $310,000 "budget" in Exhibit 1 is apparently just 1/12 the annual budget, so it is meaningless if there is any seasonality in sales—as there undoubtedly is.)

Question 3

Which type of budget should be used? A better way of asking this question may be: Was Mr. Reisman correct in believing that the variable budget technique which he had used in controlling manufacturing expenses was adaptable to the control of sales expenses?

The philosophy behind the fixed budget seems to be: since you don't know what optimum expenses are or how to judge performance precisely, you set up fixed allowances which show what you will permit the sales organization to spend. The comparison of actual to budget, therefore, shows only how well the sales organization carried out your orders regarding spending. The fixed budget has the advantage of focusing emphasis on keeping expenses within a certain dollar limit, but unless actual sales equal the budget it cannot possibly be a good standard for variable items like commissions, and it may lead to unwise action, e.g., failure to increase certain expenses when sales drop. The president evidently likes the variable budget because he assumes that sales expense is a function of sales; therefore, he will permit the organization to spend as much as they want provided they show results in terms of sales volume. Actually, for many items the apparent correlation between sales ad costs really reflects only the fact that when sales increased the organization was *permitted* to spend more. There is no reason to believe that, with respect to many items, it was *necessary* to spend more in order to get increased sales.

The variable budget handles commission easily, but—

a. It may legalize an apparent, but fallacious, correlation between sales and expense unless it is understood. (Most of the variable allowances should mean, "We will permit you to spend more when sales increase because we can afford it, not because it *is necessary* that you spend more.")

b.   By forcing expenses to expand the contract with sales, you may permit waste in times of high sales volume and force unwise cuts when sales drop, which may cause sales to drop even further.

But neither of these is the final answer. Either may stifle good plans (e.g., spend more money for traveling to cover a new segment of the market, which will throw the budget way off but which may produce good incremental revenues to the company. Selling is not a standard job (except perhaps at the lower levels in some organizations). You can't use a standard with the same degree of definiteness that you use them in the factory. But neither can you eliminate all control, as the quotation at the end of the case would suggest. Branch managers need to be cost conscious, but also need to feel that exercising good judgment is more important than meeting *monthly* allowances on *individual* expense items.

I prefer the present method to the new proposal. Most importantly, if the company does not now have extensive sales reports and *gross margin* variance analyses (note that Exhibit 1 is called a sales and expense report, which may suggest a lack of other sales reports), these are more important than trying to accomplish the impossible with discretionary costs.

If time permits, I ask students if they would have a preference between treating a branch as 1) a revenue center with a selling expense budget, or 2) a profit center (which requires a transfer price mechanism). In either instance, only sales volume and selling expenses are controllable, so many students don't see any real difference between these two alternatives. The revenue center approach does not give the Branch Manager a clear signal on revenue-expense tradeoffs (e.g., should $500 be spent for a local advertisement that is expected to increase revenues by $2,000?). The profit center approach tells the manager to trade off incremental selling expenses and added *contribution*, which is the relevant trade-off (e.g., the manager tries to determine if the $500 ad will increase contribution by more than $500, which is necessary for the ad to increase *company profit*).

Question 4

Since the company sells a "complete line" of calculators, including many types, sizes and perhaps qualities, it is probable that a dollar measure is the only feasible way of expressing sales activity in the branches. Some nondollar measures, such as units, might be appropriate as a measuring stick in the factory, but the possible distortions arising from the use of a dollar figure in the factory are not as likely to be important in the control of selling costs. As a matter of fact, it is often said that the job of the sales organization is to "generate dollars."

Question 5

This question is especially important if the instructor did not assign the Societa Rigazio case, or otherwise has not raised the issue of drawing inferences about monthly expenses from a regression based on annual data. The regression line is Expense = 294 + 9.2514 Sales (000), with $R^2 = .998$. Students who have learned regression mechanics in a business statistics or similar course, but have forgotten some of the underlying assumptions, will be tempted to say that the above equation implies a monthly flexible budget formula of $25 (= $294 / 12) plus $0.0093 per dollar of sales, analogous with the formulas in Exhibit 3 of the case. The fallacy with this (assuming some validity of using regression in the first place) is that short-run costs are more fixed with respect to volume fluctuations than are longer-run costs. For example, if sales fall "permanently," perhaps an office worker can be laid off; but the branch in all likelihood cannot fire and rehire such a person several times during the year as seasonality in sales (or some other factor) causes volume to fluctuate from month to month.

Even on an annual basis, interpretation of the equation must be cautious. I made up the data for this question by first assuming the expenses was purely variable with sales, and then modifying each year's expense figure with a small random error (positive or negative). The result is that expense as a percent of sales ranges from a low of 0.9268% to a high of 0.9404% for the data given. Thus, for example, if the branch had had a purely variable budget for this item at, say 0.9344% of sales, small favorable or unfavorable spending variances would have caused the regression line to have a fixed component, and for the slope to be 0.9251% instead of 0.9344%.

I feel the data in Exhibit 3 suggest both possible errors just mentioned. For example, the monthly formula for office salaries is not intuitively meaningful: assuming there are two office workers (since the *annual* budget implied by Exhibit 1 is $17,400), Exhibit 3 implies that one worker is guaranteed enough time each month to pay him or her $139, and then he or she, plus the second worker, are paid by the hour as needed for any work above this minimum, the extra work being solely a function of that month's sales dollars. (The formula is scarcely more meaningful if annualized to a $1,668 minimum.) Similarly, it is quite possible that branch managers have been told over the years to spend about one percent of annual sales for local advertising, and that the $35 indicated fixed component ($420 per year) reflects random past spending variances, as described above for the hypothetical data.

Case 4-3

Westport Electric Corporation

I usually start out by asking the class whether they think that King is right about the legal and training staffs. This brings up the problem of expertise. How can King be an expert on training programs, for example? If he is not an expert, how can he evaluate efficiency? Also, if he is right about either legal or training, how do we know that there are not even more inefficient staff operations than these two about which he does not know? I try to bring the class around to seeing how difficult it is for a manager of staff budgets to evaluate the efficiency of the different staff operations.

After we have established that the accounting staff cannot evaluate the efficiency or effectiveness of the staff officers, I ask if it is not the president's job to make this evaluation. After some discussion, we generally conclude that the president is probably even less capable of evaluating staff efficiency and effectiveness in a large company than the budget manager. First, he probably has no expertise in most staff areas. Secondly, he has not the time to oversee adequately what each staff office is doing. Thirdly, he probably receives better than average service from these offices and is not in a position to see their faults.

Finally, I ask the class what they would do about this situation if they were president of Westport. I get several different suggestions, the most important of which are:

1. Appoint an administrative vice president over all (or most all) of the staff activities. (This action was mentioned in the text.)

2. Periodically, hire outside consultants to review the activities of each staff office and give a confidential report. (I usually ask about the possible problems that might occur with this approach.)

3. Try to get information on what other companies are spending on the different staff activities. There are certain services available that provide information on the relative number of people in the various staff activities of different types of companies. (When this is suggested, I usually ask about the limitations of this data, assuming it is available. Particularly in view of the size of Westport, would other company experience be comparable?)

4. Adopt zero base budgeting. This is a system where each staff has to justify its entire proposed expenditure each year. When this comes up, I ask the class about the advantages and disadvantages of this method and whether it really solves the basic question.

After the above points (as well as any other suggestions) have been put on the board and discussed, I summarize the alternatives. Then, I explain that there is really no pat answer to this case. The important point is for management to be aware that the problem of goal congruity exists at the staff level and to try to take some actions to at least mitigate the problems. My own preference for action is to appoint an administrative vice president.

JD

Case 4-4

Grand Jean Company

Question 1

Corporate: Generate profits (maximize revenues/minimize costs), earn satisfactory rate of return on owners' investment, meet customers' needs, maintain price and quality, grow or maintain market share, promote employee welfare & community relations, maintain loyal and reliable outside suppliers to supplement internal capacity (invisible to customer), long-term contracts minimize capital investment and provide stability to product demand allowing internal flexibility to change product mix to meet short-term market variations.

Internal Mfg Plants: Maintain cost efficient operations, meet market demands, maintain reliable and quality standards, keep employees happy & good community relations. Compare to most efficient outsiders.

Marketing: Maximize sales revenue, maintain market share, sales mix, and price effectiveness.

Question 2

Strengths: Clear assignment of responsibility for sales revenue/marketing and manufacturing output/costs, encourages product development and awareness of customer needs, integrated budget with monthly revisions to reflect market changes, realistic and timely standards for productivity assessment and cost control, reasonably clear and objective measures of performance, bonus determined by overall performance encourages all managers to strive for higher corporate profits, timely feedback on plant performance, internal production flexibility to meet changing market demand.

Weaknesses: No clear statement of corporate goals and objectives, consistently failing to meet customer demand, top-down setting of plant targets with no plant manager participation, emphasis on monthly quotas and performance measurement leads to manipulation of output reporting, lost sales and profits, production schedule changes increase costs, corporate staff receive higher rewards than plant managers, VP Operations has bias to his past, standards and staff ratio fixation, no non-financial measures such as employee turnover, absenteeism rates, community activity, share of the market, marketing performance not linked to share of the market, old vs. new plant equipment may distort standards and targets at individual plants, lack of timely information to corporate.

Question 3

This is a tough change. Although profit center responsibility at plant level will overcome hoarding, there are other factors that the plant manager does not control such as market growth, sales price, sales mix, and production assignment. Wicks or someone else will have to integrate sales forecasts with who makes what, how much, and when? Profit center adds realism, but plant manager controls only manufacturing costs, worker assignments, training, production schedule, plant staff, and possibly investments in plant assets. Old and new assets may be a problem.

Investments in new assets will increase depreciation expenses. Managers will maximize capacity to generate more profit since all goods have market.

Rather than implement such a radical change, have Wicks change his approach on monthly quota adjustments. Once a year changes may eliminate month to month boarding.

Question 4

The choice of a transfer price is difficult. The Marketing Departments will remain revenue centers. Choice (a) is certainly objective and reliable since it is the market determined price to retailers. However, the difference between this price and the plant's manufacturing costs will be a very large gross profit. Unless other corporate expenses are assigned to the Plants, the profit margin will exceed that of the corporation. Therefore it lacks room and internal plants cannot be compared to efficient outside contractors.

Option (b) is better than (a) since it builds a fixed gross profit percentage on full-standard costs. But it adds little to cost control if plants are inefficient and standard costs/times too high. Of course, a fair percentage markup must be less than (a) and problems are what is fair and who decides? May not necessarily motivate plants to operate at capacity, since standard costs cover all manufacturing costs at different levels. It depends on how markup is determined.

Choice (c) seems best for comparison purposes and realism. The nature of the *garment* industry forces outside contractors to operate efficiently if they are to be profitable and survive. Wicks' knowledge of company owned plant standards helps him monitor contractors as well as internal plants. This is a market based wholesale selling price that competitors are likely paying. It is best for applying a realistic profit center to the plants. Gross margin is not as high as (a) and not fixed as in (b).

—Joe San Miguel

CHAPTER 5
PROFIT CENTERS

Changes from the Eighth Edition

This chapter retains the basic thrust of the eighth edition. The chapter has been rewritten to highlight three aspects: (a) considerations involved in constituting business units as profit centers; (b) considerations involved in constituting functional departments (such as manufacturing department) as profit centers; (c) considerations involved in choosing the appropriate metric to measure profit center performance (examples: contribution, profit before tax, etc.)

Cases

Profit Center Problems is new to this edition. This case introduces the considerations involved in designing profit centers.

North Country Auto case deals with the classic control problems in an auto dealership (this field base case replaces the Bultman Automobiles case).

Polysar Limited is a vehicle to discus the budgeting and performance measurement issues in setting up profit centers.

Abrams Company is a good review case in setting up responsibility centers.

Case 5-1

Profit Center Problems

The teaching plan for this set of problems can be obtained by writing to:

Dr. Anil K. Gupta
Maryland Business School
The University of Maryland
College Park, MD 20742
Tel: (301) 405-2221
        (301) 951-0162
Fax: (301) 951-0262

Case 5-2

North Country Auto, Inc.

This case has been revised to incorporate all the richness of the earlier Bultman Automobiles case. Since this case is based on a field study, this case reflects the current context of auto dealerships.

Prologue

We never thought we could replace the Bultman Automobiles case. Over the years, our students have noticed several problems with the Bultman case. One of my colleagues, Joe Fisher, developed a case on an auto dealership at Hanover, NH. The case is contemporary, raises all the control system issues that the old Bultman Automobiles case did, but avoids the problems with the Bultman case. We have had excellent success with the North Country Auto case. Students also feel better about a 1990 case!

Instructors can still benefit from the various teaching notes for the Bultman Automobiles case. We have reproduced below the detailed teaching note prepared by the author of the North Country Auto case, Joe Fisher.

I. Introduction

Some of the issues included in this case are:

A. The proper structuring of profit centers.

B. The motivational aspects of transfer pricing.

C. The motivational aspects of capitalizing vs. expensing repairs.

D. Distribution of losses on trade-in cars.

E. The best measure of profit for both motivational and compensation design.

Implicit in resolving these five issues is a definition of the mission of each department and how they contribute to achieving the mission of the dealership as a whole.

II. NCA's Competitive Situation and Mission

North Country Auto (NCA) is a small rural dealership that incurs higher cost per vehicle sold than its higher volume counterparts in more densely populated areas. The cost of operating three separate product lines with relatively low sales volume will make it difficult for NCA to compete as the low cost seller.

The exact calculation of franchise profitability by function (i.e., new, used, parts, service, body, and oil) is beyond the scope of the case, but it is important to understand that the required minimum investment in inventory, parts, technicians, showroom space, and management for each franchise will require NCA to achieve higher average gross margins to offset lower unit volume. Gross margins of 7.6 percent in the new car sales department, however, are extremely low compared with normal industry averages of 15 – 20 percent.

Given the current slump in vehicle sales, it is unrealistic to assume that NCA can substitute higher margins for lower volume.

One possible strategy for NCA in selling both new and used cars would be to offer the highest "value" to its customers by offering superior service after the initial sale. The back end serves the dual purpose of developing a base of customers who are loyal to the dealership and providing NCA with a steady stream of income to hedge against cyclical demand in the front end. In a small town where the market size is limited and the number of repeat purchases is potentially high, reputation replaces "deal" making as the key competitive advantage. NCA's back end is involved in the largest number of transactions. Its success will ultimately determine that of the dealership as a whole.

One of the toughest challenges in this case is the dual mission of the back end. On the one hand, the marketing mission of the back end of attracting and retaining customers would suggest operating the back end as a cost center, where service is treated as a break-even operation. On the other hand, the positive cash flow, or hedge mission of the back end suggests operating it as a profit center. My judgment lies with operating it as a profit center. I don't believe that this dealership can function in the long run without a service center whose mission extends beyond the scope of a mere support function. The cyclical nature of car sales demands the owners to insure a steady stream of positive cash flow to offset the depletion of working capital that occurs in times of depressed car sales.

Most students favor operating new, used, service, body, and oil change as profit centers. A majority of students argue that parts is not a profit center since most of its demand is a subset of service demands. The parts department for Ford, Saab, and VW could not exist as an independent business. I don't see a compelling managerial rationale for separating parts revenue from its derivative, revenue-generating departments. Parts income and profitability resulting from service sales should be included in service department P & L. Likewise, parts income from the body and oil should be included in these departments.

III. Transfer Pricing Alternatives

Full Retail Transfer Repairs:

	New	Used	Parts	Service	Dealership as a Whole
Sales Price	$12,850 [1]	$5,000	$235	$470	$18,555
Cost of Sales	11,420	4,455 [3]	168 [4]	134 [5]	16,177
Gross Profit	1,430	545	67	336	2,378
Fixed Allocation[2]	835	665	32	114	1,646
Net Profit	$ 595	($120)	$ 35	$222	$ 732

1. Sales Price 2,000 cash + 7,350 loan + 3,500 trade value.

2. Fixed Allocation:
   - New $396,000/474 units = $835/unit
   - Used $157,000 × .75/177 units = $665/unit
   - Parts: By # of parts ordered = $183,000/40,139 = $4.55/part × 7 parts = $32 (2 Brake kits, 1 lock assembly, 4 tune-up parts)
   - Service: By # of service orders = $371,000/9,765 = $38/repair × 3 repairs $114.

3. Used Cost = $3,500 transfer price + $705 repair + $250 commission $4,455.

4. $235 ÷ 1.4 = $168.

5. $470 ÷ 3.5 = $134.

Direct Cost as Transfer for Repairs:

	New	Used	Parts	Service	Dealership as a Whole
Sales Price	$12,850	$5,000	$168	$134	$18,152
Cost of Sales	11,420	4,052 [1]	168	134	15,774
Gross Profit	1,430	948	-0-	-0-	2,378
Fixed Allocation	835	665	32	114	1,646
Net Profit	$ 595	$ 283	($32)	($114)	$ 732

1. 3,500 + 250 + 168 + 134 = $4,052

With Full Cost as Transfer Price:

	New	Used	Parts	Service	Dealership as a Whole
Sales Price	$12,850	$5,000	$200	$248	$18,298
Cost of Sales	11,420	4,198	168	134	15,920
Gross Profit	1,430	802	32	114	2,378
Fixed Allocation	835	665	32	114	1,646
Net Profit	$ 595	$ 137	-0-	-0-	$ 732

IV. Which is Correct?

A. Under full retail Mark-up, used manager will have no incentive to keep car in inventory. She will instead have the new car sales manager wholesale the car at $3,500. The dealership then loses out as a whole:

	New	Used	Parts	Service	Dealership as a Whole
Sales Price	$12,850	$3,500	-0-	-0-	$16,350
Cost of Sales	11,420	3,500			14,920
Gross Profit	1,430	-0-			1,430
Fixed Allocation[2]	835	184	-0-	-0-	1,019
Net Profit	$ 595	($ 184)	-0-	-0-	$ 411

($157,000 × .25)/213 used cars wholesaled = $184/unit.

The $184 could be charged to the new car department, who will realize a profit of only $411.

The lost profit is $732 – $411 = $321 for the dealership as a whole.

Under the direct and full cost methods of transfer pricing, the parts and service departments make no profit. Under either of these two methods, it obviously does not make any sense to operate the departments as profit centers.

Note: The direct and full cost transfer prices for service labor do not account for down time in service. Technicians and mechanics are paid for 40 hours per week.

V. Capitalizing used car repairs into used car inventory creates the incentive for the used car sales manager to defer potential losses in her department by holding on to cars in inventory that she believes will generate negative gross margins. Since she is not charged for interest on used investment, there is no incentive to maximize asset turnover. The $59,000 loss in wholesaling used cars is most likely a result of holding losses on used inventory. Currently, the supply of used cars is high at 53 days. As used inventory ages, it loses value at a much faster rate than new. George Liddy has had to pressure the used manager to liquidate inventory to generate cash. The current system of capitalizing repair costs while not charging for carrying cost may require constant management override in controlling used inventory levels.

VI. Liddy's method of measuring performance on the basis of gross profits instead of net profits may lead to incorrect managerial signals. In a business where inventories constitute such a high percentage of total assets (55 percent for NCA), management accountability of both level and mix is key. Without accountability for financing charges, the incentive for both the new and used managers to invest inventory dollars wisely is low. NCA owners have had to step in and force the new managers to reduce new inventory by $1.5 million. The need for such an override should be eliminated.

High inventory levels pose a twofold risk to NCA: excess interest burden and greater risk of devaluation with changes in model year.

Current days supply are: (Inventory × Days/COGS)
Ford (773 × 300/2921) = 79.40 days
Saab (253 × 300/1412) = 53.80 days
VW (243 × 300/1677) = 43.47 days
Used (231 × 300/1315) = 53 days

Industry average is 75 days for new cars and 45 days for used cars. In addition to the inventory problem, measuring performance at the gross profit level reduces incentive to control other discretionary expenses such as indirect labor, advertising, rework and supplies. To the extent that the owners give their department managers authority to control these line items, they should have responsibility for them.

VII. Distribution of Losses on Erroneous Used Car Valuations

The central question here is, should the new car sales department be charged back if a trade-in is overvalued? The answer to this question will depend on how one defines the mission of the used car department. If the used department functions as a profit center, then it should bear the inventory risk of transfers from new—particularly since the used manager has initial control over valuations—and whether she will accept the trade-in from the new manager or force the new manager to wholesale it (or charge the new car manager back for wholesaling cost as done in this note).

If the used car sales department functions as a means to dispose of cars solely for the purpose of enhancing new car sales, then, by definition, it becomes a marketing cost center for the new department. The new car sales department would then assume the risk of overvaluations and "recoveries" from undervaluations.

The alternative selected by management depends on the marketing strategy pursued by a dealer. There are dealerships that run used car operations that consistently outperform their new operations and there are dealerships that take losses in used car operations as a means of generating new car volume. The choice will depend on the market for the new franchises. For higher-end cars, such as Saab, the used operation can be set-up to lower the price point for first-time Saab buyers and generate long-term customer relationships through a well-run back end and repeat purchasers. For medium to low-end cars such as Ford and Volkswagen, the used car department would lend itself more to functioning as an economy car operation that markets lower priced second cars to value-conscious customers who buy Fords and VWs. The question is, can NCA do both?

North Country Auto

Risks of Business

- High financial leverage

- High asset depreciation risk (new, used, parts)

- Cyclical demand in front end (often very fickle)

- Uncertain labor supply in back end with high training costs

- Low control over product quality and manufacturer service warranties $\Rightarrow$ quality problems pushed down on dealers with extended warranties

- Lower margins due to more dealerships and a wider variety of better products

- More sophisticated customer and higher expectations

Hedges Against Risk

- New sources of capital to reduce interest burden and factory subsidies for inventory financing

- Minimal inventory levels $\Rightarrow$ use of technology to trade between dealers

- Profitable back end

- Competitive wages and compensation

- "Redefine" business

    Is this a business we want to be in? How do we compete?

North Country Auto, Inc.

Profitability of Transaction

Use the following fixed cost allocations to compute profitability:

New: $835/veh. = $396K/474 veh.

Used: $665/veh. = $157K × .75/177 veh.

Parts: $32 = $183K/40,139 parts = 4.55/part × 7 parts
          (2 brake kits, 1 lock assembly, 4 tune-up parts)

Service: $114 = $371K/9,765 orders × 3 orders
          (lock, brakes, tune-up)

Joe Fisher

NORTH COUNTRY AUTO

Vijay Govindaraian

Professor of Strategy and Control

The Amos Tuck School of Business Administration

Dartmouth College

Hanover, NH 03755

Prevalence of Profit Centers
Among Fortune 1000 Firms

	Reece & Cool (1978)	Govindarajan & Chitkara (1993)
% of firms in Fortune 1000 with two or more profit centers	<u>96%</u>	<u>93%</u>

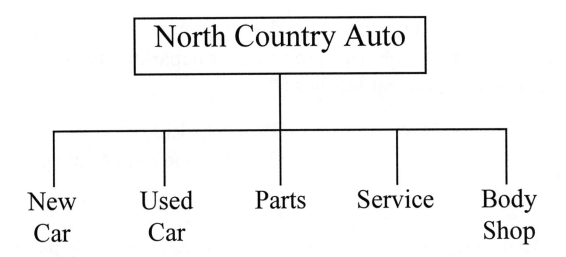

Current System

- All are profit centers

- Profit = Gross Profit

- But move towards full cost profits

- Transfer Prices = Retail or Blue Book

"I have instructed each of the department managers (new, used, service, body, parts) to run their departments as if it were an independent business."

—George Liddy
Owner & General Manager

"My department should not have to subsidize the profits of the new car sales division."

—Used Car Manager

"It is ridiculous that service department should make a profit on jobs it does for the rest of the dealership. The company can't make money when the left hand sells to its right."

—New Car Manager

North Country Auto
Issues

- How much profit did the company make on the deal?

- How much did each individual department make?

- How many businesses is the company in?

- How many profit centers should it have?

- Performance Metric?

  - Gross Profit vs. Full Cost Profit

  - Capitalizing Repairs

  - Why $59,000 Loss in Wholesaling Used Cars

  - Valuation Errors?

Strategy Issues

How does North Country Auto compete?

What is its strategy?

What is the mission of each department and how do they contribute to achieving the mission of the dealership as a whole?

Control System Issues

Should the five departments be profit centers?

How should the transfer prices be set?

Should repairs on used cars be capitalized?

How should losses on trade-ins be handled?

Should profit be calculated at Gross Profit or Full Cost Profit level?

What to do about valuation errors?

Why is there a $59,000 loss in wholesaling used cars? Is there a problem with current controls?

	New	Used	Parts	Service	Total
Sales Price					
Cost of Sales					
Other Costs					
Net Profit					

North Country Auto

*Possible Strategic
Alternatives*

*Control System
Implications*

I.   <u>Balanced Dealership</u>

     Emphasize new, used &
     "back end"

II. <u>Emphasize New Car Sales</u>

     Used car sales & "back
     end" support new car sales

III. <u>Emphasize Used Car Sales</u>

     New car sales & "back
     end" to support used car
     sales

IV. <u>Emphasize "Back End"</u>

     Low ball "front end" to
     make money on "back
     end"

	New	Used	Service	Body	Total
Sales	$6,558	$1,557	$2,089	$186	$10,390
Gross Profit	502	189	741	100	1,532
	33%	12%	49%	6%	100%
Gross Profit ÷ Sales	7.6%	12%	36%	54%	
Number of Vehicles Sold	474	390	—	—	

Case 5-3

Polysar Limited

Case History

In November, 1985, I met Pierre Choquette at a cocktail reception for AMP students. When he learned that I was teaching the first-year Control course in the MBA program, he shared with me problems that he had encountered repeatedly in his company due to managers not understanding the concept of volume variance and the problems this caused him in explaining the relative performance of his operating division. This case focuses on these issues and is motivated by the relevance of accounting variances to Polysar managers.

During 1986, the material for the case was collected. Interestingly, this was a time of some change at Polysar as the top layer of management prepared succession plans in anticipation of senior level retirements within the next 3 to 4 years. It was anticipated that Dudley, President, and Ambridge, Group Vice-President of Rubber (the largest Division), would retire in the near future since both men were approaching 65 years of age.

From my conversation with managers at Polysar, Bentley, Henderson, and Choquette were in contention to succeed Dudley. All were considered high potential and the company had sent all three to AMP on consecutive years.

Choquette was interviewed at Harvard in 1985 and at Sarnia in 1986; Henderson was interviewed at Harvard in 1986 while in attendance at AMP.

On September 1, 1986 a series of promotions and moves were announced:

Ambridge was moved laterally to the newly created position of Group Vice-President—Corporate Development;

Choquette was promoted to Group Vice-President—Rubber;

The top job in Diversified Products was upgraded from a Vice-President to a Group Vice President; Henderson was promoted to this position and returned to Sarnia from Europe;

Beaton moved laterally to Europe to take over the position of Vice-President EROW vacated by Henderson;

Bentley remained in his position as Group Vice-President—Basic Petrochemicals.

This case was prepared by Robert L. Simons.

Teaching Objectives

1. Provide a strong understanding of the relationship between capacity utilization and the absorption of fixed costs. Illustrate why accountants have developed the volume variance. Through assignment questions, motivate students to formulate a presentation to explain volume variances to others.

2. Reinforce student abilities to use budgets, pre-set standards, and ex post income statements to evaluate performance. Reinforce understanding of flowthrough relationship between production, inventory, and sales.

3. Explore the interaction between performance measurement of divisions and performance measurement of managers.

4. Provide an opportunity for students to propose improvements to a functioning information and control system based on their knowledge of the structure and functioning of the business.

Assignment Questions

1. Prepare a presentation for the Polysar Board of Directors to review the performance of the NASA Rubber Division. Pay particular attention to questions that may be raised concerning the accuracy and meaning of the volume variance.

2. What is the beat sales and production strategy for EROW Division? NASA Division? Rubber Group in total?

3. What changes, if any, would you recommend be made in the management accounting performance system to improve the reporting and evaluation of Rubber Group performance?

Teaching Strategy

The case can be taught by covering three broad topic categories: (1) mechanics of calculating volume variance, (2) evaluation of NASA Division, and (3) consideration of system improvements. The inclusion and time spent on each of these segments will depend on the students' previous exposure to volume variances and the placement of the case in the course.

If this case represents the first exposure of volume variances in class, the bulk of class time should be spent on the mechanics, perhaps using simple graphs to illustrate the procedure. However, enough time should be left in the class to discuss the evaluation of NASA Division since the case demonstrates that an understanding of accounting techniques is necessary for general managers to discharge their operating responsibilities. At the end of the class, instead of leading a discussion of possible system improvements, the instructor can reveal the changes made in the system by Pierre Choquette (to be discussed at the end of this note).

If the mechanics of volume variances has already been covered by students, the class time can be split between an evaluation of NASA performance and a discussion of possible system improvements. Since much of this discussion will focus on the volume variance and capacity issues, it is a good idea to spend 10 minutes at the beginning of class to review the calculation of the volume variance (by asking a student to review his calculation?) to ensure that all students enter into the discussion on the same footing. During the student discussion, the instructor may wish to push students to show that they understand the mechanics that underlie the accounting statements.

I. MECHANICS[1]

This segment can be structured by the instructor by asking a series of questions:

Starting with Exhibit 1, Statistics and Analyses,

a. What is the purpose of this statement?

The top half of the statement shows volume statistics and the bottom half reveals fixed costs of production?

b. Why is this important?

Volume statistics are important in any business because they are simple indicators of the physical throughput of the business and do not become clouded with accounting allocations and approximations.

Fixed costs are important in this business because it is a capital intensive, continuous process industry. As suggested in the case, even direct labor is treated as fixed since the labor component of the plant does not vary significantly with the level of production. Just as Eskimos have 11 different words to describe different types of snow, Polysar uses three different descriptors for fixed costs—direct, allocated cash, and allocated non-cash.

c. How are fixed costs accumulated in the company's accounting records?

Each of the Fixed Cost lines (Direct, Allocated Cash, and Allocated Noncash) represents the *debit* side of accounts which have been accumulating charges throughout the year. For example, the Allocated Noncash line reports the depreciation expense account which has been built up during the year by a series of entries which sum to

Dr. Depreciation expense	$15,625	
Cr. Accumulated Depreciation		$15,625

Other examples include payroll costs in direct labor and allocation of service center costs in Allocated Cash; these can be illustrated by T-accounts if necessary.

Note that the company has structured the statements so that positive figures increase profit and negative figures decrease profits. Note also that Canada uses the metric system of weights and measures and that 'tonne' signifies a metric or long ton 1,000 kilogrammes (2,204 lbs). The American 'ton' refers to a short ton of 2,000 lbs.

d. What does the line, "Fixed Cost to Production," represent?

In the budget column, this is the amount of *total* fixed costs that were budgeted for the first nine months of the year. If we assume level spending[2], the *annual* budgeted amount of total fixed costs is

$$\$44,625 / (9/12) = \$59,500$$

In the actual column, $44,127 represents the amount actually spent to date. Subtraction indicates that the Division has spent $498 less than budget (is this good?—it depends on what has been cut back).

e. Can someone explain why the "Fixed Cost of Sales" on Exhibit 1 agrees exactly with "Total Fixed Costs" on Exhibit 2? Doesn't the "Fixed Cost to Production" line of Exhibit 1 represent *total* fixed costs?

Exhibit 1, Statistics and Analyses, presents total fixed costs, both budgeted and actual, that were spent to support a certain level of *production* (in this case 55,000 tonnes budget and 47,500 tonnes actual). However, not all of these fixed costs go to the income statement since not all of this production was sold by NASA. Some products (and costs) go to/from inventory on the Balance Sheet and some products (and costs) are transferred to/from EROW. The remaining fixed costs represent the production that was sold by NASA and this cost is properly *matched against sales* on the income statement.

f. What are the mechanics by which fixed costs are transferred to the income statement?

Polysar, like many other companies, uses a standard cost system to allocate fixed costs to its products. The formula is described in the case as,

$$\text{Standard Fixed Cost per tonne} = \frac{\text{Estimated Annual Total Fixed Costs}}{\text{Annual Demonstrated Plant Capacity}}$$

$$= \frac{\$59,500}{85,000 \text{ tonnes (case p. 7)}} = \$700/\text{tonne}$$

We can trace these costs through the statements quite easily,

Statement of Net Contribution:

Sales: actual = 35,800 tonnes × $700 = $25,060
        budget = 33,000   × 700   23,100

---

[2] The analysis in this note assumes that spending and production for the last three months of the year will equal 1/3 of that recorded in the first nine months. This assumption is not unrealistic for this business.

Statistics and Analyses:

Transfers[3]
- inventory
    actual $= 1,600^1$ tonnes $\times \$700 = 1,120$
    budget $= 3,500 \qquad \times \quad 700 \quad 2,450$

$^1 47.5$ (prod) $- 35.8$ (sales) $- 12.2$ (to EROW)
    $+ 2.1$ (from EROW) $= 1.6$ addition to inventory.

- to EROW $= 12,200 \qquad \times \quad 700 = 8,540$

The transfer from EROW has a different costs allocation per tonne based on the unique fixed costs and capacity of the Antwerp plant. It is,

$$2,100 \text{ tonnes} \times Y = \$1,302$$
$$Y = \$620 \text{ /tonne}$$

g. What is the denominator of the allocation equation, "Demonstrated Capacity"?

Demonstrated capacity, as used by Polysar, is described in Exhibit 5, an excerpt from the Controller's manual. Companies must choose a production base over which to spread fixed costs. Choices may range from actual past production (which may include correctable inefficiencies) and theoretical capacity (which may never be met due to design constraints, shutdowns, maintenance, etc). Polysar has chosen "demonstrated capacity" which they define as the annualized extrapolation of what the plant has achieved in short periods of high, but unsustained, throughput.

Clearly, the choice of the denominator will affect the magnitude of the volume variance.

Let's now look at the Fixed Cost section of the Statement of Net Contribution;

h. We have identified the origin of the Standard Fixed Costs, what could be included in Cost Adjustments?

The origin and calculation of this amount is not obvious from the statements and need not be pursued in class. The adjustment represents the difference in fixed cost per unit for EROW sourced butyl sold by NASA (all units sold have been coated at NASA standard cost of $700/tonne; the EROW units, however, have only $620/tonne allocated fixed cost).

$$2,100 \text{ tonnes} \times [\$700 - \$620] = \$168,000$$

---

[3] Note that transfers to/from EROW are effected through the inventory accounts of the respective Divisions and are therefore not reflected on the income statements.

i. What does the spending variance represent?

The spending variance is the difference between the amount of total fixed costs which were budgeted to date and the actual spending. We have seen this number before on the statement of Statistics and Analyses, Fixed Cost to Production.

j. What is the volume variance and how is it computed?

The volume variance represents over(under) absorption of fixed cost due to actual production not coinciding with the denominator (in this case, demonstrated capacity) used to allocate fixed cost. It is calculated,

	Actual	Budget
Demonstrated capacity		
annual	85.0	85.0
9 months (9/12)	63.75	63.75
Production	47.5	55.0
Shortfall	16.25	8.75
Fixed cost / tonne	× $700	× $700
Underabsorbed F.C.	$11,375	$6,125

Using demonstrated capacity instead of budgeted production to allocate fixed costs is somewhat unusual. This method results in two volume variances being rolled into one,

Variance due to excess capacity (budgeted in advance)		$ 6,125
Variance due to production less than budget:		
Shortfall due to EROW (7.3 * 700)	$5,110	
due to other (0.2 * 700)	140	$ 5,250
Total Volume Variance as reported		$11,375

II. EVALUATION

This segment can be opened either by leading a general discussion on the performance of NASA or by asking (calling upon?) one or more volunteers to act as Choquette and Devereux NASA Controller, in making a presentation of Division performance.

Points to be raised include the following:

Analysis of NASA Performance

Sales revenue is up due to increased volume with slightly lower prices.

Volume	$[35.8 - 33.0] \times \$1850$	=	$5,180
Price	$[\$1840 - \$1850] \times 35.8$	=	– 358
Net increase			$4,822

Variable cost efficiency variance is favorable (241) indicating that the plant operated more efficiently than expected (we cannot, however, tell from the case if the Sarnia plant is more efficient than Antwerp—to do this we need input utilization factors).

Fixed cost spending variance is favorable (498) which suggests overhead costs have been carefully managed (although this would require more information to ensure that timing differences or cut backs on maintenance, etc. were not the cause).

Volume variance is highly unfavorable ($11,375). This is due to expected excess capacity of the plant and underproduction of 7,500 tonnes. Underproduction is due to EROW taking 7,300 tonnes less than budget. This shortfall seems large both in an absolute sense and compared to past years. Perhaps EROW makes up its butyl production shortfall at year end and transfers during the last three months will be correspondingly larger.

NASA's budgeted profit was $2 million; it has recorded a loss of $.9 million. Eliminating the volume variance would yield an adjusted budgeted profit of $8 million and an adjusted actual profit of $10.5 million.

Comparison of NASA and EROW[4]

The EROW operation is more profitable than NASA. Revenue per tonne is higher due to reduced competition. Variable costs are lower due to lower European feedstock prices. Fixed costs per tonne are lower (as per analysis in Section I).

	NASA		EROW	
Net Revenue/tonne	$1,766	(63,239/35.8)	$1,879	(89,920/47.85)
Variable cost/tonne	623	(22,294/35.8)	599	(28,662/47.85)
Contribution/tonne	1,143		1,280	
Gross margin	64.7%		68.3%	
Fixed costs/tonne	700		620	
Gross profit margin	8.2%		35.7%	

The fixed cost per tonne of Sarnia 2 is *not* $700, but really much higher if fixed costs are spread across budgeted production. The $700 figure is based on a "demonstrated capacity" of 85,000 tonnes. Based on budgeted production of 73,000 tonnes (55 × [12/9]), *actual* fixed costs per ton are approximately $815 ($59,500 / 73,000).

The capital cost structure of the two plants is very different. The Antwerp plant has charged only $4,900 of depreciation against its butyl sales. This is because the plant, built in 1964, is probably close to fully depreciated; current depreciation charges probably represent amortization of the 1979/80 refit (remember also that depreciation charges in Antwerp are split between butyl production and halobutyl production; the case, and Exhibit 7, show only

---

[4] Foreign currency accounting may change the results of the analysis. We have no information on this.

butyl production. A depreciation charge of a like amount was probably charged against the halobutyl statement).

The Sarnia plant has $15,600 of depreciation charged against operations. If depreciated on a straight line basis, the plant (original cost $550 million) is probably being depreciated over approximately 25 years (550 / (15.6 × (12/9)]).

Given the cost structures of the two regions, it is preferable to produce in Europe rather than in Canada. Contribution per tonne is higher in Europe. It should be noted that evaluation of respective Divisional performance is even more critical when the Corporation overall is hovering around the breakeven point. Managers may be considering divestitures.

Incentives for managers

Henderson and Choquette have moved up together quickly to senior positions. They are both ambitious and capable individuals. Their sequenced attendance at AMP suggests they are being considered for more senior responsibilities in the near future (of which there are only 2 levels—Group VP and President [Exhibit 3]). With similar backgrounds, Henderson and Choquette are rivals for these promotion slots.

Bonuses (and presumably advancement) for Henderson and Choquette depend significantly (50 percent) on how much profit they deliver as compared to budget. Employees at all levels also have an interest in Divisional profits and any accounting allocation that may affect profits and, hence, bonuses.

What do you think Henderson's strategy was? As he told me with a chuckle, he tells his people to sell more at higher prices and produce more in Europe." For every extra tonne that Henderson produces, his profit increases in two ways: his fixed costs are already covered so that the *contribution* goes right to net profit; and, he avoids having to receive a tonne from Sarnia with high variable and fixed costs. Sarnia's fixed cost are variable costs to Henderson and he will be willing to spend up to $700/tonne to boost Antwerp yield and avoid having to take product from Sarnia. In the longer term, there is incentive for Henderson to add capacity in Europe when the Rubber Group has considerable excess capacity.

For every tonne that Henderson does not take from NASA, Choquette's profit falls by $700 as the volume variance increases. NASA is also charged for any excess inventory (working capital charge from corporate) due to EROW not taking budgeted volume.

Since Henderson arrived at EROW in 1982, EROW has taken less butyl than budgeted each year [Exhibit 6]. What are Henderson's incentives to work to beat accurate budgets (or, more cynically, to overstate budgeted transfer estimates)?

Other

Is NASA really a profit center? The significant transfers (1/3 of production) to EROW are not acknowledged in NASA's income statement and Choquette has only partial control over the effects of the volume variance on profits. Although selling almost a third of NASA's output, EROW is not paying a proportionate share of the capital investment in NASA.

Note: Transfers at cost between inventory accounts of NASA and EROW are for internal management reporting only. For legal entity reporting, profits on shipments are split between the two countries.

III. SYSTEM IMPROVEMENTS

Pierre Choquette, in his new role of Group Vice-President, says that he is unwilling to talk in presentations and reviews of NASA and EROW as separate businesses. He now talks in global product terms. As he claims, "it is meaningless to separate the two Divisions when assets are in one place and revenues are in another." The amount of cross shipment of product between Divisions and directly to customers suggests that this approach has merit.

Choquette still maintains that the Divisions be treated as profit centers due to their size. This being the case, consideration can be given to having transfers at a price which splits the profit between the two Divisions rather than having the profit rest with EROW and the unabsorbed fixed costs with NASA.

Choquette also believes that NASA should continue to show the volume variance on their books, "I won't hold them accountable in the same way as things they can control, but I want them to know and worry about it."

The bonus plan is problematic and has been changed for employees in 1986 to reflect overall corporate performance only. Division managers are still rewarded based on division performance. It seems that more thought can be given to developing a bonus scheme for managers. Options include factoring in global product line performance, Group performance, and correcting the results for items such as the portion of the volume variance due to actions of other Divisions.

However, it is important to recognize that the Company is not rewarding based on absolute results, but rather based on budgeted results. Bonuses are based solely on the increment over budget. Thus, to the extent that excess capacity is budgeted through the volume variance, the manager is not being held responsible for it. The issue becomes how much stretch to build into the budget. Perhaps it makes sense to hold NASA responsible for underabsorbed fixed costs if so doing will cause actions to boost production to compensate for the unexpected efficiencies of EROW.

As for the volume variance, the company has chosen to divide fixed cost by demonstrated capacity (85,000 tonnes) and charge the volume variance to the plant P&L. Another possibility would be to divide fixed costs by budgeted production (which would increase per unit fixed cost). A preferred solution, in my opinion, is to charge off the fixed costs due to overcapacity as a period cost at the Group level. Using this method, Divisions would be charged only with fixed costs used in production.

Wrap-Up (announce September 1, 1986 promotions)

It is up to Choquette to explain the above information, to the extent it is not obvious, to those who must evaluate his performance and that of NASA Division. Can we assume that managers, the recipients of accounting reports, understand the calculations that lead to accounting numbers such as the volume variance? Choquette and Henderson have made it their business to understand. In fact, in the interviews, Choquette stated that he believed that he and Henderson were the only senior managers who truly understood the volume variance and its effect on performance measurement.

Note

The following assignment is used by Prof. Julie Herten.

Case — Polysar Limited

Assignment

The class will be divided into three groups for this class. Depending on the group to which they belong, students will assume the roles of the NASA management team; the EROW management team, or the Polysar Board of Directors.

Each of the two management teams will prepare a presentation to the Board of Directors to review the performance of their operating profit center within the context of the overall performance of the Rubber Group. The presentations should explain in detail the reasons for the strengths and weaknesses of your profit center's performance. Pay particular attention to the meaning and implications of the volume variance.

Members of the Board of Directors will organize the Board Meeting, and will prepare to review the performance of the two divisions and the Rubber Group as a whole. They must thoroughly understand the information about each of the two groups so they can analyze the presentations, ask questions, and make suggestions to enhance the overall success of the Rubber Group, and Polysar Limited.

All participants should keep the following in mind:

> What is the best sales and production strategy for the EROW Division? The NASA Division? The Rubber Group in total?

> What changes, if any, would you recommend be made in the management control system to improve the Rubber Group's performance, and the reporting and evaluation of that performance?

Case 5-4

Abrams Company

Using the assigned questions, this case can easily be covered in one and one half hours of class time. It has also been used as a 100 minute exam following the first seven chapters of the **Management Control Systems** text. The case was adapted from a case written by Professor J.S. Reece of the University of Michigan.

This rich case provides students with ample opportunity to apply their knowledge of design issues in management control systems including the motivational impact of particular management choices.

Question 1

The issues raised at the end of the case provide a good basis to organize the class discussion: setting transfer prices between the manufacturing plants and the AM Marketing Division on strictly AM Division parts; treating the AM Marketing Division as a captive customer; and, excessive inventories during the year. These items provide the students with opportunities to discuss alternatives and defend their positions. Below are some of the major points discussed for each issue.

Transfer Pricing

The transfer price problem pertains to only those aftermarket parts for which OEM plants have no prior experience. Few students want to continue the current negotiation and CFO arbitration methods, but they have difficulty justifying alternatives. Part availability is a critical success factor in the AM Division's business and AM cannot control the cost of goods from the OEM divisions. Some of the students will advocate no change in the system because interference by top management will harm the autonomy and decentralized responsibility given to the OEM plant managers. It is the plant managers who must develop new products and use plant capacity to primarily serve OEMS. It is the OEMs that literally drive the automotive parts industry. This then creates the aftermarket opportunity that Abrams' management want the AM Division to maximize and increase market share. If the AM Division wants non-OEM products made, they must convince OEM plant managers. Most students want Abrams' management to set corporate transfer policy for all non-OEM products. Recommendations include cost-based measures, cost plus profit measure, a dual or split pricing scheme, and an outside or market price for similar products. Clearly, there is no one dominant solution. Students have a lot to say, so you have to cut off the discussion after several recommendations have been discussed.

Captive Customer

I start by asking what is the company's strategy in seeking both OEM and aftermarket sales? What I really want them to discuss is the aftermarket strategy. The company strategy is to expand AM business because AM has a healthy gross margin, hence, AM's 50 percent goal for outside sales. The manufacturing plants must be kept busy with OEM products, and sales in the aftermarket are good business to fill up the remaining plant capacity. The 'image' concern from AM's sales of outside products is not clear. Perhaps Abrams is a top quality manufacturer and fears quality problems if the AM Division buys parts from outsiders.

Manufacturing plants have the expertise to deal with technical product questions, but the AM sales people may not have similar skills. If plants are near capacity with OEM work, top management might consider letting AM deal with outside suppliers. The plant manager's budget includes profits from forecasted sales to the AM Division. Because of ROI targets, plant managers are motivated to accommodate more sales to AM Division in the budget. At AM's high gross margin, this should improve Abrams, profit. Are the lost sales of non-OEM products worth the effort to find outside suppliers, etc.? This is a question for top management. The plant manager should recognize the profit opportunity from AM sales if they have the capacity. Because of the lack of control for major business decisions, ROI responsibility for AM Divisions may be perceived as unfair. Making the AM Division a revenue center still does not improve AM's options. Sales on non-OEM products would still have to be resolved.

Excessive Inventories

Students are quick to point out that large mid-year inventories are not goal congruent, and that delivery and part availability pressures lead to excess inventory. There are usually recommendations to modify ROI to include a better measurement of investment in inventory, such as using average investment in inventory or a capital charge as in residual income. Like the Cummins Engine case, more MRP or JIT type of controls could be implemented to help manage the inventory. Using residual income instead of ROI still requires a modification of the inventory measure. Some might suggest different rates of return for different assets.

Overall Evaluation

The discussion on the first question can consume a lot of time. At least 20 minutes should be saved to discuss this last question which focuses on the overall control system and its strengths and weaknesses. Abrams has a product division organization that focuses on specific OEM product categories. These divisions are responsive to OEMs' product development and innovation in order to keep up with competitors. These product divisions constitute the core business. The Aftermarket Division carries existing products into the parts market which is made up of distributors who buy the full-line of Abrams' products. This constitutes a further exploitation of the product line development.

The Aftermarket Division could be a revenue center with the share-of-the-market measure for performance. This is consistent with the 50 percent outside sales goals, but AM has no control over cost of goods sold and can't buy outside.

The ROI measure uses book value for fixed assets which inflates performance as assets age. This is illustrated in the profit and ROI statements in Exhibit 2. Also, the age and mix of assets may differ among the divisions. Thus, ROI may not be fair when applied across divisions. Different ROIs may be necessary for different divisions. The AM Division has smaller asset base and could be changed to a profit or revenue center. The one-year lag in counting capital investments may be a good compromise to encourage modernization. There remains the problem of division managers with high ROIs not making investments that are overall good for Abrams' ROI. The allocation of corporate overhead costs and taxes may be a good idea as long as managers are not penalized for these noncontrollable costs.

The incentive plan is based on seniority, includes staff as well as line, and is subjective. These are potential problems. Also, the amount of the bonus pool is tied to the corporate reported net income and EPS. While this is intended to promote corporate teamwork, there may be insufficient long-term focus. Adjusting the OEM Plant manager's profit for the AM sales variance seems fair in that the AM Division's commitment to buy OEM goods was included in the OEM Sales budget.

Overall, this is a very good management control system.

Joe San Miguel

CHAPTER 6
TRANSFER PRICING

Changes from the Eighth Edition

This chapter retains the basic thrust of the eighth edition. The chapter has been rewritten to highlight three aspects: (a) Market prices represent the best transfer prices, in general; (b) How to set transfer prices when market prices don't exist or can't be approximated; (c) Transfer pricing for corporate services; (d) Implementation issues in transfer pricing.

Cases

Transfer pricing problems provide practice in using the various transfer pricing methods. The final problem involves behavioral considerations, in addition to mechanics.

Birch Paper Company is a classic case in transfer pricing. Although it is only 2¼ pages, it contains almost all of the principal issues in intracompany relationships.

General Appliance Company is a challenging case on setting interdivisional prices.

Strider Chemical Company is a fairly straightforward case in transfer pricing.

Medoc Company deals with considerations involved in managing "pseudo" profit centers.

Case 6-1

Transfer Pricing Problems

Approach

Assignment of all these problems for one meeting will probably involve more preparation time than the instructor wishes. The relative time for each problem can be judged by looking at the solutions.

With the exception of Problem 9, these problems do not involve behavioral considerations. They therefore differ fundamentally from the cases in this chapter. Problem 9 does involve behavioral considerations.

Problem 1

	Product X	Product Y	Product Z
Outside Material	2.00	3.00	1.00
Inside Material		8.00	17.60
Direct Labor	1.00	1.00	2.00
Overhead	4.00	5.00	3.00
Total Std. Cost	7.00	17.00	23.60
10% of Inventories Per Unit	1.00	.60	
10% of Fixed Assets Per Unit			
Transfer Price	8.00	17.60	

Problem 2

Transfer Prices:

Product X: 4.00 per unit transferred
Monthly Charge: $30,000 + .1(100,000)/12 = 40,000/12 = 3,333$
Product Y: $5.00 + 4.00 = 9.00$ per unit transferred
Monthly Charge: $40,000 + .1(60,000)/12 + 3,333 = 7,166$

Standard Cost:	Product Y	Product Z
Outside Material	3.00	1.00
Inside Material	4.00	9.00
Direct Labor	1.00	2.00
Variable Overhead	1.00	2.00
Variable Cost Per Unit	9.00	14.00
Fixed Cost:		
Incurred within the Division	4.00	1.00
Transferred to the Division	4.00 *	8.60 **
Total Standard Cost	17.00	23.60

* $30,000 + .1(100,000) + 10,000$ units $= 4.00$ per unit
** $[40,000 + .1(60,000)/10,000] + 4 = 8.60$

Problem 3

Per Unit			Total	
Competitive Price	Variable Cost	Contribution	Volume	Contribution
Full Cost Transfer—Lower Price				
27.00	22.60	4.40	10,000	44,000
26.00	22.60	3.40	10,000	34,000
25.00	22.60	2.40	10,000	24,000
23.00	22.60	.40	10,000	4,000
22.00	22.60	(.60)	10,000	(6,000)
Full Cost Transfer—Maintain Price				
27.00		5.40	9,000	48,600
26.00		5.40	7,000	37,800
25.00		5.40	5,000	27,000
23.00		5.40	2,000	10,400
22.00		5.40	0	0
Variable Cost Transfer—Lower Price				
27.00	14.00	13.00	10,000	130,000
26.00	14.00	12.00	10,000	120,000
25.00	14.00	11.00	10,000	110,000
23.00	14.00	9.00	10,000	90,000
22.00	14.00	8.00	10,000	80,000
Variable Cost Transfer—Maintain Prices				
27.00		14.00	9,000	126,000
26.00		14.00	7,000	98,000
25.00		14.00	5,000	70,000
23.00		14.00	2,000	28,000
22.00		14.00	0	0

	COMPANY CONTRIBUTION: ($000)		
Competitive Price	Maintain Price at 28.00	Lower Price	Difference
27.00	126	130	4
26.00	98	120	22
25.00	70	110	40
23.00	28	90	62
22.00	0	80	80

Problem 4

Expense	Volume	Additional Using Unit Cost Transfer Unit	Total	Marginal	Using Var. Cost Transfer Unit	Total	Marginal
100,000	10,000	5.40	54,000	(46,000)	14,000	140,000	40,000
200,000	19,000				14,000	266,000	25,000
300,000	27,000				14,000	378,000	12,000
400,000	34,000				14,000	476,000	(2,000)
500,000	40,000				14,000		

Under the full cost transfer price system, the manager of Division C would not advertise at all. Under the variable transfer price system, he would spend $300,000 and increase profits by $78,000. The ABC Company, therefore, would have had an opportunity loss of $78,000 if the manager of Division C did not undertake the television advertising.

Problem 5

a. The Intermediate Division would maximize its profits as follows:

Product	Volume	Contribution Per Unit	Total Profit
A	10,000	7.00	70,000
B	10,000	4.00	40,000
C	30,000	10.00	300,000
			410,000

b. The Final Division would try to maximize the production of Product Y.

Product	Volume	Unit Contribution	Total Profit
X	10,000	13.00	130,000
Y	30,000	15.00	450,000
Z	10,000	7.00	70,000
			650,000

c. The optimum company production pattern would be as follows:

	Product X	Product Y	Product Z
Price	28.00	30.00	30.00
Variable Costs:			
Intermediate	3.00	6.00	5.00
Final	5.00	5.00	8.00
Total	8.00	11.00	13.00
Contribution per Unit	20.00	19.00	17.00
Volume	30,000	10,000	10,000
Total Contribution	600,000	190,000	170,000
Total		$960,000	

The profits of the Intermediate Division and the Final Division at the optimum company pattern is as follows:

Product	Volume	INTERMEDIATE DIV. Unit Contribution	Total	FINAL DIV. Unit Contribution	Total
A or X	30,000	7.00	210,000	13.00	390,000
B or Y	10,000	4.00	40,000	15.00	150,000
C or Z	10,000	10.00	100,000	7.00	70,000
			350,000		610,000

Therefore, the Intermediate Division would have profits of $60,000 less and the Final Division would have profits of $40,000 less at Company Optimum than at Divisional Optimum. In this instance, I would make the Final Division pay $60,000 to the Intermediate Division.

The reason is that the shortage is in the products produced by the Intermediate Division. The Intermediate Division is required to sell all of its products to the Final Division. If it were independent, it probably would not sell exclusively to the Final Division but would sell its optimum pattern to whoever would buy it.

The Final Division, on the other hand, might well have to reduce production or pay a premium if it were independent. The Final Division is the one benefiting from the executive decree that all of the Intermediate Division's products should be sold to it. Consequently, it should pay the premium costs of this action.

Problem 6

The only change that the absence of a competitive market price would have on the answers to Problem 5 is the distribution of the less-than-optimum profits of the Intermediate Division. If there is no outside market, this means that the Intermediate Division is essentially a captive supplier. This being the case, I would not make the Final Division reimburse the Intermediate Division for the opportunity loss of $60,000, since the Intermediate Division would not have had the option of selling its optimum pattern.

Incidentally, if there were no outside markets, it would be better if a two-step transfer price were used. In this way, the Final Division's optimum sales pattern would be the same as the Company's.

Problem 7

(a) The Intermediate Division would produce the full 12,000 units because they can pass on all excess costs.

(b) The Final Division would have the following production pattern:

	Product X	Product Y	Product Z
Original Units	10,000	30,000	10,000
Original Contribution (000)	130	450	70
Additional Units	1,000	2,000	—
Additional Contribution (000)	13	30	
Additional Costs (000)	10	24	
Revised Units	11,000	32,000	10,000
Revised Contribution (000)	133	456	70

(c) The optimum production pattern for the Company would be:

	Product X	Product Y	Product Z
Original Units	30,000	10,000	10,000
Original Contribution (000)	600	190	70
Additional Units	2000	2,000	4,000
Additional Contribution (000)	40	38	68
Additional Costs (000)	25	24	50
Revised Units	32,000	12,000	14,000
Revised Contribution (000)	615	204	188

Problem 8

There would be no difference. The existence of an outside market is important *only* if the Final Division could buy all of its requirements from outside suppliers and the Intermediate Division could sell all of its products to outside customers. In this instance, the transfer price would be the marginal cost and the Final Division's contribution would be equal to the total company contribution. In this case, with or without an outside market, the Intermediate Division must sell all of its production to the Final Division by executive decree. Consequently, the marginal cost to the company is the total variable costs of the two divisions involved.

Problem 9

1. Division A should be willing to accept any transfer price that was higher than its $500 cost for the first thousand units plus $100 for each additional thousand = $800 for 4,000 units. This is $.20 per unit. At any higher price, it will make some contribution to its profit.

2. Division B should be willing to pay Division A any amount lower than its revenue of $3,700 less its costs of $2,000 = $1,200. At any lower amount, it will make some contribution to its profit.

3. If the managers of Division A and B got together, they would realize that it was in Kappa company's best interest to sell 4,000 units, rather than 3,000, because the company profit is $900 at that quantity. Also, each division could make its maximum profit at that quantity if the total were divided fairly between them. The fairest transfer price would be to split this profit between the two divisions, probably in proportion to their respective

costs. A's proportion would be $800/$2800 = 28.6 percent; 28.6 percent of $900 = $257.14. $257.14 added to its cost of $800 makes a transfer price of $1,057.14 = $.264 per unit. At this transfer price, B's profit would be $3,700 revenue, minus $2,000 B's cost, minus $1,057.14 transfer price from A, or a total profit of $642.86 for B. The combined profit for the Kappa Company would be $257.14 plus $642.86 = $900.

If one assumes that the division managers discuss the matter, there will be a sale of 4,000 units, not 3,000 and the company profit will be $900, not $850 (or zero, if the sale is refused). The author of the example says that this is "unlikely," but the student can judge whether two managers, each out to maximize his or her profit, would be unlikely to carry on such a discussion. The example, as stated, suggests that the transfer price policy motivates Division B to accept an order for 3,000 units, whereas Kappa Company would make more profit if Division B accepted an order for 4,000 units. If, however, we assume that the division managers discuss this matter, the results should be quite different. Division A should realize that it is in its best interest to reduce its normal transfer price rather than lose the additional 1,000 of volume, and Division B should realize that it is better to sell 4,000 units and make $642, rather than sell 3,000 units and make the $100 that is calculated in Exhibit 1. They then will arrive at a solution that is optimum for each of them and for the company. (The split of the $900 profit might be based on something other than the division's relative cost, depending on the persuasiveness of each manager, but it would be in the neighborhood of the numbers derived above; the total would be $900, however it was split.)

Birch Paper Company

This is a classic case in transfer pricing and it is a very good one to introduce the subject. Although it is only 2¼ pages, it contains almost all of the principal issues in intracompany relationships. I generally discuss this case at three levels and try to confine the discussion at each level to the issues at that level. These levels are:

1.   The immediate economic impact to the company of sourcing the product to either West Paper or Eire.

2.   The possible solutions to the immediate issue.

3.   The changes, if any, that should be made in the system in the long run.

Economic Impact

		Per 1,000 Boxes
West Paper Company: Out-of-pocket cost to Birch......................		$430
Eire Paper, Ltd.:		$432
Less: Profit to Southern ($90 × .4).................................	$ 36	
Profit to Thompson ($30 − $25)	5	41
Out-of-pocket cost to Birch		$391
Thompson:		$480
Less: Profit to Southern ($280 × .14)...............................	$112	
Profit to Thompson ($480 − $400)	80	192
Out-of-pocket cost to Birch		$288

or

Thompson out-of-pocket cost ($400 − $280)	$120
Southern out-of-pocket cost ($280 × .6).................................	168
Total Out-of-pocket Cost..	$288

Potential Opportunity Loss $430 − $288 = $142   opportunity loss to company
                                 $430 − $400 = $ 30   opportunity loss to Thompson

---

This case was prepared by William Rotch (under the direction of Neil Harlan).

Copyright © 1957, 1985 by the President and Fellows of Harvard College. Harvard Business School case 158-001.

Immediate Issue

After we have the figures on the board, I ask the class how the commercial vice president should settle the issue. The answer that I usually get is to make Thompson take the business. There are two issues that I discuss here: First, isn't the commercial vice president interfering with Brunner's independence in running his business? If it were not for the fact that Southern makes a significant profit, a case could be made for leaving Brunner alone. After all, without Southern, there is goal congruity. The contribution to Thompson is the same as to the total company. Consequently, at this point, I divide the question into two parts: (a) If Southern were not involved, should the commercial vice president require Thompson to accept the business? (b) Is the answer different under the conditions of the case? The objective of this questioning is to bring out the problem of independence where profit responsibility has been decentralized and to show how a division can maximize its own profit while suboptimizing the total company profit. For Thompson, a $30 loss in contribution may well be too small to warrant changing Brunner's earlier directive to bid full costs plus profit. On the other hand, the company's loss of $142 might well make it desirable to make the boxes within Birch.

Second, after discussing at length the question of whether to source the boxes inside, I ask the following question: "Assuming that it is decided to source the boxes to Thompson, what price should be charged?" The usual answers are as follows:

a. Competitive prices: $430 for the boxes; $280 for the paper supplied by Southern. The argument for this is the maintenance of competitive prices and profits.

b. Divide the total contribution between Southern and Thompson:

1. Equally:

	Price	Decrease from Bid
Southern ($168 + $71)	$239	–$41
Thompson ($239 + $120 + $71)	$430	–$ 9

2. As a percent of out-of-pocket cost:

	Price	Decrease from Bid
Southern (1.495)($168)	$251	–$17
Thompson 251 + (1.495)($120)	$430	–$33

c. Divide the $50 reduction amongst all three divisions equally or in some other combination.

d. Let Thompson sell at $480 and Northern buy at $430. The difference is charged to some central office account.

e. Persuade the divisions to keep the business inside and ask them to agree among themselves on a division of the total company contribution.

f. Adopt a variable cost per unit plus a fixed monthly amount to cover fixed costs and profit.

None of these solutions is satisfactory and this is one of the main reasons why Birch Paper is such a good case. It shows the possible conflicts that can occur between divisions and, also, shows how difficult it may be to settle intracompany price disputes equitably. All divisions would be in favor of (d) above except that this solution avoids the issue. The (a) solution is the most theoretically correct, assuming that the Southern prices are really competitive. However, you are still forcing Brunner to make a decision that may not be in his best interests. (b) and (c) are compromises that Southern could rightly oppose if its selling prices were competitive. (e) would be all right if it could be done. I, personally, question whether it wold work, but it might. Although (f) might be appropriate for a general policy, it would not solve this problem because two-step prices applies to, more or less, captive inside sales. It is because of the difficulties in settling disputes such as this that many companies adopt the policy of making the divisions independent in their dealings with each other. As this case demonstrates, however, this policy can be expensive.

Changes to System

It seems to me that Birch Paper has a problem of suboptimization of profits. The first thing it should do is to recognize that this problem exists and decide what, if anything, should be done about it. The case does not give enough information to come up with a definite plan. It may be that the organization should be changed to combine some of the divisions (e.g., Thompson and Southern). The fact that Thompson's bid is so much higher than competition is an indication that other, integrated companies are bidding on the basis of company cost. At $430, Birch would still have a markup of 50 percent over out-of-pocket cost. This would lead me to conclude that the transfer prices were resulting in Thompson's costs being out of line with its competition.

If the organization is to remain as it is at present, Birch should certainly make a study to see the extent to which the system is creating suboptimum decisions and then take some steps to correct these situations. Perhaps the two-step pricing described in the text might be appropriate for some of the products. Also, it might be appropriate to set up a system to monitor some of the principal intracompany relationships to be sure that the best companywide decisions were being made.

JD

Additional Comments

After establishing the idea that this case really deals with a judgmental marketing problem, I next ask the class to accept a quite different set of circumstances so that we may analyze the situation in a logical manner. First, I ask them to assume that Thompson Division is a completely separate unit in a large diversified corporation, i.e., that Thompson is the only division concerned with paper and box manufacture and has no interdivision sales or purchases. Assuming the same market conditions that Thompson is currently facing, I ask if it is perfectly obvious that Thompson should be pricing its products at market ($430) rather than at some higher price. Some students think it is obvious, but others begin to wonder whether Thompson's marketing strategy might not be more profitable for it. We usually end up with a set of figures something like these:

Price Policy	Price	Volume	Contribution to Thompson	Total Contribution
Full cost	$480	400	$80	$32,000
"Shaved"	430	1,000	30	30,000

Although these numbers are purely fictitious, there are several shreds of evidence in the case to support the contention that the Thompson Division is following a marketing strategy something like that illustrated above: (1) Mr. Brunner says that he has been using this "full cost" policy "for weeks now," and it is probably fair to assume that he has received at least a few orders during that period or he would quickly abandon such a policy. And he only needs to receive 40 percent as much business to be as well off. (2) The Thompson Division did some development work for Northern "at cost," and it may be that this is part of the Thompson Division's strategy for all its customers. In any event it is possible to sow sufficient seeds of doubt in the minds of the class that they will generally agree that we lack sufficient evidence to condemn Mr. Brunner at this time.

I then ask what they would do if they were Mr. Brunner's boss in the situation assumed above. Specifically, who should be charged with the responsibility of determining the marketing strategy and pricing policy for this division? The class will generally agree that, although they would be interested in discussing the matter with Mr. Brunner, it is Mr. Brunner who is closest to the situation and has the necessary "feel for the market." Under a decentralized organization, Mr. Brunner should have the authority to test out such a marketing strategy if it appears to be a workable one.

Having established this point, I then ask the class to revert to the original set of case facts and to pinpoint the ways in which their conclusions reached above would be changed because Thompson happens to be the middle division in a chain of three integrated divisions. The discussion then typically turns to the following two items, either one of which may be discussed first.

The Opportunity to Re-Bid

Because the customer in this case (Northern) is another division of Birch, Thompson has the opportunity to lower its original bid, an opportunity which may not exist in dealing with outside customers. Some students, converts to the "hands off" policy as a result of the analysis above, will agree that the commercial vice president should not force Mr. Brunner to lower his bidding procedures to outside customers, but point out that a different pricing policy could be used on inside business. This line of reasoning leads to several problems: (1) Will Northern continue to be able to get bona fide bids from outside suppliers if the inside division always has a chance to match the lowest bid? (2) Should the inside transfer price between Northern and Thompson be $430? (3) Should the price at which Thompson buys from Southern also be renegotiated?

In raising these questions, the students again are making an implicit assumption that the Northern Division always prefers to buy at the lowest price, and once again I ask them to look at this same situation from the point of view of an outside customer. Why has the Thompson Division been successful in winning some orders during the last few weeks at a "full cost" price? Are the customers who place these orders stupid? If, in fact, some customers are willing to pay a premium for Thompson because of the development services and other attributes of its marketing program, then is it not also possible that the Northern Division may decide to buy from Thompson at a price of $480 even though it has received lower bids? In fact, it may be that the manager of the Northern Division is merely trying to take advantage of the fact that Thompson Division is a captive supplier by appealing to the commercial vice president to force Thompson to quote a lower price.

We have never managed to resolve this re-bidding question in class, but it is possible to bring out enough arguments on the other side to leave some students with the question of whether or not the "hands off" policy might not still be the better one.

Thompson's Restricted Point of View

The other issue is perhaps even more fundamental. The marketing strategy adopted by Mr. Brunner may in fact be better for his division but still not in the best interests of the Birch Paper company. Brunner is not recognizing the fact that the Southern Division makes a contribution of $112 on each unit that Thompson sells. The following calculation illustrates the point:

Price	Volume	Contribution to Birch	Total Contribution
$480	400	$192	$ 76,800
430	1,000	142	142,000

One way to correct this picture would be for Mr. Brunner to inform Southern of the strategy that he is using so that Southern might be aware of the implications that Brunner's strategy has for its own pricing policies. If Southern were totally dependent on the Thompson Division, the manager of Southern should make a calculation for his division similar to Thompson's; a calculation like the following:

Price Policy	Price (by Southern to Thompson)	Volume	Contribution to Southern	Total Contribution
Full cost	$280	400	$112	$44,800
"Shaved"	230	1,000	62	62,000

Looking at these figures, the manager of the Southern Division would then realize that he is better off lowering his price to Thompson in order to get higher volume. And Thompson, accepting the new prices from Southern, would then be able to make the following calculation:

Price	Volume	Contribution to Thompson	Total Contribution
$480	400	$130	$52,000
430	1,000	80	80,000

Based on this analysis, Mr. Brunner would be better off to lower his price to $430, thus increasing both his own volume and the volume of the Southern Division.

The fault with this analysis is in assuming that the Southern Division will (or should) follow the same marketing strategy that Thompson is using. Southern is operating in a somewhat different market, and this market has apparently not "weakened" to the extent that Thompson's market has. At least, the fact that Southern has not yet lowered its prices is an indication of this fact. It may be that the picture, seen through the eyes of the division manager of Southern, is something like the following:

Price (by Southern to Thompson and others)	Volume	Contribution to Southern	Expected Contribution
$280	600	$112	$67,200
230	1,000	62	62,000

If Southern's current demand curve is roughly along the lines shown above, then Southern's manager is correctly holding his price up. He is probably getting somewhat more volume than Thompson simply because Southern may be supplying some of Thompson's competitors who are operating with a different pricing strategy.

I have never actually pushed all these figures all the way through in class because starting down this path is usually sufficient for the students to see that each division is faced with a complex problem in pricing strategy. It is unquestionably true that Mr. Brunner is not looking out for the best interests of the entire company, but given the complexities of the situation, the company may, in fact, be better off if Brunner just does a good job of running his division while the manager of the Southern Division tries to do a good job of running his.

RFV

Further Comment

The analysis made above can be used to emphasize the central point about the goal congruence of a management control system. Assume that Mr. Brunner is (a) as knowledgeable as a first-year student about the desirability of making contributions to his profits, and (b) that he has a better feel than anyone else for the situation of the market. Then if he decides to reject the Northern offer, it is because he expects to get additional business from the outside at $480. If he is correct in this decision, the income statement of his division will show a higher profit than otherwise would be the case (which is his personal goal) and so would the income statement of the Birch Paper Company. If he is incorrect, his income statement would be lower, and so would the income statement of the Birch Paper Company. The system that reflects decisions made to achieve his personal goals (i.e., Thompson Division reported profits) also achieves corporate goals. What is good for the Division is good for the Birch Paper Company.

This is easiest to see in connection with the West bid. The situation with respect to Erie is more complicated, but even here if each manager acts in his own self-interest and is free to negotiate with other managers, the decisions they make in their own best interests are also the best decisions for the company. (I usually do not have time to trace through the negotiations, and hence rule out the Erie bid, at least until near the end of the class.)

It can be shown, I think, that goal congruence will exist under all conceivable circumstances (at least all that students have been able to conjure up over the past 20 years.)

The circumstances that make this happen may be worth noting:

1. Managers are competent.

2. Managers are informed.

3. Managers can negotiate with one another.

4. There is a mechanism for arbitration.

5. Market prices exist, and managers are free to buy and sell outside.

Transfer price systems get into difficulty when one or more of these conditions is absent.

RNA

Birch Paper Company—Additional Comments

Approach

This case is one of my favorites. At first look, it appears to be a routine problem in figuring marginal income. Further analysis shows that the solution reached by the marginal income approach does not in fact solve the problem. At this point, the situation appears to illustrate a conflict of interests between divisional management and corporate management, but it turns out that the interests of these two parties are in fact identical. The question that finally emerges is quite different; it has to do with the soundness of a proposed marketing policy, which is clearly set forth in the first sentence of the case, but which gets overlooked as students worry about the figures.

Analysis

I find it useful to diagram the three alternatives, labeling them with prices and differential costs. The diagram is shown on page ??? as Exhibit A.

The obvious first question is: For this particular order, what is the most profitable thing to do? This question is answered by calculating the marginal cost to Birch Paper Company if (1) Northern obtains the boxes from Thompson Division or (2) if Northern buys the boxes from Erie. The alternative of buying from West usually can be dismissed quickly. The difference between West and Erie is only $2, and placing an order with Erie involves more than this of additional income to Birch. However, a profit center "hard liner" may argue Kenton should take the lowest price to his division, West's $430.

If the boxes are made by Thompson, the cash costs to the Birch Paper Company are a follows:

Thompson cash	$ 120
Southern cash costs ($280 × 60%)	168
Total, Birch Paper Company	$ 288

If the boxes are purchased from Erie, the net cash flows for the Birch Paper Company are as follows:

Payment to Erie	$4432
Southern's cash costs ($90 × 60%)	54
Thompson's cash costs (given)	25
Total Birch cash outflows	$ 511
Less cash received from Erie	120
Net cash outflow, Birch	$ 391

If purchased from West, of course, Birch's net cash outflow is $430.

The figures show that Birch is $103 better off if the boxes are made by Thompson than if they are purchased from Erie, and $142 better off than if bought from West.

After the first student puts forth this conclusion, it may be interesting to ask whether the Commercial vice president should, therefore, instruct Northern to buy from Thompson, and the answer will probably be "yes." Then, one can ask innocently, "If this is done, at what price should the transaction be booked?" Then there is consternation, for it is apparent that if the price is $480, Northern's income is being penalized for a decision which was imposed on it, since Northern can in fact obtain the boxes for $432. But if the price is $432, Thompson's income will be affected by a figure which Mr. Brunner argues strenuously is unreasonable.

After some discussion of this question, students may begin to assert that there is something wrong with the system. Apparently, it leads Mr. Brunner to a course of action which is against the best interests of the company as a whole. Now, we are at the heart of the case: Is this so? Does the system motivate Mr. Brunner incorrectly?

There are various ways of exploring this question. The most careful is to examine the effect of possible decisions on the income statement of both the Thompson Division and the whole Birch Paper Company. It will be seen that if the order goes to Erie, the effect on Birch as a whole will be unfavorable, but so will the effect on Thompson, for Thompson will lose business on which it can make some marginal income. Conversely, if Thompson makes the boxes, the total Birch income will be improved, and so will the reported income of Thompson Division. There is, therefore, no conflict of interest in this situation; it is *not* true that Brunner wants to do something that will help his division but hurt the company this is not true in the *short* run.

If desired, this type of analysis can be extended to other divisions and other types of problems, and it will be seen that if (1) the division managers have full information, (2) they are free to negotiate with one another, and (3) they are competent, they will almost always reach decisions which, when in the best interests of their own divisions, are also in the best interests of the company as a whole.

How, then, do we account for the fact that a controversy is raging? The answer must be either that Brunner does not have a good argument, perhaps because he does not understand the marginal income idea; or that he is competent and is perfectly willing to lose this business in order to put teeth into his new pricing policy. This is what he says in the first paragraph of the case, and the simple answer may be that he is right.

It is, of course, also possible that he can implement his pricing policy to the outside world and still make these boxes at $432. If so, he would be wrong to refuse the business at $432. But Brunner might reason the other way: "Let Erie fill up its plant at $432 business, and I'll gamble that by waiting, I can get enough business at $480." In any event, the correct decision turns on a judgment about the market. To illustrate this point, I put the following hypothetical figures on the board:

Price Policy	Price	Volume	Unit Contribution	Total Contribution
"Shaved"	$430	1,000	$30	$30,000
"Full"	$480	375	80	30,000

This shows that with "full" pricing, Brunner's division can earn a given profit with only 37.5 percent of the volume needed to earn that profit with "shaved" prices. Moreover, the case states that "Brunner had on occasion in the past few months been unable to operate the Thompson Division at capacity" it does not say that Thompson has chronic and severe overcapacity. If Brunner's new pricing policy were out-of-step with the market, wouldn't his sales for a commodity-type item have fallen by now?

Moreover, the case states that the new profit center approach at Birch "had been successfully applied and that the company's profits and competitive position had definitely improved." Yet up to this point in the discussion, a majority of students are prepared to abandon this approach and/or to fire Brunner. I always ask them, "How did Brunner get to be a division manager if he's so unenlightened?"

Personally, as commercial vice president, I would make sure that Brunner understands the situation; and that he has sound reasons for feeling the way he does about his new pricing policy. Then, I would let him make up his own mind whether to refuse the business or accept it at $432. I would not be at all surprised if he immediately accepted it at $432, which could confirm my suspicion that actually, he is asking me to intervene simply to get a higher price for the Northern boxes. But neither would I be surprised if he stuck to the line enunciated in the first paragraph of the case. If the commercial vice president intervenes on this and similar situations, the whole divisional profit measurement system will soon be meaningless.

Similarly, I would not force the Southern Division's manager to cut his price on materials. Why should he go below the market price, if that's what Thompson would have to pay anyway? I often have two students role-play Brunner and the Southern Division manager. If Brunner threatens to buy outside at $280 to "spite" the Southern manager, if the latter is shrewd he'll call this bluff, with an offhand comment about how Brunner will explain to top management his (Brunner's) decision to buy outside when there is no price advantage in doing so.

— Jim Reece

Exhibit A

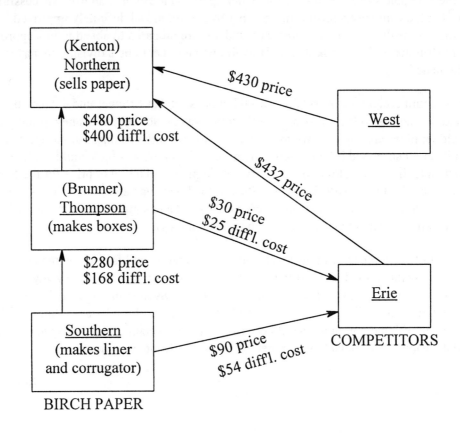

BIRCH PAPER

BIRCH PAPER COMPANY:

TRANSFER PRCING—THE ACHLLES HEEL OF PROFIT CENTER MANAGEMENT

Vijay Govindaraian

The Amos Tuck School of Business Administration

Dartmouth College

Hanover, NH 03755

Fortune 1000 Companies

% of companies
with two or more
profit centers   93%

Of these, % of companies
that transfer products
between profit centers   80%

Key Issue

A year from now, you will be working for multi-divisional, decentralized companies with transfer of goods and services taking place across divisions. Clearly, if at all divisional control is to make any sense, the question of transfer pricing becomes very important. The central question in designing a transfer pricing policy is:

> How should the transfer prices be set so that
> the actions taken by division managers in their
> *own interest* will also be in the best interest of
> the *overall company*? "Goal congruence"

Birch Paper Co.

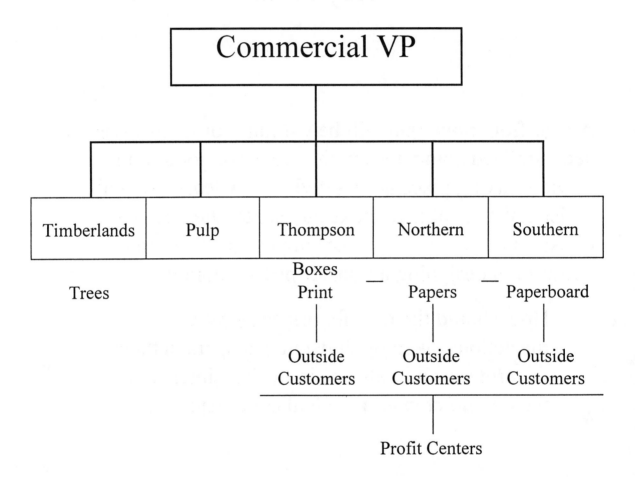

Transfer Price = Arm's Length Market Prices

Thompson Division

Price	Profit	Volume	Total Profit
$480	$80	400 (40%)	$32,000
$430	$30	1,000 (100%)	$30,000

Thompson Division

Price	Profit	Volume	Total Profit
$480	$80	400 (40%)	$32,000
$430	$30	1,000 (100%)	$30,000

Company's Results

Price	Profit	Volume	Total Profit
$480	$192	400 (40%)	$76,800
$430	$142	1,000 (100%)	$142,000

Southern Division

Price	Profit	Volume		Total Profit
$280	$112	400	(40%)	$44,800
$230	$62	1,000	(100%)	$62,000

Thompson Division

Price	Profit	Volume		Total Profit
$480	$130	400	(40%)	$52,000
$430	$80	1,000	(100%)	$80,000

Southern Division

Price	Profit	Volume		Total Profit
$280	$112	600	(60%)	$67,200
$230	$62	1,000	(100%)	$62,000

Box Plant

$$\frac{\text{Profit after tax}}{\text{Sales}} \times \frac{\text{Sales}}{\text{Investment}} = \frac{\text{PAT}}{\text{Investment}}$$

$$5\% \qquad \times \quad 3 \text{ Times} \quad = \qquad 15\%$$

Profit Margin (Before Tax) = 10%

Selling Price		$ 480
Variable Cost	$ 400	
Fixed Cost	$ 32 (7% of sales)	
	$ 432	
PBT	$ 48 (10% of sales)	

Paperboard Mill

$$\frac{\text{Profit after tax}}{\text{Sales}} \times \frac{\text{Sales}}{\text{Investment}} = \frac{\text{PAT}}{\text{Investment}}$$

$$10\% \qquad \times \quad 1.5 \text{ Times} \quad = \qquad 15\%$$

Profit Margin (Before Tax) = 20%

Selling Price		$ 280
Variable Cost	$ 168	
Fixed Cost	$ 56	(20% of sales)
		$ 214
PBT		$ 56 (20% of sales)

Transfer price between Thompson and Northern:

$430 vs. $480

What is Thompson's strategy?

Low cost vs. Differentiation

Price	Profit	Volume	Total Profit
$480	$80	400 (40%)	$32,000
430	30	1,000 (100%)	30,000

Some Evidence In Support Of Differentiation

1. This policy, in effect for four weeks, must have received some orders

2. "Development" work as the basis for differentiation "specialty box"

3. Quality, dependability

4. Price is not the only way to compete

Should Thompson Division have a strategy ("Differentiation") which is different from the other divisions of Birch Paper Company?

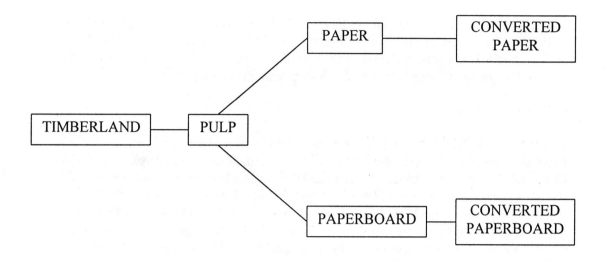

This depends upon Birch Paper's Strategy:

"One Business"

vs.

"Separate Businesses"

Case 6-3

General Appliance Corporation

Approach

This case requires two days (or sometimes three). One method is to use the "Stove Top Problem" for the first day and "Thermostatic Control Problem" and "Transmission Problem" for the second day. Another way is to discuss the solutions to the immediate issues on the first day and to take up the problem of changes in the overall system on the second day.

A. Stove Top Problem

This is a very difficult case because (as usual in transfer price problems) there is no really satisfactory answer. The discussion tends to be involved, heated, and fairly evenly divided. One group favors the Electric Stove Division because they had not been consulted on the change and, therefore, were not responsible and should not have to pay for it. Others believe that the change was made for the good of the company and should be paid for by the division that received the benefit of the change—the Electric Stove Division. They argue that the Chrome Products Division was providing better quality at an added cost and should, therefore, be reimbursed.

These arguments will go on as long as the instructor permits. I like to stop the discussion as soon as the main points are brought out and try to summarize where we stand.

1. The vice president of the Manufacturing Staff has been assigned line responsibility by the president and has exercised this responsibility. Thus, a limitation has been placed on divisional autonomy.

2. We do not know whether the action taken was in the best interests of the company. The Electric Stove Division would oppose paying for the change in quality even if it believed it to be necessary. If the division agreed to the change, it would have to pay for it. By opposing it, it may get out of paying for it. (One of the problems with decentralization is that frequently people are not above "playing games" to increase divisional profitability.)

3. The controller must settle the dispute. Consequently, the solution to the problem cannot be to fire the manufacturing vice president or something equally drastic.

This case was prepared by John Dearden and Robert N. Anthony.

Copyright © 1959 by the President and Fellows of Harvard College. Harvard Business School case 160-003.

The real issue is whether the change in quality should have been made or not. One possible solution would be to have a group consisting of a representative of the Electric Stove Division, the Chrome Products Division, and the Manufacturing Staff restudy the decision and decide whether the change in quality standard was necessary or not. If the group decides positively, then the Electric Stove Division pays for it. Otherwise, the production processes revert to the old quality standards. This may not be feasible, however, because such a study has presumably already been made. The Electric Stove Division representative would have to follow the position already taken by the division. Likewise, the Manufacturing Staff representative could hardly contradict his boss.

As controller, therefore, perhaps the only solution is to look at it this way:

1. Either the action was correct or it was not.

2. If it were the correct action, it would be equitable to charge the Electric Stove Division for the better quality.

3. If it were not the correct action, it should be charged to the division best able to change the decision. In this case, it was the Electric Stove Division.

4. Consequently, charge the Electric Stove Division for the quality change. If this division sincerely believes that the quality difference is not worth the cost, they would be able to get it changed as soon as the emphasis on quality is relaxed.

Incidentally, this case was written up in the May-June 1964 issue of the *Havard Business Review* under the title of "The Case of the Disputing Divisions."

B. Thermostatic Control Problem

In the classification given in the text, the thermostatic control unit would be a Class 2 part. It would, therefore, be priced at $2.40 because this is the long-range competitive price. This price, however, would appear to be unjust to the Refrigeration Division because, if it had not agreed to buy the part inside, it could still obtain it on the outside for $2.15. If the Refrigeration Division pays $2.15, it does not seem to make much sense for the Laundry to pay $2.40 when its requirements are five times as great as the Refrigeration Division.

The answer to this case depends on the transfer price policy of General Appliance and this case will force the company to meet this issue squarely. If the policy is long-term competitive price levels, the price would be $2.40, with possibly some relief to the Refrigeration Division. (For example, the price could be $2.15 for the next year. After that it would go to $2.40.) If the policy is to transfer parts within the company at short-term competitive prices, the price to the Refrigeration Division would be $2.15. The problem would be rationalizing a system that uses two different prices for the same product, with the higher price being paid by the division with the largest requirements.

I personally prefer a transfer policy similar to that described in the text. Under this policy, the price would be $2.40. The Refrigeration Division would have to accept the fact that there are other advantages to being part of General Appliance that offset the disadvantage of being unable to profit from a temporary depression in prices.

C. Transmission Problem

This case involves the question of whether or not a penalty should be assessed against the Laundry Equipment Division for failing to speak out when they were quoted as agreeing to a transfer price that was the basis for a capital investment decision. However, the Gear and Transmission Division was also not without fault. They must have known that the $12 price would be unacceptable to the Laundry Equipment Division and, consequently, they should have made more of an effort to negotiate a price that was acceptable.

The first consideration is whether or not a mistake had been made. That is to say, would the plant have been built if a valid transfer price had been used. If the investment would have been approved even using the lower transfer price in the capital investment analysis, then the solution to this problem is easy. The transfer price would be $11.25 because that is the price that would have resulted if everything had been done correctly. Neither division would be suffering a penalty.

If, however, the plant would not have been built, had the correct transfer price been used in the capital investment analysis, the problem becomes more difficult. There is a penalty and the question is: Who should absorb this penalty? It is my opinion that the penalty should be divided equally between the two divisions. That is, the price should be halfway between $11.50 (the $12 price minus the $.50 error) and $11.25. "Splitting the difference" is the most unsatisfactory way to settle transfer price disputes but, in this case, both divisions appear to be at fault in creating a mistake.

Obviously, company policy should be changed to require formal approval of any transfer price included in a capital investment proposal.

JD

General Appliance Corp
Some Fundamental Issues

- Why decentralize?

- How can decentralization work most effectively?

- What is top management's role in a decentralized organization?

Three Specific Disputes

- What decisions should be made in the three disputes?

- Could the problems have been avoided in the first place?

- How should manufacturing/marketing interdivisional pricing be handled?

- How should sourcing decisions be handled?

Current System

- Profit Centers

- Transfer Price = Market Price

- Sourcing constrained

Case 6-4

Strider Chemical Company

Approach

This is a fairly straightforward case in transfer pricing. The system described has some fairly obvious weaknesses, and the case is a good vehicle for giving practice in locating these weaknesses and suggesting practical ways of overcoming them.

Discussion

There are two basic reasons that explain why the Strider system is not a very good one as of the time of the case. First, is the speed with which the company introduced divisionalization. Less than a month was allowed to get ready, and in this brief time it is unrealistic to expect that the divisions could work out a good structure of transfer prices. Second, in this company there are a great many products, many of them probably having a small volume. Being a chemical company, it is also one in which joint costs are prevalent. Therefore, even if more time had been allowed, there would be more than an average amount of difficulty in arriving at good transfer prices.

The policy laid down by the president is perhaps defensible as a temporary, stopgap measure, but it has some clear weaknesses and should be changed immediately. The president evidently sought to tie the transfer prices to market prices. He starts out with a market price and adjusts this by subtracting costs that would not be incurred internally. Actually, it is debatable whether these adjustments should be made at all or at least to the extent that he suggests.. The costs, or at least some of them, may in fact be incurred on internal transactions. An easier alternative might be simply to use the external market price; however, there are arguments on both sides here, and we do not have enough facts to make a firm conclusion. If the elements of cost are, in fact, absent in internal transactions, there are good grounds for reducing the price accordingly.

The policy statement should also provide a mechanism for building a price up from cost when no market price exists. The present statement is silent on this kind of problem.

The policy statement clearly should provide for a means of negotiation between the divisions concerned. It should also provide for an arbitration mechanism, and such a mechanism should not send disputes immediately to the president for resolution. Rather, they should first go to someone below him, such as the controller, and should go to the president only on appeal. (A possible argument in favor of having disputes go to the president initially is that he might want to use this as a device for finding out about the problems involved in getting the transfer price structure going; however, what has actually happened is that disputes are piling up in his office without resolution, and this is not good.)

This case was prepared by Robert N. Anthony.

Copyright © 1965 by the President and Fellows of Harvard College. Harvard Business School case 166-016.

This case may not be reproduced. Separate copies for classroom and other use should be ordered from Harvard Business School Publishing, Customer Service, Boston, MA 02163. An order form with information on how to order cases will be found at the back of this manual. The availability of cases is subject to change.

The Williams Division did not actually follow the president's policy. Instead, it used a cost build-up. This Williams procedure superficially appeared to take the elements discussed in the president's policy, but these elements were to create a profit margin that was added on to cost, rather than to make a reduction from the market price; the latter is what the president intended. Furthermore, the Williams Division adds its margin to actual cost rather than to standard cost, thus guaranteeing itself a profit on interdivisional sales. The motivation provided by such a structure is wrong, especially when there is no provision for negotiation between the divisions. As a stopgap, there might be an argument for a *standard* profit margin, computed in the way the Williams Division computed it, but it should be added to standard cost rather than to actual cost. Of course, it is conceivable that standard costs were not available.

The practice of the Johnson Division was even worse. It has all the faults of the Williams Division practice, and in addition the fault that it took the Williams Division markup rather than one based on Johnson's own experience. There is no justification for using the Williams Division markup. If the Johnson Division is, in fact, a low-earning division, this fact should be highlighted, rather than hidden by the transfer price mechanism.

The specific problem between the Williams Division and the International Division could probably be settled by negotiation. If the Williams Division wants the business badly enough, it should be willing to reduce its domestic price to a price equal to what the International Division would have to pay if it went elsewhere. If it was unwilling to reduce the price this much, then the company would be better off if the International Division went elsewhere for the product. The exception to this statement is that headquarters might possibly want the Williams Division products to be handled by the International Division for strategic reasons. If so, it should direct that the transfer be made, and headquarters division must then set the selling price itself, because negotiation would not arrive at an equitable price under these circumstances; the divisions have no bargaining power when headquarters directs the action.

The argument between the Williams Division and the Western Division could also probably be settled by negotiation. If the Williams Division was unwilling to reduce its price to the point that the Western Division thought comparable with its own manufacturing costs plus profit, then the Western Division has good reason to build its own facilities. It should, of course, submit a capital budgeting proposal for these facilities, and in the justification for this proposal, Western would have to demonstrate that it could make an adequate return on investment from manufacturing chemical B itself, as compared with the lowest price that the Williams Division was willing to sell chemical B for. I would guess that the Williams Division would prefer to reduce the price by 15 percent rather than to have the Western Division build manufacturing facilities, but this is only a guess. In any event, the mechanism should work in such a way that the final decision would be in the best interests of the Strider Chemical Company.

Sometimes students get an impression from the problems described in a situation of this type that transfer pricing causes an undue amount of friction. The problems described here do indicate that friction exists, but the controversies bring to light policy questions which should be solved, and which might not have been brought to light in the absence of a transfer price mechanism. If these questions are resolved without undue delay (and it is not good for them to sit on the president's desk for several months without action), then the results should be good for the overall company.

RNA

Case 6-5

Medoc Company

The Milling Division is a classic example of what I call a "pseudo" profit center. A pseudo profit center is one where the divisional manager has limited control over profitability. In this case, the manager of the Milling Division has no control over 50 percent of his purchases and 80 percent of his sales. Therefore, it seems to me that it is completely illogical to treat it was a profit center. Also, even organizationally it appears illogical. Why does it have a marketing department for 20 percent of its sales?

A very simple solution would be to transfer all of the marketing responsibility to the Consumer Products Division and make the Milling Division into a cost center. Flour would be transferred to the Consumer Products Division at variable standard cost per unit plus a monthly charge for the standard fixed and nonvariable costs. The Consumer Product Division would be allowed to review and comment on any proposed capital expenditures by the Milling Division that would affect this charge.

The case, however, precludes this action. Consequently, we are faced with establishing a transfer pricing system to overcome the possible dysfunctional effects of an apparently illogical organization and a profit center with little control over profits. In this case, some adaption of the variable cost per unit plus a monthly fixed charge would be the best way to handle their problem. I would recommend a somewhat different method of calculating both the variable and fixed charges.

1. I think the variable per unit charge should be at *standard* cost, adjusted for *actual* grain prices. Otherwise, there is little incentive for the Milling Division to control manufacturing costs. The Milling Division's efficiencies or inefficiencies will be reflected in the Consumer Product's profit performance.

2. Instead of changing the percentage of capacity chargeable to the Consumer Product Division each year, I would keep it constant and change it only when:

   a. capacity was changed because of added facilities, or

   b. there was a significant and permanent change in the markets in which the flour is sold.

3. Instead of 10 percent profit on investment, I would use the average percentage earned by the Milling Division on its outside sales.

This case was prepared by Robert N. Anthony.

Copyright © 1971 by the President and Fellows of Harvard College. Harvard Business School case 171-284.

4. The above system would be in effect only as long a there was no shortage of capacity. Once the Milling Division reaches capacity, some mechanism should be set up to be sure that the flour is allocated to the areas of maximum profitability to the company. Such a mechanism might be a committee with representatives from both divisions and central staff (or, perhaps, just an executive from central staff) to review the alternatives and decide on the optimum allocation of the flour.

    Also, I would provide for the Consumer Product Division to review and comment on any facility projects initialed by the Milling Division.

Classroom Strategy

Since this is a very short case with a single problem, I try to be nondirective in teaching this case. I open the class by asking what the Medoc Company should do about the transfer price problem. I try to separate the discussion into two parts:

1. What should be done, if there were no constraints on management action; and

2. What should be done, if given the constraints in the case.

I try not to spend too much time on the first question. I believe, however, that it is useful for the class to think about a rearrangement of profit responsibility. We spend most of the time on the second question. Hopefully, I end up with most of the above analysis on the blackboard.

JD

CHAPTER 7
MEASURING AND CONTROLLING ASSETS EMPLOYED

Changes from the Eighth Edition

This chapter retains the basic thrust of the eighth edition. We now consistently use the term "Economic Value Added" instead of "Residual Income."

Cases

Investment Center Problems (A) and (B) give practice in using the various techniques and also explore how small differences in approaches can produce large differences in results.

Quality Metal Service Center relates the measurement of investment center performance to an incentive bonus calculation.

Industrial Products Corporation focuses on the problems of defining the individual items that are to be included in the investment base. This case is an update of Diversified Products Corporation.

Marden Company sets up a simple set of accounts that can be used to study the effect of alternative definitions of the investment base and of income.

Lemfert Company is a short case that discusses transfer prices that include a return on assets.

Case 7-1

Investment Center Problems (A)[1]

Approach

These problems require more time than the instructor probably wants to spend on this topic. If you don't want to examine the effect of different depreciation methods, eliminate Questions 2(A) and 2(B); similarly, eliminate Questions 3(A), 3(B), and 3(C). Each of the later problems has a different message. Any can be omitted, except that if you omit Question 6, you can't assign Question 7.

There follows a worksheet that Prof. James S. Reece uses for problems 1, 2, and 3. One copy is blank so that you can reproduce it; the solution to the worksheets is provided.

If you assign Questions 2 and 3, students may need an explanation of composite and unit depreciation.

Some conclusions that can be derived from these problems are as follows:

1. Marketing divisions tend to have fewer assets than manufacturing divisions. This affects their relative ROI's.

2. Use of balance sheet asset values favors divisions with older assets.

3. If a division uses gross book value, it can increase its ROI:

   a. By scrapping useful assets whose ROI is lower than the divisional ROI.

   b. By making an investment in new equipment whose incremental cost produces a satisfactory ROI. (Incremental cost is the cost of the new equipment less the cost of the superseded equipment.)

4. If the division uses net book value,

   a. Its ROI automatically increases the older the equipment gets.

   b. If it uses unit depreciation, the loss is shown in the year the asset is scrapped.

   c. If it uses composite depreciation, the real division profits usually are overstated, compared with not taking depreciation into account.

Questions 1 and 2

See worksheet.

---

[1] The solution to these problems benefited by comments from Jim Reece, University of Michigan.

Investment Center Problems

Note: To save space, round figures to the nearest thousand dollars; e.g., show $2 million as $2,000. Ignore taxes throughout.

Question 1

ROI Calculations	Division A	Division B	Division C
Profit before depreciation and market development	$200	$ 200	$200
Depreciation	—	100	50
Market development expense	100	—	50
Profit	$100	$ 100	$100
Total assets	$100	$1,100	$600
ROI (nearest tenth of a %)	100.0%	9.1%	16.7%

Conclusion: Marketing division have lower investment; therefore, higher ROI.

Question 2

A. New Project ROI: (gross book, composite)	(a)	(b)
New investment	$2,000	$2,500
Less: Old Investment	1,500	1,500
Δ Investment	$ 500	$1,000
Savings (before depreciation)	$ 300	$ 200
Less: Depreciation on new	(200)	(250)
Plus: Depreciation on old	150	150
Net savings	$ 250	$ 100
ROI	50.0%	10.0%

Conclusion: Optimism on capital budgeting proposals can result in ROI significantly lower than "promised"; therefore, need for capital expenditure controls.

New Division Budget	Original Budget	Δ for Investment	Adjusted Budget
(a) Profits	$ 1,000	$ 250	$ 1,250
Assets	$10,000	$ 500	$10,500
ROI	10.0%	50.0%	11.9%
(b) Profits	$ 1,000	$ 100	$ 1,100
Assets	$10,000	$1,000	$11,000
ROI	10.0%	10.0%	10.0%

Conclusion: Not achieving "promised" return shows up as ROI of 10% (no worse than before) instead of 11.9 percent. Hence, other things being equal, ROI *does* signal lack of "promised" results; but it does *not* indicate that project in (b) is unsound.

B. ROI Calculations: (gross book, unit)

	(a) 1987	(a) 1988	(b) 1987	(b) 1988
New investment	$2,000	$2,000	$2,500	$2,500
Less: Old Investment	1,500	1,500	1,500	1,500
Δ Investment	$ 500	$ 500	$1,000	$1,000
Savings (before depreciation)	$ 300	$ 300	$ 200	$ 200
Less: Depreciation on new	(200)	(200)	(250)	(250)
Plus: Depreciation on old	150	150	150	150
Net savings	$ 250	$ 250	$ 100	$ 100
Less: Book loss on old	(450)	—	(450)	—
Net profit impact	$ 200	$ 250	$ (350)	$ 100
ROI	(40.0)%	50.0%	(35.0)%	10.0%

Same as in Problem b.

Conclusion: Using unit depreciation gives accounting loss in the first year; manager may not propose attractive investment in (a).

Impact on 1987 Division ROI
(1988 same as in problem b):

	Original Budget	Δ for Investment	Adjusted Budget
(a) Profits	$ 1,000	$ (200)	$ 800
Assets	$10,000	$ 500	$10,500
ROI	10.0%	(40.0)%	7.6%
(b) Profits	$ 1,000	$ (350)	$ 650
Assets	$10,000	$1,000	$11,000
ROI	10.0%	(35.0)%	5.9%

Conclusion: Same as above—book loss on disposal may discourage manager from proposing new investment.

Question 3

ROI Calculations: (EOY net book, unit)

	(a) 1987	(a) 1988	(b) 1987	(b) 1988
Net Δinvestment*	$1,500	$1,450	$1,950	$1,850
Gross savings	300	300	200	200
Less: Depreciation on new	(200)	(200)	(250)	(250)
Plus: Depreciation on old	150	150	150	150
Less: Loss on disposal	(450)	—	(450)	—
Net savings	$ (200)	$ 250	$ (350)	$ 100
ROI	(13.3)%	17.2%	(17.9)%	5.4%

*Deriving these figures is not straightforward; try to determine how the amounts shown were calculated. (Hint: Work the next part, analysis of divisional fixed assets, and compare with balances had old machine been kept.)

Conclusion: Same as Problem 2; only year 1 and year 2 "swing" less severe.

Analysis of Divisional Fixed Assets:

	(a)				(b)		
	Gross	Deprec.	Net		Gross	Deprec.	Net
As of 1/1/87	$6,000	$3,000	$3,000		$6,000	$3,000	$3,000
New investment	2,000	—	2,000		2,500	—	2,500
Old retired	(1,500)	(1,050)	(450)		(1,500)	(1,050)	(450)
New base	$6,500	$1,950	$4,550		$7,000	$1,950	$5,050
1987 depreciation	10%	650	—		10%	700	—
Balance, 12/31/87	$6,500	$2,600	$3,900		$7,000	$2,650	$4,350
1988 depreciation	—	650	—		—	700	—
Balance, 12/31/88	$6,500	$3,250	$3,250		$7,000	$3,350	$3,650

Worksheets for Investment Center
Problems 1, 2, and 3

Note: To save space, round figures to the nearest thousand dollars; e.g., show $2 million as $2,000. Ignore taxes throughout.

Question 1

ROI Calculations:	Division A	Division B	Division C
Profit before depreciation and market development	$	$	$
Depreciation			
Market development expense	_____	_____	_____
Profit	$_____	$_____	$_____
Total assets	$_____	$_____	$_____
ROI (nearest tenth of a %)	%	%	%

Question 2

A. <u>New Project ROI: (gross book, composite)</u>	(a)	(b)
New investment	$	$
Less: Old investment	_____	_____
Δ Investment	_____	_____
Savings (before depreciation)	$	$
Less: Depreciation on new		
Plus: Depreciation on old	_____	_____
Net impact on profit	$_____	$_____
Δ ROI	%	%

New Division Budget:	Original Budget	Δ for Investment	Adjusted Budget
(a) Profits	$	$	$
Assets	$	$	$
ROI	%	%	%
(b) Profits	$	$	$
Assets	$	$	$
ROI	%	%	%

Question 2

B. ROI Calculations: (gross book, unit)	(a)		(b)	
	1987	1988	1987	1988
New investment	$	$	$	$
Less: Old investment	_____	_____	_____	_____
Δ Investment	$_____	$_____	$_____	$_____
Savings (before depreciation)	$	$	$	$
Less: Depreciation on new				
Plus: Depreciation on old	_____	_____	_____	_____
Impact on profit	$	$	$	$
Less: Loss on disposal	_____	_____	_____	_____
Net impact on profit	$_____	$_____	$_____	$_____
Δ ROI	%	%	%	%

Impact on 1987 Divisional ROI (1988 same as in Problem b):	Original Budget	Δ for Investment	Adjusted Budget
Profits	$	$	$
Assets	$	$	$
ROI	%	%	%
(b) Profits	$	$	$
Assets	$	$	$
ROI	%	%	%

Question 3

A. ROI Calculations: (gross book, unit)

	(a) 1987	(a) 1988	(b) 1987	(b) 1988
New Δ investment*	$ 1,500	$ 1,450	$ 1,950	$ 1,850
Gross savings	$	$	$	$
Less: Depreciation on new				
Plus: Depreciation on old				
Less: Loss on disposal	_____	_____	_____	_____
Net impact on profit	$_____	$_____	$_____	$_____
Δ ROI	%	%	%	%

*Deriving these figures is not straightforward; try to determine how the amounts shown were calculated. (Hint: Work the next part, analysis of divisional fixed assets, and compare with balances had the old machine been kept.)

Analysis of Divisional Fixed Assets:

	Gross	(a) Deprec.	Net	Gross	(b) Deprec.	Net
As of 1/1/87	$	$	$	$	$	$
New investment						
Old retired	_____	_____	_____	_____	_____	_____
New base	$_____	$_____	$_____	$_____	$_____	$_____
1987 depreciation	_____	_____	_____	_____	_____	_____
Balance, 12/21/87	$_____	$_____	$_____	$_____	$_____	$_____
1988 depreciation	_____	_____	_____	_____	_____	_____
Balance, 12/21/88	$	$	$	$	$	$

Note to students: If you are short of time, skip the next page.

Analysis of Divisional Fixed Assets:

	(a) Gross	(a) Deprec.	(a) Net	(b) Gross	(b) Deprec.	(b) Net
As of 1/1/87	$	$	$	$	$	$
New investment						
Old retired	_____	_____	_____	_____	_____	_____
New base	$	$	$	$	$	$
1987 depreciation	_____ =	_____	_____ =	_____ =	_____	_____ =
Balance, 12/31/87	$_____	$_____	$_____	$_____	$_____	$_____
1988 depreciation	_____ =	_____	_____ =	_____ =	_____	_____ =
Balance, 12/31/88	$	$	$	$	$	$

Revised ROI Budget:	Original Budget	Δ for Investment	Adjusted Budget
(a) 1987 Profits	$	$	$
Assets*	$	$	$
ROI	%	%	%
1988 Profits	$	$	$
Assets*	$	$	$
ROI	%	%	%
(b) 1987 Profits	$	$	$
Assets*	$	$	$
ROI	%	%	%
1987 Profits	$	$	$
Assets*	$	$	$
ROI	%	%	%

Revised ROI Budget:	Original Budget	Δ for Investment	Adjusted Budget
(a) 1987 Profits	$	$	$
Assets*	$	$	$
ROI	%	%	%
1988 Profits	$	$	$
Assets*	$	$	$
ROI	%	%	%
(b) 1987 Profits	$	$	$
Assets*	$	$	$
ROI	%	%	%
1987 Profits	$	$	$
Assets*	$	$	$
ROI	%	%	%

*Assume current assets of $4 million throughout.

	(a)		(b)	
ROI Calculations:	1987	1988	1987	1988
New Δ investment*	$ 1,950	$ 1,900	$ 2,400	$ 2,300
Gross savings	$	$	$	$
Less: Depreciation on new				
Plus: Depreciation on old	_____	_____	_____	_____
Net impact on profit	$_____	$_____	$_____	$_____
Δ ROI	%	%	%	%

*See note to Question 3.

| | (a) | | (b) | |
ROI Calculations:	1987	1988	1987	1988
Net Δ investment*	$ 1,554	$ 1,282	$ 1,963	$ 1,609
Gross savings	$	$	$	$
Less: Depreciation on new				
Plus: Depreciation on old	_____	_____	_____	_____
Net impact on profit	$_____	$_____	$_____	$_____
Δ ROI	%	%	%	%

*Do *not* take the time to verify these amounts.

Question 4(a)

Year	Investment Beginning	Investment Ending	Investment Average	Profits	Rate of Return
1	100,000	80,000	90,000	5,000	5.6%
2	80,000	60,000	70,000	5,000	7.1%
3	60,000	40,000	50,000	5,000	10.0%
4	40,000	20,000	30,000	5,000	16.7%
5	20,000	0	10,000	5,000	50.0%
Average			50,000	5,000	10%

(b)

Year	Depreciation	Investment Beginning	Investment Ending	Investment Average
1	33,333	100,000	66,667	83,333
2	26,667	66,667	40,000	53,333
3	20,000	40,000	20,000	30,000
4	13,333	20,000	6,667	13,333
5	6,667	6,667	0	3,333
Total	100,000			183,332
Average	20,000			36,667

Year	Profits before Depreciation	Depreciation	Profits after Depreciation	Investment	ROI
1	25,000	33,333	(8,333)	83,333	(10.0%)
2	25,000	26,667	(1,667)	53,333	(3.1%)
3	25,000	20,000	5,000	30,000	16.7%
4	25,000	13,333	11,667	13,333	87.3%
5	25,000	6,667	18,333	3,333	550.0%
Total	125,000	100,000	25,000	183,332	
Average	25,000	20,000	5,000	36,667	27.3%

Question 5

Year	Earnings before Depreciation	Return on 10% on Investment	Depreciation	Investment End of Year
0				100,000
1	16,275	10,000	6,275	93,725
2	16,275	9,373	6,902	86,823
3	16,275	8,682	7,593	79,230
4	16,275	7,923	8,352	70,878
5	16,275	7,088	9,187	61,691
6	16,275	6,169	10,106	51,585
7	16,275	5,159	11,116	40,469
8	16,275	4,047	12,228	28,241
9	16,275	2,824	13,451	14,790
10	16,275	1,479	14,790	—

Question 6

ROI	Division J	Division K	Division L
Budgeted Profit	90	55	50
Budgeted Assets	500	600	800
ROI	18.0%	9.2%	6.2%
Actual Profits	80	60	50
Actual Assets	490	640	900
Actual ROI	16.3%	9.4	5.5
Act. over/(under) Budget	(1.7)	(.2)	(.7)
RI			
Budgeted RI	45.0[a]	5.0[b]	(15.0)[c]
Actual RI	35.5[d]	5.5[e]	(22.5)[f]
Actual over/(under) Budget	(9.5)	.5	(7.5)

[a] $90 - .05(100) - .1(400) = 45.0$

[b] $55 - .05(200) - .1(400) = 5.0$

[c] $50 - .05(300) - .1(500) = (15.0)$

[d] $80 - .05(90) - .1(400) = 35.5$

[e] $60 - .05(190) - .1(450) = 5.5$

[f] $50 - .05(350) - .1(550) = (22.5)$

Question 7

ROI	Division J	Division K	Division L
Budgeted ROI	18.0%	9.1%	6.2%
ROI after Situation 1	16.7	9.2	6.7
Increase/(Decrease)	(1.3)	.1	.5
ROI after Situation 2	16.1	8.9	6.3
Increase/(Decrease)	(1.9)	(.2)	.1
ROI after Situation 3	18.1	9.1	6.0
Increase/(Decrease)	.1	–	(.2)
ROI after Situation 4	19.4	9.1	5.9
Increase/(Decrease)	1.4	–	(.3)
Residual Income			
Budgeted RI	45.0	5.0	(15.0)
RI after Situation 1	45.0	5.0	(15.0)
Increase/(Decrease)	–	–	–
RI after Situation 2	42.0	2.0	(18.0)
Increase/(Decrease)	(3.0)	(3.0)	(3.0)
RI after Situation 3	42.5	2.5	(17.5)
Increase/(Decrease)	(2.5)	(2.5)	(2.5)
RI after Situation 4	45.0	5.0	(15.0)
Increase/(Decrease)	–	–	–

JD

Case 7-2

Investment Center Problems (B)

Authors: Elaine Luttrell and M. Edgar Barrett

Substantive Issues Raised

These exercises comprise a series of computational problems to illustrate the nature of return on investment and residual income measures and factors that affect their use in performance evaluation. Effects of asset valuation, gross or net, income, and effects of investments under alternative conditions are illustrated.

Pedagogical Objectives

Any or all of the exercises can be assigned depending on the lessons about return on investment and residual income you wish to, teach. The exercises provide both computational practice and lessons in factors that affect ROA, ROI, and residual income.

Opportunities for Student Analysis

Suggested solutions to the exercises are included as Exhibits TN-1 through TN-15, with the number of each exhibit corresponding to the exercise number.

Briefly, the exercises teach the following lessons.

Exhibit TN-1. Return on assets (ROA) is a function of asset valuation and income. Units with the same income will have different return on assets if the assets employed are different. More assets means lower ROA.

Exhibits TN-2 through TN-5. Adding new equipment changes ROA, and whether ROA goes down, up, or stays the same depends on the cost of assets replaced, added, and their respective profitability as well as whether gross or net value of assets is used.

Exhibits TN-6 through TN-8. Reported ROA on the same economic event can be very different. Each example describes a project with an IRR of 7.93 percent, but ROA's differ dramatically depending on when assets are measured and the depreciation method used.

Exhibit TN-9. The annuity method gives a consistent rate of return on assets through the life of an asset. This exercise provides practice in calculating annuity method depreciation and in evaluating the resulting stream of income flows. The advantages of the method would include the fact that ROA does not increase as assets age. Its disadvantages usually include the fact that the resulting net book values of assets decline more slowly than current values of like assets. The 10 percent ROA can be found by solving for the internal rate of return on the project.

Exhibit TN-10 and 11 allows a comparison between budgeted and actual ROI's and residual incomes. The interactions of changes in assets and changes in profits can be interesting to analyze. By introducing a cost for the use of assets, residual income encourages economy in asset usage and efficiency in operations.

Exhibits TN-12 through TN-15. These exercises explore the possible motivational effects of ROI vs. residual income. Exhibit TN-12 shows that divisions A and E, if evaluated on ROI, would be unlikely to add an asset with a ROI of only 10 percent because it would reduce their ROI; on the other hand, if residual income were used, and a capital charge of 10 percent on fixed assets was made, all divisions would find the investment acceptable.

Exhibit TN-13 shows how a low return proposal would be only acceptable to Division C, while it would increase the residual income of all divisions by an equal amount.

Exhibit TN-14 shows that an inventory reduction that would reduce all divisions' residual income equally improves ROI in divisions with high rate of return and reduces ROI in divisions with lower rates of return.

Finally, Exhibit TN-15 shows how sale of a plant could increase residual income equally, at all plants, but this action will look least desirable to the division with the lowest ROI (Plant C).

Suggestions for Classroom Use

I usually prepare and use transparencies of assigned exercises, and then allow students to compare their answers to mine while discussing differences and conclusions they have drawn.

William J. Bruns, Jr.

Divisional Performance Evaluation

Exhibit TN-1

Complete Office Company
(thousands of dollars)

	Layout and Marketing	Office Furniture	Office Supplies
Gross profit	$400	$ 400	$ 400
Operating expenses	200	100	150
Depreciations	—	100	50
Net profit before tax	$200	$ 200	$ 200
Total assets	$200	$1,200	$ 700
Net profit (BT)/Assets	200/200 = 100%	200/1200 = 16.7%	200/700 = 28.6%

Divisional Performance Evaluation

Exhibit TN-2

Big Spender Division
(thousands of dollars)

Assets	Jan 1 1984	New Equip.	Dec. 31 1984	Dec. 31 1985
Current	$12,000	$12,000	$12,000	$12,000
Fixed	18,000	19,500	19,500	19,500
Accum. depr.	(9,000)	(5,850)	(7,800)	(9,750)
Net book value	$21,000	$25,650	$23,700	$21,750
Gross book value	$30,000	$31,500	$31,500	$31,500

Income		1984	1985
Budgeted profit		$ 3,000	$ 3,000
Add: Savings on New Equipment		950	900
Added depreciation		(150)	(150)
Loss on old machines		(1,350)	—
New budgeted profit		$ 2,400	$ 3,750
ROA		2400/31500 = 7.6%	3750/31500 = 11.9%

Divisional Performance Evaluation

Exhibit TN-3, 4, and 5

Big Spender Division
(thousands of dollars)

Assets	Jan 1 1984	New Equip.	Dec. 31 1984	Dec. 31 1985
Current	$12,000	$12,000	$12,000	$12,000
Fixed	18,000	21,000	21,000	21,000
Accum. depr.	(9,000)	(5,850)	(7,950)	(10,050)
Net book value	$21,000	$27,150	$25,050	$22,950
Gross book value	$30,000	$33,000	$33,000	$33,000

Income	1984	1985
Budgeted profit	$ 3,000	$ 3,000
Add: Savings on New Equipment	600	600
Added depreciation	(300)	(300)
Loss on old machines	(1,350)	—
New budgeted profit	$ 1,950	$ 3,300

ROA (gross book value)	1950/33000 = 5.9%	3300/33000 = 10.0%
ROA (net book value)	2400/23700 = 10.1%	3750/21750 = 17.2%
ROA (net book value with cost overruns)	1950/25050 = 7.8%	3300/22950 = 14.4%

Divisional Performance Evaluation

Exhibit TN-6

Diamond Division
(thousands of dollars)

Year	Beg. Of Year Book Value	After Tax Cash Flow	Depreciation	Profit	ROA
1	$10,000	$2,500	$2,000	500	5.0%
2	8,000	2,500	2,000	500	6.2
3	6,000	2,500	2,000	500	8.3
4	4,000	2,500	2,000	500	12.5
5	2,000	2,500	2,000	500	25.0
Average ROA					11.2%

Manager's bonus:

Year 1	$ 500
2	625
3	833
4	1,250
5	2,500

Internal Rate of Return = 7.93%

Divisional Performance Evaluation

Exhibit TN-7

Spade Division
(thousands of dollars)

Year	End Of Year Book Value	After Tax Cash Flow	Depreciation	Profit	ROA
1	$8,000	$2,500	$2,000	500	6.2%
2	6,000	2,500	2,000	500	8.3
3	4,000	2,500	2,000	500	12.5
4	2,000	2,500	2,000	500	25.0
5	—	2,500	2,000	500	∞

Average
ROA   ∞

Manager's bonus:

Year 1	$ 625
2	833
3	1,250
4	2,500
5	N/A

Internal Rate of Return = 7.93%

Divisional Performance Evaluation

Exhibit TN-8

Heart Division
(thousands of dollars)

Year	Beg. Of Year Book Value	After Tax Cash Flow	Depreciation	Profit (Loss)	ROA
1	$10,000	$2,500	$3,333	(833)	(8.3%)
2	6,667	2,500	2,667	(167)	(2.5%)
3	4,000	2,500	2,000	500	12.5
4	2,000	2,500	1,333	1,167	58.4
5	667	2,500	667	1,833	274.8
Average ROA					67.0%

Manager's bonus:

Year 1	$ —
2	—
3	1,250
4	5,840
5	27,481

Internal Rate of Return = 7.93%

Divisional Performance Evaluation

Exhibit TN-9

Ace Corporation
(thousands of dollars)

Year	After Tax Cash Inflow	Depreciation	Beg. Of Year Net Book Value	Net Profit	ROA
1	$1,627.5	$ 627.5	$10,000	1000	10%
2	1,627.5	690.3	9,372.5	937.2	10
3	1,627.5	756.3	8,682.2	868.2	10
4	1,627.5	835.2	7,922.9	792.3	10
5	1,627.5	918.7	7,087.7	708.8	10
6	1,627.5	1,010.6	6,169.0	616.9	10
7	1,627.5	1,111.7	5,158.4	515.8	10
8	1,627.5	1,222.8	4,046.7	404.7	10
9	1,627.5	1,345.1	2,823.9	282.4	10
10	1,627.5	1,479.6*	1,478.8*	147.9	10

*Difference due to rounding.

Divisional Performance Evaluation

Exhibit TN-10 and 11

Ultima Company
(thousands of dollars)

BUDGETED

Division	Average Assets	Profit	ROI	5% Charge Cur. Assets	10% Charge Fixed Assets	Residual Income
A	500	90	18.0%	5	40	45.0
B	600	55	9.2	10	40	5.0
C	800	50	6.2	15	50	(15.0)
D	1,000	100	10.0	10	80	10.0
E	1,200	150	12.5	20	80	50.0

ACTUAL

Division	Average Assets	Profit	ROI	5% Charge Cur. Assets	10% Charge Fixed Assets	Residual Income
A	490	80	16.3%	4.5	40	35.5
B	640	60	9.4	9.5	45	5.5
C	900	50	5.6	17.5	55	(22.5)
D	1,000	105	10.5	10.0	80	15.0
E	1,000	155	10.0	10.0	80	60.0

Divisional Performance Evaluation

Exhibit TN-12

Ultima Company
(thousands of dollars)

Effect of adding fixed assets of $100,000 for profits of $10,000/year

Division	New Budgeted Profit	Average Assets	ROI	Previous Budgeted ROI	Difference
A	100	600	16.7%	18.0%	(1.3%)
B	65	700	9.3	9.2	.1
C	60	900	6.7	6.2	.5
D	110	1,100	10.0	10.0	—
E	160	1,300	12.3	12.5	(.2)

Division	New Budgeted Profit	5% Charge Current Assets	10% Charge Fixed Assets	Budgeted Residual Income	Previous Budgeted R.I.	Difference
A	100	5	50	45	45	—
B	65	10	50	5	5	—
C	60	15	60	(15)	(15)	—
D	110	10	90	10	10	—
E	160	20	90	50	50	—

Divisional Performance Evaluation

Exhibit TN-13

Ultima Company
(thousands of dollars)

Effect of adding fixed assets of $100,000 for profits of $5,000/year

Budgeted ROI

Division	Profit	Average Assets	ROI	Previous Budgeted ROI
A	97	600	16.2%	18.0%
B	62	700	8.9	9.2
C	57	900	6.3	6.2
D	107	1,100	9.7	10.0
E	157	1,300	12.1	12.5

Budgeted Residual Income

Division	Profit	5% Charge Cur. Assets	10% Charge Fixed Assets	Budgeted Residual Income	Previous Budgeted R.I.
A	97	10	40	47	45
B	62	15	40	7	5
C	57	20	50	(13)	(15)
D	107	15	80	12	10
E	157	25	80	52	50

Divisional Performance Evaluation

Exhibit TN-14

Ultima Company
(thousands of dollars)

Effect of reducing inventories by $50,000 at a cost of $5,000 in profit.

Budgeted ROI

Division	Profit	Average Assets	ROI	Previous Budgeted ROI
A	85	450	18.9%	18.0%
B	50	550	9.1	9.2
C	45	750	6.0	6.2
D	95	950	10.0	10.0
E	145	1,150	12.5	12.5

Budgeted Residual Income

Division	Profit	5% Charge Cur. Assets	10% Charge Fixed Assets	Budgeted Residual Income	Previous Budgeted R.I.
A	85	2.5	40	42.5	45
B	50	7.5	40	2.5	5
C	45	12.5	50	(17.5)	(15)
D	95	7.5	80	7.5	10
E	145	17.5	80	47.5	50

Divisional Performance Evaluation

Exhibit TN-15

Ultima Company
(thousands of dollars)

Effect of selling plant, reducing assets by $75,000 at a cost of $5,000 in profit

Budgeted ROI

Division	Profit	Average Assets	ROI	Previous Budgeted ROI
A	85	425	20.0%	18.0%
B	50	525	9.5	9.2
C	45	725	6.2	6.2
D	95	925	10.3	10.0
E	145	1,125	12.9	12.5

Budgeted Residual Income

Division	Profit	5% Charge Cur. Assets	10% Charge Fixed Assets	Budgeted Residual Income	Previous Budgeted R.I.
A	85	5	32.5	47.5	45
B	50	10	32.5	7.5	5
C	45	15	42.5	(12.5)	(15)
D	95	10	72.5	12.5	10
E	145	20	72.5	52.5	50

Case 7-3

Quality Metal Service Center

Purpose of Case

QMSC buys metals from original manufacturers (such as USX) in large quantities and supplies them, in smaller lots, to users of metals. Customers are thus freed from ordering directly from mills in large quantities—and from maintaining heavy inventories. QMSC is not simply a middleman, but adds value—through preprocessing capabilities and technical know-how. The company has a highly interdependent network of 4 regions and 23 districts. Both the regional and district managers are on an incentive system which is based solely on achieving budgeted levels of Return on Assets.

This is a very "rich" case in management control which raises a number of key issues.

1.   The need to tie controls to strategy;

2.   The rationale and criteria used to set up investment centers;

3.   The motivational issues involved in evaluating managers on Return On Assets vs. Residual Income;

4.   The different ways "profits" can be defined while calculating ROA or RI and the associated behavioral ramifications;

5.   The different ways "investment" can be defined and valued and the attendant motivational issues;

6.   The considerations involved in designing an incentive system that ties bonus to financial performance.

Assignment Questions

1.   Is the capital investment proposal described in Exhibit 3 an attractive one for Quality Metal Service Center?

2.   Should Ken Richards, the Columbus District Manager, send that proposal to home office for approval?

3.   Comment on the general usefulness of ROA as the basis of evaluating district managers' performance. Could this performance measure be made more effective?

4.   In deciding the investment base for evaluating managers of investment centers, the general question is: What practices will motivate the district managers to use their assets most efficiently, and to acquire the proper amount and kind of new assets? Presumably, when his return on assets is being measured, the district manager will try to increase his ROA, and we desire that the action he takes towards this end be actions that are in the best interest of the whole corporation. Given this general line of reasoning, evaluate the way

This teaching note was prepared by V. Govindarajan and John K. Shank as an aid to instructors in classroom use of Quality Metal Service Center (B). Copyright © 1989 V. Govindarajan and John K. Shank.

Quality computes the "investment base" for its districts. For each asset category, discuss whether the basis of measurement used by the company is the best for the purpose of measuring district's Return on Assets. What are the likely motivational problems that could arise in such a system? What can you recommend to overcome such dysfunctional effects?

5. While computing district profits for performance evaluation purposes, should there be a charge for income taxes? Should corporate overheads be allocated to districts? Should profits be computed on the basis of historical costs or on the basis of replacement costs? Evaluate these issues from the standpoint of their motivational impact on the district managers.

6. Evaluate Quality's incentive compensation system. Does the present system motivate district managers to make decisions which are consistent with the interests of the firm? If not, make specific recommendations to improve the system.

Case Analysis

1. Strategy

   One of the themes of our book is that financial control systems in a business are a major part of the formal structure designed to implement strategy through the people of the organization (the Human Resource) to achieve targeted results (see Figure 1 to this note). The key ideas underlying this theme are: (i) different organizations typically have different strategies; and (ii) different control systems are needed to effectively implement different strategies. Thus, one has to evaluate the control systems of a company in the context of that company's strategy.

   This teaching note was prepared by V. Govindarajan and John K. Shank as an aid to instructors in classroom use of Quality Metal Service Center(B). Copyright a 1989 V. Govindaraian and John K. Shank.

   QMSC is an excellent case to explicate the framework linking controls to strategy. We will first identify the strategy of QMSC prior to the evaluation of its control systems. The starting point for identifying QMSC's strategy would require an understanding of the metal distribution industry. Based on the five-force analysis (a la Porter) given below, one can conclude that metal warehousing is a tough business where the average returns are likely to be low.

   a. **Supplier Power** is high:

      i. Few, concentrated suppliers.

      ii. They are large and have lots of resources.

      iii. They have the ability to forward integrate.

   b. **Buyer Power** is high:

      i. Undifferentiated product.

ii.   Customer loyalty is low. Though some loyalty can be built through fast delivery and full-line inventory, it does not allow distributors to charge significantly higher prices.

iii.   Large size buyers (i.e., Fortune 500 companies) can exert tremendous leverage since they have the ability to buy directly from the mills.

iv.   Small to medium-sized companies have relatively less power for the following reasons:

-      They do not have the ability to lift mill-level quantities; hence they are more dependent on the distributors;

-      They do not buy large enough volumes to justify pre-production processing equipment.

c.   **Threat of Substitutes** is high:

i.   There is a substitute for the distributor's service, which is suppliers selling to customers directly.

ii.   Steel distributors have to contend with the substitute metal, aluminum.

iii.   Metal distributors have potential threat from other materials such as plastics, paper, glass, and fiber-foil.

d.   **Entry Barriers** are low:

i.   Low capital intensity due to:

-      Leased space;

-      Moderate working capital (Inventory + Accounts Receivable – Accounts Payable).

ii.   Distribution expertise is not proprietary.

e.   **Rivalry Among Existing Players** is high:

i.   Lots of competitors; fragmented industry

ii.   Low product differentiation.

iii.   Thin margins due to low value added and few ways to add value.

iv.   Low customer loyalty.

v.   Very price sensitive $\rightarrow$ low margins $\rightarrow$ high volume is critical $\rightarrow$ commodity product — heavy price competition.

vi.   Derived demand; growth tied to economy; cyclical.

vii.   Availability of substitutes.

viii.   High buyer power.

ix.   High supplier power.

x.   Low entry barriers.

Though it is true that metal distribution is a tough business, the instructor should point out that a few trends in the industry are enhancing Service Centers' growth potential.

a.   Given the high cost of ownership and maintenance of inventory, most metal users are attempting to reduce their costs by lowering their levels of raw material inventories ("Just-in-time" inventory management). This has resulted in a need for smaller order quantities and more frequent deliveries. This implies that metal users are not able to directly access mills that sell their products in large lots. Metal service centers have, therefore, a natural advantage in that inventory management is their stock in trade.

b.   In their efforts to become more cost competitive, most of the major domestic metals producers have scaled back their product lines, eliminating the low volume, specialty items. Full-line service centers, recognizing that many customers prefer to deal with only a few primary suppliers, have profited from this trend by maintaining wide product lines.

c.   Further, in order to address profitability problems, metal producers have reduced sales force size and technical support. This has provided an opportunity for distribution centers which can provide the sales and technical service.

Given this background, what should QMSC do strategically to earn a reasonable ROI? Students typically suggest that QMSC adopt a combination of low cost (for some areas of their operations) and differentiation (for other areas of their operations) strategies:

a.   Low Cost, especially while distributing commodity steel

     –   Key is purchasing economies

     –   Effective inventory management (20,000 products; stockouts = lost sales; but excess inventory = cost disadvantage).

b.   Differentiation, especially while distributing specialty metals

     –   Value added opportunities (both for commodity and specialty metals)

     –   Emphasize specialty metals (stainless steel, nickel alloys, copper, carbon alloys)

     –   Sales and engineering support

–   Full product line

–   On-time delivery

c.   Focus on small-to-medium size metal users (to benefit from better leverage with this buyer group)

2. Control Systems

The focus of the case is on the control systems used over the district managers and the broad issue is: Are these controls consistent with the strategy of QMSC? The present performance evaluation and incentive compensation system over the district managers can be summed up as follows:

Control Systems Dimension	QMSC's Current Choice on the Specific Dimensions
Responsibility Structure	Investment Center
Performance Criteria	Return on Assets (ROA)
Formula-based vs. Subjective Bonus Determination	Formula-based
Mix of Salary and Bonus	Maximum Bonus is 75 percent of Base Salary
Degree of Profit Sharing	Bonus Basis: 75 percent on District ROA 25 percent on Regional ROA

At present, these controls are applied *uniformly* across all 23 districts. The next section will evaluate the choices made by QMSC in its control systems, in the context of the company's strategy.

2.1 Responsibility Structure

Should districts be investment centers? Some possible alternatives would be to designate them as standard cost centers, or revenue centers, or profit centers. Students would easily eliminate the cost center idea since districts have authority over sales. The revenue center concept is inappropriate as well since the district manager has control over selling prices. As a revenue center, the district manager will not be charged for the cost of the inventory purchased from internal sources; this might, therefore, motivate him—incorrectly—to ignore the inventory cost in setting selling prices.

Should the districts be profit centers or investment centers? District managers have authority to alter their investments in inventory and accounts receivable—almost on a daily basis—to generate sales and profits. Under a profit center system, since the district manager is not accountable for investment, the manager could potentially <u>over</u>-invest in working capital to generate profits. Thus, students will conclude that the investment center idea makes sense to properly control district managers' actions.

The key idea in a responsibility center design is: What decisions are decentralized to the manager of that responsibility center and are the results of those decisions captured in the performance metric? Since the district manager has decision-making authority over costs, revenues, <u>and</u> investments, the manager has to be controlled on all of these three variables—leading to the argument for the investment center concept.

The instructor might want to drive home these points by putting up the following performance indicators for two districts, Milwaukee and Columbus:

	Milwaukee	Columbus
Profit As A Percent of Sales	5%	4%

The instructor can then ask the class: Which district is more successful? Student comments like "we want to know the performance of the districts over the past few years" could be answered simply by stating that the districts have performed at about the same levels over the past several years. Obviously, Milwaukee has a higher profit margin than Columbus? Does it imply that Milwaukee is more successful than Columbus. This does not follow since this ignores sales volume, among other things. Put another way, if we use profit margin as a criterion to evaluate districts, the district manager might just sell a few items at very high margins. This clearly does not constitute good performance.

The instructor might now provide the following information:

	Milwaukee	Columbus (000's)
Profit Margin	5%	4%
Sales	$5,000	$25,000
Profit	$ 250	$ 1,000

The instructor can again ask the class: Which district is more successful? Some students might think that the Columbus District is more successful since it has made a profit of $1,000 as compared to the profit of only $250 for the Milwaukee District. Soon, some student is likely to point out that a higher profit does not necessarily imply better performance since a district can increase profits by a more than offsetting increase in investment. This points out the need to consider profits in relation to investment (or the use of "investment center" concept) while evaluating the performance of district managers.

The instructor can now add the following to the illustration:

	Milwaukee	Columbus (000's)
Profit Margin	5%	4%
Sales	$5,000	$25,000
Profit	$ 250	$ 1,000
Investment	$1,000	$ 5,000
Return on Investment	25%	20%

Again, the instructor can ask: Which district is more successful? Many students might, at first glance, think that the Milwaukee District is more successful since it has the higher ROI of 25 percent. A smart student is likely to point out that it might be better to evaluate the districts on "residual income," i.e., after deducting all expenses including a capital charge on the investment tied in the district.

The instructor can now supply the following:

	Milwaukee	Columbus (000's)
Profit Margin	5%	4%
Sales	$5,000	$25,000
Profit	$ 250	$ 1,000
Investment	$1,000	$ 5,000
Cost of Capital	15%	15%
Capital Charge	$ 150	$ 750
Residual Income	$ 100	$ 250
ROI	25%	20%

We like the above, rather simple, illustration since it gives contradictory rankings of the districts under various performance criteria. Witness the following:

	Milwaukee	Columbus (000's)
Profit Margin	First	Second
Sales Dollars	Second	First
Profit Dollars	Second	First
ROI	First	Second
Residual Income	Second	First

By now, students are clear that, if we were looking for a single comprehensive measure of a district manager's performance, it cannot be profit margin or sales dollars or profit dollars. The district manager should be evaluated as an investment center. Now, the question is: should a district's success be decided based on ROI or Residual Income? Or in other words, should the district manager's incentive bonus be based on ROI or Residual Income. This is the topic we turn to next.

2.2 Performance Criteria

The instructor should use the "incident" in the case to raise the issue of whether ROA is an appropriate performance criteria to calibrate district managers' performance.

A good lead-off question would be: Is the capital investment project described in Exhibit 3 attractive for the company? If the students have already had a finance course, they will be quick to point out that the project is an extremely attractive one for the company. Notice the following:

Payback Period	= 4.5 years (criteria = 10 years)
IPR	= 21.8% (criteria = 15%)
NPV at 15% discount rate	= $486,000

A few relatively minor points can be noted here:

1. Though the district's performance is evaluated on a pre-tax basis, the district has to still evaluate the capital project on an after-tax basis. The theme "different costs for different purposes" that is usually introduced in the early sessions on cost accounting can again be emphasized.

2. The payback period of 4.5 years considers only the initial equipment investment of $1,200,000. If one considers also the working capital investment, the payback period would be about 7 years but is still well within the criteria of 10 years. The point to note here is that the sales manager, who is probably anxious to get the proposal approved, might have a tendency to bias the data to show a more favorable picture.

3. If the Columbus District is currently getting the preprocessing done by other districts, the capital investment analysis would be different. Under this scenario, the processing revenue for the company would not change, even though the processing revenue for the Columbus District would go up and there would be a corresponding reduction in the processing revenue in some other district. The case states that the Columbus District currently does not satisfy the demand in its area for pre-production processing through transfers from other districts. Thus, the analysis done in Exhibit 3 holds for the entire company as well as for the Columbus District.

The discussion up to this point should be to get an agreement among students that the project described in Exhibit 3 is very attractive financially for QMSC. The instructor should be careful not to get too deeply involved in capital budgeting since this is not the focus of the case.

Next, the instructor could ask: Does the project have "strategic" fit? Students will readily agree that this project fits very well strategically since one of the key competitive strategies of QMSC is to emphasize value added business. Thus, the instructor can summarize this part of the discussion as follows:

The Project	For QMSC
"Financial" Fit	High
"Strategic" Fit	High

At this point, the instructor could ask: Is the project described in Exhibit 3 attractive for Ken Richards, the manager of the Columbus District? Students are likely to refer to Exhibit 4 and point out that the incentive bonus for Ken Richards in 1989 would go down from 11.1 percent of salary to 4.28 percent of salary, if the manager undertakes the project. With a reduction in the bonus of about 7 percent of salary (for a base salary of $100,000, it works out to $7,000), it is unlikely that Ken Richards would look upon this proposal with favor.

This brings the class to the central issue: Why is a very attractive project for the company not attractive to one of its district managers? Even though capital investment decisions above $10,000 are approved at headquarters, it is the district manager who identifies opportunities, develops the economics of the project, and sends it to head office for approval (a "bottom up" process for generating capital proposals). Thus, the district manager controls which capital projects are seen by head office. If improperly motivated, the district manager might suppress proposals for new investments which are "good" for the company as a whole.

There is something in QMSC's control system which is forcing Ken Richards to forego an excellent investment opportunity. This ties in with the concern expressed by Ed Brown in the first page of the case that the company is missing out on growth opportunities. Why is Ken Richards not making "goal congruent" decisions? What can be done to correct the situation?

By now, students will clearly see that something is wrong with QMSC's incentive compensation procedure. Why does a project with a high positive net present value (at the company's cost of capital) lower the incentive bonus for the district manager? (Note: the calculations in Exhibit 4 use a figure of $240,000 for working capital investment. This is the working capital buildup by the end of 1989. A shrewd student might point out two things: (1) The company does not typically deduct "accounts payable" from a district manager's investment base; and (2) Current Assets are included at an average value and not at the end of the period value. Though these observations are correct, it still does not contradict the basic message of Exhibit 4 that the incentive bonus for Ken Richards would appreciably decline in 1989 if the new project is undertaken).

At this point, it might be useful to continue with the simple example introduced in Section 2.1 relating to the Milwaukee and Columbus districts, before returning to the case. We left the simple example with the question: should the district's success be based on ROI or Residual Income?

After some discussion, students are likely to point out the problems with using ROI as a performance evaluation tool. Given an investment opportunity whose ROI is <u>above</u> the cost of capital but <u>below</u> a district's current ROI, the district manager may forego this opportunity since this investment, while economically sound, will lower the district's ROI below the current level. This point can be fixed in students' minds by expanding on the earlier example as follows.

Let us assume that the Milwaukee and the Columbus districts hit upon a similar investment opportunity to make an additional investment of $1,000,000 to return $220,000/year for 10 years. How would these two managers view the new investment under ROI and Residual Income methods of performance evaluation?

After the New Project:

	Milwaukee	Columbus (000's)
Profits	$ 470	$ 1,220
Investment	$2,000	$ 6,000
ROI	23.5%	20.3%
Residual Income	$ 170	$ 320

From the corporate point of view, the new investment project is attractive since its return of 22 percent is much higher than the cost of capital of 15 percent. However, the two district managers would view the new investment differently under the ROI system. The Milwaukee district manager would probably reject the investment opportunity since it reduces his ROI to 23.5 percent. On the other hand, the Columbus district manager would look upon it favorably since it increases his ROI to 20.3 percent. Thus, the same investment opportunity would not be equally attractive (or otherwise) to the two districts under the ROI system. This motivational problem is corrected under the Residual Income (RI) method. Both Milwaukee and Columbus managers would find the new investment attractive since the RIs for both managers increase exactly by $70,000 if they undertake the new project.

The ROI evaluation system can, therefore, cause serious problems in resource allocation decisions, especially if several districts are earning different ROIs. Consider the following situation:

District	Current ROI
A	4%
B	15%
C	25%

Let us assume that the company as a whole earns 15 percent ROI. In this situation, where will all of the capital funds go? To District C? Not likely! In the eyes of C, "good" projects must earn at least 25 percent. C's managers are motivated to spurn 20 percent return alternatives because C's performance measure, ROI, will decrease, even though a 20 percent return on the project will improve total company ROI. At the other extreme, a 5 percent project, while falling well below the average company ROI, looks very attractive to District A. Unless the capital budgeting system has been designed to thwart this tendency, District A may request funds for just these projects. Since there are always more low return ideas than high return ones, District A may very well end up with the bulk of new capital funds.

Synchronizing the capital budgeting system's required rate of return with the capital charge used in calculating RI makes the two systems compatible. Under RI measurement, a high-earnings district, as in the case of Milwaukee, is motivated to invest in projects below 25 percent but above 15 percent since any investment returning higher than 15 percent will increase RI. This is exactly how the Milwaukee manager ought to behave.

New getting back to QMSC, their incentive methodology creates a problem in that the current ROA of a district becomes its hurdle rate (refer to Step 1 in Exhibit 2). Thus, the Columbus District which is currently earning a very high ROA of 38 percent (before tax) does not find a project earning the cost of capital of 15 percent (after tax) attractive. One possible solution would be to change Step 1 where the asset over- or under-employed would be multiplied by the pre-tax cost of capital of 30 percent. In other words, we can calculate Residual Income as follows:

RI = Profit − (30% × Investment)

The managers can then be evaluated on a comparison between actual RI and budgeted RI.

Some students might wonder whether we are too quick to conclude that Ken Richards is unlikely to send the investment proposal to the corporate. No doubt, his incentive bonus goes down in 1989 if he undertakes the project. But what about years 1990 − 1998? Is it possible that the bonus for Ken Richards would in fact increase over the time horizon of the new project. There are at least three points that are worth noting here:

1.   This assumes that Ken Richards will be in his current job for the next 10 years. This might not be true. This is probably one reason why managers tend to focus on short payback projects and focus greater attention to cash flows in the first few years of the project.

2.   Even assuming that Ken Richards will be in his current job for the next 10 years and his ROA target during that period will remain at 38 percent, let us see what will happen to his incentive bonus during 1990 – 1998.

	1983	1984	1985	1986	1987	1988	1989	1990	1991
Profit Before Tax (000's)	$460	548	620	680	700	740	768	780	800
Investment:									
Fixed Asset	$1,200	1,200	1,200	1,200	1,200	1,200	1,200	1,200	1,200
Working Capital	$550	600	670	730	800	890	970	1,070	1,180
Total	$1,750	1,800	1,870	1,930	2,000	2,090	2,170	2,270	2,380
ROA (Pre-tax)	26%	30%	33%	35%	35%	35%	35%	34%	34%

As can be seen from the above table, the ROA for the new project is not above 38 percent in any of the years between 1990-1998, if he goes ahead with this new project. Thus his incentive bonus will go down in every one of the next 10 years, if he undertakes the new project.

1.   Even if Ken Richards were to receive an additional incentive bonus during 1990-98 on account of this new project, its value to the manager today would be lower due to the time value of money.

To sum up the discussion so far, it can be pointed out that since the district managers are *evaluated* on their ability to increase ROA, they will be *motivated* to do so which, as argued earlier, might go contrary to corporate goals. An alternative measurement approach, Residual Income, overcomes the deficiencies inherent in the ROA system.

After the above summary, the instructor might ask: Does RI really overcome the problems which we noted in the context of the ROA system? Students who have done additional analysis will realize that even with the use of RI concept, the incentive bonus for Ken Richards goes down in 1989 if he undertakes the project. Why does this happen? This is because the pre-tax ROA in 1989 is only 6 percent ($80,000/$1,440,000), whereas the pretax cost of capital is 30 percent. Therefore, even synchronizing the performance evaluation system with the capital budgeting system does not provide enough incentive for Ken Richards in 1989. This problem would occur in 1990 as well since the pretax ROA in 1990 is 26 percent. ($460,000/$1,750,000) , which is again below the cost of capital of 30 percent. This problem would cease to happen from 1991 onwards when the project's ROA exceeds the cost of capital.

It is quite typical for the project's ROA to be below the cost of capital in the first few years of the project (in our case, this happens in the first 2 years). Even the use of RI system does not address this issue. What else can be done? Some possibilities are presented below:

1.   One might "protect" the district manager's bonus for a certain period (e.g., 2 years) in cases where he has made a new capital investment. One difficulty with this approach

would be that managers might then "save" deferrable expenses for those years when their bonus would be paid anyway.

2. Instead of using a strict formula based incentive system as done by QMSC, one might introduce some subjective element into the system which could take into account the type of inequities mentioned above during the initial periods of new investment.

3. Another possibility would be to exclude "fixed assets" from the investment base. This possibility, which is considered in detail later, might mitigate the above noted problem.

At some stage during this discussion, students might suggest that the Columbus District Manager would go ahead with this project even under a ROA system, if he is able to re-negotiate the ROA target from its current level of 38 percent to a lower level based on the ROA for the district with this new project. This possibility for re-negotiation is available since the district manager has to go to headquarters anyway to obtain funds for this new capital project. As a response to this line of reasoning, the instructor may want the student to react to the following scenario:

New York District's current ROA is 40 percent.

This district manager is contacted by a large customer who is willing to buy extra quantities of metal if the district will give the customer a longer credit period over and above the district's normal credit policies.

This decision involves *incremental* accounts receivable investment of $500,000.

This decision, however, will yield additional sales which, let us say, will yield <u>additional</u> profit of $150,000.

This new business opportunity yields an ROA of 30 percent ($150,000/$500,000).

The cost of capital is 15 percent.

Is this a good business opportunity for the company? YES.

Is this a good business opportunity for the district manager? "NO" under the ROA-based control system since this new business will lower the district's overall ROA below its current level of 40 percent.

Will re-negotiation of ROA targets solve the problem? "NO" since accounts receivable (and inventory) decisions are made by districts <u>without</u> consultation with the head office. To require re-negotiated goals for such decisions will not only make a mockery of decentralization but also severely overload the corporate office (since districts make working capital investment decisions on a daily basis and there are 23 such districts!).

The Residual Income metric will provide the correct signal for the New York District Manager in this scenario.

Further, we noted earlier that RI might still not solve the problem for multi-year capital projects where ROA for the initial years will typically be below the cost of capital. This limitation of RI will not apply to working capital investments (such as the scenario described for the New York District) since the impact of extending extra credit must produce extra profit within a fairly short period, certainly less than a year.

Thus, the net conclusion is that RI is the correct metric to guide district managers' working capital investment decisions. Clearly, these are the most frequent decisions—day-to-day, year-in-year-out decisions—that the district managers will make. This still does not address how to deal with the limitations of RI vis-a-vis long-term capital investment decisions. This is a topic we address later on in this note.

To sum up, the class by now should see the definite merit in moving to a RI system. The RI concept, however, requires proper definitions of "profit," "investment," and "cost of capital." These issues are considered below.

2.2.1 Defining "Profit" for Calculating RI

Profit, for a district, could be calculated in several ways. Given below are some possibilities:

Income Statement for a District

Sales		
Less Variable Costs (Controllable Expenses)	_____	
CONTRIBUTION		(1)
Less District-Fixed Expenses (Uncontrollable Expenses)	_____	
DISTRICT DIRECT PROFIT		(2)
Less Allocated Corporate Overhead	_____	
PROFIT BEFORE TAX		(3)
Less Income Taxes	_____	
PROFIT AFTER TAX	_____	(4)

QMSC uses the line "Direct District Profit" as the basis to calculate ROA. Clearly, this is only one alternative. The instructor should highlight several points: (a) None of these alternatives are inherently right or wrong; (b) Each alternative will induce different managerial behaviors; (c) An MBA is expected to have a reasoned opinion on each alternative.

Some class attention should be focused on the distinction between controllable and noncontrollable expenses. The company seems to imply that variable expenses such as warehouse labor and sales commissions are controllable whereas fixed expenses such as rent, utilities, and property taxes are noncontrollable. Some students might feel that such distinctions are of little value from a managerial viewpoint. After all, fixed costs depend upon managerial discretion and can be controlled; in any case, even if an expense such as administrative salaries cannot be reduced in the short-run, the district manager can certainly control the efficiency and productivity of the employees. For these reasons, some students might argue that all costs under the authority of the division/district are controllable and it might be inappropriate, from a motivational standpoint, to label some of the district costs as "noncontrollable."

The next question is: should the corporate overheads be allocated to the districts? At this point (or even sometime earlier), it is better to point out that we possibly need two sets of data: one to evaluate the district manager and the other to evaluate the district itself. Top management might want to "fully allocate" all costs to a district to see whether that district is viable as an economic entity. This computation need not have to be performed frequently, or even regularly. The other question is: From a motivational standpoint, is it desirable to allocate corporate overheads while evaluating the performance of a district manager? There are two arguments against such allocations. First, the costs incurred by corporate staff departments such as Finance, Accounting, and Human Resource Management are not controllable by the district manager. Therefore, he should not be held accountable for what he does not control. Second, it is possibly very difficult to find acceptable bases of allocating the corporate staff services that would properly reflect the relative amount of corporate costs that are caused by each district.

There are, however, some equally compelling arguments for allocating corporate overhead to districts in their performance reports:

a. If an operating manager pays for a service whether he uses it or not, he will be more likely to use it.

b. If corporate overheads are allocated to districts, there is a greater possibility that the district managers will raise questions about the amount of corporate overhead; this helps to keep the head office spending "in check."

c. District profits would be more realistic and comparable to competitors because the competitors would have. to pay for similar services.

d. The district manager is given the message that the district has not earned a profit unless it recovers all costs, including a share of allocated corporate overhead. Thus, the district manager would be motivated to take his long-term marketing decisions (pricing, product mix, etc.), keeping in mind that he has to recover his share of the corporate overhead. This is desirable since, otherwise, the company will not be viable in the long run.

If students feel that QMSC should allocate corporate overheads to districts, it should be emphasized that when overheads are allocated, the budgeted costs, not the actual costs, should be allocated. This would ensure that the district managers would not complain either about the arbitrariness of allocations or the lack of control over allocated costs since, in their performance reports, no variances would be shown for allocated overheads; rather, the variances would appear in the reports of the responsibility center that incurred the costs.

The next issue is: should districts be evaluated on a pre-tax or after-tax basis? (Again, for evaluating the district as an economic entity, top management might compute an aftertax return for the district; here the issue relates to using the after-tax profits for performance evaluation purposes). The argument against computing after-tax profits for the districts is that decisions that have an impact on income taxes are made at headquarters, and that district profits should not be affected by these decisions. The following arguments can be supplied for evaluating districts on an after-tax basis:

a. This basis would put the district on a comparable basis with an independent competitor.

b. The sum of the profits of the districts would equal the "bottom line" of the company.

c. This would motivate district managers to be conscious of the tax consequences of their decisions, and in particular, would motivate them to seek opportunities to minimize taxes.

d. This would equate the way profits are computed for performance evaluation purposes with the way profits are computed for capital budgeting purposes.

2.2.2 Defining "Investment" for Calculating RI

It is best to consider the way individual assets are handled by QMSC while computing the investment base and raise the issue: What practices will motivate the district managers to use their assets most efficiently, and to acquire the proper amount and kind of new assets?

The class attention could be first directed at working capital items. Cash is excluded from districts' assets since the amounts are trivial. QMSC, like most companies, has a centralized cash management function; this explains the low levels of cash at the districts. One alternative would be to allocate the cash held at head office to the districts on some basis (e.g., GM uses 4.5 percent of sales; DuPont uses 2 months' cost of sales less depreciation). This would both state district's ROA realistically as well as put the district on a comparable basis with outside firms.

There will be very little disagreement among students that accounts receivable and inventory should be included in the investment base. The district manager has direct control over these two items and probably makes decisions, almost on a daily basis, which affect the investment in these two asset categories; by including them in the asset base, the district manager would constantly make trade-off decisions between increased investments in inventories and receivables versus incremental sales and profits. A few points could be highlighted at this stage. First, QMSC uses average balance for the period instead of the end of the period balance. Though this adds to bookkeeping, this is probably worthwhile since district managers can more easily manipulate end of period balances (also, an average figure is a conceptually better measure). Second, it is probably a good idea to include inventory at replacement costs (certainly, better than a LIFO valuation). Third, the students could be asked whether the accounts receivable should be included at selling prices or at cost of goods sold. After all, QMSC's real investment in accounts receivable is only the cost of goods sold and it is probably enough if the district managers make a satisfactory return on this investment. On the other hand, it is possible to argue that QMSC can potentially reinvest the money collected from accounts receivable; therefore, it should be included at selling prices.

QMSC handles accounts payable in an interesting way. If a district manager negotiates a credit period in excess of the company's credit standard of 30 days, inventory assets are reduced for the excess credit period. This gives the correct motivational signal to the district manager: all other things being equal, seek out the supplier with most favorable credit terms. However, QMSC does not penalize a district manager if he negotiates a credit period less than the 30-day company standard. This is probably undesirable; the company should just deduct the average accounts payable balance from current assets while computing the investment base. This would provide the proper motivation to the district manager to seek the most favorable credit terms. The students should again be reminded that we recommend reducing the current assets by accounts payable because the district manager has the authority to locate and negotiate terms with the suppliers. If the district manager did not have this authority, there would be little merit in deducting accounts payable. Some students might argue that if we deduct accounts payable from the investment base, the district manager might have a tendency to make accounts payable as large as he could, so as to increase his ROA; such an action might not be in the best interest of the corporation because of its possible bad effect on the company's credit standing. Though this argument might be generally true, it is not a problem in QMSC's case since it is the head office, not the districts, who controls payments to suppliers; districts only locate and negotiate with suppliers and do not have the authority to "stretch" supplier payments.

Now, attention could be turned to the group of fixed assets "Land, Warehouse Building, and Equipment" which are included in the asset base at gross book value. Including these fixed assets at gross book value can cause district managers to make certain incorrect decisions. E.g., in a district whose current ROA is 30 percent, its overall ROA can be increased by disinvesting in an asset whose ROA is 20 percent; yet, this is clearly inappropriate if the cost of capital is only 15 percent. The following illustration captures this point:

Suppose the Columbus District has two fixed assets yielding the following ROAS:

	Asset 1	Asset 2	Total (000's)
Profit	$100	$200	$ 300
Investment	$500	$500	$1,000
ROA	20%	40%	30%

The Columbus District can Increase its overall ROA (from its current level of 30 percent) to 40 percent by divesting "asset 1." This is not in the corporate interest if the cost of capital is 15 percent.

An alternative would be to use "net book value." This could lead to a potential problem since the investment base of a district will be automatically reduced as the asset ages (due to depreciation). Thus the rate of return will increase simply by the passage of time. This can result in very high returns on older assets. Thus, new investments are discouraged because they will reduce a district's ROA, at least in the short run. The following numerical example illustrates why the "net book value" approach creates such distortions:

Suppose the Milwaukee District has an asset with an outlay of $1 million and which yields a profit of $200,000 per year for 10 years. Let us assume that this asset is depreciated on a straight-line basis. The following would be the financial details of this asset for the Milwaukee District:

	1	2	3	4	5	6	7	8	9	10
Profits	$200	200	200	200	200	200	200	200	200	200
Asset	$1,000	900	800	700	600	500	400	300	200	100
ROA	20%	22%	25%	30%	33%	40%	50%	67%	100%	200%

Suppose the Milwaukee District gets a similar opportunity to invest $1 million in year 7. Probably, the district manager would turn it down since his ROA in year 7 will go down (from its current level of 50 percent), if he undertakes this project. Of course, this problem would be more severe if some form of accelerated depreciation is used by the company.

Annuity depreciation method could possibly mitigate some of these problems; however, it seems to have very little support from practitioners.

Another alternative might be the use of "replacement costs." However, the difficulty in estimating replacement costs, coupled with the subjectivity inherent in such a valuation, needs to be considered in implementing replacement-cost-based systems for management control.

Given some of the motivational problems inherent in fixed asset valuation, the instructor might ask: Is there a need to include fixed assets at all? A good question to focus student attention on this issue would be to ask them: how frequently does a district manager make a decision to build a warehouse or relocate his warehouse? Probably, once in his career! There is no particular advantage in designing a management control system such that a district manager would make the correct decision once in 50 years; one could probably ensure this in other ways. Thus, one could make a good argument to exclude Warehouse, Land, and Buildings from the investment base. The instructor could again compare the nature of current assets and the nature of Warehouse, Land, and Buildings, from the standpoint of the frequency with which district managers can invest or disinvest in them.

Equipment decisions are typically made once in 10 years, except for some routine replacements. Again, one could argue that there is not much to gain (and probably something to lose) by including equipment in the asset base.

We earlier noted that RI might still not give the right signal to the Columbus District Manager since his ROA for the first 2 years is less than the cost of capital. This problem would be avoided if fixed assets were not included in the investment base while calculating RI.

Investments in warehouse facilities and equipment can be carefully controlled by the corporate office at the point when these decisions are made. Corporate office might still want to know when capital investment decisions have turned "sour" both because some action may be appropriate with respect to the person responsible for the mistakes, and also because some safeguards to prevent a recurrence may be appropriate. Some form of post-completion audit might be adequate to control capital investments in warehouse facilities and equipment (instead of including them in the operating evaluation system).

Next, attention could be focused on "leased trucks." The company does not include the capitalized value of the leased trucks in the investment base; rather, lease expenses on trucks are deducted in the income statement. The financial statements of the district would be affected differently under these two alternatives:

Capitalize Leases	Expense
Income Statement	Income Statement
Depreciation Expense	Lease Rental
Balance Sheet	Balance Sheet
Leased Asset	No Asset Recorded.

If leases are expensed, district managers will be motivated to lease trucks, rather than own them, as long as the interest charge that is built into the rental cost is less than the cost of capital that is applied to the district's investment base (income taxes are ignored here since the district manager is evaluated on a pre-tax basis). The point here is that district managers might not consider lease vs. buy decisions in the way finance literature recommend. This problem is less likely to happen if leases are capitalized since that would be equivalent to the way the district's financial statements would look like under the "buy" alternative. Even though all leasing decisions are centrally approved at QMSC, we desire that the control system be so designed that district managers would send to the head office only those lease proposals which are economically sound.

QMSC does not deduct any long-term liabilities from the district's asset base; this is proper since capital structure decisions are taken at the head office.

To summarize, the "investment base" for a district can be defined as follows:

Accounts Receivable
Inventory
Replacement Equipment
Less Accounts Payable

The above represents an "investment base" over which the district managers have considerable amount of control, at fairly frequent time intervals.

If QMSC were to adopt this recommendation, this would imply that the RI targets for the districts would be much higher than what they are at present (since fixed assets will be excluded from the investment base). The budgeting system of the company needs to be adjusted to reflect this change.

2.2.3 Definition of "Cost of Capital" for Calculating RI

There are several issues here:

a. Should QMSC use a single hurdle rate or multiple hurdle rates across districts?

b. Should QMSC use one rate on working capital items and a higher rate on fixed assets?

c. How to estimate cost of debt? Is it past cost or future cost?

d. How to estimate cost of equity? How to allow for business risk? How to allow for financial risk? How to incorporate inflation?

e. How to estimate the debt percent and equity percent in the overall capital structure? How to establish debt-equity mix for each district, if multiple hurdle rates are used?

These are, of course, very relevant questions if QMSC were to adopt a cost of capital framework to evaluate the performance of its districts. Finance courses would cover these issues in considerable detail. The instructor might just list these issues and point out that these need to be resolved before RI can be implemented.

3. *Formula-Based vs. Subjective Bonus Determination*

Incentive bonus for any manager can either be strictly formula-based (example: bonus is some fixed percent of net profits) or it can be strictly subjective or it can be some combination of the two approaches. Each of these alternatives would have different motivational effects on the manager.

In the context of QMSC, the incentive bonus for the district manager is strictly formula-based. There is only one thing that matters viz., improving ROA. No qualitative factors or discretionary elements are provided for in the performance evaluation system. Students might perceive this as a "harsh" system, especially since the budget setting process seems to be "top down" and further, that the managers are evaluated against the original budget and not against the revised budget. However, students will understand the need for a tight financial control system if they consider it in the context of the earlier discussion on the structure of the industry in which QMSC operates. As discussed earlier, the metal distribution industry is not "glamorous." In fact, it is quite difficult to make handsome profits in this industry due to intense competition, greater bargaining power of suppliers and customers, relatively low barriers to entry, and presence of substitutes. Under these conditions, a tight financial control system seems appropriate for QMSC, given its industry and competitive situation.

Also, a strict formula-based system forces managers at all levels to be focusing on ROA; under such circumstances, there is a greater probability that QMSC, as a company, can deliver the desired ROA to its stockholders.

With a formula-based bonus system, students might want to change QMSC's budget setting process. Some class time could be devoted to this topic. Budget processes are typically characterized as either "top down" or "bottom up." With top down budgeting, higher levels of management set the budget for the lower levels. It is a way of saying, "Here's what we want you fellows to do." With bottom up budgeting, on the other hand, the lower levels say, "Here's what we think we can do." QMSC seems to employ a "top down" process. This insures that budgets will be acceptable to the corporate management. This approach has a cost, however. It might lead to a lack of commitment on the part of district managers who are, in fact, responsible for achieving the budget targets, thereby endangering the plan's success. Bottom up budgeting, in which district managers participate in setting their own budget goals, is most likely to generate commitment to meeting those goals. This system also has a cost in that those goals may be too easy or may not match the company's overall ROA objective. A "good" blend of the two approaches along the following lines might be more appropriate:

a. Corporate management first assesses the market and business environment, and then sets a strategic framework including statements of targeted profits and ROA for the next 3-5 years for the overall company. This is the framework within which the annual budgeting process will begin.

b. The district managers (after receiving a statement of the overall corporate goals as well as a statement of the corporate assumptions regarding the overall industry environment, growth, competitive factors and so on) will work on a detailed plan for the next year and arrive at an operating budget for the district.

c. The regional managers would then review and critique the budget of the districts reporting to them. A "tough" approval process would ensure that the district managers do not "play games" with the budgeting system.

d. The regional budgets would similarly be reviewed and approved at the corporate level. If the overall corporate expectations are not met at this stage, a process of negotiation should take place between the corporate and the regional managers to find out ways and means of sharing this "gap" among the regions (if this were not possible, corporate expectations will have to be revised down).

The whole purpose of having a blend of the top down as well as bottom up approaches to budgeting is to ensure that QMSC comes up with a budget which both meets the corporate expectations and simultaneously leads to greater commitment on the part of regional/district managers. QMSC can then tie the incentive bonus of their managers to attaining these budgeted RI targets.

4. Mix of Salary and Bonus

There are two basic philosophies on incentive compensation. Some companies argue that they recruit good people, pay them well, and then expect performance (Figure 2a). These companies emphasize high salaries (fixed component of total compensation) and not incentive bonus. Under this system, pay is not linked to performance and is, therefore, not at risk. This raises the following issue: What happens if the person does not perform well?

Another group of companies (example: Nucor Steel) subscribe to the philosophy that we recruit good people, expect them to perform well, and pay them well, if performance is actually good (Figure 2b) . These companies who practice "performance-based pay" emphasize incentive bonus (variable component in total compensation) and not salary.

These two control philosophies have very different motivational implications. QMSC puts a cap on incentive bonus-bonus cannot exceed 75 percent of salary. To that extent, they do not fully subscribe to the "performance-based pay" philosophy. Why put any caps on incentive bonus? Under QMSC's system, what will a district manager do when the manager, during the first 6 months of the year, has already reached the 75 percent limit? Is this functional? Class time should be devoted to pursuing these issues. Some students would argue for no caps on bonus as a way to motivate district managers to continually improve RI.

5. Degree of Profit Sharing

A district manager's bonus can be based solely on the district's performance or solely on the region's performance or on some combination of both. Each of these arrangements send different signals to the district manager regarding inter-district cooperation. QMSC ties 25 percent of the district manager's bonus to regional performance and 75 percent to district's performance.

The fact that 25 percent of the district manager's incentive bonus is tied to regional performance would encourage the district manager to consider overall regional interest while making decisions. This design feature, which fosters goal congruence, is particularly desirable given the high degree of interdependence between the districts and the regions, especially in the area of efficient inventory management.

6. Uniform versus Differentiated Controls

QMSC does not differentiate its controls across the 23 districts. Clearly, some districts are in high growth areas (suggesting "build market share" strategy) and others are in mature markets (suggesting "harvest for cash flows" strategy). Similarly, some districts might be primarily dealing in commodity metals with a cost leadership focus and others might have a value leadership focus. Should QMSC differentiate its controls across districts with build versus harvest strategies; low cost versus differentiation strategies?

The instructor might pursue the motivational effects on a "build" district manager whose performance evaluation is strictly based on RI. Students would suggest that district managers be evaluated based on RI and sales growth. However, the weights assigned to these criteria should be differentiated depending on the strategy pursued by the district—for a build strategy, greater weight should be placed on sales growth whereas, for a harvest strategy, greater weight should be placed on RI.

7. Summary

QMSC provides a good setting to motivate the discussion on the topics of "investment centers" and "incentive compensation" design. The key question in constituting districts as investment centers is: does the district manager control "profits" and "investments"? Again, the term "investment center" does not have uniform and consistent meaning across firms. By this, we mean that in some firms, divisional managers are held accountable only for current assets, in others for total assets, in some others for total assets less current liabilities; yet, all the three types are termed "investment center" control. Therefore students have to address two interrelated issues: should district managers be evaluated as investment centers? If so, what is the best way to measure "profits" and "investments"?

As noted earlier, students should recognize the distinction between evaluating the manager vs. evaluating the venture. The "investment center" concept could be used for both types of evaluations or just for evaluating the venture.

The considerations involved in designing control systems for evaluating managerial performance have less to do with accounting and more to do with human behavior. Managers will have a tendency to maximize those yardsticks which are bases on which their incentives are decided. The control system should, therefore, be so designed that it elicits the behavior from a district manager which maximizes his own profits and simultaneously maximizes QMSC's profits. The ROI-based control system does not do this whereas the RI concept does. The instructor, at some point, might refer to arguments made by Hayes and Abernathy[1] and others as to how financial control systems used by the U.S. corporations might have led to their lack of international competitiveness. Students might get a feeling, after reading Hayes and Abernathy's article, that financial controls are bad (though we do not think the authors intended that). It needs to be emphasized that U.S. corporations might not be over-controlled; it might just be a case of mis-control. We can, in fact, suggest better ways to control QMSC's business. The fact that current financial control systems in the U.S. might be focusing managers' attention on short-time performance does not imply that control systems ought to be de-emphasized. Quite the contrary, controllers should design "smart" management systems which would help plan and control decentralized operations, while allowing the divisional managers to be innovative and maintain global competitiveness.

Teaching Strategy

Positioning of the Case

We have used this case in the first year required Managerial Accounting course as an introduction to the topic of "investment centers." We have also used the case in the second year elective course on "Management Control Systems." The case raises a comprehensive list of issues in evaluating investment center managers, all of which can be meaningfully discussed with either an introductory or an advanced group of students. The case has plenty of issues to fully utilize two class periods (of 90 minutes each). However, the case can be covered in one class period, if the instructor cannot allot two class sessions for this topic. If used for one session, the instructor has to be somewhat more structured and might want to decide what major issues to focus on in class. Our preference is to at least cover the following topics: (1) the rationale and criteria used to set up investment centers; and (2) the motivational issues involved in evaluating managers on Return on Assets vs. Residual Income; we cover the other issues in whatever depth time allows. If the case is used for two sessions, the instructor will be able to cover all of the issues discussed in this teaching note.

Classroom Strategy

We have provided below a set of teaching questions (with approximate time allocation) that are designed to facilitate a discussion of the case over two class sessions.

Day 1

1. Discussion of the metal distribution business and QMSC's strategic positioning in this industry. (20 minutes)

2. Responsibility structure. (15 minutes)

    a. What is a cost center, profit center, investment center?

---

[1] Hayes and Abernathy, "Managing Our Way to Economic Decline," *Harvard Business Review*, July-August, 1980.

b. What criteria are useful in allocating financial responsibilities?

c. Should districts be investment centers?

3. ROA vs. Residual Income (50 minutes)

a. Is the project described in Exhibit 3 attractive for QMSC? Why?

b. Is the project attractive to Ken Richards? Why not?

c. Why does the district manager reject a proposal which is good for the company?

d. Does the incentive bonus for Ken Richards go down only in year 1 of the project? What happens to his bonus over the duration of the project?

e. Can you suggest an incentive system for QMSC which would overcome the deficiencies found in their current system?

f. Would RI solve the problem? If not, what else can we do?

4. Summary and wrap-up. (5 minutes)

<u>Day 2</u>

1. Introductory comments on ROA vs. RI. (5 minutes)

2. Definition of "profit" in calculating RI. (10 minutes)

a. Should corporate overheads be allocated?

b. Should district managers be evaluated on pre-tax or after-tax profits?

3. Definition of "investment" in calculating RI. (20 minutes)

a. Should "cash" be included? If so, at what value?

b. How do you evaluate the way receivables, inventory, and payables are handled by QMSC?

c. Should Warehouse Land, Buildings, and Equipment be included in the asset base? If so, what valuation basis (gross book value, net book value, or replacement cost) should be used?

d. How should leased trucks be handled?

4. Formula-based vs. subjective bonus determination. (10 minutes)

5. Mix of salary and bonus. (15 minutes)

6. Degree of profit sharing. (15 minutes)

7. Uniform vs. differentiated controls. (10 minutes)

8. Summary. (5 minutes)

    a. Reiterate goal congruence theme.

    b. Some comments on Hayes and Abernathy's article.

    c. Emphasize the need for a fit between QMSC's control systems, the industry in which it operates, and its strategy.

VG

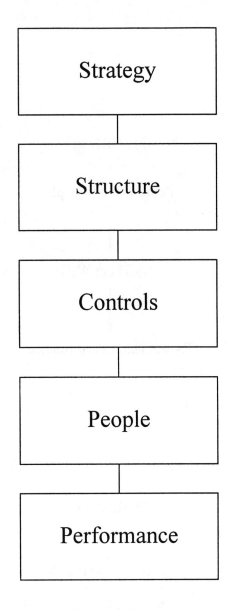

FIGURE 1

Framework For Control System Design

FIGURE 1a

Recruit Good People

↓

Pay Them Well

↓

Expect Good Performance

FIGURE 1b

Recruit Good People

↓

Expect Good Performance

↓

Pay Them Well, If Performance is Actually Good

QUALITY METAL SERVICE CENTER
MANAGEMENT CONTROL SYSTEMS

Vijay Govindaraian

The Amos Tuck School of Business Administration

Dartmouth College

Hanover, NH 03755

(603) 646-2156

Objective of Session

1. Responsibility center issues—profit center and investment center concepts.

2. Rona management issues.

3. Balancing short-run and long-run tradeoffs and financial/non-financial tradeoffs.

4. Implementing strategy through formal controls—pros and cons.

Responsibility Centers

Inputs		Outputs
	Process	

"Investment"

Cost Centers	→	Measure Inputs (Engineered or Discretionary)
Revenue Centers	→	Measure Outputs <u>Less</u> costs directly controlled by the responsibility center
Profit Centers	→	Measure Inputs and Outputs
Investment Centers	→	Measure Inputs and Outputs in Relation to Investment

1. Any responsibility center can be made into a cost, revenue, profit, or investment center.

2. Managers typically worry about the items on which they are controlled.

3. What do you want the managers to worry about?

Survey of Fortune 1000 Firms

Companies with one or more
investment centers   78%

Of these, companies using
    Residual Income   36%
    Return on Investment   64%

Economic Value Added (EVA) Definition

Net Operating Profit After Tax (NOPAT)

– Charge for invested capital

$$\boxed{\text{= Economic Value Added (EVA)}}$$

- Economic Value Added represents the return on the assets invested in a business in excess of the financial cost of those assets

- EVA = [ROIC (%) – Cost of Capital (%)] × Capital Employed

EVA Approach

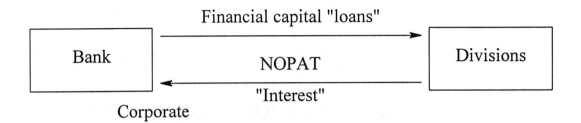

Objectives:

- Establish target financing structure

- Obtain low cost capital

- Allocate capital to divisions

- Buy/sell businesses:

  - Increase division competitiveness

  - Eliminate low return business

- Improve operating profits without tying up additional capital

- Eliminate low return assets

- Identify projects with return greater than "interest":

  - Grow

EVA: Correlation to Shareholder Wealth

- Economic Value Added is the measure most closely tied to shareholder value creation

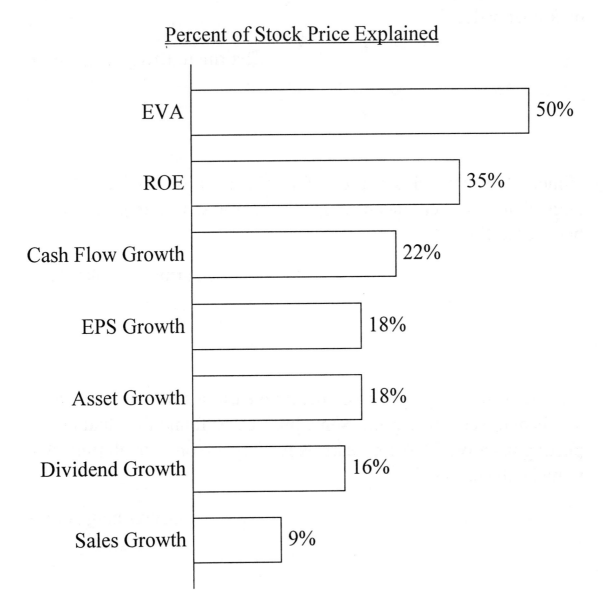

Percent of Stock Price Explained

EVA	50%
ROE	35%
Cash Flow Growth	22%
EPS Growth	18%
Asset Growth	18%
Dividend Growth	16%
Sales Growth	9%

Source: Stern Stewart
14034hub1304
Talisman

EVA as a Management Tool

"We believe that this measurement, with incentive compensation linked to it, can effectively encourage management decisions that maximize value."

—Chairman, Briggs & Stratton

"Since EVA is the closest proxy for value creation, we have aligned management incentives with shareholder interests by tying bonuses to EVA."

—Chairman, Quaker Oats

"'Good' is no longer positive operating earnings. It's only when you beat the cost of capital. Some businesses found they had been posting negative EVA for years. Now they are on a tough timetable to make the hurdle."

—Chairman, AT&T

EVA Represents a Single Financial Measure Which Links all Decision Making

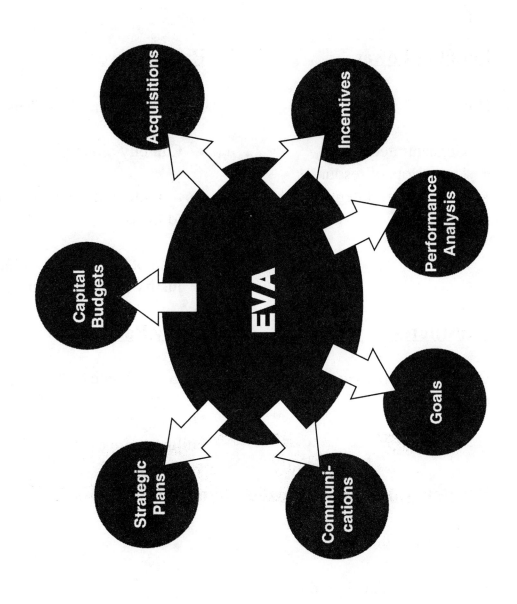

Metal Distribution Industry

A.M. Castle

Supplier Power

High

- Concentrated
- Large; lots of resources
- Can forward integrate

Buyer Power

High for Fortune 500 firms

- Can buy directly

Low to medium for small and mid-sized firms

- Do not buy enough volume to justify preproduction equipment

Substitutes

Buyers and sellers getting together directly

Entry Barriers

High working capital

High capital for fixed assets, if buildings are owned

Rivalry Among Existing Companies

Price rivalry high

- Undifferentiated product
- High supplier and buyer power
- Many rivals; fragmented industry
- Low customer loyalty
- Low value added (thin margins)
- Availability of substitutes

Strategic Planning Associates

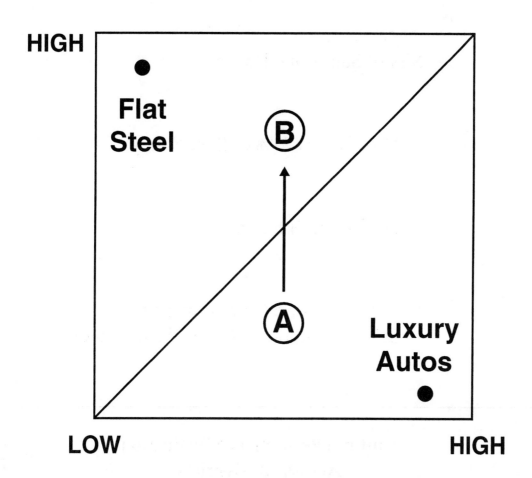

PRICE SENSITIVITY OF CUSTOMERS

PERCEIVED PRODUCT DIFFERENTIATION

Control Systems

- Performance Evaluation Criteria

  ROA; No Non-Financials

- Mix of Salary and Bonus

  Max. Bonus 75% of Base Salary

- Degree of Profit Sharing

  75% on District's Performance
  25% on Corporate/Region Performance

> Uniform Performance Evaluation
> Across All Districts

Is this a good project for the company?

"Strategic" Fit

"Financial" Fit

Should Columbus District Manager send it to
Head Office for approval?

$$K = 15\% \text{ (AT)}$$

$$K = 30\% \text{ (BT)}$$

	1982	1983	1984	1985	1986
PBT	$40	230	274	310	340
Investment	720	875	900	935	965
ROI	5.5%	26%	30%	33%	35%

	1987	1988	1989	1990	1991
PBT	$350	370	384	390	400
Investment	1,000	1,045	1,085	1,135	1,190
ROI	35%	35%	35%	34%	34%

	('000s)	
	New York	Boston
Profit as a % of Sales	5%	4%
Sales	$5,000	$25,000
Profit	$250	$1,000
Investment	$1,000	$5,000
Return on Investment	25%	20%
Cost of Capital	15%	15%
Capital Charge	$150 (15% on $5,000)	$750 (15% on $5,000)
Residual Income	$100	$250

New investment $1,000,000 to return $220,000 per year for 10 years.

Profit	$470	$1,220
Investment	$2,000	$6,000
ROI	23.5%	20.3%
Capital Charge	$300	$900
Residual Income	$170	$320

New York

A New Business Opportunity

Δ Accounts Receivable $500,000

Δ Profit $150,000

Δ ROI = $150,000/$500,000 = 30%

Current ROI = 40%

Cost of Capital = 20%

Investment Centers

Residual Income

How to Define:

- Profit

- Investment

- Cost of Capital

Types of Profitability Measures

Sales Revenues
Less Variable Costs   _____

        CONTRIBUTION   (1)

Less Division's Fixed Expenses   _____

        DIVISION DIRECT PROFIT   (2)

Less Allocated Corporate Overhead   _____

        PROFIT BEFORE TAXES   (3)

Less Income Taxes   _____

        PROFIT AFTER TAXES   (4)

                                                   _____

How to Define "Investment"

I. Working Capital Items

Cash

Accounts Receivable

    End of period vs. average balance
    Cost of goods sold vs. sales revenue

Inventory

    End of period vs. average balance
    LIFO, FIFO, replacement costs?

Accounts Payable

II. Fixed Assets

    Net book value

    Gross book value

    Replacement cost

Fixed Assets Valuation

Net Book Value

Year	1	2	3	4	5	6	7	8	9	10
Profit	$200	200	200	200	200	200	200	200	200	200
Net Book Value	1,000	900	800	700	600	500	400	300	200	100
ROI	20%	22%	25%	30%	33%	40%	50%	67%	100%	200%

Gross Book Value

	Asset 1	Asset 2	Total
Profit	$100	200	300
Investment	500	500	1,000
ROI	20%	40%	30%

How to Define "Cost of Capital"

- Single Rate or Multiple Rates Across Divisions?

- Different Rates Across Working Capital and Fixed Assets?

- Estimation of Cost of Debt and Cost of Equity

    Business Risk

    Financial Risk

    Inflation

- Capital Structure (Debt-Equity Mix) for Each Division

Performance Evaluation

District: _____   Manager: _____

	Actual	Target
Return on Controllable Assets:		
Customer Service Rating:		
Internal Efficiencies:		
Inventory Turnover		
S&A as % of Sales		
Gross Margin		
Product Availability (number of stockouts)		
Delivery Performance:		
New Customers:		
New Business:		

AM Castle

Some Organizational Changes

1. Districts constituted as <u>separate businesses</u> (with complete sourcing & marketing authority)

2. Residual income measure on controllable assets

3. Reduction in salary; no caps on bonus ("Incentive-Based Pay")

4. Different controls across different districts with different strategic contexts:

| Residual Income Market Share Sales Growth | weights on these criteria varied across districts |

A.M. Castle

	1982	1985
Tons Sold	211,000 tons	210,000 tons
Sales	$200 million	$305 million
Margin	15%	26%
Profit	$30 million	$80 million

80/30 Dilemma

80% of us typically believe we are in the upper 30% of performers.

Research Examples

Interpersonal Skills

> 100% believe they were about average.
> 60% believe they were in the top 10%.
> 25% believe they were in the top 1%.

Leadership

> 70% believe they were in the top 25%.
> 2% believe they were below average.

Engineers

> 100% believe they were above average.
> 86% believe they were in the top 25%.

Consequence:

This nonrational aspect of human nature—the average is above average—is a major reason why purely rational appraisal is primarily a demotivating process.

Accounting As:

- *Applied Economics*

   Or

- *Applied "Behavioral Science"*

A "Good" Control System Must Consider:

- *The Nature of the Business (KSFs)*

- *Competitive Strategy Being Followed*

<u>Investment Center</u> Management Ideas

Case 7-4

Industrial Products Corporation

Purpose

This case can be used to explore the use of return on investment (ROI) to measure divisional performance. If the use of ROI is compared with the use of profit alone, the difference is having investment in the denominator. One use of performance measures is to influence behavior. So including investment in the measure means top management wants to influence the division manager's behavior with regard to investment.

The question then arises, in what ways can the division manager influence investment? The case describes the make-up of the division's investment (or in this case its assets) and enables students to consider in some detail how the division manager can, or might, influence the level of investment.

Synopsis

Baker Division was one of a number of divisions of Industrial Products Company. For many years rate of return on investment had been used to measure divisional performance. The case describes the several components of Baker Division's assets and the ways in which Mr. Brandt, the division manager, could influence the size of investment in each.

Assignment

The two questions at the end of the case ask students to think about how much Mr. Brandt can influence the level of investment in the various asset classes of the division and whether ROI is a good measure of divisional performance.

Analysis

Careful review of case information shows that Mr. Brandt influences the level of investment in Baker Division through the following decisions and actions:

- choosing whether to pay dividends (cash);

- using the EOQ formula, which includes a cost of capital figure, and applying a constant to modify the forecast of future usage (inventory); and

- capital expenditure management, including deciding which projects to propose to top management, and how to set the hurdle rate to the extent that the rate was within his jurisdiction (machinery, land and buildings).

This case was prepared by Professor William Rotch, Johnson and Higgins Professor of Business Administration, University of Virginia. Copyright © 1996 by the University of Virginia Darden School Foundation, Charlottesville, VA. All rights reserved.

These are rather specialized decisions. Mr. Brandt might consider using Economic Value Added internally to broaden the application. To do so effectively would probably require an extensive educational campaign. Nevertheless, there still remains a question whether including investment in ROI or EVA will significantly influence the behavior of many managers like Mr. Brandt of Baker Division.

Given the narrow range of Mr. Brandt's influence, in practice, should ROI be dropped in favor of the simpler profit measure? Two considerations can be brought up here. One is that even though the range of influence is narrow, the division manager does have some influence and if only profit were measured, those important trade-offs between revenue, expense and investment might be forgotten. Inventory could expand to ensure there would never be a stockout. Idle time might be used to build inventory and thereby avoid negative variances. So having investment in the measure provides an important discipline.

The other consideration is the need for an ROI measure (or EVA) to evaluate the merits of the business. Are IPC's funds being well used? This is a sort of portfolio perspective, in which the Baker Division is one of many investments.

Thus the case provides an opportunity to explore how the ROI measure can influence a division manager, and separately, how the measure is useful in measuring Baker Division's performance as one investment in a portfolio of investments.

Diversified Products Corporation

Prologue

We have also reproduced the teaching note for the earlier Diversified Products Corporation since the issues are similar to Industrial Products Corporation.

Approach

In order to discuss the investment base problem adequately, each of the main items on the balance sheet must be discussed separately. Although several of the cases in this section of the book describe all the balance sheet items, I prefer to focus on certain items in one case, and other items in another, rather than covering each item briefly in each case. I use Diversified Products Corporation as a basis for discussing the current assets because there are several interesting aspects to the current asset treatment in this case, and I prefer to use Antol for a discussion of the fixed assets. These notes will be structured in this fashion.

In all cases, the general question is: What practices will motivate the division managers to use their assets most efficiently, and to acquire the proper amount and kind of new assets? Presumably, when his investment is being measured, the division manager will try to increase his divisional return on investment, and we desire that actions he takes toward this end be actions that are in the best interest of the whole corporation. In addition, but as a subsidiary point, we would like the return on investment measure to be perceived as being fair and equitable.

Discussion

In the discussion that follows, the principal current asset items will be discussed separately.

Cash

Diversified Products does not attempt to charge actual cash to the divisions. This is a common practice. The actual cash balance in a division, i.e., bank accounts, is a fairly meaningless measure of the cash resources necessary to support divisional operations because the division has quick access to the cash of the whole corporation and, therefore, does not need the cash "safety factor" that would be necessary if the division were a separate corporation. In Lemfert, cash is recorded at an arbitrary amount, 18 percent of manufacturing costs, and in Antol, the amount of cash charged to the division is fixed by agreement between the division and the head office. In Diversified, the formula is especially interesting. There is an agreed-upon fixed amount of cash that is intended to correspond to the minimum needs of the division; the division can keep cash in excess of this amount, and on the excess it receives a 3 percent credit. (The excess is called marketable securities," but this term has no special meaning; it does not correspond to any physically identifiable marketable securities.) Since the division undoubtedly earns more than 3 percent on its total assets, it can increase its return on investment by voluntarily returning excess cash to corporate headquarters. The system, therefore, motivates the division to do this, which is good for the corporation as a whole.

Accounts Receivable

The division is charged with its actual accounts receivable. Since it has no real control over either credit terms or collections, this theoretically could mean that it is being charged with a noncontrollable item. As a practical matter, there is probably little, if any, complaint about this charge; the amount of the asset will tend to vary with the sales volume of the division, and this is probably perceived as being equitable. Note that in Lemfert, the accounts receivable was a standard percentage of manufacturing costs in order to avoid the charge of noncontrollability. This may well be considered as a small improvement over the practice used by Diversified.

Inventory

The text describes how the general policy of inventory control is tied with the specific rules for figuring inventory requirements for individual items. It also illustrates how the formulas found in textbooks are modified in practice. The example worked out in Exhibit 1 is based on the conventional Economic Order Quantity formula, but two "correction factors" are inserted in it. Apparently, these factors distort the formula. Actually, I think they are better viewed as a way of introducing the judgment as to current needs and conditions into the straight mechanical application of the formula. The 4½ percent cost-of-capital charge used in the formula is obviously too low, but the correction factor of 0.6 tends to bring it up to what it probably should be. From the example it can be calculated that the implicit capital charge is actually 15 percent, and deducting 4½ percent for the cost of insurance, inventory, taxes, and obsolescence leaves about 10 percent as a cost-of-capital figure, which seems reasonable.

Calculations from which the above conclusions were drawn are given in Exhibit A.

Exhibit A

EDQ Computations

A. Demand (dozen)

Current Quarter	83×3	249
Previous Quarter	$54 \times 1/4$	54/303

$$303 \div 4 = 76$$

76 dozen per quarter $\times 4 = 303$ per year

B. EDQ without adjustment

$$Q = \sqrt{\frac{2\ RS}{KC}} = \sqrt{\frac{2.303 \cdot \$3.14}{.09 \cdot \$1.77}}$$

$$= \sqrt{\frac{1.900}{.16}} = \sqrt{11,800}$$

$$= 110$$

C. With .6 adjustment

$$\sqrt{\frac{1.140}{.16}} = \sqrt{7,100}$$

$$= 84 \text{ (as given)}$$

D. Original demand: what implicit interest rate?

$$1,900/x \cdot 1.77 = 7,100$$

$$1,900 = 12,567x$$

$$x = .15 = 15\% \text{ implicit rate}$$

The quantity discount analysis is another example of how specific rules are used to implement the general policy. Note that the widgets used in this example are <u>not</u> the same as the gremlets used in Exhibit 1; students unfortunately are often misled by trying to relate these two examples.

In general, inventory is controllable, it should be included in the asset base, and the way in which Diversified Products does this is probably satisfactory.

Current Liabilities

Diversified does not deduct current liabilities from the asset base; some companies do. They are not deducted here presumably because the division manager has little, if anything, to say about the amount of short-term bank loans or the promptness with which his current bills are paid; these are corporate decisions. If current liabilities were deducted, the manager would be encouraged to make current liabilities as large as he could, because this would decrease his asset base and therefore increase his return on investment. This might not be in the best interest of the corporation because of its possible bad effect on the company's credit standing. Companies that do deduct current liabilities usually lay down specific rules that are designed to prevent such abuses of credit privileges.

RNA

Case 7-5

Marden Company

This case can be taught at two levels. Using level 1, Chapter 8 or the equivalent reading is not assigned. The purpose is to get the students thinking about measuring the performance of a profit-center manager. You may have to be somewhat directive because the class may not have much background in the principles and techniques of ROI. In any event, there are three things that have to be discussed and I ask the questions listed below and make the class stay on one issue at a time. The questions are as follows:

1. What should be the basic measure of managerial performance?

   I get alternatives and explanations of alternatives and write them on the board. With a little direction I obtain a list of alternatives somewhat as follows:

   > Return on investment
   > Profit after a capital charge
   > Profit against budget
   > Absolute profitability

   I do not worry too much about the pros and cons of each method because there is not time. I do, however, ask for a vote to find out the class sentiment and to get them committed to a method.

2. How should profit be measured?

   I get a series of alternatives and write them on the board and take a vote. The series usually have some resemblance to the measures described in Chapter 6, particularly if Chapter 6 had already been assigned.

   Again, I do not spend too long on the pros and cons because of time constraints. (If, however, you do find that the class is reacting more quickly to the questions than I have anticipated, there is certainly some worthwhile discussion on the advantages and disadvantages of the different profit measures.)

3. If it is decided to use return on investment, what balance sheet items should be included in the investment base and at what value?

   I then take each balance sheet item in turn and ask whether it should be included and, if so, at what amount. The main areas of contention are:

   > Cash (because of lock box system)
   > Fixed Assets (gross or net)
   > Current Liabilities (whether to include or not)
   > Debt (whether to include or not)

   It is necessary to move the class along to complete the above discussion in a class period. At the end of the period, I tell the class to read Chapter 8. This approach has been successful as introduction to measurement systems. It is a way of getting them intrigued with the subject before introducing the technicalities.

The case can be taught at level 2 if the class has read Chapter 8. I ask the same questions but handle the discussion differently. First, I go over the alternatives quickly and try to make the class tell what they would do about each of the issues and why. For example, when I get no student to take a position, I ask the class if everyone agrees. Since agreement is rare, it is easy to get an animated discussion (otherwise known as an argument) going.

The main purpose of this approach is to make sure that the class understands Chapter 8 and to see that the issues are far from simple.

JD

Case 7-6

Lemfert Company

Approach

This case can be used either in the profit center section or in the investment base section. Its place in this book suggests its use as a case for pulling together the ideas developed in both of these sections. Although short, it has enough information to furnish the basis for a good discussion of many points.

Discussion

Profit center or not. Perhaps the most interesting question is whether Division F should be a profit center. We submitted this case to 14 leading public accounting and management consulting firms, asking them essentially the questions that appear at the end of the case. Only two of these firms thought that Division F should be a profit center, and 12 thought Division F should be operated as an expense center. Of course, students need not side with the majority; I, for one, do not.

The arguments made by these firms in favor of having Division F as a profit center are summarized below, in approximately the words used by them:

- With a profit center, you make better long-run decisions.

- A profit center keeps a division on its toes.

- Division managers in a profit center are entrepreneurs; they are first-class citizens. Managers of expense centers are cost operators; they are second-class citizens.

- A profit center increases aggressiveness and a competitive spirit.

- You can't really measure the performance of the divisions without a profit center.

- Expense control is not adequate here. There is no way of checking whether the output is satisfactory.

Those who argued against having Division F as a profit center made the points listed below:

- The transfer price is arbitrary and hence the profit of the division is arbitrary.

This case was prepared by Robert N. Anthony.

Copyright © 1963, 1964 by the President and Fellows of Harvard College. Harvard Business School case 118-116.

- You can exercise adequate control through an expense budget; a profit center is unnecessary.

- This is a captive plant. The company can't go outside for type K items; thus it doesn't have decisions to make.

- The objective of cost minimization is as good here as the objective of profit maximization.

- The whole process in Lemfert is interrelated. Chopping it up into pieces is arbitrary—a bookkeeping game—hanky panky. There will be too much argument, friction, bad feeling, over the transfer price.

- Not everyone is or should be an entrepreneur.

- In this system there will be a problem of assigning responsibility for defective products.

- This system must cost an enormous amount to operate.

- The costs of type K items include a fictitious profit and thus hide the "total corporate variable cost." The company should focus on the total cost of production, not the cost of segments.

- They really can't estimate the cost of "efficient producers."

- There should not be a transfer price unless there is at least one outside price to check against.

- This system gives too much power to the controller.

Transfer price. Most of the elements of the transfer price, including the elements entering into the investment base, have been discussed in connection with earlier cases, and the discussion will not be repeated here. One new aspect is the fact that the material, labor, and overhead cost components of the transfer price are those that would be incurred by "efficient processing on modern equipment." This is a sound concept, although difficult to apply in many situations.

Division F makes only ten type K items, and probably the volume of each of these items is substantial. Therefore, it can afford to spend a substantial amount of effort in arriving at a good transfer price. In situations where the number of items was large or the dollar value of items was small, the work involved in arriving at a transfer price might cost more than its value. Even in this situation, some adequate substitute for a price built up on each item might be feasible; for example, the "time and material" pricing formula used by many job shops, such as printing plants. In other situations a cost build-up may be unduly influenced by factors noncontrollable by the division manager, and therefore unsatisfactory as an expression of the results of their decisions. It is for this reason that most petroleum companies have abandoned the attempt to make a transfer price for refined products going from the refinery to the marketing division. Other situations where a transfer price should not be used are given in the "Note on Transfer Pricing."

The president of a medium-size, profitable company once told a visitor: "Our executive team is one big happy family. If we put in profit centers and transfer pricing, we would surely increase friction, competition, and argument. I'm not sure we want to do this." The visitor thought to himself that this executive team might indeed be one big happy family, but that it might at the same time be a *complacent* family, that eventually would lose out in the competitive struggle.

RNA

CHAPTER 8
STRATEGIC PLANNING

Changes from the Eighth Edition

Because there is a chapter on strategies, the strategic material in Chapter 8 has been reduced. The chapter has been rewritten. The title of the chapter has been changed from "programming" to "strategic planning." This change reflects better the actual practice.

Cases

Codman & Shurtleff is an excellent case on strategic planning and its use as an interactive control to develop new strategies.

Copley Manufacturing Company describes the problems of introducing a strategic planning system.

Allied Stationery Products, adapted from Allied Stationery Products (A), (B), and (C), deals with activity-based costing in a service business context; further, this case focuses on customer profitability analysis (as opposed to product profitability analysis).

Emerson Electric describes the company's strategic and annual planning process and their role in implementing its low-cost strategy.

Case 8-1

Codman & Shurtleff, Inc.

Teaching Objectives

1. To illustrate the use of a comprehensive formal planning and control system in formulating and implementing strategy in a large decentralized company.

2. To introduce the concept of organizational learning and illustrate how this can be institutionalized through formal process.

3. To consider the relationship between organizational innovation and formal control.

4. To consider the relationship between organizational reward practices, organizational learning, and formal systems.

Possible Assignment Questions

1. Evaluate the planning and control system in use at Johnson & Johnson. What are its strengths and weaknesses?

2. In the 1980s, surveys of CEO's of the 250 largest U.S. companies repeatedly ranked Johnson & Johnson as one of the most innovative and well-managed firms in its industry. What role, if any, do you believe that J&J's management planning and control systems play in achieving (or hindering) innovation?

3. From information provided in the case, suggest how you would design a reward/incentive system for Roy Black and the Codman & Shurtleff Board to capture maximum benefit from planning and control procedures. How would you deal with relating pay to performance in rapidly changing environments?

4. Roy Black states that decentralized management is "unequivocal accountability for what you do" (last paragraph of this case). Do you agree with his statement?

Case Background

This case was prepared by Robert L. Simons.

Copyright © 1987 by the President and Fellows of Harvard College. Harvard Business School case 183-081.

This case was written as part of an ongoing research project designed to increase our understanding of the relationship between business strategy and formal control systems. An earlier study[1] using statistical tests on a large sample of firms had produced a paradoxical result: firms that were following innovative, "Prospector" strategies used their formal control systems more intensively than firms following cost-oriented, "Defender" strategies. This result differed from the widely held view that innovation is best achieved in organizations that minimize formal control and allow creative individuals to work in an unconstrained environment.

To gain more understanding about this paradox, I decided to study in detail an organization that was widely regarded as both well-managed and highly innovative; through this research, I hoped to understand if the statistical results were valid and, if so, gain some insight into the processes in organizations that linked innovation with formal control.

Using the annual *Fortune* magazine surveys of the most admired corporations in America, I chose Johnson & Johnson to study because it was widely believed to be both innovative and well managed by CEOs in its industry and by those in other industries. Moreover, J&J operated in 75 countries; employed 75,000 people; and competed successfully in a wide variety of highly competitive markets.

Conducting the study involved interviewing many J&J corporate managers including the president and other members of the Executive Committee; visiting major operating subsidiaries; and attending strategic planning meetings and budget meetings at Codman & Shurtleff, a Boston-based subsidiary[2].

I was amazed and intrigued by the incredible amount of organizational effort that went into the formal planning and control process at J&J. It was clear that the results of the previous statistical study were not an anomaly.

At Johnson & Johnson, formal control systems are not seen as an end in themselves, but are very much a part of the management process. Operating managers are intimately involved in the formal control process on a regular basis. These systems are used to set agendas throughout the organization to debate strategies, competitor actions, environmental developments, and tactics. There are several key features in the way these systems are used at J&J to activate learning throughout the organization and, as a result, a high level of innovation. The remainder of this note addresses these features and classroom pedagogy.

Pedagogy

The class can be structured into two segments: first, work with students to trace through the planning and control processes on the board; second, elicit an analysis from students of the strengths and weaknesses of the process before them. At the end of the session, students will have a solid understanding of the process and will, typically, be impressed by its power.

---

[1] Robert Simons, "The Relationship Between Business Strategy and Accounting Control Systems: An Empirical Analysis," Accounting, Organizations and Society, July 1987, (pp. 357 – 374).
[2] A description of the study and its results can be found in Robert Simons, "Planning, Control, and Uncertainty: A Process View," in W.J. Bruns, Jr., and R.S. Kaplan, (eds), Accounting and Management: Field Study Perspectives, (Boston: Harvard University Press, 1987).

In the first part of the class, ask students to describe the formal process and record their analysis on the board. Use colored chalk, feedback loops, and arrows to build up a picture to illustrate the complexity and interactive nature of the process. Before class, set up the board with J&J hierarchical levels down the left side and the months of the calendar year along the top. (See Appendix A of this note to give an idea of how the board may look by the time you are finished.)

Three formal processes can be considered in sequence: long range planning; profit planning; and revisions and reforecasts. The class could proceed as follows:

Long Range Planning

Question

Let's look at the long range planning system first. When does the process start and what are the inputs?

Answer

The process starts in January and takes 6 months to complete. Inputs include: (1) the 5/10 year plan from the previous year, and (2) the mission statement (it is necessary to stress the importance of a well thought out and current mission statement in this process).

Question

What happens next?

Answer

Business plans are developed by segment, competitor activity is analyzed through the preparation of pro forma income and strategy statements, and each department prepares plans based on marketing plans.

Question

Next?

Answer

Then, over a series of meetings in May, the top functional managers sit down with Roy Black to begin a process of review, challenge, and adjustment. All this is in anticipation of the June meeting with Stolzer.

Question

What happens at the Stolzer meeting?

Answer

Again, review, challenge, discussion of changes since previous years, analysis of action plans, revision, commitment, and approval.

Question

And then?

Answer

Black sends a two page summary letter to Jim Burke, CEO, and this is discussed in a "heated" session at the November Executive Committee meeting.

As you work through this process and fill in the board, many questions will arise and students can be challenged to answer them. For example:

- How does the 5/10 year plan work? What are its advantages?

Students can be asked to fill in a table such as this to demonstrate how the planning horizon changes over time. Start with 1983.

Question

In 1983, what years do managers focus on in developing plans? What years do they focus on in 1984? When does the 5/10 year planning horizon shift from 1990/1995 to 1995/2000?

Year	Profit Plan	2nd year Forecast	5/10 Year Planning Years	
1982	1983	1984	1985	1990
1983	1984	1985	1990	1995
1984	1985	1986	1990	1995
1985	1986	1987	1990	1995
1986	1987	1988	1990	1995
1987	1988	1989	1990	1995
1988	1989	1990	1995	2000
1989	1990	1991	1995	2000
1990	1991	1992	1995	2000

etc.

By focusing on the same two long range planning years over a five-year horizon, managers are forced to reconsider repeatedly how the competitive environment has changed and what steps they should put in place now (e.g., manpower planning) to compete effectively when the planning year arrives. Also, planning is taken seriously because everyone knows that the day will arrive when you have to live with the 5/10 year forecast as part of your current profit plan.

Focusing on change and the continual revisiting of the same planning years motivates learning and information sharing throughout the organization.

- Won't managers try to bias their estimates 5 and 10 years out to avoid being committed to tough profit plans in the future?

A number of features make this unlikely:

1. The same planning years are analyzed repeatedly over time by many people so multiple perspectives are considered;

2. Managers cannot obtain incremental resources for future opportunities unless they identify opportunities in their plan;

3. The 5/10 year plan is limited to four financial estimates. The real focus is on markets, customers, competitors, and strategies and tactics. The financials provide a common denominator to frame these discussions and point to problems and opportunities;

4. Stolzer, and all senior managers, have been in the business for a long time (Stolzer has 35 years experience). J&J promotes from within—all senior managers have worked as operating company presidents. Stolzer has a lot of "street savvy" and can push hard to make sure plans are realistic; and,

5. Managers are not rewarded on a formula basis for hitting profit plan targets.

- Isn't 6 months too long to be spending on this process?

If we are merely filling out forms, 6 months is too long. If we are engaged in an interactive set of discussions among various levels of management, if we are in a complex business with many business units, if we must undertake market assessments and technology reviews, it may not be too long. Is this not managing?

- But do we really need these formal systems to force managers to think strategically? Won't good managers do this without having to go through this formal process?

Good question for class discussion. A competing view is that managers are often too busy fighting fires to do long range business planning.

- What is the role of the Executive Committee in this process? It appears that this process is very bottom-up; is the Executive Committee just a rubber stamp?

We are told that Executive Committee meetings are heated and challenging. The challenging of proposals will ensure that plans throughout the organization have sufficient stretch. Stolzer is coming to a public forum and must be able to demonstrate that he has done his job well. Once Black and the Codman Board have sold their plan to Stolzer, he is their partner. It is his job to fight for them at the Executive Committee. By implication, knowing that he must face tough Executive Committee challenge, we can expect that Stolzer is a tough taskmaster at the advance meetings that he holds with the Codman Board.

In addition, the Executive Committee will play a critical role in integrating this highly diversified organization by considering market opportunities not contained in individual operating plans. This may involve enlarging the mission of certain companies, considering structural realignments, and authorizing acquisitions and divestitures.

Financial Profit Plan and Revisions

A similar approach can be followed to fill in the remainder of the board for the details of the profit plan and the various revisions. Note the following:

1. The Executive Committee focuses on revisions of *both* the profit plan and the second year forecast in March, June, and November. The June revision is a full-blown rebudgeting from the lowest expense center. The March and November updates involve all departments but with less detail. Although we only have dates of the Executive Committee review, draw in the interactive process of review that works from the bottom up before each of these three meetings.

2. The case depicts the Codman managers preparing to discuss the June revision with Stolzer on May 14.

3. Stolzer is also receiving weekly sales numbers and monthly variances from Black. Remember to draw these on the board.

By the time all formal processes have been traced, students should be asked to consider the tremendous overlap of activities at any point in the year. Choose a month, and draw a vertical line down the board to get a sense of the concurrent planning and control activities that are taking place within the organization.

Evaluation of System

Now that the board is filled with a maze of chalk, students will appreciate the complexity and amount of effort that J&J Puts into formal planning and budgeting.

Students are now ready to venture overall impressions and evaluations. Points that may be raised include the following:

<u>**Strengths**</u>

Forces busy managers to do strategic planning

Causes constant interaction among all managers in the company

Sets agendas for the debate of strategies and tactics

Motivates organizational learning about markets, competitors, etc.

High level of involvement builds commitment

Managers are constantly developing action plans. Very action-oriented.

Tight linkages between various types of plans causes realistic targets and a high degree of effort

The reward system is well suited to the process (more on this below)

Allows J&J corporate manage great diversity and uncertainty

Provides training to managers

Weaknesses

Costly in terms of the management time tied up in the process. High opportunity cost.

Overkill for a small business with 800 employees

Plans are too tightly linked to budgets

Can Executive Committee members like Stolzer be competent to review 17 businesses?

Focus on short-term action plans risks sacrificing long-term strategic objective (e.g., R&D cuts)

After the strengths and weaknesses of the system have been considered, several general points should be made in summary or as part of general student discussion.

Formal Systems and Innovation

Formal systems need not hinder innovation; formal systems can empower innovation by bringing focus and energy to organizational problems and opportunities. To do this, systems must be interactive and organizational rewards must be allocated in a way that complements desired management processes.

Formal Systems and Interactive Processes

In large complex organizations, formal procedures such as the J&J planning and control systems are used to motivate management process. To the extent that these procedures are effective, they are not just an aid in running the business, but rather an integral part of managing.

J&J has made its formal planning and control systems interactive by the following conditions:

1. The process requires frequent and regular attention from operating managers at all levels of the organization.

2. The role of staff specialists is limited.

3. Data derived in the process are interpreted in face-to-face meetings.

4. Information generated in the process represents agenda items for the highest levels of management.

5. The process relies on continual challenge and debate.

Interactive control procedures, which have high opportunity costs for the managers involved are appropriate when decision activities (1) are non-routine and unstructured and (2) affect significant portions of the organization. Interactive control causes organizational learning (organizational learning is the process by which an organization influences the learning of its individual members and the manner in which this knowledge is stored and transmitted).

Reward systems — (why does J&J go to such tremendous trouble to track performance and then back off and not reward people based on achieving targets?)

Johnson & Johnson rewards its managers on effort rather than on outcomes. Rewards are subjectively determined by superiors and are not tied in to a predetermined formula. This has several implications:

1. Managers are shielded from the variability in outcomes due to uncertain environments. Individuals will share information since their personal rewards will not be threatened as might be the case if information was used to, say, increase output targets.

2. To gain recognition and rewards, managers will try to make their effort visible to superiors by informing them of changing conditions and the actions that they have taken to deal with these changes.

3. To evaluate properly the efforts of subordinates, superiors must understand changes in the competitive environments, potential opportunities and constraints, and the range of action alternative available to subordinates. Subjective evaluation, therefore, reinforces information gathering and organizational learning.

Managers may be evaluated on their effort not only in increasing sales, net income, or ROE, but also on their efforts in increasing market share, and in new product introductions. Managers can also be rewarded for efforts that will help the business long term but which have little immediate return. Managers are held accountable to manage innovatively in rapidly changing circumstances.

CODMAN & SHURTLEFF

Vijay Govindaraian

Earl C. Daum 1924 Professor of International Business

The Amos Tuck School of Business Administration

Dartmouth College

Hanover, NH 03755

(603) 646-2156

J&J

Operated in 46 countries

75,000 employees

155 autonomous business units

Three product groups

J&J

Consumer Products

43% of Sales
↓   ↓
60% U.S. 40% Non U.S.

New products key to growth
Advertising and Promotion as % of
  Sales high
Key uncertainties:
  Product innovation
  Competitors' actions

Pharmaceutical Products

23% of Sales
↓   ↓
54% U.S. 46% Non U.S.

Prescription Drugs
R&D as % of Sales ≈ 15%
"Discovery, Testing, Approval"
  cycle is key
Marketing and Distribution is key
Competition from generic products

Professional Products

34% of Sales
↓   ↓
70% U.S. 30% Non U.S.

Key uncertainties:
  Hospital reimbursement practices
  Decrease in hospital admissions
  Physician's requirements

New product introduction
Pricing → Cost effective
Manufacturing involves advanced
  technologies in metallurgy,
  electronics, and optics

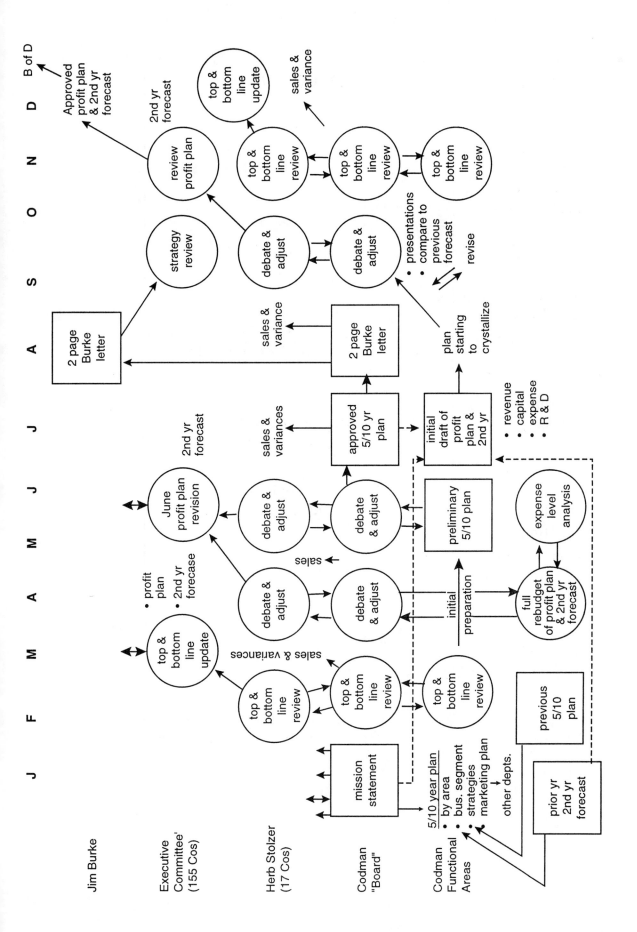

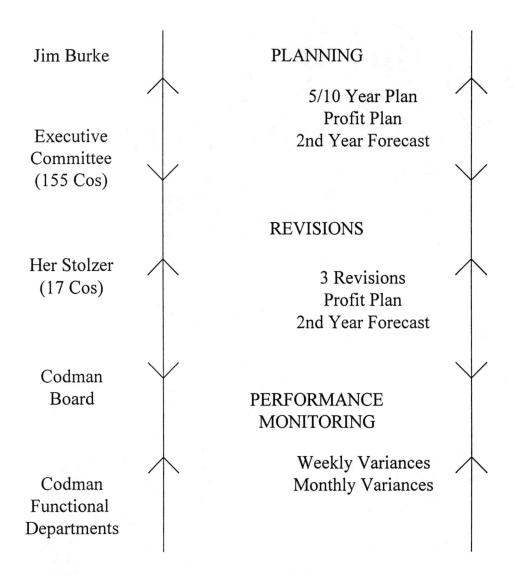

Jim Burke

Executive
Committee
(155 Cos)

Her Stolzer
(17 Cos)

Codman
Board

Codman
Functional
Departments

PLANNING

5/10 Year Plan
Profit Plan
2nd Year Forecast

REVISIONS

3 Revisions
Profit Plan
2nd Year Forecast

PERFORMANCE
MONITORING

Weekly Variances
Monthly Variances

Time Horizon

Year	Profit Plan	2-Year Forecast	5/10 Year Planning Years	
1983	1984	1985	1990	1995
1984	1985	1986	1990	1995
1985	1986	1987	1990	1995
1986	1987	1988	1990	1995
1987	1988	1989	1990	1995
1988	1989	1990	1995	2000
1989	1990	1991	1995	2000

J&J
Formal Planning & Control Systems

Strengths	Weaknesses
• Forces busy executives to do planning	• Too much time
• Causes constant interaction among managers	• Too financial
• Facilitates organizational learning	• Focus on short-term; no risk-taking
• Helps eliminate "slack"	• Overkill for 800 employee business
• High involvement leads to high motivation	• Can J&J top management review 155 SBUs?
• Communication tool	• Reward systems lets "managers off the hook"
• Very action-oriented	• No one worries about synergies
• Allows J&J to manage diverse businesses	
• Training tool	
• Strategy formulation tool	

Overall, does the formal planning & control hurt or facilitate innovation and profitability?

The Core Issue

Do formal planning and control systems hurt or facilitate innovation?

- Long Range Planning

- Profit Planning

- Plan Revisions

- Performance Evaluation

- Management Compensation

At the moment, we can't get more price. My expenses are cut to the bone. Further cuts will mean letting staff go.

— Marketing Manager

It is a bad idea. If we cut the volume any more, the unit material cost will double.

— R&D Manager

OK. We'll stick to 100 prototypes.

— General Manager

The next round of cuts will be the programs themselves, and we know we don't want to do that.

— R&D Manager

Yes. I agree.

—General Manager

Management Compensation

"Bonuses are not tied to achieving budgeting targets. They are subjectively determined... They are intended to reward efforts, not results."

Why subjective bonus is best for J&J:

1.   Not penalized for sharing information ("bad news")

2.   Incented to discuss uncertainties candidly

3.   Superior has the ability to do subjective evaluation

Implications of Subjective Rewards for the Success of J&J's Management Control Systems

1. Managers are shielded from the variability in outcomes due to uncertain environments. Individuals will share information such as worsening demand conditions since their personal rewards will not be threatened as might be the case if information was used to, say, increase profit targets.

2. To gain recognition and rewards, managers will try to make their effort visible to superiors by informing them of changing conditions and the actions that they have taken to deal with these changes.

3. To evaluate properly the efforts of subordinates, superiors must understand changes in the competitive environments, potential opportunities and constraints, and the range of action alternative available to subordinates. Subjective evaluation, therefore, reinforces information gathering and organizational learning.

J&J

1950 – 1990

Sales Growth @ 14% p.a.

EPS Growth @ 17% p.a.

Twice the Average for <u>Fortune 100</u> Firms

1970 – 1990

Ranked #1 in a nationwide survey of successful new product introductions among 18 major health and beauty aid companies over a 20-year period.

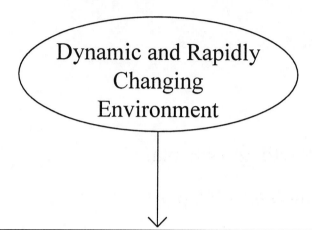

Dynamic and Rapidly Changing Environment

Key Management Challenge is to
Create a Learning Organization

Encourage managers at all levels to indulge in
continuous search activity, on-going scan and sharing
of critical environmental changes, and continuous
experimentation in order to respond to the
environmental changes.

"You won't get innovation without pressure. We must empower employees to continually experiment—but in a controlled way."

— CEO, 3M

Characteristics of J&J's Management Control Systems

1. Information generated by the system is an important and recurring agenda addressed by the highest levels of management.

2. The systems require frequent and regular attention from operating managers at all levels of the organization.

3. The role of staff specialists is limited.

4. Profit plans have contingency buffers.

5. Data derived in the process are interpreted and discussed in face-to-face meetings of superiors, subordinates, and peers.

6. The process relies on continual challenge and debate.

7. Managers are rewarded on effort rather than on outcomes.

Will J&J's management control systems contribute to success in a rapidly changing environment where innovation is key?

Some Issues to Think Through

- Is J&J truly "decentralized"?

  "Decentralized management is unequivocal accountability for what you do."

- Is "profit center" idea inconsistent with exploiting "synergies and core competencies" across business units?

- Is formal planning and control systems and "innovation" oxymorons?

Concluding Thoughts

- Formal systems need not hinder innovation

- Organizational learning ($\approx$ innovation) can actually be facilitated

- Some enabling conditions:

  - Long tenure of executives

  - Promotion from within

  - Reward system based on "Effort," not "Outcome"

  - Long-term incentives awarded as stock options

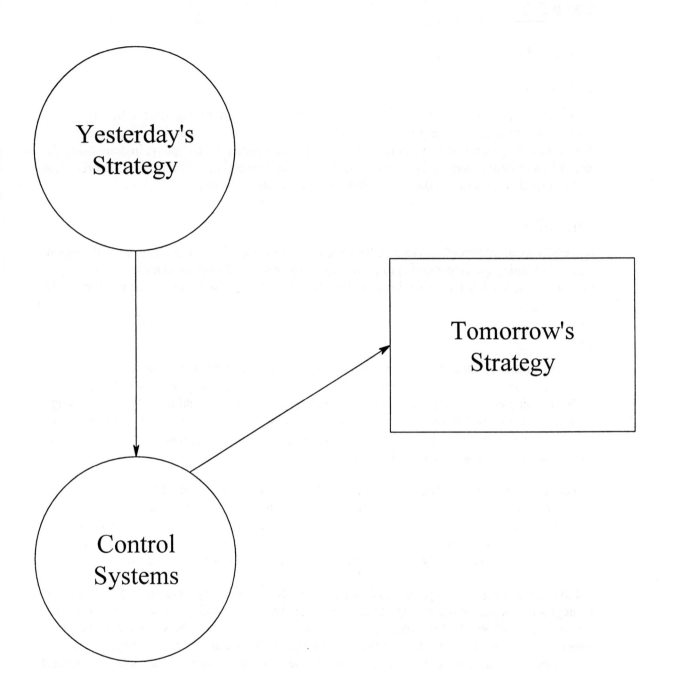

Case 8-2

Copley Manufacturing Company

Objectives

This case describes a company's efforts to install and use a programming system. Several attempts were made over the period 1966 – 1969, but at the end of that period the company still did not have a system that contributed significantly to managing the company. In diagnosing the strengths and weaknesses of the various approaches, the student should increase his appreciation of the steps that need to be taken if a system is to work satisfactorily.

Discussion

Since it is apparent that efforts to install a programming system have been unsuccessful, a good way of beginning the discussion is to go back over the several attempts and try to decide why they are unsuccessful. This is the intent of Question 1. The text discussion can be used as a guide to this analysis.

1966

The 1966 effort corresponded in some ways to the description in the text: guidelines, assumptions and an economic forecast were disseminated early in the year, both as to the nature of the planning effort and, in the case of the financial part of it, an actual format for submitting the plan. These were discussed in meetings between headquarters and divisional personnel. The plans were reviewed in top-level meetings, and the executive vice president sent a memorandum summarizing the results of these meetings.

Nevertheless, there is not much indication that the process actually affected the way the company was managed. In the Cutting Tool Division, which was singled out as the best division, the job of formulating the program was turned over to a staff man, Mr. Volante. Mr. Tyler, the division manager, said he was "too busy" to participate actively. Since a programming effort should involve line managers heavily, this attitude is a sufficient reason for the lack of success.

Although guidelines, assumptions, and formats were distributed, they were not based on a set of strategies developed by top management; rather, they were produced by a committee consisting primarily of staff people (two members of line management were members). One gets the impression that the divisions thought they were supposed to extrapolate the existing programs for five years, rather than to think deeply about desirable shifts in programs. (This is how I interpret

---

This case was prepared by Robert N. Anthony.

Copyright © 1976 by the President and Fellows of Harvard College. Harvard Business School case 176-189.

the reference to a "numbers game.") Indeed, in the description of the financial plan (Exhibit 1) there is no mention of adding new product lines.

Good practice requires that when the programs are initially submitted to headquarters, they be given a preliminary analysis by staff, and that a preliminary corporate program be prepared by putting the individual plans together. From this program, the planning gap is identified. This was not done. Instead, each divisional plan was presented to the management group in a meeting. Evidently, the corporate management mostly listened, because the division managers emerged from this meeting with no clear idea as to what parts of their program were acceptable and what parts were not acceptable.

A second series of meetings was held to reach some agreement, and a memorandum of agreements reached was distributed after this meeting, signed by the Executive Vice President. This helped remedy the lack of decision in the earlier meetings, but by then the year was over, the budgets for 1967 presumably had already been prepared, and these decisions could not impact the budget preparation process. It is essential that the approved program form the basis for the budget, and this requires that the programming process be completed by the fall.

1967

In 1967, the intention was to devote more time and thought to strategy development in the spring, and this was good. The steps outlined in Exhibit 2 are much better than those used in 1966, but (1) there was no provision for headquarters staff analysis of the plans prior to the meeting (but staff did participate in the meetings), and (2) the timetable ended too late to permit the approved program to be used in preparing the budget.

In July 1967, the programming effort was halted and all efforts were focused on the short-term problem of coping with a recession. Some students argue that this was not a valid reason for discontinuing the programming effort, because "firefighting" activities should not be permitted to supplant efforts with long-run implications. Personally, I find the termination of programming quite understandable. Not much good had come of the effort so far, it was regarded by some as a number-pushing exercise, and it is quite natural that managers would conclude that when the recession hit they had more important ways to spend their time.

The product line evaluations started in 1967, although not a part of the formal programming process, were perhaps the most important development of the general principles of programming that occurred that year. Unfortunately, this was viewed as a "one-shot study." It is really the heart of programming.

1968

The programming process was resumed in 1968, along the same general lines as those planned for 1967, but with a better timetable; the first cut of the program was to be completed by June 30, and this allowed time for revision of the program in time to use it in budgeting. The quantitative part of the program was kept quite simple, so simple that probably not enough data were provided to permit staff analysis, even if a staff analysis were contemplated, which did not seem to be the case. Major emphasis was focused on the development of strategies, primarily in a nonquantitative way.

The outcome of this effort could not be a formal program for the whole company which identified a planning gap. This emphasis on nonquantitative aspects, and the informality of the whole process probably reflects the management style of John Tyler.

1969

In 1969 a formal programming process, as such, was to all intents and purposes abandoned. There was no staff participation at all. The guidelines were strictly those set forth orally at a meeting in Bermuda. The programs were described at a series of meetings held throughout the country, to which all division managers were invited, and at which no thorough analysis of programs would be possible. The reason for this, I believe, is that Mr. Tyler, who seems to be the chief executive, was not temperamentally inclined to use a formal programming system.

Summary of weaknesses

Looking back over the whole history, we can identify these weaknesses:

1. There never was a clear statement of corporate goals. Efforts to develop such a statement started in 1962, and they had not been successful through 1969. The chief executive should not have permitted this situation to exist. It is possible to argue forever about what the goals should be and to disagree both on the wording and on the quantitative aspects, such as the appropriate return on investment and growth in sales. Nevertheless, there comes a time when these arguments should cease, and someone should say: "these are our goals." The chief executive officer should have done this in 1966 when the programming effort started.

2. Top management did not back the effort with deeds. Although there is a nauseous repetition of the phrase, "planning is a way of life," there is little evidence that planning actually was a way of life. We see Tyler, who at the end of the case is the chief executive, turning the whole operation over to a staff in 1966. We see no indications of positive changes in direction that resulted from the programming effort. We do not see firm, perhaps unpleasant, decisions being made by top management as a result of the effort.

3. There were no clear guidelines. There were forecasts for the economy as a whole, but no statement of divisional charters, or of the types of activities that top management wanted to encourage and the types it wanted to discourage.

4. There was no analysis by a planning staff; in fact, in 1969 there was not even a planning staff. A program should be subjected to intensive analysis before it is reviewed by line management to insure that it is consistent with the guidelines and is internally consistent. Such analysis develops the question that top management needs to raise during the review process.

5. There were no firm decisions resulting from the review and analysis.

6. The timetable was not correct. The process should have been completed by September so that it could influence the preparation of the budget.

Prognosis

From the above we get the strong impression that Mr. Tyler does not want a formal programming system, with a set timetable, thorough staff analysis, resulting in important decisions. His management style, as strongly indicated by the quotations at the end of the case, is to rely on his line managers to run their own show and to give them direction through relatively unstructured meetings. This is a perfectly acceptable management style. It is not, however, compatible with formal programming, and I would expect that the company would not devote much if any attention to such a process.

Possible System

Question 3 asks the student how he would handle formal planning at Copley. If he has the same temperament as Mr. Tyler, he would undoubtedly continue with the informal procedures used in 1969. If, however, he wanted to use a formal system in an important way, these are the steps that are indicated.

1. A statement of corporate goals and strategies and of the charters of each division should be decided on by the chief executive. This statement might be worked on by a committee, but the committee effort should not be permitted to get bogged down; at a certain point, the chief executive says, "this is what I have decided."

2. In December or January, guidelines are published. These include the statement mentioned above, assumptions about the economy, and format for submission of the program. Possibly there is a "summit meeting" of division managers at which top management convinces them that the programming effort is to be taken seriously.

3. Divisions submit a tentative plan in the Spring. It is not worked out in great detail, but gives enough information on overall direction so that the next step can be carried out.

4. From the tentative plans, the headquarters staff develops an overall program and identifies the planning gap. Management decides how to close the gap. Discussions are held between top management and division managers to agree on the broad outlines of an acceptable program, including revisions necessary to eliminate the planning gap.

5. Divisions prepare a detailed program and submit it by early summer.

6. Headquarters staff analyzes this program for conformity with the guidelines and for internal reasonableness and consistency. Each division then has a long session (at least 1/2 day) with top management to discuss the program. Top management makes decisions at this meeting. This process is finished by October 1.

7. Divisions prepare next year's budget, based on the approved program.

RNA

Case 8-3

Allied Stationery

Overview

The topic for this case is Activity Based Costing and Activity Based Management. The setting is a company which sells inventory management services as an add-on to the business forms business. The company's strategy is simple—differentiate a "commodity" product—business forms—with value-added services—forms inventory management.

The case provides practice in ABC calculations (in a non-manufacturing setting) as well as practice in transitioning from ABC to ABM, and in transitioning further from ABM to an SCM perspective on the business and the business problem.

Answers to Assignment Questions

Question 1

One suggested solution to the question is shown in Exhibits A and B here. Requisition handling could also be charged per line rather than per requisition. Data Entry could also be charged per requisition rather than per carton line. These changes would not alter the overall result materially.

Some class time should probably be devoted to the fixed/variable cost behavior issue and to the capacity utilization issue. Very probably, most of the costs in column 2 are fixed across fairly wide volume swings. Thus, the per unit amounts in column 5 represent "long-run variable costs," not short-run incremental costs. Also, volume growth could reduce the per unit costs until a new "step cost" increase is necessary.

Also, related to the prior point, the specific calculations in column 5 represent current cost divided by current volume. They do not explicitly deal with the cost of excess capacity. How to best treat capacity utilization in unit cost calculations is a very rich topic, but it is beyond the scope of this commentary.

Question 2

One suggested solution to the question is shown in Exhibits C and D here.

Question 3

Exhibit E here is a summary of customer profitability under the "old" and "new" accounting systems. The Exhibit ends with the question of which is the better customer. The answer is not easy.

This teaching commentary was prepared by Professor John Shank of the Amos Tuck School at Dartmouth College.

Customer A now appears much more profitable than before and dramatically more profitable than Customer B. But, Customer A is much more vulnerable to a competitor who would charge use-based prices. And, Customer A does not fit the business—TFC cannot build a business around customers who don't use its services!

Customer B now shows losses. But, they are a heavy user of the services—they like what TFC offers. Of course, they may only like it as long as they don't have to pay for it!

So Customer B really uses the services TFC offers, but they don't pay for them. Customer A is very profitable for TFC, but they don't use much of the service which is the basis for TFC's business.

Question 4

This question moves the focus of the discussion from accounting issues to management decisions. Should TFC adopt "menu pricing"?

This is a very rich question which will support at least 30 minutes of class discussion. The basic themes are as follows:

1. Yes for menu pricing.

   a. Logically, the heavy users should pay more than light users.

   b. Pricing should allow the customer to decide which services to use, based on a cost-benefit trade-off.

   c. Right now, B is getting a "free ride" and A is being overcharged.

2. No for menu pricing.

   a. Lowering prices to the A's will not make them happy.

   b. Why drop a price when A is happy now at the higher price?

   c. Raising prices to the B's will encourage them to change suppliers. This will drive our unit costs even higher.

   d. What is the *justification* for a price increase? Blaming it on a "new accounting system" won't impress most customers.

   e. Analysis of case Exhibits 5 and 6 shows that pricing is already higher than normal for the "A's" and lower than normal for the "B's."

	Revenue	Cost	Normal Revenue (Cost × 1.586)	% of Normal
Exhibit 5	$1,279	$779	$1,231	104%
Exhibit 6	$717	$486	$768	93%

3. "Maybe" for menu pricing.

    a. The real issue is value to the customer. Cost is not directly relevant for the user; value is.

    b. What do we know about customer perceptions of value here? Not much!

    c. SBP is a variation on old-fashioned cost based pricing. It may or may not represent good value to customers.

The key idea for this question is that TFC needs to understand more about customer value before it imposes a new and more complex cost-based pricing system.

Question 5

Exhibits F, G, H and I are summaries of the managerial issues facing the senior management team of TFC. Exhibit F is the overall summary.

Trying to describe here the richness of these issues would result in at least a book-length manuscript! Since most accounting professors (me included) don't have much explicit expertise in these broader management topics, I believe the best approach in class is just to put up the exhibits, solicit student input and comments, and broker the discussion (nodding wisely once in a while!). The basic idea behind the question is to encourage students to see the problem much more broadly than just an exercise in ABC or even ABM.

My best judgment in 1996, based on Exhibit 1, is that *nothing* TFC does (with the possible exception of desk top delivery) really adds value for the *customer*. The business really adds value for the old style manufacturing plants who want standard quantities and long runs.

The customer *should* want the right number of forms, delivered directly to the user, at the time of use—"right number, right time, right place." TFC only adds value to the customer if the customer must accept the conventional approach to manufacturing and sales in the Forms Division.

"PickPack" is only necessary because of standard packaging (500 units per box). Inventory financing is only necessary because the factories don't practice JIT and Flexible Manufacturing. The inventory belongs to TFC, *not* the customer.

An "EDI" link between the forms user and the manufacturing plant (Exhibit 1) would constitute a much more innovative business response by Allied. But the General Manager of the Forms Division probably does not want to hear that, especially not from the General Manager of TFC.

Teaching Strategy

I use this case to introduce ABC in the required managerial accounting course at Tuck. The ABC part of the case is fairly easy for students, so it constitutes good reinforcement of the basic calculational approach summarized in Exhibit A here.

The case can be covered in one class period. In class, I go through the questions one by one, following the approach outlined in this commentary.

The concept of ABM, as an extension of ABC comes in as part of question 3 or 4. Exhibit H here is a good tool for reinforcing the concept of "value-adding" versus "non-value adding" processes. It is easy for students to miss the idea that none of these stages is really value adding (except desk top delivery).

I try to save at least 20 minutes for question 4 and 10 minutes for question 5.

Exhibit A

ABC—Seven Steps

1. Define cost pools—the value chain steps

2. Assign costs to the pools

3. Determine the "driver(s)" for each pool

4. Measure aggregate activity units for the "drivers"

5. Divide costs (step 2) by driver units (step 4) to get cost per driver unit

6. Measure cost driver units for each customer for each cost pool

7. Activity Based Cost for the customer equals: cost driver units (step 6) × cost per driver unit (step 5), summed across all cost pools

Exhibit B

Activity Based Costs
Calculation of Service Costs

(1) Value Added Activities Defined as:	(2) Total FY92 Expense per Activity (000)	(3) Cost Driver Defined	(4) Cost Driver Units FY92 Plan	(5) Service Costs	
Storage	$1,550	Cartons in Inventory	350,000	$0.37	per carton per month
Requisition Handling	1,801	Requisitions	310,000	$5.81	
Warehouse Activity	761	Carton Lines	775,000	$0.98	
Pick Packing	734	(PP) Lines	700,000	$1.05	
Data Entry	612	Carton Lines	775,000	$0.79	
Desk Top Delivery	250	Per Time	~8,500	$30.00	
	$5,708				

Freight--Charge Actual Cost---

Inventory Finance--Inventory Value × Capital Charge*--------------------------------

*Assume Cost of Capital = 13.5% If prime rate is ~10%, Weighted Average Cost of Capital would be at least 13%. Careful attention to WACC here is beyond the scope of this commentary

Exhibit C

A Saga of Two Customers (Step 6)

	Customer A	Customer B
Annual Revenue	$79,320	$79,320
Requisitions	364	790
Requisition Lines (all "pick pack")	910	2,500
<u>Average Inventory</u> at the Centers—Cartons	350	700
$	$15,000	$50,000
<u>Per carton</u>— Cost	$43.	$71.
Average Revenue*	$68.	$113.
<u>Shipments</u>— Number	52	156
"Desk Top"	0	26
Freight. $	$2,250.	$7,500.
Freight/Shipment	$43.	$48.
Revenue/Line	$87.+	$32.–
∴Each Requisition Line =	1.2 Cartons	.3 Cartons
	(87/68)	(32/113)

*Cartons shipped = $50,000 ÷ $43 = 1,163. Revenue of $79,320 ÷ 1,163 = $68. (A)
  = $50,000 ÷ $71 = 704. Revenue of $79,320 ÷ 704 = $113. (B)

Conclusion?

Exhibit D

Calculation of Service Costs—ABC (Step 7)

	Customer A	Customer B
Storage	350 Cartons	700 Cartons
	× $.37/carton/month	× $.37/carton/month
	× 12 months	× 12 months
	$1,554	$3,108
Requisition Handling	364 requisitions	790 requisitions
	× $5.81/requisition	× $5.81/requisition
	$2,115	$4,590
Warehouse Activity	910 lines	2500 lines
	× $.98/line	× $.98/line
	$892	$2,450
Additional "Pick Pack" Charge	910 pick-pack lines	2500 pick-pack lines
	× $1.05/line	×$1.05/line
	$956	$2,625
Data Entry	910 lines	2500 lines
	× $.79/line	× $.79/line
	$719	$1,975
Desk Top Delivery	0 times	26 times
	× $30/time	× $30/time
	$0	$780
Freight Out	$2,250	$7,500
Inventory Financing (Estimated)	$15,000 inventory	$50,000 inventory
	× 13.5%	× 13.5%
	$2,025	$6,750
Inactive Inventory Surcharge (A proxy for obsolescence cost borne by TFC)	$0 inventory	$7,000 inventory
	× 1.5%	× 1.5%
	× 3 months	× 3 months
	$0	$315
Total Service Charges—ABC Basis	$10,510	$30,093

The idea here is simple. One customer (A) is a light user of the services and one customer (B) is a heavy user. Average costing camouflages this difference. ABC clearly shows the differences.

Exhibit E

Customer Profitability Analysis

Old Method	Customer A	Customer B
Sales	$79,320	$79,320
Product Cost	(50,000)	(50,000)
Service Fees	(16,100)	(16,100)
Gross Profit	$13,220	$13,220
Gross Profit %	17%	17%

Activity-Based Analysis	Customer A	Customer B
Sales	$79,320	$79,320
Product Cost	(50,000)	(50,000)
Service Fees	(10,510)	(30,093)
Gross Profit	$18,810	(773)
Gross Profit %	24%	Negative

Which is the better customer?

Exhibit F

Moving from Analysis to Action

- "Value-Engineer" The Cost Structure

- Marketing Strategy Decisions

  – Customer Selection

  – Pricing

- Additional Analysis Possibilities

  – Value Chain Analysis

  – ABC for Manufacturing Costs

Exhibit G

Marketing Strategy Decisions

- Pricing

  – SBP Pricing?

  – Implementation Issues

    Raise Prices for "B's"?

    Lower Prices for "A's"?

- Customer Selection

  – Do we want more As or Bs?

  – What kind of new customers to seek?

  – What to do with the current customers?

Exhibit H

"Value-Engineer" The Cost Structure

Cost Pools	Activity Drivers
Storage	Number of Cartons Stored
Requisition Handling	Number of Requisitions
Warehouse Stock Selection	Carton Lines
"Pick-Pack" Activity	Pick-Pack Lines
Data Entry	Carton Lines
Desk Top Delivery	Number of Deliveries
Freight Out	Distance Traveled
Inventory Financing	Inventory Turnover and Cost of Capital

- Which of the activities in the Distribution Center is non-value added?

- Is Allied's cost structure in each of the value-adding activities competitive?

- How should the company prioritize activity drivers for management attention?

Exhibit I

The Value Chain Concept

The Business Forms Chain

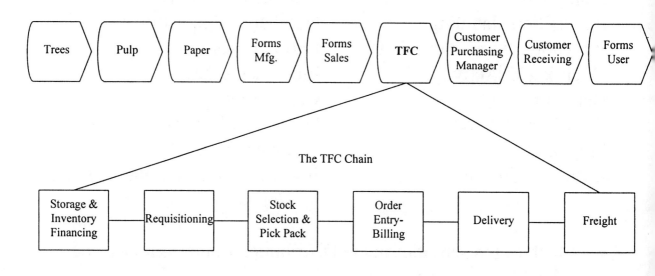

The TFC Chain

Case 8-4

Emerson Electric Company Teaching Strategy

This case presents the planning and control system used at Emerson Electric Company and developed by its Chief Executive Officer, Charles F. Knight. Because of the variety of issues discussed in the text and exhibits, this case can be used to introduce strategic planning, as a differentiated strategy illustration, or as a wrap-up case at the end of the course. It also has been used as a final examination. It fits with other formal planning cases such as Quaker Oats, Galvor, Texas Instruments, Litton, and General Electric. The assigned questions are one way to organize the classroom discussion. There are no real decisions in the case, just a fascinating company and a very unique planning system that I have not seen elsewhere.

If not assigned previously, the article "Balance 'Creativity' and 'Practicality' in Formal Planning," by John K. Shank, et al. *Harvard Business Review*, January-February, 1973, may be assigned. This article discusses the linkages between the strategic plan and the budget in terms of content, organizational, and timing linkages.

Background

As an $8 billion company, Emerson has a very conservative, and lean organization. There is very little debt. Corporate staff is kept very small and there is no organization chart. Knight's personal attention and style have guided the company for over twenty years with high returns to shareholders. Consistency of results for such a long period is quite an achievement, especially in the last 5 years. Yet this is not a technology driven company. The successful strategy is efficient, quality, and low cost production. R&D does not get a great deal of attention from top management as OST gets at Texas Instruments. Cost control and reduction get a lot more attention.

Question 1

To start the discussion, a student can be asked to describe the planning process at Emerson. This could be a month-by-month detailed description listing the major players, decisions, and documents, or a narrative on each step. The planning system is not a complicated one but it deserves close scrutiny. Clearly, planning is top-down with CEO Knight actively involved from the start of the process. If the students have read material on linkages between the long-range plan and the one year budget, then the organization, content, and timing linkages can be explored.

The case exhibits are information rich. The first four exhibits capture the essence of the planning system. The value measurement chart contains comparisons in five-year increments for investments, operating profit, return on invested capital, sales, operating capital turnover, capital charge, and economic profit. Discussion of the capital charge based on the cost of capital should be introduced. In addition to NOPAT, Emerson uses a measure of "economic profit" which is similar to residual income. The chart reflects the sales and return on total capital targets set by top management.

The division sales targets that are set by top management are optimistic. The purpose of the sales gap chart and the line chart is to identify the sources of five year sales growth and to highlight the sales shortfall. Exhibit 2 illustrates a 15% target growth rate for sales which results in shortfalls for each year. of course, division presidents must provide action plans for closing the gap.

The comparative profit and loss statements for eleven years in Exhibit 4 seems like overkill. One advantage is that they show trend. Included at the bottom is the return on total capital.

The strength of the Emerson process is that it gets commitment from the division presidents. Certainly, they participate in the planning process to a great degree. There is no reliance on planning staff. Division presidents are given full responsibility and accompanying authority.

The linkage between the plan and the detailed forecast (the one-year operating budget) is extremely tight. Top management must approve any changes from the approved plans. In addition, divisions are expected to prepare contingency plans at lower level of sales. Top management may request that a division switch to contingency plans if forecasted performance falters.

The key document to the control process is the president's operating report (POR). This represents an unusual approach to monitoring performance. There are only six items of data on this report: intercompany sales, sales, gross profit, SG&A expenses, operating profit, and earnings before interest and taxes. Monthly reporting during a quarter can lead to a change in the forecast data for that quarter. The CEO and senior managers review performance. Divisions are expected to meet the annual forecast performance.

Question 2

Advantages include heavy involvement of division presidents in the planning process and the cost reduction programs. There seems to be a lot of discussion and interaction between division managers and top management. While there are a lot of numbers in the planning documents they don't seem to be a great burden as for example at Geneen's ITT planning system. A desktop computer spreadsheet can handle the documents. The linkage between the long-range plan and the one-year forecast is rather loose. Controllers are not very involved in the planning process. One major report seems to be used in the control process. Both the short-range and long-range compensation systems reinforce the planning and control system.

Disadvantages include the possibility of overly optimistic top-down directives on sales and return on investment targets. The tight linkage of numbers between the plan and the one-year budget may lead to budget rigidity. With a lean corporate staff, some services to divisions may be lacking. Division staff may be large to provide assistance with analyses of competition, new products, and marketing forecasts. It is difficult to distinguish between operational and strategic decisions. There is no explicit data on market share or other non-financial measures of performance. Also, the cost of capital may not be adjusted for risk when applied to different divisions.

Question 3

When questioned on the role of the new business segment managers, a top Emerson official remarked that it was a good observation. Evidently the planning system does not explicitly involve the business segment managers. What might their role be? Emerson consists of forty divisions organized into eight business segments. This is an average of five divisions per business segment. The case says the reason for this new organization were distribution channels, organization capabilities, and technologies. As Emerson moves into foreign markets more aggressively and forms new international alliances, business segments may be needed to coordinate related product divisions across international boundaries. Knight should include business segment managers in the planning process as a means to keep information flowing smoothly at all levels.

Joseph C. San Miguel

CHAPTER 9
BUDGET PREPARATION

Changes from the Eighth Edition

This chapter is reorganized as follows. The first part of this chapter highlights the technical aspects in developing the operating budget. The second part highlights behavioral aspects of developing budgets.

Cases

Sound Dynamics focuses on the considerations involved in budget revisions during the operating year. This case replaces the earlier National Motors case.

Pasy Company describes the detailed steps involved in developing profit budgets. This case replaces the earlier case entitled Empire Glass Company.

Boston Creamery is a re-write of Midwest Ice Cream Company and it deals with the development and implementation of an operating budget.

Case 9-1

Sound Dynamics, Inc.

Notes: This case is a rewrite and update on National Motors. The basic issues remain unchanged.

Objectives and Approach

This is an extremely difficult case to analyze. The difficulty arises primarily because the arguments made by the two parties rest on slightly different premises, and the figures therefore do not quite collide head-on with one another. Despite this difficulty, the case is an extremely valuable one. It shows both the problems involved in attempting to control managed costs and the possibilities for good controls in a tough-minded, sophisticated organization. It also permits a good discussion of the proper role of the controller.

Discussion

I break the discussion into two general parts, the first dealing with the specific issue raised in the case, and the second dealing with broader questions. Unless the first part is arbitrarily kept to a specified time, there will be no time for the second part. (Of course, it is possible, and perhaps desirable, to use this case on two days, the first day discussing only the specific issue and the second day discussing the more general questions.)

As a way of coming to grips with a specific issue, I put on the board at the beginning of class the following little table that summarizes the difference between the two parties:

	People	Money
Manufacturing Position	54	$ 1,458,000
Controller Position	42	1,128,000
Difference	12	$ 330,000

In introducing these figures, I point out that the controversy has been going on for some months now and the parties have not retreated at all from the positions they took initially. I ask what are the general explanations of the difference of 12 people and $330,000 and elicit the following list: the parts count, the salary mix, the cost of the computer, and "other." Then I attempt to get students to discuss each of these to decide how much of the difference is attributable to each element and whether the amount is justified.

The easiest element to discuss is the salary mix. This seems to be a justifiable argument on manufacturing's part because it is indeed reasonable to expect that the consolidation would result in a higher average salary. The only question is whether the amount of $92,000 is too high. An argument can be made that the amount should be $1,600 × 42 people, or $67,000. However, I do not want to spend too much time on this, and therefore am willing to put down as the amount that should be allowed the total amount of $92,000, in order to shut off the argument.

With respect to the parts count, there does seem to-be an additional work load that is properly attributable to the parts count. Again, there can be great debate as to what the amount of the increase should be, and students can make rather sophisticated analyses from the various figures that are given in the case. Without trying to settle on what is the best way of putting together the figures (and it must be remembered that all figures rest on the tenuous assumption that there is validity to the various ratios that are proposed), I am willing to accept the argument that the parts count justified five people and $94,000. This leaves seven people to be explained.

The next item is the cost of implementing the computerized system. Here, the controversy can be great indeed. My personal opinion (which not all my colleagues share) is that the manufacturing people were too optimistic in estimating the savings that would be obtained from computerization and that the first-year costs are going to be six people and $112,000 more than they originally anticipated. If this is so, then the computer is not going to make the savings that were contemplated when its use was originally proposed, and its acquisition may, therefore, have been a mistake. The question then arises: What should be done in view of this mistake? On the one hand, it can be argued that the company should face facts, and the budget should reflect the actual situation, even if the original estimate turned out to be overoptimistic. This is not the view that the Sound Dynamics people would actually take, however, although not set forth in the case, their attitude is that when a department makes a proposal that shows a certain estimated saving, the acceptance of this proposal involves a commitment by the department to earn the promised savings. If the situation does not work out as planned, it is up to department to find the savings somewhere else in its operation. The merits of this approach can be taken up in the second part of the discussion. My estimate of the magnitude of the computerization argument is six people and $336,000, although others can arrive at different figures. This leaves only one person and $96,000 to be accounted for and frankly I have never gotten this far in the discussion in class and would not attempt to go into any depth on where these residual amounts come from.

Having looked at the details of the argument, the next question is what attitude the controller should take. This largely depends, I think, on the attitude toward the computerization area. If the controller is willing to give on this, and if he accepts (as I think he should) the proposition that the parts count and salary mix arguments are justified, then he might as well agree with the manufacturing people and not argue about the relatively small remaining difference. If, however, the controller sticks to the philosophy indicated above, then he should probably refer the controversy to the general manager for resolution since it is unlikely that the manufacturing people are going to budget from their position. This is the course of action that the controller actually did take, and the memorandum which he submitted to the general manager is given as a supplement to this commentary.

General Questions

I now turn to the general questions which can be discussed in connection with this case.

First, there is the question of whether this is the best method of arriving at and analyzing a budget. The method here is to take as a bench mark the situation in the preceding year, to adjust it for changes in the job to be done, for changes in techniques, for changes in prices and mix, and to use the adjusted figure as the current year's budget. Students often suggest that a better way would be to use some kind of work measurement or job analysis technique. Actually, in a managed-cost situation of this kind, it is highly doubtful that such techniques would produce any better results. Furthermore, in the particular controversy shown here, there simply would not be time for the use of such techniques.

Another question is whether the controller has exceeded his proper role here. I don't think that he has. He is arguing vigorously with the manufacturing department, but he is never implying that he is going to make a line decision that requires the manufacturing department to adhere to a certain figure. If the controller cannot persuade the manufacturing people of the soundness of his views, he sends the matter up to a line executive for decision; he does not make the decision himself. He, therefore, is acting as a staff agency, which is his proper role.

Third, there is the question of whether the whole procedure is worth all the trouble involved. It requires a large analytical staff, it evidently results in considerable friction, and the controller people are clearly in the position of challenging the so-called experts in the manufacturing organization. Nevertheless, in the absence of some mechanism like this, the company's only alternative would be to accent, pretty much without analysis, the budget submitted by the line organization and this could quickly lead to a loose kind of operation. When the whole organization understands that their budgets are going to get the very careful scrutiny that is illustrated in this case, they should take a somewhat different attitude toward the preparation of the budgets than would otherwise be the case.

Summary

I use this case to point out some rather important matters dealing with the control of discretionary costs, as indicated below.

1. Note the tie-in with the capital budgeting procedure. The manufacturing people promise savings of 11 people and $138,000 if they are permitted to acquire a computer. The operating budget is automatically changed to reflect these savings as soon as the capital proposal is approved. This type of closed loop is not customary in business, but it has the great advantage of making certain that promised savings do not get lost from view and hence leads to more realistic estimates. It is an excellent practice.

2. Note that there really can be no standard in this situation. There is no way to knowing how many people you need to do this job. In the absence of such a standard, the company assumes that if the job was done at a certain cost last year, it can be done at the same cost this year, with due allowance for changes in the situation. Both parties to the controversy agreed to this general philosophy; their differences come in quantifying the difference between this year and last year. This is not a scientific way of deciding on the proper cost, but there simply is no scientific way in this type of situation.

3. Some changes are unavoidable, and the controller shouldn't argue about them. He overlooked the salary mix change of $84,000 in his original analysis, but it is a fact, and it should be admitted as a fact.

4. Note the force of the commitment principles. Once an amount has been agreed to, it becomes a bilateral commitment as set forth in the appendix to the case.

5. Note that the success of this whole operation depends entirely on management backing. If the management is not willing to give a good hearing to the controller views, then the manufacturing people would not bother to make the careful rejoinders that they have made to the controller.

Supplement

The controller's department did not concur in the adjustments to the costs of the manual control system proposed by the Manufacturing Office. Their final recommendations to Ms. Larson included the following comments:

Increased Parts Count ($94,000)

Increased parts counts are significant in determining workload only if the additional parts generate additional specification requests or otherwise increase the level of workload. Manufacturing has not provided an indication of the increase in specification requests or other workload generated by the additional parts. Moreover if the increased number of parts did, in fact, generate additional workload, Manufacturing was apparently able to absorb the increase in the initial months of 1990 inasmuch as they did not request a budget supplement until April 1990.

Increased Average Salaries ($92,000)

Manufacturing has indicated that the average salaries of the personnel retained in the operations control department increased approximately $800 per year as a result of retaining high seniority personnel transferred from the San Reno Division and terminating low seniority Reichard personnel.

In our opinion, the Reichard Division should not be expected to incur increased costs as a result of the consolidation. Consequently, we suggest the increase in salaried expense resulting from this rate differential be charged to San Reno Division.

Non-Recurring Cost Penalties

Although we would agree that implementation costs are probably required during the initial year of the computer system, Manufacturing's proposal to computerize the parts control system indicated that a substantial savings would be achieved during the first year including full recovery of any first year implementation costs. Manufacturing has departed from this commitment without any detailed explanation or justification.

Summary

The proposal to computerize the Reichard operations control system was approved on the basis of a substantial cost savings. Manufacturing has now indicated that a computer system increases the Division's costs rather than achieving the committed savings.

In our opinion, the total cost of the consolidated operations control activity should not exceed the original Reichard budget for a manual system plus the cost of San Reno workload computed at Reichard manual standards. On this basis, the total 1990 budget would be $1,220,000 (including $92,000 for the increased average annual salaries) and 55 personnel. If Manufacturing wishes to continue using a computer system, it will be necessary to reduce the salaried personnel level to 42 or 12 less than has been proposed in order to achieve this savings. Consequently, we recommend a combined Reichard-San Reno level of $1,220,000 and 42 personnel.

Additional Comments on Sound Dynamics, Inc.

After identifying the general explanations for the difference of 12 people and $330,000, I ask: would you allow the supplemental budget? Some students will point out the line in the case which states; "Supplemental budgets must be justified on the basis of changed conditions from those existing when the original budget was approved" (if no student points this out, I usually do so). Then use this criteria to evaluate the following three items individually:

1. Increased average salaries.

2. Increased parts count.

3. Over-estimation of the dollar benefits of computerization.

Usually there is considerable controversy on each item. Shouldn't the manufacturing manager have anticipated, *at the time the original budget was approved,* that average salaries would go up after consolidation? Shouldn't the manufacturing manager have anticipated, *at the time the original budget was approved,* that parts counts would go up (since car model decisions are made far ahead of time)? And so on.

I let students argue about this for a while, I then disclose what the company did. I then ask: What are the behavioral effects of such a control system?

Case 9-2

Pasy Company

Note: Pasy Company is identical to NorthAm Company from the Eighth Edition. We have reproduced below the teaching commentary for NorthAm Company.

Prologue

This case replaces the earlier Empire Class Company. The major change is to set the case in aluminum container industry as opposed to the glass container business. Aluminum containers are a more realistic context for current times. Further, we have added more industry data on the metal container industry. The new case retains all the issues from the earlier Empire Glass Company case.

This is a classic case on management control. It serves to highlight two topics:

1. Detailed discussion on the development of profit budgets.

2. Constituting manufacturing manager as a profit center.

I start the class by taking a vote on the following questions: "How many students like to treat manufacturing manager as a cost center? How many like the system the way it is?" In my experience, 90 percent of the students like to treat manufacturing as a cost center. I take a similar vote at the end of class. If the discussion goes well, 90 percent of the students like to treat manufacturing as a profit center by the end of class! This is what I call a good class!

Instructors might want to refer to Chapter 3 of *Strategic Cost Analysis* (John Shank and VG, Irwin, 1989) for an analysis of the industry in which North Company competes. For case of convenience, this analysis is provided at the end of this teaching note. The industry analysis will sharpen NorthAm Company's strategy. It is in the context of NorthAm's strategy that students feel convinced that manufacturing must be responsible for profits.

Reproduced below is the detailed teaching note prepared by Chuck Christenson as well as additional comments on the case.

VG

NorthAm Company (A)

Primary Teaching Note

Charles Christenson
April 1988

The purpose of the case is to illustrate the role of the budgetary process in assigning decision rights and in encouraging the sharing of information that is distributed throughout the organization.

Assignment Questions

1. Trace the steps in the budget formulation process of NorthAm Company. Which steps do you think can be eliminated. Why?

2. Examine Exhibit 1 (the main Profit Planning and Control Report). What does this report tell you about the responsibility of the plant manager in NorthAm's management control system?

Organization and Timing

Analyze specifics of budgetary process	30 minutes
Responsibility structure	40 minutes
Summary	10 minutes

Teaching Approach

I generally open the class by asking someone to give a summary evaluation of the NorthAm system. I then invite comments from others, keeping notes of the comments on the left hand side board.

The Budget Formulation Process

After a few minutes at this level of generality, I suggest that it would be useful to examine some of the specific features of the system and that we might start with the process of preparing the budget (assignment question 1). *Let's look at the budget formulation process step by step. Who is involved in each step? What function does the step serve? Could it be eliminated?*

There are several ways of organizing this discussion. One approach would be around a flow chart of the process similar to that shown in Exhibit TN-1. The flow chart can be developed from student remarks on the middle front board or, to conserve time for discussion of other issues, a transparency of Exhibit TN-1 can be projected on the screen during the discussion.

An alternative approach would be to sketch an organization chart similar to Exhibit TN-2(a) on the middle front board. As students describe the process, use words, circled numbers, and arrows to trace the flow. Exhibit TN-2(b), from Tom Piper's teaching notes, gives the major steps. While the end result will be a messy board, this approach does bring out vividly the complexity and interactive nature of the process and will help the students to understand why it takes seven months.

During the discussion of the process, I like to make certain that at least the following questions are raised. These have mainly to do with the distribution of specific knowledge in an organization and/or the allocation of decision rights.

1. There are three separate projections made of sales for the budget year: by divisional general managers, by the corporate market research group, and by the district sales offices. Why? How do the methods used in these three projections compare?

2. How is the plant budget built up?

   a. Use of standard costs.

   b. Planned methods improvements.

3. What is the purpose of the visit of the corporate controller, his assistant, and other members of the corporate staff to the plants as described on page 7 of the case?

4. A distinction is often drawn between "top down" and "bottom up" approaches to budgeting. How would you characterize the NorthAm approach?

5. What changes, if any, would you make in the NorthAm budget formulation process?

The Responsibility Structure

The fact that the plant is responsible for profits will have come up earlier in the class, if not in the opening discussion then in the analysis of the build-up of the plant budget, but I ask the class at that time to defer discussion of the desirability of this approach until later.

To open this part of the class I ask the simple question, *should the plant managers be evaluated as profit center managers?* The initial reaction of most students will be "No," on the grounds that the plant managers should not be evaluated on something over which they have no control, namely sales.

After a few minutes, if it has not happened spontaneously, I steer the class into a "key success factors" analysis. The main points that should come out are summarized in the following paragraphs.

Environmental Factors

Aluminum cans have become a staple product in recent years; NorthAm was once able to command premium price because of superior quality but can do so no longer. Product quality and customer service (meeting delivery commitments) are now the key competitive factors. Given the nature of the customers, it is unlikely that personal selling is much of a factor; the company's sales force is probably primarily a communications link with the customers, taking orders and communicating special requests to the plants.

The manufacturing process is highly automated and relatively inflexible; this implies a need to plan ahead and minimize short-run changes. Working conditions are not good, the production jobs are machine-paced, but wages are relatively high.

Corporate Goals

At the corporate level, the orientation toward profit is manifested by the way in which the corporate staff reviews plant-level budgets. Yardley says that "the review is a way of giving guidance to the plant managers as to whether or not they are in line with what the company needs to make in the way of profits [emphasis supplied]. When budgets are cut, it is not because "the company cannot afford the program."

It may be inferred from this that NorthAm begins the annual budget formulation cycle with some targeted profit figure for the budget year in mind. In order to meet this targeted figure, it is sufficient that (1) all of the individual budgets of the company's component units "add up" to the target, and (2) each component lives up to its obligation as spelled out in its budget. on the other hand, the ability of a component to deliver on its part of the bargain may depend upon what other components do. Thus, coordination of the components is required during the budget execution cycle.

Key Success Factors

What must this company (or more particularly its Aluminum Can Division) do well in order to earn its target profit? I find it useful to think in terms of a system model such as that shown in Exhibit TN-1, which interrelates the various factors influencing profit. There are four "instrumental variables" in the model as depicted: sales effort, unit price, quality and schedule performance, and costs. Of these, we can observe the following:

1. Sales effort probably has little demand-stimulating effect. As noted earlier, it is concerned primarily with sensing customer needs and communicating them to the plant.

2. Unit price is now largely market-determined and not within the control of anyone within the company.

3. Quality and schedule performance are controlled by plant personnel subject to pressures from the sales force.

4. Costs are controlled by plant personnel.

The rather complicated interrelationships involving quality and schedule should also be observed. High performance on these factors may, on the one hand, increase sales volume and hence profits but may also, on the other hand, increase costs and hence decrease profits. There is, therefore, a tradeoff to be made here and it involves both sales and manufacturing. The sales force will usually have the best specific knowledge about customer needs but the cooperation of the plant will be required in meeting those needs. Also, plant personnel will have the best specific knowledge about the costs of responding to customer requests.

Organization Structure

The Aluminum Can Division is organized on a functional basis, with separate manufacturing and marketing organizations. There are probably several reasons for this. First of all, given the nature of the technology, the manufacturing plants probably specialize by type of product, whereas it would be more natural for the sales force to specialize by customer. Second, the continual need for process and methods for a strong manufacturing staff at the Division level; if the functional breakdown did not occur until a lower level in the organization, there might be a dissipation of scarce manufacturing talent.

Given the functional organization, the ability of the hierarchy to coordinate sales and manufacturing dynamically during the budget execution cycle will be limited. The company has instituted two other mechanisms to help achieve this coordination: one structural (the plant production control department shown in case Figure C) and the budgetary control system.

Control System

Mr. Yardley, the corporate controller, states (case page 4) that "the budget is the principal management tool used by the head office to coordinate the efforts of the various segments of the company toward a common goal." Despite the "common goal," which we have seen to be earning the target profit, Yardley is quite explicit about the message the budgetary system is intended to send to subordinate managers (case page 7). Sales managers are responsible for volume, price, and sales mix; sales offices are revenue centers. Plant managers are responsible for profits, not costs, "even if actual dollar sales drop below the budgeted level"; plants are profit centers. You might ask: What consequences would you expect from this assignment of responsibilities? The fact that Yardley is explicit on the points mentioned earlier should alert the reader to the fact that the consequences of the control system are not entirely unintended.

You might ask: *What would be the consequences of making the plant a cost center rather than a profit center?* In terms of the vital tradeoff between service and quality on the one hand and cost control on the other, the consequence would almost certainly be to make the plant extremely reluctant to exert itself to meet unexpected customer requirements. Making the plant a profit center gives plant management an objective that is more consistent with that of the sales force and thus should help to encourage cooperation.

The corresponding question regarding the sales force is: *What would be the consequences of making the sales force a profit center rather than a revenue center?* Presumably it would make the sales force more concerned with the costs of responding to unusual customer requests and therefore less sympathetic with those requests. Do we want that? I would think not. The sales force can't control those costs. What we want the sales force to be in this system is a vigorous advocate of the customers' requirements. Making it responsible for revenue helps to insure this.

Although the students will probably not remember this detail, in the Continental Can Company of Canada (B) case, it is revealed that making the plant responsible for profits is a relatively recent innovation. Prior to this change, the plant bonus was tied to plant-wide efficiency and prior to that to departmental efficiency.

NorthAm Budget Process

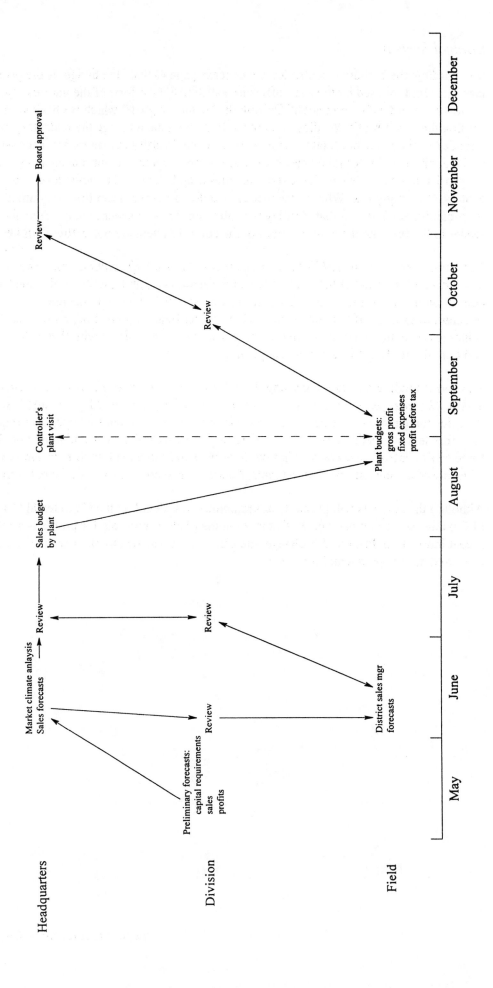

May	June	July	August	September	October	November	December

Headquarters

Division

Field

Market climate anlaysis
Sales forecasts

Review

Sales budget
by plant

Controller's
plant visit

Review

Review

Board approval

Preliminary forecasts:
capital requirements
sales
profits

Review

District sales mgr
forecasts

Review

Plant budgets:
gross profit
fixed expenses
profit before tax

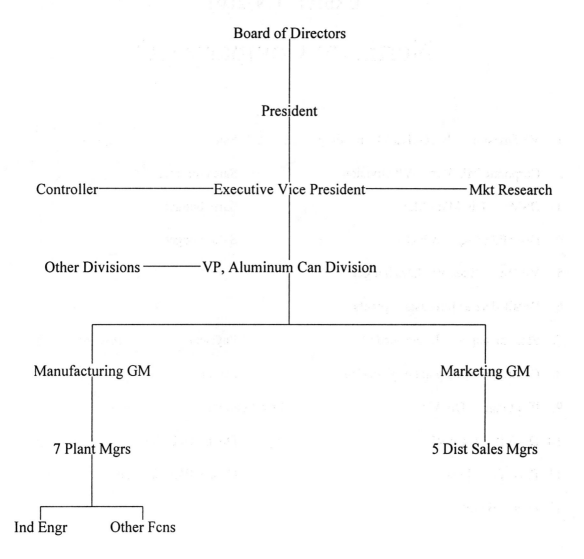

NorthAm Company (A)

1. VP Division   Executive VP spending   Sales   capital

2. Corporate Mkt Res   VP Division   Sales forecast

3. DSMs   Div Mktg Mgr   Sales budget

4. Div Mktg Mgr   VP Div   Sales budget

5. VP Div   Exec VP Sales budget

6. Detailed sales forecasts   plants

7. Plant manager   Depts needs   Physical   resource

8. Controller visits plant engineering   gaming   on

9. Plant mgr   Div VP   Profit budget

10. Div VP   Exec VP   Div profit budget

11. Exec VP   Pres   Consol P&L, BS, CF

12. Pres   Board

How NorthAm Makes a Profit

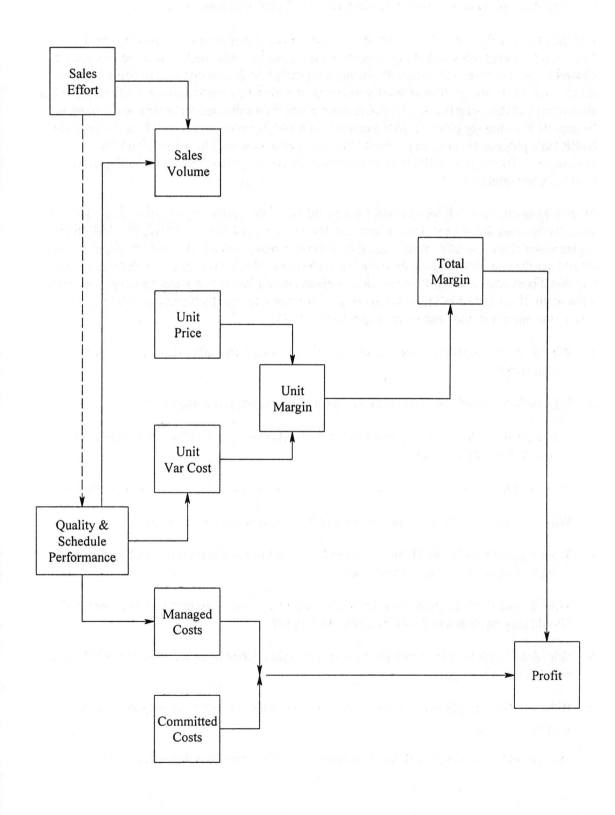

Additional Comments on NorthAm Company

This is a very "rich" case, which easily can be used for two class sessions. Though the nominal issue is whether plants should be expense centers or profit centers, the case also includes an excellent description of the profit budgeting process and of performance reporting.

I let the class briefly respond to question 1. It will come out that we don't explicitly know NorthAm's strategy, although some broad statements can be made, such as that the company has chosen to operate in related businesses (containers and packages) as opposed to being broadly diversified. There also is little case information on the strategy planning phase. Only rarely will a student note at this point that the four objectives given for a sales budget review really seem to be aspects of a strategy planning phase rather than a budget review. This may be a weakness in NorthAm's procedures, or it may indicate that in a stable, mature, low-growth industry environment, the program stability is so great that the strategy planning and budgeting phases tend to be intermingled.

I then turn to question 2. Prior to class, I put on the board the partial organization chart. Then as students describe the process, I use words, circled numbers, and arrows to trace the flow on this organization chart. The end result is too messy to show here, which is the desired effect: students should see the complexity of the process, and understand why it requires seven months. I have had this discussion go for an entire session, without getting into the expense versus profit center issue at all. If students don't raise all the issues I feel are relevant, I have in my notes a list of discussion questions that I can raise at appropriate points:

1. Why does the budgeting process begin with the division VPs, rather than at corporate headquarters?

2. Why do these initial forecasts (May 15) go out three years, rather than just one?

3. Why have the VPs do this step at all, since the market research staff seems to start from scratch in their forecasting?

4. Do you want market research to start from scratch, or to modify the division VPs' forecasts?

5. Why have a centralized forecasting group rather than one in each division?

6. What types of people would you expect to find in NorthAm's market research staff today? What techniques would they likely use?

7. What do you think the marketing general manager does with market research's forecasts? Should they be shown to the district sales managers?

8. Why does NorthAm get sales budgets from the DSMs, when there are already the VP's and market research's figures?

9. If there a difference between a sales *forecast* and a sales *budget*? Who prepares which in Empire?

10. How should top management decide whether market research is doing a good job?

11. Plant managers receive, in effect, a tentative monthly production schedule. Explain how they transform these data into a profit budget.

12. What are the stated purposes of the controller's plant visit during the budget process? Are those the real reasons?

13. Are these visits a good idea? How would you feel about these visits, (a) as a plant manager? (b) as the executive VP?, (c) as a NorthAm shareholder?

14. As plant manager, would you want the visit to last longer than it now does? Can anything really be accomplished in a half day?

15. How likely is it that the budget will be rejected by the president? by the board?

16. Why does NorthAm spend 7½ months preparing a budget that could probably be prepared centrally by a group of forecasters, engineers, and accountants in two to three weeks?

Discussion of these issues, in my experience, results in a fairly short list of suggested improvements, given how negative students (including many experienced business people) tend to be about NorthAm after reading the case and discussing it in their study groups. This list may include:

1. Issue the budget guidelines and basic assumptions prior to the VPs' preparation of their initial forecasts, rather than after.

2. Let the plant managers defend their own budgets at meetings at the head of office, rather than relying on the corporate controller to answer questions about them.

3. Have the head of plant industrial engineering report to the head of a higher-level IE department, rather than to the plant manager.

On day 2 I turn to the question of what type of responsibility center the plants should be. Students will come down hard on the existing system, and insist that the plants should be expense centers. In defense of their position, they will argue that "you shouldn't hold someone responsible for what he or she can't control," saying. (or implying) that it's obvious that in a functionally organized company like NorthAm, Marketing controls revenues and Manufacturing controls expenses. Usually a few students will suggest that the present system seems to be working satisfactorily, but they tend to get shouted down by the majority *unless* they base their statement on an analysis of the "key success factors" in this business.

If a better student does not do this "key factors" analysis, then after the consensus seems to be to change the plants to expense centers, I ask, "What must NorthAm do well to be economically successful in the aluminum can business?" With some coaxing, the students will come up with three factors: cost, quality, and delivery. Cost control is important, because cans are a commodity with an established market price; hence the opportunity to increase unit margins rests in cost control, not pricing. Quality here means two things: no defects that could result in an end-user product liability claim; and cans exactly the specified size and shape so that they don't foul up the customer's (canner's) highly automated lines. Delivery is important because canners don't want to inventory a bulky yet cheap item like cans. (One container industry person has told me that it is not unusual for a semitrailer full of bottles to be left at the canner's loading dock for a day or two, and then unloaded from the truck and put directly onto the canning line.)

With this list on the board, it begins to dawn on the students that in this company, the sales force are essentially order-takers. This stuns some students, as they realize they have been using a stereotype that assumes selling *anything* involves strong *personal* selling, as with encyclopedias. They also see, of course, that the key variables are most significantly influenced by decisions and activities made within the plant.

Students will not immediately be won over to the point of view that treating the plants as profit centers is more appropriate than treating them as expense centers. So I ask two more questions. First, "How difficult is it to forecast sales in this business?" If you previously have traced through the budgeting process, the students recall that the nature of the industry was such that the Market Research group put together a forecast, which sounded like multivariate regression tempered with judgment. I also bring out the fact that cans are used primarily for beverage and food products, and that demand should therefore be relatively easy to project. Also it should be remembered that Marketing is held responsible for revenue variances: price, volume, and mix. (The case is fairly clear on this, I think, yet students seem to think Marketing has no performance measures.) In developing the sales budget, would the marketing people be motivated to submit pessimistic (easily attainable) or optimistic sales figures? I think the former, and feel that the reason the forecasts of Market Research seem to go into the division management's "top drawer" and apparently are not seen by the district sales managers is that division management uses these "independent" *forecasts* as a test of whether the sales force has put enough "reach" in their sales *budgets.* In sum, I feel that the combination of the underlying industry economics and the sales forecasting/budgeting process makes it very unlikely that a plant manager will be laboring under an overly optimistic volume estimate, as the students have worried about up to this point. (In fact, NorthAm's sales budgets essentially always are met within plus or minus 5 percent.)

Second, I ask, "Suppose the plant sends out a shipment of cans too late, and/or delivers an off-standard (in terms of quality as defined above) shipment—how long will it be until NorthAm knows the customer is unhappy?" The answer is "within a few days." Thus if a plant manager doesn't maintain service and quality, the plant's sales will begin to drop *this* year, and he will be unable to meet the profit goal and earn a bonus for himself and other members of plant management. I have the students contrast this situation with the auto industry, where falling down on quality may not have much impact on sales until two or three years later when owners start to trade in their cars for new ones. Again, the point is to get the students to think about the appropriateness of profit centers in *this* company in *this* industry, rather than to deal in generalities.

As a "clincher," I ask students to compare how a plant manager might react to a request for a rush order if (a) the plant is a profit center and (b) it is an expense center with a flexible budget. If the plant is a profit center, management must trade off possible lost gross margin on this and future orders from the same customer against increased production costs from added setups and interrupting long production runs. If the plant is an expense center, if the order is lost, the plant volume stays the same (or fails in the future), but the plant should be able to meet the expense budget because of efficient production scheduling. On the other hand, if the rush order is accepted, the cost budget increases, but probably not by enough to compensate for the inefficiencies of interrupting production schedules. Thus, I maintain that the profit center approach is more likely to foster the needed sales-manufacturing cooperation than is an expense center approach. The case hints that in fact the present system is achieving the desired trade-off: "The sales force are supposed to know their customers well enough to judge whether or not the customer *really* needs the product" (emphasis added). One can imagine that if the sales force "cried wolf" too often, a plant manager would ignore all rush order requests.

As a matter of fact, NorthAm formerly treated the plants as expense centers, and changed to the profit center approach because of a lack of sales-manufacturing cooperation. The instructor would also be interested in seeing—and perhaps teaching—Empire Class Company (B) (Case 125), in which the pressures this system creates at the plant level are described. It turns out that, as one might guess, the ulcer-producing job is that of the production scheduler (Production Control in Exhibit 2 of the case).

I should add that even my strong feeling that the present system is appropriate will not be shared by all students—nor perhaps even by the instructor. The total set of alternatives which can be defended effectively under a given set of assumptions (and without the benefit or bias of my firsthand knowledge of NorthAm) include the following:

1. Status quo. Note that although I have referred to this as the *profit* center approach, the bottom of Exhibit 3, PPCR #1, suggests the plants actually are *investment* centers.

2. Treat the plants as expense centers, and move profit responsibility up to the division level.

3. Treat both the plants and sales districts as profit centers, with transfer pricing between the two.

4. Reorganize the division, redefining five sales districts aligned with the five plants, and treat the new sales district-plant pair as a profit center.

5. Maintain the present system, but tie part of the sales force compensation to plant profitability.

6. Have separate plant bonuses for sales and expenses, but do not combine these into a profit bonus.

This range of alternatives makes the case a good one for an examination on management control issues.

If time permits (and it seldom does), I ask what is gained by treating the plants as investment centers rather than just profit centers. Since this is primarily a produce-to-order business, finished goods and work-in-process inventories are not significant. And the case indicates that receivables are not included in the plants' investment base (although they are included—appropriately—at the division level). It's also possible that major raw materials purchases are handled at the division level, although this is not clear, because there is a plant purchasing agent shown on Exhibit 2. The point is that if plant mangers have little influence over current assets, then the capital budgeting process can control fixed assets without using an investment center approach at the plant level. In fact, if not implemented with care, the ROI approach may motivate a plant manager to "drive the plant into the ground," letting depreciation increase accounting ROI. In NorthAm's case, this risk is mitigated because (1) emphasis on the P/V ratio should motivate productivity improvement capital expenditure proposals, and (2) fixed assets are valued at replacement costs, not at net book value.

Structural Analysis of the Metal Container Industry[1]

According to Porter,[2] industry profitability is a function of the *collective strength* of *five* competitive forces: bargaining power of suppliers, bargaining power of buyers, the threat of substitutes, the entry of new competitors, and the rivalry among the existing competitors. To quote Porter: "The five forces determine industry profitability because they influence the prices, costs, and required investment of firms in an industry—the elements of return on investment. Buyer power influences the prices that firms can charge, for example, as does the threat of substitution. The power of buyers can also influence cost and investment, because powerful buyers demand costly service. The bargaining power of suppliers determines the cost of raw materials and other inputs. The intensity of rivalry influences prices as well as the costs of competing in areas such as plant, product development, advertising, and sales force. The threat of entry places a limit on prices, and shapes the investment required to deter entrants.[3]

The profit potential in the metal container industry is analyzed using the five-forces framework.

Bargaining Power of Suppliers

A. Aluminum Companies

   1. There are only four suppliers of aluminum (Alcoa, Alcan, Reynolds, and Kaiser); further, these companies are much more concentrated than the metal container industry.

   2. These firms have vast resources and pose credible threat of forward integration (in fact, Alcoa and Reynolds have already forward integrated into can manufacture).

   3. Can manufacturers do not pose any threat of backward integration.

Net Conclusion. Aluminum companies can exert considerable amounts of bargaining power over metal can manufacturers in negotiating raw material prices.

B. Steel Companies

   1. There are few suppliers of tin plated steel.

   2. Steel companies pose a credible threat of forward integration but have not actually done so yet.

   3. Can companies do not pose any threat of backward integration.

Net Conclusion. Steel companies can exert a good deal of bargaining power over metal can manufacturers.

Bargaining Power of Buyers (80 percent of metal containers are purchased by food and beverage companies)

1. Buyers of cans are very large and powerful.

---

[1] Discussions on the metal container industry are based on data as of 1977.
[2] Michael E. Porter, *Competitive Strategy* (New York: Free Press, 1980)
[3] Michael E. Porter, *Competitive Strategy* (New York: Free Press, 1980), p. 5.

2. The cost of the can is a significant fraction of the buyer's costs (the container constitutes about 45 percent of the total cost of beverage companies).

3. Customers buy in large quantities.

4. Customers buy an essentially undifferentiated product and face no switching costs.

5. Customers typically keep two sources of supply. Poor service and uncompetitive prices are punished by cuts in order size.

6. Can manufacturers typically locate a plant to serve a single customer so that the loss of a large order from that customer could greatly cut into profits.

7. There is low customer loyalty.

8. Buyers pose a credible threat of backward integration. In fact, several food and beverage companies already make their own cans (e.g., Campbell soup is a major producer of three-piece steel cans). The proportion of "captive" production increased from 18 percent to 26 percent between 1970 and 1976. It is important to note that this backward integration has taken place primarily in the three-piece cans. The buyers do not possess the technical skills to develop their own two-piece lines.

9. Can manufacturers have no ability to forward integrate into the food and beverages industry.

Net Conclusion. Buyers can exert a great deal of power over metal can producers.

Pressure from Substitute Products

A. Aluminum

1. Its lighter weight could help in transportation costs.

2. Aluminum is easier to lithograph, producing a better reproduction at lower cost.

3. Aluminum is favored over steel as a recycling material, because the lighter aluminum can be transported to recycling sites more easily, and recycled aluminum is far more valuable.

4. Aluminum is known to reduce the problems of flavoring, a major concern of both the brewing and soft drink industries.

Net conclusion. Aluminum is a very great threat to the traditional, tin-plated steel (notwithstanding the fact that aluminum is about 20 percent more expensive than steel).

B. Plastics

1. It is lighter.

2. It is resistant to breakage.

3. It has design versatility, thereby lowering shelf-space requirements.

Net Conclusion. Plastics pose a significant threat to tin-plated steel in many user segments.

C. Fiber-Foil

1. It is 20 percent lighter than steel cans.

2. It is 15 percent cheaper than steel cans.

Net Conclusion:. In certain user segments (particularly for motor oil and frozen juices), fiber-foil is a significant threat to tin plated steel.

Overall Conclusion. With the exception of food cans, steel faces a significant threat from substitute materials such as aluminum, plastics, and fiber foil.

Threat of Entry

1. Economies of scale in this industry are quite low and as such cannot be used as an entry barrier; for example, the minimum efficient plant size for two-piece can lines is two to three lines.

2. Capital investments are certainly not an entry barrier (especially for suppliers and buyers); for example, for two-piece can lines the per-line cost is about $10 – $15 million.

3. Technology is not an entry barrier for three-piece containers. However, the canning technology for the two-piece lines is not available with buyers such as Campbell Soup.

4. Brand loyalty is absent and is not available as an entry barrier.

Net Conclusion. Metal container industry has very low barriers to entry, as evident from the fact that this industry is characterized by a large number of small players.

Intensity of Rivalry among Existing Competitors

Notwithstanding the fact that there are only four major players in this industry (Continental Can, American Can, National Can, and Crown Cork and Seal), price rivalry is intense due to the following factors:

1. This is a slow growth, mature industry (3 percent annual growth rate).

2. Metal container is largely an undifferentiated product, forcing the customers to choose on the basis of price, if service is comparable.

3. Presence of close substitutes keeps the lid on prices.

4. Low entry barrier puts a cap on selling prices.

5. Presence of very powerful buyers and very powerful suppliers keeps the container prices down (as otherwise they will enter the industry).

Net Conclusion. Price competition is quite intense.

Overall Conclusion. Given the very high supplier power and buyer power, low barriers to entry, availability of close substitutes, and intense price competition among existing players, the profit potential in the metal container industry is expected to be low. In fact, the *Forbes* magazine ranks this industry at 24 out of the total of 31 industries in the United States on the criterion of return on equity.[4]

Appropriate Overall Competitive Strategy

Given the commodity nature of the product, it is imperative that, to be successful, a firm in this industry must gain competitive advantage in relative costs. That is to say, a high performer must have the *lowest cost* in the industry. How can a firm cut costs in a commodity product? It can be done if cost analysis and strategic thinking are brought closer together.

The average cost structure in the metal container industry is estimated as follows:

Raw material	64%
Labor	15
Depreciation	2
Transportation	8
Research and development	2
General Administration	9
Total Cost	100%

---

[4] *Forbes*, January 13, 1986, pp. 256 – 58.

Case 9-3

Boston Creamery, Inc.

Overview

This is one of the "classic" cases in conventional managerial accounting. It has been used over the years in many of the leading business schools in the world (Harvard, Stanford, Chicago, Wharton, HEC, INSEAD, IMD, IESE, ...). It was published in 1974, along with a commentary, in the leading academic journal in accounting (*The Accounting Review*). At one time in the 1970s it was voted the best accounting case of the year by Stanford's first-year MBA class. It has been reprinted and translated many times in many places. The current version has been updated to reflect many of the teaching issues which have surfaced over the years.

For most of its life, the case has been seen as a good example of good management control theory in action—"formal profit planning and control systems," with an emphasis on "managerially relevant profit variance analysis." Unfortunately, my best assessment of the case from a 1995 perspective is that it is a *good* example of *bad* management control in action! *Sic Transit Gloria*! It is still a clear practical example of a formal profit planning and control system in action. I no longer believe that conventional "profit planning and control" is a useful management control tool.

The teaching commentary in this book for the Kinkead Equipment case presents the logic for arguing that conventional profit planning and control is now outdated because of the lack of a "strategic dimension." The poignant memo appended to this teaching commentary further illustrates the shortcomings of the system described in the case.

This teaching commentary takes the case at face value and describes the teaching strategy that has worked very well for the case for twenty years. The fifth question has been added to the case to explore the SCM perspective on the case. The instructor is referred to the Kinkead Equipment commentary if that perspective is to be covered with this case.

Teaching Strategy

To teach this case in one class period, it is necessary to keep moving through the numbers and not spend "too much" time on any one calculation. *We do not recommend going through the assignment questions in order*. For this case, it is better to start with an overview framework for profit variance analysis. First, work through the concept of the variance calculations, one step at a time.

This teaching commentary was prepared by Professor John K. Shank of the Amos Tuck School of Business.

One approach here which many students find helpful is the "spin one dial at a time" framework shown below:

Spin One Dial At A Time

I. Conceptually	(1)	(2)	(3)	(4)	(5)	(6)
Market Size	P	A	A	A	A	A
SOM	P	P	A	A	A	A
Mix	P	P	P	A	A	A
Sales Prices	P	P	P	P	A	A
Costs	P	P	P	P	P	A

II. For the Case	(1)	(2)	(3)	(4)	(5)	(6)
Sales	9,220	9,815	9,619	9,645	9,657	9,657
Variable Costs	6,629	7,056	6,915	6,936	6,936	
Contribution Margin	2,591	2,759	2,704	2,709	2,721	8,940*
Fixed Costs	1,946	1,946	1,946	1,946	1,946	____
Profit	645	813	758	763	775	717

Variance Due To:

Market Size	168F	
SOM	55U	
Sales Mix	5F	
Sales Prices	12F	
Costs	58U	

72F

*No fixed/variable breakdown is given in the case.

This format emphasizes five key points: 1) There are several components to the plan; 2) Each one can vary between plan and actual; 3) Each component thus contributes to the overall profit variance; 4) In measuring the separable impact of any one component, it is necessary to hold the other components fixed, spinning only one dial at a time; and 5) The total variance is the sum of the components. We start the class by working through this schematic, beginning with column 1 filled in.

We work through columns 2 to 6, in order, showing students the conceptual segment (part I) and asking them to fill in the numbers below (part II).

We then show a transparency of the following table to present an overview of the profit planning process and show where profit variance analysis fits in. The idea is to emphasize the iterative nature of the process and the key role of meaningful variance analysis in facilitating the iteration.

Formal One Year
Profit Planning and Control

The Planning Cycle

1. Set standard costs and prices (variable costs only) for all products.

2. Sales forecast.

3. A fixed cost budget.

4. Pull the parts together and iterate if necessary.

The Control Cycle

1. Adjust the budget to actual volume (the "flexed" budget).

2. Measure flexible budget vs. actual results.

3. Analyze the variances—profit variance analysis.

4. Take appropriate corrective actions.

After discussing this schematic, we note that there are many different ways to organize a profit variance analysis. We tell the students we are going to illustrate a second format that "peels the onion," one level at a time, and shows a specific calculational formula for each of the components. We emphasize that the components are the same as in the "spin the dial" format—they are just arrived at differently. We then go through the following analysis for levels zero through four:

Level 0

	Original Plan	Actual	Variance
	$645,400	$717,100	$71,700F

Level 1—Income Statement Line Item Comparison

	Original Plan	Actual	Variance
Revenues	$9,219,900	$9,657,300	$437,400F
Expenses	8,574,500	8,940,200	365,700U
	$ 645,400	$ 717,100	$ 71,700F

(THIS IS USELESS IN ANY MANAGERIAL SENSE!)

Level 2—Introduce the Flexible Budget Concept

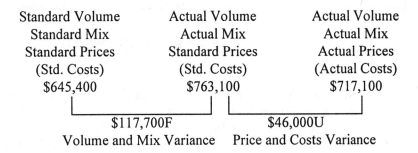

Standard Volume	Actual Volume	Actual Volume
Standard Mix	Actual Mix	Actual Mix
Standard Prices	Standard Prices	Actual Prices
(Std. Costs)	(Std. Costs)	(Actual Costs)
$645,400	$763,100	$717,100

$117,700F
Volume and Mix Variance

$46,000U
Price and Costs Variance

Level 3

3A.—Separate Sales Volume and Sales Mix Variances

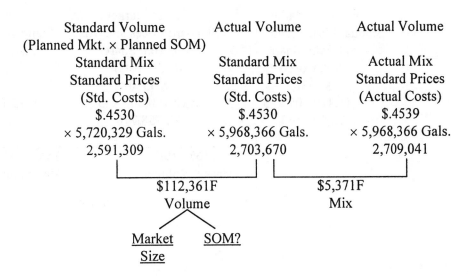

Standard Volume	Actual Volume	Actual Volume
(Planned Mkt. × Planned SOM)		
Standard Mix	Standard Mix	Actual Mix
Standard Prices	Standard Prices	Standard Prices
(Std. Costs)	(Std. Costs)	(Actual Costs)
$.4530	$.4530	$.4539
× 5,720,329 Gals.	× 5,968,366 Gals.	× 5,968,366 Gals.
2,591,309	2,703,670	2,709,041

$112,361F
Volume

$5,371F
Mix

Market Size   SOM?

3B.—Separate Sales Price Variances From Operating Cost Variances

1. Sales Prices

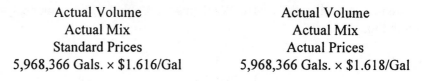

Actual Volume Actual Mix Standard Prices 5,968,366 Gals. × $1.616/Gal	Actual Volume Actual Mix Actual Prices 5,968,366 Gals. × $1.618/Gal
$9,644,879	$9,656,816

Sales Price Variance

$11,937F

2. Operating Costs

	Actual	Flex Budget	Spending Variance
Cost of Goods Manufactured	$6,824,900 –	$6,725,900 =	$99,000U
Delivery 706,800 –		760,800 =	54,000F
Advertising	607,700 –	578,700 =	29,000U
Selling	362,800 –	368,800 =	6,000F
Administrative	438,000 –	448,000 =	10,000F
			58,000U

$$1 + 2 = \$12F + \$58U = \$46U$$

Level 4— A. Sales Volume Variance Separated By Market Share and Total Market Volume
B. Mix Variance—By Products
C. Sales Prices—By Products
D. Operating Costs—By Line Item in Each Dept. and with Price vs. Quantity for Key Line Items

4A. Market Volume and Market Share

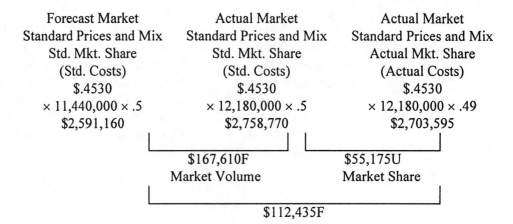

Forecast Market Standard Prices and Mix Std. Mkt. Share (Std. Costs) $.4530 × 11,440,000 × .5 $2,591,160	Actual Market Standard Prices and Mix Std. Mkt. Share (Std. Costs) $.4530 × 12,180,000 × .5 $2,758,770	Actual Market Standard Prices and Mix Actual Mkt. Share (Actual Costs) $.4530 × 12,180,000 × .49 $2,703,595

$167,610F
Market Volume

$55,175U
Market Share

$112,435F

4B. Mix Variance By Products

Act. Gal × ΔMargin (Product Standard Margin – Average Standard Margin)

Vanilla	49,000U
Chocolate	1,000F
•	•
•	•
•	•
Total	<u>$5,340F</u>

4C. Sales Prices By Products

(Actual Price – Standard Price) × Actual Volume

Vanilla	•
Chocolate	•
•	•
•	•
•	•
Total	<u>$12,000F</u>

4D. Manufacturing Department Cost Variances—Key Line Items

Milk	QV	$31,400U
	PV	57,300U
Sugar	QV	3,100U
	PV	23,400U
Flavoring/Additives	QV	35,300F*
Labor-Cartons	QV/PV	34,400U
All Other, Net		<u>15,300F</u>
		$99,000U

*Apparently there is no price variance for flavorings/additives. If so, it would be shown in a separate line item, as is done for milk and sugar.

Summary of the Calculations

Following is a recap of the "peel the onion" approach down through four levels:

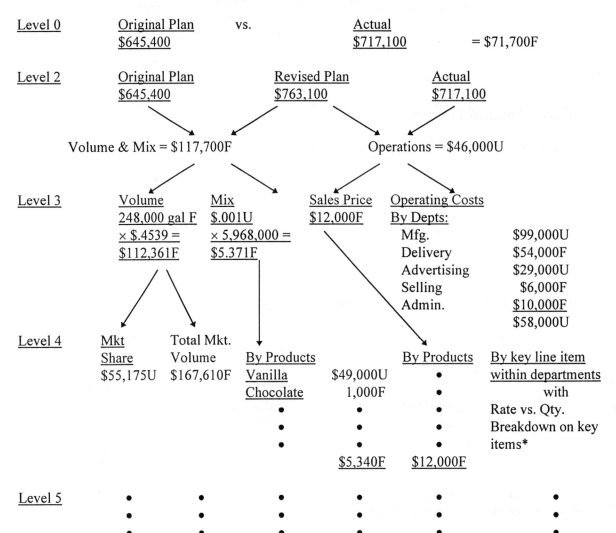

Recap of Multi-Level Profit Variance Analysis

Level 0   Original Plan   vs.   Actual
           $645,400 $717,100   = $71,700F

Level 2   Original Plan   Revised Plan   Actual
           $645,400 $763,100 $717,100

           Volume & Mix = $117,700F   Operations = $46,000U

Level 3   Volume   Mix   Sales Price   Operating Costs
           248,000 gal F $.001U $12,000F   By Depts:
           × $.4539 =   × 5,968,000 =   Mfg. $99,000U
           $112,361F $5.371F   Delivery $54,000F
                                                         Advertising $29,000U
                                                         Selling $6,000F
                                                         Admin. $10,000F
                                                                       $58,000U

Level 4   Mkt   Total Mkt.   By Products   By key line item
           Share   Volume   By Products   within departments
           $55,175U $167,610F   Vanilla $49,000U   •   with
                                 Chocolate 1,000F   •   Rate vs. Qty.
                                     •   •   •   Breakdown on key
                                     •   •   •   items*
                                     •   •   •
                                            $5,340F $12,000F

Level 5   •   •   •   •   •   •
             •   •   •   •   •   •
             •   •   •   •   •   •

Level "n"

*Level 4 variance breakdown for manufacturing:
           Dairy Yield $31,400U
           Milk Price   57,300U
           Sugar Yield   3,100U
           Sugar Price   23,400U
           Labor-Cartonizing   34,400U
           Flavors/Additives   35,300F
           All Other (net)   15,300F
                                 99,000U

There is no right answer as to how many levels is "enough." Each level breaks down the preceding level with one more layer of detail. The idea is to stop when you stop getting managerially useful insights.

We try to cover all of the above calculations in no more than an hour, to save thirty minutes for the "so what" question. After discussing these two different approaches to calculating the variance components we note that we are only half finished. Calculating the components is half the task, but the other half is to put the components together to tell a meaningful story about what happened.

Telling a Story from the Calculations

What story do the components tell for Boston Creamery for 1973? The case shows one possible story—Frank Roberts' preliminary report. Jim Peterson, however, has raised several questions about this format. A "level four" analysis in the "peel the onion" format addresses most of Peterson's concerns. But how can the pieces be put back together most meaningfully? The following table present three very different stories, all drawn from the same components:

From the Calculations to the "Story"
Three Versions of the "Story"

I. Per Marketing VP		II. Per Operations VP		III. Per Controller		
Favorable variance due to Sales		Uncontrollable		Uncontrollable		
Sales Volume	117,700F	Market Growth	167,600F	Market Growth		167,600F
Prices	12,000F			Delivery System. Change		
				Delivery	54F	19,600F
Unfavorable variance due to		Unfavorable Marketing Variances		Mfg. Labor	34.4U	
Operations		Market Share	55,300U			187,200F
Manufacturing	99,000U	Mix	6,000F			
Delivery	54,000F	Poor Margin Control		Marketing		
Advertising	29,000U	Sales Prices		Margin Control		68,700U
Selling	6,000F	vs.	68,700U	Market Share		55,300U
Administrative	10,000F	Purchase Prices		Selling & Advert.		23,000U
		(12F vs. 80,700U)		Mix		6,000F
NET	71,700F	Selling & Advert.	23,000U			141,000U
			141,000U			
		Favorable Operations Variances		Operations		
		Delivery	54,000F	Poor Dairy Yield		31,400U
		Administrative	10,000F	Poor Sugar Yield		3,100U
		All other operating		Poor Quality Control		
		variances—NET		on Flavors and		
		(.2% of Costs)	18,900U	Additives		51,300F
			45,100F	All other		8,700F
						25,500F
		NET	71,700F	NET		71,000F

Conclude?	Conclude?	Conclude?
Marketing—*Good*	Marketing—*Poor*	Marketing—*Poor*
Operations—*Poor*	Operations—*Good*	Operations—*Poor*
		Uncontrollable—*Good*

*Note that *putting the pieces back together* intelligently is just as important as tearing the pieces apart. There is as much *management philosophy* here as accounting.

From the "Story" (Which One?) to the Recommendations for Action

The first column is Frank Roberts' preliminary report in which Marketing looks good and Operations looks bad. The middle column is the report which John Parker constructed to "neutralize" Roberts' version. In Parker's version, Operations looks good and Marketing looks bad. This version is one answer to question three in the case. The third version is one produced by the controller when Jim Peterson asked him to comment on the other two conflicting versions. His shows both Marketing and Operations doing poorly with "uncontrollable" factors getting the credit for the favorable overall variance. This third version probably comes closest to answering question one in the case.

Which of these is "right"? Obviously, none of them. Telling the "story of the numbers" is a management task, not an accounting calculation. The real problem here for Boston Creamery is that none of the three versions deals *at all* with the strategic issues of a "cost control" based management lens used to analyze a business facing major competitive threats (the rise of "designer" ice cream). The *internal* focus of the variance analysis system misses the major *external* forces at work in the ice cream business in the mid 1970s.

As a last issue for class discussion we show a transparency of the following memo about the company on which this case was based.

This is a disguised version of a memo written to me, and subsequently shared with Tuck MBAs, from "John Jones," a Tuck graduate and great, great grandson of the founder of "J.P. Jones Dairy."

We spend whatever time we have left discussing the issues raised in the memo. We try to close by asking students what would have been a more "strategically astute" management control system for the company in 1973.

We say we will try to present some ideas on this topic in later classes (A.B. Thorsten, Tuck Industries, and Brunswick Plastics). Having thus left a nice big challenge for ourselves, we close the discussion!

The Boston Creamery case takes place at the beginning of the final stage in J.P. Jones' career as head of the Jones family business.

The Company evolved out of a Chester Vermont dairy farm owned by John Paul Jones, grandfather of the current (1973) CEO of the same name. Jones specialized in local delivery of premium quality milk. Paul Jones, son of the founder, took over the company early in the twentieth century, and established Jones as the premier dairy producer in the Hartford area. He established a large fleet of delivery vehicles (initially horse drawn), established large bottling operations, and began to buy most of Jones milk and other raw materials from outside dairy farms.

The second John Paul Jones took over the Company in 1928 at the young age of thirty. Under his direction, Jones expanded their operations throughout much of New England, expanded product offerings to include a greater variety of dairy products and orange juice, and developed Jones reputation for superior customer service.

For over two decades after World War II, Jones enjoyed almost a monopoly in large parts of New England. Jones enjoyed strong relationships with the majority of the "Mom and Pop" type of stores which dominated the retail grocery business during this period. Jones' competitive advantage was their premium product, distribution network (there was never a middleman between Jones and the retailer), and strong relationships with the retailers, allowing them to price at a premium level.

The sixties saw the rise of the supermarket as a major force in grocery retailing and the narrowing of differentiation in most dairy products. Rather than lower their prices to the levels which supermarkets demanded, Jones made a strategic decision to keep prices at their high levels so as not to undercut the prices of their primary customers, the "Mom and Pop" stores, and so that their healthy margins could be retained. Unfortunately the company did not perceive the relevance of the supermarket trend until it was too late. By the mid-1970s the majority of "Mom and Pops" had been driven out of business by the supermarkets, and Jones had alienated the major supermarkets and their distributors. The competition was now firmly entrenched in supermarkets with their own products and through private label products, both of which were now comparable in quality to Jones products.

The situation facing Jones in the mid-1970s was not unlike the situation facing IBM in the early 1990s. Jones had been the innovator and dominant player in the dairy business for years, and believed their name and quality would allow them to hold their ground with continued high pricing and select customers. But as competitors learned to make a comparable product and the nature of how the product was sold changed, Jones began to lose significant market share. Profits decreased steadily through the early seventies. "Formal controls" were instituted to control costs more carefully. By the end of the decade, the company was showing annual losses, in spite of its "modern" approach to planning and control.

J.P. Jones II had run the company for so long that he never properly considered how to hand it over to new, younger managers who would understand the changes happening in the marketplace. He retired from active operations in the early 1970s. But even then, major decisions were never made without him. He died in 1978 and the company was sold to a competitor in 1980.

CHAPTER 10
ANALYZING PERFORMANCE REPORTS

Changes from the Eighth Edition

We first discuss variance analysis—the technical aspects of performance assessment. We then discuss how variance reports are used—the behavioral aspects of performance assessment.

Cases

Variance Analysis Problems gives students practice in the mechanical aspects of variance analysis.

Solatronics describes the variance analysis under full costing. This case replaces Cotter, Inc. This case also raises behavioral effects of using the variance reports in evaluating managerial performance.

Galvor Company is a classic case on the use of tight financial control in a highly diversified corporation.

Captain Jamie Tolten deals with performance evaluation issues and the need for "fit" between management control and organization's and individual's goals an objectives.

Case 10-1

Temple Division

Variance Analysis Problems

Problem 1

Part A

February, 1988
(000)

Question 1—Variance Analysis Assuming Direct Costing

Revenue Variance

Price

	Product A	Product B	Product C	Price Variance
Actual volume	120	130	150	
Actual price	$ .95	$ 1.90	$ 2.80	
Budget price	1.00	2.00	3.00	
Variance: Per unit	$ (.05)	$ (.10)	$ (.20)	
Total	$(6)	$(13)	$(30)	$(49)

Mix

Product	Actual Volume at Budget Mix	Actual Sales	Difference	Unit Contribution	Mix Variance
A	133.3	120	(13.3)	$ .20	$(2.7)
B	133.3	130	(3.3)	.90	(3.0)
C	133.3	150	16.7	1.20	20.0
Total	400	400			$14.3

Volume

Product	Actual Volume at Budget Mix	Budget Volume	Difference	Unit Contribution	Volume Variance
A	133.3	100	33.3	$ .20	$ 6.7
B	133.3	100	33.3	.90	30.0
C	133.3	100	33.3	1.20	40.0
Total	400	300	100		$76.7

Variable Cost Variances

	Units Produced	Material	Labor	Overhead	Total
Standard costs					
Product A	150	$ 75.0	$15.0	$ 30.0	$120.0
Product B	130	91.0	19.5	32.5	143.0
Product C	120	180.0	12.0	24.0	216.0
Total	400	$346.0	$46.5	$ 86.5	$479.0
Actual cost		361.0	56.0	105.0	522.0
Variance		$(15.0)	$(9.5)	$(18.5)	$(43.0)

TEMPLE DIVISION

Performance Report—February, 1988
($000)

Actual profit	$ 59
Budget	80
Variance	$(21)

Analysis of Variances

Revenue variances		
Price	$ (49.0)	
Mix...	14.3	
Volume	76.7	$ 42
Variable cost variance		
Material..	$ (15.0)	
Labor..	(9.5)	
Overhead..	(18.5)	(43)
Fixed cost variances		
Manufacturing overhead expense...........................	$ (5)	
Selling expense	(7)	
Administrative expense	(8)	(20)
Net variances		$(21)

TEMPLE DIVISION
Performance Report—February, 1988
($000)

	Actual	Budget*	Actual Better/(Worse) Than Budget
Sales	$781.0	$830.0	$ (49.0)
Cost of sales			
Std. Variable cost of sales..........................	509.0	509.0	—
Material variance	15.0		(15.0)
Labor variances..	9.5		(9.5)
Variable overhead variance	18.5		(18.5)
Total cost of sales	$552.0	$509.0	$ (43.0)
Contribution..	$229.0	$321.0	$ (92.0)
Fixed overhead	80.0	75.0	(5.0)
Gross profit	$149.0	$246.0	$ (97.0)
Selling expense...	57.0	50.0	(7.0)
Administrative expense...................................	32.0	25.0	(8.0)
Net profit at actual volume and mix	$ 59.0	$171.0	(112.0)
Mix variance...			14.3
Volume variance			76.7
Net variance...			$ (21.0)

Question 2—Variance Analysis with Full Cost Systems

Revenue Variances
Price variance = $(49) unfavorable

Mix

Product	Actual Volume at Budget Mix	Actual Volume	Difference	Unit Contribution	Mix Variance
A	133.3	120	(13.3)	$ (.05)	$ .7
B	133.3	130	(3.3)	.65	(2.2)
C	133.3	150	16.7	.95	15.8
Total	400	400			$ 14.3

Volume

Product	Actual Volume at Budget Mix	Budgeted Volume	Difference	Unit Contribution	Volume Variance
A	133.3	100	33.3	$ (.05)	$ (1.6)
B	133.3	100	33.3	.65	21.7
C	133.3	100	33.3	.95	31.6
Total	400	300	100		$ 51.7

---

* Budget at standard prices and costs but actual sales volume and mix.

Manufacturing Cost Variances

Standard Costs	Units Produced	Manufacturing Costs			
		Material	Labor	Overhead	Total
A	150	$ 75.0	$15.0	$ 67.5	$157.5
B	130	91.0	19.5	65.0	175.5
C	120	180.0	12.0	54.0	246.0
Total		$346.0	$46.5	$186.5	$579.0
Actual costs		361.0	56.0	185.0	602.0
Variance		$ (15.0)	$ (9.5)	$ 1.5	$(23.0)

Overhead Variances

Actual overhead cost	= 185.0
Absorbed overhead	= 186.5
Budgeted overhead	$= 75 + [(150 \times .20) + (130 \times .25) + (120 \times .20)]$
	$= 75.0 + 30.0 + 32.5 + 24.0 = 161.5$
Spending variance	$= 161.5 - 185.0 = (23.5)$ unfavorable
Volume variance	$= 186.5 - 161.5 = 25.0$ favorable
Net variance	= 1.5

Standard Cost of Sales

Product	Volume Sales	Standard Cost/Unit	Total Standard Cost of Sales
A	120	$1.05	$126.0
B	130	1.35	175.5
C	150	2.05	307.5
Total	400		$609.0

TEMPLE DIVISION

Performance Report—February, 1988
($000)

Actual profit	$ 59
Budget	80
Variance	$ (21)

Temple Division (continued)

Analysis of Variances

Revenue variances

Price	....	$ (49.0)	
Mix	....	14.3	
Volume	....	51.7	$ 17

Manufacturing cost

Material	....	$ (15.0)	
Labor	....	(9.5)	
Overhead—spending	....	(23.5)	
Overhead—volume	....	25.0	(23)

Other costs

Selling expense	....	$ (7.0)	
Administrative expense	....	(8.0)	(15)
Total variances	....		$ (21)

TEMPLE DIVISION

Performance Report—February, 1988
($000)

	Actual	Budget*	Actual Better/ (Worse) Than Budget
Sales	$781.0	$830.0	$ (49.0)
Cost of sales			
Std. manufacturing cost	609.0	609.0	—
Material variance	15.0		(15.0)
Labor variances.........................	9.5		(9.5)
Overhead variance			
Spending	23.5		(23.5)
Volume..................................	(25.0)		25.5
Total cost of sales	$632.0	$609.0	$ (23.0)
Gross profit	$149.0	$221.0	$ (72.0)
Selling expense	57.0	50.0	(7.0)
Administrative expense	33.0	25.0	(8.0)
Net profit..............................	$ 59.0	$146.0	$ (87.0)
Mix variance			14.3
Volume variance........................			51.7
Net variance			$ (21.0)

---

* Budgeted cost and prices at actual sales mix and volume.

Question 3—Variance Due to Market Penetration and Industry Volume

Calculation of Actual Market Penetration

	Product A	Product B	Product C
Industry volume—Feb.	600	650	1,500
Actual sales volume	120	130	150
Market penetration—actual..........................	20%	20%	10%
Market penetration—budget	12%	20%	6%

Market Penetration Variance

	Product A	Product B	Product C	Total
(1) Actual sales.................................	120	130	150	400
(2) Budget penetration at industry volume	72	130	90	292
(3) Difference (1) – (2).................................	48	—	60	108
(4) Unit contribution.....................................	$ .20	$ .90	$1.20	
(5) Variance due to market penetration...........	$ 9.6	—	$72.0	$81.6

Industry Volume Variance

	Product A	Product B	Product C	Total
(1) Industry volume—Feb..............................	600	650	1,500	2,750
(2) Budgeted industry volume........................	833	500	1,667	3,000
(3) Difference	(233)	150	(167)	(250)
(4) Budgeted market penetration....................	12%	20%	6%	
(5) (3) × (4)	(28.0)	30.0	(10.0)	
(6) Contribution—unit	$ .20	$ .90	$1.20	
—total	(5.6)	27.0	(12.0)	9.4
Net variance				$91.0

Part B

March, 1988
(000)

Question 1—Variance Analysis Assuming Direct Costing

	Price			
	Product A	Product B	Product C	Price Variance
Actual volume	90	70	80	
Actual prices	$ 1.10	$ 2.10	$ 3.15	
Budget prices	1.00	2.00	3.00	
Variance: Per unit	$ .10	$ .10	$ .15	
Price Total	$9	$7	$12	$28

Mix

Product	Actual Volume at Budget Mix	Actual Sales	Difference	Unit Contribution	Mix Variance
A	80	90	10	$ .20	$2
B	80	70	(10)	.90	(9)
C	80	80	—	1.20	—
Total	240	240			$(7)

Volume

Product	Actual Volume at Budget Mix	Budget Volume	Difference	Unit Contribution	Volume Variance
A	80	100	(20)	$ .20	$ (4)
B	80	100	(20)	.90	(18)
C	80	100	(20)	1.20	(24)
Total	240	300	60		$(46)

Variable Cost Variances

	Units Produced	Material	Labor	Variable Overhead	Total
Standard costs					
Product A	90	$ 45	$ 9	$18	$ 72
Product B	80	56	12	20	88
Product C	100	150	10	20	180
Total	270	$251	$31	$58	$340
Actual cost		245	26	54	325
Variance		$ 6	$ 5	$ 4	$ 15

TEMPLE DIVISION

Performance Report—March, 1988

Actual profit	$ 85
Budgeted profit	80
Variance	$ 5

Analysis of Variances

Revenue variances
Price	$ 28	
Mix	(7)	
Volume	(46)	$ (25)
Variable cost variance		
Material	$ 6	
Labor	5	
Overhead	4	15
Fixed cost variances		
Manufacturing overhead expense	$ 5	
Selling expense	5	
Administrative expense	5	15
Net variances		$ 5

TEMPLE DIVISION
Performance Report—March, 1988

	Actual	Budget*	Actual Better/ (Worse) Than Budget
Sales	$498	$470	$ 28
Std. variable cost of sales	293	293	
Material variance	(6)		6
Labor variances	(5)		5
Variable overhead variance	(4)		4
Total cost of sales	278	293	15
Contribution	$220	$177	$ 43
Fixed manufacturing cost	70	75	5
Gross profit	$150	$102	$ 48
Selling expense	45	50	5
Administrative expense	20	25	5
Net profit	$ 85	$ 27	58
Mix variance			(7)
Volume variance			(46)
Net variance			$ 15

---

* Budget at standard prices and costs but actual sales volume and mix.

Question 2—Variance Analysis with Full Cost Systems

Revenue Variances
Price variance = $28 favorable

Mix

Product	Actual Volume at Budget Mix	Actual Volume	Difference	Unit Contribution	Mix Variance
A	80	90	10	$ (.05)	$ (.5)
B	80	70	(10)	.65	(6.5)
C	80	80	—	.95	
Total	240	240			$(7.0)

Volume

Product	Actual Volume at Budgeted Mix	Budget Volume	Difference	Unit Contribution	Volume Variance
A	80	100	(20)	$ (.05)	$ 1
B	80	100	(20)	.65	(13)
C	80	100	(20)	.95	(19)
Total	240	300			$(31)

Manufacturing Cost Variances

Standard Costs	Units Produced	Material	Labor	Overhead	Total
Product A	90	$ 45.0	$ 9.0	$ 40.5	$ 94.5
Product B	80	56.0	12.0	40.5	108.0
Product C	100	150.0	10.0	45.0	205.0
Total	270	$251.0	$31.0	$125.5	$407.5
Actual costs		245.0	26.0	124.0	395.0
Variance		$ 6.0	$ 5.0	$ 1.5	$ 12.5

Manufacturing Costs (spanning Material, Labor, Overhead, Total columns)

Overhead Variances

Actual overhead cost	= $124.0
Absorbed overhead cost	= $125.5
Budgeted overhead cost	= 75 + [(90 × .20) + (80 × .25) + (100 × .20)]
	= 75 + 18 + 20 + 20 = 133
Spending variance	= 133 − 124 = 9 favorable
Volume variance	= 125.5 − 133 = (7.5) unfavorable
Net overhead variance	= 1.5 favorable

Standard Cost of Sales

Product	Volume Sales	Standard Cost/Unit	Total Standard Cost of Sales
A	90	$1.05	$ 94.5
B	70	1.35	94.5
C	70	2.05	164.0
Total	240		$353.0

TEMPLE DIVISION

Performance Report—March, 1988
($000)

Actual profit	$ 92.5
Budget	80.0
Variance...	$ 12.5

Analysis of Variances

Revenue Variances

Price	$ 28.0	
Volume	(7.0)	
Mix..	(31.0)	$ (10.0)

Manufacturing Cost

Material..	$ 6.0	
Labor...	5.0	
Overhead—spending	9.0	
Overhead—volume...	(7.5)	12.5

Other Costs

Selling expense	$ 5	
Administrative expense	5	10.0
Net volume..		$ 12.5

TEMPLE DIVISION

Performance Report—March, 1988
($000)

	Actual	Budget*	Actual Better/ (Worse) Than Budget
Sales	$498.0	$470.0	$ 28.0
Standard cost of sales	353.0	353.0	—
Material variance	(6.0)		6.0
Labor variances	(5.0)		5.0
Overhead variance			
Spending	(9.0)		9.0
Volume	7.5		(7.5)
Total cost of sales	$340.5	$353.0	$ 12.5
Gross profit	$157.5	$117.0	$ 40.5
Selling expense	45.0	50.0	5.0
Administrative expense	20.0	25.0	5.0
Net profit	$ 92.5**	$ 42.0	$ 50.5
Mix variance			(7.0)
Volume variance			(31.0)
Net variance			$ 12.5

Question 3—Variance Due to Market Penetration and Industry Volume

Calculation of Actual Market Penetration

	Product A	Product B	Product C
Industry volume—March	500	600	1,000
Actual sales volume	90	70	80
Market penetration—actual	18%	11.7%	8%
Market penetration—budget	12%	20%	6%

Market Penetration Variance

	Product A	Product B	Product C	Total
(1) Actual sales	90	70	80	240
(2) Budget penetration at industry volume	60	120	60	240
(3) Difference (1) – (2)	30	(50)	20	—
(4) Unit contribution	$ .20	$ .90	$1.20	
(5) Market penetration	6	(45)	24	$(15)

---

* Budgeted cost at standard prices and costs but actual volume and mix.

** Note that the profit using standard full cost is $7,500 higher than the profit using standard direct cost.

· This is because the production volume is greater than the sales volume by 30,000 units. This means that the inventory has been increased by this number of units and that fixed costs of $7,500 (30,000 × .25) were capitalized in inventory.

Industry Volume Variance

	Product A	Product B	Product C	Total
(1) Industry volume—March	500	600	1,000	
(2) Budgeted industry volume	833	500	1,667	
(3) Difference	(333)	100	(667)	
(4) Budgeted market penetration	12%	20%	6%	
(5) (3) × (4)	(40)	20	(40)	
(6) Contribution—unit	$ .20	$ .90	$1.20	
—total	(8)	18	(48)	$(38)

Revenue Variances

	Price			Actual	
Product	Standard	Actual	Variance	Volume	Total
E	$.15	$.13	(.02)	1,000	(20)
F	.20	.22	.02	1,000	(20)
G	.25	.22	(.03)	4,000	(120)
H	.30	.31	.01	3,000	30
					$(90)

Analysis of Variances, January, 1988

	Favorable/ (Unfavorable)
Actual profit/(Loss)	$ (70)
Budgeted Profit	210
Variance	$(280)

Analysis of Variances

Revenue Variances

Price		(90)
Volume		(88)
Mix		38
Net Revenue Variances		(140)
Cost Variances		
Material	10	
Labor	(20)	
Variable Overhead	(20)	
Selling Expense	(40)	
Administration	50	
Research and Development	10	
Net Cost Variances		(10)
Overhead Volume Variance		(130)
Total Variance		$(280)

Solartronics, Inc. (B)

Substantive Issues Raised

John Holden, president and general manager of Solartronics, Inc., was concerned about the fact that his firm has just reported a loss on its internal books for the month of January. While he knew that sales had been down and that production had been scaled back somewhat to help reduce the level of inventory, he was still surprised to find that the firm's profit was some $38,400 below that of an "average" month for the budget year.

Pedagogical Objectives

This case is quite similar to the Cotter Company, Inc. case which was included in the first edition of this book. As such, it allows the student to analyze such things as the existence of multiple "break-even" models, the use of profit models, and some of the many implications of absorption costing.

It can also be used to allow the students to develop and/or strengthen their understanding of the meaning or significance of such things as a volume variance. Students who master this case should carry away a much clearer idea of what the volume variance represents. In particular, they should understand how it differs from other variances, particularly those caused by spending.

The case discussion should prove to be particularly useful as a device for exploring some of the implications and limitations of employing a "full cost" standard costing system. Other concepts, including the idea of their being a "contribution margin" at both the production and sales level in a full cost system and some of the other implications of fixed and variable expenses, are easily introduced and reinforced.

Opportunities for Student Analysis

This case will prove to be much more difficult than expected for most students. It is short, contains a relatively limited amount of financial data, and "looks" easy. It. however, is not easy to solve. A thorough, comprehensive analysis requires that the student have both a good grasp of basic cost accounting and a good deal of both patience and common sense. In fact, and as noted later in this teaching note, the instructor may wish to provide the class with a set of highly structured assignment questions.

Author: M. Edgar Barrette

One way to initiate the analysis of this case is to create a simple economic model of the company:

	Dollars in an "Average" Month	Per "Equivalent Unit"	Per Sales Dollar
Sales	$250,000	$600	$ 1.00
Less Variable Costs:			
Direct Labor	$ 35,000	$ 84	$ 0.14
Direct Materials	65,000	156	0.26
Variable Factory Overhead	30,000	72	0.12
Sales Commissions	25,000	60	0.10
Total	$155,000	$372	$ 0.62
Contribution (to fixed cost & profit)	$ 95,000	$228	$ 0.38
Less Fixed Costs:			
Fixed Factory Overhead	$ 35,000	$ 84	$ 0.14
Selling Expenses	10,000	24	0.04
General Corporate Overhead	20,000	48	0.08
Total	$ 65,000	$156	$ 0.26
Expected Monthly Profit	$ 30,000	$ 72	$ 0.12

Under the economic model just derived, the firm can be "seen" to earn a budgeted or standard profit of 12 cents per sales dollar, or $72 per equivalent unit. Unfortunately, however, the design of a "full cost" accounting model is such that the *reported results* will not be generated in quite such a straightforward manner. This is due to the fact that the firm can be said to earn a "profit"—at least under the terms of a conventional standard full cost absorption system—in two ways. First, it will report a "profit" by producing goods and selling them to inventory. Second, it will also report a "profit" by selling goods (from inventory) to the customer. Using one sales dollar as our standard for comparison, the following "profit margins" can be derived:

Production: Inventory is carried at 66% (66¢) per sales dollar, but only costs 52% (52¢) to produce. Thus, each unit *produced* will yield a 14% (14¢) contribution to overhead and profit.

Sales: One dollar is received (on average) for each 66 cents worth of inventory (at standard full cost). The sales commission (10¢) reduces the contribution to 24% (24¢).

The Effect of Decreased Sales. With the data just derived, attention might be turned back toward an analysis of what happened in January 1984. For example, one question that might be addressed is the one of how much an increase of $85,000 in the monthly sales (up to the "average" monthly level of $250,000) taken by itself would affect the bottom line. Answers ranging from $10,200 (.12 × 85,000) to $40,800 (.48 × 85,000) are likely. The point can then be made again (or prompted) that each dollar of sales, *taken by itself*, generates 24¢ in additional "bottom line" (before tax) profit. Thus, the extra $85,000 in sales would have generated $20,400 in additional profit.

The Effect of Decreased Production. At this point, the missing $38,400 has been reduced to $18,000. We have not, however, looked at the issue of how much the production level was cut back from normal. As noted in the case, there was a negative volume variance of $17,500 for the month of January. This piece of data, when combined with the monthly amount of budgeted fixed overhead of $35,000 (derived in the "economic model"), allows one to determine the actual production volume (*as measured in equivalent sales dollars*).

Absorbed Overhead/Budgeted Overhead = Actual Production/Budgeted Production

or

$$\$17,500/\$35,000 = x/\$250,000$$

Therefore, $x = \underline{\$125,000}$

At this point, we have enough data to fully explain $37,900 of the $38,400 profit shortfall. A format such as the one shown below might be used to illustrate progress to date.

Table TN-1

	Volume (Measured in Sales Dollar Equivalents)		Contribution		Variance
	Budgeted	Actual	Budgeted	Actual	
Sales	$250,000	$165,000	$60,000 [1]	$39,600 [2]	20,400 U
Production	$250,000	$125,000	$35,000 [3] $95,000	$17,500 [4] $57,100	17,500 U 37,900

Notes:

[1]$250,000 at 24%.	Direct Labor Variance	3,500 U[5]
	Direct Material Variance	(500)F[5]
[2]$165,000 at 24%.	Variable Factory Overhead Variance	1,500 U[5]
	Fixed Factory Overhead Spending Variance	(2,000)F[5]
[3]$250,000 at 14%.	Reduction in General Corporate	
	Overhead	(2,000)F[6]
[4]$250,000 at 14%.		$38,400

[5]Taken from the body of the case.

[6]This is derived by subtracting the $18,000 shown in Case Exhibit 1 from the $20,000 shown in our "economic model."

Some General Conclusions. The analysis to date, while not exhaustive, would allow one to draw some general conclusions. For example, the biggest single issue has to do with what caused the dip in sales. If the downturn is purely seasonal, then the only area that would seem to warrant management attention is the remainder of the operating variances. In fact, one could even argue that the loss for the month is overstated as the production level was less than the sales level—resulting in some $5,600 (40,000 × .14) of "lost contribution" at the production level. On the other hand, if the drop in sales is caused (at least in part) by other than seasonal factors, then there is real cause for alarm.

The operating variances, which are both alluded to above and shown in Table TN-1, deserve at least some attention from management. For example, one would want to ascertain the underlying causes for both the unfavorable variance in direct labor and the unfavorable variance in variable factory overhead. Quite possibly, they are both caused in large part by the very dramatic (50%) cutback in production relative to a "normal" month. It would also be helpful to know what caused the two large favorable variances (fixed factory overhead-spending and general corporate overhead).

Other Possible Issues. There are several other questions that might be addressed in a full-blown analysis of this case. The more obvious (at least to the author) of these are listed below:

- How much did the finished goods inventory change in January?

- What were the actual factory overhead costs in January?

- What is the monthly break-even volume for Solartronics, Inc.?

Finished Goods Inventory. The firm sold $165,000 worth of product (measured in terms of the final sales value) in January. It only produced at the sales level, however, of $125,000. Thus, the final sales value of the *drop* in inventory was $40,000. We have already concluded that the inventory is carried at an average of 66% of the final sales dollar. Therefore, the decrease in inventory valuation terms was $26,400 (.66 × 40,000).

Actual Factory Overhead Costs. As derived earlier, the budgeted monthly factory overhead is $35,000 plus 12¢ per sales dollar equivalent of the production level attained. On a production level of $125,000 (sales dollar equivalent), the firm's flexible budget would have allowed an expenditure of $50,000 ($35,000 + .12 × 125,000). The two factory overhead variances not related to volume (variable factory overhead and fixed factory overhead-spending) net to a favorable variance of $500. Thus, the total expenditure must have been $49,500. This can be further disaggregated into a $33,000 expenditure for fixed factory overhead and a $16,500 expenditure for variable factory overhead.

Monthly Break-even Volume. In the Cotter Company case, Professor John Shank suggested that an interesting extra twist to the class discussion would involve asking the students to compute (and interpret) the firm's break-even volume as traditionally computed. Such an approach can be used in this case as well. The results of such an extended analysis follow:

(a) Compute the traditional break-even volume

Fixed Costs divided by Contribution equals Break-even Volume

or

$65,000 ÷ .38 = $171,053

(b) Using the earlier data in respect to the "contribution" earned at both the production and sales levels, it is now possible to demonstrate how it is possible to report a loss, a zero profit, and a positive profit—all at the alleged break-even volume.

Table TN-2

Various Profits at the Same Break-even Volume

	Situation One		Situation Two		Situation Three	
	Absolute	Contrib.	Absolute	Contrib.	Absolute	Contrib
Sales (24% Contrib.)	$171,053	$41,053	$171,053	$41,053	$171,053	$41,053
Production (14% Contrib.)	150,000	21,000	171,053	23,947	200,000	28,000
		62,053		65,000		69,053
Less: Fixed Costs		65,000		65,000		65,000
Profit Reported		($2,947)		– 0 –		$ 4,053

Several interesting points can be made as a result of deriving an example such as that shown in Table TN-2. The most obvious, perhaps, is that the traditional concept of a break-even volume presupposes that the sales and the production function are operating at the same unit volume figures. In any one month, this is most unlikely for the average firm.

The second point is that a firm employing a standard, full absorption costing system can induce an increase in reported profit simply by increasing its level of production. Thus, the example is a nice illustration of both "selling to" and "buying from" inventory. Finally, one can use the example that there exists a different cost accounting system (direct or variable costing) wherein the level of reported profit is tied only to sales and not to a combination of production and sales.

Suggestions for Classroom Use

It is a rare class that will develop the insights suggested in the above section of this note without a good deal of direction from the instructor. Thus, the instructor must make an initial decision as to whether the class discussion is to be highly structured or reasonably unstructured. The assignment questions shown at the end of the case presuppose the latter approach. Under this approach, the class discussion might be initiated by merely asking for a volunteer ("military" or otherwise) to deal with the first question at the end of the case. This may well lead to one or more fairly mechanical comparisons of planned versus actual amounts for the various categories of the firm's summarized monthly income statement. If it does, the instructor will need to be prepared to steer the discussion somewhat by introducing either selected data or pointed questions at various junctures during the class hour. The previous section of this teaching note contains a number of issues or aspects that might be employed in such a manner.

The alternative way of approaching the class discussion process involves the use of a set of highly structured assignment questions. These questions, which are shown in the next section of this teaching note, are designed to "force" the student to direct attention to many of the discussion issues outlined earlier.

Suggested Assignment Questions

As noted in the preceding section, the instructor has at least two basic choices as to the assignment questions provided to the students. Those instructors desiring to employ a relatively unstructured format should probably simply use the questions included with the case. Those instructors wishing to employ a relatively more structured format might wish to use the assignment questions listed below instead.

1. How much of the $38,400 difference between the January 1984 profit and the average monthly budgeted profit is attributable to decreased sales?

2. What was the production level obtained by Solartronics, Inc. in January?

3. How much did the firm's finished goods inventory change in January?

4. What was the total of actual factory overhead costs in January?

5. What is the monthly break-even volume for Solartronics, Inc.?

6. What are the primary causes for the decreased level of profit relative to an average month? Please identify and comment on each of at least three *major* categories of causes.

M. Edgar Barrett, with acknowledgements to W. J. Bruns, Jr., J. K. Shank, and R. F. Vancil

Galvor Company

Prologue

This is a classic case on the use of tight financial control and the attendant behavioral effects.

My preference is to break the disguise of the case *before* class. I say something like this in the homework assignment: "This case is based on ITT under Harold Geneen who was the CEO from 1959 to 1976. The system as portrayed is easy to dislike. Be sure you understand what the system is intended to achieve before you begin to criticize it." I also assign the following additional reading:

"The Case for Managing By the Numbers," *Fortune*, October 1, 1984, pp. 73–81.

The following two teaching commentaries on Galvor Company case by Richard Vancil and John Dearden are self-explanatory.

VG

Teaching Note

Substantive Issues Raised

Universal Electric, a U.S. based conglomerate, has acquired a small company in France, and has imposed a new planning and control system on it. Whereas previously the subsidiary had been managed by one owner-manager, the new system uses elaborate and extensive planning and reporting forms and processes.

Pedagogical Objectives[1]

Galvor is more than "just" another case on strategic planning systems; in particular, the exchange of TELEXs provides us with a richer set of behavioral data than is available in most cases. Thus, I use the case to attempt to achieve two pedagogical objectives: (1) To wind up the section on situational design, with an opportunity to review each of the critical design parameters, and (2) To stretch the students' thinking beyond the issues of planning systems design so that they will attempt to relate their conclusions about such issues to other elements of the management systems and procedures employed by a company.

Assignment Questions and Suggestions for Classroom Use

That's a lot to attempt in just one class, but a great deal can be covered in a short period of time if a structured set of assignment questions are used. Alternatively, the case is so rich and flexible that it can be taught in a great many different ways. A simple assignment, such as "what do you

---

[1] We wish to express our gratitude to Richard F. Vancil for permission to include this teaching note, which was prepared by him, in this *Instructor's Manual.*

think of Galvor's planning system?" and a non-directive discussion leader can produce an exciting 80 minutes in the classroom. This approach works particularly well when the class consists of mature executives from a variety of companies who each have their own experiences to bring to the problem. For M.B.A. students, the following more detailed set of assignment questions also works very well:

This is a case on the situational design of strategic planing systems, and we'll want to examine many of the specifics of the UE system. The case also permits us to appraise UE's system in the broader context of that company's entire set of management systems and its management processes. To the extent feasible, we'll attempt to discuss the following four questions in the sequence given below:

1. What is your general assessment of the effectiveness of the UE planning system as it is applied to Galvor?

2. Identify, in as much detail as possible, all of the new management systems and techniques that UE has required Galvor to establish.

3. What is your evaluation of the effectiveness of the working relationships between Hennessy and the UE executives in Geneva? What do you infer from the TELEXs about Hennessy's autonomy as a Managing Director?

4. What specific changes, if any, would you make in the UE planning? In its other management systems? If the management processes need improving, how would you change them?

The first and last questions above are obviously relevant to a discussion on strategic planning systems, but I devote only about one-third of the class time to those two questions, dividing the other two-thirds evenly between questions 2 and 3. The instructor must manage the class time quite carefully in order to cover all four questions and still leave five minutes at the end for a surprise (don't peek ahead) and some closing remarks.

Opportunities for Student Analysis

General Assessment of the System

Most students (either M.B.A.s or executives) come into the classroom with a quite negative reaction to the Galvor situation. Some of them are almost vehement in criticizing the massive requirements that UE has laid on poor little Galvor, and they're also quite sympathetic for the plight of Mr. Hennessy. I start the class by asking each student to give me one or two sentences reflecting their general assessment of the situation, and I try to get such reactions from six or eight students. From each one I lift out the most loaded words of criticism and catalog them on the blackboard.

It's important not to let this discussion run too long—and not only because we're going to end up short of time. If you go much beyond a half dozen students, then pretty soon a student is going to feel the need to leap to UE's defense and may start saying something positive. I'm not really looking for positive comments at this point, but if I get one sooner than expected, I'll go on to one more student who, hopefully, will be negative, and then close off the discussion as follows: Well, it looks like a clear consensus that there's a lot wrong with what Universal has done for (or to) Galvor. Let's move right on to question 2 and try to get very specific about what some of these requirements are.

Management Systems

As I move to the second assigned question, I point out that there is a distinction in my mind between question 2 and question 3. One way of talking about this difference is the difference between structure (the form and content) of the management systems used by a company and the *process* by which the managers in a company use those systems to improve the ways that they work together. A planning system, for example, has a formal structure consisting of many of the design features that we have discussed in earlier cases, but the purpose of the system is to improve the planning process in the company, thus permitting the managers collectively to arrive at a better set of strategic decisions. We'll want to discuss both structure and process in Galvor, but let's discuss the management systems first. What systematic requirements has UE imposed on Galvor?

With a little prodding, it only takes a few minutes to get a list similar to that shown in the middle column of Exhibit TN-1. The topic headings are probably not necessary, but it is useful to group the items into categories. I then put a heading on that column of systems, labeling it Systems Under Hennessy, and then put the heading on the next column (Systems Under La Tour) and ask a student to fill in the column in parallel fashion.

The stage is now set for an interesting, if brief, discussion. Assuming that Galvor were an independent company, which set of management systems would you recommend? As a consultant, what would you advise Mr. Hennessy? That question can be sharper even more with the following: Assuming that 42 people are required in Accounting Department to operate all the systems that Hennessy now has, how many people do you think should be cut from the accounting staff, and which systems would be eliminated? Mr. La Tour managed quite well with less than 20 people in his Accounting Department; would you like to return to the good old days?

Most students can't bear to part with any of the goodies UE has laid on, and the implications begin to dawn on them of what it means to be trained to be a professional manager. The good old days are gone.

A useful, more general question that makes sure that they all see the point is to ask: Why do management systems differ between two companies in the same industry? They quickly see that the answer has something to do with the style (and training) of the manager, his aspirations for the company, the strategy he's pursuing, and, of course, the size of the business. Hennessy's business is somewhat larger than La Tour's was, and plans to make it a great deal larger so that he will eventually need more sophisticated management tools.

At about this point, it is useful to switch back to the opening comments and ask whether anyone is still critical of Galvor's systems, particularly if we now recognize the fact that it is a subsidiary of Universal Electric. The discussion immediately returns to the issue of the quantity of detailed reports which Galvor submits to Geneva, and the way those reports are used, as evidenced by the exchange of TELEXs. At that point, I try again to get the students to recognize the difference between the *design* of management systems and the *use* that management makes of those systems. Most students are in favor of having most of the design elements shown in

Exhibit TN-1; their real concern is for the way some executives at Geneva are using the data made available by the systems.

UE's Management Process

The way to start this discussion is to first get the class to agree on what the organizational structure of UE looks like. The necessary information to construct an organization chart is imbedded in the case, but I have found that asking students to derive it is more time consuming than it's worth. Instead, I simply put up a chart like the one shown in Exhibit TN-2, saying that it represents my understanding of the organizational relationships in UE and then asking the class if this chart jibes with their interpretation of case facts. The ensuing brief discussion will establish three points: (1) Forrester in Geneva is Hennessy's "line" superior. Forrester's title sounds rather modest (in the United States he might be called a group vice president), but it is clear that the eight product line managers are the ones that summarize profit responsibility at the intermediate level between the operating units like Galvor and UE's European Headquarters. (2) There are several functional staff directors, and Poulet is one of those, in charge of manufacturing. (3) The European controller, Boudry, has a direct relationship with the controllers in the operating units. The line between Boudry and Barsac need not be drawn when the chart is put up, but at some point it's important to note that Galvor's monthly package of reports goes from Barsac to Boudry and that the narrative letter that is prepared is written by Barsac and read first by Boudry's assistants in Geneva.

Once the organization chart has been validated by the class, I then suggest we turn directly to the TELEXs. What's going on here between Hennessy and Poulet?

Now is the time for the instructor to stand back and let the students pour out their wrath. The contents of the TELEXs from Poulet (the French word for chicken?) may be described in rather graphic language by some students. I like to allow such comments to run on for a few minutes, and then I start needling with questions like: Who's really running Galvor, Hennessy or Poulet? What is it in the TELEXs that makes you think that Poulet is interfering with Hennessy's authority? What operating decisions have to be made to deal with the problem at hand? who is making those decisions? The key to the answer to that line of question is imbedded on the ninth line of the last TELEX, where Hennessy refers to "my decision." Sometimes a student will find that or, if pressed for time, I will point it out to them. When the chips are finally down, it's Hennessy who makes the operating decisions.

Discovering that makes it possible to raise the level of discussion by one notch. Even if Hennessy is the decision maker, the students are still disturbed by the exchange of TELEXs. Either or both of two lines of questioning may help the students to think more concretely about what disturbs them. One line of questions begins: What does "autonomy" mean in a hierarchical organization? Why and how is Hennessy's role different as a general manager in the UE system than it would be if he owned Galvor? Why is Poulet sending these TELEXs? What do you think that he's trying to accomplish? The other line of questioning also works fairly well: Why doesn't Hennessy quit? Why does he continue to participate in this charade that he is really the "managing director" of Galvor? Does Hennessy believe that he *is* managing director of Galvor? What do you think that Hennessy thinks that Poulet is trying to do in this exchange of TELEXs?

If the class is composed of experienced executives, they won't need these kind of leading questions, but less experienced students eventually come to about the same conclusion. Hennessy is a successful young executive in UE, on the rise and loving his work. He faces a tremendous challenge in "turning Galvor around," and he needs a lot of help. UE gives him a lot of help in two forms: a package of management systems and techniques (standard costs, etc.) and a diverse group of staff functional experts in Geneva who can provide specific technical assistance when needed. Hennessy stays with UE because he can sense that he is growing in his development into a professional general manager. The pressures that he must bear are a part of this development process, and he is aware of that. He is only getting TELEXs from Poulet because he, Hennessy, is not meeting the objectives that he laid down for himself a year earlier.

The picture painted just above may be viewed through rose-tinted glasses, but at least some students find that they can buy into that conclusion. The decision is a personal one. Once I think that the class understands the UE management process, it's fun to ask how many of you would be willing to go to work for UE in a job like Hennessy's? The show of hands makes the point that some would like it and some not. The executives who stay at UE must be those who like it, and the result is that the UE system works.

Moving to the next level of abstraction, I then ask the students to try to generalize about the critical elements of a management *process*. We're now on very squishy ground, but it's useful to ask the students to try to pinpoint the aspects of UE's procedures that produce the results that we see in Galvor. I can identify four items: (1) Setting objectives (Forrester's role vs. Hennessy's vs. UE's Headquarters in the United States), (2) Allocating resources (the decision made by UE Europe in September 1966 to cut Galvor's proposed capital expenditures by 34 percent). (3) Analysis of performance (the frequency and degree of detailed information which Galvor reports to Geneva on a monthly basis), and (4) The role of staff (the fact that specialists like Poulet are on the payroll in Geneva). UE is manipulating these four variables, and others, to affect Hennessy's behavior, and through him, the performance of Galvor.

What did UE bring to Galvor? More, surely, than a few people like Hennessy and Barsac. More simply than a package of management technology, all of which was imposed on Galvor and some of which it maybe didn't need. In addition, UE brought a sense of urgency for better management, forcing more rapid change in Galvor than would have occurred under a less aggressive owner. And UE also brought a sense of pressure for better management, forcing more rapid change in Galvor than would have occurred under a less aggressive owner. And UE also brought a sense of pressure for better performance by Galvor. There is a cost of urgency and a cost of pressure, but there are also benefits to be won. UE does have a unique management "style" (a synonym, really, for management process). Its managers have created a climate in which a manager like Hennessy gets a lot of help when he is in trouble, but UE's managers also have high morale because they think they are high performers. Hennessy believes that he has some autonomy, that Poulet's comments are those from a coach rather than from a critic, and it's Hennessy's perception that counts.

There are no data in the case to support the comments made just above. Occasionally, however, I may include comments such as these as a part of my closing summary for this case.

Planning Issues

Class time is now running out, but it's important to devote a few minutes to look at the way that UE has handled some of the planning design issues that we have been discussing in other cases.

By now, the students should have no trouble identifying these issues and appraising UE's approach. I will tick off some of them briefly:

1. **Goal-setting.** UE's process is clearly top down, with the initiative resting with the product-line managers in Geneva. This process may be a little rough on Galvor for its first two or three years as a part of UE, but UE's planning process is mature, and goals are negotiated between Geneva and the operating managers.

2. **Focus of Planning.** There is a lot of financial detail included in the business plan, but it also requires the general manager to identify the actions that he is going to take to achieve his plan. If you're lucky, some student will point out that UE's planning system is the antithesis of the concept of situational design. There are a massive number of forms to be filled out, and each operating unit like Galvor must follow the same set of forms. Even worse, all data to be submitted must be in dollars and in English. Viewed from the Geneva perspective, however, the first summary page of each unit's business plan is a marvelous management tool. In effect, that page is a financial model of a manufacturing company, making it easy for a product-line manager like Forrester to compare and contrast critical operating ratios for the plants that produce his product lines. I also like to point out that UE is an extremely diverse company, and that while it does have a planning guide that applies to all manufacturing companies, it has a separate guide for finance companies, for hotels, etc.

3. **Role of the Planner.** There is no mention in the case about a separate planning department at Geneva, but the issue about the role of the planner can easily be broadened to the role of staff. UE makes heavy use of staff, and the staffs are powerful in terms of their access to detailed information and their prerogative of dealing directly with operating units. This approach is inconsistent with our generalized model of strategic planning for diversified companies, but is certainly consistent with UE's management style.

4. **Linkage to Budgets.** UE has certainly solved this problem. Minor differences between the first year of the business plan and the subsequent operating budget are not permitted. If a major change is necessary, an entire new business plan must be resubmitted to Geneva.

In a broader sense, UE's planning system is not all that unconventional. As sketched out in Exhibit TN-3, the system does involve three cycles, and they are approximately equivalent to "business planning," "programming," and "budgeting" defined in the readings. While some students may be unhappy with UE's planning system taken by itself, my conclusion is that the system is completely consistent with the entire set of management systems that UE has developed. I would not attempt to change the structure of the system unless that change were a part of a much more sweeping set of changes in UE's systems and processes.

The final part of the fourth assigned question directs the students to the issue of how management processes change. There is really no good answer to this question, but it's an important one to think about. In UE, the only way that major change could occur would be if the company had new chief executive officer. As discussed below, the style of UE flows directly from the personality of its president. A new CEO might make many changes, including a reduction in the quantity of detailed financial information that flows up the hierarchy. Making that change would help to reduce the power of the technical staff groups, and that would lead to a whole series of other changes. Engineering the entire set of changes in systems and procedures is a complex process in itself.

Breaking the Disguise

I like to save the last five minutes or so of class to break the disguise of this case. In executive groups, it's common for one or more students to guess that UE is really ITT, and indeed it is. As of the date of the case, Harold Geneen had been president of ITT for about seven years and was well along on his development of a most effective management team. Starting in 1960, Geneen put together 12 successive years of increases in earnings per share, all the more impressive because for nearly 50 successive quarters ITT reported an increase in earnings over the same quarter of the preceding year. Earnings per share rose from 97 cents in 1960 to $4.17 in 1973, while sales revenues increased from $811 million in 1960 to over $10 billion in 1973.

Stories about ITT are legend, but I like to tell a couple of them as I'm winding up the Galvor case. ITT managers regard themselves as an elite core of professional executives, and ITT's policy is to pay 30 percent over the market for executives. Such men do not lack for ego. The senior V.P and comptroller of ITT came to lecture to my class on a couple occasions in the early 70s. He liked to be introduced as the highest paid financial executive in the world (and he was), and he also pointed out to the class that all of the financial people in ITT worldwide report up a chain of command directly to him—that amounts to more than 20,000 financial people.

Geneen's capacity for work was enormous. He put in very long hours and had a voracious appetite for financial detail. He crossed the Atlantic with great frequency, and the stories have it that he traveled with assistants, each of whom carried two bulging brief cases which Geneen devoured during the trip. It was his personal drive that energized the entire ITT management system that we see in Galvor.

My favorite story about Geneen is as follows: One day he was returning from Europe, and got aboard the airplane with no brief cases. Sitting down next to a fellow passenger in the first-class section, they struck up a conversation and chatted amiably all the way across the Atlantic. As the plane began to circle Kennedy airport, his companion said, "Well, this has been an extremely pleasant conversation, and I've enjoyed chatting with you. I'm rather embarrassed that we didn't introduce ourselves at the beginning." To this, Geneen replied, "Well my name is Harold Geneen." The companion replied (mispronouncing his name), "Well, Mr. Geneen, it's been a real pleasure meeting you." "No," Geneen replied, "the name Geneen—it's not a hard G as in God, it's a soft G as in Jesus."

Richard F. Vancil

Management Systems — Before and After

Topic	Under Hennessy	Under La Tour
Planning	Plan for the first, second and fifth years, including R&D and product planning	No formal planning
Budgeting	Tight, formal commitment, with a contingency plan	None
Cost Accounting	Standard product costs	No product costs?
	15 factory costs centers	One overhead rate
	9 perpetual inventory accounts	No formal inventory control
Analytical Tools	Market and sales forecasts	?
	EOQ for production scheduling	None
	Product profitability to eliminate low margin items	?
	Variance analysis of performance deviations	?
Reporting	Detailed monthly reports by departments and for Galvor Co.	Annual tax return
Size of Accounting Dept.	42 people	Less than 20 people

Exhibit TN-2
The Galvor Company

Rudimentary
(and partial) Organization Chart

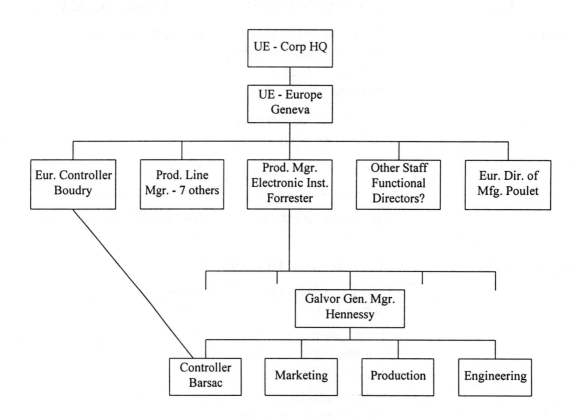

Teaching Note: Galvor Company

Reproduced below are the assignment questions and my teaching note for Galvor. The note indicates the questions that I ask and the order in which I ask them. After each question, I have written my answer, There are several reasons for preparing for class in this manner; first, I do not like to ask questions that I have not thought through myself. This makes sure that I have done so. Second, it is a guide in handling the case discussion. Third, it gives me some assurance that the questions are not too vague nor the answer too obvious for adequate discussion. Note that I do not try to lead the class to these answers, nor do I treat answers that are different from mine as incorrect. As in most of these discussions, the correct answer is the one consistent with the assumptions.

Question 1

What are the purposes of Universal Electric's accounting and financial control system? That is, what is this system supposed to accomplish for either Universal Electric or Galvor?

The following three criticisms have been made of Universal's financial control system as it applies to Galvor:

a. There is too much detail. The system requires too much management time. It is also too expensive for such a small company.

b. The system does not leave enough initiative to management. There is too much staff interference and too much control by headquarters.

c. The system encourages short-term action that may not be in the best long-run interests of the company.

Question 2

Review the reports that Galvor is required to prepare. In what ways would you modify Galvor's reporting requirements?

Question 3

What is Universal Electric trying to accomplish with their "tight" control system? What price do they pay for such a system" What are the alternatives? What would you do?

Question 4

What action, if any, should M. Boudry take?

Question 1 — Purposes of System

Q. What are the purposes of Galvor's accounting and financial control system?

That is, what is this system supposed to accomplish for either Universal or Galvor?

(a) It forces management to plan ahead.

(b) It requires operating units to set up good internal accounting and control systems.

(c) It forces management's attention to critical areas.

(d) It provides a basis for overall company planning.

(e) It provides a basis for evaluation operations management.

(f) It provides a basis for early warning. It allows headquarters to get into operations if they believe something is going wrong.

(g) It motivates the operating manager by requiring him to set tight short-term objectives and then, do his best to meet these objectives.

(h) It provides a basis for consolidating Galvor's financial statements into Universal's financial statements.

(i) It trains managers.

To summarize, then, the purposes of the accounting and control system that Universal is installing in Galvor has three principal functions:

(1) To enable Universal to *control* Galvor. This includes such activities as: (a) management action: *evaluation* and *motivation* of Galvor's management; (b) resource commitment expenditures; (c) corporate planning of *future activities*, and (d) *early warning* of problems and the taking of appropriate corrective action where required.

(2) To *train* Galvor's management to develop and use internal planning and control systems. This includes planning systems, financial accounting systems, cost accounting systems, inventory control systems, etc.

(3) To provide information to *headquarters* that are required by the *fiscal accounting and planning activities*. For example, tax reports, consolidated financial statements, headquarters planning, etc.

Criticisms of Systems

The assignment sheet listed the following three criticisms of Universal Electric's system:

(1) *Too much detail*; too much management time; too expensive.

(2) Not enough initiative left to operating management; *too much staff interference*; not enough freedom to plan and execute; oppressive management control. In short, too much control of the operating manager by headquarters.

(3) *Incentive towards short-term action* to meet goals that may be out-of-date or suboptimum at the date of action. Commitment to courses of action ahead of the lead time.

Let's look at each of these criticisms to decide on their validity and to consider changes or modifications to the system.

Question 2 — Too Much Detail

First, let us look at a list of reports submitted to Galvor on pages 485 and 486. Let us go over each of these items to see which ones can be eliminated in light of the objectives listed above.

Statement	Use
Accounting Statements	
Preliminary Net Income	Consolidation and control
Income Statement	Consolidation and control
Balance Sheet	Consolidation and control
Changes in Retained Earnings	Consolidation
Cash Flow	Consolidation and control
Employment Statistics	Management
Status of Orders Received Cancelled and Outstanding	Management
Intercompany Transactions	Consolidation
Transactions with Headquarters	Consolidation
Analysis of Inventories	Management
Analysis of Receivables	Management
Status of Capital Projects	Management and control
Budgets and Plans	Control
Controller's monthly financial review	Control

Conclusion

You really cannot eliminate any of the reports. Each is necessary for either accounting consolidation, local management, or control. (The controller's monthly report could be shorter, perhaps, and many would assert that it should be prepared by the manager.) This will always be true any time a large company acquires a small company, particularly if the acquired company is managed by its owner.

First, *a control system must be superimposed* on the company to replace the owner-manager's personal control and decision making. Decisions (such as capital investments) that could be made on the basis of calculations on the back of an envelope must now be formalized. Further plans must be reviewed and approved formally and so forth.

Second, the acquired company's accounting system must be made consistent with the acquiring company's. This usually involves considerably more sophistication than was previously necessary.

Third, new management techniques (for example, better cost accounting) are often required both to support the control system and to provide managers with better information than is often available in the acquired company.

Question 3 — Not Enough Management Initiatives

Let's look at question 3 next.

Q. First, what is Universal Electric trying to accomplish with this control system?

Universal Electric has what I call a *tight* control system. This means that budget commitments are firm goals that must be met if at all possible. If they cannot be met, detailed explanations of "why" are required. The rationale behind a tight system are:

1. Divisional management will accomplish more if it is given specific, short-term goals that it is expected to meet.

2. It allows central management (in this case the Geneva staff) to get into operations and take action where they believe conditions at the operating level could be improved. (In other words, an early warning system.)

3. It provides a basis for evaluating the divisional manager.

4. In Universal Electric's case there is also an element of corporate profit planning. Headquarters wants to know the amount of profits that are expected from the division in time to do something about corporate earnings per share if subsidiary profits fall below expectations.

Q. What price does Universal Electric pay for this "tight" system?

A. First, in management initiative and even in the managers they are able to hire and retain. Many managers can not and will not work under such a system. Second, it requires an extensive and expensive financial group at all levels of operation.

Q. What are the alternatives to the Galvor System?

A. The alternative is a "loose" system where the budget is more of a plan than a firm management commitment. One of the problems with a loose system is that it frequently is not an adequate early warning system. Also, it may not be a basis for evaluating management.

Conclusion

The choice of a "tight" or "loose" system is a matter of managerial choice. Both have their advantages and disadvantages. There appears to be a trend during the past few years towards a tight system.

Note that the paperwork would be much the same under either a tight or loose system. (Under a loose system, however, you would eliminate the TELEXs.)

Question 4 — Short-term Action

This is one of the toughest problems in "tight" management control systems. There is no really satisfactory answer to this problem. It is important, however, to be aware of its existence. Top management should review proposed actions of operating managers for correcting underbudget situations with this in mind. However, this would not help short-term actions taken by operating management to *avoid* an underbudget condition. The same is true of changing plans when it is clear that the original plan was suboptimum. Certainly Poulet's attitude would encourage operating management to freeze into a plan once it was approved.

J.D.

GALVOR:

DIVISIONAL PLANNING

AND CONTROL SYSTEMS

Vijay Govindarajan

The Amos Tuck School of Business Administration

Dartmouth College

Hanover, New Hampshire 03755

ITT Under Geneen

	Sales	Earnings
1958	$750 million	$50 million
1963	1.5 billion	
1968	3.0 billion	
1973	6.0 billion	
1978	12.0 billion	800 million

Double four times in 20 years!

Compound growth rate of 15%

for 20 years starting from

$750 million base in

"stable" business.

Galvor (R-3)

Rudimentary
(and partial) Organization Chart

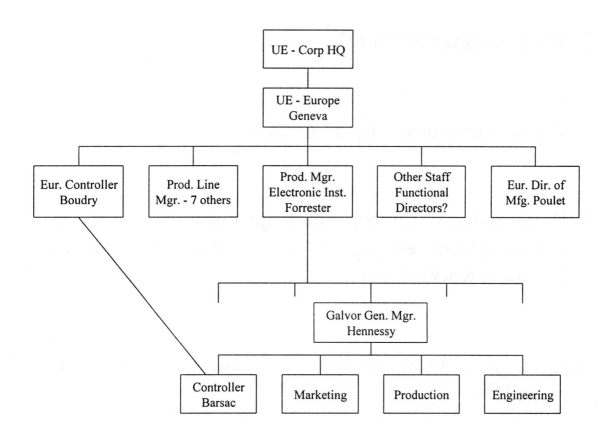

The Goal Setting Process

1. Why does it take 4 months to get agreement on five numbers: sales, earnings, assets, employees, and capital spending?

2. What is Forrester's role?

3. Where does Forrester get his cues?

4. How can the U.S. management get away with changing something Hennessy spent 4 months thinking about and 2 months working on?

5. Is the goal setting "top down" or "bottom up"? Does it matter?

Performance Evaluation and Control Phase

1. What is going on in the TELEXs between Hennessy and Poulet?

2. Who is really running Galvor—Hennessy or Poulet?

3. Even if Hennessy is making the final decisions, why all these TELEXs?

4. What does autonomy mean in a hierarchical organization?

5. Why and how Hennessy's role is different as a General Manager in the ITT system than it would be if he owned Galvor?

6. Why is Poulet sending these TELEXs? What is he trying to accomplish? What does Hennessy make of them?

7. How do you rate the control phase on a scale from "tight" to "loose"?

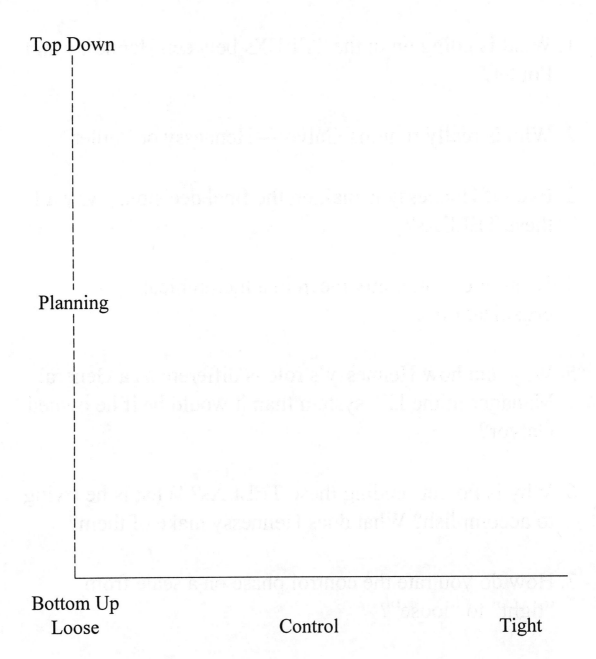

Top Down

Planning

Bottom Up
Loose   Control   Tight

The Galvor Company

Management Systems — Before and After

Topic	Under Hennessy	Under La Tour
Planning	Plan for the first, second and fifth years, including R&D and product planning	No formal planning
Budgeting	Tight, formal commitment, with a contingency plan	None
Cost Accounting	Standard product costs	No product costs?
	15 factory costs centers	One overhead rate
	9 perpetual inventory accounts	No formal inventory control
Analytical Tools	Market and sales forecasts	?
	EOQ for production scheduling	None
	Product profitability to eliminate low margin items	?
	Variance analysis of performance deviations	?
Reporting	Detailed monthly reports by departments and for Galvor Co.	Annual tax return
Size of Accounting Dept.	42 people	Less than 20 people

Issues:

1. Assuming Galvor was an independent company, which set of systems would you now cut out?

2. Mr. La Tour managed quite well with 20 accountants. Would you like to return to the good old days?

Which of the planning and control systems components would you give up? I think "none." Why?

1. Is ITT interested in Galvor for its present contributions? No! It must grow aggressively. How to infuse this sense of urgency?

2. If Galvor grows, they will more clearly need the full-blown system. Laying it on now and letting them grow into it is not necessarily worse than starting with one system and then changing it when they get bigger. (Issue: Do you design a system for the division's current needs or do you let the division grow into the system?)

3. Geneen can't afford to allow a personalized approach to planning and control in the divisions under his "tight rein" approach to management. (Issue: Do you tailor the system to the division's needs or to the chief executive's needs?)

Characteristics of a "Good" Acquisition Candidate for Geneen

- Good growth potential

- Can be acquired at a bargain price

- Seller doesn't demand cash

- A business where the "Geneen System" can be the lever to create the growth

The value added is the

management system.

CEO's Style

- Control systems are an extension of CEO's personality

- CEO's style affects the way control systems will be operated

- Need to tailor control systems to CEO's style

Tight Financial Control

Benefits:

- Prevents managers from being wasteful

- Motivates managers to take initiatives to meet the profit targets

Shortcomings:

- Encourages wrong short-term actions

- Discourages right long-term actions

- Encourages data manipulation

- Degree of tightness of financial controls depends upon the situation

- Every situation should have both financial and non-financial controls; the relative emphasis might be different from one situation to the next.

Concluding Thoughts

1. Do you design a control system for division's current needs or do you let the division grow into the system?

2. Do you tailor a system to division's needs or CEO's needs?

3. Control systems are an extension of CEO's personality.

   Geneen: Sense of pressure for better management
            Sense of urgency for better performance

4. Not every MBA can or would like to work for every company.

Case 10-4

Captain Jamie Tolten

I. Synopsis of Case

The Company B commander, CPT Jamie Tolten, of a Basic Combat Training unit (B-3-3), has recently installed a Company Performance Control System. The system uses quantified measures to assess the performance of individual recruits and their respective platoons on four dimensions of performance. While the system appeared to be working fairly well, a recent incident involving "cheating" on the rifle range (scores on the rifle range were used in the performance-measurement system) suggests that the system may be inducing dysfunctional behavior.

In addition, an inventory-control system developed by CPT Tolten appears to be working "too well" and has caused CPT Tolten to overspend his equipment budget. While CPT Tolten is not evaluated on adherence to budget, his immediate superior [and performance rater (evaluator)] is. CPT Tolten is responsible for his superior's only variance from budget.

The performance control system is described in the case, and the events leading up to the rifle-range and inventory problems are outlined. Additionally, the formal officer evaluation procedures are presented in enough detail for students to assess those evaluation and staffing procedures.

II. Purpose/Issues

My students tell me that this is one of the most enjoyable cases involving management control systems. I find it equally enjoyable to teach. A major reason for these feelings is that the case allows one to explore a variety of performance-evaluation issues.

First, it gives enough detail for the student to evaluate the "fit" of the performance control system with both the organization's and CPT Tolten's goals and objectives. Both the structure of the system (performance-measurement mechanics) and the behavior it induces are subject to student critique.

Second, it permits a rare opportunity to review a well-designed subjective performance-evaluation system (the officer-evaluation system). Unlike many subjective evaluation systems, this system does much to reduce rater bias in the overall assessment of performance.

Third, it permits an opportunity to explore the issue of internal competition. The system, as designed, works only because it puts platoons in competition with each other. In some organizational situations, this practice may not be healthy. The case permits the opportunity to explore the factors that are important when competitive approaches to control-system design are considered.

Last, it addresses some of those subtle implementation and application issues that are so important to the success of any management control system. In so doing, it allows students to identify constraints under which the system was designed.

Because it encompasses so many issues, I use this case relatively late in either a module or course on management control systems. I normally use it as an integrative case. With careful direction on the part of the instructor, the case can be used to explore those issues important to the *design* (i.e., goals and strategies, management style, culture, and organizational structure) of a management control system. At the same time, issues surrounding the *process* of management control systems (i.e., definition and understanding of purpose, consistency between system components, rewards valued, appropriate performance measures, etc.) can be addressed. It is also a useful case to demonstrate some implementation techniques, particularly, participative ones, that help not only in the design of the management control system, but also in its acceptance and use.

III. *Case Analysis*

The description of the officer-evaluation system presented in the case, along with case Exhibits 2 and 3 indicates that the performance-evaluation system used by the U.S. Army is very good. In fact, many large corporations could learn much from careful study of this system. While Exhibit TN-1 summarizes the strengths of this system, I will briefly expand on them here.

In essence, this system is an MBO system in which the objectives are rarely quantitative in nature. Although many diverse subgoals are found in a military organization, very few of these subgoals lend themselves to easy quantification. It is appropriate, therefore, that subjective measures of performance be used. Review of Part III of the OER Support Form shows that, in many cases, responsibilities, objectives, and contributions can be described in an explicit manner, which makes using an MBO system that much easier.

The objectives are defined jointly by the rater and the rated officer. The system prescribes that verbal and written feedback on performance be given to each rated officer by his or her rater on a frequent (one year or less) basis. Mutual agreement on objectives and frequent feedback are positive features of the system, in that they *force* the communication that is all too often neglected in formal performance-appraisal systems.

Unlike the private sector, the military has a distinct superior-subordinate hierarchy. Technically all captains, for example, are subordinate to all majors. Since there may be several hundred officers on a base the size of Ft. Dix, it becomes important to know the direct "chain of command" in order for an officer to know "who his/her boss is and who is his/her boss's boss." The published rating scheme serves this purpose. It lets officers know who will ultimately be responsible for their evaluation.

A number of system features help the rated officer ensure that a "fair" evaluation was performed. The first of these is the OER Support Form. Because the objectives and responsibilities (Parts III a and b) are defined in advance and the contributions (Part IIIC) completed at the end of the rating period and then *submitted along with the OER,* the rater is reminded of the agreed objectives and the activities of the rated officer during the rating period. In effect, this form "refreshes" the rater's memory.

Multiple raters are used, thus reducing the possibility of an unfair evaluation resulting from personality conflicts or other subjective factors. In addition, the use of histograms (see Part VII of the OER) permits senior raters' rating tendencies to be tracked over time (i.e., Are they easy or hard raters?), which, in fact, is done.

All officers are rated under the same system. Therefore, they should understand it from both sides (as a rater and as a rated officer). Since they are all rated under the same system they have no inducement to "play games" when rating an officer, because they would not want to be subject to the same game playing when they are the rated officer.

If an officer feels he or she has been given an unfair rating he/she may challenge the evaluation and, if successful, have it removed from his/her personnel file (OMPF). In addition, only in rare instances would one subpar evaluation have an effect on future appointments. [As an aside, the OMPF if also a strong feature of the system in that it focuses on long-term performance as the basis for critical appointments rather than (as in many companies) the most recent performance assessment.]

The system also has several features that permit the rater to give an honest assessment of the rated officer's performance. The performance of the rated officer is to be rated primarily *but not exclusively* on the achievement of the stated objectives, this feature permits the rater to include other things in the overall evaluation. This "escape hatch" is, of course, necessary, as dimensions other than achievement of stated objectives determine the effectiveness of an officer. For this reason, Part IV of the OER, also gives the rater latitude in performance assessment; while much of the report focuses on the achievement of specific objectives, this part is concerned with the congruency of the rated officer's activities with the mission of the Army and the qualities necessary for effective leadership.

The first level of critique of CPT Tolten's performance and inventory-control systems should be concerned with whether the systems are consistent with organizational (U.S. Army) goals. Assuming that the Army desires to keep equipment-replacement purchases to a minimum and identify and hold accountable those responsible for equipment losses, CPT Tolten's inventory-control system is goal congruent. Furthermore, if it is assumed that a soldier is "better" if he/she can shoot accurately, or has physical stamina, etc., then the performance control system is also goal congruent. In addition, these systems are consistent with Tolten's own personal goals: graduating well-trained, disciplined soldiers; maintaining high appearance and maintenance standards; and eliminating equipment losses and damage.

On a lower level of analysis, it is even easier to see just how well designed these systems are. First, three of the four performance measures are based on existing tests required of all trainees. Two of those three award trainees' numerical scores, which are used in the performance control system. CPT Tolten thus did not have to develop surrogate performance measures for two of the performance dimensions.

The system not only rewards good performance, but it penalizes poor performance. This is particularly true of the rifle and PT tests. In the former, points are subtracted for any soldier failing to qualify on the rifle range, and only the *passing* scores are included in the numerator of the PT ratio.

Since scores are converted to ratios and then summed and divided by four, none of the performance dimensions dominates the score.

The mechanics of the system are simple and easy to understand and, therefore, can be used effectively to direct the behavior of the DIs. In addition, because most of the scoring is done by individuals outside the Company, the system is relatively free from bias.

Awards are made to the platoons rather than to individuals; this platoon cohesion and cooperation is encouraged. If, for example, a trainee scores low on the first round of tests, it will be in the best interests of the Trainee's platoon leaders and members to help him/her become more proficient because of the way in which the scores are aggregated. While this aim was a stated purpose for developing the barracks-inspection ratio, it is also a subtle aspect of all the measures.

In addition to being well designed, the performance control system has been well implemented. Since implementation of any organizational change or system can have a great impact on the effectiveness of the system, it is worthwhile exploring some of the implementation and system-development issues. First, however, the management style or philosophy underlying the system needs to be defined and conditions for its use explained.

CPT Tolten explained to me that he based the system on a very simple philosophy: "an organization does best those things a 'boss' checks," and "people love to excel." Clearly, the system, as designed, is consistent with this philosophy. Whereas the efficiency of his inventory-control system is in large part a result of his responsibility-accounting system and periodic inventory counts, the success of the performance control system is based primarily on the competitive nature of the DIs and the platoons.

The use of a competitively based performance control system in the case begs the more general question: When are competitive approaches to management control systems appropriate? Clearly, there are many times when competitive approaches to management control can be used, but I feel that there are five key items to its successful implementation:

- The competitors must not compete in a "zero-sum" game.

  By this I mean that Division A's gain should not be achieved at the expense of Division B's loss. Zero-sum games can lead to uncooperative behavior on the part of the divisions as well as jealousy, cheating, and distrust—things that are not conducive to good organizational functioning.

- Organizational success should not depend on careful coordination or integration of competing divisions' activities.

While this item may be considered related to the first issue, it makes the subtle distinction that, even when the divisions do not compete in zero-sum games, cooperative behavior may suffer because information may not be shared or provided on a timely basis. This may occur when a division recognizes that one way to enhance its relative standing is to "help" its internal competitors perform at a suboptimal level. If withholding information can give a division this advantage, the managers may do so.

- A climate that fosters competition should exist.

The job tasks, the motivation of the personnel, the extent to which "effort" is translated into results, the support given by top management, the extent to which the "rewards" are valued by the affected personnel, etc.—all are important determinants of the success of a competitively based control system. For example, if the personnel affected have a culture that discourages "rate busting" and extra effort, a competitive approach to control is highly unlikely to work. Similarly, if the personnel believe that a disproportionate share of the fruits of their extra effort accrue to the firm rather than themselves or their group, or if they do not value the rewards offered, then competitive approaches will not work.

- "Rules" for playing the game should be well defined.

Competition implies that there is a "game" being played. For any game to be successful requires that the objective of the game be understood, that the way in which the winner is chosen also be understood, and that well-defined rules govern the play of the game. If the participants are allowed to make their own rules, the game may not achieve the desired results.

- Activities or behavior should be observable.

Rule enforcement requires that the enforcers be able to observe whether the players are playing within the rules. In an organizational setting, it also requires that the actions of the affected personnel be observable (although perhaps with some effort) to ensure that the actions are congruent with organizational objectives (and the purpose for establishing the game). If only results or outcomes of the activities are observable, an attitude of "the end justifies the means" is fostered and the game may break down into just that—a game with no concern for the true purpose of the competition.

Does Company B meet these criteria? For the most part, YES! Each platoon is essentially a stand-alone unit. Whereas intra-platoon cooperation and teamwork are required for it to be an effective military unit, inter-platoon cooperation is not. Likewise, when one platoon scores high on any of the measures, it does not do so at the other platoons' expense; all platoons are encouraged to excel on the performance dimensions. A competitive spirit already exists among the DIs, and this is translated by the DIs to the trainees. (CPT Tolten mentioned that DIs are constantly comparing/bragging about their platoons among themselves in the NCO club. Great pride is taken in having the top-rated platoon at graduation; this is an important determinant in a DI's relative "status" with the other DIs.) Because all the performance dimensions but the barracks inspection (conducted by CPT Tolten) are "scored" by individuals outside Company B, the measurement "rules" are well defined and easily enforced. There is little chance of manipulating the scores. In addition, even though a problem has arisen on the rifle range (discussed later in this note), if CPT Tolten suspected that any cheating is going on, he can observe each of the events and prevent or discover its occurrence if he so desires.

While the incorporation of DIs' competitive nature in the design of his performance control system was clearly the most obvious manner in which CPT Tolten relied on or worked within existing cultural and organizational norms to implement his system effectively, other mechanisms played an important part in the successful implementation of the system. The use of a quantitative system that was easily understood by the DIs made acceptance much easier. Since the DIs understood that it would be difficult for any of them to "fiddle with" the scores and since the scores were relatively free from rater bias (objective rather than subjective), the DIs could be easily "sold" on the system.

Participation of the DIs in the design of the barracks-inspection checklist was another clever use of implementation strategy: the one measure that had some element of subjectivity in it was the one in which the DIs had the most design input. In addition, by letting the DIs develop the checklist, Tolten was also working within the cultural norms of the organization. The barracks is the province of the DIs. Officers are only "tolerated" inside the barracks. Any attempts to manage the barracks on the officer's part is usually met with a "we'll take care of it" response by the DIs. Thus it was important that the checklist have significant input from DIs. (An interesting side note is that the checklist designed by the DIs turned out to be tougher and more thorough than CPT Tolten would have designed himself!)

Another issue related to the successful implementation of the control system is the elimination of the "eight-ball award." As mentioned in the case, this award was eliminated because of the demoralizing effect it had on the platoon. (CPT Tolten mentioned that, in one instance a DI actually cried when his platoon received the "award.") Tolten realized that there was little benefit and possibly great cost in terms of platoon cohesion and teamwork in continuing the practice—particularly when it is considered that the platoons in Company B were out-performing almost all of the other platoons involved in BCT.

The two immediate problems faced by CPT Tolten offer some insights into his managerial abilities and how even the best control systems can be circumvented at times. The incident on the rifle range indicates the amount of effort individuals will give to circumventing a management control system. Unless Tolten acts swiftly and appropriately, this incident will open the door for the other DIs to try to manipulate scores to their advantage. If they do so, neither CPT Tolten's nor the Army's goals of graduating well-trained soldiers will be met. CPT Tolten does not want to set a precedent for "game playing." Instead, he is as much concerned with the "process" of training soldiers as he is with the results of the training process (scores on the tests) . He could let the DIs handle the situation, but that might result in trouble (recall the "counseling about the head and shoulders"), or it might not result in any direct action on the part of the other DIs (except to act as an encouragement for them to cheat), because direct action might violate accepted group (NCO) norms. Tolten's solution to this problem was to confront the DI in question and simply tell him to stop it. He did!

Solving the supplies problem (overspending the equipment budget) required a much different approach. As CPT Tolten mentioned in the case, the purpose of his inventory-control system was consistent with Army objectives but not consistent with the manner for which equipment expenditures and reimbursements were accounted. He was getting penalized for doing the "right" thing. The long-range fix would be either to change the accounting procedures so that reimbursements for expended equipment got credited to the company account (highly unlikely, since it would require fundamental changes in the Army accounting system) or to have better forecasts that took into account a better inventory-control system (possible, but would not help CPT Tolten during his meeting with LTC Daniels). Instead, Tolten had to educate LTC Daniels about the purpose of and procedures used for inventory control. In effect, he had to convince LTC Daniels that the system is sound and establish his credibility as a manager (which, in fact, is what he did).

IV. Assignment Questions

Since I use this case as an integrative case, I do not assign questions on the officer-evaluation system, even though, as mentioned in Section III, I do spend some time on system critique. Instead, I focus student attention on the system designed by CPT Tolten and his current problems.

1. Evaluate CPT Tolten's control system for B-3-3.

2. Do you believe CPT Tolten's system is appropriate and/or necessary in this type of environment?

3. What alternative systems or system modifications would you suggest to CPT Tolten?

4. How would you deal with the "rifle-range" and "supply" problems?

5. What problems do you foresee during the discussion with LTC Daniels?

V. Agenda

I begin class with a brief introduction of the structure and purpose of the Basic Combat Training Brigade at Ft. Dix. I often ask if anybody in the class has ever gone through basic training and get them to describe their experiences briefly. I make sure the students understand that there might be as many as 10 companies, each with 4-6 platoons and up to 2,500 recruits. I also make sure students understand the chain of command (organizational structure) of Company B.

Once the chain of command has been described, I ask a student to describe the officer-evaluation system. I make sure the student describes the system in detail (particularly the OER, OER Support Form, and the OMPF) and try to discourage the student from making any critical assessment of the system until I feel comfortable that all students have a good understanding of the system. During the description, I list some of the relevant dimensions of the system (such as those on the right-hand side of Exhibit TN-1) on the board. I then spend approximately 15–20 minutes eliciting student opinions about the system. I have found that there is a natural tendency for students to evaluate the system harshly. I believe this happens because we are discussing *military* procedures and, as one student said, "If its the military, it (the system) must be worthless!" However, I find that most of the harsh comments lack any real substance, and when pressed to defend their criticisms, students find it difficult to do so. As the discussion proceeds, I write in relevant comments about each of the items used to describe the system (see left-hand side of Exhibit TN-1). Faced with this information, the students conclude that the system is fairly well designed.

I then move on to a description of CPT Tolten's performance control system, prefaced by a description of the mission of B-3-3 and CPT Tolten's personal goals for the Company. I ask a student (or students) to outline the performance measures and describe the mechanics of "scoring" the performance dimensions. I also ask how the measures were developed and whether there was any evolution in the development of the current performance system (i.e., elimination of the "eight-ball award").

At this point, it becomes necessary for the students to see that, for the system to work right, a strong competitive environment is required. I use this opportunity to explore the issue of building competition into a management control system. While I do not spend a lot of time on this issue, I try to get the students to think of factors that are necessary in order for competitive approaches to work.

I then get the students back to the case issues by asking them if they feel that this particular environment is well suited to a competitively based performance control system. At this time I also elicit student opinions about the performance control system in general. As outlined in Section III, it is usually difficult for students to defend a position that is highly critical of the system.

Because the system is difficult to criticize on technical and structural grounds, I then ask the students if they feel it was poorly implemented. I write on the board issues the students identify that are pertinent to CPT Tolten's use of an implementation strategy, including factors that limited his choice of implementation techniques.

I find that, once the discussion about implementation strategy is completed, most of the class time has expired and it is necessary to address the rifle-range and supplies problems. I ask a student if he/she believes the rifle-range problem is serious. I couch this question in terms such as "Weren't the results *good* for CPT Tolten?" Most often, students seem to feel that the problem is serious for some of the reasons mentioned in Section III. I then ask if CPT Tolten should let the DI's "solve" the problem themselves. Students quickly realize that this is not an appropriate way to handle the problem; instead CPT Tolten must act to stop the cheating before the entire performance control system is put in jeopardy.

The supplies problem is addressed next and, as outlined previously, it proves to be a considerably more difficult problem to solve. Because I usually try to leave 5–10 minutes for summary, I often find it necessary to discuss this issue during the case wrap-up. At that time, I summarize the good things about the performance control system, show the results achieved by CPT Tolten, and identify the long-term benefits to the base (Ft. Dix) of the system (see the Appendix).

Additional Comments on Captain Jamie Tolten

Approach

This case has its own issues, but it is also interesting as a contrast with (a) business companies, and (b) managers of large units. Captain Tolten is an Army officer, commanding (managing) approximately 200 enlisted personnel.

There are 100,000 officers in the Army. Most of them start as second lieutenants. The next step is first lieutenant, then captain. Most are promoted from within, and unless an officer performs poorly, he or she can count on staying in the Army for at least 20 years (when retirement with a moderate pension is earned), or for 30 years (when the pension is considerably larger). Selection boards meet at regular intervals. Competition is keen, both for promotion, and for selection to one of the special schools, such as the Army Command and General Staff college mentioned in the case. Most officers of the rank of colonel and above are graduates of this College. Only one of these at a time will reach the top: Army Chief of Staff.

The Officer Evaluation Report (Exhibit 1) is an important document in making these decisions. Over the years, much effort has gone into making refinements in this report. As is the case with many business companies, its preparation starts with an agreement between the officer and his or her superior as to the objectives that the officer is to accomplish during the rating period. This agreement is reduced to writing. The officer is rated by the superior, and also by that superior's superior, according to his or her success in meeting the agreed upon objectives, and the rater discusses the ratings with the person being rated. In some businesses, the process is less formal, with no prescribed format or list of criteria, and the ratings are not based on stated objectives. In some businesses, the ratings are entirely subjective. But in all businesses, managers are judged on their performance.

In the Army, officer compensation is based (with a few exceptions) on rank and years of service. Unlike any other case in this book, there is no incentive compensation plan. How can this be? I think the answer is that the officer Evaluation Report has an important role in promotion and assignment decisions, and therefore provides strong motivation to career officers.

Although rating is essential, if the system is not operated properly, the consequences can be unfair, or even dysfunctional. Examples are given in the case. For example, overemphasis on the rating caused punishment which resulted in hospitalization.

CPT Tolten has made a personal extension of the prescribed system; he developed a system for rating his own subordinates, even though there was no requirement that he do so.

Question 1

CPT Tolten has three types of ratings, each related to the nature of the measurement data that were available. The marksmanship and physical fitness ratings are *scalar*; that is, the rating was based on a numerical scale. The proficiency test is *discrete*; that is, performance either met a prescribed standard or it did not. The discipline measure is a *surrogate*; that is, the attribute could not be measured directly in quantitative terms, so a substitute that could be measured was developed, with the expectation (or at least, hope) that performance of the substitute would correlate reasonably well with performance of the desired attribute. In this case, the surrogate was a point system based on the appearance of the barracks. He did *not* use a judgmental rating, that is, a rating based on personal judgment (either his own or the judgment of others) as to how good performance was.

Students probably can relate these types of ratings to various types of grading systems with which they are familiar, and they usually have strong feelings about the strengths and weaknesses of the various types. If a scalar system actually measures the attribute, it is the best way of arranging the subjects in order from best on down. Students can point out, however, that questions on a multiple choice test may not actually relate to knowledge of the subject, or they may not be clearly worded; if so, the number of questions answered correctly is not a valid measure of performance. A go no-go measure separates the group into two classes, but tells nothing about how well the person did compared with others in the class. Also, wherever the line is drawn, questions can be raised about performance that is very close to the line; that is, was the performance actually above or below it? In such systems, therefore, an appeal by a person who slightly below the line is often permitted. A surrogate measure, of course, is no better than the surrogate; if it is not a good representation of the attribute whose measurement is sought, it is not worth much. A judgmental measure is open to bias; however, an individual's judgment may actually be a better way of measuring performance than any numerical test that can be devised. The more the attributed departs from a strictly observable amount (such as rifle scores in hitting a target), the more necessary it is to rely on a judgmental measure (and note that even an observable measure can be affected by cheating).

In general, developers of performance measurement systems attempt to find attributes that are both important and measurable in some way that does not involve judgment; their next best rating is discrete; and they are least comfortable with a measure that is heavily influenced by judgment.

All of the above relates to the measurement as an accurate reflection of the attribute being measured. Of at least equal importance is the effect of the measurement on the person being measured. If good performance, as the person views performance, is rewarded with a high rating, the person is motivated toward good performance. If the measurement is unfair, as the person perceives unfairness, it may be dysfunctional. Also, as illustrated in the case, if too much emphasis is given to the measurement, it is dysfunctional.

Students probably will conclude that the marksmanship and physical fitness measures are sound, although some may argue that the scores reflect the innate ability of the individuals, rather than the drill instructor's influence (but is there any better way?). On the physical fitness test, some may argue that successful performance the second time should be given more weight than performance the first time, on the grounds that it reflects the instructor's ability to overcome obstacles. (However, if the weighing were reversed, instructors would be motivated not to achieve good results on the first test.) Students may question whether any numerical measure is an adequate surrogate for the discipline attribute.

Question 2

The question asks what you believe, and this is the key to its importance. People differ in their attitude to formal rating schemes. The officer who preceded CPT Tolten did not use one. There is therefore no "right answer" to this question. A show of hands may indicate this legitimate difference of opinion although there may be a tendency to conclude that the system is too complicated, especially with students who tend to have an aversion toward grading.

Question 3

The discussion in Question 1 suggests alternatives.

Question 4

Probably the "rifle range" problem will correct itself. The "show" that the platoon sergeant put on should be recognized as a show before too long. If so, no action is needed. Dressing down the platoon sergeant may be difficult, because he will of course deny what he has done, and the "Unwritten code of ethics" inhibits the collection of evidence. (Note the importance of *this* code in affecting the reliability of the measurement system.) If the problem does not go away, CPT Tolten must act. A system that is regarded as being unfair is dysfunctional.

The "supply" problem illustrates how rules can be dysfunctional. The system does not give CPT Tolten credit for the money collected from those who have lost equipment; it should do so. (A similar problem exists in various other places in the military. It stems from legislation that requires that receipts go directly to the Treasury, rather than to the responsible unit. In recent years this problem has been corrected in some areas.) But the system defect exists, and CPT Tolten can't do anything about it. Many students probably will conclude that he should go along with the system, cease his efforts to collect funds, and cover the shortages by the time-honored practice of scrounging. This depends heavily on the attitude of LTC Daniels, as discussed in Question 5.

Question 5

CPT Tolten's performance also affects LTC Daniels' rating; for example, LTC Daniels has exceeded his budget because of CPT Tolten's diligence in identifying shortages and causing them to be replaced. LTC Daniels is likely to be unhappy about this fact. However, he is leaving, so the discussion affects only the current evaluation report, (unless Daniels brings Tolten's conduct into his conversation with his successor.)

The discussion depends heavily on LTC Daniels' attitude toward the system, and CPT Tolten should try to judge what Daniels' attitude is. If Daniels regards Tolten as an "eager beaver," who has developed a fancy system that results in criticism of Daniels, and who is unwilling to go along with the way the Army does things, his attitude may be negative. If so, CPT Tolten perhaps should be contrite, even to the point of agreeing to modify, or perhaps abandon, his system. If, on the other hand, LTC Daniels appreciates someone who thinks up innovations, CPT Tolten may decide to explain the situation, and hope that LTC Daniels will approve his actions. CPT Tolten perhaps should be willing to compromise if LTC Daniels indicates strong disapproval. He may, however, decide to ride out this criticism and hope that his next superior will appreciate what he has done.

RNA

CHAPTER 11
PERFORMANCE MEASUREMENT

Changes from the Eighth Edition

This chapter is new to the 9th edition. This chapter discusses two topics: (1) The design of a balanced scorecard to implement strategies; (2) The use of a subset of management control system as an interactive control to develop new strategies.

Cases

Analog Devices is given credit for pioneering the balanced scorecard concept. The case describes the company's evolution in implementing the balanced scorecard during 1984–1996. This is an excellent case. This is new to this edition.

Warren Insurance Company is a case on measuring intellectual. This case is new to this edition. The case describes in detail the experience of Skandia, a Scandinavian company, in measuring intellectual capital.

General Electric Company (B) describes the company's effort during the 1950s to develop a balanced scorecard. This case reminds the students that the concept of blending of financial and nonfinancial metrics is not new.

Enager Industries can be either used with Chapter 7 or with Chapter 11. Used with Chapter 11, students can be made to not only understand the limitations of ROI but can also be challenged to develop a balanced scorecard for the 3 divisions of the company.

Analog Devices Case[1]

Objective

The main objectives of this case are:

1. to illustrate a number of approaches to measuring the performance of an organization.

2. to examine how these measures change over time as the organization changes

3. to evaluate the strengths and weaknesses of the different systems and how a system can degrade over time

4. to examine how reliance on financial measures alone can cause unintended results.

Synopsis

Analog Devices is a leading manufacturer of analog integrate circuits. Since 1983, Analog Devices has been using total quality management techniques as part of its management process, which it refers to as Quality Improvement Process (QIP).

ADI has received the most attention for a management development that evolved from the QIP process—the corporate scorecard. The corporate scorecard was introduced in 1987 by Art Schneiderman, Vice President of Quality and Productivity Improvement. The corporate scorecard was the result of a customer survey conducted by Schneiderman that indicated what areas were important to customers. He then developed measures for these areas, as most were not directly financial and applied a theory that he had developed, the half-life system, to come up with a series of targets for ADI. Combining the measures the targets, and ADI's current state, Schneiderman created a one-page report that listed 16 different measures. It is this basic scorecard which was later repackaged and refined to become the popularized balanced scorecard.

This scorecard was then introduced to the entire company, being used as both a goal-setting and performance-measurement device, as well as a communication tool. While the scorecard contributed greatly to quality improvements at ADI, financial performance barely improved and after 3 years with the corporate scorecard, ADI experienced a loss and then a 10% workforce reduction in 1991. At this time, Ray Stata, CEO of ADI, became more personally involved in the QIP effort. As a result, ADI introduced new systems, Hoshin and key success factors, that would provide a stronger growth focus than ADI's corporate scorecard. This was combined with efforts to decentralize the planning and strategy activities to increase commitment and aid in the challenge of repositioning ADI to more effectively compete in the new and growing markets, automotive and consumer electronics. Under these systems, ADI has returned to growth after a stagnant period from 1988 to 1992.

---

[1]This teaching note was prepared by Kirk Hendrickson, Tuck '97. Copyright © Osceola Institute 1997.

Discussion

The discussion is going to focus on the five questions asked. These five questions address the central themes of this case and should provide sufficient focus for a 90-minute discussion. Before beginning though, you may want to have the students determine what Analog Devices strategies were for the period before 1991 and from 1991 to the present. They may be something like:

Prior to 1991 Analog Devices pursued a strategy of differentiation through quality leadership. Emphasizing new products and improved quality as a way to decrease costs and improve customer satisfaction and derive higher revenues from the existing customer base.

After 1991, Analog Devices pursued a strategy of targeting growing industry segments and providing high quality specialty products for these growing segments.

Question 1

Critically evaluate the "half-life" concept, in light of Analog Devices' strategy during the second half of the 1980s. What are the potential and limitations of the half-life concept? How would a company develop the half-life for different processes?

Anyone familiar with experience curves will probably see some similarity when they look at the half-life concept. In effect it is just another form of an experience curve replacing the axis of units produced with an axis of time. If we had the data, we would probably find that ADI's half-life graphs would change only marginally if we substituted units for time. While this is speculation, the idea of half-life as an experience curve is a good way to understand it. Effectively, every time that ADI doubles the amount of time it has been consistently working on TQM for a particular product, it should improve the quality by a certain percentage. The math between the two is interchangeable.

As a result, we find many of the same pitfalls with half-life as we did with experience curves. The first limitation is that the numbers may just be wrong. They are estimates that can change over time. More importantly, they focus the company on incremental improvements over innovation, while incremental improvements are important, this approach does not prepare a company for fundamental shifts in the nature of competition in the industry, something that occurs frequently within IC's. Smooth improvement ignores these important discontinuities. The strength of the half-life approach is that it stretches the experience curve concept to an area that is less likely to be used as the thrust of the company's strategy and more likely to be a supporting part of the overall plan. While you can try to become the cost leader through experience and base your strategy on this, becoming the defect-free leader is unlikely to be the key feature of your strategy.

This brings us to ADI and its use of the half-life system. Because of Schneiderman's evangelism of half-life, ADI was using half-life for everything from incremental improvement steps to fundamental breakthroughs. They were following a strategy of becoming the quality leader. ADI did become a quality leader. The quality improvements were fantastic as the half-life drove stretch goals and gave employees a framework where they could see that these quality improvements were possible.

Unfortunately, no one was willing to pay for ADI's quality. In addition, ADI understood that its quality improvements came from employee commitment, causing great reluctance by management to rationalize the workforce to take advantage of productivity gains. Effectively what ADI found was that it had improved its capacity without increasing demand and all of the money that it had invested was like investing in a new plant when you had no new sales. The result was that ADI's reliance on the half-life system distracted ADI from the major objective, growth.

Question 2

Identify the conflicts which exist between the QIP measures and the measures reported by the financial system. Which numbers should we believe? Can they be reconciled?

As already mentioned, ADI's financial position deteriorated while its quality improved. When looking at its QIP measures, every measure was improving, yet financials were getting worse. The issue is that QIP measures were being used as predictors of future results, yet the correlation between improvements in QIP measures and actual results was never verified until it was too late and ADI discovered that QIP measures had little correlation with financial results, or even future financial results. The problem was that in and of themselves, improved QIP measures gave no distinctive competitive advantage to ADI. Thus, the QIP measures had no way of being translated to the financial statement unless some area of investment was being reduced. As the property, plant and equipment to produce these products hadn't changed, and the labor was still being employed at the same level, the only thing left were the wasted material, which was actually a small part of the overall expense of these systems. While costs associated with waste materials can be eliminated with relative ease, eliminating labor and equipment costs were much more difficult. Thus, unless the company has a mechanism for translating QIP measures to the financial statements, the financial statements are likely to be more reliable. However, with a mechanism, then the QIP measures can start to provide predictive abilities that no financial statement could.

Question 3

Critically assess the usefulness of the information contained in the corporate scorecard in Exhibit 3 as a way to implement Analog Devices' strategy as of 1988. What role does each set of measures play? What should be the relative importance of financial versus non-financial measures? What additional information would you like to see included in the scorecard?

ADI's measures can be broken down into three areas: measures of past success, current success and future success. While financial statements are well understood measures of past success, New Products and QIP are tenuous measures of current and future success. They are complementary measures that supplement financial statement reports to give a more complete picture of how well the company is performing. Assessing the information in Exhibit 3:

Financial (Past Success)	The financial information is relevant at the general management level, though it tells you how you did and gives little feedback on where going.
New Products (Present Success)	A category that gives substantial air time to developing and introducing new products. Unfortunately, the concentration here encourages many incremental changes without understanding the cannibalization effect of these new products or the need for breakthrough steps. This is very key as most of the measures are self-reinforcing, time to market, number of introductions, time to break-even. This encourages low investment, quick breakeven lots of products. While this isn't bad, it can cause an imbalance.
NP Introductions	Encourages lots of new products to be introduced
NP Bookings	Follows whether the new products actually make any money
NP Break-even	Considers the investment side of the equation
NP Peak Revenue	Tracks what the highest revenue point is for NP
Time to Market	Indicates what is the average time to bring these new products to market
QIP (Future Success)	These measures are taken on face value as predictors of future success. Unfortunately, it is nearly impossible to link them to actual future success. The major problem with the QIP measures is that they are very internally focused. They do not have an external component, such as satisfaction with the on-time delivery.
On-time delivery	Important first step in creating a proxy for customer satisfaction
Cycle-time	Combined with other measures provides information about ability to rapidly respond to changing environment. Still leaves issue of was anything actually improved during this cycle.
Yield	Measure of how much waste is occurring in the process. Important to consider if there are targets or standards that might actually be inhibiting further improvements.
Outgoing Defects	These are problem components that the customer sees. The goal should be zero outgoing defects.
Cost	Aggregate cost of quality
Employee Productivity	Illustrates increased capacity of each employee. Unfortunately, ADI didn't use it this way. They used it more as a benchmark of whether quality improvement was working.
Turnover	Employee turnover is a measure of both employee satisfaction and an internal perception of the opportunities and rewards within the company.

If this scorecard was to be extended, the key areas that it would need to consider are measures for customer satisfaction and competitor capability. ADI's viewpoint on the corporate scorecard is purely internal, as a result, there is no evident measurement of how the customers perceive these changes nor where the competitors are at with their own quality programs and innovation efforts. While these are more difficult areas to gather information, it is critical that they be given the same level of importance as the other scorecard measures. Some specific measures might be the rate of new product introductions by competitors, the level of satisfaction with the quality of ADI's products, especially in comparison to ADI's competitors.

Question 4

Evaluate the evolution of the corporate scorecard and related management planning and control systems at Analog Devices during 1988-1995.

ADI went through a process where it:

- Recognized that there was a problem

- Tried to fix it internally, failed

- Sought outside help, introducing a fresh player with fresh ideas into the mix

- Learned what it could from the outsider

- Developed its own way of doing business

- Realized that the outsider was preventing further progress as he allowed the CEO to avoid direct evangelism

- Incorporated the CEO more heavily in the process

- Determined that focus was on shrinking cost, not growing business

- Found new tools that could assist in growth

- Implemented these new tools

- Refined the tools as they developed more experience with these tools

- Altered the old systems to serve a new purpose

When all things are considered, it would have been nearly impossible for ADI to have moved from the stage of identifying a problem to developing systems for monitoring and assisting in company growth without having gone through the discovery process. This example provides us a fundamental lesson in how when we are trying to make major changes to the company, we are making a big jump. Rather than making the jump all at once and risking falling short or missing the mark, it is easier to take a series of little jumps. After we complete each little jump, we can determine where the next jump needs to be to take us to our desired goal.

This may be one of ADI's biggest failings in the development of QIP, it did not have a consistent vision of where the company was going. Schneiderman took it one way, Stata another, and now Suttler will have his opportunity to move it a different way. Hoshin is a step in the right direction as it has focused the improvement process on two key areas: new products and delivery.

Question 5

Describe Analog Devices' 1996 strategy. How should the corporate scorecard change in 1996 to best fit the strategic needs of the company?

The corporate scorecard has evolved into a communication tool for ADI. Its purpose is to indicate to employees what are the most important aspects of their jobs. The corporate scorecard requires constant updating as the employees achieve goals and make one measure obsolete by performing it so well that improvements in it will result in marginal improvements in performance, while improvements in another measure that has been left off of the scorecard has been allowed to flounder and could drive substantial increases in performance from just concentrating on it.

In addition, the scorecard needs to be consistent with the company's strategy. While it is often looked at in the light of what measures can we take that will be a proxy for customer satisfaction or improvements in the process, what is lost is that they may be proxies for areas that don't matter to ADI's strategy.

Finally, the scorecard can be used as a method for not only communicating expected performance, but also for communicating benchmarks and external results. There is no reason why a division's scorecard cannot have measures of competitors successes and direct customers' opinions. The value here is that while the employee is being empowered to make process changes that improve quality and lower cost, they are not being fed the information that will allow them to understand the linkages between their actions and the company's success with regards to the competitors and customers. In fact, if you think about the groups that were improving yields and preventing defects for 3 years prior to 1991, thinking that everything was going great as the QIP measures kept improving, they were probably very surprised by the layoffs. While a focus on what the division's competitors were doing would have shown competitors with improving quality, increasing market share, and customers who were unwilling to pay for the additional quality. If this had been done, not only would the results in 1991 not have been surprising, but they might have been totally different had the employees been given the information to change the industry.

Additional Materials

Teaching note for "Analog Devices: The Half-Life System," prepared by Professor Robert Kaplan, Harvard Business School. This can be ordered directly from Harvard by referring to No. 5-191-103.

Case 11-2

Warren Insurance Co.

Objective

The purpose of Warren Insurance is to expose students to the idea of managing intellectual assets. In particular, we want the student to understand how intellectual capital can be defined, how companies are trying to measure it, and what companies are doing to manage it. Finally, the student should develop an opinion on what value intellectual capital can bring to a company and how the management systems in a company have to change in order to support the development of intellectual capital.

Synopsis

Warren Insurance Co. is about a fictional insurance company where the controller is looking for insights into managing intellectual capital. The main focus of the case is on Skandia Insurance Company, a worldwide insurance company based in Sweden. In 1994, Skandia issued a supplement to its annual report, "Visualizing Intellectual Capital in Skandia." This supplement contained a discussion of Skandia's philosophy with regard to intellectual capital. In the supplement, Skandia shows a tool that it calls the Skandia Navigator to use as a framework for measuring intellectual capital. In addition, Skandia provided summaries of how certain business units are developing processes to enhance organizational capital and cause positive business effects.

Along with the discussion of Skandia's Navigator, Warren Insurance also presents examples from Canadian Imperial Bank of Commerce (CIBC), Dow Chemical, and Hughes Space & Communication Division. CIBC divides intellectual capital into human capital, structural capital and customer capital. Dow Chemical is actively managing its patent portfolio. Hughes Space & Communications is developing methods of speeding access to information and retaining intellectual capital.

Additional Resources Available from Skandia

Two video tapes:

Future Accounting & Intellectual Capital — best piece is near end where the controller of Skandia discusses the navigator.

Reflections on Intellectual Capital — This is a 20-minute tape with a good discussion of Skandia's philosophy and some of what Skandia is doing. The drawback with this tape is that it is very dry.

This note was prepared by Kirk Hendrickson (Tuck '97). Copyright © Osceola Institute.

CD-ROM:

Skandia and the Intellectual Capital Development — pretty comprehensive with short QuickTime™ movies.

Note: You can obtain the abovenoted three materials by contacting: Skandia, Marketing Communications, tel: 46-8-788-1000; fax: 46-8-788-2685.

Class Session

The class case discussion can go something like the following:

- Define intellectual capital

- Watch portions of Skandia videos on intellectual capital

- Discuss Question 1: evaluation of Skandia's approach

- Briefly discuss what CIBC, Dow and Hughes are doing

- Discuss Question 2

- Summarize

Defining Intellectual Capital

The case contains Skandia's definition of intellectual capital—the aggregate sum of the intangible values in knowledge-intensive operations. The students (like the case writer) will probably find this definition to be a little impenetrable. Instead, of trying to work with it, it is important for the students to develop their own definition of intellectual capital. While they can probably all tell you what physical capital is, there will be some disagreement on what intellectual capital is. Thus, it would be worthwhile to try to get the students to define intellectual capital; after all, we can't measure what we can't define.

The definition could include items such: intangible, invisible, hard to quantify, valuable, inimitable, subjective, flexible, leverageable, appreciates with use, related to people, human resources, not on the balance sheet. Another approach would say that intellectual capital is the systems, the organization, the culture, the learning, the knowledge of the company.

Other definitions than Skandia's include:

"Intellectual capital is 'intellectual material that has been formalized, captured, and leveraged to produce a higher-valued asset.'"[1]

"Intellectual capital is something that you cannot touch but still makes you rich."[2]

A working definition of intellectual capital could be something like:

---

[1] Larry Prusak, Principal, Ernst & Young, as quoted by Thomas Stewart in "Your Company's Most Valuable Asset: Intellectual Capital," *Fortune*, October 3, 1994, p. 68.
[2] Leif Edvisson, *Reflections on Intellectual Capital*, Skandia, 1996.

Intellectual capital is the valuable, intangible assets that result from the interaction of the organizational structures, processes, and philosophies with the human capabilities of the organization.

Using a definition like this focuses the students on what piece of the company that we are really trying to understand how to measure, value, and manage.

Discussion of Question 1

The first response to this question might be something along the lines of Skandia's intellectual capital sell being marketing over matter. While there is definitely an element of that, as Skandia's performance has been inconsistent and they needed something to try to tell to the market how great the company's future is going to be, the level to which Skandia is pursuing this indicates that they believe that they need to be better at managing non-financial assets.

Skandia, as with many other companies, is saying that financial information is not sufficient to make decisions about the future direction of the company. Being historic, financial measures are inherently backward-looking, while what Skandia would like is better predictors of the future. While the idea that intellectual capital is a better predictor of future results than financial indicators is common sense, it is not common practice to attempt to quantify intellectual capital. Thus, Skandia's attempts to measure and define intellectual capital are at least a step in the right direction.

The navigator, in particular is not a very insightful innovation. In fact, it is an outgrowth of the balanced scorecard. As with the balanced scorecard, the navigator has some problems. The students will probably point out that the measures shown for some of the divisions are either subjective, like the empowerment index, or irrelevant, such as the number of full-time employees being a measure of the level of human focus in Skandia. Is the implication of the number of full-time employees that you should have more or less? Obviously, these holes create some cynicism in the student. In addition, students might point to companies, such as 3M, which have been effectively measuring and managing their intellectual capital for years. Thus, suggesting that this is nothing new, combining this with the idea that the measures shown are not relevant in capturing results or motivating improved intellectual capital performance, the navigator appears to be no more than marketing hype.

On the other hand, the Skandia Navigator is just one manifestation of Skandia's changing attitude towards intellectual capital and the need for the organization to recognize it, measure it and manage it. Current strategic concepts, such as core competencies, are more oriented towards the value of the intangibles that you possess as being the best predictors of future success than the level of hard assets that you have today.

What Skandia has done is:

- Developed a company wide framework for focusing on intellectual capital

- Analyzed what processes create value for the customers

- Linked value-creating processes to the resulting organizational capital

- Examined the business effect of these change in organizational capital

- Used the Navigator as a tool for developing a continuous improvement culture

Combining all of these items illustrates how Skandia is making an attempt to shift the company culture to focus on developing intellectual capital. While Skandia has by no means done it right, it has taken the first steps in that direction. Whether Skandia is being too aggressive in its attempt to quantify these intangible assets is yet to be seen.

Before moving on from Skandia, it is interesting to see in the 1995 supplement that Skandia has broken down the building blocks of intellectual capital even further. Figure 1 shows Skandia's breakdown from market value all the way to innovation and process capital. Skandia feels that these additional levels of breakdown help focus employees and management on the elements that are crucial for Skandia's future. Interestingly, Skandia believes that there is an additive relationship between the different types of capital. I would suggest that the relationship is actually multiplicative. First, a lack of any one type of capital makes all of the other capital worthless. Second, a deficiency in one area is likely to result in a deficiency throughout the organization. As a result of this, using a multiplicative relationship would be more appropriate, requiring the organization to maintain and improve all of these forms of capital in order to build its overall intellectual capital.

Figure 1
Intellectual Capital and Its Component Pads

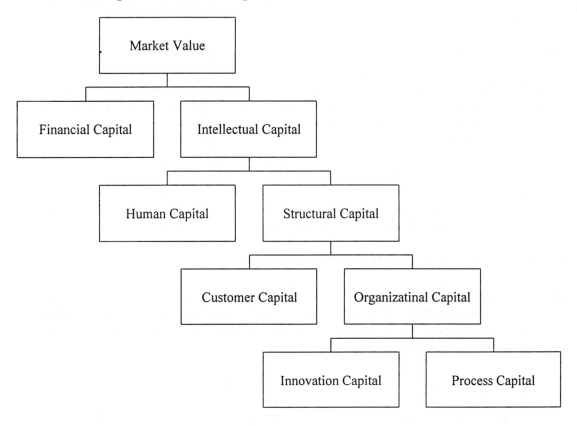

SOURCE: "Value-Creating Processes," *Supplement to Skandia's 1995 Annual Report*, p. 5.

Discussion of CIBC, Dow Chemicals and Hughes Space

While also pursuing the goal of managing intellectual capital, CIBC, Dow Chemicals and Hughes Space approach the process differently than Skandia.

CIBC has a well-developed system for understanding its intellectual capital. While not as public about it as Skandia, CIBC has created a rich intellectual capital framework. CIBC began developing this framework after the savings and loan collapse and the failure of a number of major financial institutions. In both cases, CIBC saw a series of banks owning hard assets, yet these hard assets held little value. At the same time, CIBC was watching companies, such as Microsoft, which had few hard assets yet they were creating value at an unprecedented rate. As far as CIBC was concerned, they were lending against the wrong thing, hard assets, and what they need to be lending against were the intellectual assets. In order to do this, CIBC needed to be able to define what the intellectual assets were and be able to value them. While there is only a limited list of measures shown for CIBC, the student should see how these measures are more closely linked to intellectual capital than some of the measures in the Navigator. Hopefully giving them some ideas to put to work in question 2.

Unlike CIBC, Dow Chemical has developed a process for managing intellectual assets. It is applying this process to its large bank of patents, which it had been expending millions of dollars on, yet not leveraging in an appreciable way. This six-step framework has been very effective in helping Dow rationalize its patent portfolio and developing a new portfolio of intellectual assets. The interesting area that Dow Chemical adds that Skandia and CIBC don't discuss at length is an examination of the competitors' intellectual capital.

Hughes Space, instead of developing an overall framework or process for managing intellectual capital, has focused instead on trying to understand how innovation capital can be retained. The concept that people learn through stories and that stories convey wisdom and experience faster and more meaningfully than facts, can be seen in the success of other companies. At Nordstrom, the true stories of the heroics of employees in serving the customers leads to a deeper understanding by the sales associates of how customer service can be done.

Skandia describes itself as a knowledge organization, one focused on both teaching and learning. In addition, Skandia suggests that a company's IQ increases as the time between the time that the organization learned how to do something and the time that the organization can teach someone else how to do something decreases. This relationship can be written as:

$$\text{Organization IQ} = 1/\text{Time}_{teach} - \text{Time}_{learn}$$

Thus, an organization that can learn and then teach instantaneously would have an infinite IQ. In Hughes' case, the introduction of contextual knowledge reduces the time between learning and teaching, as the story can be internalized faster than facts and spread more quickly. Thus, the move to contextual knowledge will increase Hughes' IQ.

Discussion Question 2

What advice do you have for Allen in terms of measuring intellectual capital for Warren Insurance?

Our advice would be:

- Intellectual capital will be a critical part of your success in the future

- Measuring intellectual capital is essential

- First step is in defining what intellectual capital means to Warren Insurance

- Next, Warren Insurance must determine what are the critical success factors that help create intellectual capital within Warren Insurance

- Then, Warren should establish a framework for how it wants to measure improvements in intellectual capital, company IQ, a Warren Navigator, or others. The critical factor here is that the framework must include all of the factors that create intellectual capital.

- With this framework, Warren Insurance needs to develop a series of measures no matter how rudimentary that start to get at the key factors supporting the intellectual capital framework.

- Finally, Warren Insurance needs to develop a mechanism for refining and improving these measures. At this point, they are very rough, but in the future they will get better.

Additional Books

Leif Edvisson, *Intellectual Capital*, Harper Collins, 1997.

Case 11-3

General Electric Company (B)

Objectives

I use this case as a device for describing the totality of the management control problem. Used in this way, one can spend only a small amount of time on each aspect of the problem, and it should be made clear to the student that subsequent cases will go into more depth on each of these aspects.

Discussion

The two questions suggest the two general parts of the class discussion. The first part relates to the best way of measuring those financial aspects of performance that can be measured, and the second part relates to why even the best financial measurement is inadequate as a real measure of performance.

I.   I start the discussion of the measurement of profitability by getting agreement on the criteria that should be used in judging what approach gives the best measure. I believe there are two essential criteria: (1) goal congruence; that is, the system should motivate division managers to act in the best interests of the company; and (2) feasibility, that is, the system should be workable, and the figures should be obtainable without too much difficulty. Students often want to add a third criterion, comparability, that is, the figures for one division should be comparable with those of another division. I try to avoid this criterion in this case, partly because we do not have any information which can be used to judge whether it is a good criterion, and partly because I am by no means sure that it is necessary to achieve comparability for the purpose that the system is supposed to serve. In any event, I would like to postpone a discussion of comparability until later; if it comes in here, the students can get involved in trying to list factors that can make one division noncomparable with another.

Having established the criteria, I ask how profitability should be measured in terms of these criteria. The first problem is to agree on exactly what method GE does use. For this purpose, I use a model divisional income statement and balance sheet as shown in Exhibit A. I put this on the board before class, except that I stop the income statement with the profit-after-taxes figure. Students are supposed to see that the income statement must have the capital charge in order to conform to GE's method, but when they are pushed as to exactly how the capital charge is to be figured, they quickly see that the case does not tell them which of several possibilities is actually used.

This case was prepared by R.H. Caplan (under the direction of Robert N. Anthony).

This directs our attention to the balance sheet and to a preliminary discussion of what possibilities are available. For example, the current items could be omitted, they could be shown at the gross amount of $400, or they could be shown at net working capital amount of $200. These alternatives would, respectively, lead the division manager to not worry about either current assets or current liabilities, to worry only about current assets, and to worry about both current assets and current liabilities. There can be some discussion of the extent to which top management wishes the division manager to be concerned with some or all of the working capital items. For example, if current liabilities are subtracted, the division manager may be expected to incur a larger amount of current liabilities than is good for the company as a whole.

A similar discussion can be carried on with respect to the fixed assets. Here the question is on whether the valuation should be at gross book value, at net book value, or at some figure outside the books, such as replacement value. Obviously, there can be only an introductory discussion at this point, since there will be presumably much more on this topic later on in the course. In connection with this discussion, there can be a question as to whether the inclusion of depreciation on the income statement as well as the capital charge is double counting the fixed assets. The answer is that there is no double counting; depreciation recovers the cost of the assets, and the capital charge has to do with an amount in excess of cost.

II. Having established that the capital charge approach is a good one in that it broadens the division manager's attention to include both items affecting income and the management of assets, the next question is whether this method is the best for General Electric. It can be compared. first, with a return-on-investment-percentage method. The example in Exhibit A can be used to demonstrate that the return-on-investment percentage has a conceptual weakness; namely, it would lead the division manager to reject proposals that promise a return between 6 percent and 10 percent because these would lead to a decrease in his divisional return on investment. Nevertheless, such proposals presumably are good for the GE company as a whole because they earn more than the 6 percent which is presumably the desired minimum.

Another alternative, profit as a percent of sales, will presumably be rejected out of hand. It does not focus on control of assets at all, and it has the additional weakness of leading the manager to seek high-margin business and reject business that contributes dollars of profit to GE even though the percentage margin is below average.

Finally, it is possible to consider a measure based on direct cost, rather than full cost. This is the so-called contribution profit, which can be used in connection with the other measures discussed above. Personally, I think that the actions the division manager takes are, or should be, in no way influenced by the inclusion or exclusion of indirect cost and that, therefore, it cannot be argued that there is any advantage or disadvantage from a goal congruence standpoint in including indirect cost. This is especially so if care is taken in designing the system to insure that actual indirect costs are always the same as budgeted indirect costs so that no variance develops. Since, by definition, the division manager cannot influence this item, it does not, or should not, affect his actions. An advantage of including indirect costs is that it shows the division manager a better picture of the real profitability of his division, since the division must, in fairness, assume a fair share of the total corporate expense. Also, if the division manager is charged with this cost, he may be motivated to raise questions about the cost of headquarters operations, and it is good to have someone raising these questions. I would be inclined, personally, to include indirect costs in the system, but do not feel strongly about this one way or the other.

My own conclusion, therefore, is that the GE system is the best system.

III. Turning to the second question, one can make quite a point of the fact that we have gone to great lengths to bring as many items as possible into the profitability measure, and we therefore wonder why GE feels it needs seven additional measures of divisional performance. There are good reasons for at least some of the other measures, and it is quite important that these be brought out, at least in an introductory way. The principal reasons are, I believe:

1. **Long run vs. short run**. Profitability measures current performance, and there are many actions that the division manager can take to improve current performance at the expense of future performance. The corporation is interested in long-run performance. Examples are, a decrease in advertising or research expenditures, which automatically improves current profit, but which probably will hurt future profit. The key result area on market position presumably attempts to measure whether the division manager is taking short-run actions that affect his market position and hence will show up in the future, and the measure on product leadership has a similar purpose with respect to research. Another example is the personnel development item. This is an item which is an expense in the short run and hence cuts short-run profits, but an expense incurred for the good of the corporation.

2. **External forces**. The division's current profitability may be affected by external forces which the division manager cannot control. For example, in good times, profits will almost automatically increase, but perhaps not as much as they should. An examination of market position, for example, will show whether the division manager is maintaining his share of the market, whatever the total size of the market may be. The productivity item will also show whether plant efficiency is being maintained, which may be masked by the high profits that arise in good times.

3. **Inadequacies of accounting**. The division manager may have various opportunities to manipulate accounting figures, such as deferring expense to some future period. The nondollar measures may overcome this tendency, or at least help to overcome it.

4. **Ethical considerations**. General Electric Company is interested in aspects other than straight profitability, and several of the measures bear on these aspects.

Summary

The residual income approach is good for the General Electric Company. There are many specific problems to be solved in deciding exactly how to measure profitability. These are best solved by applying the criteria of goal congruence and feasibility. The residual income method is better than alternative ways of measuring profitability in GE. (I would like to ask whether it is better in other types of situations, but I never seem to have time to get to this point.)

Nevertheless, profitability alone does not describe the general manager's responsibilities adequately or completely. For the reasons given above, we must use a broader basis of measurement. General Electric attempts to reduce these other measures to numbers. Very few companies do this, but whether they make a numerical measure or whether they use judgment in interpreting the profitability measure, the fact is inescapable that profitability alone is not enough.

EXHIBIT A

Model
(000 omitted)

Income Statement

Revenue		$1,000	
Less: Direct Costs..........	$ 400		
Depreciation	100		
Other Overhead	300	800	
Profit before taxes...........		$ 200	
Taxes		100	
Profit after taxes..............		$ 100	
Capital charge*		60	
Residual Income		$ 40	

Balance Sheet

Current Assets		$ 400	Current Liabilities............................	$ 200
Fixed Assets, Gross................	$1,500			
Depreciation.....................	700		Fixed Debt	300
Fixed Assets, net..............		800	Equity	700
Total Assets...........................	$1,200		Total Equities	$1,200

Return on investment 100/1,000 = 10%

Return on equity 100/700 = 14.3%

RNA

---

* Assume Corporate ROI = 6%

Case 11-4

Enager Industries

Note: This case is rewritten and updated to 1993. However, the issues are essentially the same.

Prologue

Enager Industries is an excellent case on investment center management. To capture the richness of the case, we have reproduced below the teaching notes of four professors—Joe Fisher (Indiana University), Barrett (SMU), Reece (Michigan), and John Shank (Dartmouth).

VG

Enager Teaching Note by Joe Fisher

The participants have now been sensitized to the problems with financial control. Enager is a divisionalized firm with little apparent synergies among the three divisions. The corporation controls the divisions using the financial metric, return on investment (ROI). However, this control metric leads to tension among the divisions and between corporate headquarters and the divisions. The case questions ask participants to analyze why this tension exists and to think about remedies to the tension. The case deals with the following topics:

Objective of Session

1. Responsibility center issues—profit center and investment center concepts

2. ROA management issues

3. Balancing short-run and long-run tradeoffs and financial/nonfinancial tradeoffs

4. Implementing strategy through formal controls—pros and cons

One underlying key to the case discussion is to note that different divisions typically have different strategies. Different strategies imply different organizational structures, and different control systems should be tailored to the strategy and structure of the division.

However, individually tailored control systems lead to increased complexity at the corporate level. It is much easier to control a limited number of "objective" financial measures.

The Enager Case

There are many aspects to this case and which ones to emphasize is a matter of taste. We will give our outline, with other broad issues presented at the end of the case.

The first issue we like to ask is "How is the company doing?" Between 1992 and 1993 sales increased by 5%, net income increased by 11% and assets increased by 18%.

The issue is, did company performance improve? Profits did increase. We raise this issue by asking, "What is the overriding economic objective of a business?" Typically the first answer is "profit maximization." We then ask if that means a firm earning over $100 million net income is twice as profitable as one earning $50 million. Participants soon realize that the profit should be linked with the investment required to generate it, and we arrive at the conclusion that return on investment is a more meaningful measure of a firm's profitability. Most participants will realize that profits should be related to the investment.

ROA calculation:	Profit Margin	× Turnover	= Return on Assets
	NI/Sales	× Sales/Assets	= ROA
1992	5.14%	× 1.105%	= 5.68%
1993	5.46%	× 0.9841%	= 5.37%

What does this imply? Asset management is deteriorating. The overall result is a decreasing ROA.

However,

EPS

1992	1993
$7.27	$7.37

How is it that ROA is down but EPS is up?

One possible cause of this phenomenon is the fact that generally accepted accounting principles ignore the cost of equity capital in calculating net income. For example, a project returning (before interest) 6 percent on assets, which was financed with 8 percent debt, would diminish e.p.s. But, the same project financed by retention of internally generated funds would increase reported e.p.s., even if the project's ROA were less than the overall ROA would have been without the project (thus reducing overall ROA despite the increase in e.p.s.).

In Enager's case, this phenomenon occurred because ΔEBIT ($3,093)[*] exceeded ΔInterest ($1,200), thus increasing e.p.s.; but ΔEBIT + ΔAssets = 9.1%, which was lower than the previous year's average of 9.5%.

The general conclusion is that while *profits* are increasing, *profitability* is decreasing. The company is under pressure to improve performance which is probably why the hurdle rate has been increased.

- Ask the question, "Why was McNeil's proposal rejected?"

The following shows an analysis of McNeil's proposal:

$390,000 Pre-tax
Tax rate 34%
After tax $257,400
$257,400/1,650,000 shares = 15¢ increase in EPS

---

[*] EBIT is a jargon term for "Earnings Before Interest and Taxes."

What does this analysis assume?
    How financed?
    Equity-
    Debt-

This analysis assumes that no stock is issued for the new proposal. Since the participants have been exposed to capital budgeting techniques, they quickly should point out that a discounting technique should be used to evaluate Ms. McNeil's new product proposal. Despite the normative truth of that statement, it is nevertheless quite conceivable that a manager might feel that a project which will improve e.p.s. (and accounting ROI!) should be acceptable.

Another aspect of capital budgeting in an investment center setting (or company-wide setting, for that matter) which often puzzles participants is this: Why is the "hurdle rate" used in evaluating a new project higher than the division's ROI target? One reason is that a Significant portion of a company's capital budget funds must be used for projects which will not (in any obvious way) increase profits—e.g., pollution control equipment. Thus projects which *will* improve profits have to "carry more than their fair share of profitability contribution" in order to compensate for the nondiscretionary (necessity) investments which tend to lower ROI. Other reasons include allowance for risk/uncertainty, and the desire to improve ROI fairly rapidly.

The following overhead calculates the 13% return.

REV:	$18.00 × 100,000 =	$1,800,000
VC:	$9.00 × 100,000 =	900,000
	CM	900,000
	Differential FC	510,000
	Profit Before Tax	390,000
	Tax	132,600
	Profit	$ 257,400
	"Gross" Return	390,000/3,000,000 = 13%

Previous Target 12%

- However, since Enager is already under-performing, management has given new projects a 15% hurdle.

- Estimated 10 year IRR = 10.2%

    yr. 1   (3,000,000)
    yr. 1–10   PAT = 257,400 + Depreciation (150,000) = Cash Flow (A/T) of $407,400
        yr. 11   Return of WC = + 1,500,000

Question the participants, what will ROA on this project look like over time (assume 10 year life)?

At end year 1: 390,000/2,850,000 = 13.7%
                  2: 390,000/2,700,000 = 14.4%
                  10: 390,000/1,500,000 = 26%

So, if we compute ROA, should the asset base consist of book value, replacement cost or some other measure? As can easily be seen, the ROA for the project increases over time as the asset base depreciates. However, any other measure of the asset base also has deficiencies. For example, if replacement cost is chosen, the valuation of the assets becomes problematic.

As a side point, ask the participants, "Is McNeil's project well managed? How can we tell?"

A/R Turnover:

Sales/AR = 1,800,000/450,000 = 4

360/4 = 90 days = Very High!

Inventory Turnover:

CGS/Inv = 1,410,000/900,000 = 1.57

360/1.57 = 230 days = Very High!

This project does not appear to be well managed. The low inventory and accounts receivable turnover reflect this fact. The decreasing asset turnover for the firm as a whole also reflects this problem.

Does the industrial product manager have a legitimate complaint? The industrial products manager may have a legitimate complaint, since his assets are all rather new and would thus deflate his ROA in comparison with a division that had an older asset base. The issue involves definition of assets and profits. If the industrial products manager has recently purchased a lot of equipment which is not yet fully contributing to earnings, ROA is artificially reduced. This is a penalty which may directly contradict the desirability of the investment.

Why might the professional services ROA be so high? The professional services asset base includes mostly human resources. Human assets (expertise) is not recorded on the balance sheet. Therefore, the asset base is understated and the ROA high. ROA is, in general, a poor measure of success in people intensive businesses. Does this argue for *individual* SBU ROA targets? Although it is seemingly self-evident that different investment centers will have different strategies, risk profiles, and ROI potentials, it is nevertheless true that some companies use the same "across-the-board" ROI target percentage for divisions in quite different businesses, as was done by Enager. This phenomenon occurs because the firm may confuse what is a *desirable* economic return for the overall company with what is a reasonable return for the manager to achieve, given conditions in the industry, efficiency of the division's equipment, and so on. For purposes of *managerial* evaluation, a division's ROI target should (may) be negotiated between the division manager and his or her superior, as part of the budgeting process.

ROI versus residual income. Residual income (RI) may be introduced here. If so, an attempt should be made to convey the conceptual advantage of RI over ROI—that having to do with how a division manager would react to a project whose ROI is higher than the cost of capital but lower than the investment center's overall target ROI. This RI concept could also be raised earlier in the context of how to define "profit," since RI essentially corresponds to the economist's view of what constitutes profit.

How should a multi-divisional firm control its assets?

Use of investment centers. Having established that ROI is a measure of interest to top corporate management, it is easy to see that responsibility for earning a reasonable return can be segmented and delegated, just as is profit responsibility delegated to profit center managers. However, if the measure is to be used in evaluating the investment center manager's performance, equitability requires that the manager be able to significantly influence both profit and investment. In many companies, this degree of responsibility is found only at the "division" level and above (where we are using "division" to connote an essentially self-contained business within the corporation).

Enager's top management fell into essentially every trap lurking behind the simplicity of the ROI fraction. In addition to the conceptual flaws, the top-down imposition of the new approach with little explanation or training for the managers was not a good way to introduce a major organizational change, and it's no wonder that "there seems to be a lot more tension among our managers the last two years."

It is a good idea to have an off-site retreat. However, it appears that the top management first should find an expert to discuss ROI and investment center implementation complexities with them to help them understand the causes of the current "tension"; perhaps this same person could then be engaged to play a major role in the retreat and subsequent training sessions.

Other Issues in this Case

Ask the participants how they would control the three divisions, and what impact division strategies have on your answer. This is not an issue that is easily solved or resolves to a unique solution. One group of participants tried to deduce the strategies of the three divisions and then attempted to build controls that were congruent with the strategy. The strategy set we use is the growth-maturity-harvest-divest set. They made the following guesses:

Consumer Products	Perhaps should be growth strategy, but seems to be "Harvest" (reluctant to invest in new ventures; lots of old assets).
Industrial Products	Mature to Harvest Strategy may be appropriate, but growth seems to be stressed (lots of new assets).
Professional Products	Growth (Star?)

The case does not give enough information to answer this question fully, however the participants' best guess is good enough for our purposes here. The important issue is the link from the strategy to the control system. For a given strategy, ask participants how they would control the division (or if ROI measurement is appropriate).

The following response is typical:

Growth Strategy	Control of market share, growth measures and new product development.
Harvest Strategy	Cash flow measures. ROI is probably more applicable here when compared with the growth strategy.

Participants will probably point out that ROI is difficult to implement with a service organization. The real assets of the professional products division (people) are not on the balance sheet. Many service organizations control on billable hours, utilization and new customers, but these are indirect measures of success, at best.

Moral: ROI is conceptually simple but difficult to implement. We will not find a simple solution but, we should be aware of the difficulties in controlling a divisional firm.

Problems With ROI Control

1. Turn down profitable projects because of a high current ROI?

2. Not invest in new assets, which would show good long-term return?

3. Games played increasing income and decreasing investment?

4. Too aggregate for effective control?

Enager Teaching Note by Edgar Barrett

Substantive Issues Raised

Sarah McNeil, product development manager of the Consumer Products Division of Enager Industries, Inc., is upset because a new product proposal that she had developed has not been accepted by top management. The principal reason for rejection seems to be that the project does not have as high a rate of return as has been chosen as a hurdle rate by the corporate vice-president of finance. At the same time, both the vice-president of finance and the president have been calling for projects which would raise return on investment and earnings per share, and McNeil is sure her project meets these criteria.

For two years, each division at Enager Industries has been measured on the basis of its return on assets. The asset structure of each division is markedly different, and therefore it is not surprising that division managers are not equally pleased with the new performance criterion that has been adopted. Furthermore, results in the two most recent years, 1992 and 1993, have provided confusing signals to corporate officers.

Pedagogical Objectives

This case focuses on the broad range of problems that arise when profit, investment, and return on investment are selected as criteria for project approval, measurement of economic performance, and evaluation of the manager's performance. The detail in the case allows a thorough discussion of the use of return on investment as a measurement criterion.

The project proposal described in the case is simple enough to raise a variety of issues about project analysis and whether or not criteria of contribution and income or some other criterion such as internal rate of return is the best measure of whether or not a new project should be accepted. The case also allows discussion of the impact of acceptance of a project on earnings per share and return on investment. Finally, the case allows a focus on the issues involved in the implementation of a new performance measurement and management control system in a divisionalized corporation.

Opportunities for Student Analysis

Student analysis of the case most profitably moves from specific to general issues. Consequently, the first question (included at the end of the case) is designed to induce the student to ask whether the project proposal developed by Sarah McNeil meets the criterion set by management when they adopted the return on investment measurement system. There are several ways to approach this analysis.

The Economics. Looking first at the economics of the proposal, we should test McNeil's statement, "No matter how we price this new item, we figure to make $390,000 on it pre-tax." Using the price and volume estimates in the case the analysis presented in Exhibit TN-1 confirms that this is true (if the price/volume estimates are correct). Thus, the only apparent reason for rejection of the project is that its gross return on invested capital falls below the target rate of 15% that has been established for new investments.

$390,000 + 3,000,000 = 13$ percent < 15 percent

Further analysis by the student might lead to an investigation as to how this project would affect other measures of corporate performance. For example, would it increase corporate return on assets? Divisions are evaluated by return on assets, which is defined as:

Profit before Tax[*] – Allocated Corp. Tax/Division Assets + Allocated Corp. Assets = R.O.A.

(Since this project is expected to increase both the division's revenue and profit, it may well increase the Consumer Product Division's allocated share of administrative expenses, corporate tax and corporate assets. In this instance, we have assumed that the other two divisions will grow enough to keep pace with the growth in Consumer Products, so we are not allocating it any greater percentage of corporate expenses, taxes or assets.)

$390,000 - (390,000 \times .34)/3,000,000 = 257,400/3,000,000 = 8.58\%$ R.O.A.

It is clear that the 8.58% R.O.A. figure compares favorably with the 5.37% for the corporation. Thus, the project *would* increase return on assets.

Another measurement of performance noted in the case is the so-called "Gross Return." As is stated there, this number is derived as follows:

Corporate Earnings Before Interest & Taxes (EBIT)/Total Corporate Assets = Gross Return

---

[*] The Divisional "Profit before Tax" figure will have already been reduced by that division's allocated share of corporate administrative expenses.

Comparing the gross returns for the corporation as a whole and by divisions, we find that Sarah McNeil's new project would increase gross returns for both the corporation and her own (or any other) division:

Company Average	=	9.4%
Professional Services Division	=	14.6%
Consumer Products Division	=	10.8%
Industrial Products Division	=	6.9%
"Project Return"	=	13.0%

Finally, if debt is used to finance this project, the interest expense would reduce net income and owner's equity (via retained earnings), but the greater amount of debt would lower the owner's equity percentage of sources of funds, so that the return on equity should be increased if the return on the project is higher than the interest rate paid to finance it.

All of the above analysis leads to the conclusion that this project looks good compared to current performance. It apparently fails only because it does not meet the 15% gross return target decreed by Henry Hubbard. Before we could offer a definitive judgment as to whether Hubbard was wise to reject this investment, we would need to know two things: 1) what other projects are available and the returns they offer; and, 2) the cost of capital to finance this project. By this point in the analysis, however, all students should quite clearly understand why Sarah McNeil is bitterly disappointed with management's rejection of her project.

Return on Investment Criteria. At this point, the class analysis should probably turn to the construction and use of the return on investment criteria. The DuPont formula chart shown in Exhibit TN-2 shows the components that build to form an ROI number. With these interrelationships in mind, it is easier to understand the problems faced by management at Enager Industries. Obviously there are two component parts of Return on Investment, the measurement (or definition) of "Return" and the measurement (or definition) chosen of "Investment." Some of the more common problems arising on the denominator side are noted in the following paragraphs:

1. **Use of Gross Assets for Permanent Investment.** One might employ historical purchase price values for assets without consideration for depreciation, or current replacement or salvage values. This is a stable number, not declining from year to year, although with inflation the stated return on assets may climb over the years, giving the impression of a slightly increasing return. If, through obsolescence, the production by these assets falls, the ROI number falls and managers are encouraged by the system to get rid of assets, even if they could be marginally productive or it might be wise to keep them for other uses later.

2. **Use of "Net Book Value" for Permanent Investment.** One might also employ historical purchase price less accumulated depreciation values. This method of determining an asset base leads to constantly declining values for any given set of assets. Thus, it will normally lead to a higher ROI figure each year even if the actual profit number remains the same. Keeping old, depreciated, lowly-valued assets makes managers look good (possibly, even in the face of increasing repairs necessary with older equipment, which are expensed in each period). This may lead managers to retain old assets and defer the purchase of new assets (even if the new assets would be more efficient or more cost-beneficial).

3. **Use of Replacement Costs of Assets for Permanent Investment.** This method, for simplicity's sake, might be seen as being the same as fair market values for assets. This represents a good concept, since it may seem to be a fair valuation to all concerned. As is well known, however, it is very difficult to calculate because of the problems of evaluating a current price for a similar machine less physical depreciation and functional obsolescence, or a percentage of current value for a better machine (which was not available when this one was bought but which one would decide to purchase if the purchase decision were made today).

Depending upon the sophistication of students, they will consider a variety of alternatives including gross assets, replacement costs of assets, or other arbitrary measures of investment. Depending upon the sophistication of their analyses, the defects of each of these are likely to come out in their conclusions, as well as in the classroom discussion.

A second set of issues arises because the company has chosen to use the same criterion for all divisions or for comparisons of divisions. The divisions at Enager are substantially different from each other. Professional services is not capital intensive and, therefore, will always find it easy to meet a return on investment or return on asset criterion. In contrast, both the consumer products and the industrial products divisions require producing assets. Consumer products, however, has older assets which, when treated net of depreciation, inevitably will make the manager of that division look better than the manager of the industrial products division which is not only capital-intensive but also has newer assets which are valued at much nearer their acquisition costs.

Using the same criterion of ROA to evaluate performance of all three divisions or performance of the managers of all three divisions is simply not fair, unless a different *target* ROA is set for each division, and then evaluation is in comparison to this goal. The target ROA should be set by agreement between top management and the manager of each division with consideration given to the conditions specific to each division, e.g., the relevant asset base, expected growth of the economy in that area, etc.

Any criterion is acceptable for evaluation as long as it is individualized to the situation in each division, and a series of personal conferences held with the head of each division to set this goal is certainly preferable to imposition of a 12% company-wide goal from the top. Not only might the goals become more realistic through individual conferences but the morale of the managers will probably rise. In setting goals, several methods should be considered by management, such as residual income, ROA, ROI, and net profit defined in various ways. Once a realistic goal has been agreed upon between top management and divisional managers, the percentage by which it is accomplished or exceeded could be used for comparison between divisions, if a comparison needs to be made.

Other Analytical Issues. The fact that gross return (EBIT divided by assets) has fallen from 9.5% to 9.4% in 1993 is probably due to the fact that new assets were added faster than income increased. This is not an unusual result if the new assets involved an expansion. The corporation may simply have to give those assets time to pay off.

Likewise, return on assets (net income divided by assets) fell from 1992 to 1993 for the same reason of increased investment in assets. An examination of the financial statements in these two years reveals large increases in plant and equipment, investments, accounts receivable, and inventory which are being financed through long-term debt, common stock, and apparently efficient use of current liabilities, such as accounts payable.

At the same time, return on invested capital has dropped from 6.9% to 6.6%, and return on owner's equity has increased from 9.1% to 9.2% because a higher proportion of debt than equity was used to finance asset expansion.

Action Steps. Concerning what to do at Enager now, the first objective should probably be for the president (and possibly also Henry Hubbard) to become much more aware and knowledgeable in respect to the various performance measurements available, what they mean, how they can be influenced, and how they can influence (motivate) the performance of managers. Once educated, top management should realize they are running three separate businesses, and possibly even divide the financial statement into three divisions, summarized by a consolidated set of financial statements. This realization of being in three separate businesses should make it easier for top management to set different profitability goals for each.

Once the basic educating of the top management is accomplished, and the same information has been distributed to divisional managers, the one-day, off-site "retreat" of both corporate and divisional managers to discuss new goals for each division and the means to achieve them could be quite profitable for both financial returns *and* personnel morale, but such a retreat is not essential. *Any* re-evaluation of divisional goals by top management at this point would be beneficial if it is done with knowledge and the cooperation of divisional managers.

Having decided upon different objectives for each division, top management probably will be more open to accepting projects that will yield a greater than current ROA even if they are less than desired ROA, in order to raise the total current ROA. Knowing when to override a criterion is one of the most important judgment calls of a good top manager.

Suggestions for Classroom Use

This case is rich with issues. As a result, it can be used from the undergraduate level to the executive program arena. Discussion may be very structured or range widely over the issues discussed above. If students are unfamiliar with the use of return on investment measures, an additional reading assignment which discusses the problems with such measurements or kinds of responsibility centers and their use in controlling divisional operations will prove helpful. Two good articles are:

John Dearden, "The Case Against ROI Control," *Harvard Business Review*, May–June, 1969.

James S. Reece and William R. Cool, "Measuring Investment Center Performance," *Harvard Business Review*, May–June, 1978.

Return on investment or return on assets are complex measures because they require both the measurement of income and the determination of the investment for which we hold managers responsible. Using such a measure for evaluating economic performance is quite different from using it to evaluate managers themselves, particularly if managers have little or no control over investment. Also, the results given by a measurement such as return on investment will not always agree with the results promised by an investment proposal analyzed using discounted cash flow techniques. Finally, systems for evaluating management performance must be designed and used carefully to achieve the results that management wants. Attention should be paid to the measurements employed, the targets which are communicated to managers, the way in which divisional performance is measured, the way in which divisional managers' performance is measured, and how rewards are allocated.

Suggested Questions

The questions included with the case have proven effective in many contexts in stimulating student discussion across the broad range of issues discussed above. More specific questions on return on investment might be included in the assignment if the articles mentioned in the preceding section have been assigned.

Elaine Luttrell, under the supervision of M. Edgar Barrett with acknowledgments to William J. Bruns, Jr., 1981 James S. Reece, 1977

Enager Industries

"Project Return" from McNeil's Consumer Product Proposal

Price per unit	$18.00	$21.00	$24.00
Variable cost per unit	9.00	9.00	9.00
Contribution per unit	$ 9.00	$12.00	$15.00
Estimated Volume (units)	100,000	75,000	60,000
Total contribution	$900,000	$900,000	$900,000
Differential fixed costs*	$510,000	$510,000	$510,000
"Project Return"	$390,000	$390,000	$390,000

Investment required = $3,000,000

*Depreciation expense is included as part of "Differential Fixed Costs." Therefore, if one were to define the "Project" return as *cash*, the number would be greater than $390,000.

Exhibit TN-2
Enager Industries
Formula Chart

Relationship of Factors Affecting Return on Investment

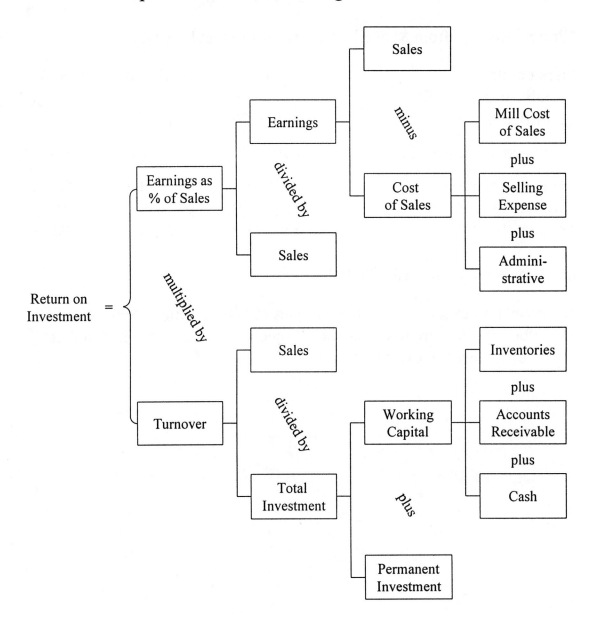

Enager Industries, Inc.: Teaching Note by James Reece

This case was written for use in a required one-semester course in management accounting, where usually only a single session is devoted to investment centers. Whereas most available cases on investment centers focus in detail on narrower issues, such as proper valuation of fixed assets for an investment center, this case is intended to raise both the rationale for having investment centers and some of the broader issues surrounding ROI and an investment center structure for a responsibility center.

Broad Case Issues

As different instructors will choose to emphasize different aspects of this case, I will simply describe sequentially the various issues the case raises.

1. **Profit versus profitability**. I raise this issue by asking, "What is the overriding economic objective of a business?" Typically the first answer is "profit maximization." I then ask if that means a firm earning $100 million net income is twice as profitable as one earning $50 million. Students soon realize that the profit should be linked with the investment required to generate it, and we arrive at the conclusion that return on investment is the more meaningful measure of a firm's profitability.

2. **Use of investment centers**. Having established that ROI is a measure of interest to top corporate management, it is easy to see that responsibility for earning a reasonable return can be segmented and delegated, just as is profit responsibility delegated to profit center managers. However, if the measure is to be used in evaluating the investment center manager's performance, equitability requires that the manager be able to significantly influence both profit and investment. In many companies, this degree of responsibility is found only at the "divisional" level and above (where I am using "division" to connote an essentially self-contained business within the corporation).

   At this point I draw the very important distinction between using ROI to measure economic performance of a responsibility center and using it to measure the performance of the center's manager. (In my experience, this distinction is too frequently missing in industry.) There is really no need to treat a responsibility center as an investment center if the manager doesn't influence asset levels; this does not mean, of course, that the center's ROI can't be computed for analytical purposes (e.g., for consideration for discontinuing that responsibility center's activities)-but this computation does not need to be performed frequently, or perhaps even regularly.

   I also tell the students that the profit center/investment center distinction appears more in textbooks than in practice: most managers I have met call both types of responsibility center simply "profit centers."

3. **Definition of ROI**. By now, the students are aware that ROI is (simplistically) defined as profits divided by investment. I now ask, "What is investment?" I am not trying at this point to get into valuation of specific assets, but rather the broader notion that to businesspersons the word "investment" variously means total assets, invested capital (total assets minus current liabilities, or equivalently, long-term liabilities plus owners' equity), or owners' equity.

I point out that none of these concepts is right or wrong—it depends on the perspective of the person considering ROI. A shareholder (and probably also securities analysts) would be most interested in return on equity. Corporate financial officers seem to focus on return on invested capital (the apparent notion being that current liabilities are both "free," and "take care of themselves.") Operating managers don't really care how the assets they manage were financed (nor can they usually tell, since "all money is green"); they (and their superiors) are concerned about how well the assets are utilized, leading to a return-on-assets perspective.

Exhibit 4 contains several ROI measures, to highlight the fact that the term ROI itself is extremely ambiguous. The calculation of return on invested capital has been adjusted for interest, whereas return on assets has not (because this is the way Enager is calculating ROA).

4. **ROI growth and e.p.s. growth not necessarily equivalent**. I point out to students that it is possible to increase earnings per share while decreasing ROI. Indeed, Enager presents an example of this: from 1992 to 1993 e.p.s. increased, but return on assets (ROA) went down. I must confess that this possibility had never occurred to me until I read Frederick Searby's article in the March–April 1975 *Harvard Business Review*, "Return to Return on Investment." (Instructors may wish to consider using reprints of this article with the Enager case.)

One possible cause of this phenomenon is the fact that generally accepted accounting principles ignore the cost of equity capital in calculating net income. For example, a project returning (before interest) 6 percent on assets, which was financed with 8 percent debt, would diminish e.p.s. But the same project financed by retention of internally generated funds would increase reported e.p.s., even if the project's ROA were less than the overall ROA would have been without the project (thus reducing overall ROA despite the increase in e.p.s.). In Enager's case, this phenomenon occurred because ΔEBIT exceeded interest, thus increasing e.p.s.; but ΔEBIT $\div$ ΔAssets was lower than the previous year's average.

5. **Setting ROI targets**. Although it is seemingly self-evident that different investment centers will have different risk profiles and ROI potentials, it is nevertheless true that some companies use the same "across-the-board" ROI target percentage for divisions in quite different businesses, as was done by Mr. Hubbard of Enager. I think this phenomenon occurs for a reason alluded to earlier—confusing what is a *desirable* economic return for the overall company with what is a reasonable return for the manager to achieve, given conditions in the industry, efficiency of the division's equipment, and so on. For purposes of *managerial* evaluation, a division's ROI target should be negotiated between the division manager and his or her superior, as part of the budgeting process.

6. **Defining "profit" in ROI**. Whatever degree of detail the instructor wishes to get into here, at a minimum students should realize that defining "profit" as "net income calculated using the same generally accepted accounting principles as are used for reporting to shareholders" is only *one* of many ways of defining profit for ROI computations. For example, depreciation can be based on replacement costs rather than historical costs; or a variable costing approach can be used instead of full costing. Also, a company can use the notion of *controllable* profit for calculating ROI.

In general, I think a definition involving controllable profit is best for calculating ROI for purposes of *managerial* evaluation, but that a "net" figure after including noncontrollable allocations is better for *economic* performance analyses. Again, in my experience, companies usually do not make this distinction, and tend to use a GAAP net income figure in the ROI calculations. (See James S. Reece and William R. Cool, "Measuring Investment Center Performance," *Harvard Business Review*, May–June 1978.)

7. **Valuing "investment" in ROI.** Whether one regards "investment" as total assets, invested capital, or owners' equity, asset valuation affects the indicated amount of investment once again, in my experience, companies tend to value assets for ROI computation the same way they report asset amounts to shareholders. Students should realize that this is only one alternative, as they are more likely to realize these days given all the discussion of replacement-cost accounting.

8. **ROI versus residual income.** While I feel this is too advanced for a one-session shot at ROI, some of my colleagues feel that residual income (RI) should be introduced here. If so, an attempt should be made to convey the conceptual advantage of RI over ROI—that having to do with how a division manager would react to a project whose projected ROI is higher than the cost of capital but lower than the investment center's overall target ROI. This RI concept could also be raised earlier in the context of how to define "profit," since RI essentially corresponds to the economist's view of what constitutes profit.

9. **New project proposals in an ROI system.** This is the "lead-off" issue in Enager. If your students have been exposed to capital budgeting techniques, they quickly will point out that a discounting technique should be used to evaluate Ms. McNeil's new product proposal. Despite the normative truth of that statement, it is nevertheless quite conceivable that a manager might feel that a project which will improve e.p.s. (*and* accounting ROI!) should be acceptable. (See Lerner and Rappaport's "Limit DCF in Capital Budgeting," *Harvard Business Review*, September–October 1968.)

    Another aspect of capital budgeting in an investment center setting (or companywide setting, for that matter) which often puzzles students is this: Why is the "hurdle rate" used in evaluating a new project higher than the division's ROI target? One reason is that a significant portion of a company's capital budget funds must be used for projects which will not (in any obvious way) increase profits—e.g., pollution control equipment. Thus projects which *will* improve profits have to "carry more than their fair share of profitability contribution" in order to compensate for the nondiscretionary (necessity) investments which tend to lower ROI. Other reasons include allowance for risk/uncertainty, and the desire to improve ROI fairly rapidly.

10. **Overall "moral."** ROI is conceptually simple, but complex to implement (if one recognizes the pitfalls, as Hubbard and Randall did not). Students should not be left with the feeling that ROI should be avoided, but rather that its implementation should be approached with great care.

Issues Specific to Enager

1. **What is the incremental ROI on the proposed project?** The case numbers are "rigged" so that the incremental EBIT percentage at any of the three prices is 13 percent ($390,000 +

$3,000,000). A variation on this calculation is to say that, at least in an accounting sense, the *average* plant and equipment investment over the life of the project is only $750,000, giving an ROI of 26.0 percent ($390,000 + $1,500,000). We do not know the potential life of this project; its payback period will be approximately 5.5 years [(390,000 + 150,000 depreciation) + 3,000,000]. (Assume ten year straight line depreciation.) I ask the students this question: Suppose Enager was committed to go ahead with this project—would you suggest a price per unit of $18, $21, or $24? Students cannot choose on the basis of incremental profit, which we have seen is the same ($900,000 contribution less $510,000 fixed costs = $390,000) at all three prices. Some will say $18, because it gives the largest market share (a point of view which may have validity, if one believes the Boston Consulting Group's experience curve hypothesis). Others will say $24, since that has the lowest break-even volume; however, in my opinion, one cannot choose based on break-even volume, since at each of the three prices the break-even volume is 56 2/3 percent of the estimated sales volume at that price, and profits are the same at the three estimated sales volumes.

Eventually a student will realize that the *current* asset investment should not be assumed to be the same at all three prices (as I have let them implicitly assume to this point in the discussion): certainly a volume of 100,000 units ($1,800,000 revenues) will require more cash on hand, receivables, and inventories than would a volume of 60,000 units ($1,440,000). Therefore the price chosen on short-term ROI analysis should be $24. This discussion of variability of current assets with volume may also cause some students to notice that the projected level of current assets seems excessive. If volume = 100,000 units, average unit cost = $14.10; $150,000 cash is 39 days' expenses (really more, after considering depreciation); $450,000 receivables is 3 months' sales; and $900,000 inventories is 233 days' worth. Based on the company's average ratios, the current asset picture at a price of $18 and volume of 100,000 units would be:

Cash = $1,410,000/365 days × 8 days' cash =	$ 30,900
Receivables = $1,800,000/365 days × 75 days' cash A/R =	370,000
Inventories = 100,000 units/365 days × 160 days × $14.10 =	618,000
Total Current Assets	$1,018,900

Avg. ROI = $390,000/($1,018,900 + $750,000) = 22.0% (v. 26.0%)

Not only does projected ROI improve: note that the three current asset utilization ratios used in this adjusted projection do not represent very laudatory current asset management. And again, the ROI (short-run, at least) would be still higher at the higher-price/lower-volume combinations.

2. **Explain Enager's 1992 versus 1992 results**. This is best done, I feel, using a "DuPont chart" approach. Essentially all of the numbers for this analysis (on a return-on-assets basis) are included in the case. This is a very useful approach, in my opinion, because it demonstrates how ROI is impacted by decisions made throughout the organization.

3. **Enager's implementation of ROI**. The preceding discussion in this commentary should make it rather clear that Enager's top management (i.e., Hubbard and Randall) fell into essentially every trap lurking behind the simplicity of the ROI fraction. In addition to the conceptual flaws, the top-down impositions of the new approach with little explanation or training for the managers was not a good way to introduce a major organizational change, and it's no wonder that "there seems to be a lot more tension among our managers the last two years."

Personally, I feel Ms. Kraus has a good idea in the off-site retreat. However, it appears that Hubbard and Randall first should engage a consultant to discuss ROI and investment center implementation complexities with them to help them understand the causes of the current "tension"; perhaps this same person could then be engaged to play a major role in the retreat and subsequent training sessions.

Enager Industries: Teaching Note by John Shank

Prologue

John Shank has retitled the case as Tuck Industries. All the financial numbers in "Enager Industries" have been based on "Tuck Industries" (multiplied by a factor of three).

Overview

Tuck Industries is not a real company. Rather, it is a composite of many component issues and ideas, each of which is taken from real companies in the "soaring 60s." The case is an excellent vehicle for reinforcing problem recognition and for reviewing many basic financial analysis techniques. Problem recognition is emphasized in the sense that the company has a great many problems of all kinds—how many can the student see? Technique areas covered include contribution analysis, project economics, ABC, cash flow analysis, ROI analysis, ratio analysis, performance measures, capital structure, and takeover maneuvers.

The case is fun for students and fun to teach. It will clearly support a full class period of discussion, or more, depending on how deeply the instructor wants to delve into each area. We see the exercise as essentially broad and shallow. That is, we try to cover as many issues as possible but don't try to cover any of them very deeply. The case isn't rich enough to go very deeply on any issue, but, it is broad enough to support a wide-ranging "review" class.

We use the case at or near the end of the required management accounting course. We have also used it as a final exam case, with a 3- or 4-hour time limit.

Teaching Strategy

We go through the assignment questions in order. The questions are arranged to build upon each other. We try to save at least 10 minutes at the end for the classic "what would you do?" question. However, we don't push hard in this case for the students to "put themselves in the

---

This teaching commentary was prepared by Professor John K. Shank of the Amos Tuck School of Business.

shoes of management." The case is rigged so that it is legitimately very difficult to generate much empathy or sympathy for the president or the CFO.

We plan to spend no more than 10 or 15 minutes on any one question, but the instructor should be aware that any one of the questions can absorb 30 minutes or more if you let it. We "cold call" very strong students for this day to maximize the chance that we get good coverage across the issues and do not get bogged down along the line. The instructor should keep in mind that the case is intended as a review and not as the first exposure by students to any of the ideas which emerge.

Answers to Assignment Questions

The following analyses go as deeply as possible into each of the questions. We would not expect students to go this deeply on any one question.

Question 1

A) EBIT

	As Shown	+	Add Back Corporate Allocation	=	Gross Margin	−	Sales & Marketing "ABC"[1]	−	Corporate General Expense[2]	=	Revised EBIT
Consumer	3.6		3.6		7.2		(6.2)		(.6)		.4
Industrial	2.5		3.6		6.1		(.3)		(.6)		5.2
Professional	1.1		3.6		4.7		(2.5)		(.6)		1.6
	7.2		10.8		18.0		(9.0)		(1.8)		7.2

B) Investment

	A/R + Inventory	−	Less Current Liabilities[3]	+ Cash[4] +	Gross Fixed Assets[5]	=	Revised Total	Revised Gross ROA
Consumer	20.3		(6.7)	.7	21.2		35.5	1.1%
Industrial	14.8		(4.8)	.5	24.5		35.0	14.6%
Professional	6.0		(1.9)	.2	—		4.3	37.2%
	41.1		(13.4)	1.4	45.7		74.8[6]	9.5%

Notes:

1. Probably about 25% of sales for a marketing-intensive customer products business
   10% of sales is *given* for professional services
   Plug industrial at .3 — A job shop like this should have very little "Sales & Marketing" expense

2. Assign corporate overhead based on sales—The *real* issue here is whether *any* value is added by corporate!

3. Deduct current liabilities, allocated based on current assets.

4. Assign cash based on current assets and *exclude* corporate investment.

5. Use *gross* fixed assets rather than *net* — A better rough proxy for "replacement cost"?

6. Reconciliation to the balance sheet:

Total assets	75.4
Add back depreciation	16.0
Less current liabilities	(13.4)
Less corporate investment	(3.2)
"Gross Assets"	74.8

C. Inferences

1. Consumer

   a. Working Capital (WC) Assets = 82% of Sales = Terrible!

   b. Gross Margin (GM) = 7.2/24.8 = 29% = Far too low!

   c. Gross ROA = 1+% = Dismal, even with benefit of assets brought at lower price levels.

This business *sucks* and is just *soaking up wasted* WC as it grows. *Why do we keep it?*

2. Industrial

   a. WC Assets = 60% of sales = too high. Probably excess WIP inventory (no FG).

   b. GM% = 6/24.7 = 24+% = OK for a "lean/mean" job shop.

   c. Gross ROA = 14.6%, in spite of heavy asset additions in 1968 for the future = *pretty good.*

3. Professional

   a. This is a "people" business for which ROA doesn't mean much.

   b. Receivables at 89 days is way too high—may be a *"customer value"* problem on billing.

   c. Should be higher than 37% ROA/heavy Sell/Mktg. investment in the future?

   d. Could be a good business, but not *clear.*

Question 2

A) Corporate Level, Aggregated

		Sources		Uses	
PAT	2.9				
Dep'n	+3.3	Operations	6.6	+ΔAR	1.9
Def tax	+ .4	Sell Stock	2.1	+ΔInventory	3.3
		+ΔLTD	4.4	+ΔInvestment	1.1
		+ΔCL	2.5	Dividends	.9*
			15.6	Buy Property	8.4
					15.6

*$900,000/550,000 = ~$1.60/share
Yield = 1.60/42 = ~4%

Or

1. Operations $(6.6 + 2.5 - 1.9 - 3.3)$ = 3.9   ⎫
2. Financing $(4.4 + 2.1 - .9)$ = 5.6   ⎬ Net $\underline{0}$ (By Definition!)
3. Investing $(8.4 + 1.1)$ = (9.5)   ⎭

B) Division Level Cash Flow—1968

	Consumer	Industrial	Professional	Total
Revised EBIT	.4	5.1	1.6	7.1
− Interest[1]	(.3)	(.7)	—	(1.0)
− Taxes	(.05)	(2.35)	(.8)	(3.2)
PAT	.05	2.05	.8	2.9
+ Depreciation[2]	1.6	1.7	—	3.3
+ Def. Tx	—	.4	—	.4
Cash flow from Operations	1.65	4.15	.8	6.6
+ ΔA/R	(.5)	(.4)	(1.0)	(1.9)
+ ΔInventory	(1.8)	(1.5)	—	(3.3)
Capital Expenditures	(.4)	(8.0)	—	(8.4)
Net Before Financing	(1.05)	(5.75)	(.2)	(7.0)

Recap

		+ ΔFinancing		
Net from Operations—As Above	(7.0)	Trade Payables[3]	2.5	← (75+ days seems very suspect
Corporate Investments	(1.1)	Issue Debt	4.4	← (marginal interest rate = .4/4.4 = 9%, vs. 5% average last year)
Dividends	(.9)	Sell Stock	2.1	← (sale price = $42/share vs. $80 book value)
Total to be Financed	(9.0)		9.0	

Notes:

1. The 1967 debt of $12.6M spread equally to 2 divisions, at 5% interest. The new debt in 1968 charged to industrial division at 9%.

2. Allocated based on gross assets in 1968.

3. <u>Days Purchases Outstanding</u>

Cost of goods sold	56.3		
– Depreciation	(3.3)		
+ Corporate Expenses	<u>11.8</u>	64.8	13.4/64.8 = 20.7 = 75.5 days

Observations

1. Inventory & AR growth exceeded sales growth 5.2 vs. 3.5) → Lousy WC management. (AR & Inventory for C and I together *up* on *flat* sales!)

2. Sold stock at 50% of BV = Very bad form!
   $2.1M/50,000 = $42 vs. $44M/550,000 = $80
   They must have been desperate for cash to accept this kind of equity dilution.

3. Heavy *external* financing at *steeply higher* interest rates (5% in 67 vs. 9% on new debt) to grow business where the net mix does not seem to be earning a reasonable WACC—*WHY*? *Marginal Cost of Debt* = 9% vs. 5% for '67 → Lenders see problems!

4. Apparently still conglomerating since "investments" still growing—WHY?

5. 30% dividend payout in spite of major growth. Why not *retain more* to self finance growth? (4% dividend yield seems "OK")

6. Could have financed capital expenditure without new outside financing if could hold down Accounts Receivable, Inventory, and "Investments."

7. Only the Industrial Division shows positive operating cash flow before capital expenditures. Weak cash flow for consumer and professional.

Question 3

First, note that *corporate* financial ratios aren't very meaningful here because they are an amalgam from three disparate businesses.

1. <u>Balance Sheet—1968</u>

   <u>Accounts Receivable</u>
   Consumer = 6.2/24.8 = 90 days = very high
   Industrial = 3.4/24.7 – 50 days = about OK
   Professional = 6.0/24.7 = 89 days = very high (may be indicative of poor
         customer satisfaction)

   <u>Inventory</u>
   Consumer = 14.1/17.6 = 80% = 292 days = very high
   Industrial = 11.4/18.7 = 61% = 222 days = very high, since a job shop should
         have zero finished goods

Payables and accruals

At 75+ days expenses outstanding, Tuck is probably viewed as a slow pay, bad customer by its suppliers

Long Term Debt

ΔDebt = 4.4 million and ΔInterest = .4, a 9% rate versus 5% average last year (.6/12.6). Apparently, lenders see problems in the extra leverage.

Leverage at D/D of 17/17 + 4 = 28%
and Interest Coverage = EBIT/I of 7.1/1 = >7x
Means Tuck is still *not* heavily leveraged.

Owners Equity

a. ΔCommon Stock of $2.1 million for Δ50,000 shares implies Tuck sold stock at $42/share, with book value of $80/share. This was a remarkably low issue price. This suggests Tuck was in *desperate* need of new equity. Why?

b. ΔRE of +$2.0 versus PAT of $2.9 implies a $.9 million dividend. Why is Tuck paying out 30+% of earnings (.9/2.9) when there is such heavy investment need?

2. Earnings Statement—1968

	EBIT as shown	Add Back Corporate Expenses	Gross Sales	%Sales	Comment
Consumer	3.6	3.6	7.2	29%	Very low for a marketing intensive business
Industrial	2.4	3.6	6.0	24+%	Seems OK for a job shop
Professional	1.1	3.6	4.7	19%	Very low for a consulting firm unless there is substantial "investment" in people ahead of presumed sales growth

Sales growth = $3.5 million, with +20% for Professional = $+4.1(24.7/1.2 = $20.6), we can infer that sales for Consumer and Industrial actually *dropped* $.6 million!

Question 4

1. Lousy W/C Management (90 days AR & one inventory turn) → *Poor Management of the Division*

2. Cannot possibly be *indifferent* to price/volume choices

a. As a small niche player, only $8 would make sense for us—*Diff'n vs. low cost* strategy

b. $8 also means *lower* WC investment for *same* cash flow

$6 price makes very little sense for Tuck, but the 60K volume at $8 is only half the capacity—this suggests: *build smaller* scale equipment (unless expect growth, which *isn't* in the proposal).

Lousy Strategic Thinking

3. Apparently, the analysis *excludes* any ΔSell/Marketing Expense. Division *gross* margin is 29%, overall. For this project the margin is 22% or 27% depending on sales price. This seems too high for *net* margin—more likely a gross margin, before selling and marketing.

4. IRR as shown (with zero Δ selling and marketing expense)

   a. Year 0 (1000)
      Years 1–10 = 112.4 in After Tax Cash Flow
      Year 11 = +500 (WC recovery + salvage value)
      IRR = ~7.5% = pretty thin (WACC?)

   b. With $8 price and (120 + 180 = 300 WC) & half used plant!

      Year 0 (850,000)
      Years 1–10 = 112,400   IRR = 9.2%
      Year 11 = +350,000   Probably > Weighted Average Cost of Capital

5. No *apparent* awareness of basic project economics by management.

Overall, they don't seem to be a good bet for good management of the project.

Rejection seems *reasonable.*

And, per Q1, Q2, and Q3, whole consumer products business is a *dog!*

Why try to expand a loser?!

Question 5

1. Stock price at $42 vs. BV of $80 implies the company is worth more *dead* than *alive* (assume assets liquidated at book value). [Let *me* kill it, for a *fee* of course.]

2. Company is investing heavily in the Industrial Products Business, using low value stock & running up the leverage—why dissipate the borrowing capacity?

3. Lousy control over A/R & Inventory → lax management of working capital.

4. Still, not highly leveraged: D = 17, E = 44, D/D + E = 28%

5. Good cash flow, pre capital expenditures & pre corporate overhead = ~6.6 + .9 = 7.5 = >10% of sales, after tax. EBIT/Interest = 7.1/1 = 7X coverage.

<u>Takeover strategy</u>:

1. Tender (at 20% premium?) $42 \times 1.2 = \$50.4$/share
   Purchase price $= \$50.4 \times 550,000 = \$27.7$ million

2. Receivables "dividend" (down to 45 days $= \$9.5$ vs. $\$15.6$) $= \$6.3$ million.

3. Inventory "dividend" $= \$14.8$ million

   > Consumer CGS $= 17.6$ |
   > Industrial CGS $= 18.7$ | (4X on $\$36.3 = \$9.1$ vs. $\$25.5$)
   > Sell $\$16.4$ *Excess* inventory at *80%* $= \$13.1$. Tax loss of 3.3 saves 1.7 in taxes.
   >   [$\$13.1 + 1.7 = \$14.8$]

4. Can also strip out excess cash & "investment" of ~$4 million.

5. After the "dividends," equity $= \$17.3$ $[44 - 6.3 - 14.8 - 1.6 - 4 = 17.3]$. This is 1:1 with debt.

6. New owner's net investment now is $27.7 - 6.3 - 14.8 - 4 = 2.6$

7. Billy Bob winds up with control of $6.6 million annual cash flow for $2.6 million! Higher if drop useless 1.8 of corporate overhead.

8. Divest Consumer Division for some multiple of operating cash flow?

Question 6

[3 different business, 3 different hurdle rates, 3 different performance packages]

A. <u>Consumer</u>: Using ROA is OK, but a *high risk* business with *low* leverage implies a goal of 9% AT, at least

   > ROA $= 9\%$
   > A/E $= 2$X
   > ROE $= 18\%$

   <u>"KSFs"</u>? Only a niche/differ strategy is plausible

   > SOM in niches
   > New customers
   > New products
   > Must manage A/R & Inventory
   > Quality & Service measures
   > Manufacturing margins must be ~50%
   >   •
   >   •
   >   •

B. Industrial: Using ROA is OK, with *normal* risk & *normal* leverage → goal = 5%, AT

       ROA = 5%
       A/E = 3X
       ROE = 15%

"KSFs"? The key is *winning* enough *high margin* bids

       Worker Skill Level (Turnover?)
       Design Capability (R&D spending?)
       Capacity Utilization at Bottlenecks
       Hit Rate on Bids
       # of Bids Placed
       Cycle Time/Lead Time
          •
          •
          •

C. Professional: No ROA—Not meaningful for this business

"KSFs"?

       Growth in Revenue
       Attract & Retain Good People/Staff Utilization
       Margins on Jobs—How allow for spending *ahead* of growth?
       Proposals Hit Rate
       # of Proposals Made
       Manage Receivables (a measure of customer satisfaction)
       Develop New Ideas
          •
          •
          •

Question 7

A. Sell or disband Consumer, unless can get much better achieved margins, cash flow, and ROA.

B. Better WC management for Industrial and Professional. This gets ROE way up.

C. Professional looks shaky.
       Too high A/R
       Margins are pretty thin at 19% before S, G & A. Why so low?
       Spending ahead of growth?
       Pricing too low in order to get 20% growth?
How can corporate add any value here?

D. Industrial seems OK if get inventory down. Watch growth plans carefully ($8 million spending vs. $~3.9 cash flow). Flat sales is a red flag.

E. What real value is added by "corporate"? Why not split up Tuck into three separate companies and let investors build their own portfolios? Firing Richards and Hosbein seems no great loss!

CHAPTER 12
MANAGEMENT COMPENSATION

Changes from the Eighth Edition

In the first part of the chapter, we discuss considerations involved in designing incentive contracts tied to annual performance and contracts tied to long-term performance. Next, we discuss incentive contract design for corporate executives. This is followed by motivating business unit executives through incentive contracts. Finally, we discuss the potentials and limitations of agency theory in incentive contracting.

Cases

The Lincoln Electric Company (A) focuses on performance-based incentive compensation in this highly successful company.

Lincoln Electric Company (B) brings this case updated to 1993.

Anita's Apparel, new to this edition, focuses on the compensation practices at Nordstrom, very good at customer service.

Wayside Inn, new to this edition, focuses on the compensation system used by Wayside Inn in respect to their Inn Managers and its behavioral impact on decisions.

Mary Kay Cosmetics, new to this edition, considers the strategy, structure, and the unique compensation systems in this cosmetics company.

Case 12-1 and 12-2

Lincoln Electric Company (A) and (B)

Note

These two cases should be assigned for the same day. Bulk of the class discussion (about 80% of the class time) should be devoted to the (A) case; here, the focus should be to understand why the management controls works so well at Lincoln Electric. In the remainder of the class, the instructor should turn to the (B) case which describes Lincoln Electric's expansion outside the U.S.; here, the focus is on understanding whether Lincoln Electric would be able to export its successful control systems from the U.S. to foreign locations.

Prologue

Lincoln Electric Company is a very successful company in a relatively non-glamorous industry. The company's "pay-for-performance" type of management control is largely credited with the success of the company. Instructors might wish to show the following two video tapes at the beginning of class;

1. "The Lincoln Electric Company" (10 minutes). Date made 1979.

   Instructors can secure this video tape from CBS; the title of the video is called "Mr. Rooney Goes to Work" (Phone (212) 975-2875).

2. Lincoln Electric Company (12 minutes). This was also produced by CBS 60 minutes. But this tape was made in 1992. It is useful for students to see both tapes.

Teaching Note

Approach

Cases, journal articles, and even books on the Lincoln Electric system date back to the 1940s. (See James F. Lincoln, *Lincoln's Incentive System,* New York: McGraw-Hill, 1946.) The situation poses an interesting question: Lincoln Electric's compensation system with bonuses approximating 100 percent of base pay, seems to have been highly successful over a period of many years; but not many other companies have successfully used such a system. Why? Instructors who have used some version of a Lincoln Electric case for many years continue to try to put their finger on the answer.

As the case describes, Lincoln Electric was an investor in many respects in addition to its compensation plan: "advisory board," now common in several European countries, but not in the United States; stock purchase plans (employees own 50 percent of stock); suggestion system; promotion from within; formal job evaluations; employee participation without a union; Just in Time; emphasis on quality; work cells ("factory within a factory"); guaranteed employment (since 1958).

The company also differs from many others in its reluctance to have formal organization charts, in its nonuse of debt financing, its stock control by management, and its widespread use of piece rates, as well as in the compensation system described in the case. The span of control (100 workers per supervisor) is quite unusual.

Its success is not based on patent protection; patents on some of its most profitable products expired years ago, but the company continues to have a high market share. It is not based on an entrenched brand name (e.g., Bayer Aspirin) because for industrial products, brand names are not of great importance (although a general reputation for quality and on-time delivery is important). It is not because it operates in a low-cost section of the country; labor rates in Ohio are high. It is not because of government subsidies, defense contracts, protective tariffs, or other government assistance.

CAUTION: Before taking an enthusiastic approach to this case, prudence suggests that the instructor should look up Lincoln Electric's current performance. If it has deteriorated, we have a new question in addition to those raised in the case: what went wrong?

Question 1

Its strategies are described at length in the case, and are summarized in the statement "build a better and better product at lower and lower prices." Some specifics are summarized briefly: The company has few and narrow product lines and chooses not to diversify very much. It gives great emphasis to increasing productivity and passes along the savings as reductions in prices holders (in contrast with the typical message in texts and in company reports to stockholders and investment analysts that a company's basic goal should be to "maximize shareholder value"). It finances primarily from retained earnings, thus reducing the risks associated with debt financing. It spends relatively little on advertising.

Question 2

Elements of its approach to organization and control are described in the case and above. Judgments as to which are the most important will differ. It seems clear that the extraordinarily high bonus is one factor. The plan is structured in ways that encourage teamwork, suggestions for improvement, and hard work. There does not appear to be the dysfunctional emphasis on individual or divisional profits that is described in other cases (although the case is silent on the use of profit centers.)

It seems clear that the mechanisms fit the company's strategies.

Question 3

This is the basic question raised in the approach to the case. If we knew the answer, American productivity and profitability might be considerably improved. (Alternatively, Lincoln Electric's actual performance may be overstated in this case and in the books and articles about it; however, I know of no article that claims that the situation as described in the case is overly laudatory.)

A similar question may be asked about the performance of certain Japanese companies, both their operations in Japan and in factories that they operate in the United States. Also German, Swiss, and Swedish companies.

One important factor, I believe, is the elusive term "culture." Lincoln Electric has operated this way for decades. It is a way of life, and the favorable publicity (plus the monetary rewards) convinces everyone that it is the best way of life.

Question 4

As with questions in other cases that refer to "you," the answer to this one is highly personal. Points that come out in the discussion, perhaps concluded by a show of hands, should demonstrate that people's preferences differ. At Lincoln Electric, employees start at the bottom (with some exceptions), they receive relatively little supervision, they cooperate with one another, they work hard (and slackers probably are not tolerated), their performance is carefully evaluated, their suggestions are given attention, they are well paid, and they are assured of lifetime employment. If their potential is good, they are promoted (although there are not as many steps on the promotion ladder as is the case in many companies). Probably, as implied in the brief comment about the 1982 recession, their compensation fluctuates widely with the business cycle (because the bonus depends considerably on volume).

RNA

Additional Comments on the Lincoln Electric Companv

Case Description

This case describes one of the world's most efficient manufacturing companies and the way it recruits, motivates, involves and rewards its employees.

Case Objectives

Primary objectives include:

1. Understanding how strategy relates to organizational elements.

2. Understanding the elements of motivation and reward systems.

3. Relating success to the 7 S's.

Assignment Questions

1. Why has Lincoln Electric been so successful?

2. What role does their merit rating system serve?

3. What changes are needed for the future?

Teaching Questions

1 Why has Lincoln Electric been so successful?

   a. How important is their product-market strategy? What is it?

   b. What role does leadership play?

   c. Does their structure help?

   d. How good are their people? Why?

e.   What are their skills?

f.   What systems are important?

g.   How do you describe their goals?

h.   Who can compete with them? Why?

2.   What role does their merit rating system serve?

a.   What are its components?

b.   What do you want it to do?

c.   What is quality for?

d.   What is dependability for?

e.   What are ideas and cooperation for?

f.   What is output for?

g.   What do firms normally stress?

h.   How does this system work?

i.   Is there anything missing?

3.   What changes are needed for the future?

a.   What problems are there?

b.   What growth do you predict?

c.   Can you change strategy?

d.   What if growth slows?

e.   How involved is the president?

f.   How does he see his role?

g.   Can they continue to reduce costs and increase volume in a no-growth economy?

h.   Can they compete with the Japanese?

i.   Can they diversify? How?

j.   What implications would change have? How about a second factory?

Case Discussion

1. Why has Lincoln Electric been so successful?

    You can basically go through the seven S's here to identify Lincoln's well integrated strategy. They are the low cost producer and are able to increase demand by lowering prices. Their management reinforces the cost and quality values through the rewards given. The structure is shallow (almost everyone having access to the president) to facilitate communication and problem solving. Only highly motivated personnel join the company and their promotion is based on how well they internalize and perform in the merit system. The ability to communicate well (i.e. the management advisory board and walking around), to track costs and quality, and to motivate employees are critical skills. No one has been able to compete with them.

2. What role does the merit rating system serve?

    If you look carefully at the five elements in Lincoln's merit rating system, you will see how it causes each worker to "act as a worker and a manager." Individual output is tempered by good quality. Overall output requires people to be "on-the-job" and to "cooperate" with other workers. Generating "ideas" to save costs, increase productivity, or improve quality, supports the goals and values of the organization. If people do these things, they will be rewarded. In this way, personal goals are directly tied to organizational goals.

3. What changes are needed for the future?

    There are several ways to approach this question. You can begin by assessing if the environment will allow them to continue to grow. If not, then there will have to be some changes in strategy which will affect the other "S's." You can also look at the impact that growth has on an organization—the new plant's distance from headquarters. If the seven S's have to be balanced, what changes are needed to achieve that balance?

The cyclicality of the industry and the reduction in steel usage or construction could have a significant impact on welder sales. Now, this could also drive competitors out of the market to give Lincoln a still larger share. However, guaranteed employment could cause the work force to age if growth were to slow. This has happened in Japan as robotics is applied to production.

The president's closeness to the work force has been important in keeping a family spirit and open communications. Willis leads by example and pays attention to details. Shared values and goals are perpetuated from within the organization. The only difficulty may be that the president is spread thin as outside facilities are established. However, he needs to also look outside.

New technology and robotics could cause a problem for Lincoln. Routine welding is being turned over to robots. Factory automation could also take labor out of welding equipment and allow the Japanese to compete. The strong internal culture could make it difficult to bring in new skills. However, we do reward new ideas!

Profits require continued integration as costs decline. If we stop pursuing our strategy, though, the overall "fit" will decline.

We can question which of these skills can be transferred to other industries or organizations. Answers might include:

a. non-union organizations

b. organizations that trust their workers

c. use of management advisory boards (or QC circles?)

d. training in knowledge and skills

e. relating rewards to behavior in key areas

f. use of piece rate.

Much of this also requires growth.

Mr. Willis sees his role as perpetuating and maintaining their current system. He needs to plan his succession and ensure that the values continue. He also needs to worry about the future of his industry and its maturity. If less developed countries grow, this may require a movement into international markets. It so, how will the system need to change?

Lincoln Electric Company

I break the discussion of Lincoln into four parts, encompassing two 90-minute class periods.

The first part, to which I devote about 45 minutes, is to focus on external to Lincoln, to understand the industry as well as Lincoln's product-market strategy.

Lincoln competes to be the cost leader, the quality leader, and the service leader. We find that ultimately what contributes to Lincoln's success is not a function of industry structure or Lincoln's unique strategy.

What I try to do is eliminate the various factors which often contribute to profitability.

The welding products industry is not one where high profits should be common. The industry is mature. In terms of Porter's Five forces, suppliers and buyers are powerful, scale-type barriers to entry exists but technology and patents do not present significant barriers, there are many substitute products, and direct rivalry among participants is intense.

Lincoln's success is not a function of its product-market strategy:

- Goal hierarchy—employees, then stockholders

- Competitive advantage (i.e., why should customers buy Lincoln products)—quality, price, service leadership

- Functional area strategies: marketing, R&D, finance

In **the second part**, I focus on organization and control, which is strategy implementation.

I show two videos (one by Andy Rooney, from the early 1980s and the later 60 Minutes video). Both were made during difficult periods at Lincoln, major sales decline in 1982–83 and losses during 1992–

93. Yet it is clear employees evidence a high degree of commitment. Few companies experience high output and high commitment, as Lincoln does, although there are many examples of one or the other.

I use the McKinsey Seven-S framework to pull out from students what Lincoln does relative to implementation. The strategy is cost, quality, service. But the strategy is ultimately not implemented unless you pay attention to the other S's. I draw the boxes in, say, green and the connecting lines in red. Then, I ask, "Which is more important, the red or the green. After some discussion, students realize the connecting lines arc more important, at least at Lincoln. That is, the relationships, for example, of systems to structure, of style to skills, and of each "S" to shared values are the determining factors which generate high output and high commitment.

How do you design the internal organization so that it promotes high quality, low cost, and high service? You have a portfolio of tools: piece rates, bonus, dividends, promotion policies, stock ownership. But each must be related to quality, cost, or service.

Take piece rates. I ask, "What do you like about them?" Usual answers include, "focuses you on maximizing the number of units," "leads to self-management" and so forth. For each response, I ask students to show how quality, cost, or service is improved.

Next, I ask, "What are the toxic side effects of piece rates?" Students may say, "You may eliminate jobs," "Employees don't help others," or "You eliminate older people, because they cannot keep up."

Then, I ask, "How has Lincoln gone about minimizing the toxic side effects?"

We engage in the same treatment of the bonus component: "What do you like about it?" "What are the side effects?" "How has Lincoln minimized the side effects?"

This segment of the class can be extended as long as one likes, by treating each of the "tools" mentioned earlier.

The third part of the class is devoted to the question, "Is Incentive Management exportable to other companies?" I treat this domestically then internationally, keeping the distinction clear. My goal here is to clarify what makes the Lincoln system work or not work in other contexts.

Let's say Lincoln's sales were to drop by 50 percent, as was almost true in the early 1980s. The typical reaction would be to lay off half the workers, keeping unit labor cost the same. Lincoln's option is to keep everyone, but to guarantee only 75 percent employment. Piece rate totals drop by half—because half as many units are produced. The bonus pool may also be cut in half. This means the average Lincoln worker's pay has gone from twice the Cleveland area average to about equal to it. This is brilliant! While people in other companies are being fired right, left, and center, Lincoln employees keep their jobs at the area average wage.

What are the reasons other companies don't do it? First, it has to do with culture, which cannot be created overnight. Second, Lincoln's industry has had stable technology which allowed maximum learning curve and experience curve effects. Most industries are not like that. This heightens the sustainability of Lincoln's cost, quality, service advantage internationally—and to a lesser extent domestically—the work-leisure tradeoff is different than in Cleveland. Social entitlements— "Government will support me"—keep people from being willing to put forth the required effort.

How do unions play in this? In this country we have messed up our relationship with unions in many companies. There is a lot of suspicion—"What angle is management playing this time?" It is very hard to build back the trust. But, in the face of such a problem, do you give up or do you play harder.

These are all alibis. They can be overcome. It is not impossible for other companies to use much of the Lincoln system, and I recommend my clients do it. There are examples: Motorola, GM, Corning Glass all employ the broad spirit—quality, empowerment—although not the exact nitty gritty.

Human effort is the core competence of most companies and you have to treat employees as partners.

In the fourth and final part of the class, I discuss national competitiveness. The goals there are productivity, savings, and full employment. If the Lincoln plan is used by all companies, it instantly solves all three problems. Lincoln productivity is twice the industry average. Because the employees get high pay and half as bonus, much of if will be saved. Also, the Employees Stock Purchase Plan encouraged saving through stock ownership—I am troubled by its discontinuance. Finally, Lincoln never lays anyone off due to lack of work. If other companies followed that example, there would be full employment.

VG

Lincoln Electric Company

When I teach the case, I start by summarizing on one sheet of newsprint the nature of Lincoln's business and its basic competitive strategies. I ask the participants in the class not to reflect inward during this early discussion of the case; but to look from the perspective of Lincoln Electric out toward competitors and other customers. When I am done with the first 10–15 minutes of the class, which focuses on the questions of what business is Lincoln in and how it competes in this business, I have created one page of newsprint which has something like the following on it:

Nature of Business/Strategy

Arc welding — *focus*

Equipment plus consumables (rods)

Bases of competition:

1. Cost – Price
2. Quality
3. Service – Problem Solving,
   Applications Engineering

Not basic R&D

Not delivery

Customer mix: primarily small contractors

No debt policy

What I want to establish in the first 15 minutes of class is that Lincoln has a very focused business strategy. It competes extremely well on several competitive dimensions, while not attempting to be the best at absolutely everything. It also has some other policy choices it has honored over time, namely, internal financing and a focus on a primary target market of small customers. I attempt to make the point that very few firms have this strategic clarity and focus, and that very few strategies fit the customer base so well. I generally conclude by saying this is a classic defender strategy; the best of the breed, because the service function provides a much needed adaptive mechanism.

Next, I show the five-minute CBS video tape featuring Andy Rooney. I tell them that the compensation figures mentioned in the film have basically doubled since the time of the film in 1979 or so. I tell them that the film will help them see the kind of meaning that workers attach to being part of this organization and that it will give them a sense of what the working conditions are like.

Following the video tape, I ask them to tell me what the most important factors are in their Organization & Management/Human Resource systems that help explain why they have been able to implement their strategy so successfully for such a long period of time. They focus on a number of things. Some focus on the company's founding philosophy and value system. Others focus on the compensation system. Still others focus on various human resource management systems and so forth. At some point in this discussion, I begin to start showing how all of these different elements of the design of Lincoln are mutually reinforcing and internally consistent; how they are not just good ideas in isolation. Then I often delve into one or two specific areas in the case such as the compensation system. I end up showing them that workers are held accountable in a very serious way for the factors that drive the strategy of the firm. Indeed, I say to the participants that firms don't have strategies unless you can find people on the shop floor who are focusing their attention on and getting heavily reinforced for exerting effort toward factors over which they have control that are part of the strategy statement of the firm.

Finally, I focus on the potential threats to a system like this and explain some of the adaptive mechanisms inside Lincoln that help them deal with these threats so long as they don't come at large magnitudes. It is here that I sometimes wait to offer the defender strategic classification.

The discussion of Lincoln Electric usually takes an hour and fifteen minutes to an hour and a half, because I find having taught it for quite awhile I can really get into it. I was also a small aerospace contractor in Norfolk, Virginia when I first came across a Lincoln sales rep, so I really got sold on the firm at that time, and I have a few stories that I can tell. But regardless of how much time and how much depth you get into the case, the primary purpose it serves for me is an illustration of the total systems concept. I usually illustrate this with the simple 7-S framework, and I occasionally make reference to and sometimes teach in tandem the "Human Resources at Hewlett Packard" case, which illustrates a total systems solution for the prospector strategic type of firm.

Lincoln had sales of $800–900 million in 1990. Has gone overseas in a big way. I hand out a recent article, "Fine-tuning a Classic" (enclosed) as a "B-case."

—Bob Miles

Lincoln Electric Company

Overview

Lincoln Electric has pursued the most powerful of competitive strategy approaches—that of *simultaneously* being the industry's low-cost producer and the industry's highest quality producer. In effect, Lincoln Electric manufactures the best quality products in the arc-welding market and sells them at quite low prices relative to competitors; it is known as the industry leader on both high quality and low price. This is a very tough strategy to beat. Over the years, the company has performed very well. It has become the world's largest manufacturer of arc-welding products and has roughly a 40 percent market share in the U.S.; profits have been consistently good.

The case relates how Lincoln's management has successfully implemented the company's high-quality/low-price strategy. Lincoln's employees work in an environment dominated by incentive compensation, employment benefits, labor-management cooperation, and a well-articulated set of beliefs and values. It is a strong culture company with a deeply ingrained array of policies, procedures, and practices. The strategy implementation approach at Lincoln has produced productivity levels about double that of competitors, plus it has enforced strict attention to quality control and reliable product performance.

The case lays out what Lincoln's management has done to achieve all these results. When you finish discussing Lincoln Electric, you will be in a position to pose a very interesting question for the class to ponder: Is Lincoln Electric one of the best manufacturing companies in the world? Why?

Suggestions for Using the Case

The Lincoln Electric case should be used to illustrate the importance of incentive compensation, corporate culture, and values and beliefs in facilitating successful strategy implementation. The Lincoln Electric, Mary Kay Cosmetics, and Wal-Mart cases (along with the Nucor case in Section B) can be used to form a module on corporate culture, motivation, incentive compensation, and strategic leadership. These cases all involve application of the material in Chapter 10.

We like to start the class discussion by writing the essence of Lincoln's competitive strategy on the board: Produce the industry's highest quality product and sell it at prices equal to or below that of rivals. We then bring out the point that such a strategy is the most powerful competitive approach a company can employ; it is a strategy which cannot be defeated, provided it is implemented and executed successfully. It is obvious from reading the case that Lincoln Electric has done a fine job of making the strategy work. We then proceed to develop how Lincoln Electric has approached the strategy implementation task—what policies and procedures have been used to undergird implementation, how the corporate culture has been shaped, what role incentive compensation has played, and what Lincoln Electric's senior managers have done to lead the implementation/execution process. In effect, we use this case to force students to search out and explain the significant reasons for Lincoln's exceptional success. The lesson to be learned here is that Lincoln's success is due mainly to great strategy implementation rather than great strategy.

Data from case Exhibit 3 has been loaded onto STRAT-ANALYST to make it easy for students to check out some of the financial numbers. With STRAT-ANALYST students will be able to generate Lincoln's compound growth rates over the 1979–1987 period, percentage compositions of the income statement and balance sheet, and an assortment of financial ratios.

Assignment Questions

1. How would you characterize Lincoln Electric's strategy for competitive success? Has the strategy been successful?

2. What are the key policies, procedures, and management practices which have contributed to the success of Lincoln Electric's strategy? What has Lincoln Electric's management done to implement the company's strategy in a successful manner?

3. What is the "corporate culture" like at Lincoln Electric? What type of employees would be happy working at Lincoln Electric?

4. What key values, beliefs, and attitudes underlie the corporate culture at Lincoln Electric? Where did these come from?

5. Why do Lincoln employees have such high productivity levels? What is Lincoln's human relations strategy? How well has it been implemented? What strengths and weaknesses do you see?

6. Why are Lincoln's employees not interested in joining a union?

7. To what extent is the corporate culture at Lincoln Electric aligned with Lincoln's overall strategy? Evaluate the "fits" in terms of the McKinsey 7-S framework.

8. What could cause Lincoln's strategy implementation approach to break down? What are the threats to Lincoln's continued success?

9. What are the implications for Lincoln's human relations strategy and incentive compensation approaches if sales and earnings do not grow fast enough to permit the payment of attractive bonuses?

10. What recommendations would you make to Lincoln's management to keep strategy implementation on track?

Teaching Outline and Analysis

Before class starts we like to go over to a corner of the board and write a quote taken from the opening of the old Harvard case on Lincoln Electric: "We are a manufacturing company and I believe we are the best manufacturing company in the world." Under the quote we write "George Willis, CEO, Lincoln Electric" who made the statement to the Harvard casewriter some years ago. Without any comment, we proceed to call on students to tell the class what the Lincoln strategy is and then we methodically draw out in detail just what Lincoln's management has done over the years to make the strategy work.

1. What is Lincoln Electric's strategy?

The core of the company's business strategy is to make a very high quality product (the best in the industry) at the very lowest possible cost (Lincoln seems to be the industry's low-cost producer) and to sell the product at as low or lower prices than competing companies (Lincoln is the undisputed industry leader on low price). This is a very, very powerful strategy (how, in fact, can such a strategy be defeated if it is well-executed?). No other company we know of has pursued such a strategy–usually companies which manufacture a premium quality product charge a premium price to cover the extra costs associated with premium quality. But a strategy of selling a premium quality product at rock-bottom prices relative to competitors is almost unheard of. A company which can execute such a strategy and still make respectable profits has an almost unassailable competitive advantage.

As the power of Lincoln's strategy begins to sink in to the class, we like to toss out the remark that the case we are discussing today is perhaps the most important of the whole term because we get a chance to learn how Lincoln's management has been able to implement the most powerful competitive strategy there is—perhaps the "secrets" used at Lincoln can be applied elsewhere. This remark usually perks everyone's ears up a bit and heightens the interest in the discussion that follows.

2. **What are the key policies, procedures, and management practices which have contributed to the success of Lincoln Electric's strategy?**

This question goes to the heart of what the case is all about and you need to draw out the answers patiently and in some depth, always probing for *why* the particular policies, procedures, and practices that students come up with have been important and the role they play in the overall implementation scheme.

Our list of key policies, procedures, and policies would include the following:

- The reliance upon and use of incentive compensation (the payment of the annual bonuses and the widespread use of piecerates).

  — Piecerate compensation causes production workers to be very attentive to the *volume* they turn out during each work shift (this is why there are no coffee breaks, no idle chatter, etc.—workers are busy working!).

  — Regular compensation via piecerate provides workers with a wage/income comparable to that earned by other similarly skilled workers in the area.

  — The annual bonus (based on how well the company as a whole does and how well each individual worker performs) provides them with an above-average income. The bonus has averaged about 90 percent of the annual wage. In 1988, the average bonus was $21,258— an amount quite large enough to attract every employee's attention and an amount definitely large enough to prompt each worker to (1) work hard, (2) observe all the "rules," and (3) strive to get an above:-average individual performance rating.

    Conclusion: Lincoln's use of incentive compensation has produced high levels of employee commitment and high levels of employee productivity. The high productivity levels have contributed to the achievement of Lincoln's low-cost producer status.

- The policy of lifetime employment security

  — Lincoln's employees don't have to worry about the possibility of working themselves out of a job; at many companies union practices discourage hard work and "eager beaver" behavior since it can mean fewer jobs. At Lincoln, hard work and "eager-beaver" behavior puts more money in workers' pockets–the higher their performance ratings and the better the company does, the better off workers are monetarily. Loss of job is not really a factor;

neither is the fear of being laid off. If times get really hard, work hours can be cut back and bonuses may not be as high, but workers really don't have to worry about job security or loss of their paychecks.

- The methods used to recruit and select entry level employees

  — Emphasis on personal interviews and screening of candidates by the Personnel Department, the management committee, and the supervisor with the job opening helps to ensure that only people who like to work hard, who are motivated by strong monetary incentives, and who have a work ethic compatible with Lincoln Electric's work climate and corporate culture will ultimately be hired. Even if a mistake in hiring is made (a person is hired who really doesn't fit in), the person's co-workers are likely to exert strong peer pressure to make it uncomfortable for "misfits"—especially if they are not hard workers and don't pull their weight. Worker inefficiency penalizes everyone because it reduces the total size of the bonus pool.

- The practice of soliciting employee suggestions, providing for employee participation in decision-making, and having joint labor-management committees meet regularly

  — Giving more responsibility to employees and letting them participate in decisions they are most knowledgeable has worked exceptionally well at Lincoln, probably due to the serious, concerted effort on management's part to make it work.

  — The Advisory Board, elected by workers, meets with the Chairman and the President every two weeks to discuss ways of improving operations.

- The tough, but fair, system of performance evaluation

  — Evaluations are done twice a year.

  — Each supervisor's evaluation must average out to 100 for all the employees evaluated; this prevents a supervisor from rating all employees above average and forces them to a bell-shaped distribution that separates the weak performers from the strong performers

  — Each worker's performance score matters a lot in terms of their pocketbook because it determines whether they get a below- or above-average bonus (the difference can amount to several thousand dollars).

- The policy of tracing each warranty claim to the individual employee whose work caused the defect. The worker may have to repay the cost of servicing the warranty claim or the worker's performance evaluation score may be reduced.

  — This policy undoubtedly contributes mightily to making Lincoln Electric's strategy of superior product quality a reality.

3. **What role have these policies and practices played in shaping the corporate culture at Lincoln Electric?**

Obviously, a very big one. The point of asking this question is simply to hammer home how and why the policies and practices used by management act to create a particular work climate and organizational atmosphere. They are part and parcel of the corporate culture.

4. **What else besides these policies and practices make the corporate culture at Lincoln Electric what it is?**

The remaining drivers of the corporate culture at Lincoln Electric relate mainly to the strongly imbedded values and beliefs that are much in evidence:

- The customer's interest comes first.

  — Top priority is given to "How do I make this better, cheaper, more useful?"

  — Lincoln's goal is "to build a better and better product at a lower and lower price."

  — Lincoln's pricing approach is to price on the basis of cost and to keep pressure on driving costs lower and lower, year after year after year.

- The employee's interest comes second.

  — Indeed, employees are very, very well-served by the way Lincoln Electric is run.

  — The company's strong concern for the welfare of employees is reflected in the various benefits that employees have, the participative role given to employees, and the overall attitude the company has towards employees.

- The stockholders, come third.

  — Lincoln Electric cannot be accused of running the company solely for the benefit of the stockholders. This has worked well because the ownership of stock is closely held (mainly by employees) and the stock is not regularly traded on the open market.

  — The contribution of "absentee stockholders" is seen as minimal and, thus, as deserving of minimal reward.

- Labor and management should not be in warring camps; they should cooperate fully and happily.

  — Organization charts are unnecessary and undesirable because they create formal lines between managers and workers.

- Employee performance and productivity are the primary means by which the customer's needs are fulfilled.

- The use of formal authority is quite strong—management runs the company.

— Management "must have complete power."

— "Management is the coach who must be obeyed."

— When employees "bring up something that management thinks is not to the benefit of the company, it will be rejected."

— Management has authority to transfer workers.

— Supervisors have authority to assign individual workers to specific parts.

5. **Why is it that a production foreman supervises as many as 100 workers? Why is it that supervisors are busy with record keeping and planning duties rather than watching the actions of the workers they supervise? How can such an unconventional approach work?**

This is an important question to ask because it demonstrates the motivating power and the behavioral controls of a well-designed incentive compensation system. The piecework rates and the bonuses (based on the twice-a-year evaluations) make it unnecessary to supervise workers closely to see they are doing what they are supposed to be doing. To begin with, all employees are carefully selected–so that only highly industrious, money-motivated people are hired. Second, workers are paid based on strictly defined and strictly measured performance criteria. Each worker ends up knowing exactly what they need to do and how they will be evaluated. There is every incentive for a worker to try to perform up to their best ability. Everyone works hard; there is no goofing off, no wasted time, and no toleration of inefficiency. So what is there to supervise? There's no need for supervisors to spend the majority of their time supervising–they have ample time to take on other duties.

6. **Why is there no union at Lincoln Electric?**

Students ought to come up with several key reasons:

- Management treats employees honestly and fairly.

- Any grievances and concerns can be immediately taken up with the chairman and the president by the employee-chosen Advisory Board at the bi-weekly meetings.

- Employees are very well compensated.

- From the interviews at the end of the case, it seems clear that workers are quite satisfied with pay and with working conditions; many know the senior officers personally and believe they can and do get fair treatment when issues and problems come up.

In short, there's nothing to be gained from unionization.

At some point in the discussion, we always like to ask students what they think the parking lot at the Lincoln Electric plant looks like. Most students quickly observe that it will be filled with late-model cars, trucks, and vans, not a bunch of aging, dilapidated vehicles that came off cheap used-car lots.

7. **What is your assessment of the company's financial performance since 1979?**

A quick review of case Exhibit 3 makes it clear that Lincoln Electric's performance during the 1980s has been less than sparkling. Revenues and profits dropped off sharply in 1982 and have yet to recover to the levels realized in 1981. The gross amounts paid out in incentive bonuses peaked at $56 million in 1981 and were only $39 million in 1987.

Table 1 presents a series of financial calculations which students can obtain using the STRAT-ANALYST software package. The first section of Table 1 shows the percent composition of Lincoln Electric's income statements. Despite the roller coaster ride in revenues between 1979 and 1987, the percentages remained very stable, fluctuating within a very narrow range; this is indicative of tight controls and tight management, and it was accomplished without employee layoffs and without unraveling the incentive bonus arrangements.

The second section of Table 1 presents a series of financial ratios for the company. As might be expected, there has been a significant falloff in ROA and ROE since 1981. Stockholders have definitely not fared as well lately—an outcome consistent with the company's longstanding philosophy that stockholders come third.

The last section of Table 1 shows compound average growth rates for the nine-year period.

8. **To what would you attribute this weak performance?**

There are really just three basic causes of weak performance in any kind of business:

- weak strategy

- problems in strategy implementation

- unfavorable market and competitive conditions beyond management's ability to rectify

Plainly, the difficulties at Lincoln Electric relate to the third cause. We've already discussed that Lincoln Electric has a powerful strategy and that management has done an excellent job of implementing and executing the strategy. Otherwise Lincoln could hardly be the acknowledged market leader with a 40 percent market share. The case does not say much about the nature or the causes of market weakness for Lincoln Electric's products, but the presence of weakness is amply reflected in Lincoln's revenues.

The downturn has resulted in reduced bonus payments per worker during most of the 1980s:

Year	Total Amount of Year-end Incentive Bonus	Number of Employees Eligible for Bonus	Average Bonus per Eligible Employee
1980	$43,249,000	2,637	$16,400
1981	55,718,000	2,684	20,760
1982	36,870,000	2,634	14,000
1983	21,914,000	2,561	8,560
1984	32,718,000	2,469	13,250
1985	38,000,000	~2,400	15,800
1986	33,000,000	~2,400	14,000
1987	39,000,000	~2,400	16,000
1988	unknown	unknown	21,258

Table 1
Financial Performance Indicators for Lincoln Electric 1979–1987

Percent Composition of Income Statements

	1979	1980	1981	1982	1983	1984	1985	1986	1987
Revenues	100%	100%	100%	100%	100%	100%	100%	100%	100%
Cost of prod sold	63%	65%	62%	65%	65%	67%	64%	66%	63%
Selling and admin	11%	11%	11%	14%	16%	14%	14%	15%	14%
Incentive bonus	11%	11%	12%	11%	8%	10%	11%	10%	10%
Pretax income	15%	13%	15%	10%	11%	9%	10%	8%	13%
Income taxes	7%	6%	7%	5%	5%	4%	5%	4%	6%
Net income	8%	7%	8%	5%	6%	5%	6%	5%	7%

Financial Ratios Calculated from Exhibit 3

	1979	1980	1981	1982	1983	1984	1985	1986	1987
Pretax ROA	30%	25%	29%	15%	13%	14%	17%	14%	21%
Net ROA	16%	14%	16%	8%	7%	8%	9%	8%	12%
Return on equity	19%	16%	19%	9%	9%	10%	12%	9%	15%
Current ratio	3.7	4.4	3.7	5.1	4.4	4.6	4.4	4.3	3.4
Total asset turnover	2.0	2.0	2.0	1.5	1.2	1.5	1.6	1.7	1.7
Inventory turnover	10.1	11.1	10.2	8.7	8.9	9.0	10.1	12.5	9.4

Compound Average Annual Growth Rates Calculated from Exhibit 3

	1979–83	1982–87	1979–87
Revenues	-7.9%	8.0%	-0.3
Pretax income	-14.4%	12.5%	-1.9%
Net income	-13.2%	12.3%	-1.3%
Total assets	4.7%	0.0%	2.3%

Source: Calculated from case Exhibit 3 using STRAT-ANALYST.

9. **Do you see any other factors (besides market saturation or decline for arc-welding products) which could pose a significant threat to Lincoln Electric and to the success of its policies, practices, and cultural orientation?**

Perhaps the biggest threat concerns technological breakthroughs which either make current products obsolete or nullify Lincoln's low-cost advantage. As the case states, both technology and the products themselves have remained unchanged for years and years. This has made it feasible for Lincoln to spend little on R&D, to invest minimally in plant and equipment, and to pursue relentlessly becoming more and more efficient in its work methods and work practices. However, a sudden technological innovation in arc-welding which made Lincoln's products, equipment, or work methods cost inefficient could prove immensely disruptive. With the strong policy of promotion from within and the vested interest in preserving present work practices, it would be very difficult to adapt to new technologies and new procedures. Lincoln's cost advantage would be lost, at least initially. The introduction of new technicians and new work practices could be the undoing of the culture and could force important revisions in Lincoln's strategy and compensation system (a piecerate system might or might not fit the new technology and production process).

— Art Thompson
A.J. Strickland

Teaching Manual to Accompany
The Lincoln Electric Company

As The Lincoln Electric Company celebrated its centennial in 1995, it had just reported record profits after two straight years of losses stemming from a seemingly disastrous foray into Europe, Asia, and Latin America. The case "The Lincoln Electric Company, 1995" culminates in CEO Don Hastings decisions surrounding his goal to reduce Lincoln's debt while continuing to modernize and expand the company so as to give future employees a "very solid, secure company in which to place their lives." Earlier Lincoln cases by the same author were adopted for dozens of college textbooks and used in hundreds of universities and executive development programs worldwide. One, "The Lincoln Electric Company, 1989," was published by the Case Research Journal twice, the second time as a "NACRA Classic Case." "The Lincoln Electric Company, 1995" had not been classroom tested as of May 1995, but was scheduled for use at several universities, including the Southwestern University of Finance and Economics in Chengdu, the People's Republic of China.

Intended Courses and Audiences

"The Lincoln Electric Company, 1995" is designed mainly for use in the business school class variously called "strategic management," "integrative," or "policy." The case describes a failed—or did it fail?—attempt at international expansion and thus may be scheduled for sessions on international business strategy. Past Lincoln cases in this series were mainly viewed as "strategy implementation" cases, without a particular decision focus, and this one will probably be no exception. However, this case does present strategies which have already been formulated, so it will be useful to evaluate them and suggest alternative ones. Thus, the case may be used as a "strategy formulation" case. Of course, "The Lincoln Electric Company, 1995" may be used in executive development programs. The Lincoln Incentive Management System is featured in many organizational behavior, personnel, human resources management, and production management courses, so the case will find use in such classes and texts.

Topics Covered

Data are provided to address four specific topics, which raise many "teaching points." The first topic is *the priority management at Lincoln and elsewhere, should place on serving its various constituencies.* Teaching points which might be raised here include common rationales for stockholder wealth maximization, the power positions of various management constituencies at Lincoln, and the legal and ethical issues faced by the new public company and financial directors at Lincoln.

The second topic is *the factors which explain the high employee productivity at Lincoln.* Suggested teaching points include the following: the degree to which Expectancy Theory and Needs Theory help explain Lincoln employee behavior, the effect of pay as a motivator, the relationship between employee motivation/competence and span of control, and the effect of accountability and statistical control on motivation.

Topic three is *the relationship between promotion from within and "inbreeding" in organizations.* Of particular interest here are the new outside directors and managers recruited by Lincoln and their probable impact—positive and negative—on company performance.

The final topic is *evaluation of recent Lincoln strategies and evaluation of those Hastings has set forth for the future.* Is Lincoln better or worse off because of Willis' "mistakes"? Does Lincoln really need to modernize? Expand? Pay off the debt?

Teaching Objectives

Every honestly-written business case is a *window* on the world. Students gain *familiarity* with the world of work by just looking through such a window, reading the case. But case teaching seeks *involvement,* to make classes a *door* to the world. Both goals are often furthered if a case teacher establishes specific objectives for a class. The four below are recommended for sessions on "The Lincoln Electric Company, 1995" and serve as a framework for the succeeding analysis.

1. To discuss the priority management, at Lincoln and elsewhere, should place on serving its various constituencies.

2. To discuss the factors which might explain the high productivity at Lincoln.

3. To discuss the possible relationship between promotion from within and "inbreeding."

4. To evaluate Lincoln's recent strategies and those Hastings has set forth for the future.

Associated Theoretical Material

This Teaching Manual aims to make the teaching job easier by presenting the author's initial analysis of the case as a starting point for preparation of a class plan by the instructor.

Perhaps the most lucid and influential text on discussion teaching is C. Roland Christensen, David A. Garvin, and Ann Sweet, eds., *Education for Judgment: The Artistry of Discussion Leadership,* (Boston: Harvard Business School Press, 1991). Perusal of the fine essays in this book will likely make any case teacher better at the task.

Any of the literature of motivation and leadership can be—and has been—discussed in the context of the Lincoln experience. This includes McGregor's Theory X-Y, Herzberg's two-factor theory, Maslow's and McClelland's needs theories, expectancy theory, and so forth.

No study of Lincoln can be complete without notice of James Lincoln, *A New Approach to Industrial Economics* (New York: The Devin-Adair Company, 1961). In that book Lincoln sets forth his theory of management based in part on the Christian Gospel—as a solution to a company's as well as a country's problems. Lincoln's approach is almost secular, with the Gospel presented more as philosophy than religion.

Arthur Sharplin and Lonnie D. Phelps, "A Stakeholder Apologetic for Management," *Business and Professional Ethics Journal*, 8, 2 (Spring 1990), 41–53, discuss Agency Theory as a rationale for management representation of various constituencies. Sharplin and Phelps write that if "there are adequate incentives for managers to maximize shareholder wealth, financial theorists have no theoretical imperative to look further into the black box [as the firm is represented in The Theory of the Firm]—a firm's production function will not differ by virtue of its being widely or closely held." They add,

> But strategic management (or business policy) theorists do have such an imperative. They are concerned with distributional as well as efficiency issues and have long recognized that corporate executives represent a variety of groups besides shareholders, among them creditors, employees, customers, and the multiple communities in which a firm operates.

Arthur Sharplin, *Strategic Management* (New York: McGraw-Hill, 1985), presents a model of strategic management which highlights environmental facets such as those affecting Lincoln. On page 153 Sharplin presents a matrix illustrating how the size and complexity of an organization, on one hand, and its cultural homogeneity, on the other, affect the difficulty of changing organizational culture. As Sharplin's model predicts, the Lincoln culture, being large and homogeneous, survived trauma which would have decimated weaker company cultures.

Michael E. Porter's books *Competitive Advantage* (New York: The Free Press, 1985) and *Competitive Strategy* (New York: The Free Press, 1980) remain good sources of guidance on all aspects of strategy. In particular, Porter counsels seeking leadership in market share or cost, or both. Lincoln had both until Miller and ESAB overtook it in machines and consumables, respectively. Whether Willis overreacted by deserting profound Lincoln principles to expand internationally is debatable especially if employee bonuses are viewed as a division of profits, rather than a cost. Even with the high employee compensation, Lincoln's labor cost were low and it probably remained the world's low-cost producer of both machines and consumables.

Another important source book for the case is Michael E. Porter, *The Competitive Advantage of Nations* (New York: The Free Press, 1990). In the section, "Selective Foreign Acquisitions," starting at the bottom of p. 611, Porter says the two reasons for making foreign acquisitions are "to gain access to a foreign market or to selective skills" and "to gain access to a highly favorable 'national diamond.'" The first of these justifications seem to apply to Willis' overseas acquisitions. And Lincoln was able to retain some of the acquired technology and much of the market penetration, even after retrenching.

Synopsis of Case

As The Lincoln Electric Company celebrated its centennial in 1995, it had just reported record profits after two straight years of losses stemming from a seemingly disastrous foray into Europe, Asia, and Latin America. Lincoln was a leading producer of arc-welding products and also made electric motors. Company patriarch James Lincoln had been dead 30 years in 1995. His protege Ted Willis had retired from Lincoln's top post. And Don Hastings, a Harvard MBA and former marketer, was Chairman and Chief Executive Officer.

Lincoln was founded in 1895 and James Lincoln took over in 1914. A stream of management innovations from then to 1960 included an employees stock purchase plan, company paid life insurance, an employees association for athletic and social programs and sick benefits, piece rates adjusted for inflation, a suggestion system with cash awards, a pension plan, a policy of promotion from within, lifetime employment, formal job evaluation, merit rating which affected pay, and paid vacations.

From 1986–92 CEO Ted Willis bought up foreign welding products operations, incurring large debts. Willis retired in 1992 and Don Hastings closed and wrote off many of the plants, reporting losses in 1992 and 1993 but record profits in 1994.

The welding products market of the mid 1990s was classified as "mature and cyclical." By 1995, at least 75 percent of machine and consumables sales could be attributed to Lincoln and three other firms. Lincoln's made about twice as many different products in 1995 as it had ten years earlier. Instead of outsourcing components, Lincoln made them from basic industrial commodities Almost all components were made by numerous small "factories within a factory." Electrode manufacture was highly capital intensive and teams of Lincoln workers who made electrodes shared group piece rates. Lincoln required most suppliers to deliver raw materials just as needed in production. A new Lincoln electric motor factory was almost complete in mid 1995. Adjacent to the electric motor factory was a smaller building housing Lincoln's new robotics unit.

The Lincoln Incentive Management System was said to be a "comprehensive philosophy," based on the Christian Gospel, along with "rules, regulations, practices, and programs which have evolved over a 70-year period." It involved treating customer interests as paramount, paying only modest dividends, and distributing any residual profits to employees. Employee bonuses from 1934–94 equaled 90% of base wages and product prices lagged inflation.

Hastings brought in several outside directors and managers in 1992–95. Two levels of management, at most, existed between supervisors and the president and supervisors typically had 60–100 subordinates. Lincoln borrowed no money until the 1980s. But during 1986–92, Willis spent far more on acquisitions than net income could fund, and the company's total debt went from $4.5 million to $248.6 million. The common shares had begun a steady rise in 1992, doubling in price, to $39, by late 1994. In March 1995, Lincoln canceled the employee ownership plan and announced it anticipated engaging in a public issue of non-voting stock. And Hastings said Lincoln needed to expand, modernize, and pay off the debt.

Assignment Questions and Analysis

One comprehensive question is given below for each teaching objective. The author has placed an asterisk (*) before each sentence he feels relates to ideas which will only be addressed by better students. This is prediction, rather than research, and the author himself may have missed important issues.

Assignment Question 1 with Analysis

Discuss the priority management, at Lincoln and elsewhere, should place on serving its various constituencies.

Aside from the following rather heretical essay, the author will leave it to professors and students to analyze this issue. Most students as well as professors and managers rationalize any behavior which appears to serve a constituency other than shareholders as if the *real effect* is to maximize shareholder wealth. But it is the author's firm conviction that this is a totally misguided view.

Maximize shareholder wealth has stood for two centuries as a description of what managers do, a prescription for what they *should* do, and a favored object of public policy. James Lincoln decried this idea and placed shareholders dead last among managerial constituencies. *Clearly, the proposition is based upon a faulty simile: that shareholders own the private property of the corporation just as the proprietor owns that of a sole proprietorship. Eugene Fama wrote,

> Dispelling the tenacious notion that a firm is owned by its securities holders is important because it is a first step toward understanding that control over a firm's decisions is not necessarily the province of security holders. The second step is setting aside the equally tenacious role in the firm usually attributed to the entrepreneur.

Harvard's Michael Jensen agreed that public firm shareholders are not owners and apologized for making the "semantic misstep" of referring to them that way.

Aside from semantics, shareholder wealth maximization is neither descriptive of public firm behavior, defensible as a management norm, nor necessarily efficient. This is not quite what R.P. Rumelt referred to as "the standard attack on neoclassical theory," a disputation of *profit* maximization. Rather, it is mainly a disputation of popular arguments for *shareholder wealth* maximization as the *raison d'etre* of public firm management. *All* categories of stakeholders seek profit and, *ceteris paribus*, undoubtedly prefer that their profit be large. There seems a consensus among managers and employees at Lincoln that employees there work largely because they seek profit—but for themselves, not shareholders.

*Lincoln's new outside directors will undoubtedly worry about lawsuits if they favor employees over shareholders. Actually, though, organizational economists hardly claim any legal basis for the maximize shareholder wealth norm. Instead they often imply that shareholders are more *deserving* of management allegiance or more *interested* in the corporation than are other stakeholders. For example, Williamson wrote, "Suppliers of finance bear a unique relation to the firm: The whole of their investment is potentially placed at hazard" (1984: 1208). In a similar vein, Fama and Jenson claimed that shareholders bear *residual risk*, "the risk of the difference between stochastic inflows of resources and promised payments to agents." Comments throughout the Lincoln case, especially by Hastings (If we don't reduce the debt, we are sowing the seeds of our own destruction) and by several interviewees, show that the employees realize they bear the lion's share of Lincoln's risk, as is true in most large companies.

In contrast, public firm shareholders typically diversify their holdings, so have little of their wealth tied up in a particular firm and experience little firm-specific risk. In fact, it is illogical to refer to current public firm shareholders as "suppliers of finance." Few ever made any exchange through the firm, let alone contributed to it, as James Lincoln remarked.

Other stakeholders generally have neither such mobility nor such diversification and they do transact business through the firm. For example, employees furnish labor and receive pay. Their mobility is typically limited by the value of their firm-specific skills and knowledge and their "golden handcuffs" in the form of pensions, contingent compensation plans, and other non-portable benefits. A large percentage of a typical employee's wealth consists of the present value of expected job benefits and wages from a particular firm, especially if that firm is Lincoln. Consequently, employees experience a great deal of firm-specific risk. Similarly, many communities have invested millions in amenities such as roads, housing, and trained labor forces tailored to one or a few firms, not to mention various tax breaks and subsidies. The loss of a major plant or headquarters is often devastating to such a community.

Jensen wrote, "Shareholders are the only constituency of the corporation with a long-term interest in its survival". And The Working Group on Corporate Governance stated, "Shareholders should recognize and respect that the only goal common to all shareholders is the ongoing prosperity of the company." But long-term survival of a particular public company is of no interest at all to rational and opportunistic shareholders. For example, given a choice between a perpetual dividend d per year and a liquidating dividend, such a shareholder with discount rate r will elect to receive any liquidating dividend (or accept any share price) exceeding d/r. In fact, institutional investors may create a conflict of interest if they discourage actions which maximize share price, whatever the effect on the firm's "ongoing prosperity." And when shareholder power is concentrated, as through an LBO, the new "owners" frequently break up the firm. If the Lincoln family were willing to "cash out" its investment, how much could LBO association KKR get for the company? Certainly a lot more than $40 a share, the trading price in early 1995.

*If there is a distinction among stakeholders here, it is that a typical shareholder has the least, not the most, interest in the longevity and success of a particular firm; bears less risk than does, say, a midlevel, longtime employee of that firm or a leading official of the host city; and, in contrast to certain other stakeholders, has never contributed wealth to (or through) the firm. In addition, it seems clear employees, members of communities, and perhaps even suppliers and creditors, are more likely than shareholders to compromise their own interests for corporate success and survival. So organizational economists could certainly choose a more interested stakeholder—and probably a more "deserving" one as well.

James Lincoln suggested that public shareholders have much less moral claim to management fealty than do customers and employees. At Lincoln in 1994, as the company reported losses, the employees got $55 million in bonuses while shareholders got $7 million in dividends. This after decades of relatively minuscule returns to equity.

It was possible to sustain Lincoln's view as long as most stock was also owned by employees and Lincoln family members and as long as public shareholders were unrepresented. Even in 1995, his descendants may be able to keep majority control in friendly hands, by selling nonvoting stock, for example. *But the genie may be out of the bottle because the board of directors now includes outsiders, who may deem themselves legally bound to assure shareholders get much more than they have received in the past. Also, Hastings has disengaged the bonus amount from the company's bottom line by paying bonuses when the company lost money. He thus has prepared employees for a looser connection in the future.

Assignment Question 2 and Analysis

Discuss the factors which might explain the high productivity at Lincoln.

This is the issue for which Lincoln is most famous. With average wage levels roughly double the average in other industrial companies, Lincoln workers are obviously highly productive. Otherwise, the company could not long pay such wages. We may need look no further than the case itself to understand the employees motivation. Sabo wrote of employees, "They must feel secure, important, challenged, in control of their destiny, confident in their leadership, be responsive to common goals, believe that they are treated honestly and with integrity, have easy access to authority and open lines of communication in all possible directions."

And James Lincoln is quoted as follows:

> The greatest fear of the worker, which is the same as the greatest fear of the industrialist in operating a company, is the lack of income.... The industrial manager is very conscious of his company's need of uninterrupted income. He is completely oblivious, evidently, of the fact that the worker has the same need.

> He is just as eager as any manager is to be part of a team that is properly organized and working for the advancement of our economy.... He has no desire to make profits for those who do not hold up their end in production, as is true of absentee stockholders and inactive people in the company.

> If money is to be used as an incentive, the program must provide that what is paid to the worker is what he has earned. The earnings of each must be in accordance with accomplishment.

> Status is of great importance in all human relationships. The greatest incentive that money has, usually, is that it is a symbol of success.... The resulting status is the real incentive.... Money alone can be an incentive to the miser only.

> There must be complete honesty and understanding between the hourly worker and management if high efficiency is to be obtained.

In terms of needs theory, it is clear several interviewed employees believe their higher-order needs motivate them, although James Lincoln explains, above, how money can appeal to such needs. One is left with the impression, however, that security, a lower-order need, plays a big part and that pay plays the main part.

Expectancy theory seems to offer the most complete answer. Oversimplifying, this theory holds that,

Motivation = Expectancy × Valence

Perhaps mainly because of the 70-year history of management faithfulness at Lincoln, employees see a very high probability (Expectancy) they will benefit individually from increased output—and suffer from decreased output or decreased quality. The interviewees, at least, appear to value highly (Valence) the outcomes achieved, such as money, approbation of peers and superiors, and security. So, one might reason, motivation is high.

Well, students often ask, if it is this simple, why doesn't every company employ piece rates and bonuses and guarantee employment, at least. Sabo gives a partial answer: "It is not easy.... It requires tremendous dedication and hard work." Also, there can be honest disagreement about who deserves the lion's share of profit, or whether any single constituency does.

*Piece rates, in particular, often do not work well as motivators because they will almost inevitably be lowered if employees start earning "too much." I illustrate this by letting a student play the role of a supervisor in a clothing factory, where piece rates are common. A new employee reports for work and soon far exceeds standard, earning twice the norm. Assuming the employee resists the "binging" and ostracism which peers often impose in such cases, my student-cum-supervisor usually insists the employee should be allowed to earn the high pay. When the supervisor bids a new batch of work and realizes just a 1 percent reduction in costs may make the difference, the worker may be asked to compromise, perhaps reducing pay to only 50 percent above norm. Other pressures can be brought to bear on the supervisor, but many resist approaching the worker at this point. However, when the worker is reassigned, promoted, or quits, most student/supervisors agree they would cut the rate for the successor.

Assignment Question 3 and Analysis

Discuss the possible relationship between promotion from within and "inbreeding."

*The genetics metaphor, although often cited, may not be completely valid. Inbreeding, in genetics, involves a closed population and is often employed to fix desirable genetically-transmitted traits. An unwanted effect is that it also fixes undesirable traits and sometimes results in decreased vigor, size, etc. of the species over time. In management, hiring from within may not bring in needed diversity in the short term, but new employees from diverse backgrounds are continually fed into the system at the bottom. And there is nothing to prevent managers from adopting views and knowledge from without the organization. Still, Hastings decided Lincoln needed "new blood," and recruited several managers and directors from outside. He also promoted several managers to vice president, which put internal talent in succession to the top offices.

Assignment Question 4 and Analysis

Evaluate Lincoln's recent strategies and those Hastings has set forth for the future.

Recent Strategies. *Doing exactly what Lincoln did, including buying *and* closing the foreign plants, could as well have been explained as a planned strategy as an ill-advised reaction. The recession in Europe was fortuitously timed to justify the restructuring—which might have been a good strategy even if the recession had not occurred. There seems a consensus at Lincoln that the company is better off than if Willis had not expanded overseas. In fact, buying the plants and other assets abroad may have been the only way to get the related marketing structures and governmental facilitation, which will probably justify the total cost of the expansion. It is clear that shutting down facilities and retrenching otherwise did not affect sales much.

The extra debt gave Hastings good justification to seek new equity and the losses were the reason given for terminating the Employee Stock Ownership Plan. This along with the prospect of substantial public trading in the stock and the presence of outsiders on the board probably had much to do with the doubling of share price between 1992 and 1995. It is also noteworthy that among the 75 percent of Lincoln employees who own 40 percent of the shares, the average one owns about 1,700 shares (10 million shares/[3,000 employees × 75%]), worth perhaps $68,000 at 1995 prices. So employees might favor any action which causes share price to rise. This may be important, because if the issue of non voting shares does not merit the desired price, as appears likely, selling voting shares may need to be justified.

There is every reason to think Hastings is sincere in attempting to get the debt to a very low level and to return to following James Lincoln's principles insofar as practical. The table below provides credit ratios, as presented by McDonald and Company except for the last column. It is easy to see that interest coverage is far below historical levels. The main relevance of this is probably that zero debt facilitates guaranteed employment. Sabo's idea that there is a level of debt which is a "tax advantage" may be bogus. But his suggestion of achieving 22–25 percent debt to equity is probably conservative enough for most tastes.

Alternatives for the Future. Much has already been committed. Lincoln clearly plans to attempt a public issue of non voting shares. The Employees' Stock Purchase Plan is gone. Employees now may purchase shares just like anyone else. The company will try to expand, but by letting marketing lead production. It appears unlikely that Hastings will try to get debt to zero, as both James Lincoln and Bill Irrgang would counsel if they were alive. Still, he is right to treat the present situation as an emergency—debt to total assets is 38.2 percent, much higher than all-industry averages. This is up from 1.9 percent in 1986. Porter would say he is also right to continue modernizing and expanding.

Credit Ratios

	12/86	12/87	12/88	12/89	12/90	12/91	12/92	12/93	12/94
Assets / Equity (Y-E)	1.3	1.4	1.8	1.9	2.3	2.4	3.0	3.9	2.9
LT Debt / Capitalization (%)	0.0	0.0	7.2	11.0	30.0	37.1	52.7	60.2	50.1
Ttl Debt / Total Assets (%)	1.9	2.3	14.1	15.7	26.2	32.2	41.2	44.7	38.2
Ttl Debt / Cap+ST Debt (%)	2.5	5.7	20.2	22.7	37.1	43.8	55.6	63.6	52.3
Ttl Debt / Eqty Mkt Val (%)	2.5	6.0	NA	NA	NA	NA	NA	NA	0.53
EBIT / Interest Expense	30.41	39.26	22.76	7.40	3.74	3.19	-0.84	-1.65	6.1
Oper Funds / Int Expense	22.84	33.79	20.60	7.66	4.57	2.55	-0.30	1.47	
Fixed Chg Cover Incl. Rents	NA	16.86	9.29	5.04	2.90	2.55	-0.19	-0.70	

Hastings has decoupled employee bonuses somewhat from the level of profitability, by paying bonuses in 1992 and 93, when the company incurred losses. Will he return to past practices: set aside seed money; pay modest dividends; divide the remainder of net profit among employees as bonus; grow slowly? Or will the company continue to evolve toward more conventional approaches—perhaps by increasing dividends and using more and more of profit to expand production operations abroad. The escalation in share price which added debt might promise will be very tempting to major holders.

Teaching Plan

A good approach to teaching the Lincoln case is to role-play a directors meeting. Directors include Emma S. Lincoln, David C. Lincoln, and G. Russell Lincoln, family members who each own scads of shares. There are also Don Hastings, Fred Mackenbach, and Harry Carlson (Vice Chairman) who are corporate officers with substantial holdings of shares. Other directors include Ed Hood, former executive and director of General Electric, Paul Lego, former Westinghouse CEO, Hugh Libby, CEO of a company which makes diesel/gas turbine generator sets, Henry Meyer, CEO of Society National Bank (Lincoln's lead lender), Lawrence Selhorst, CEO of American Spring Wire Corporation, Craig Smith, CEO of Ameritrust banking corporation, and Frank Steingass, Chairman and President of a commercial printing company. Simply having Hastings present his strategies, listed at the end of the case, will be enough to occupy several hours. Emma Lincoln and Fred Mackenbach, credibly, might decry recent Hastings strategies which appear to subvert James Lincoln's ideals. And the outside directors might favor moving even faster than Hastings proposes toward leveraging financially, if not operationally, expanding, and de coupling pay from net profit.

Research Basis for Gathering Case Information

Case information was accumulated over a 14-year period culminating in site visits and interviews during April 1995. The author is an experienced welder and steel fabricator and once owned a Lincoln distributorship, so has some personal knowledge of the industry and of Lincoln in particular. Financial reports (annual reports, 10Qs, 10Ks) were obtained both from the company and from Disclosure, of Baltimore, MD.

—Arthur Sharplin

Implementing Strategy:
The Single Business Context

LINCOLN
ELECTRIC COMPANY

Vijay Govindarajan

Professor of Strategy and Control

The Amos Tuck School of Business

Dartmouth College

Hanover, NH 03755

Phone: (603) 646-2156

Fax: (303) 646-1308

Key Questions

- What is Lincoln Electric's product-market strategy? What business is Lincoln in and how does Lincoln develop competitive advantage in this business?

- How well do Lincoln's organization and control fit the company's strategic requirements?

- Is Lincoln ahead or behind current good management practice?

- How difficult would it be for Lincoln Electric to implement its unique control systems in the manufacturing plants it has opened abroad or the companies it has acquired in the U.S.?

- What ideas would you transplant from Lincoln to other companies?

- Would you like to work in an environment like Lincoln Electric?

Discussion Topics

- Lincoln Electric's product/market strategy

- Lincoln's implementation approach

- Applications of Lincoln's approach to other companies

Strategy Implementation:
Conceptual Framework

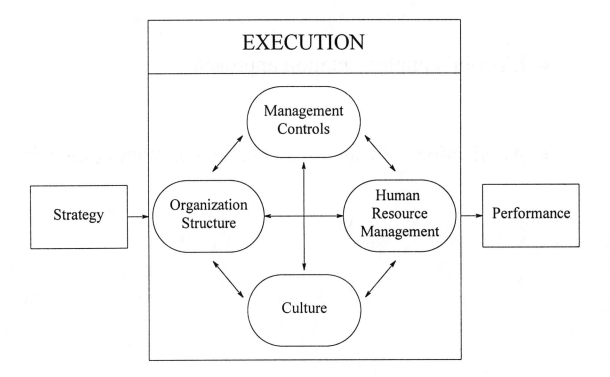

Company Background

- Founded 1895 in Cleveland, Ohio

- CEOs:

1895–1914	John Lincoln
1914–1965	James Lincoln
1965–1986	William Irrgang
1986–	George Willis

- Often termed as one of the best manufacturing companies in the world

Top Management Team

Year joined

1947	George E. Willis, CEO
1948	Don F. Hastings, President
1954	Harry Carlson, Vice-Chmn
1953	John Gonzalez, Sr VP, R&D
1932	W.I. Miskoe, Sr V-P, Int'l
1942	E.F. Smolnik, Sr V-P & CFO
1950	Roger F. Young, Sr V-P
?	Paul J. Beddia, VP, HR
?	David J. Fullen, VP
?	Harry C. Handlin, VP
1936	Al S. Patnik, VP, Sales
?	John R. Velliky, VP

Industry Characteristics

- Not a very glamorous industry

- Mature, cyclical market

- Buyers are in capital goods industries; linked to fate of US capital goods manufacturers

- Evolutionary change in technology so far

- Little patent protection

- Brand names largely irrelevant

Lincoln's Strategy

- Essentially single business company: arc welding machines and electrodes (87%), motors (13%)

- Till recently, mainly US-based, some exports; now expanding aggressively abroad through JVs and acquisitions

- "Give customers more and more of a better and better product at a lower and lower price"

- Clear cost leader

- Competitively superior product reliability and customer service

Explanation for
Lincoln Electric's Success

Industry Effect

Lock on Technology

Brand Name

Low Cost Labor

Government Subsidies

Protectionism

Unique Strategy

Strategy Implementation

Organization and Control

- Functional, very flat structure

- 2600 employees (incl. 400–500 design, process, and sales engineers)

- Avg. age — 40 years
  Avg. tenure — 17 years

- Pay-for-performance system:

  Pay = Wages + Bonus
       = Wages (1 + Merit Rating * Bonus Factor)

  Wages = f(Piece rate, productivity)
  Piece Rate = f(Cleveland area wages, production standards)

  There are 70,000 piecework prices; piecerate changes only if company introduces new technology or production method

  Merit Rating = f(Output, dependability, quality, ideas & cooperation)
              = Must equal 100 for all employees
              = Range 45 to 160

  "We believe in sharing profits but not in sharing them equally"

  Bonus Factor = f(company profitability)
              = Target: 100% of wages

- Average blue-collar 1990 pay: $45,000 (peak over $90,000)

- No pay for defective products; warranty repairs at worker's own time

- No paid holidays

- Mandatory overtime; job re-assignments cannot be refused; seniority is irrelevant

- Entry level hiring only (shop-floor worker, sales trainee, engineering trainee) coupled with internal promotions

- Guaranteed employment after 2 years' seniority: at least 30 hours/week

- No mandatory retirement

Organization and Control (cont'd)

- 75% of employees own stock (50% of company) "Restricted stock"

- Advisory board of elected employees

- Suggestion system:
    3000 suggestions/year
    500 implemented
    3 full-time methods engineers to follow-up

- No management perks

- Very spartan/frugal culture: "We don't spend money on anything that we don't have to"

- No unions; labor turnover rate: 6% (vs. 36% for Industry)

"Fixed" Pay

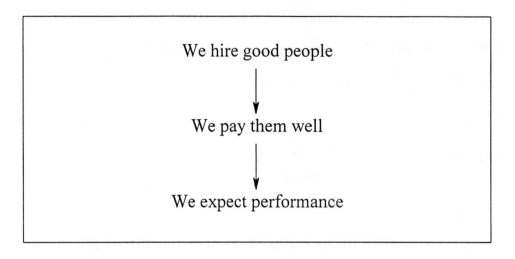

We hire good people

↓

We pay them well

↓

We expect performance

"Performance-Based" Pay

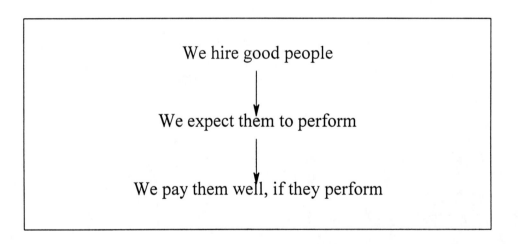

We hire good people

↓

We expect them to perform

↓

We pay them well, if they perform

Implications

- Speed of cost reduction (flexible bonus system)

- Continuous process improvement (detailed analysis of process, life-long tenures)

- Very high current productivity (pay-for-performance)

- Very low administrative infrastructure costs (self-management)

Performance

	1970	1981	1988	1990
($millions)				
Revenues	118	542	585	811
Net Income	10	40	34	11
EPS		$29	$33	$10

Market Share:

- 1980: US – 40%, non-US – insignificant

- 1990: US – over 50%
  1995 goal: Global – 40%

Implications for Public Policy

- National Competitiveness

- Achieving Full Employment

- Improving National Savings Rate

The Seven "S" Model

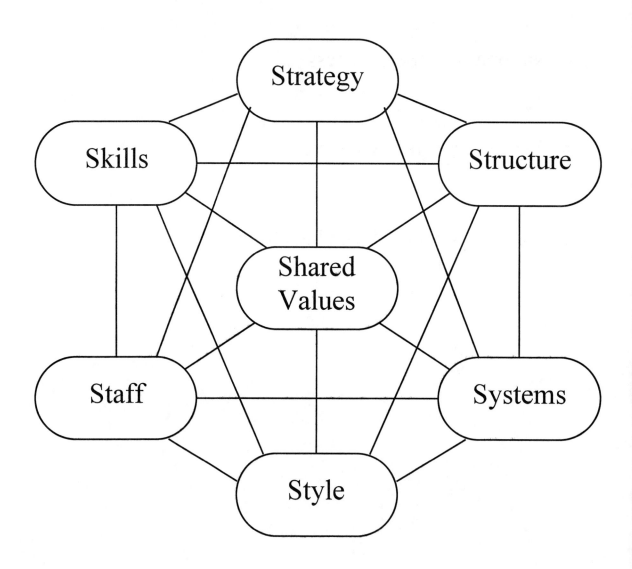

Seven "S" Model

1. **Strategy** — Plan or course of action leading to the allocation of a firm's resources to reach identified goals.

2. **Structure** — How people and tasks relate to each other. The basic grouping of reporting relationships and activities. The way separate entities of an organization are tied together.

3. **Shared Values** — The significant meanings or guiding concepts that that give purpose and meaning to the organization.

4. **Systems** — Formal processes and procedures including management control systems, performance measurement and reward systems, planning and budgeting systems, etc. and the ways people relate to them.

5. **Skills** — Organizational competencies. These include the abilities of individuals as well as management practices, technological abilities and other capabilities that reside in the organization itself.

6. **Style** — The leadership style of management and the overall operating style of the organization. A reflection of the norms people act upon and how they work and interact with each other, vendors and customers.

7. **Staff** — Recruitment, selection, development, socialization and advancement of people in the organization.

After Richard Pascale, *Managing on ilte Edge,* Simon & Schuster, 1990

Seven "S" Implications

1. Many factors influence organizational effectiveness. Not just strategy.

2. These factors are interrelated. Leadership involves managing the constantly changing "fit" of these factors without finding a too-comfortable "rut."

3. Changes in one factor are likely to trigger reactions in other areas. A "total systems" approach to change is necessary.

4. The traditional management realm of the more tangible (hard) "S's" is where we are most comfortable and most inclined to operate.

   - Strategy
   - Systems
   - Structure

5. Companies with sustained high performance, however, are noted for their attention to the less tangible (soft) "S's."

   - Skills
   - Style
   - Staff
   - Shared Values

Anita's Apparel

Objectives

- To examine how different compensation and reward mechanisms influence behavior.

- To understand how management control systems can be translated from one company to another.

- To examine the difficulty in changing corporate culture.

Synopsis

Anita's Apparel—a fictional retail apparel store—is wrestling with how to improve sales per square foot. The case uses this reference frame to look at Nordstrom. Nordstrom has the highest sales per squarefoot in the retail apparel industry and is well known for its outstanding customer service. The case describes a selection of the compensation and incentive systems which Nordstrom uses. In addition, the case discusses union problems that Nordstrom had as a direct result of one of these systems. While the complaints of the union are understated because of the eventual outcome, they do point to the potential abuses when mangers and employees try to game the performance measurement system.

Structuring a class

While the question asked is discussed below and it will give students a great deal to think about when preparing the case. The discussion will be more fruitful if it is started with a little more structure. The goal of this discussion is to see how different management control systems will effect employees' behavior and change the level of customer satisfaction. The process will be to begin by developing three lists:

- Service Differences

- Impact on Sales

- Mechanism for influencing employee behavior

These lists play into each other and help guide the student into thinking about how a specific mechanism can cause employees' to behave one way and how a group of mechanisms working in concert can align an employees' actions closely with the goals of the company.

The next step is to take this learning and apply it to the question for Anita's Apparel. From this, you are likely to get a rich discussion of not only the mechanics of compensation, but also the different systems that must be in place to support the compensation system. One of the key lessons when discussing the Anita's Apparel compensation system is that the compensation system and the supporting systems must themselves be consistent with the company's strategy. Commission selling may not be the best approach to compensating sales clerks in a bargain basement type store. The sales and marketing

---

This teaching note was prepared by Kirk Hendrickson, Tuck '97.

expenditures might be better made elsewhere. From Anita's Apparel's business strategy and the understanding of the mechanism of behavior influence, the students should be able to develop a detailed description of a possible compensation system for Anita's Apparel.

Service Differences:

Begin by getting a feel for the number of people in the class who have shopped at Nordstrom. Then ask how is customer service different at Nordstrom than it is at Macy's or Dillards or any of the students other favorite or least favorite retail stores and list these on the right hand side of the board. This list is likely to include:

- Personalized thank you notes

- Sales clerks that move with you from department to department

- Willingness to take anything back, no hassles

- Personal, yet not overbearing attention.

- Good quality merchandise

- Reasonable price for the quality

- Wide selection

- Pleasant atmosphere

How do service differences impact sales?

Next, taking each of the points of the above list, ask how do each of these differences in customer service impact sales? List the responses in the center of the board showing the connection between the specific differences and the impact on sales.

Some of the general themes that should come out of this are that they increase customer loyalty and a customer's willingness and desire to shop at Nordstrom's again. In addition, you feel that the quality is good but not overpriced. Also, they are likely to sell you more items because you can always return it, and the sales associates aren't stopped by the store's department boundaries from selling you everything that you need. In fact there is one example of a Nordstrom sales associate getting out petty cash, going to a competitor and buying a specific pair of pants for a customer because Norstrom didn't have this customer's size, and then selling it to the customer at a discount because it was during one of Nordstrom's semiannual sales.

The question: "Do returns increase or decrease sales" is always a tough one. On one side, a student would argue that the unconditional return policy allows people to return items they would never return elsewhere, thus causing costs and losing revenue. On the other hand, many people will see Nordstrom's return policy as an option and thus be willing to pay a premium price for the clothes because they are purchasing both the clothes and a put option on the clothes. If the clothes do not perform to expectations, then they can be returned, giving the customer the benefit of having the clothes without the cost. As with most options, it is rarely exercised, yet people are still willing to pay for them. Taking a different approach, the unconditional return policy creates prima-facia credibility between the sales associate and the customer. The reason is that the customer knows that the sales associate has little incentive to sell you things that you don't want because they will come back. This credibility allows the customer to have a more positive, cooperative relationship with the Nordstrom sales associate. This positive relationship results in higher sales. Also, even if a customer went to return some items, this increases "traffic" in stores and the customer might purchase other items.

Mechanisms that influence employees' behavior

Now that we have an idea of how different customer service methods have an impact on sales, the big question is what management control mechanisms are necessary to cause employees to act in ways consistent with the customer service differences?

There is a split between policies that Nordstrom has that the employees follow, unconditional returns, and suggested activities that Nordstrom sales associates perform but are not required to, thank you notes, going from department to department. In all of these cases, Nordstrom is trying to motivate improved customer service to create brand loyalty among its customers. Nordstrom is able to trade on this brand loyalty to charge premiums, increase repeat sales, and have customers select Nordstrom over other stores when they need to make a purchase. The intensity of this brand loyalty is demonstrated by a common Seattle license plate holder that says, "I'd rather be shopping at Nordstrom." This fierce loyalty is a source of sustained competitiveness and the direct result of deliberately selected policies and activities of Nordstrom.

Policies:

Unconditional returns:

> As discussed above, Nordstrom's policy of unconditional returns has several ways in which it influences the behavior of sales associates to improve customer satisfaction. The main motivation is that it is a stick that will punish sales associates who antagonize customers. Items will be returned and the sales associate will lose that commission. This encourages the sales associate to act in a manner that is consistent with the customer's best interest so that the customer is happy about their purchase and does not return it. This actually encourages sales associates to take steps to provide after sales service, something that is unheard of in the retail apparel industry.

Promotion from within:

> This policy influences behavior by ensuring that the managers and buyers who are supporting the sales associates understand the conditions that the sales associate are working in and what can be done to improve those conditions. This also provides a direct path for progression for high performing sales associates. At many other department stores, the store managers, etc. come from the ranks of the buyers or other positions, not the sales clerks. The sales clerks in these stores are completely transient with little career opportunities.

Commissions:

The more you sell, the more you make. There are no limits. Low performance results in termination. Therefore, only those who are able to sell stay.

Inventory:

While not discussed in the case, Nordstrom makes a conscious decision to keep higher inventory than its competitor including more sizes and variety. This allows for rare out of stock circumstances and allows Nordstrom sales associates to serve a wide variety of customers.

Suggested Activities:

Contests:

These occasional events provide additional motivation for sales people to improve certain aspects of their performance. It is not always sales, often it is directly related to customer service. The contests provide for the employees to make customer service innovations because they tell what it is that the employees need to do: provide the best customer service, but not how they are to do it. Many of the actions taken by current sales people were during previous contests.

Recognition:

Recognition provides direct praise to the sales associates as to what is good and bad behavior. While behavior requirements can be spelled out in a policy manual, the recognition programs of Nordstrom prove an anecdotal example of what is and is not exemplary performance and how exemplary performance can be tied to special rewards. The exemplary performance comes in two areas, how much did you sell and how well did you serve the customers. By recognizing and rewarding these two activities, Nordstrom focuses the sales associates' efforts on selling and customer service.

Heroics:

Heroics are something that Nordstrom sales associates can aspire to and imitate. By imitating these heroics, the sales associates will be acting in manners consistent with Nordstrom's desired outcome of improved customer service. In addition, heroics often get into the public domain and add to Nordstrom's mystique, encouraging customers to shop at Nordstrom because the service they will receive will be legendary.

Finally, Nordstrom is very careful to make sure that the heroics are all about what someone did to improve customer service and show the proper face to the customer. They were never stories about how much money someone saved the company.

Now that we have looked at the different types of control mechanisms and their effect on employees behavior, we want to shift gears to Anita's Apparel and the idea of translating control systems across corporate cultures.

Question: **How would you advise Anita Lamont about compensating her employees?**

When considering the issue of compensating her employees, Anita Lamont is in a position where she can make a big mistake. The big mistake that she could make is in concentrating on answering exactly the question that was asked. Anita Lamont's compensation system does need to be changed. She is paying employees a high hourly wage and expecting this to be sufficient incentive to align her employees' goals with her goals of increasing sales and revenues. Considering Nordstrom, Anita Lamont is presented with a very different approach to compensating sales clerks, which Nordstrom carefully refers to as sales associates and not clerks. Nordstrom uses 100 percent commission compensation. As mentioned in the case, this allows sales associates to earn almost twice what their counterparts do at other stores. In fact, it is not unheard of for a Nordstrom sales associate to make over $80,000 per year, about five times the industry average. In order to achieve these earnings, the Nordstrom sales associates had to sell anywhere between 7 and 13 times their compensation. As the class will have already discussed, these sales associates' actions are clearly in line with Nordstrom's goal of increasing sales.

Looking at Nordstrom from a myopic viewpoint, another store might conclude that introducing a commission system is sufficient, as the sales clerks compensation system will encourage high achievement. This is exactly what some of Nordstrom's competitors, such as Macy's, May and Bloomingdale's, thought when they tried to duplicate Nordstrom's commissions policies and found little change in sales yet higher selling costs. In one case, "Carter Hawley Hale Stores invested more than $30 million in its commission program but failed to realize any extraordinary productivity gains and continued to lose market share to Nordstrom."[1] Commission selling could dramatically increase selling expenses at Anita's Apparel without necessarily increasing sales.

So what does Anita Lamont need to do?

The first step in developing the compensation system is to determine what her business strategy is and how the compensation system will support this strategy. In Nordstrom's case, they have limited advertising and promotion, choosing instead to spend its sales and marketing dollars on the sales associates. While this works well for Nordstrom, it may not work well for Anita's Apparel. While this is not a marketing case, we can make some assumptions about Anita's Apparel's market and derive a possible strategy, other assumptions will lead you to a different strategy.

As a retailer of high-end women's business apparel in the Midwest with four stores, Anita's Apparel is likely to have customers who are:

- well educated and well read

- time sensitive

- expecting a high level of service

While there are many other likely characteristics of its customers, these few start to form the picture that Anita's Apparel's customers are a select segment who are unlikely to be reached through television or other mass media advertising. They may be drawn in by promotions, but more like they will be

---

[1] Robert Spector and Patrick D. McCarthy, The Nordstrom Way, (New York: John Wiley and Sones, 1995), p. 115.

drawn in by the service and selection as these customers will be shopping for clothes they will need on a regular basis. This suggests that Anita's Apparel's customers will be looking to purchase when they have a need and will make a purchase at this time rather than waiting for a promotion. In addition, Anita's Apparel's customers are probably not very price sensitive.

From this, it would seem that Anita's Apparel should expend its sales and marketing budget on in store sales and service rather than advertising or promotions. This leads us to asking what is the best way to develop in store sales and service. It would appear that Anita's Apparel's current approach of high fixed wages isn't working. Customer complaints are up, though they are up in proportion with the number of stores, and sales per square foot is down.

I suggest a plan that looks something like:

- Place all sales clerks on a commissioned compensation system.

- Change the job title from sales clerk to sales associate.

- Train the sales force in customer service and what the new commission system means to them.

- Change the buying to support the new customer service approach. Inventory management is important, but inventory stinginess will keep this plan from working.

- Add a complete money back guarantee. As discussed, this is an option, price accordingly yet imbed the price in the price of the clothing not as a separate fee.

- Introduce sales and service contests that reward high sales and high service performance.

- Start creating a record of heroics. These heroics should be careful to demonstrate customer service as the prime motivation.

- Require the current store managers to sell on the floor. While we can't grow this generation of store managers, we can at least get them close to the customers.

- Aggressively weed out under-performing sales people through 30 day and 90 day reviews. Under-performance after 90 days is cause for termination.

Viewing this suggested solution, we see many similarities with Nordstrom's approach. While these control systems might work for Nordstrom, they may not work for Anita's Apparel. If this is true, then what can Anita's Apparel do?

Nordstrom itself and many other companies have had trouble altering existing control systems. First, in 1975, Nordstrom made its last purchase of an outside department store.

The former president of Nordstrom indicated that trying to adopt the corporate culture of another organization to that of Nordstom's was just too difficult and costly and that it is much more cost beneficial to just start our own Nordstrom's from the ground up.

While the above suggestion attempts to address issues of what makes sense for Anita's Apparel, its design has to be based on Anita's Apparel's business strategy. As the students devise their own plan, it will be worthwhile to ask:

What is the goal of the plan?

- Is this goal consistent with business strategy?

- Does it encourage behavior in alignment with the goal?

- Is it comprehensive?

- Does it consider the balance between the effects of the different systems?

- Does it prevent gaming of the system?

- Can it be adopted within the Anita's Apparel culture?

These questions will lead to a rich discussion of how can Anita's Apparel in particular and in company in general can introduce a management control system.

Finally, there is the issue of the union dispute. While briefly mentioned in the case and not dealt with at length in this teaching note, what the union dispute points out is that control systems can have negative side effects and that it is important as managers not to ignore these side effects. While Nordstrom's position in the dispute was strong, the negative impact it had on the company and its publicity could have been devastating to a less loved company. A company such as Anita's Apparel would be unlikely to survive such a lambasting. This suggests that the students strongly consider how Anita's Apparel's performance measurement system could be gamed and whether these games would compromise the integrity of the system either legally or ethically.

Additional Materials

1. *60 Minutes* video on Nordstrom. Order this directly from CBS (Phone: 212/975-2875). This 15-minute video should be shown during class discussion prior to discussing the applicability of Nordstrom's system to Anita's Apparel.

2. Teaching Note on "Nordstrom: Dissention in the Ranks? (A) and (B)" 5-192-026. Order this directly from Harvard (617/495-6117).

3. Teaching Note on Nordstrom 5-594-052. Order this directly from Harvard.

Wayside Inns, Inc.

Author: Charles T. Sharpless, under the supervision of M. Edgar Barrett

Substantive Issues Raised

Kevin Gray, Regional General Manager for Wayside Inns, Inc., was reviewing his file on Layne Rembert's compensation package and on his related performance evaluation. Rembert, Inn Manager of the Memphis Airport Wayside Inn, had expressed some concern about how a proposed 40-room expansion at his location would affect his total compensation.

The case contains a significant amount of data in respect to the firm's strategy, the proposed investment in expanded facilities at the Memphis airport location, and the compensation system used by Wayside Inns in respect to their Inn Managers. In addition, some additional ideas as to how Inn Managers might be evaluated are included.

Pedagogical Objectives

Due to the multiple issues mature of the case, it is particularly useful as either an overview or a summary case in either the management control systems module of a broader course or in a course devoted to the topic of management control systems. Alternatively, the case might be, used as a partial or whole basis for the discussion of incentive compensation systems.

In either event, the nature of the case is such that the firm's strategy, the proposed investment, and the compensation system will all need to be discussed.

Opportunities for Student Analysis

The Firm's Strategy. If one presumes that decisions about such things as expansion and the type of compensation system that is appropriate should be made in the overall context of the firm's corporate strategy, then a brief discussion and analysis of that strategy would seem to be in order. The firm, in fact, has positioned itself in a most interesting market niche.

As stated in the case, "The company's fundamental strategy was to cater to those business travellers who were generally not interested in elaborate settings." In addition, the firm has consciously chosen to play a very minor role in the restaurant business. Thus, the prototypical clientele of the firm consists of business (as opposed to convention or holiday) travellers who are interested in clean rooms, dependable service and rates below those of such other national chains as Marriott, Hilton, Hyatt and Sheraton.

The firm has also consciously opted for multiple locations. This provides them with at least three distinct advantages. First, they can keep the properties small enough that they can be managed by a live-in management couple. Second, they can disperse their locations in such a way that they have an Inn near each of a variety of commercial districts, industrial facilities and/or educational or shopping areas in any given metropolitan area. Finally, they can hedge their risks by limiting their exposure to any one neighborhood.

While the firm generally stayed out of the restaurant business—which made its managerial tasks and structure much simpler, it did profit from the presence of the adjoining restaurant. As seen in Case Exhibit 4, the restaurant rental revenues (which typically covered the ground lease only) could amount to ten percent of operating income. Finally, the firm's overall strategy allowed them to charge 15 to 20 percent less than their major competitors. This, among other things, resulted in an occupancy rate 10 to 20 percent higher than these same competitors.

Evaluation of the Investment. Drawing firm conclusions in respect to whether the proposed investment is likely to be a good one for Wayside Inns, Inc. is not easy in this case. There are a variety of reasons why one could argue either the "pro" or the "con" case, although the pro case would appear to be more convincing over the long run.

A set of data derived from Case Exhibits 4 and 6 is shown in Exhibit TN-1. As shown there, the ROI for the overall inn is projected to fall from 27.1 percent to 24.3 percent. The data in this exhibit, however, are based on the assumptions made by Kevin Gray, which ignore a number of major issues both pro and con.

On the pro side are several strategic factors—the proposed expansion appears to meet the firm's stated expansion criteria and the expansion may be needed to preempt competition; several market factors—any customer growth projections based on either a trend line or the "turnaway" data are bound to look good and the existing inn is clearly operating at or near its practical capacity; and several financial factors—the analysis is based on one year only (and inflation helps an already constructed motel with a fixed mortgage payment) and it ignores the fact that the management and reservations fees (at least in part) stay within the overall firm. In total, these factors combine to argue reasonably persuasively for the project.

On the con side, the three biggest issues have to do with the incremental ROI, the turnaway count and the increased risk that one might be hurt by either a downturn in the economy or overbuilding in the local market. The incremental ROI, as shown in Exhibit TN-1, is projected to be 20.5 percent on a pre-tax basis. If one considers the relatively high interest rates of 1981 and 1982 (prime in the 15 to 20-percent range), this can be seen as a very disturbing piece of data.

The turnover count is even more interesting. If one considers how these data are collected, and the fact that the competitors are likely to be working with similar data, then one could get nervous here as well. The basic problem here is that the same person—in reality representing *one* turnaway—could show up on the turnaway count of several motel chains and more than once on one or more of those. All the person has to do is call several reservation services and then drive down the highway, stopping at each of several motels to see if the motel is, in fact, fully booked. Thus, the turnaway counts *might* be grossly overstated.

The increased risk of being hurt by either a downturn in the economy or overbuilding in the local market is due largely to the incremental fixed costs and the resulting higher breakeven point. The parent company's managers, however, think that they are reasonably well positioned for an economic downturn as people can, and do, "trade down" from the more expensive competitive locations in times of economic uncertainty.

Layne Rembert's Concern. Understandably enough, Layne Rembert is concerned about how the proposed expansion is likely to affect his overall level of compensation. As shown in Case Exhibit 6, a 34 percent increase in the size of the property managed would result in only a 13.7 percent increase in compensation. Taken literally, this would appear to be somewhat unfair. The fact that the data shown in Case Exhibit 6 are the result of "...a rough calculation" may need to be stressed, however, as the base salary is unlikely to be left untouched from one year to the next.

Appropriateness of Current Compensation Package. Assessing the appropriateness of a compensation plan is a task where the relevant criteria are sometimes far from obvious. Nonetheless, the issue is a crucial one in any management control system.

One way to attack the problem is to assess how controllable the various causal factors lying behind the four components of income really are. The results of such an assessment are shown in Exhibit TN-2. As can be seen, much of the compensation earned by a management couple is in no sense of the word controllable by them.

If most of the causal factors lying behind the current compensation scheme are not controllable by the management couple, then the obvious question becomes, "What factors are controllable and how, if at all, should they be related to the compensation scheme?" Enter the items shown on Case Exhibit 7.

The management couples *are* Wayside Inns, Inc. as far as most of the firm's customers are concerned. They, or their direct reports, are the people with whom the client deals. In addition, they are the line managers most directly responsible for such factors as the internal and external appearance of the motel, the cleanliness of the rooms and the attitude of the front desk personnel.

In addition, the management couples do have some influence over direct costs (through efficient utilization of both labor and supplies), over administrative and financial costs (through the prompt depositing of funds and the timely and accurate submission of reports), and over the volume of business (through sales calls and through the ability to retain existing clients). Thus, one could argue quite persuasively for the inclusion of the *Performance Evaluation Report* as one of the determinants of compensation.

Other issues that might be raised in respect to the current compensation package include: (1) the key role of the regional general manager and how that might raise the anxiety level of the management couples; and, (2) the inherent unfairness of an ROI-based system that is tied to an historical cost measurement system.

In respect to the former, one might argue for the need to ensure some uniformity of evaluation techniques across the various inns. A traveling inspector, for example, might be employed to periodically check such things as room cleanliness, exterior appearance and the courtesy and efficiency of the front desk personnel. McDonald's is reported to use that procedure in evaluating their unit managers.

In respect to the latter, the fact that an older property has a higher ROI (lower depreciation and a lower investment base) may more than offset the fact that its investment base is somewhat smaller. This problem, in addition, will make almost any expansion proposal look less favorable than it should.

Similarity of Performance Measurement System across Levels of the Organization. Asking whether the performance measurement system for a Regional General Manager should be focussed upon the same variables that are used to evaluate and compensate an Inn Manager is tantamount to asking how the managerial roles vary as one moves up in the organization. In the case of Wayside Inns, Inc., several things are clear.

First, the ability to directly affect the more strategic decisions—such as site selection, market segmentation policies, and the size of the inn to be built increases as one rises in the organization. Second, the appropriate time period for evaluation tends to lengthen as one rises in the organization. Inn managers can be measured on short-term results almost exclusively (assuming, of course, that the variables are controllable), but the senior management should be assessed, at least in part, on the basis of long-range objectives. Third, the immediate supervisor of a particular line manager should be held accountable for those aspects of that line manager's behavior which the supervisor can and should influence. For example, the regional general manager should be held accountable—at least in part—for the cleanliness of the inns within his geographical area.

Suggestions for Classroom Use

As noted earlier, I usually use this case as either an overview or a summary case in a management control systems module. As a result, the focus of the class discussion is broad rather than narrow.

The flow of the class discussion can easily follow the sequence outlined in the preceding section. The portion of the discussion dealing with the evaluation of the investment, however, can occur almost anywhere during the hour.

Suggested Questions

1. Is the proposed investment likely to be a good one for Wayside Inns, Inc.?

2. Is Layne Rembert's concern justified?

3. Is the current compensation package for Inn Managers an appropriate one? If not, what would be?

4. Should the performance measurement system for a Regional General Manager be focussed upon the same factors that are used by Kevin Gray and Wayside Inns to evaluate and compensate an Inn Manager? (An RGM has responsibility for a geographical area containing anywhere from 10 to 15 motels.)

Exhibit TN-1
Wayside Inns, Inc.

Financial Evaluation of the Proposed Investment

Revenue	Status Quo[1]	Post Investment[2]	Increase
Room	$ 998,277	$1,420,238	$421,961
Restaurant	32,304	40,571	8,267
Other	19,148	25,050	5,902
	$1,049,729	$1,485,859	$436,130
Variable Costs			
Room	229,520	326,700	97,180
Mgmt Fees[3]	49,914	71,012	21,098
	279,434	397,712	118,278
Contribution	770,295	1,088,147	317,852
(%)	<73.4%>	<73.2%>	<72.9%>
Fixed Costs			
Op. Exp.	310,991	376,832	65,841
Depr.	58,320	82,400	24,080
Mgmt Fees[3]	3,480	4,680	1,200
	372,791	463,912	91,121
EBIT	$397,504	$624,235	$226,731
Investment	1,468,789	2,573,789	1,105,000
R.O.I.	27.1%	24.3%	20.5%

Notes:

[1]Data taken from Case Exhibit 4.
[2]Data taken from Case Exhibit 6.
[3]5% of room revenue (variable); and $30 per room, per year (fixed).

Exhibit TN-2
Wayside Inns, Inc.

Controllability of Components of Compensation

Causal Factors

Type of Compensation	Not Controllable — Degree of Controllability by Inn Manager — Controllable			
Base Salary	– Decree of Competition –	– Relative Sales Volume –		– Years of Service –
Sales Volume Incentive	– Degree of Competition – – Chain-wide Effects – – Economic Conditions –	– Price –	– Sales Efforts –	– Level of Service –
ROI Bonus – PF	– Size of Investment –			
– EBIT	– Indirect Expenses –	– Price –	– Sales Efforts –	– Efficiency –
– Investment	– Fixed Assets –	– Current Assets –		– Level of Service –
Fringe Benefits	** Constant for All Inn Mangers **			

Case 12-5

Mary Kay Cosmetics

Note

Instructors should contact Mary Kay Cosmetic Company and obtain videotape of Mary Kay's philosophies. Students enjoy seeing such videos in class.

Overview

This case describes the corporate culture of one of the 100 best companies to work for in America. The case is written around the issue of how the company has dealt with its first real slowdown in recruiting Mary Kay beauty consultants to market the company's cosmetic lines. The drop off in recruiting jeopardized MKC's reputation as a growth company.

Management responded to the problem by instituting changes in its sales incentives and sales policies, by quadrupling its recruiting budget, raising prices, and staging a nationwide closed-circuit telecast to entice new recruits to the MKC ranks.

The case contains extensive detail on the company's sales force organization, its incentive and compensation policies, its motivational practices, how the company's culture was established and nurtured, and Mary Kay Ash's unique role as inspirational leader.

Suggestions for Using the Case

The case has a wealth of detail on how the company operates, the strategy implementation approaches that have been used, Mary Kay Ash's management philosophy, and in particular its motivational approaches for stimulating the efforts of its 195,000-person force of beauty consultants. The case is an in-depth portrayal of the corporate culture of MKC and how this culture undergrids and shapes the company's strategy. It should be used to drive home the points made in Chapter 10 of the text.

The Wal-Mart, Lincoln Electric, and Mary Kay Cosmetics cases form a module on corporate culture, the role of values and beliefs, the role of incentives and motivation, and the importance of good strategic leadership in successfully implementing the chosen strategy. We recommend you use at least two of the three cases (if not all three) so as to give students a basis for comparing and contrasting the approaches to implementation in successful companies. All three cases are intended to serve as lessons/examples of how to do a good job of implementing strategy. As indicated in the Nucor teaching note, you can use the Nucor case for this module as well.

Depending on your own preferences, you can spend one or two days on the Mary Kay case. The case is longer than average and contains enough material to drive a two-class-period discussion. On the other hand, it is easy enough to focus on the key points efficiently and get through the case in one day.

The information in Exhibit 2 has been loaded on the STRAT-ANALYST disks to make it simple and quick for students to explore MKC's rapid growth and financial performance. There is also a "what-if" exercise for projecting future performance. Otherwise, this is not really a number-crunching case and most of the student's attention needs to be focused on how MKC had tackled the task of implementing strategy and building a strategy-supportive organizational climate with a network of incentives, compensation policies, motivational practices, and managerial approaches.

This case is well-suited for outside written case analysis and group presentations.

Suggested Written Case Assignment

1. Prepare a report to Mary Kay Ash giving her (a) your appraisal of the strengths and weaknesses of the company's approach to recruiting, retaining, motivating, rewarding, and organizing its 195,000-person sales force and (b) recommending improvements in how the company can implement its direct sales strategy.

Assignment Questions

1. What are the key practices and policies used at Mary Kay Cosmetics to implement the company's direct sales strategy?

2. What impresses you most about this company? Do you think MKC is justifiably included on the list of the 100 best companies to work for in the U.S.? What kinds of people are attracted to become Mary Kay beauty consultants?

3. What are the important components of the corporate culture at MKC? What has Mary Kay Ash done personally to build, shape, and reinforce this culture? How important has her role been? Is Mary Kay a leader or a manager? What's the difference?

4. How important is MKC's corporate culture in accounting for the company's success to date?

5. What problems do you see arising at MKC? Can the company continue to be successful with its strategy and its strategy implementation practices?

6. What changes do you think need to be made in the way things are done at MKC? Is it time to change the strategy or should the company concentrate on improved strategy execution?

Teaching Outline and Analysis

A good way to open the class discussion is by asking the class what impresses them most about the company. Students ought to mention several things here:

*   Mary Kay Ash—her style of leadership, her philosophy about how to manage people, her ability to motivate and inspire, the image she has created of herself and her company, and so on.

*   The company's elaborate motivational and incentive compensation practices (the singing, the prizes, the monetary rewards, the use of emotion, the elaborate staging of events—National Guest Night and the annual Seminars in Dallas).

*   The company's growth and performance.

*   The careful detail paid to treatment of people—the people-oriented climate.

*   The company culture and atmosphere.

You also may want to probe for negatives about the company; some students are "turned off" by direct selling, by some of the things the company does, and by the fact that they personally would not want to work for this kind of company (being a beauty consultant won't likely appeal to female students as a career path). Even so, these negatives should not override a key point of the case: the Mary Kay approach works well and is producing very good results. Probing into "why" should be the next step.

1. What are the primary practices and policies used at Mary Kay to implement the company's direct sales strategy?

Several techniques have been developed and adeptly applied at Mary Kay:

- Incentives given to beauty consultants to bring in more recruits

- The hierarchical network of prizes and monetary rewards given to beauty consultants

- The elaborate efforts to recognize (as well as reward) people for their individual accomplishments

- The accentuation on "the positive" approach to motivation and reward (all carrots, no sticks)

- The strong appeals to emotion, to ego, to the yearning of individuals for success

- The staging of big events to stimulate interest, excitement, and sales activity

- The use of images (pink Cadillacs) and singing (to build up positive emotions and reinforcement)

- Mary Kay's personal charisma, leadership, and undeniably superior ability to inspire the rank-and-file

- The constant emphasis on values, beliefs, and stories of individual accomplishment

- Development of policies and practices that have particular appeal to women (flexible work hours, the nature of the prizes and recognition for achievement—cars, furs, diamonds, and other success symbols, understanding the needs of women to have ample time to deal with unexpected family problems, etc.). It's really a woman-dominated company, run by and for women

2. What are the important components of the corporate culture at MKC?

All of the previously mentioned policies, practices, and approaches contribute to the company's culture. All are important in their own way. Students need to see and appreciate that corporate culture is made up of many pieces and has many facets and elements, each of which has a role and plays a part in creating the atmosphere and work climate. What makes the Mary Kay case so useful is that students ought to be able to see the extent to which management has left virtually no stone unturned in how to nurture and enhance the internal company climate. There are some very important drivers of the corporate culture at MKC:

- Mary Kay's own role and style as inspirational leader and keynoter.

- The values and beliefs that Mary Kay herself espouses and practices.

- The strong emphasis on individual achievement and recognition for this achievement.

- The women-oriented policies and practices.

- This is a good spot to bring in the McKinsey 7-S Framework. Ask the class how well the 7-S's fit together at MKC; their answer should be a "very, very good."

3. What has Mary Kay Ash done personally to shape and nuture the culture at MKC? How important have her actions and philosophies been?

It is difficult to overemphasize the importance of Mary Kay Ash to this company. Her performance on National Guest night (Salute to the Stars) provides a vivid example of her inspirational and motivational role and the reaction she evokes from the rank-and-file. She is the organization's role model. And she plays out her role to the hilt; every detail is well-orchestrated. She is every bit as dominant a force at MKC as Ted Turner at TBS, Ken Iverson at Nucor, and Sam Walton at Wal-Mart. But her style provides quite a contrast (it's more compatible with Sam Walton's than the other two). It is important for the class to see why she is held in such high esteem and reverence by the beauty consultants. One big reason is that she has been where they are, done what she's asked them to do, and been successful at it. A second reason is her strong people-orientation, her impressive skills in dealing with people, and her ability to project empathy, sincerity, and concern; the beauty consultants respond to this strongly because many of them have lived hard lives and yearn for some of the success that Mary Kay has achieved. Thus they are able to identify with her and are receptive to her message and the way she delivers it. A third reason is that Mary Kay Ash has the presence, the poise, and the communication skills to be effective as the company's central figure and leader. Part of "the secret" is the positive approach she takes to everything and the positive system of reinforcement that permeates the company's system of incentives and rewards. It should be clear that Mary Kay understands the great importance of all the itty-bitty, teeny-tiny things (like her personal design of the birthday cards) that, when taken together, count for more than one sees at first glance. And she is a master in employing symbols of success and in image-building (the use of pink, the selection of prizes and awards, the first-class approach in staging events, the "star" treatment given to achievers).

A telling point to bring out in this discussion is that Mary Kay is a leader in every sense of the word but she is not a professional manager. If time permits you may want to get the class to explore the differences between managers and leaders or you might interject a mini-lecture on the subject.

Before you move on, be sure that students see the significance and appreciate what Mary Kay Ash has done personally to build, shape, and reinforce the company's culture. Get them, if necessary, to cite specifics (there are many mentioned in the case).

4. How important is MKC's corporate culture in accounting for the company's success to date?

By this point in the class discussion, there should be broad consensus that the answer is "very important." It's the culture that glues the rest of the 6-Ss together. And Mary Kay Ash has been instrumental in building this culture and in leading the day-to-day actions that reinforce this culture. MKC is definitely a "strong culture" company.

5. What is your appraisal of all the sales force incentives rid the structure of the sales force organization?

The case contains a wealth of information about how the sales force is organized, motivated, compensated, and rewarded. The system is quite well-conceived; some of the strategy-supportive features need to be highlighted:

- There are strong financial incentives for beauty consultants to recruit more people into the sales force ranks (a bigger sales force is crucial to MKC's growth, as is replenishment of the supply of consultants lost through turnover).

- There are strong financial incentives, prizes, and recognitions given for reaching ever higher sales plateaus (the more productive each beauty consultant is in terms of sales, the faster MKC grows).

- None of the sales contests involve 1st, 2nd, or 3rd place winners; each contest is geared so that prizes are awarded to every beauty consultant who achieves targeted performance levels. This produces a stronger across-the-board motivation because there can be hundreds or thousands of winners rather than just a few—an important consideration in a sales force of 195,000 persons.

- Everybody in the sales-force organization is compensated by commissions—including those designated as managers. This keeps everybody's efforts trained directly on selling and on recruiting—the two dominant key success factors.

- The prizes for the sales contests are chosen to excite and motivate a female sales force; all of the prizes and awards are symbols of status and success.

This is a good point to ask the class what it thinks of the weekly Monday night sales meetings. How important are they? How important are the sales directors? What is their role in the organization? Does a highly productive beauty consultant necessarily make a good sales director? How long will it take for a beauty consultant to have "burn out" on showings? Is it necessary to offer productive beauty consultants the chance to become a sales director in order to retain them? Are you impressed with the way Jan Currier, senior sales director, conducted the weekly sales meeting? What would it be like to be a sales director at MKC? What kind of person would find this type of job attractive?

6. What kinds of people are attracted to become Mary Kay beauty consultants?

This is an important question and the answers provide good insight into the Mary Kay organization and culture. The class should identify the following characteristics of the typical Mary Kay consultant:

1. Comes from an upper-lower/lower-middle class background.

2. Aspires to a much better lifestyle.

3. Is motivated by monetary incentives and prizes that denote status and success.

4. Wants to be seen as a professional.

5. Has a self-starting, entrepreneurial streak but needs regular, positive reinforcement.

6. Is hungry for a better lifestyle and income level.

Plainly enough, a lot of people are not cut out to be Mary Kay beauty consultants and would not see such a career as attractive despite however much they might earn relative to other career endeavors. That a Mary Kay career is not universally attractive is strategically unimportant to the company; all that is needed is for a sizable enough number of people to be attracted to pursue a Mary Kay career—so far the numbers have been there.

7. What problems do you see arising at MKC over the next 5 years? What strategic issues face the company as of 1984?

A number of problems and issues seem to be lurking as of 1984:

- Can the company recruit adequate numbers of new beauty consultants to sustain its growth?

- Will the company's approach to sales incentives and compensation continue to appeal to women, given the broader career opportunities women now have and the changing attitudes of women about careers, work in the home, lifestyles, and part-time vs. full-time employment?

- Will Mary Kay products continue to have their appeal, given the trend to upscale, high quality products and the negatives associated with direct selling?

- Can the company adequately cope with the eventual loss/retirement of its spiritual and cultural leader, Mary Kay Ash?

The issue of whether the company can sustain its good performance is an important one. Table 1 shows the growth rates which the company has achieved over the past ten years. Table 2 shows various performance measures calculated from the financial summary presented in case Exhibit 2. The data in these two tables indicate a good solid performance on the part of the company:

- a 30.7 percent compounded average annual revenue increase over the 1973–83 period.

- 26.9 percent compound growth in operating income and net income (despite declining trends in the operating profit margin and net profit margin).

- very high times-interest-earned coverages and low levels of long-term debt.

- excellent returns on assets and stockholders' equity.

The increasing percentages for selling and administrative expenses are at least partly a reflection of the commission structure for the sales force organization. The higher the proportion of sales directors the company has and the bigger percentage of people in the other ranks above beauty consultants, all of whom earn commissions on the sales of those they have recruited, the more the overall percentage paid on commissions tends to be. The pyramiding of commission earnings, of course, also accounts for the high earnings of the company's top performers. Also pushing up selling and administrative percentages are (1) the costs of recruiting so many new consultants and (2) the growing list of winners of big prizes and big awards. In other words, the greater the percentage and number of high-achieving sales people in the organization the greater are MKC's costs for commission fees and contest awards.

Table 1
Growth Rates, Mary Kay Cosmetics, 1973–1983

Annual Growth Rates

	1973–74	1974–75	1975–76	1976–77	1977–78	1978–79	1979–80	1980–81	1981–82	1982–83	10-yr. Compound Avg.
Net Sales	36.1%	15.7%	28.4%	6.7%	12.3%	70.1%	82.6%	40.9%	29.3%	6.4%	30.7%
Cost of Sales	41.2%	16.1%	34.5%	3.0%	20.3%	57.5%	90.3%	35.5%	23.5%	1.3%	63.8%
Selling, G&A Exp	35.7%	14.6%	27.5%	11.5%	28.1%	66.1%	91.1%	38.9%	27.6%	9.5%	33.1%
Operating Income	31.5%	16.9%	22.9%	3.1%	–25.8%	107.4%	50.0%	57.8%	44.0%	5.9%	26.9%
Interest and Other Inc	14.9%	–53.3%	148.0%	–65.1%	277.1%	–25.3%	44.4%	108.6%	86.1%	35.1%	25.8%
Interest Expense	–6.9%	11.1%	–28.3%	393.0%	137.7%	90.1%	–33.7%	59.7%	26.6%	124.8%	47.8%
Income Before Income Tax	31.0%	13.2%	25.9%	–1.1%	–24.3%	98.6%	54.3%	59.0%	45.8%	4.8%	26.4%
Provision for Income Tax	30.9%	12.8%	30.7%	–2.4%	–28.0%	99.7%	51.1%	58.3%	45.0%	6.2%	25.8%
Net Income	31.0%	13.5%	21.7%	0.1%	–21.4%	99.1%	57.1%	59.6%	46.4%	3.6%	26.9%
Earnings Per Share	22.2%	18.2%	23.1%	6.3%	–11.8%	120.0%	57.6%	57.7%	43.9%	3.4%	29.8%
Dividends Per Share	200.0%	0.0%	66.7%	0.0%	20.0%	0.0%	50.0%	11.1%	10.0%	9.1%	28.2%–
Total Assets	26.2%	13.1%	22.6%	2.3%	3.4%	40.2%	46.2%	35.7%	51.0%	18.5%	24.9%
Long-Term Debt	–88.5%	–51.7%			–36.4%	12.4%	–25.0%	–21.1%	97.3%	–16.1%	17.9%

Source: Calculated from case Exhibit 2 using STRAT-ANALYST.

Table 2
Selected Performance Measures, Mary Kay Cosmetics, 1973–1983

	1973	1974	1975	1976	1977	1978	1979	1980	1981	1982	1983
Cost of Sales as % of Sales	28.9%	30.0%	30.1%	31.5%	30.4%	32.6%	30.2%	31.4%	30.2%	28.9%	27.5%
S, G, & Admin. As % of Sales	43.6%	43.4%	43.1%	42.8%	44.7%	51.0%	49.8%	52.1%	51.3%	50.6%	52.1%
Operating Profit Margin	27.5%	26.6%	26.9%	25.7%	24.9%	16.4%	20.0%	23.5%	18.4%	20.5%	20.4%
Int Expense as % of Sales	0.3%	0.2%	0.2%	0.1%	0.4%	0.9%	1.0%	0.4%	0.4%	0.4%	0.9%
Net Profit Margin	15.3%	14.7%	14.5%	13.7%	12.9%	9.0%	10.5%	12.9%	10.3%	11.6%	11.3%
Times-Interest-Earned	111.9	156.8	159.8	280.0	57.0	18.8	19.6	44.4	44.2	50.7	24.2
L-T Debt/Assets	3.9%	0.4%	0.2%	0.0%	15.9%	9.8%	7.9%	4.0%	2.3%	3.1%	2.2%
Return on Total Assets	17.3%	18.0%	18.0%	17.9%	17.5%	13.3%	18.9%	20.3%	23.9%	23.2%	20.3%
Total Asset Turnover	113.3%	122.1%	124.8%	130.7%	136.3%	148.0%	179.5%	157.1%	233.0%	199.6%	179.2%
Ret on Avg Stkhldrs' Equity			21.0%	23.0%	24.0%	20.0%	38.0%	48.0%	48.0%	45.0%	32.0%
Dividend Payout Ratio	11.1%	27.3%	23.1%	31.3%	29.4%	40.0%	18.2%	17.3%	12.2%	9.3%	9.8%

Source: Calculated from case Exhibit 2.

8. What recommendations would you make to the company regarding its strategy implementation efforts?

Students are likely to find little in the way of substantive changes to recommend. The consensus recommendation is likely to be "continue doing things pretty much as they are being done now." There are no big flaws in what the company is doing already and there are substantial risks in making big changes. Richard Rogers responded to the downturn in the rate of sales force growth with a rather aggressive program; the adjustments he announced are hard to fault. The short-term priorities at MKC need to be (1) trying to reduce the high turnover of consultants, (2) attracting higher caliber people into the sales force ranks, and (3) boosting the annual sales per consultant. However, tightening up the recruiting standards very much will hurt the company since one-third or more of total company revenues come from the orders placed by new consultants.

Most of the recommendations for action will probably fall into the area of fine tuning the approaches it is already using to implement its direct selling strategy:

- Trying to upgrade the image of Mary Kay products and Mary Kay beauty consultants

- Coming out with fresh products to keep the Mary Kay line competitive with what other cosmetics companies are offering

- Adjusting the array of prizes so as to continue to stimulate the sales efforts of beauty consultants

- Gradually raising the requirements for reaching sales director status

- Boosting, from time to time, the minimum order sizes required of beauty consultants

- Pushing to develop even more effective sales training aids and sales training methods

- Maintaining, even boosting, research and development expenditures so as to add to the performance features and effectiveness of Mary Kay products

Table 3 shows the results of "what if" projections of MKC's operating performance for 1984–1988. The projections incorporate modest revenue growth of 6–10 percent to allow for the possibility that 1983 signals a permanent growth slowdown rather than just a temporary one-year downturn. The cost of goods sold projections were fixed slightly below the revenue growth to reflect an improving gross margin (see the trend in line I of Table 2); the selling and administrative expense growth rate was set above the revenue growth rate in reflection of the rising percentage trend shown in line 2 of Table 2. If these projections prove prophetic of MKC's situation and long-run outlook, then the company's future performance will not begin to match past growth. In essence, the strategy will have "matured" and MKC will no longer qualify as a growth company.

Table 3
"What If" Projections of MKC's Performance, 1984–1988

"What If" Growth Rates

	1983-84	1984-85	1985-86	1986-87	1987-88
Net Sales	6.00%	8.00%	10.00%	10.00%	10.00%
Cost of Sales	5.90%	7.90%	9.80%	9.80%	9.80%
Selling, Gen, & Admin Exp	6.10%	8.10%	10.20%	10.20%	10.20%
Operating Income	5.88%	7.88%	9.75%	9.75%	9.75%

Projected Performance

	1984	1985	1986	1987	1988
Net Sales	$343,183	$370,638	$407,702	$448,472	$493,319
Cost of Sales	94,209	101,651	111,613	122,551	134,561
Sell, Gen, & Adm	179,051	193,554	213,297	235,053	259,029
Operating Income	$ 69,924	$ 75,433	$ 82,792	$ 90,868	$ 99,730
Oper Prof Margin	20.38%	20.35%	20.31%	20.26%	20.22%

Source: Calculated using the capabilities of STRAT-ANALYST.

The possibility of a low-growth scenario raises several strategic issues:

• Should the company diversify?

• Should the company expand its product line?

• Should the company merely accept its slow-growth fate and simply follow a "hold and maintain" strategy?

We tend to favor the last option of continuing as is, because of the enormous risks of trying to meddle with the "Mary Kay" formula and the strong culture and traditions that have been institutionalized. Top management may not be skilled enough to execute any other basic strategy than the one it has developed and pursued all along.

Epilogue

Since the case was researched the one really big development of significance is that MKC was taken private on a leveraged buyout by the company's senior management in 1985. This move, of course, has limited the amount of publicly available information about the company. Also, as of early 1986, the size of the company's sales force had shrunk from a high of 195,000 in 1983 to about 155,000.

— Art Thompson
A. J. Strickland

Original Teaching Note, Section 1: Mary Kay Cosmetics, Inc.

Case Summary

The business of Mary Kay Cosmetics is manufacturing and marketing cosmetics. Sales are by independent beauty consultants educated to serve the needs of the individual consumer for skin care and makeup instruction. Consumers "try before buying" through participation in demonstrations in homes.

The company was founded in 1963 and achieved early expansion and success both in the United States and in limited areas of Canada and Australia. Sales totaled $53.7 million in 1978 and assets were $35.3 million. The marketing system was designed by the founder, Mary Kay Ash, and implemented by her son, Richard Rogers, both of whom are still active in the company.

Case Objectives

1. To consider the relationship of financial strategy to overall strategy.

2. To look at strategic implications of short-term performance.

3. To consider the role of managerial values and experience in formulating strategy.

Issues

1. Have the financial restrictions accompanying the stock repurchase tied the company's hands strategically?

2. Do the experience and values of management fit the needs of a growing company?

3. How can the declining profits be interpreted, and what should be the company's response?

Questions

Early

1. How would you assess the company's performance between 1974 and 1978?

2. What differentiates Mary Kay from other cosmetics manufacturers? From other direct sales companies?

3. How does Mary Kay compare with Avon?

Later

1. Is Mary Kay selling anything besides cosmetics?

2. Would the distribution system work with another product? Why or why not?

3. Would you rather buy the firm's stock or buy the firm?

4. What is being done about management succession?

This teaching note was prepared by Phyllis G. Holland, Valdosta State College.

Case Analysis

Mary Kay Cosmetics produces and markets a limited line of skin care and makeup products. The company depends on its program of recruiting and motivating its independent sales force. to "push" the line in home demonstrations. The company was fifteen years old at the time the case was written.

Financial data are provided to assess performance trends in recent years. The following percentages (derived from income statements) indicate that cost control is becoming a problem:

	Percent of Sales			
	1978	**1977**	**1976**	**1975**
Cost of sales	32.5%	30.4%	31.5%	30.0%
Selling, G&A expenses	50.9	44.7	42.7	43.0
Operating income	16.0	24.7	26.7	27.2
Net income	9.0	12.8	13.7	14.4

In three years, operating income has been cut almost in half. Costs and selling expenses are gradually rising as a percent of sales, and pressure on prices or profits or both are likely.

While total sales have grown, the increase has been in number of consultants (as indicated below) rather than in sales per consultant.

	Percent Increase (Decrease) from Previous Year				
	1978	**1977**	**1976**	**1975**	**1974**
Net sales	12.0%	6.6%	28.4%	15.7%	36.0%
Net sales per consultant	(5.0)	(3.0)	18.0	(1.2)	(0.6)

Stock prices have also declined in recent years. Earnings per share have increased, but the purchase of stock by the company has inflated this figure.

Methods of recruitment, motivation, and support for sales personnel at Mary Kay and Avon are compared in the following table.

	Avon	**Mary Kay**
1. Incentive for recruiter	Cash or prize for successful referral sales	Continuing commission for recruiter on recruit's
2. Initial cost to new recruit	$21	$65
3. Requirements for new recruit	none	Book 5 beauty shows in first week
4. Earnings potential	$40 for 15-hour work week	$120 in 2 hours
5. Advertising of product and company	National, extensive	None
6. Wholesale terms to sales rep	One week's order on credit	Cash in advance
7. Training	Varies with local sales directors	Local training varies; regional and national training opportunities
8. Upward mobility	Limited by number of territories	Depends on individual's goals and abilities; no territorial limits

In contrast with Avon, Mary Kay provides more long-term support for the consultant who can make the initial investment and contacts with customers through her own network of acquaintances. Avon, on the other hand, provides more start-up advantages (lower cost to sales personnel and national name recognition).

Current Position

The strategic alternatives for Mary Kay are limited by the size and financial resources of the company. Using Avon's estimated market share of 15 percent as a guide, Mary Kay's share is less than I percent. In addition, the company is entering a loan agreement which will restrict its ability to raise new capital. Another limitation on strategic change is the expressed wishes of top management to maintain the present strategy. On the other hand, environmental threats such as energy shortages, governmental regulation of the cosmetics industry, and increased competition from Avon, Amway, and other direct sales companies could make holding to the status quo less attractive.

A severe energy shortage could have several effects on Mary Kay:

1. Increased costs of new materials and packaging.

2. Increased distribution costs.

3. Increased expenses for consultants.

4. If extreme, refusal of customers to attend home shows.

Governmental regulation of cosmetics would be a more serious threat for smaller companies because increased testing and administrative costs would be a larger percentage of total sales.

Avon's productivity campaigns supported by national advertising have been successful. If Avon decided to adopt the party plan for selling some or all of its products, Mary Kay's competitive edge in customer service would be threatened.

Strategic Alternatives

Mary Kay's strategy has been to produce cosmetics for sale to an independent sales force. The company relies on training and motivation of the sales force to stimulate demand for its product line, which consists of skin care and makeup items. Sales have grown steadily as a result of additions to the sales force.

To continue the present strategy of incremental growth, the company need only continue its present emphasis on adding new members to the sales force. This involves little risk since there are few fixed costs associated with additional consultants. It is not, however, a strategy with promise for long-term effectiveness. There are limits to the size of the recruit pool, and environmental forces (more women choosing full-time careers and other direct sales companies competing for recruits) are working to contract rather than expand the pool. In the process of reaching these limits, the company might generate enough financial support to make strategic changes to cope with a saturated market. There is little to indicate that such long-term planning occurs.

One alternative that is likely to be suggested is initiating advertising to stimulate "pull" for the products rather than relying completely on the sales force to "push" them. The resources for a national ad campaign are not available. Mary Kay's total selling, general, and administrative expense spending would buy very little national advertising. The alternative would be to choose regional markets, abandoning the Northeast, Northwest, and Midwest, where the company is weak, and concentrate on the Southeast and Southwest, where the company is more established and relatively less effort would be required to stimulate demand.

Another alternative is to broaden the product line (for example, add fashion accessories) to capitalize on established customers. The requirements for this strategy are even greater than for achieving national status. In addition to financial resources, production capacity, marketing, and R&D capability would be necessary. Of these, Mary Kay could claim only production capacity. Addition of new products through acquisitions is not financially feasible.

Short-term increases in revenue could be sought through capacity utilization (sell to other distributors with different or the same brand), price cutting, or advertising. Problems with advertising have already been discussed, and with lack of product "pull" and name recognition it is unlikely that the company would be able to achieve favorable terms of distribution. Price cutting is likely to squeeze profits, and sales to other cosmetic producers would not be very profitable, nor would they continue through economic downturns.

There are few niches in the cosmetic industry available for a small company operating on a shoestring. Mary Kay has managed to occupy one (direct sales and home demonstration) but would be very vulnerable to competition from a company with greater financial resources or a national name.

On the positive side, Mary Kay seems to have built a stable sales force (the 33 percent turnover that Mary Kay has achieved is considered good for direct sales companies) and appeals to a particular kind of woman—ambitious but untrained, eager for money and/or achievement but unwilling or unable to take a job outside the home. The company has based this appeal on the values of Mrs. Ash, and top management has literally grown up with those values.

An important consideration in strategic choice is how alternatives fit with managerial values. In this case, the influence of such values is vividly illustrated. The company has been conservative financially. No financing is provided for sales personnel, probably because the company was simply unable to extend credit in the early years. There has been little use of debt until the recent purchases of stock. The management was acting to protect personal investments, possibly because ownership is concentrated among insiders and the price of stock had been steadily dropping. The long-term value of the stock would be bolstered more by increases in productivity and careful cost control than by conversion of shares to treasury stock, however.

A sell-out strategy seems promising for this firm for the following reasons:

1. Its growth is likely to slow in the next few years.

2. It cannot generate the volume needed to cut costs without financial backing.

3. It is moving into areas that will be more difficult to penetrate (Northeast, Midwest).

4. It cannot move into new products without financial backing and thus cannot capitalize on its sales force.

5. Mrs. Ash will not live forever, and the value of the company without her as a symbol and spokesperson is likely to diminish.

Problems with selling out would include:

1. The difficulty of ensuring continued loyalty of the sales force.

2. Unwillingness of Mrs. Ash to lose control of a company that bears her name and the stamp of her personality.

3. Change of management and accompanying transition problems is likely.

A sell-out could of course be accomplished while protecting Mrs. Ash's role- in the. company. Her continued presence as a corporate symbol and member of the board could be provided for in the terms of the sale. This would contribute to maintaining sales force loyalty also.

Section 2: Chapter Key

Section	Chapter in the Text
Industrial Highlight	2
Theory Applications	2, 3, 4, 11
Financial Analysis	10
In-Class Exercise	10
Current Issues and Update	

Section 3: Industrial Highlight/External Analysis—Cosmetics Industry

The Industrial Highlight on the cosmetics industry provides some important information regarding growth and profit potential for Mary Kay (MK) as well as some potential threats. Since MK has indicated its focus on growth from increased market penetration, the Industrial Highlight information can be extremely useful.

Since the case did not provide any additional industry information, the external analysis is based upon Industrial Highlight information only.

General Information

Economic

Inflation Rates

- Modest price increases for cosmetics prices since 1967.

Growth Rate

- Annual growth rate 7.3 percent from 1972 to 1978 from $4.2 billion to $6.5 billion. Growth rate for fragrances, hair preparations, and oral hygiene products are 8 percent, 6.4 percent, and 4.5 percent, respectively.

- Fragrance sales are growing rapidly due to various reasons (see Industrial Highlight).

- Ethnic cosmetics are developing into fast-selling line of products aimed at Black market.

- Outlook for continued annual growth in sales is excellent. Real growth expected to be 4.3 percent.

Social

Lifestyle

- Women will become more innovative in use of cosmetics, with more fashion coordination using cosmetics and fragrances.

- Increased consumption of a variety of cosmetics is due to changing lifestyles including half of all women working outside the home.

Political

Regulation

- Industry has embarked upon self-regulation programs to determine which ingredients can be used safely and which cannot.

- Consumer safety is of prime importance, and more federal government regulations have been proposed. Even more regulation is inevitable. Primary agency is FDA.

Technological

New Technologies

- Cost-control measures are being implemented which include improving quality, productivity, operations, and materials management.

Operating Environment

Competitive

Rivalry

- One thousand cosmetic firms make 20,000 brands.

- Ten firms account for 55 percent of market share and 65 percent of earnings.

- Brand identity is important as consumers continue to rely on known brands.

- New product development will offer growth opportunities, especially ethnic and geriatric products.

International

Exports

- Export of cosmetics increased 10 percent to $152 million in 1978. Exports have increased more than 3.5 times during 1972–1978.

- Exports expected to increase substantially as more U.S. firms look to expand international markets.

Imports

- Imports for 1978 have risen twice the 1972 level to $48 million. In 1978 exports will exceed imports by $104 million. In 1972 exports exceeded imports by only $20 million.

The potential for growth and profits in the industry is favorable. The major threat appears to be the possibility of increased government regulation. Transparency II.1 can be used for class discussion purposes. Discussion could center on what firms will have to do to take advantage of the favorable environment.

Section 4: Theory Applications

The Mary Kay case can be related specifically to Chapters 2, 3, 4, and 11. The focus of the case deals with assessing MK's current situation and determining how best to achieve growth from increased market penetration.

Chapter 2: Environmental Analysis

Internal Analysis

The internal environment is that level of an organization's environment which exists inside the organization and normally has immediate and specific implications for managing the organization. The information in Table 2.2 in the text can be utilized to assess the internal environment of MK.

Factor	MK's Situation
Organizational	
Organization structure	Simple chain of command
Record of success	Sales increases uneven
Objectives	Formulated
Management team	Family run
Marketing	
Segmentation	Specific segment
Product strategy	Stress skin care
Pricing strategy	Total price of basic line is $27.50
Promotion strategy	Mainly for incentives for sales force; little direct advertising.
Distribution strategy	Party system—simple chain
Financial	
Liquidity	Disturbing decreasing trend
Profitability	Higher than industry, but downward
Activity	Inventory turnover appropriate
Investment opportunity	Company buying its own stock
Personnel	
Training programs	Workshops, weekly unit meetings, and annual seminar
Performance appraisal	Standards set for sales directors
Incentive system	Discounts and commissions
Production	
Facilities	Automated, efficient plant
R&D	One million dollars in 1978 for product improvements

MK has been successful with its unique strategies. Discussion could focus on what has made MK successful. Students should be able to detect the change in financial situation and its implications for the stock purchase offer and future growth. Students should be encouraged to explore the reasons for the change in financial picture (increasing costs, etc.). Transparency II.2 is provided for classroom discussion.

Chapter 3: Establishing Organizational Direction

Areas of Organizational Objectives

Peter Drucker has identified eight key areas in which organizational objectives should be normally formulated. MK can be compared against these eight areas to further evaluate the effectiveness of its current position.

Area	MK's Evaluation
Marketing standing	Future growth from increased market penetration; increases in size and productivity of sales force (Exhibits 10–11 in the text)
Innovation	Stress product improvement
Productivity	Productivity gains in sales force uneven
Resource levels	Cash/inventory levels fluctuate
Profitability	Greater than industry, downward trend with increasing costs
Manager performance	Standards established
Worker performance	Sales per consultant decreasing
Social responsibility	Concerned about safe products

MK has formulated and implemented objectives in all the key areas. Discussion should focus on MK's success rate of accomplishment for its objectives. Students should be able to perceive the downward trend for the "numbers" and offer some possible explanations. Transparency II.51 is provided for classroom purposes.

Chapter 4: Strategy Formulation

SWOT Analysis

SWOT analysis is an appropriate tool to assess MK's current position.

Internal Analysis

Strengths	Weaknesses
Incentive system	Liquidity
Past record	Working capital
Product line quality	Trend in profitability
Distribution	Market segment
Sales force	Distribution
Plant facilities	Cost trends
R&D expenditures	Sales force
Profitability	Promotion
Market segment	

External Analysis

<table>
<tr><td align="center">Opportunities</td><td align="center">Threats</td></tr>
<tr><td>Industry growth rate</td><td>Government regulation</td></tr>
<tr><td>Export potential</td><td>Reaching working women</td></tr>
<tr><td>Segment growth potential</td><td></td></tr>
</table>

The SWOT analysis reveals that MK has its strengths but at the same time has some weaknesses which need attention. Students should be encouraged to discuss how some of the factors, such as distribution, sales force, and market segments, can be both strengths and weaknesses. The financial picture, with profits and costs, should be thoroughly discussed. Transparency II.5, is included for classroom purposes.

Strategy Formulation Constraints

The MK case will involve the students in formulating recommendations for MK's future, which include recommendations for the stock purchase and increased market penetration. Regarding the stock purchase, Exhibit 11 in the text should be noted and utilized. In making their decisions, students should be encouraged to address the following issues. Transparency II.6 is provided.

- Does MK have the necessary financial resources?

- How much risk is involved in your recommendations?

- Does MK have the necessary organizational resources?

- Does MK have the necessary channel relationships?

- Have you considered possible competitive retaliation?

Chapter 11: Marketing Foundations for Strategic Management

Designing the Marketing Mix Strategy

Since MK has stated growth through market penetration as one of its objectives, strategies must be formulated to achieve that end. The marketing mix is an appropriate starting place for strategy formulation. Students can be asked to consider how the marketing mix could be changed to achieve the increased market penetration. Each factor should be discussed to determine the feasibility of possible changes. The implications/consequences of each change should be addressed; that is, what effect will the change have on existing customers, other functional areas, and so on. The strategy selection constraints could also be utilized. Transparency II.44 is provided for classroom discussion.

<table>
<tr><td>Factor</td><td align="center">Possible Changes</td><td align="right">Implications/Consequences</td></tr>
<tr><td>Product</td><td></td><td></td></tr>
<tr><td>Price</td><td></td><td></td></tr>
<tr><td>Place</td><td></td><td></td></tr>
<tr><td>Promotion</td><td></td><td></td></tr>
</table>

Section 5: Financial Analysis

Financial analysis (thousands) [*]

Ratio/WC	1975	1976	1977	1978	Average	Trend	Industry 1978
Working capital	6,449	7,979	5,253	5,724	6,351	E	
Liquidity							
Current	3.05	2.57	1.90	1.94	2.37	E	3.10
Quick	1.28	1.35	0.64	0.70	0.99	E	1.89
Activity							
Asset turn	1.24	1.30	1.36	1.48	1.35	U	1.40
Invent turn	6.64	7.62	6.75	8.2	7.31	E	6.03
Ave. col P	1.11	1.09	0.90	1.40	1.13	E	67.59
Leverage							
Debt/asset	11.30	0.00	32.40	26.50	17.55	D	35.03
Debt/equity							
Profitability							
ROI	18.00	17.80	17.50	13.40	16.68	D	8.06
Margin	14.40	13.60	12.80	9.00	12.45	D	6.12

E = Erratic

Financial Recap

Ratio/WC	1975	1976	1977	1978	Average	Trend	Industry 1978
Net sales	34,947	44,871	47,856	53,746			
Net income	5,050	6,144	6,152	4,873			
Working capital	6,449	7,979	5,253	5,724			
Total assets	27,996	34,331	35,144	36,305			
Long-term debt	42	0	5,592	3,558			
Sthlers equity	24,402	28,607	22,984	25,947			
Changes							
% Sales		28	7	12			
% NI		22	0	–21			
% WC		24	–34	9			
% TA		23	2	3			
% LTD		–100	ERR	–36			
% S E		17	–20	13			

MK's liquidity and profitability are declining while its leverage picture has fluctuated.

---

[*] Source: COMPUSTAT.

Section 6: In-Class Exercise

Stock Purchase Decision

Objectives

To give students the opportunity to consider the implications and consequences of a major corporate-level decision on the stock purchase offer and to make a judgment on whether the offer is a viable one.

Procedure

Divide the class into groups of three to five students. Instruct each group to consider the stock purchase offer as illustrated in Exhibit 8 in the text. Inform the students that they are to identify the major implications/consequences of the stock purchase offer as it affects MK in the short and long run. Both positive and negative implications/consequences should be considered. Finally, the students should decide whether the stock purchase offer is a smart strategic move. Each group should make a short presentation to the class with its analysis.

Concluding Remarks

General discussion should focus on the main implications/consequences identified by the groups, especially on the long-run effects. A consensus on the wisdom of the stock purchase offer could be reached by noting how each group felt.

Section 7: Current Issues and Update

Mary Kay had sales of $324 million in 1983 with earnings of $36.7 million or a profit margin of 11.3 percent. However, the economic recovery was detrimental to MK. As more women entered the work force, the sales consultants found it more difficult to reach prospective customers at home. More working women also affected the availability of prospective sales consultants. The number of consultants decreased 22 percent from 195,000 in 1983 to 152,000 in 1984. Sales in 1984 decreased 14 percent to $287 million, with earnings falling 8 percent. In July 1985, an offer was made by a management group headed by Mary Kay Ash and her son, President Richard Rogers, to buy out public shareholders. Mary Kay went private late in 1985.*

Section 8: Supplemental Discussion Questions

1. Evaluate MK's competitive position utilizing the SWOT analysis approach.

2. What are the strengths and weaknesses of MK's current marketing strategy?

3. Which elements of the marketing mix strategy are of greatest concern in this case?

4. How would the marketing strategy have to be changed to achieve MK's objective of growth through increased market penetration?

---

* Source: Forbes, August 12, 1985, p. 12.

5. What is the major strategic issue involved in the MK case?

6. Has MK considered the impact of major environmental threats facing it?

7. How are the personal values of Mary Kay Ash reflected in the firm's objectives?

8. Does MK have the appropriate business-level strategy?

9. Discuss MK's competitive advantages.

10. How would the stock purchase offer affect MK in the short and long run?

Mary Kay Cosmetics, Inc. Teaching Note[*]

I. Overview

Mary Kay Cosmetics, Inc. (MKY) is one of the top ten firms in the cosmetics industry. Founded in 1963, the firm manufactures and distributes its own line of skin care products. During 1970–1981, the firm experienced very rapid growth. Annual sales increased from $6 million in 1970 to $235 million in 1981, for an average annual compound growth rate of 35.8 percent. By 1981, over 150,000 independent sales consultants and directors were engaged in direct selling of MKY products in the United States, Canada, Argentina and Australia.

A basic motivation underlying the formation of MKY was Mary Kay Ash's personal desire to give women an opportunity to advance to become successful, and to be rewarded for hard work. Positive motivation is instilled personally by Mary Kay. A present strategic objective of the firm is to become the largest and best skin-care company in the world.

II. Teaching Objectives

This case can be used to develop a greater understanding of factors that give rise to successful performance. Mary Kay Ash's original objective of improving career opportunities for women, together with her motivational techniques have inspired and developed a large, successful sales force. High product quality, good leadership, proper incentives, and excellent motivation of sales people are the major reasons for MKY's sales and profits growth. The organization culture focuses on managerial approaches that emphasize and optimize selling effort.

III. Teaching Strategy

This case provides an opportunity for students to consider elements of developing and operating a successful direct sales organization. Also afforded is an opportunity to learn more organization. Also afforded is an opportunity to learn more about the cosmetics industry. It is recommended that students be asked to identify and discuss what factors gave rise to the success of MKY, what actual or potential problems exist, and what recommendations the students would offer in light of these problem areas.

---

* This teaching note was prepared by Paula Walters, Richard Edwards, Robert and Marlene Carle under the supervision of Professor Sexton Adams, North Texas State University and Professor Adelaide Griffin, Texas Woman's University. Parts I, II, III, V, VI and VII were developed by the authors.

Areas appropriate for independent research and reports include an analysis of the cosmetics industry and a review of how MKY is performing since the time of the case.

IV. Discussion Questions and Case Analysis

Problem Areas

MKY faces several actual or potential problems. How these problems are handled and the actions taken to overcome them will bear significantly upon the future performance and character of the company. These problem areas include:

- A class action suit against the company with respect to a tender offer and purchase of MKY stock.

- A possible slowdown and leveling of industry growth.

- A possible slowing in sales growth for MKY.

- The implications of recent, very rapid growth at MKY.

- The question of tax status of independent sales contractors.

- The possibility of increased regulation by the Food and Drug Administration.

- Problems and prospects in international operations.

- Managerial succession at MKY.

Each of these problem areas is discussed and analyzed below.

Discussion Questions, Analysis, and Recommendations

1. **What is the status of the class action suit against the Company with respect to the tender offer and purchase of MKY stock?**

    Analysis. On November 16, 1979, George Sibley filed a lawsuit against the company and its president, Richard Rogers. This suit alleges that the company neglected to disclose from its 1979 tender offer that its sales, profit margins and net income per share for the first quarter of 1979 and succeeding quarters would be dramatically improved as compared to previous years. In addition, the plaintiff is seeking an order rescinding the company's purchase of 2,798,856 shares of Common Stock in the 1979 tender offer.

    On the other side of the coin, Mary Kay indicated in an interview that it was impossible to predict that there would be a sudden upturn and dramatic increase in sales and profit margins. It must also be taken into account that it was in 1978 that the new compensation plan was implemented. Therefore, allowing at least one year for it to run through the system, a tremendous increase in sales for the company could have resulted from the new incentive program.

    Recommendation. At the present time, this suit has not been resolved. Obviously the company will need to present the necessary documents and legal information regarding the introduction of and subsequent repurchase of the tender offer of common stock. In addition, the Company should look into the background of the plaintiff regarding past history and lawsuits that he has filed. Should the company have to make payment to the plaintiff, as Mary Kay said, "It will only cost $17 million and last year we made $458 million. And anyway, we aren't going to lose."

2. **From the articles, reports, and other documents that we obtained, it appears that the cosmetics industry is leveling off. What impact will this have on Mary Kay Cosmetics?**

Analysis. It would appear that MKY would be faced with a problem in that the cosmetics industry is possibly leveling off. Should this occur, it appears that MKY would need to take several steps to offset this potential or real problem.

Recommendation. MKY should consider diversification. Perhaps the company needs to develop fingernail polish to complete the total image that it is trying to project. The company could also look at selling over-the-counter cosmetics. We would not recommend that the Company sell the basic 5-Step Skin Care Line over-the-counter, since this would not be compatible with the philosophy of teaching skin care to consumers and the educational purposes of Mary Kay Cosmetics. However, MKY does need a new market. We would also recommend that if the industry is leveling off, the company seek a merger with another company whose line would be complimentary to Mary Kay's. Since many fashion designers are developing their own perfumes, cosmetics and luggage, it would appear that Mary Kay could diversify into another area with success.

3. **In 1982, sales growth for MKY was 28 to 30 percent. This is significantly lower than that experienced in 1980 and 1981, as shown in Part VI, Financial Analysis, below. What impact will a reduction in sales growth rate have upon the company?**

Analysis. The reader must keep in mind that Mary Kay cosmetics is primarily a *one-product* company. Therefore, the Company assumes a very high risk by investing all capital into a one-product line. Should the trend continue towards a decline in the cosmetics industry, Mary Kay Cosmetics would need to rethink its current strategy and develop new plans to reduce its reliance upon one basic line of products.

Recommendation. Diversification is one alternative, as mentioned above. To stimulate additional growth in its present line of skin-care products, MKY should reexamine its compensation program once again. If sales increases are to come from the market shares of competitors, these increases will be hard-won. The percentage compensation program was implemented in 1978. It may need restructuring in order to provide additional compensation to the independent sale consultants.

4. **One problem facing MKY is that of very rapid growth in recent years. What are the implications of this both presently and in the future for MKY?**

Analysis. When the company was started in 1963, it started with nine consultants, Mary Kay and her son, Richard Rogers. Today, some 25 years later, the company has over 150,000 beauty consultants and employs approximately 1,400 employees. In 1981 the Company grossed $235 million in sales. Already in the building stages is the company's new campus being built on 177 acres across from Texas Stadium. Almost every department will have its own building. The land cost $6.5 million while the entire project is expected to cost $100 million. Once the new facility is completed, the present building and warehouses will be sold to help finance the new project. After talking with Mary Kay and Mr. Stubbs, Vice President of Finance, both insist that the funding for the project will be generated internally. It is possible that costs for future research and development, new acquisitions and other programs could be enormous. As the result of this current expansion, funding for research, development, and other programs might be limited.

Recommendation. It may be necessary for MKY to purposely allow a reduction in growth to occur for a one-or-two year period. This would provide time to consolidate its financial obligations, finish its current facilities expansion program, and develop new strategic plans for the next round of development.

The limitations of a single product line company must be faced if MKY wishes to continue on a high growth curve. The company may work to emphasize research and development as a means of developing new products internally. The company should also consider finding a merger partner in order to diversify its product line. MKY may need to hire, new professional staff to lead these and similar activities.

5. **In the Securities and Exchange Commission report on MKY for the fiscal year ended December 31, 1981, there was a question of the independent beauty consultants and sales directors acting as independent contractors rather than employees of Mary Kay Cosmetics. The Internal Revenue Service has challenged the status of such employees. What has happened with this issue?**

Analysis. The status of beauty consultants acting as independent contractors was questioned for purposes of federal withholding and employment taxes. The Revenue Act of 1978 provided to taxpayers involved in employment tax status controversies interim relief from employment tax liabilities.

The company was then relieved of all liability for federal income tax withholding,. FICA and FUTA taxes with respect to its sales persons for any period ending before January 1, 1979. During 1980, Congress extended the period of interim relief until July 1, 1982. Mr. Stubbs said that the issue was resolved with an Act passed August of 1982 called the Tax Equity Act and Fiscal Responsibility Act.

Recommendation. According to Mary Kay Ash, Monty Barber, Vice President and General Counsel, and Mr. Stubbs, the company did not assess what an adverse ruling would have cost the company in past years and for the future. We find that hard to believe since the Direct Sales Association and Mary Kay Cosmetics were endorsing the bill. Undoubtedly, an adverse ruling would have had a negative effect on the financial status of MKY. Such a ruling would also impact negatively upon recruitment of new sales consultants. Mr. Barber's only response was that a negative ruling would have a tremendous impact upon MKY.

It is our recommendation that MKY provide detailed training on financial and tax matters to all sales force personnel. This training should include information on tax rules, legitimate allowances and deductions, money management and other financial matters. This will help ensure that the company will not be open to criticism by the Internal Revenue Service. Amway, another direct sales organization, has already started this type of training program.

6. **There is also the possibility of increased regulation by the Food and Drug Administration. What effect would this have on MKY?**

Analysis. Presently, Mary Kay cosmetics are selling in the mid-to-upper price range. Increased regulation would result in additional costs for MKY. If the firm could not increase its prices sufficiently, profit margins and return on investment would suffer. Also MKY would likely have to increase its expenditures for research and development. At present, R&D as a percentage of sales is less than one percent. This is quite low!

Recommendation. MKY should do everything possible to assure that product quality remains high and that its products are safe. As Bruce Rudy, Vice President of Quality Assurance, stated, MKY is currently working with engineering groups to ensure that the firm will meet present and future requirements.

7. **What is the possibility of MKY expanding into other foreign markets?**

Analysis. Presently, the MKY operates wholly owned subsidiaries in Australia and Argentina. The firm also distributes its line in Canada. Good potential for growth appears to exist in Australia. Political, economic, anci language problems exist in the Argentine subsidiary. At the end of this case, MKY is planning to start operations Santo Domingo, Dominican Republic.

While international expansion may prove to be an excellent avenue of growth for MKY, several problems must be addressed before the firm enters additional foreign markets. As noted above, these problem areas include the political climate of a nation, the condition of a nation's economy and overcoming language barriers. As noted by Mary Kay in an interview:

> "In the two (countries) where we have a different language, we have a language barrier that we, from the home offices find very difficult to hurdle…. We have tried to find someone who not only knows the cosmetic business well, but who is willing to come here and spend a year to a year and a half, learning *our* way of doing business.

Recommendation. MKY should expand into foreign markets as a means of maintaining sales growth. To do this successfully MKY should develop a training program for foreign nations. Preferably, some of this training should take place in their native country, as well as in the U.S.

Before additional expansion is undertaken in Latin American countries, MKY should consider first expanding to other English-speaking areas of the world. This will allow MKY to gain experience in foreign, non-English-speaking operations, while at the same time generating some new growth in international sales in more familiar cultures.

8. **The future of MKY has to be in jeopardy once Mary Kay leaves. What is the future of MKY?**

Analysis. Any direct sales company is dependent upon its ability to recruit new sales personnel and motivate these workers. MKY is no exception. Mary Kay's responsibility is to motivate and train these sales directors by example and by relationships. Right now, the plan MKY is using is effective. But these consultants and directors are being trained to be carbon copies of Mary Kay. Says Mary Kay, "You are the future of this company. When I am not here, you will be taking over. Each of you is in training to be Mary Kay." The problem is that Ms. Ash is 63 years of age. To predict how much longer she will be active in MKY is impossible. However, it is not possible for Richard Rogers to take over that aspect of the company because he has never sold and is not Mary Kay.

Recommendation. The plan that MKY is presently using is probably as effective as one could develop. It is possible that the national sales directors, who are carbon copies of Mary Kay, could lead the company for a period of five-to-ten years. But after that time, the image, the aura and the love of Mary Kay and for Mary Kay will not be existent because she has not touched their lives. There is only one Mary Kay and she can't be cloned!

Nonetheless, Mary Kay Ash and her son Richard should carefully review these sales consultants who have performed successfully at MKY, have risen through the ranks, and have given evidence of having both strong leadership ability and the same values as those held by Mary Kay Ash herself. It is from this group of individuals that the successor to Mary Kay must ultimately be chosen. It is recommended that top candidates be given opportunities for advanced management training at leading business schools, along with other professional development programs. Rotating assignments at MKY headquarters, including working closely with Mary Kay, should also be developed.

V.   Case Update

In July 1985, Mary Kay's board of directors agreed to sell the firm for $300 million to a group headed by Mary Kay Ash, chairman, and her son, Richard Rodgers, president.[1]

At that time, the sales growth rate for Mary Kay was slowing and recruitment of new sales people was getting tougher.

Earlier, profits fell from $36.7 million in 1983 to $33.8 million in 1984, while stock price reached a high almost $45 in 1983.[2]

In 1984, the stock declared to $13 per share. As recently as 1980 it was selling at $8 per share.[3]

Acquisition of the shares was completed on December 4, 1985.[4]

---

[1] "Mary Kay Paints a Private Face," *Time*, July 15, 1985, p. 50.

[2] *Ibid.*, p. 50.

[3] "The Doubts About Mary Kay," *Business Week*, March 12, 1984, p. 116.

[4] Standard & Poor's Corporation, *Standard Corporation Description*, November 19, 1987, p. 5358.

VI.   Financial Analysis

Mary Kay Cosmetics, Inc.
Selected Measures of Financial Performance
(1979–1981)

	1979	1980	1981
General Performance			
Revenues ($000)	$91,893	167,650	236,781
Annual % Change:		82.4%	41.2
Average Annual Compound Rate:		37.1%	
Net Income ($000)	9,632	15,135	24,155
Annual % Change:		57.1%	59.6
Average Annual Compound Rate		35.9%	
Profitability			
Return on Equity	n.a.	39.2	39.0
Return on Assets	n.a.	20.3	23.9
Net Profit Margin	10.5%	9.0	10.3
Liquidity			
Current Ratio		1.2	1.2
Quick Ratio		0.5	0.4
Leverage			
L.T. Debt to Equity		.08	.04
Total Debt to Equity		.89	.59
Activity			
Asset Turnover		2.3	2.3
Inventory Turnover		7.8	8.7
Accounts Receivable Turnover		151.2	86.7
Average Collection Period		2.4	4.2

VII. SUGGESTED READINGS

1. "Part-time Payoff of Direct Sales: Sampling Entrepreneurship Without Risk Can Help You Sell Your Way To More Gracious Living," Elaine Gregg, *Black Enterprise*, May 1986, p. 58ff.

2. "Behind Closed Doors: Can Public Firms That Go Private Handle Their New Freedom?," Jill A. Fraser, *Working Woman*, March 1986, p. 56ff.

3. "How Cosmetics Makers Are Touching Up Their Strategies," Christine Dugas and Amy Dunkin, *Business Week*, September 23, 1985, p. 66ff.

4. "Where's the Ding Dong Gone?," *Economist*, September 14, 1985, p. 78ff.

5. "A Tale of Three Companies," Allan Halcrow, *Personnel Journal*, September 1985, p. 14ff.

6. "Mary Kay Paints a Private Face," *Time*, July 15, 1985, p. 50.

7. "Mary Kay's Plan To Go Private," *Business Week*, June 1985, p. 44.

8. "Cold Cream and Hard Cash: Mary Kay Ash," Kim Wright Wiley, *Savvy*, June 1985, p. 36ff.

9. "All The Way With Mary Kay," David Olive, *Canadian Business*, November 1984, p. 77ff.

10. "Mary Kay's Video Analysis Keeps Packaging in the Pink," *Packaging*, May 1984, p. 84ff.

11. "The Doubts About Mary Kay," Anthony Bianco, *Business Week*, March 12, 1984, p. 116.

CHAPTER 13
CONTROLS FOR DIFFERENTIATED STRATEGIES

Changes from the Eighth Edition

The first part of the chapter discusses the planning and control requirements of different corporate strategies—single business, related diversification, and unrelated diversification. The next part discusses the planning and control requirements of different business unit strategies. The final part discusses the control implications of top management style.

Cases

United Instruments Inc. focuses on the need to link profit variance analysis to business unit strategies.

Nucor Corporation, new to this edition, focuses on their organization and control systems as they relate to their strategy execution.

Texas Instruments Inc. focuses on planning control systems that are designed to institutionalize innovation. Texas Instruments and Hewlett Packard should be assigned on the same day.

3M, new to this edition, focuses on the organization and control policies of 3M and their impact on their ability to innovate.

Case 13-1

United Instruments, Inc.

The following article provides the teaching note for the case:

Vijay Govindarajan and John Shank, "Profit Variance Analysis: A Strategic Focus," *Issues in Accounting Education,* 4, 2, Fall 1989, pp. 396-410.

For convenience, the article is reproduced below.

Profit variance analysis is the process of summarizing what happened to profits during the period to highlight the salient managerial issues. Variance analysis is the formal step leading to determining what corrective actions are called for by management. Thus it is a key link in the management control process. We believe this element is underutilized in many companies because of the lack of a meaningful analytical framework. It is handled by accountants in a way that is too technical. This paper proposes a different profit variance framework as a "new idea" in management control.

Historically, variance analysis involved a simple methodology where actual results were compared with the budget on a line-by-line basis. We call this Phase I thinking. Phase II thinking was provided by Shank and Churchill [1977] who proposed a management-oriented approach to variance analysis. Their approach was based on the dual ideas of profit impact as a unifying theme and a multilevel analysis in which complexity was added gradually, one level at a time. We believe that, the Shank and Churchill approach needs to be modified in important ways to take explicit account of strategic issues. Our framework, which we call Phase III thinking, argues that variance analysis becomes most meaningful when it is tied explicitly to strategic analysis.

Table 1
United Instruments, Inc.

Income Statement for the Year 1987

		Budget (1,000s)		Actual (1,000s)
Sales		$16,872		$17,061
Cost of goods sold		9,668		9,865
Gross margin		$ 7,204		$ 7,196
Less: Other operating expenses				
Marketing	$1,856		$1,440	
R&D	1,480		932	
Administration	1,340	4,676	1,674	4,046
Profit before taxes		$ 2,528		$ 3,150

This paper presents a short disguised case, United Instruments, Inc., to illustrate the three phases or generations of thinking about profit variance analysis. We believe it also demonstrates the superiority of integrating strategic planning and overall financial performance evaluation, which is the essence of Phase III thinking. The purpose of this paper is to emphasize how variance analysis can be, and should be, redirected to consider the strategic issues that have, during the past 15 years, become so widely accepted as a conceptual framework for decision making.[1]

United Instruments, Inc.: An Instructional Case[2]

Steve Park, president and principal stockholder of United Instruments, Inc., sat at his desk reflecting on the 1987 results (Table 1). For the second year in succession, the company had exceeded the profit budget. Steve Park was obviously very happy with the 1987 results. All the same, he wanted to get a better feel for the relative contributions of the R&D, manufacturing and marketing departments in this overall success. With this in mind, he called his assistant, a recent graduate of a well-known business school, into his office.

"Amy," he began, "as you can see from our recent financial results, we have exceeded our profit targets by $622,000. Can you prepare an analysis showing how much R&D, manufacturing, and marketing contributed to this overall favorable profit variance?"

Amy Shultz, with all the fervor of a recent convert to professional management, set to her task immediately. She collected the data in Table 2 and was wondering what her next step should be.

United Instruments' products can be grouped into two main lines of business: electric meters (EM) and electronic instruments (EI). Both EM and EI are industrial measuring instruments and perform similar functions. However, these products differ in their manufacturing technology and their end-use characteristics. EM is based on mechanical and electrical technology, whereas EI is based on microchip technology. EM and EI are substitute products in the same sense that a mechanical watch and a digital watch are substitutes.

United Instruments uses a variable costing system for internal reporting purposes.

---

[1]During the past 15 years, several books (e.g., Andrews [1971], Henderson [1979], and Porter [1980]) as well as articles (e.g., Buzzell et al [1975] and Govindarajan and Gupta [1985]) have been published in the field of strategic management. In addition, two new journals (*Strategic Management Journal and Journal of Business Strategy*) have been introduced in the strategy area during the past ten years. Also, traditional management journals such as *Administrative Science Quarterly, Academy of Management Journal, and Academy of Management Review* have, during the past decade, started to publish regularly articles on strategy formulation and implementation.

[2] This case is motivated by a similar case titled "Kinkead Equipment Ltd.," which appears in Shank [1982].

Table 2
Additional Information

	Electric Meters (EM)	Electronic Instruments (EI)
Selling prices per unit		
Average standard price	$40.00	$180.00
Average actual prices, 1987	30.00	206.00
Variable product cost per unit		
Average standard manufacturing cost	$20.00	$50.00
Average actual manufacturing cost	21.00	54.00
Volume information		
Units produced and sold—actual	141,770	62,172
Units produced and sold—planned	124,800	66,000
Total industry sales, 1987—actual	$44 million	$76 million
Total industry variable product costs, 1987—actual	$16 million	$32 million
United's share of the market (percent of physical units)		
Planned	10%	15%
Actual	16%	9%

	Planned	Actual
Firm-wide fixed expenses (1,000s)		
Fixed manufacturing expenses	$3,872	$3,530
Fixed marketing expenses	1,856	1,440
Fixed administrative expenses	1,340	1,674
Fixed R&D expenses		
(exclusively for electronic instruments)	1,480	932

Phase I Thinking: The "Annual Report Approach" To Variance Analysis

A straightforward, simple-minded explanation of the difference between actual profit ($3,150) and the budgeted profit ($2,528) might proceed according to Table 3. Incidentally, this type of variance analysis is what one usually sees in published annual reports (where the comparison is typically between last year and this year). If we limit ourselves to this type of analysis, we will draw the following conclusions about United's performance:

1. Good sales performance (slightly above plan).

2. Good manufacturing cost control (margins as per plan).

3. Good control over marketing and R&D costs (costs down as percentage of sales).

4. Administration overspent a bit (slightly up as percentage of sales).

5. Overall Evaluation: Nothing of major significance; profit performance above plan.

How accurately does this summary reflect the actual performance of United? One objective of this paper is to demonstrate that the analysis is misleading. The plan for 1987 has embedded in it certain expectations about the state of the total industry and about United's market share, its selling prices, and its cost structure. Results from variance computations are more "actionable" if changes in actual results for 1987 are analyzed against each of these expectations. The Phase I analysis simply does not break down the overall favorable variance of $622,000 according to the key underlying causal factors.

Table 3
The "Annual Report Approach" to Variance Analysis

			Budget (1,000s)				Actual (1,000s)	
Sales			$16,872	(100%)			$17,061	(100%)
Cost of goods sold			9,668	(58%)			9,865	(58%)
Gross margin			$ 7,204	(42%)			$ 7,196	(42%)
Less: Other expenses								
Marketing	$1,856	(11%)			$1,440	(8%)		
R&D	1,480	(9%)			932	(6%)		
Administration	1,340	(8%)	4,676	(28%)	1,674	(10%)	4,046	(24%)
Profit before tax			$ 2,528	(14%)			$ 3,150	(18%)

Phase II Thinking: A Management-Oriented Approach to Variance Analysis

The analytical framework proposed by Shank and Churchill [1977] to conduct variance analysis incorporates the following key ideas:

1. Identify the key causal factors that affect profits.

2. Break down the overall profit variance by these key causal factors.

3. Focus always on the *profit* impact of variation in each causal factor.

4. Try to calculate the specific, separable impact of each causal factor by varying only that factor while holding all other factors constant ("spinning only one dial at a time").

5. Add complexity sequentially, one layer at a time, beginning at a very basic "common sense" level ("peel the onion").

6. Stop the process when the added complexity at a newly created level is not justified by added useful insights into the causal factors underlying the overall profit variance.

Tables 4 and 5 contain the explanation for the overall favorable profit variance of $622,000 using the above approach. In the interest of brevity, most of the calculation details are suppressed (detailed calculations are available from the authors).

What can we say about the performance of United if we now consider the variance analysis summarized in Table 5? The following insights can be offered organized by functional area:

Marketing

Comments:

Market Share (SOM) increase benefited the firm	$1,443 F
But, unfortunately, sales mix was managed toward the lower margin product	921 U
Control over marketing expenditure benefited the firm (especially in the face of an increase in SOM)	416 F
Net effect	$ 938 F
Uncontrollables: Unfortunately, the overall market declined and cost the firm	$ 680 U

Overall evaluation: Very good performance

Manufacturing

Comments: Manufacturing cost control cost the firm $ 48 U

Overall evaluation: Satisfactory performance

R&D

Comments: Savings in R&D budget $ 548 F

Overall evaluation: Good performance

Administration

Comments: Administration budget overspent $ 334 U

Overall evaluation: Poor performance

Thus, the overall evaluation of the general manager under Phase II thinking would probably be "good," though specific areas (such as manufacturing cost control or administrative cost control) need attention. The above summary is quite different—and clearly superior—to the one presented under Phase I thinking. But, can we do better? We believe that Shank and Churchill's framework needs to be modified in important ways to accommodate the following ideas.

Sales volume, share of market, and sales mix variances are calculated on the presumption that United is essentially competing in one industry (i.e., it is a single product firm with two different varieties of the product). That is to say, the target customers for EM and EI are the same and that they view the two products as substitutable. Is United a single product firm with two product offerings, or does the firm compete in two different markets? In other words, does United have a single strategy for EM and EI or does the firm have two different strategies for the two businesses? As we argue later, EM and EI have very different industry characteristics and compete in very different markets, thereby, requiring quite different strategies. It is, therefore, more useful to calculate market size and market share variances separately for EM and EI. Just introducing the concept of a *sales mix* variance implies that the average standard profit contribution across EM and EI together is meaningful.

For an ice cream manufacturer, for example, it is probably reasonable to assume that the firm operates in a single industry with multiple product offerings, all targeted at the same customer group. It would, therefore, be meaningful to calculate a sales mix variance because vanilla ice cream and strawberry ice cream, for instance, are substitutable and more sales of one implies less sales of the other for the firm (for an elaboration on these ideas, refer to the Midwest Ice Cream Company case [Shank, 1982, pp. 157-173]). On the other hand, for a firm such as General Electric, it is much less clear whether a sales mix variance across jet engines, steam turbines, and light bulbs really makes any sense. This is more nearly the case for United because one unit of EM (which sells for $30) is not really fully substitutable for one unit of EI (which sells for $206).

Table 4
Variance Calculations Using Shank and Churchill's Management-Oriented Framework

Key Causal Factors:

Total market	Expected	Actual	Actual	Actual	Actual	Actual
Market share	Expected	Expected	Actual	Actual	Actual	Actual
Sales mix	Expected	Expected	Expected	Actual	Actual	Actual
Selling price	Expected	Expected	Expected	Expected	Actual	Actual
Costs	Expected	Expected	Expected	Expected	Expected	Actual

Profit Calculation:

Sales	$16,872	$15,836	$18,034	$16,862	$17,060	$17,060
Variable costs	5,796	5,440	6,195	5,944	5,944	6,334
Contribution	$11,076	$10,396	$11,839	$10,918	$11,116	$10,726
Fixed costs	8,548	8,548	8,548	8,548	8,548	7,576
Profit	$ 2,528	$ 1,848	$ 3,291	$ 2,370	$ 2,568	$ 3,150

Variance Analysis:

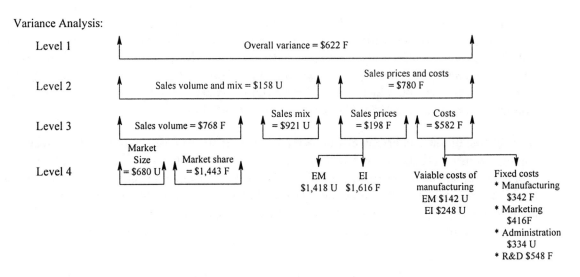

Note: F indicates a favorable variance and U indicates an unfavorable variance.

Table 5
Variance Summary for the Phase II Approach

Overall market decline	$ 680 U
Share of market increase	1,443 F
Sales mix change	921 U
Sales prices improved	198 F
EM $1,418 U	
EI $1,616 F	
Manufacturing cost control	48 U
Variable costs $390 U	
Fixed costs $342 F	
Other	
R&D	548 F
Administration	334 U
Marketing	416 F
Total	$ 622 F

An important issue in the history of many industries is to determine when product differentiation has progressed sufficiently that what *was* a single business with two varieties is *now* two businesses. Some examples include the growth of the electronic cash register for NCR, the growth of the digital watch for Bulova, or the growth of the industrial robot for General Electric.

Following Phase II thinking, performance evaluation did not relate the variances to the differing strategic contexts facing EM and EI.

Phase III Thinking: Variance Analysis Using a Strategic Framework

We argue that performance evaluation, which is a critical component of the management control process, needs to be tailored to the strategy being followed by a firm or its business units. We offer the following set of arguments in support of our position: (1) different strategies imply different tasks and require different behaviors for effective performance [Andrews, 1971; Gupta and Govindarajan, 1984a; and Govindarajan, 1986a]; (2) different control systems induce different behaviors [Govindarajan, 1986b; Gupta and Govindarajan, 1984b]; (3) thus, superior performance can best be achieved by tailoring control systems to the requirements of particular strategies [Govindarajan, 1988; Gupta and Govindarajan, 1986].[3]

We will first define and briefly elaborate the concept of strategy before illustrating how to link strategic considerations with variances for management control and evaluation. Strategy has been conceptualized by Andrews [1971], Ansoff [1965], Chandler [1962], Govindarajan [1989], Hofer and Schendel [1978], Miles and Snow [1978], and others as the process by which managers, using a three- to five-year time horizon, evaluate external environmental opportunities as well as internal strengths and resources in order to decide on *goals* as well as *a set of action*

---

[3] Several studies have shown that when an individual's rewards are tied to performance along certain dimensions, his or her behavior would be guided by the desire to optimize performance with respect to those dimensions. Refer to Govindarajan and Gupta [1985] for a review of these studies.

plans to accomplish these goals. Thus, a business unit's (or a firm's) strategy depends upon two interrelated aspects: (1) its strategic mission or goals, and (2) the way the business unit chooses to compete in its industry to accomplish its goals—the business unit's competitive strategy.

Turning first to strategic mission, consulting firms such as Boston Consulting Group [Henderson, 19791, Arthus D. Little [Wright, 1975], and A. T. Kearney [Hofer and Davoust, 1977], as well as academic researchers such as Hofer and Schendel [1978], Buzzell and Wiersema [1981], and Govindarajan and Shank [1986], have proposed the following three strategic missions that a business unit can adopt:

Build: This mission implies a goal of increased market share, even at the expense of short-term earnings and cash flow. A business unit following this mission is expected to be a net user of cash in that the cash throw-off from its current operations would usually be insufficient to meet its capital investment needs. Business units with "low market share" in "high growth industries" typically pursue a "build" mission (e.g., Apple Computer's MacIntosh business, Monsanto's Biotechnology business).

Hold: This strategic mission is geared to the protection of the business unit's market share and competitive position. The cash outflows for a business unit following this mission would usually be more or less equal to cash inflows. Businesses with "high market share" in "high growth industries" typically pursue a "hold" mission (e.g., IBM in mainframe computers).

Harvest: This mission implies a goal of maximizing short-term earnings and cash flow, even at the expense of market share. A business unit following such a mission would be a net supplier of cash. Businesses with "high market share" in "low growth industries" typically pursue a "harvest" mission (e.g., American Brands in tobacco products).

In terms of competitive strategy, Porter [1980] has proposed the following two generic ways in which businesses can develop sustainable competitive advantage:

Low Cost: The primary focus of this strategy is to achieve low cost relative to competitors. Cost leadership can be achieved through approaches such as economies of scale in production, learning curve effects, tight cost control, and cost minimization in areas such as R&D, service, sales force, or advertising. Examples of firms following this strategy include: Texas Instruments in consumer electronics, Emerson Electric in electric motors, Chevrolet in automobiles, Briggs and Stratton in gasoline engines, Black and Decker in machine tools, and Commodore in business machines.

Differentiation: The primary focus of this strategy is to differentiate the product offering of the business unit, creating something that is perceived by customers as being unique. Approaches to product differentiation include brand loyalty (Coca-Cola in soft drinks), superior customer service (IBM in computers), dealer network (Caterpillar Tractors in construction equipment), product design and product features (Hewlett-Packard in electronics), and/or product technology (Coleman in camping equipment).

The above framework allows us to consider explicitly the strategic positioning of the two product groups: electric meters and electronic instruments. Though they both are industrial measuring instruments, they face very different competitive conditions that very probably call for different strategies. Table 6 summarizes the differing environments and the resulting strategic issues.

Table 6
Strategic Contexts of the Two Businesses

	Electric Meters (EM)	Electronic Instruments (EI)
Overall market (units):		
Plan	1,248,000	440,000
Actual	886,080	690,800
	Declining Market (29 % Decrease)	Growth Market (57% Increase)
United's share:		
Plan	10%	15%
Actual	16%	9%
United's prices:		
Plan	$40	$180
Actual	30	206
	We apparently cut price to build share.	We apparently raised price to ration the high demand.
United's margin:		
Plan	$20	$130
Actual	9	152
Industry prices:		
Actual	$50	$110
	We are well below "market."	We are well above "market."
Industry costs:		
Actual	$18	$46
Product/market characteristics:	Mature	Evolving
	Lower technology	Higher technology
	Declining market	Growth market
	Lower margins	Higher margins
	Low unit price	High unit price
	Industry prices holding up	Industry prices falling rapidly
United's apparent strategic mission	"Build"	"Skim" or "Harvest"
United's apparent competitive strategy	The low price implies we are trying for low cost position.	The high price implies we are trying for a differentiation position.
A more plausible strategy	"Harvest"	"Build"
Key success factors (arising from the plausible strategy)	Hold sales prices vis-à-vis competition. Do not focus on maintaining and improving SOM.	Competitively price to gain SOM. Product R&D to create differentiation

Aggressive cost control	Lower costs through
Process R&D to reduce unit costs.	experience curve effects

How well did electric meters and electronics instruments perform, given their strategic contexts? The relevant variance calculations are given in Tables 7 and 8. These calculations differ from Phase II analysis (given in Table 4) in one important respect. Table 4 treated EM and EI as two varieties of one product, competing as substitutes, with a single strategy. Thus, a sales mix variance was computed. Tables 7 and 8 treat EM and EI as different products with dissimilar strategies. Therefore, no attempt is made to calculate a sales mix variance. The basic idea is that even though a sales mix variance can always be calculated, the concept is meaningful only when a single business framework is applicable. For the same reason, Tables 7 and 8 report the market size and market share variances for EM and EI separately, and Table 4 reported these two variances for the instruments business as a whole. Obviously, a high degree of subjectivity is involved in deciding whether United is in one business or two. The fact that the judgment is to a large extent subjective does not negate its importance. Table 9 summarizes the managerial performance evaluation that would result if we were to evaluate EM and EI against their plausible strategies, using the variances reported in Tables 7 and 8.

Table 7
Variance Calculations Using a Strategic Framework

Key Causal Factors:

	Expected	Actual	Actual	Actual	Actual
Total market	Expected	Actual	Actual	Actual	Actual
Market share	Expected	Expected	Actual	Actual	Actual
Selling price	Expected	Expected	Expected	Actual	Actual
Variable costs	Expected	Expected	Expected	Expected	Actual

Electric Meters (EM)

Sales	$4,992	$3,544	$5,671	$4,253	$4,253
Variable costs	2,496	1,772	2,835	2,835	2,977
Contribution	$2,496	$1,772	$2,836	$1,418	$1,276

Market size = $724 U	Market size = $1,064 F	Sales price = $1,418 U	Manufacturing Cost = $142 U

Electric Meters (EI)

Sales	$11,880	$18,652	$11,191	$12,807	$12,807
Variable costs	3,300	5,181	3,109	3,109	3,357
Contribution	$ 8,580	$13,471	$ 8,082	$ 9,698	$ 9,450

Market size = $4,891 F	Market share = $5,389 U	Sales price = $1,616 F	Manufacturing Cost = $248 U

Firmwide Fixed Costs (by responsibility centers)

	Budget	Actual	Variance
Manufacturing	$3,872	$3,530	$342 F
Marketing	1,856	1,440	416 F
Administration	1,340	1,674	334 U
R&D	1,480	932	548 F

Table 8
Variance Summary for the Phase III Approach

Electric Meters
Market size	$ 724 U
Market share	1,064 F
Sales price	1,418 U
Variable manufacturing cost	142 U

Electronic Instruments
Market size	4,891 F
Market share	5,389 U
Sales price	1,616 F
Variable manufacturing cost	248 U
R&D	548 F

Firmwide Fixed Costs
Manufacturing	342 F
Marketing	416 F
Administration	334 U
TOTAL	$ 622 F

Table 9
Performance Evaluation Summary for Phase III Approach

	Electric Meters "Harvest" vs. "Build"	Electronic Instruments "Build" vs. "Skim"
Marketing Comments	If we held prices and share, decline in this mature business would have cost us $ 724 U But, we were further hurt by price cuts made in order to build our SOM (our price was $30 vs. the industry price of $50). $ 1,418 U 1,064 F Net effect $ 1,078 U This is a market that declined 29 percent. Why are we sacrificing margins to build market position in this mature, declining lower margin business? We underspent the marketing budget. $ 416 F But why are we cutting back here in the face of our major marketing problems?	We raised prices to maintain margins and to ration our scarce capacity (our price was $206 vs. the industry price of $110). In the process, we lost significant SOM, which cost us (netted against $1,616 F from sales prices). $ 3,773 U This is a booming market that grew 57 percent during this period. Then why did we decide to improve margins at the expense of SOM in this fast-growing, higher-margin business? Fortunately, growth in the total market improved our profit picture. $ 4,891 F We underspent the marketing budget. $ 416 F But why are we cutting back here in the face of our major marketing problems.
Overall evaluation	Poor performance	Poor performance
Manufacturing Comments	Manufacturing cost control was lousy and cost the firm $ 142 U If we are trying to be a cost leader, where are the benefits of our cumulative experience or our scale economies? (industry unit costs of $18 vs. our costs of $21)	Variable Manufacturing costs showed an unfavorable variance of $248 U (industry costs of $46 vs. our costs of $54). Does the higher manufacturing cost results in a product perceived as better? Apparently not based on market share data.
Overall evaluation	Poor performance	Poor performance
R&D Comments	Not applicable	Why are we not spending sufficient dollars in product R&D? Could this explain our decline in SOM?
Overall evaluation		Poor performance
Administration Comments	Inadequate control over overhead costs, given the need to become the low cost producer ($334 U).	Administration budget overspent. $ 334 U How does this relate to cost control?
Overall evaluation	Poor performance	Not satisfactory

The overall performance of United would probably be judged as "unsatisfactory." The firm has not taken appropriate decisions in its functional areas (marketing, manufacturing, R&D, and administration) either for its harvest business (EM) or for its build business (EI). The summary in Table 9 indicates a dramatically different picture of United's performance than the one presented under Phase II thinking. This is to be expected because Phase II thinking did not tie variance analysis to strategic objectives. Neither Phase I nor Phase II analysis explicitly focused on ways to improve performance en route to accomplishing strategic goals. This would then imply that management compensation and rewards ought not to be tied to performance assessment undertaken using Phase I or Phase II frameworks.

Conclusions

Variance analysis represents a key link in the management control process. It involves two steps. First, one needs to break down the overall profit variance by key causal factors. Second, one needs to put the pieces back together most meaningfully with a view to evaluating managerial performance. Putting the bits and pieces together most meaningfully is just as crucial as computing the pieces. This is a managerial function, not a computational one.

Phase I, Phase II, and Phase III thinking yield different implications for the first step. That is, the detailed variance calculations do differ across the three approaches. Their implications differ even more for the second step. The computational aspects identify the variance as either favorable or unfavorable. However, a favorable variance does not necessarily imply favorable performance; similarly, an unfavorable variance does not necessarily imply unfavorable performance. We argue that the link between a favorable or unfavorable variance, on the one hand, and favorable or unfavorable performance, on the other, depends upon the strategic context of the business under evaluation.

No doubt, judgments about managerial performance can be dramatically different under Phase I, Phase II, and Phase III thinking (as the United Instruments case illustrates). In our view, moving toward Phase III thinking (i.e., analyzing profit variances in terms of the strategic issues involved) represents progress in adapting cost analysis to the rise of strategic analysis as a major element in business thinking [Shank and Govindarajan, 1988a, 1988b, and 1988c].

References

Andrews, K. R., *The Concept of Corporate Strategy* (Homewood, IL: Dow-Jones Irwin, 1971).

Ansoff, H. I., *Corporate Strategy* (New York: McGraw-Hill, 1965).

Buzzell, R. D., T. Gale, and R. G. M. Sultan, "Market Share—A Key to Profitability," *Harvard Business Review* (January–February 1975), pp. 97–106.

_____, and F. D. Wiersema, "Modelling Changes in Market Share: A Cross-Sectional Analysis," *Strategic Management Journal* (January–March 1981), pp. 27–42.

Chandler, A. D., *Strategy and Structure* (Cambridge, MA: The MIT Press, 1962).

Govindarajan, V., "Implementing Competitive Strategies at the Business Unit Level: Implications of Matching Managers to Strategies," *Strategic Management Journal* (May–June 1989), pp. 251–269.

_____, "Decentralization, Strategy, and Effectiveness of Strategic Business Units in Multi-Business Organizations," *Academy of Management Review* (October 1986a), pp. 844–856.

_____, "Impact of Participation in the Budgetary Process on Managerial Attitudes and Performance: Universalistic and Contingency Perspectives," *Decision Sciences* (1986b), pp. 496–516.

_____, "A Contingency Approach to Strategy Implementation at the Business Unit Level: Integrating Management Systems with Strategy," *Academy of Management Journal* (September 1988).

_____, and A. K. Gupta, "Linking Control Systems to Business Unit Strategy: Impact on Performance," *Accounting, Organizations and Society* (1985), pp. 51–66.

_____, and J. K. Shank, "Cash Sufficiency: The Missing Link in Strategic Planning," *The Journal of Business Strategy* (Summer 1986), pp. 88–95.

Gupta, A. K., and V. Govindarajan, "Business Unit Strategy, Managerial Characteristics, and Business Unit Effectiveness at Strategy Implementation," *Academy of Management Journal* (March 1984a), pp. 25–41.

_____, and _____, "Build, Hold, Harvest: Converting Strategic Intentions into Reality." *Journal of Business Strategy* (Winter 1984b), pp. 34–47.

_____, and _____, "Resource Sharing Among SBUs: Strategic Antecedents and Administrative Implications," *Academy of Management Journal* (December 1986), pp. 695-714.

Henderson, B. D., *Henderson on Corporate Strategy* (Cambridge, MA: Abt Books, 1979).

Hofer, C. W. and M. J. Davoust, *Successful Strategic Management* (Chicago, IL: A. T. Kearney, 1977).

_____, and D. E. Schendel, *Strategy Formulation: Analytical Concepts* (St. Paul, MN: West Publishing, 1978).

"Midwest Ice Cream Company," in J. K. Shank, Ed., *Contemporary Management Accounting: A Casebook* (Englewood Cliffs, NJ: Prentice-Hall, 1982), pp. 157–173.

Miles, R. E., and C. C. Snow, *Organizational Strategy, Structure and Process* (New York: McGraw-Hill, 1978).

Porter, M. E., *Competitive Strategy: Techniques for Analyzing Industries and Competitors* (New York: The Free Press, 1980).

Shank, J. K. *Contemporary Management Accounting: A Casebook* (Englewood Cliffs, NJ: Prentice-Hall, 1982).

_____, and N. C. Churchill, "Variance Analysis: A Management-Oriented Approach," *The Accounting Review* (October 1977), pp. 950–957.

_____, and V. Govindarajan, "Making Strategy Explicit in Cost Analysis: A Case Study," *Sloan Management Review* (Spring 1988a), pp. 19–29.

_____, and _____, "Transaction-Based Costing for the Complex Product Line: A Field Study," *Journal of Cost Management* (Summer 1988b), pp. 31–38.

_____, and _____, "Strategic Cost Analysis-Differentiating Cost Analysis and Control According to the Strategy Being Followed," *Journal of Cost Management* (Fall 1988c).

Wright, R. V. L., A *System of Managing Diversity* (Cambridge, MA: Arthur D. Little, Inc., 1975).

Case 13-2

Nucor Corporation

Teaching Note

At the end of 1986, Nucor is a U.S. company with $750 million in sales that focuses on making and fabricating steel products. Nucor has grown very rapidly and profitably despite its focus on a stagnant, capital-intensive sector with by far the lowest average profitability of any within U.S. manufacturing. F. Kenneth Iverson, Nucor's CEO for more than two decades, must now decide whether the company should, at considerable cost and risk to itself, pioneer the commercialization of a new process technology that may allow it to enter the flat-rolled sheet segment, about half the total U.S. market for steel and hitherto the preserve of integrated steelmakers.

Teaching Objectives

Nucor is meant to be an overview case and is therefore optimally positioned toward the beginning or the end of a course on strategy. (I have historically preferred the latter option.) The case facilitates discussion of four important topics:

1. Explanations of above-average performance. The Nucor case hints at the limits of aggregated explanations of above-average performance, and does so in a way that covers aggregation at the industry, intraindustry (strategic group) and country levels.

2. The links between competitive strategy and internal organization. The Nucor case contains extensive information about the company's organizational policies that can be related to its low-cost strategy, spanning the traditional distinction between strategy formulation and implementation.

3. Comprehensive analysis of a major commitment. The information in the case sorts positioning, sustainability and flexibility analyses of Nucor's decision about a new process technology that places it at a potential crossroads.

4. The role of managerial judgment in making major commitments. In a video that is meant to be shown toward the end of the case discussion, Nucor's CEO, Iverson, emphasizes that top managers must integrate case-specific analysis with judgments based on experience in making such decisions.

These areas cannot all be covered in detail in a single session. Where to focus the discussion depends, in part, on whether Nucor is being used at the beginning or the end of a course on strategy. In a single session, I typically aim for a relatively brief discussion of the first two areas in order to be able to focus on the last two and show the video. Additional time to discuss areas #1 and #2 is available when the Nucor case is taught over two sessions, or is followed by a companion case, "Continuous Casting Investments at USX Corporation [9-391-121]" that describes USX's review and rejection of thin-slab casting technology in a way that permits direct comparison of Nucor and USX. A separate teaching note for the USX case follows this one.

Professor Pankaj Ghemawat prepared this teaching note as an aid to instructors in the classroom use of "Nucor At a Crossroads," HBS case 793-039. Copyright © President and Fellows at Harvard College.

Teaching Aids

An eight-and-a-half minute video of Iverson (HBS Video #792-501), visiting my class at Harvard in December 1990 is available. I assign chapter 7 of *Commitment,* particularly pp. 135-147, as a supplemental reading on judgment (discussion area #4), and rely on previous reading of chapters 4 through 6 to supply a framework for the analysis of commitments (discussion area #3). Areas #1 and #2 are discussed in much more detail in my paper in the *Journal of Economics & Management Strategy,* "Competitive Advantage and Internal Organization: Nucor Revisited."

Teaching Questions

1. Why has Nucor performed so well in the past?

   - Is Nucor's industry the answer?

   - Is it Nucor's strategic group (minimills)?

   - Is it Nucor's home-base (United States)?

   - Is it Nucor's choice of a low-cost strategy?

   - What are the most unusual attributes of Nucor's organization?

   - How are they related to its low cost-strategy? To each other?

   - Would you like to work for Nucor?

   - How does Nucor coordinate across its plants?

   - What role does investment in physical capital play in Nucor's competitive advantage?

   - What is the logic of Nucor's financial policies?

   - Why haven't Nucor's organizational arrangements been more widely imitated?

Pedagogy

1. Nucor's Superior Performance

A. Nonexplanations

I introduce the Nucor case by emphasizing its stellar stock price performance (Exhibit B). I then lead the discussants relatively quickly through several nonexplanations of Nucor's superior performance. The average profitability of the U.S. steel industry has been poor, and while minimills have managed to outperform integrated steelmakers by a significant margin, that still leaves most of Nucor's superior performance unexplained (Exhibit 7).

It may also be worth pointing out that in terms of Porter's [1990] prominent framework for analyzing home-base effects, the United States appears to have been a bad, rather than merely mediocre, base for internationally competitive steelmakers: conservative buyers resisted the introduction of new process technologies, large, sluggish incumbents focused on propping up prices, rapacious suppliers of labor expropriated most of the proceeds from capital investment, domestic suppliers of steelmaking equipment withered away and trade restrictions didn't help. By implication, country-level effects do not explain aspects of Nucor's success such as its ranking as the second most productive steelmaker in the world (p. 9 of the case).

A less-aggregated explanation that does not fare much better, at least on its own, is Nucor's choice of a low-cost competitive strategy. This point can be surfaced by asking discussants to guess the number of Nucor's minimill competitors that were pursuing generically different strategies in 1986. The answer is not very many, as indicated by the following quote (not included in the case) of H. David Aycock, who was Nucor's COO then: "The key to making a profit when selling a product with no aesthetic value, or a product you can't really differentiate from your competitors, is cost."

B. Nucor's Internal Organization

By a process of elimination (explanations in terms of market power are also implausible in light of Nucor's limited market share), Nucor's superior performance must be explained in terms of firm-specific efficiency effects. Discussants often couch such explanations in terms of Nucor's superior strategy implementation, as opposed to its formulation of a superior strategy. It is important to get them to realize that the formulation-implementation dichotomy is not a very fruitful one: that Nucor prospered because of the fit between its organizational arrangements for administering its key resources ("implementation") and its low-cost competitive strategy ("formulation").

Another other major challenge in this segment of the discussion is to impose some structure on what might otherwise end up simply being a long list of Nucor's organizational policies with no implication more specific than the advice to get everything right. I have found that it works well, boardwise at least, to organize the discussion in terms of "People" and "Plants" since that covers the two types of resources, human and physical capital, that appear to have been the most crucial to Nucor's success. The ways in which Nucor coordinates across its plants can be bundled into the first category and its financial policies and governance structure into the second one. Arrows between the two categories can be used to highlight people-plant complementarities and arrows can be drawn between each of them and Nucor's low-cost strategy. There is, in addition scope for an interesting discussion of why Nucor's apparently superior organizational policies haven't been more widely imitated.

In this teaching note, I treat Nucor's organizational policies relatively briefly. My 1993 paper, which was cited above as a teaching aid, provides much more detail. Exhibit C is a schematic that can be used to summarize (most of) the class discussion.

<u>People</u>

Nucor's low cost strategy and the high utilization levels that it implied enabled human resource management policies that yielded (additional) operating efficiencies.

Production incentives: Production workers accounted for most of Nucor's employees and most of its compensation costs. The high-powered, explicit, output-based linear compensation formula applied to them is a staple of macroeconomic models of principal-agent problems. This formula appears to have tied into Nucor's choice of a low-cost strategy as well: Nucor would probably have been less successful with quantitative incentives if it had been following a differentiated strategy instead since quality tends to be harder to meter than quantity. (Nucor's most "progressive" minimill competitor, Chaparral, paid its workers straight salaries instead of offering them production incentives for precisely this reason.) Low costs also implied high capacity utilization, narrowing the scope for divergence between worker interest in output-maximization and managerial interest in profit-maximization. To enhance the effectiveness of its production incentive plan, Nucor offered its workers some insurance against macroeconomic downturns by shrinking bonus targets in proportion to the number of days a plant was deliberately idled by management. It relied, in addition, on self-selection by exceptionally able, motivated production workers and on peer pressure, which was fueled by group-level incentives.

Other incentives: Exhibit 8 indicates and salary data confirm that incentive intensities were significantly lower for salaried workers and department heads than production workers, but significantly higher for officers (corporate managers and plant general managers). Limited incentive-intensity for department heads and, especially, salaried employees such as accountants and secretaries, can be rationalized in terms of their limited impact on performance. The high incentive-intensity for top managers can be rationalized on the opposite grounds. Top managers did not, however, appear to be looting the corporate coffers. CEO compensation, for instance, appears to have averaged a smaller multiple of worker compensation at Nucor than at integrated steelmakers (and, it turns out, at large U.S. companies in general), and to have been significantly more risky in terms of its volatility. In addition, the fact that these incentives tied individual compensation to performance at some higher level of aggregation encouraged lateral communication, particularly across plants. Even though plant managers were compensated on the basis of corporate performance, they were held accountable for achieving a 25% pretax return on assets at their respective plants.

Participatory management: The efficacy of the sorts of monetary incentives described above appears to depend on employee participation in decision making. Nucor's top managers promoted such participation by flattening the company's hierarchy, decentralizing decision making, disclosing information widely, limiting status as well as income-related differentials among employees, guaranteeing worker rights (particularly through policies that guaranteed just-cause dismissal and no layoffs), and cultivating a reputation for considering employees' as well as shareholders' interests in the formulation of company policies. Nucor's competitive advantage and the rapid expansion that it permitted played a key role as well: it encouraged suggestions from the shop floor about how to substitute capital for labor by casting such suggestions in win-win terms. In competitively disadvantaged, shrinking firms such as the integrated steelmakers, in contrast, the substitution of capital for labor was more likely to be seen by workers as inimical to their interests (a complementarity between human and capital resource management). That was also true, to a lesser extent, of minimills that had constrained their own growth by restricting their geographic or product scope.

Coordination: Nucor coordinated across its multiple sites in ways that facilitated information transfer across plants. Plant managers were compensated on the basis of corporate ROE rather than absolute or relative plant ROA and were kept posted, by the corporate office, on each other's financial and operating performance. In addition, the corporate office regularly arranged formal interplant meetings and encouraged informal communication among them as well. It probably also intervened to make sure that employees with plant construction and start-up skills (a scarce resource for Nucor) were released from old plants to new ones. But with these exceptions, it tried to stay out of the loop in order to avoid becoming, because of its leanness, the bottleneck in information transfer. It instead placed its trust in incentives and norms

Plants

Nucor's low costs and the rapid expansion that they permitted also led, in conjunction with appropriate capital resource management policies, to investment efficiencies.

Financing/Governance: Nucor restricted its debt to less than 30% of its total financial capital and had a policy of not issuing additional equity shares to the public, indicating a preference for financing most investment out of retained earnings. Nucor's low level of debt afforded it flexibility in exploiting investment opportunities, particularly lumpy ones involving entire plants, that turned up as a result of its competitive advantage: it probably wouldn't even have been in a position to consider pioneering thin-slab casting if it had been as leveraged as most of its rivals. Nucor's competitive advantage expanded its internal supply of funds as well as increasing effective demand for them. Financial self-sufficiency also helped buffer Nucor's managers from capital suppliers in a way that promoted participatory management (another complementarity between capital and human resource management). Fears of managerial opportunism on the part of shareholders appear to have been restrained by the reputation Nucor's top managers had cultivated for doing well by them.

Investment criteria: In deciding whether to invest in a new plant, Nucor did not systematically discount cash flows. It relied, instead, on the principle that new plants had to achieve a 25% return on assets within five years of start-up. This focused *ex ante* investment analysis on the same measure that was used *ex post* to audit operating performance (another complementarity between capital and human resources). Nucor's ability to devise an effective principle of this sort appears to have been related to the characteristics of steelmaking (tangible, relatively measurable capital resources and continuous technical progress) and to its strategy (which had been stable and which involved continuously building or rebuilding plants, as discussed below). It is useful to point out that the 25% ROA target typically implied an investment benefit-to-cost hurdle greater than 1. Nucor's competitive advantage made this high hurdle practical; its rationale was related to the way in which Nucor implemented its investments.

Investment implementation: Nucor invested more steadily than its competitors and placed more emphasis on building or rebuilding entire sites. This approach allowed coherence in site design and prevented the logic of Nucor's human resource management policies from breaking down at older sites because of dated technology. Its most important effect, however, was to build up Nucor's experience at plant construction and start-up in a way that was evident in a number of the company's investment implementation policies: it designed its plants as they were being built, speeding up construction; it had learnt to configure them in ways that anticipated expansion and to minimize supplier holdup by locating them in rural areas where it had access to at least two railroads, low electricity rates and plentiful water; and it acted as the general contractor for each of its construction projects instead of relying, more expensively, on a turnkey contractor. Each construction project was managed by a "tiger team" of engineers experienced at plant construction and start-up, a scarce resource that accounted for Nucor's policy of effectively setting its investment benefit-to-cost hurdle higher than 1. Many of the construction workers that they supervised were retained as the production workforce for new plants (yet another complementarity between capital and human resource management). These policies helped reduce operating as well as investment costs in obvious ways.

<u>Lack of Imitation</u>

Explanations of why the sources of Nucor's competitive advantage weren't more widely imitated by its competitors can be grouped in terms of three types of factors: input factors that Nucor or its competitors obtained from others, organizational factors that were specific to Nucor, and precommitments by other competitors. The second and third categories turn out to have more explanatory power than the first one.

Input factors: Transferable input factors to which Nucor might have tried to tie up superior access include scrap, technology, workers, and sites. None of these is a very plausible explanation of the sustainability of Nucor's advantage. Nucor coordinated its plants' purchases of scrap through an independent purchasing agent who pooled its demands with its competitors'. For technology, it relied on suppliers who licensed their equipment and processes nonexclusively and with flow-back clauses (as SMS was insisting in the context of thin-slab casting). While Nucor did seem to attract superior workers, the success of Japanese manufacturers investing in the United States, particularly auto makers, in recruiting rurally suggests that Nucor was in no position to tie up the supply of "farm boys" (the phrase is due to Nucor's COO, John Correnti) in a way that would lock out its direct competitors. The value of spatial preemption was undercut by the low minimal efficient scales at which minimills operate and their steady expansion at the expense of integrated steelmakers.

Organizational factors: Nontradeable factors accumulated internally by Nucor suggest more plausible explanations of non-imitation. First, Nucor may have seized such a lead at accumulating plant construction and start-up experience that imitation of its investment policies, and their organizational concomitants, may have become unprofitable for its competitors. Second, the sort of reputation that Nucor's top managers had cultivated since the mid-1960s for not abusing the company's workers or its shareholders takes time to build, delaying imitation and perhaps even tipping the scales against it. Third, the complementarities among Nucor's organizational arrangements made it inappropriate to imitate them piecemeal, elevating the fixed costs and difficulty of imitation.

Competitors' precommitments: At least some of Nucor's competitors had precommitted themselves in ways that discouraged imitation of Nucor's organizational arrangements. Thus, Chaparral, Nucor's most capable minimill competitor (which is discussed in the technology and operations management course in Harvard's MBA program), was precommitted to a differentiation strategy that precluded it from offering production incentives, and to a single site that prevented it from accumulating experience at (re)building and starting up entire sites. Integrated steelmakers were even more precommitted in ways incompatible with imitating Nucor, as the case on USX, which is meant to follow this one, indicates.

Update

The video of Iverson updates the situation through fall 1990: it describes Nucor's decision to go ahead, the problems it encountered with its first plant at Crawfordsville, Indiana that its process capabilities could not prevent but did help overcome, and its decision to build a second plant, at Hickman, Arkansas—a process that has involved significantly lower start-up costs than did the first one. By the end of 1992, Nucor had decided to form joint ventures in Trinidad and the Pacific Northwest to make, respectively, directly-reduced iron (a substitute for scrap input) and flat-rolled sheet. The site in Trinidad would take advantage of cheap natural gas, labor and

Brazilian iron ore and the flat-rolled mill in the Pacific Northwest of the captive demand of the local partner, another minimills Oregon Steel, for flat-rolled sheet.

The move into the Pacific Northwest, while critical to Nucor's continued growth, poses two locational problems. The first is that it will have to compete there with low-cost Asian imports as well as some relatively efficient U.S. suppliers of flat-rolled sheet. Second, scrap inputs are not available in the Pacific Northwest in quite the same quality and quantity as in the regions in which Nucor's first two flat-rolled plants are located. Success in West Coast markets therefore depends, to an important extent, on the success of the venture for making directly-reduced iron in Trinidad.

The Trinidad plant attempts to take advantage of a relatively cheap, small-scale process for making directly-reduced iron that has never been commercialized before. Its first stage is projected, in early 1993, to cost $60 million and to have the capacity to produce 320,000 tons of iron carbides (a substitute for scrap) per year. The plant is being built so that its capacity can be doubled or even redoubled if it works well—an interesting example of the use of modularity to create flexibility value. If the Trinidad plant doesn't work well, limits to the supply of scrap may place a brake on minimill growth in general and Nucor's in particular. If it does work, Nucor may be able to achieve its target of becoming the largest steelmaker in the United States within a decade.

The stock market's assessment of these developments has, as of this writing, been quite favorable: adjusted for splits, Nucor's stock price surged from $15 at the end of 1986 to $70 by the end of 1992. Meanwhile, domestic competitors continue to talk of imitating Nucor by using thin-slab casting to enter new product segments but have yet to do so. The reasons individual minimill competitors haven't yet imitated Nucor's move reflect, to varying degrees, capital constraints, lower operating efficiency, lack of experience constructing and starting up greenfield sites, and divergent beliefs about how the U.S. steel industry is likely to evolve. The hesitations of an integrated steelmaker about thin-slab casting are described in the case (and teaching note) on USX that ideally follows this one.

Summary

Given the richness of the case, it can be summarized from a number of different perspectives: organizational, technological, competitive (as in interactive), et cetera. Whatever the perspective, the summary comments may either review the discussion or try to induce additional meditation by discussants. They are also likely to be affected by whether the USX case will be discussed next.

I tend to use Nucor and USX as a summary case series. Instead of reviewing the positioning-sustainability-flexibility-judgment framework (the subject of about two-thirds of the section on "Pedagogy") in detail, I focus on some of the broader patterns at which Nucor's history appears to hint. More specifically, I make (some of) the points that follow.

1. What is most uncanny about Nucor's early history is the way in which it *anticipates* patterns in the diversification of relatively large U.S. companies. (The terminology employed here follows Wrigley [1970] and Rumelt [1974].) Nucor's corporate predecessor, Reo, started off as a single-product firm. It started to diversify into related businesses in the 1920s. It was the target of a hostile takeover in 1955 as it tried to liquidate itself. The post-takeover entity, the Nuclear Corporation of America, attempted in the late 1950s to become a dominant firm in a cluster of businesses related to each other (via atomic physics) but unrelated to Reo's original business of car manufacture. In 1960, it became, amidst faltering results and under a new CEO, an early recruit to the ranks of the conglomerate movement. In 1965, amidst even worse results and under another new CEO, it returned to a policy of corporate specialization, anticipating what is asserted to have been a general trend in this direction by about two decades (Bhagat, Shleifer and Vishny [1990]). There is probably an important lesson about diversification follies herein.

2. Nucor's specialization and success at steelmaking over more than a quarter of a century, and particularly over a period that proved to be difficult for most of the U.S. steel industry, also hints at the important role that resources specialized to particular domains, as opposed to generic resources, play in sustaining superior performance. Such an inference is consistent with empirical evidence that stable firm-level effects (as opposed to stable effects that operate at the industry or business unit levels) account for only 1%–2% of the variation observed in business unit profitability (Rumelt [1991]).

3. Nucor's commitment to steelmaking since the mid-1960s should not be allowed to obscure the significant changes in its boundaries or scope that were subsequently effected. Nucor's geographic scope expanded steadily: in 1965, it operated two steel joist plants, at two locations (as well as a rare earth elements operation); by 1993 it operated steelmaking and fabrication plants at more than a dozen sites in the United States and was contemplating its first plant overseas (in Trinidad). So did its product scope, from joists to other low-end products and, more recently, to more demanding, higher-end products such as wide-flange beams and flat-rolled sheet. It also began to form interorganizational relationships (e.g., with Yamato Kogyo and its partners in Trinidad and Oregon). Even more strikingly, its vertical scope shifted backward as well, from fabricating steel products to making steel and, more recently, partially integrating into steel inputs (through the directly-reduced iron plant) and technology development. Forward (quasi)integration into relationship-based marketing was likely in the future if the company continued to grow. Note that all these changes had implications for Nucor's organizational arrangements. Successful specialization would therefore seem to involve adaptation instead of stagnation.

4. Nucor's ability to build steel mills cheaply and operate them economically indicates that organizing appropriately can have very large efficiency effects. In addition, its record on improvement challenges conventional wisdom in two ways. First, in steel, as in many other capital-intensive process industries (refer, for instance, to Hollander's [1966] study of rayon), ideas for improvement are not enough: implementation involves embodying them in physical capital and therefore implies attention to investment as well as operating processes.

Second, continuous improvement in small steps, while necessary for progress, also fails to be sufficient: the example of Nucor's first thin-slab caster indicates that deepening competences or building up capabilities or however else one might choose to describe the process of upgrading, tends to involve a few large steps (major commitments) as well as many small ones.

5. Major commitments deserve to be pondered in particular depth because their irreversibility sets the context for the far more numerous and less commitment-intensive choices that follow. The positioning-sustainability-flexibility framework helps systematize the analysis by imposing some structure on it; it may, in addition, highlight important considerations that might otherwise be overlooked (e.g., the option value of being able to build follow-on thin-slab casting facilities). It would, however, be jejune to pretend or prescribe a purely "objective" analytical basis for commitment decisions. While they shouldn't ignore such analysis, they shouldn't ignore subjective, experiential considerations either given the potential for both honest mistakes and deliberate distortions in the analysis.

If the case on USX's consideration of thin-slab casting comes next, it is useful to add that unlike the Nucor case, it looks at the downside of (pre)commitment.

Exhibit A

Board Plan

Small Left   Small Right

Technology	Lists
Procurement	Hurdle Rates
Operations	Monte Carlo Analysis
Marketing	Worst-Case Analysis
Finance	Scenario Analysis
(Competitor) Strategy	Option Analysis

Top Board

	(The Projected Positioning of Thin-Slab Casting vs.)					
	Unmodernized Int. capacity		Int. capacity being modernized		Already modernized Int. capacity	
	HR	CR	HR	CR	HR	CR
Operating cost differences						
Price differences						
Invest. cost differences (at 5%, 10%, and 15%)						
Net differences						

Middle Board

Nucor's Organization

People	Plants
Monetary incentives	One/Year
Participatory management	Own construction manager
(Worker) Self-selection	Tiger team
(Managerial) Reputation	Start-up

Bottom Board

Sustainability for Nucor

Imitation	Holdup
Other minimills	Buyers
Integrated steelmakers	SMS
	Railroads
	Utilities
	David Joseph

Substitution	Slack
Hazelett	Labor
Manesmann-Demag	Top managers
Driect stip casting	

Exhibit B

Cumulated Abnormal
Returns of Nucor's Stock

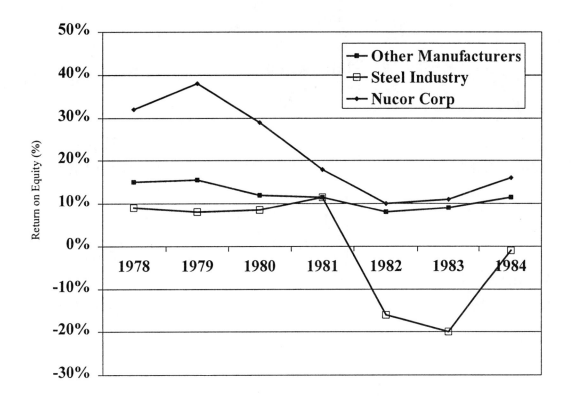

Exhibit C

Competitive Advantage
and Internal Organization at Nucor

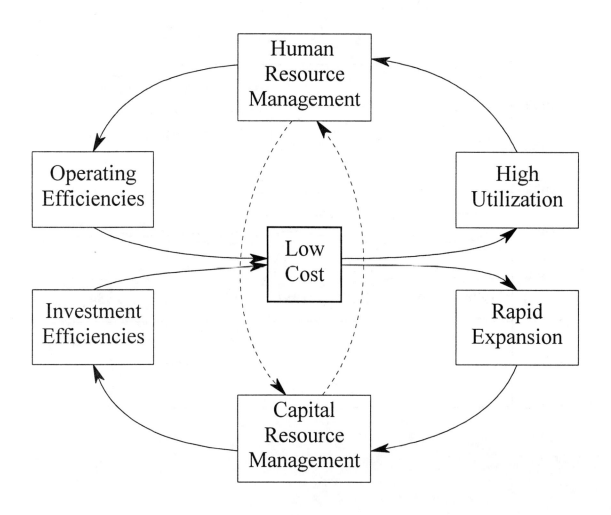

Nucor Corporation Teaching Note[*]

Competitive Advantage and Internal Organization: Nucor Revisited

Pankaj Ghemawat
Harvard Business School
Boston, MA 02163

Why does the cost of organizing particular activities differ across competitors? This article explores in detail the organization of Nucor, a steel minimill that has sustained a significant cost advantage over its competitors. Nucor's past success highlights the complementarities among organizational policies and competitive advantage as well as barrier to the imitation of apparently superior organizational arrangements. The case study also suggests avenues for additional empirical and theoretical research.

1. Introduction

Cross-industry studies suggest that there may be significant, sustained differences in the efficiency and profitability levels of direct competitors (e.g., Caves and Barton, 1990; Rumelt, 1991). But because of aggregation requirements, such studies say little about the firm-specific factors that may be at work. That leaves room for case studies, based on finer-grained data, to make a contribution.

This paper adopts the case study approach: It analyzes the superior performance of a U.S. steelmaker, Nucor. Detailed analysis of the ways in which Nucor administers the resources in its organizational coalition and comparisons with its competitors should help illustrate the links between competitive advantage and internal organization. The discussion is complementary to, and draws most on the same body of information, as Ghemawat (1993). That paper analyzed why an important process innovation, thin-stab casting, was first adopted by a steel minimill (which makes steel from scrap) instead of by integrated steelmakers (which make steel primarily from iron ore). This papers elucidation of Nucor's competitive advantage helps explain why it, rather than some other minimill, was the first to commercialize the new process technology.

Section 2 of this paper assembles evidence that Nucor has outperformed most other U.S. steelmakers over a significant period of time. Section 3 scouts various firm-level explanations of Nucor's superior performance. Sections 4 and 5 focus attention, respectively, on Nucor's organization of its human and (physical) capital resources and compare it, in these respects, to its

---

This article has benefited from the presentation of earlier drafts at seminars at Harvard University, INSEAD, Université Catholique de Louvain, the University of California at Los Angeles, the University of Michigan, and the University of Minnesota. Detailed comments from the Srinivasan Balakrishnan, David Collis, Anita McGahan, Joan Ricart i Costa, Richard Rosenbloom, Jitendra Singh, Richard Walton, an anonymous referee, and the editor proved particularly helpful. Jeffrey Arthur and John Neiva de Figueiredo generously provided access to their cross-sectional analysis of U.S. minimills. Henricus J. Stander III supplied able research assistance, and the Division of Research at the Harvard Business School supported the research financially.

Journal of Economics & Management Strategy, Volume 3, Number 4. Winter 1995, 685-717

competitors. Section 6 discusses the sustainability of Nucor's competitive advantage, and Section 7 concludes.

2. Nucor's Superior Performance

This section presents evidence that Nucor has managed to sustain superior performance over a significant period of time. Several sorts of evidence are presented: financial data, operating data, and project-specific data. This evidence steers one away from aggregated explanations (e.g., explanations at the level of the industry or the strategic group) of Nucor's success toward firm-level ones.

Financial Performance

The most dramatic piece of evidence that Nucor created and sustained a substantial competitive advantage over a long period of time is provided by the price of its common stock, which increased from a high of $2.13 in 1975 to a high of $81.75 in 1990. This performance cannot easily be ascribed to either a general rise in the stock market over that period or to the slightly above-average "systematic risk" of Nucor's stock: Between the end of 1975 and the end of 1990, the cumulated "abnormal" return multiple on Nucor's stock, adjusted for dividends, the market rate of return and systematic risk, came to a factor of approximately 14 (see Figure 1).

Figure 1
Cumulated Abnormal Stock Return

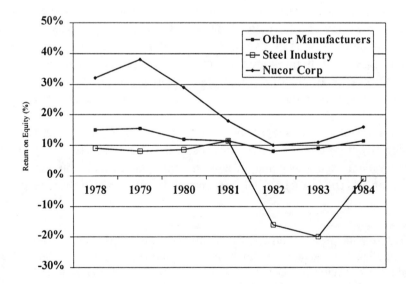

Figure 1 also plots the cumulated abnormal returns for two other steelmakers, USX (formerly U.S. Steel) and Bethlehem. These two companies were the largest U.S. steelmakers over most of the 1970s and 1980s; USX diversified substantially beyond steel in the early 1980s but

Bethlehem did not. Their records undercut the hypothesis that Nucor's exceptional performance can largely, or even significantly, be attributed to stable industry-level effects. So does evidence that between 1980 and 1988, the average stock price performance of the seven—eventually six—largest integrated steelmakers (which accounted for 79% of integrated and 64% of total steel-making capacity in the United States in 1986) substantially lagged the market rate of return (DeAngelo and DeAngelo, 1991). In fact, Federal Trade Commission (F-TC) data indicate that over the 1970s and 1980s, steel and iron ranked last among 18 two-digit manufacturing subsectors in terms of profitability, measured in terms of return on equity, assets, or sales.

A slightly less aggregated explanation of the sources of Nucor's success is suggested by the *intraindustry* structure of steel making minimills within which minimills have steadily increased their share of the U.S. market at the expense of integrated steelmakers. Might the superiority of minimills performance to integrated steelmakers' account for a substantial fraction of Nucor's excess financial returns?

Table I compares the stock price performance of Nucor, its three largest publicly held minimill competitors, and the two largest domestic integrated steelmakers, USX and Bethlehem, over a 10- rather than 20-year period. These datapoints suggest that although minimills' efficiency advantages vis-à-vis integrated steelmakers fed Nucor's superior financial performance, they accounted for less than half of the differential. In other words, Nucor's superior financial performance is better explained at the strategic group (minimill) level than at the industry (steel making) level but mostly remains unexplained, implying the importance of firm-level differences.

Table I
Comparative Steel Company Financial Performance

	Price Range of Common Stock ($)		Average % Change	Average Market-to-Book
	1976	1985	1976–1985	Ratio, 1985
Nucor Corp.	3.70–7.91	31.00–55.75	647.20	2.05
Other Publicly Held Minimills				
Texas Industries (owner of Chaparral Steel Co.)	11.00–15.38	25.75–34.38	127.94	1.33
Northwestern Steel & Wire Co	27.50–36.10	38.00–14.50	−64.64	0.44
Florida Steel Corp.	4.88–7.44	12.63–19.88	163.80	1.80
Integrated Firms				
U.S. Steel Corp.	45.68–57.50	24.38–33.00	−44.39	0.63
LTV Steel Co.	10.00–17.70	55.25–13.25	−33.45	0.72
Bethlehem Steel Co.	33.00–48.00	12.50–21.13	−58.52	0.84
National Steel Corp.	37.38–52.25	24.00–33.63	−35.71	0.64

Source: Barrett and Crandall (1986, p. 15)

Operating Performance

Satisfactory comparisons of minimills' operating performance are generally harder to come by than comparisons of their financial performance, for several reasons. Operating comparisons typically focus on labor productivity and even when they do examine total factor productivity, they reduce all input quantities to dollar amounts for purposes of normalization, making it impossible to separate technical efficiency (production of the largest possible output from a given set of inputs) from allocative efficiency (combination of inputs in cost-minimizing proportions given their prices). They are generally based on a single year of data and, because of their usual determinism, fail to allow for exogenous influences on plant efficiency—a combination that is particularly unfortunate because of the large, possibly different effects of short-run cyclical fluctuations on the efficiency with which steel plants operate. Finally, they tend to ignore differences in output mix and headcounting policies.

The one study of productivity of which I am aware that manages to overcome most of these problems, Neiva de Figueiredo's (1993), is based on proprietary plant-specific data on input requirements and standard costs assembled on a consistent basis by Donald Barnett, a leading consultant to the steel industry. Barnett's database covers selected years from 1983 to 1991 and appears to be weighted toward plants operated by the firm that are considered to have been the best performers among U.S. minimills over this period. Neiva de Figueiredo focused on a subset of these plants that produce similar categories of products, yielding an average of three years of observations on 17 plants operated by 11 firms. His sample included four plants operated by Nucor, four by Florida Steel, and one apiece by other firms.

Neiva de Figueiredo used stochastic production frontier methods to estimate the technical efficiency of these plants.[1] One Nucor plant ranked first among the 17 on this measure, another ranked fifth, and the others ranked eighth and ninth. Florida Steel's plants, in contrast, ranked third, sixth, thirteenth, and sixteenth. The unweighted average measures of technical efficiency equaled 84% for Nucor, 79% for Florida Steel, and 77% for all non-Nucor plants. When one capitalizes this difference and accounts for differing growth rates as well, it is easy to explain Nucor's high market-to-book ratio.[2]

In addition, Neiva de Figueiredo's results indicate that Nucor's superior operating efficiency stemmed in large part from its lower capital recovery costs (accounting charges for capital expenditures). This conclusion does not, however, explain why Nucor's capital recovery costs are lower even after the implementation of controls for plant-level differences in vintage, numbers of products and grades, and total output. For finer-grained data that focus more attention on these issues, consider Nucor's construction, start-up, and continued improvement of a large, strategically salient plant at Crawfordsville, Indiana, over the period from 1987 to 1992.

Project-Specific Performance

Nucor's Crawfordsville plant pioneered the commercialization of a "thin-slab casing" process developed by SMS, a leading German supplier of steelmaking equipment, which permitted steel to be cast in slabs 2 inches thick, rather than the customary 8–10 inches, reducing the labor, energy, and equipment subsequently required to roll slabs into sheets one-tenth of an inch thick. SMS developed thin-slab casting between 1983 and 1995 and began to promote it to as many steelmakers as possible. More than 100 companies sent their engineers or executives to view SMS's pilot thin-slab caster, but nothing more happened until the summer of 1986, when Nucor

---

[1] More specifically, Neiva de Figueiredo reported average technical efficiency for each plant in his sample based on the estimation procedures proposed by Battese and Coelli (1988).

[2] See, for instance, Ghemawat (1991), p. 161, footnote 3.

invited SMS to prepare a definite proposal.[3] The terms of a nonexclusive license with technology flow-back clauses were finalized in late 1986 and announced in early 1987. Nucor selected Crawfordsville, Indiana, as the site for the first thin-slab caster of commercial scale.

By the end of 1992, Nucor was reaping substantial returns from Crawfordsville despite depressed industry conditions; had completed construction of its second thin-slab casting plant at Hickman, Arkansas; and was considering building a third in coalition with Oregon Steel in the Pacific Northwestern region of the United States. Nucor's stock price surged even more sharply post-Crawfordsville than prior to it, which suggests that thin-slab casting was a clear winner for the company rather than an instantiation of the "winner's curse." So does the fact that while Nucor was the sole adopter of SMS's thin-slab casting technology by 1992, several minimills and at least one integrated steelmaker were reported to be on the verge of adopting it as well. While it is still impossible to compare Nucor's costs of adopting the new technology at Crawfordsville with adoption costs for its competitors, comparisons with other benchmarks can be made.

Crawfordsville's construction costs highlight what is perhaps the most important channel whereby Nucor obtained its capital productivity advantage. They amounted to $265 million or, including some expenditures on extra equipment to expand capacity, about $280 million in total. This figure was remarkably low given that an integrated steelmaker studied how much Crawfordsville's construction would cost Nucor, and came up with an estimate in excess of $400 million. Under average pricing assumptions and based on casting capacity of 850,000 tons per year, the implication of cutting capital costs from $400 million to $280 million is to reduce the capital-to-output ratio in thin-slab casting from 1.4 to 1.0.

Start-up costs were a second important element of the overall cost picture, amounting to $60 million. Offsetting them, however, was the fact that Nucor deliberately pursued fast-track construction by finalizing the design of the Crawfordsville plant as it was being built, breaking ground on the facility in October 1987, starting production in August 1989, and reaching operating break-even (50% capacity utilization) about a year and a half later. Assuming that Nucor thereby shaved a year and a half off steel industry norms implies savings (in the form of a shorter lag between cash outlays and inflows) of the same order of magnitude as the start-up costs. Nucor was also able to transfer learning from Crawfordsville to its second thin-slab caster, at Hickman: It held start-up costs at the latter to $30 million instead of $60 million and reduced the lag between the start of construction and operating break-even by another nine months.

By 1992, Crawfordsville's output exceeded its original rated capacity, and the labor it required to produce hot-rolled sheet had been reduced below the initial target of 1.0 man-hours per ton (mhpt) to less than 0.8 mhpt, making it one of the world's most efficient steelmaking facilities. These incremental operating improvements were being supplemented with a drastic one that would nearly double Crawfordsville's capacity by adding, at very modest incremental capital and labor costs, a second thin-slab caster to share the rolling stands with the first one.

In summary, Nucor's construction, start-up, and continued improvement of its Crawfordsville plant over the period from 1987 to 1992 suggests that the company was able to add new capacity more cost-effectively than its competitors *and* to wring extra operating profits out of that

---

[3] The matching process between Nucor and SMS is described in much more detail in Ghemawat and Stander's (1992) teaching case.

capacity, reducing capital recovery costs as a percentage of revenues recorded, and allowing the company to expand its product scope within steelmaking.

Firm-Level Explanations

The data presented in the previous section suggest that Nucor's superior financial performance cannot plausibly be attributed to industry effects and that although intraindustry (minimill) effects pack more explanatory punch, they still explain less than half of the competitive differential. By implication, firm-level explanations must be entertained. There are at least four candidates: market power, interorganizational relationships, competitive strategy and internal organization.

Explanations that involve market power are common in cross-sectional research in industrial organization economics. In the present context, one might extend Gale's (1972) finding that large firms benefit disproportionately from the collusive possibilities afforded by high levels of industry concentration to argue that as the largest U.S. minimill (at least by the end of the 1980s), Nucor could be expected to exhibit profit levels higher than its direct competitors. This explanation appears implausible, however, for a number of reasons: the toughness of price competition in the steel industry, particularly within the segments penetrated by Nucor and other minimills; the fact that in spite of its rapid growth Nucor's domestic market share is still significantly less than 10%; and the efficiency effects evident in, among other things, Nucor's ability to garner quasi-rents from the commercialization of a technology that belonged to SMS.

A second, efficiency-oriented explanation of a company's superior performance emphasizes its interorganizational relationships (Coase, 1988). In the case of Nucor, at least, this explanation is unconvincing because the company traditionally limited such relationships.[4] Nucor's dealings with its buyers tended to minimize transaction (bookkeeping) costs rather than to establish relationships with them on the basis of special deals. Nucor did not try to build direct relationships with its suppliers of steel scrap either: instead, it coordinated its plants' purchases of scrap through an independent purchasing agent who pooled Nucor's demands with several of its competitors' (including Florida Steel). In its relationships with railways, Nucor emphasized access to more than one at a new site (and, preferably, to waterborne transportation as well). For innovation, it relied, except for its shop floor "R&D," on independent upstream equipment suppliers (e.g., SMS in the case of thin-slab casting) who licensed their technologies nonexclusively and with flow-back clauses. In summary, Nucor's policies mostly restricted its vertical scope to manufacturing and made its interboundary interactions with other organizations more marketlike or transaction-oriented in order to mitigate the small-numbers bargaining problem associated with special relationships. It is difficult, therefore, to explain Nucor's superior performance in terms of its superior interorganizational relationships except in the sense that it historically eschewed them.

A third explanation of a company's superior performance highlights its choice of a particular competitive strategy. Probably the most widely used typology of this sort is Porter's (1980), which distinguishes between low-cost and differentiated strategies and allows for a focus option that cuts across the two. In his presentations to executives, Porter cites Nucor as an exemplar of successful focus, with an emphasis on low costs.

---

[4] Although Nucor is currently expending such relationships, considerations of sequencing suggest that such transformations should be seen as a consequence of its success, not at an important cause.

This characterization can be tested with the help of a data base on U.S. minimills assembled by Jeffrey Arthur. In late 1988, Arthur mailed questionnaires about competitive strategy and human resource management (the topic of the next section) to, respectively, the general managers and the personnel managers of all 54 U.S. minimill plants identified in that year's Directory of Iron and Steel Plants. The response rate was well over 50% and included four Nucor plants. Although Arthur's published work (1992, 1994) does not identify individual plants, he was kind enough to share with me the averages reported by Nucor and non-Nucor plants after being authorized by Nucor's top management to do so.

According to Arthur's data, Nucor's plant general managers considered themselves significantly less, not more, focused than their counterparts at other minimills.[5] The hypothesis that Nucor emphasized low costs fares better. Even so, there are problems in attributing its success solely to its choice of this competitive strategy. First, Arthur's (1992) cluster analysis indicates that 30% of the non-Nucor plants followed a low-cost strategy as well, making it hard to assert uniqueness for Nucor in this regard. Second, while the plants in the low-cost cluster reported significantly lower numbers of product types, sizes, and grades than the others, Nucor did not stand out along these product-related dimensions: Its plants reported about the same number of product types and significantly higher numbers of product sizes and grades than the other low-cost plants.

My own conclusion is that while it makes sense to assert that Nucor achieved a low-cost position, understanding *how* it did so requires looking beyond the product-related attributes emphasized by Porter to Nucor's organization of the factors or resources under its control *and* the alignment of its organization with its competitive strategy. The evidence presented in the last section on Nucor's operating and investment efficiency focuses attention on its human and capital resources, broadly defined. Sections 4 and 5 of this paper describe in some detail Nucor's policies in these two areas and their complementarities with each other and with the company's low-cost strategy. Much of the discussion can be summarized in terms of the two virtuous cycles depicted in Figure 2: Low costs implied relatively high capacity utilization rates and thereby enabled human resource management policies that yielded (additional) operating efficiencies; they also permitted rapid expansion that led, in conjunction with appropriate capital resource management policies, to investment efficiencies.

---

[5] This conclusion will not surprise industry participants, who regard Florida Steel, which focuses on construction markets in the southeastern part of the United States, as perhaps the most obvious practitioner of a focus strategy. Nucor, in contrast, has a broader—and expanding—product line and national scope.

Figure 2
Competitive Advantage and Internal Organization at Nucor

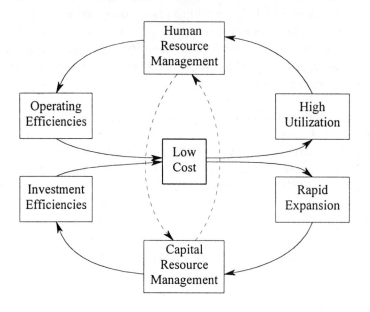

4. Human Resource Management at Nucor

The broadest characterization of Nucor's human resource management policies is the one provided by its erstwhile personnel manager, John Savage (1985, pp. 241-242): "To a certain extent we take the approach that each . . . [group of workers] is in business for itself. We supply the building, the equipment, the know-how, and the supervision. But what they earn depends directly on how much they produce."

The discussion in this section will begin by describing Nucor's incentive plan for its production workers and comparing it with other minimills on the basis of data from Arthur's (1994) survey of minimill personnel managers. It will then review other incentive programs, primarily for other employees. It will conclude by considering the ways in which Nucor ensured broad employee participation in decision making.

Production Incentives

Nucor's top management regarded its production incentive plan as the most important element of its incentive compensation program. F. Kenneth Iverson (1991, pp. 287-288), Nucor's chief executive officer for more than 20 years, described this plan succinctly:

> We take groups of about twenty-five to thirty-five people who are doing some complete task, such as making good billet tons, good roll tons, or good finish tons. We have more than seventy-five groups of this type in the company. We establish a bonus that is based on a standard. If the employee group exceeds that standard in a week, they receive extra compensation based upon the amount of increased production over the standard. Very simple. There is no maximum. It is never changed unless we make a large

capital expenditure that significantly changes the productivity opportunities for the employee.

Each production group included a foreman and maintenance workers as well as production workers; quality inspectors were, however, excluded. Standards were defined in terms of anticipated production time or tonnage produced and were based on historical experience. Base pay for Nucor's nonunionized workforce was less than that of steelworkers at most other minimills and integrated steelmakers, but incentive bonuses averaging 80–150% of their base pay lifted their cash compensation to comparable levels (see Table II). These incentives were reinforced by stiff penalties: Anyone late for a shift lost a day's bonus, and anyone who missed a shift lost the bonus for the week. No bonus was paid when equipment did not operate. When market downturns forced Nucor to limit its capacity utilization, the production bonus remained in place but might be based on one two fewer days of work, reducing the average worker's total pay 15–20%.

Such explicit, objective, output-based linear compensation formulas that provide high-powered performance incentives as well some insurance to effort- and risk-averse workers have attractive theoretical properties and are, therefore, a staple of microeconomic models of efficient incentive contracting. They tend, however, to be rarer in practice than in theory (Mitchell et al., 1990). Nucor's minimill competitors, in particular, did not offer their production workers such high-powered, output-based incentives (see Table II).

Table II
Comparative Human Resource Variables

	Nucor Plants		Non-Nucor Plants		
	Number	Mean	Number	Mean	T Statistic
Number of production workers per supervisor	4	10.37	26	6.05	3.43
Total employment cost per production/maintenance worker ($/hour)	4	21.69	24	19.34	1.27
Bonus or incentive payments as a % of total employment cost	4	56.25	22	15.52	7.27
Turnover rate of production/ maintenance workers (% per year)	4	2.66	25	5.82	0.98

Source: Adapted from Arthur (1994) on the basis of a private communication.

The effectiveness of high-powered, output-based compensation for production workers at Nucor appears to have been related to its low-cost strategy. It would have been less successful with an output-based compensation formula if it had been following a differentiated strategy instead since quality tends to be harder to meter than quantity.[6] Nucor's low costs also increased its optimal capacity utilization level relative to its competitors, narrowing the scope for divergence between output and profit maximization. In addition, the reputation that Nucor's management

---

[6] Chaparral, for instance, placed more emphasis on differentiation and preferred to have its production workers perform an essential part of the quality control function.

had developed over several decades for not unfairly ratcheting up standards and the participation of its workers in decision making (discussed toward the end of this section) probably helped facilitate high-powered incentives as well.

An aspect of Nucor's production incentive plan that appears more heterodox in terms of macroeconomic theory is its emphasis on rewarding groups of workers, rather than individuals, for exceeding predetermined productivity standards: Although the base pay would differ from a foreman to a general laborer, they would receive the same percentage bonus if they belonged to the same production group. This arrangement simplified the measurement of output and encouraged teamwork (e.g., on-the-job training of new workers by more experienced ones). Its most important effect, however, seems to have been to create peer pressure for individual workers to exert themselves for the good of the group. For instance, if a group missed its weekly production target because of a few workers' absenteeism, *all* its members lost their bonus for that week. By harnessing peer pressure, Nucor's managers were largely able to delegate the monitoring of production workers' activities to each production group without worrying about free-rider problems (although other groups engaged in similar activities yielded useful performance yardsticks). As a result, Nucor was able to get by with a higher ratio of production workers to supervisors than most other minimills (see Table II).

A second potential problem with group-level incentives may stem from heterogeneity in the skill or motivation levels of group members. Nucor addressed this problem by emphasizing the recruitment and retention of relatively homogenous, motivated workers ("farm boys," in the words of Nucor's COO, Correnti). To be specific, Nucor offered its production workers, most of whom were novices at steel making, the prospect of making significantly more than other workers in the rural areas where it built its plants. This led to an excess supply of job applicants and let Nucor use psychological and other tests to screen applicants for goal orientation, self-reliance, and, one would guess, aversion to unionization. In addition, the combination of "stretch" standards and substantial payoffs to surpassing them induced less able or motivated workers to self-select themselves out of the organization over time even if they mistakenly signed up with it. The importance of self-selection as opposed to screening—and, by implication, of the hidden heterogeneity of workers—is indicated by the change in turnover rates at the Darlington, South Carolina, mill since its start-up, from 35% in 1969 to 20% in 1970 (Marshall, 1975), and a more gradual decline, to 2–3%, since then. Steady-state turnover rates appear to have been somewhat lower at Nucor plants than at plants operated by other minimills (see Table II).

Other Incentives

Nucor's incentive compensation plans for nonproduction employees resembled the production incentive plan in that they involved explicit linear compensation formulas based on some measure of collective performance (see Figure 3). Base compensation began below industry norms for all employee groups except salaried employees (accountants, engineers, secretaries, etc.) whose base was supposed to be 100% of comparable local rates. Performance measures for nonproduction employees were based on financial performance rather than tonnages and varied across groups: Officers (corporate managers and plant general managers) were rewarded on the basis of corporate return on equity, department heads (an average of six per plant) on the basis of their plant's return on assets, and salaried employees on the basis of plant (or occasionally, corporate) returns.

Figure 3
Nucor Incentive Structure

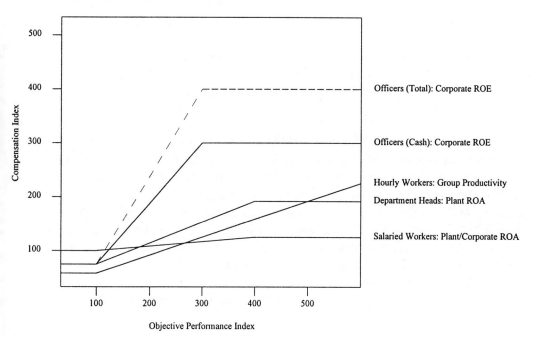

Source: Casewriter's estimates based on Nucor compensation schedules.

Incentive payments under these programs to nonproduction employees were capped (unlike payments to production employees). These programs were topped off with others that shared 10% of each year's pretax profits among nonofficers (including production workers) and awarded them discretionary bonuses in years when corporate performance was particularly strong; granted stock options to officers and other key employees, such as engineers experienced at plant construction and start-up; and offered a childrens' college education allowance to all employees.

The incentive intensities of these programs can be compared with those for production workers, whose bonuses averaged 80–150% of base pay. For department heads, incentive bonuses were capped at a level of 75%, which was rarely realized. The cap for salaried employees was only 20% and similarly elusive. Senior officers, in contrast, stood to make several times their base salaries in bonuses in a good year. The relatively low intensity of the incentives for department heads and by salaried employees can be rationalized in terms of the limited impact of their efforts on performance and, perhaps, measurement problems. The greater intensity of incentives for officers compared with production workers seems to reflect the officers' greater risk tolerance (their total compensation tended to fall by 60–70% during recessions, compared with 15–20% for production workers) and the arguably wider discretion that they exercised in making their choices. In addition, the fact that payments to officers accounted for only 1–3% of total compensation, whereas payments to production workers accounted for close to two-thirds of it may have restricted the intensity of the incentives that could be offered to workers, because of the constraint that incentive-induced improvements should not entirely be dissipated in the form of increased compensation costs.

The compensation package for Nucor's CEO, Iverson, is of particular interest because Iverson essentially dictated the terms of his own compensation through his control of Nucor's board of directors: All other board members either worked under him or had done so in the past. Iverson's compensation was related in a transparent way to the compensation of other officers. More specifically, a portion of each year's pretax earnings in excess of a preset earnings base was set aside for all officers and allocated among them in proportion to their base pay and was split, again in a preset way, between cash and deferred stock compensation. Since the institution of this incentive compensation plan, just after Iverson became president in 1965, the earnings base had been revised 13 times, from $500,000 to $80,000,000, which is suggestive of self-restraint on his part.

Additionally Iverson's compensation package was substantially lower and more incentive-intensive than his counterparts at integrated U.S. steelmakers.[7] Under the brunt of a recession, for example, Iverson's compensation shrank from $276,000 in 1981 to $107,000 in 1982. Despite the posturing they were then engaged in vis-à-vis unionized production workers, the average compensation of the CEOs of the seven largest integrated steelmakers dropped only from $708,000 to $489,000 over that time. Since Nucor's nonunionized production workers earn only slightly less than unionized steelworkers, Nucor appears to have compressed its vertical span of compensation relative to integrated steelmakers (as well as other large U.S. companies, for which Blinder and Krueger (1993) report a CEO-to-worker wage ratio of 17.5). Such vertical compression may have promoted participatory management, which is the subject of the next subsection.

A final point that should be emphasized in this subsection is that although Nucor's plant general managers were compensated on the basis of corporate performance measures, they were primarily held accountable for the performance of the plants they managed. Plant-level accountability involved sticks instead of carrots: The corporate office focused much of its attention on assuring that each plant general manager achieved an annual contribution equal to at least 25% of the net assets employed at his plant, or was able to explain the shortfall adequately. Although several plant managers had been dismissed over the years for failing to clear this hurdle, judgment was exercised in its application: At least one manager was fired for clearing the hurdle by cutting back on investment (thereby compressing the plant's asset base). In addition, exceptions to the 25% ROA rule were entertained for new plants and for depressed market conditions—conditions under which other plants making the same products provided useful yardsticks. The purpose of supplementing the plant ROA stick with the corporate ROE carrot seems to have been to foster communication and cooperation among plants scattered at about a dozen distinct sites by forcing plant general managers to attend to interplant as well as intraplant concerns. Note that Nucor applied this principle of tying individual compensation to performance at some higher level of aggregation to nonofficers as well.

Participatory Management

The discussion in this section has focused, so far, on Nucor's incentive schemes. Broader evidence suggests, however, that the efficiency of such schemes may depend on employee participation in decision making (e.g., Blinder, 1990). In addition to supporting this suggestion, Nucor's human resource management policies shed light on the specifics of participatory

---

[7] Comparisons with other large minimills are precluded by their privately held status or clouded by their dissimilar governance structures.

management, which is useful in view of the vagueness of the term. Nucor promoted participatory management by flattening its hierarchy, decentralizing decision making, disclosing information widely, limiting nonpecuniary as well as pecuniary differences among employees and guaranteeing individual rights. The first three of these policies, which are cited (among others) by Walton (1992), made worker participation possible, and the last two, which are discussed by Levine and Tyson (1990), made such participation desirable by forging more trust and cooperation between workers and managers than purely pecuniary incentives would. Each of these policies deserves to be described in more detail.

Nucor restricted supervisory personnel to four layers: the chief executive and chief operating officers (the latter position was added in 1984 to cope with rapid growth), plant general managers, department heads, and foremen. Integrated U.S. steelmakers tended, in contrast, to sport as many as a dozen layers of management. And even Chaparral, which was celebrated for its participatory human resource management, employed five supervisory layers at its single plant. Since Nucor operated plants at about a dozen sites and had several times as many employees as Chaparral, the flatness of its hierarchy cannot be ascribed to the limited scope or scale of its operations. As Iverson (1991, p. 286) explained it, "The fewer [layers] you have, the more effective it is to communicate with employees and the better it is to make rapid and effective decisions."

To make this flat hierarchy work, Nucor tried to decentralize as many decisions as the next layer down could manage. This meant that individual plants operated as independent divisions. All decisions except capital expenditures, major organizational changes, hiring and firing at or above the department head rank, and pricing were made at the plant level.[8] Nucor can be contrasted in this regard with Florida Steel, which centralized purchasing, sales, credit collections, and engineering. In addition, Arthur's (1994) data indicate that Nucor's plants scored higher on a categorical measure of decentralization than did non-Nucor plants, although the difference was not statistically significant. As far as Nucor's corporate office was concerned, it focused, in order of importance, on monthly operating reports, weekly tonnage reports, and monthly cash management reports from each plant. The standardization of these reports and the simplicity of Nucor's low-cost/high-utilization strategy prevented the wide span of control at the corporate office from breaking down even though the ratio of corporate employees to plants approximated unity.

For the local decision making built into decentralization to work well, information had to be communicated from other parts of the organization to the locus of decision. Communication within plants was facilitated by the informal ceiling of 500 employees per plant. Some communication across plants occurred through formal channels, such as the three meetings with corporate officers that all plant general managers attended each year. The bulk of it took place, however, through informal channels, such as one-to-two day visits that managers and workers frequently made to other plants. The corporate office encouraged information transfer by disseminating monthly operating statements for all plants to each plant manager, by setting up an incentive system that, as described in the last subsection, motivated plants to beat the performance targets set for them instead of each other and to take an interest in overall corporate

---

[8] Centralization of the first three types of decisions is common in multidivisional organizations according to Markham (1973). The centralization of pricing decisions can be interpreted as an efficient response to situations in which changes in process must respond to global shocks, such as general economic downturns or upturns, rather than just local ones. See Aoki (1988), especially Chapter 2.

performance as well, and by ensuring that experienced engineers and operators from existing plants were tapped for the construction and start-up of new ones.

The efficiency of informed decentralization depended, in addition, on trust and cooperation between workers and management. The compressed vertical span of compensation described earlier encouraged such a climate, as did Nucor's strenuous efforts to minimize nonpecuniary, status-related differences among employees. All employees received the same benefits in such respects as insurance and holidays. On the factory floor, everybody wore green spark-proof jackets and hardhats (unlike integrated mills, where different colors signaled different levels of authority). There were no assigned parking places or company cars, boats, or planes. Everybody who had to travel by air flew coach class, and frequent flyer awards earned on business travel were redeemed for future business travel. Each year's annual report listed all employees on its cover in alphabetical order. Iverson and other officers answered their own phones and promised to respond to questions from any employee within a day.

Nucor also fostered a climate of trust and cooperation by safeguarding worker's rights in a number of ways, particularly through a just-cause dismissal policy and a policy of never laying off workers during economic downturns. The credibility of these policies was reinforced by the reputation forged by Nucor's top managers for living up to the spirit as well as the letter of implicit contracts with workers. The practicality of these policies, especially the latter one, can be related to Nucor's low costs. Low costs were of additional importance because they permitted rapid expansion: Nucor's steelmaking capacity had grown 20-fold in as many years despite a decline in U.S. steel shipments over that period. Rapid expansion encouraged workers with specific knowledge (in the sense of Hayek [1945]) to suggest ways of improving efficiency, particularly labor productivity, for reasons articulated by Milgrom and Roberts (1992, p. 280): "For a growing firm, jobs may be best protected by ensuring that the company's costs are low enough to allow the growth to continue. In comparison, when output in a company is shrinking, the interests of capitalists and laborers in finding labor-saving, cost-reducing production methods may become sharply divergent."

Participatory human resource management could, therefore, be predicted to prove more of a win-win solution for Nucor's suppliers of capital and labor than for the stakeholders in competitively disadvantaged, shrinking integrated steelmakers or even in other minimills that had constrained their own growth by restricting their geographic or product scope.

5. Capital Resource Management at Nucor

The last section focused on Nucor's interactions with its human resources, particularly those responsible for operating its capital resources. It is appropriate to work backward at this point, to investments in capital resources that, according to Iverson (as well as Savage, who was cited at this point in the previous section), defined the potential for subsequent operating improvements. The discussion in this section will begin by describing Nucor's financial policies. It will go on to discuss how financial capital resources were allocated among opportunities to invest in specialized physical capital resources. It will conclude with a review of how Nucor actually implemented its investments, particularly in new plants.

Financial Policies

Nucor's financial policies involved restricting long-term debt to less than 30% of total financial capital, not issuing additional equity shares to the public, and trying to increase per-share cash dividends from year to year while limiting payouts to a modest fraction of net income. This subsection begins with an examination of Nucor's debt-to-capital ceiling, the policy on which its top managers placed particular emphasis.[9] It will then consider the collective implication of Nucor's financial policies: its preference for financing most of its investment out of retained earnings.

Nucor typically stayed well below its debt-to-capital ceiling of 30%: Its level of indebtedness amounted to 8% in early 1992. Perhaps the most common way to explain why low financial leverage may be a value-maximizing choice in a particular case is to invoke industry (or strategic group) characteristics. The steel industry is marked by high cyclicality, fixed costs, and competitive intensity, characteristics commonly held to imply low optimal debt-to-capital ratios. There is a problem, however, with this generic explanation for Nucor's low leverage: Other steelmakers, minimills as well as integrated ones, typically had higher levels of leverage and lower debt ratings than Nucor (see Table III).

A more satisfactory explanation of Nucor's low debt level is suggested by the fact that all the competitors listed in Table III found their investment programs in real (physical) capital constrained, to a degree, by their debt levels. Such constraints on overall investment at the three integrated steelmakers, USX, LTV, and Bethlehem, are well known. Of the minimills listed, both Northwestern Steel and Wire and Florida Steel suffered financial distress subsequent to 1986 (the latter as a result of an overleveraged buyout). Chaparral felt somewhat constrained through the mid-1980s by the financial weakness of its 50% owner, Co-Steel; it subsequently had to cover several years of losses at the cement operations of Texas Industries, the other original co-owner, that bought out Co-Steel's interest in 1985.

In fact, one can argue that Nucor might not have invested in thin-slab casting when it did if it had been as leveraged as other minimills. By the time the thin-slab casting opportunity arose, Nucor was already committed to a joint venture to produce wide-flange beams. Simultaneous pursuit of the two opportunities was projected to require capital expenditures (including start-up costs) of $100 million in 1987, $250 million in 1988, and a balance of $60 million or more in 1989. If Nucor, a company with three-quarters of a billion dollars in sales at the time, had been as highly leveraged as other management would probably have thought much harder about borrowing the money they did to pursue both projects.

---

[9] For value-maximizing explanations of corporate reluctance to cut dividends and to issue additional equity, consult the signaling-based models of Bhattacharya (1979) and Myers and Majluf (1984), respectively.

Table III
Comparative Steel Company Debt Ratings in 1986

Company	Debt Rating
Nucor Corp.	Aa
Other Publicly Held Minimills	
Texas Industries	Ba2
(Owner of Chaparral Steel Co.)	
Northwestern Steel and Wire Co.	Caa (Subordinated debt)
Florida Steel Corp.	Caa (Subordinated debt)
Integrated Firms	
U.S. Steel Corp.	Baa3
LTV Steel Co.	Ca
Bethlehem Steel Co.	Ba2

Source: Moody's Rating Service.

By implication, Nucor's generally low level of indebtedness can be interpreted as a value-maximizing response to its competitive advantage. This interpretation rests on the idea that debt is a relatively binding commitment to pay out future cash flows and therefore limits managerial discretion to invest. For this reason, it has been argued that a company with a very limited menu of profitable investment opportunities should take on high levels of debt (Jensen, 1986). By a symmetric argument, a company that enjoys a rich stream of such opportunities, perhaps because it has a competitive advantage, might be expected to keep its leverage low most of the time—especially if it doesn't want to tap the equity markets either.

This benefit must, of course, be weighed against the potential costs of limiting debt levels and, more generally, of self-financing most investment. The attention paid to self-sustaining growth equations by *Fortune 500* companies in the United States indicates that one of the principal concerns with a self-finance constraint is that it may limit growth for financial, rather than competitive, reasons. Since Nucor expanded its capacity 20-fold over as many years, this constraint appears not to have pinched much: Its competitive advantage expanded its internal supply of funds about as rapidly as it increased effective demand for them by unlocking profitable investment opportunities. While either the supply-side or the demand-side effects may dominate in a particular case, Morone and Paulson's (1991) interviews of top managers at 15 U.S. firms (including Nucor and three other firms from the steel sector) suggest that firms with competitive advantages manage to strike a stable balance between inside and outside sources of financial capital, while firms without such advantages are apt to complain about the availability and cost of outside capital.

Another potential problem with low debt levels in particular and self-finance in general is the one originally emphasized by Jensen (1986): Financial self-sufficiency buffers managers from capital markets and may, therefore, end up expanding the scope of the agency problem between managers and capital suppliers, particularly shareholders. Several governance-related indicators that are supposed to aggravate concerns about such an agency problem (Jensen and Warner, 1988) would seem to raise alarms about Nucor. Nucor lacked large outside stockholders to monitor its top managers through most of the 1970s and 1980s: Iverson was the single largest stockholder, with holdings of 1.3% in 1986, more than the median but less than the mean for CEOs of large U.S. corporations (Jensen and Murphy, 1990). Over most of that period, the board consisted of either insiders who served under Iverson or "outsiders" who had previously done so. Iverson himself enjoyed enormous clout as the manager who had presided over Nucor's steady, surprisingly successful climb out of near bankruptcy since he took its helm in 1965. He had worked with the other top corporate managers, David Aycock, who retired as chief operating officer in 1988, and chief financial officer Sam Siegel, over an even longer period of time. Under their stewardship, Nucor had steadily added anti-takeover amendments to its corporate charter.

Figure 1 suggests, nonetheless, that Nucor's powerful management did well by the company's much less powerful shareholders. The reputation developed by top managers for not abusing their discretion at the exception of the company's (other) stakeholders—its suppliers of capital and of human resources—seems to have kept fears of managerial opportunism within reasonable bounds through 1992. The company's competitive advantage enhanced the credibility of a reputation for nonabuse by generating substantial rents that could (partially) be passed on to stakeholders. Note that the lack of a narrow focus on capital suppliers is consistent with a central feature of participatory management: "The body of employees is, together with the body of shareholders, explicitly or implicitly recognized as a constituent of the firm, and its interests are considered in the formation of managerial policy" (Aoki, 1987, p. 265).

Investment Definition and Approval

The allocation of capital resources at Nucor was an informal, iterative process. Ideas for new investments had to relate to steel—a boundary system by which top managers influenced their definition—but could come from anywhere. Participatory management ensured a steady stream of investment proposals, mostly modest ones, from the factory floor. Larger or more radical investments were, however, more frequently defined at higher levels. The investment at Crawfordsville, for example, can be traced to a search initiated by Iverson in 1983, a year after Nucor experienced its first decline in annual sales since he took charge, for ways to enter the flat-rolled sheet segment. Nucor's managers also tried to build a new plant or rebuild an old one every year, for reasons described in the next subsection.

Investment proposals were first evaluated at the organizational level at which they surfaced. The three top corporate officers, CEO Iverson, COO Aycock (subsequently, Correnti), and CFO Siegel, signed off on all capital expenditures, but their actual level of involvement in the approval process depended on the size and the radicality of the commitment being contemplated. Relatively small, incremental projects were routinely approved if they satisfied the criteria described in the next paragraph. To evaluate large, risky commitments such as the thin-slab caster at Crawfordsville, the three senior officers formed a task force to which other personnel were deputed as necessary—a pattern that fits well with process models of capital resource allocation (e.g., Bower, 1970).

Nucor contradicted conventional wisdom, however, by not using net present value (NPV) analysis or internal rates of return (IRR) to evaluate investment proposals. Investments in new (rebuilt) plants had to achieve a 25% ROA within five years of start-up (refurbishment). Investments in capacity expansion had to achieve payback over a shorter time horizon and investments in cost reduction over an even shorter horizon. The limited number of investments in technology development were not subject to such financial criteria. The use of different criteria for different types of investment projects appears to reflect both dissimilarities in their risk-return characteristics and measurement constraints.

Nucor's investments in new or refurbished plants merit particular attention because of their magnitude and complexity. The use of a 25% ROA rule focused ex ante financial analysis on the same measure that was used ex post to audit investment performance. While that commonality probably simplified postaudits, it begs the question of how Nucor was able to come up with a fairly specific principle that did not systematically discount cash flows, yet served it fairly well in evaluating them. Nucor's ability to devise such an effective principle can be explained in several different ways: The resource the steel industry used most intensively, physical capital was tangible and therefore relatively easy to measure; technological progress in steel making had been continuous rather than discontinuous, permitting a degree of reliance on the historical averages, as did the stability of Nucor's cost-based strategy and the inertia of the integrated steelmakers that it tried to take business away from; so too had Nucor's practice, discussed below, of continuously building or rebuilding its plants. Morone and Paulson's (1991) study, cited earlier, may tie in here as well because it suggests that discounted cash flow analysis is emphasized by disadvantaged competitors but may be deemphasized by competitors with advantages.

The 25% ROA hurdle is of interest parametrically as well as an instance of an apparently effective principle. Given Nucor's typical cash flow profiles on new (or completely rebuilt) plants, its accelerated depreciation schedules and its cost of capital, the target of a 25% ROA within five years implies an investment benefit-to-cost hurdle significantly higher than 1. Conventional financial theory insists, in contrast, that the investment hurdle should always equal 1. To understand this divergence, it is necessary to understand the investment implementation process at Nucor.

Investment Implementation

The financial policies and investment definition and approval procedures described above resulted in an investment pattern at Nucor that differed from most minimill competitors' in its somewhat greater steadiness and its emphasis on building or rebuilding entire sites rather than partially upgrading existing ones. As noted above, Nucor tried to build or rebuild one plant per year. This was a relatively high frequency: Of its four largest minimill competitors in 1986, North Star, which was then larger, had acquired four of its five steel plants, and two others, Northwestern Steel and Wire and Chaparral, operated only one plant each, which limited their opportunities for complete refurbishment. Most of the smaller competitors tended to be single-plant operations as well.

Nucor's clean-slate approach allowed coherence in site design in a way that could not have been achieved by jamming new technologies onto old ones. The emphasis on rapid refurbishment also helped ensure that the logic of Nucor's human resource management policies did not break down at the older sites because of the limited potential for improvement afforded by relatively dated technologies. The most important implication, however, of building or rebuilding a plant annually seems to have been the accumulation of a level of experience at investing in entire plants that could not have been attained had the frequency of such events been much lower. Nucor's investment implementation policies combined with its demonstrated investment efficiencies suggest that that experience allowed it to build up exceptional capabilities at plant construction and start-up.

Nucor designed its new plants as they were being built, speeding up construction. It had learned to configure them in ways that anticipated both expansion and the information ceiling of 500 employees per plant, and to minimize supplier holdup by locating them in rural areas where it had access to at least two railroads, low electricity rates, and plentiful water. Instead of relying on a turnkey contractor, as was common in the steel industry, Nucor acted as the general contractor for each of its construction projects. Contracting with individual suppliers tended to be quick and informal and usually involved, in another departure from industry norms, fixed-price contracts. Exceptions were occasionally made for new, untried equipment, such as SMS's thin-slab caster: Nucor then tried, in such cases, to build in performance incentives for key suppliers. Each construction project was managed by a core group of experienced engineers and operators drawn from other Nucor operations who worked alongside construction workers—many of whom were retained as the production workforce for the new plant. Organizing along these lines forged close work relations and an intimate understanding of each plant's physical character, facilitating further operating efficiencies.

According to Iverson, the key carriers of Nucor's experience at construction and start-up from one plant to the next were the experienced employees who were transferred to supervise those processes: "We can only train the skilled core needed to start up a new plant so quickly. For a new plant, they all come from other plants, so we have a time/person optimization problem. We have to ask ourselves if we have the people we need to build and run a new plant and, at the same time, do we have the quality people left when these people go to start up the plant."

The implication that such specialized resources, instead of fungible financial ones, were the key constraints on Nucor's growth in the operational short run helps explain why the company effectively imposed a benefit-to-cost hurdle significantly higher than 1 on its new or refurbished plants with its requirement that they yield a 25% ROA within five years. The affinities with Penrose's (1959) theory of the short-run constraints on the growth of firms are striking.

6. The Sustainability of Nucor's Advantage

The last two sections explored the associations between Nucor's internal organization and its competitive advantage. They touched only in passing, though, on the reasons why Nucor's organizational arrangements were not more widely imitated by its competitors if they made such clear sense in the context of steel making. Possible explanations can be grouped in terms of three types of factors: input factors that Nucor or its competitors could purchase or otherwise obtain from others, organizational factors that were specific to Nucor, and precommitments by Nucor's key competitors. The second and third categories seem more compelling than the first one.

Input Factors

Input factors are defined here as factors that firms purchase or obtain from others. Such factors are not initially specialized to particular firms, although they may become so through investment or contracting. Input factors can garner rents when they are in fixed or limited supply. Scarcity of at least three types of inputs, labor, land, and capital might be cited as explaining Nucor's sustained superior performance. Specifically, it might be argued that Nucor sustained its competitive advantage by building up superior access to relatively able workers, to relatively superior sites, or to a relatively abundant pool of financial capital. Consider each of these explanations in turn.

The hypothesis that Nucor sustained its advantage because it attracted and retained workers of high ability (or amenability to incentives) does not appear compelling. Even if it is true, as some authors (e.g., Klein, 1984) have asserted, that "farm boys" tend to have a superior work ethic, the success of Japanese manufacturing firms investing in the United States, particularly automobile companies, in recruiting workers rurally suggests that one relatively small U.S. steelmaker was in no position to tie up their supply in a way that would lock out its direct competitors.

The hypothesis that Nucor sustained its advantage because it preempted superior sites does not fare much better. While markets for raw material inputs and product output are indeed regionalized in the steel industry, the value of spatial preemption by minimills is capped by their low minimal efficient sales. In addition, the steady expansion of minimills at the expense of integrated steelmakers makes maneuvering to lock minimill rivals out of attractive regions more problematic than the stagnant overall demand for steel might suggest. Finally, this explanation, like the previous one, presumes unique foresight (or luck) on the part of Nucor: Otherwise, competition for superior workers or sites would presumably have bid up their costs, with scarcity rents being passed through to the respective suppliers and, from a firm-level perspective, being dissipated.

Third, it might be hypothesized that Nucor sustained its advantage because it had built up superior access to sources of financial capital. While this hypothesis presumes imperfections in capital markets, it is, as indicated in Section 5, a moderately plausible explanation of why at least some of Nucor's smaller minimill competitors did not more quickly imitate its move into flat-rolled sheet via thin-slab casting. It seems rather less plausible in the context of less lumpy investment opportunities, which predominate in competition among minimills. And even in the specific context of thin-slab casting, it fails to explain why much larger integrated steelmakers, with access to the absolute amount of cash required, didn't imitate Nucor's move more quickly. I will revisit the importance of capital constraints in the last part of this section.

Other types of input factors such as scrap and technology seem much less likely explanations of Nucor's sustained superior performance. As noted in Section 3, Nucor coordinated its plants' purchases of scrap through an independent purchasing agent who pooled its demands with its competitor and for technology, it relied on suppliers who licensed their equipment and processes nonexclusively and with flow-back clauses.

Organizational Factors

Organizational factors are defined here as factors that firms accumulate internally. This tends to make them more firm-specific than input factors. Two kinds of firm-specific organizational factors seem to have played particularly important roles in sustaining Nucor's superior performance: its superior experience at plant construction and start-up, and the reputation its top managers had developed for not abusing their considerable discretion.

Section 5 assembled evidence of the superiority of Nucor's experience at plant construction and start-up (the virtuous capital resource management cycle introduced at the end of Section 3). Such experience tends to be a relatively sustainable source of competitive advantage when it is held collectively by an organization instead of being vested in a few individuals who can cart it off to competitors. This condition seems to have been satisfied at Nucor in the past, although it will be tested by the departure, in August 1993, of three top managers from Nucor's Crawfordsville plant to set up their own thin-slab casting minimill. And the credibility of threats to imitate Nucor by rapidly accumulating experience internally—as opposed to poaching it— may have been compromised by competitors' poor relative positions: Footrace models of competition reveal that when one player gets far enough ahead of the pack, its competitors may rationally elect not to try to catch up. More generally, a head start at getting the virtuous experience-based cycle going may allow a competitor to outpace its rivals thereafter. In addition, as the next subsection shows, imitation of Nucor's strategy of accumulating experience at investing in entire plants was at least partially precluded by precommitments that key competitors had made.

Another organizational factor that appears to have mattered at Nucor was the reputation its top managers had cultivated since the mid-1960s for not abusing the company's workers or its shareholders, with ramifications for its human resource and financial policies, which were discussed, respectively, in Sections 4 and 5. Section 4, in particular, concentrated on the virtuous human resource management cycle introduced at the end of Section 3. In terms of sustainability, the idea is that it may be very hard to get such a virtuous cycle going unless a firm starts out with the "right" reputation. In addition, Nucor probably benefited from its reputation as a tough product market rival willing to slash prices in order to increase volume—a reputational effect also enhanced by its low-cost position. Reputations can be relatively sustainable sources of competitive advantage because of the long lags that competitors may face in imitating them, lags that may even tip the scales against imitation.

A third kind of organizational explanation of Nucor's sustained superior performance turns on the possibility that superior organizational forms may be *intrinsically* inimitable. Three sources of such intrinsic inimitability have been articulated in the literature on strategic management: unique historical circumstances, causal ambiguity, and the social complexity of organizational phenomena that may make it impossible for firms to systematically manage or influence them (e.g., Barney 1989). The three arguments deserve to be sketched and assessed.

Unique historical circumstances evoke explanations such as the following: Iverson inherited the idea of a production incentive plan from Vulcraft's joist division and was simply the first manager to apply it to steel making as well as steel fabrication. But to argue, as is sometimes attempted, that unique historical circumstances straitjacket managerial behavior is to imply that irreversibilities render imitation intrinsically infeasible. Such a position emphasizes the dead hand of the past at the expense of the visible hand of managerial coordination; it would surely be useful to supplement it with some consideration of the possibility that imitation may be costly but not intrinsically infeasible.[10] Causal ambiguity is a more subtle construct, one that focuses on ambiguity about the connections among policy choices and outcomes. It would not, however, seem to characterize the case being considered: Nucor's organizational choices complemented its competitive strategy simply but powerfully and were well known to its competitors given the relatively free interfirm flow of information in the steel industry, especially among minimills. Finally, the idea of social complexity is useful in that it calls attention to complementarities and how they may render piecemeal imitation of superior organizational arrangements inappropriate. Once again, however, its more extreme interpretations stress the strict infeasibility of imitation at the expense of the possibility that imitation may be feasible but regarded as undesirable, a possibility implied by two of Nucor's key competitors, as described in the next subsection.

---

[10] For a general treatment that tries to integrate irreversibilities and autonomous strategic behavior, see Ghemawat (1991).

Competitors' Precommitments

The preceding inferences about the sustainability of Nucor's competitive advantage were supplemented by interviews with managers at the U.S. Steel division of USX and Chaparral. While other competitors might also have considered imitating Nucor, these two seemed, for different reasons, to figure toward the head of the queue: U.S. Steel was still the largest integrated domestic steelmaker and was, therefore, disproportionately affected by Nucor's thin-slab casting plant at Crawfordsville, which allowed it to enter the last bastion of integrated steelmakers, flat-rolled sheet; and Chaparral was considered Nucor's leading minimill rival in terms of its organizational capabilities. Given the salience of Nucor's commitment to make flat-rolled sheet via thin-slab casting, interviews at both companies focused on why they hadn't more quickly imitated that particular move. Both turned out to have considered doing so within five years of first adoption by Nucor. Both had held back because of precommitments they had made as well as some of the factors that have already been considered.

U.S. Steel, the traditional industry leader and still the largest, most financially healthy integrated steelmaker, was first prompted to compare twin-slab casting and conventional continuous casting after the 1987 settlement of a six-month strike that committed it to modernize casting at its mill in Monongehela River Valley (henceforth referred to as Mon Valley). Conventional continuous casting appeared more attractive to it than did thin-slab casting for several reasons. The 10 miles that separated the steel-making facility and the rolling mill at Mon Valley posed no particular problem for conventional continuous casting but penalized thin-slab casting since it was supposed to be a continuously coupled process. Mon Valley's target capacity of 3 million tons per year meant that several thin-slab casters would have to be placed in parallel and their output continuously merged into a single stream passing through the rolling mill. Additionally, the labor savings that SMS was promoting as an important advantage of thin-slab casting would be limited by the inflexible work rules built into U.S. Steel's union contract. These economic precommitments combined with U.S. Steel's limited experience at implementing unfamiliar manufacturing technology to make it adopt conventional casting technology at Mon Valley.[11]

The failure of Chaparral, a minimill, to adopt thin-slab casting technology more quickly appears to reflect a strategy it had precommitted to instead of factor precommitments. Although Chaparral was starting to feel cramped at its single site and lacked recent experience at constructing and starting up new ones, it was an R&D-oriented organization with technological capabilities that were generally regarded as comparable or even somewhat superior to Nucor's. Its financial resources weren't quite as ample, but according to its top managers, that wasn't the key reason that it had refrained from thin-slab casting. The key reason seems, instead, to have been Chaparral's pursuit of a more differentiated competitive strategy that placed more emphasis on high margins and less on high volumes than did Nucor's. From Chaparral's perspective, SMS's thin-slab casting technology did not offer a large enough cost advantage over conventional methods for making flat-rolled sheet to be used to enter that large segment.

Chaparral concentrated, instead, on developing a proprietary process for thin-slab casting that would permit it to enter attractive but smaller niches with more substantial cost advantages. Interviews at Chaparral indicated that its competitive strategy influenced not only its decision not to adopt SMS's thin-slab casting technology but a panoply of organizational policies and procedures as well. Chaparral's top management had a harmonious relationship with the

---

[11] For additional information on U.S. Steel's choice at Mon Valley, consult Christensen and Rosenbloom (1991), and for additional interpretation, Ghemawat (1993).

company's production workers and paid them about as much on average as did Nucor, but without output-based bonuses: Production incentives appeared to be inconsistent with both Chaparral's relatively differentiated strategy (which had production workers performing their own quality control) and its top managers' personal values. In terms of capital investment, Chaparral emphasized investments in building up technological capabilities that were supposed to buffer the company from an intensification of rivalry in steel making: Its top managers professed no interest in propelling themselves down the experience curve by pursuing a "cookie-cutter approach that would have involved building the same basic plant over and over again at new sites.[12]

Such precommitments by key competitors complement Nucor's organizational advantages, discussed in the last subsection, as explanations of Nucor's sustained superior performance. The complementarity can be clarified by noting that stylized models of races among competitors, such as the models of competition to accumulate learning or experience referred to in the last subsection, typically feature competitors who pursue the same strategic position (unless, of course, they rationally elect to drop out of the race). Comparisons of U.S. Steel and, particularly, Chaparral, with Nucor suggest, however, that precommitments may lead at least some competitors in the same industry to pursue quite different positions within it. Such competitive heterogeneity provides an additional, albeit partial, explanation of why organizational arrangements that appear to be associated with a particular firm's superior performance aren't more widely imitated by its rivals: Some rivals may be pursuing alternate strategic paths.

7. Conclusions

Section 1 of this paper claimed that the case studies with a competitive slant can help advance our understanding of the links between competitive advantage and internal organization. The rest of this paper tried to validate that claim in a way that would interest researchers in both economies and management strategy.

To be more specific, Section 2 illustrated the extent to which competitors' performance levels may diverge even in "mature" industries, a possibility to which economists, in particular, need to be more sensitive. Sections 3–5 sorted through various explanations of superior performance and linked them to Nucor's internal organization in a way that was meant to interest researchers of both stripes and to induce them to think about organizational issues in a way that transcends the unidimensional treatments (e.g., types of products to be produced, workers' incentives, centralization versus decentralization, managerial predispositions, governance structures, etc.) that are traditional in larger-sample studies. Section 6 evaluated hypotheses about Nucor's historical ability to sustain its competitive advantage—a hot topic in management strategy but one that is often approached without the benefit of any data.

Having said as much, I should add that the case study raises questions as well as answering them. At a theoretical level, there are obvious opportunities for research into some of the organizational elements highlighted by the Nucor case. Perhaps the most obvious one concerns group (as opposed to individual) incentives, which Kandel and Lazear (1992) have made a start at studying, but which could benefit from additional work. Other topics include capital budgeting rules that do not systematically discount expected cash flows and the role that reputation can play in solving agency problems.

---

[12] For additional information on Chaparral's strategic orientation, consult Leonard-Barton (1992).

In regard to Nucor itself, it will be interesting to see how long the company can continue its record of rapid, profitable growth. Whether that record will survive the recent departure of the three top managers from Nucor's Crawfordsville plant or the age-related turnover of Nucor's original triumvirate of top managers that is likely to be completed soon should shed some light on the extent to which key organizational factors are vested in particular individuals. And if Nucor's growth does slacken for these or other reasons—such as constraints on the availability of either inexpensive scrap or expensive integrated steel-making capacity from which to wrest market share—that will afford an opportunity to examine the extent to which organizational arrangements optimized for rapid growth can be adapted to slower growth without disrupting profitability.

A final question that may linger on in the minds of readers is whether the benefits of such case studies justify the substantial fixed costs that must be incurred in undertaking them. Without wishing to discount the concerns about generalizability that motivate this question, I think that the answer is unambiguously affirmative. Our understanding of the details of internal organization is still confined to a very few companies, which is why the example of Lincoln Electric (Berg and Fast, 1975) is so widely bandied about by researchers in both organizational economics and management strategy. A few additional case studies can, therefore, contribute significantly to our understanding of the issues. Given the low-cost orientation of both Nucor and Lincoln Electric, detailed case studies of the internal organization of companies that successfully follow strategies of either horizontal or vertical product differentiation would seem to be a particularly high priority.

References

Aoki, Masahiko, 1987, "The Japanese Firm in Transition," in Kozo Yamamura and Yasukichi Yasuba, eds., *The Political Economy of Japan, 1: The Domestic Transformation*, Palo Alto, CA: Stanford University Press.

_____, 1988, *Information, Incentives, and Bargaining in the Japanese Economy*, Cambridge, UK: Cambridge University Press.

Arthur, Jeffrey B., 1992, "The Link Between Business Strategy and Industrial Relations Systems in American Steel Minimills," *Industrial and Labor Relations Review*, 45, 488-506.

_____, 1994, "The Effects of Human Resource Systems on Manufacturing Performance and Turnover," *Academy of Management Journal*, in press.

Barnett, Donald F. and Robert W. Crandall, 1986, *Up From Ashes: The Rise of the Steel Minimill in the United States*, Washington, DC: The Brookings Institution.

Barney, Jay, 1989, "Firm Resources and Sustained Competitive Advantage," *Journal of Management*, 17, 99–120.

Battese, G.E. and T.J. Coelli, 1988, "Prediction of Firm-Level Technical Efficiencies with a Generalized Frontier Production Function and Panel Data," *Journal of Econometrics*, 38, 387–399.

Berg, Norman and Norman Fast, 1975, "The Lincoln Electric Company," Harvard Business School case #376-028.

Bhattacharya, Sudipto, 1979, "Imperfect Information, Dividend Policy, and 'The Bird in the Hand' Fallacy," *Bell Journal of Economics*, 10, 259–270.

Blinder, Alan S., ed, 1990, *Paying for Productivity: A Look at the Evidence*, Washington, DC: The Brookings Institution.

_____ and Alan B. Krueger, 1993, "International Differences in Labor Turnover. A Comparative Study with Emphasis on the United States and Japan," in M. Porter, ed., *Capital Choices: Changing the Way America Invests in Industry*, Boston: Harvard Business School Press.

Bower, Joseph L., 1970, *Managing the Resource Allocation Process*, Boston: Harvard University Graduate School of Business Administration, Division of Research.

Caves, Richard E. and David R. Barton, 1990, *Efficiency in U.S. Manufacturing Industries*, Cambridge, MA.: The MIT Press.

Christensen, Clayton and Richard S. Rosenbloom, 1991, "Continuous Casting Investments at USX Corporation," Harvard Business School case #9-391-121.

Coase, Ronald H., 1988, "The Nature of the Firm: Influence," *Journal of Law, Economics & Organization*, 4, 33–47.

DeAngelo, Hary and Linda DeAngelo, 1991, "Union Negotiations and Corporate Policy," *Journal of Financial Economics*, 30, 3–43.

Nucor Corporation

Analysis of the U.S. Steel Industry

The U.S. steel industry is in the mature phase of its product life cycle. The industry grew rapidly from 1920 to W.W. II as the U.S. government invested billions developing an infrastructure for modern society on projects such as bridges, railroads, and power plants. At the same time, a wealthier U.S. population was purchasing consumer durables, such as automobiles and metal appliances, that used significant amounts of steel.

Since approximately 1950, the U.S. steel industry has been various states of a seminal decline. Two major factors contributing to this decline have been:

Lower Demand. Demand increased slowly through 1973 when it reached 130 million tons. Slower economic growth and substitution to lighter and stronger materials, such as plastic and aluminum, have resulted in a 40% decline in domestic demand since then.

Globally, the steel market is experiencing uneven growth. However, U.S. manufacturers have been unable to benefit from this growth given their high cost position. See Exhibit 1 at the end of this note.

Stronger global competitors. Lower-cost imports take 20% of the U.S. market. Without protectionist legislation, import levels would be even higher. Comparative cost data for global producers is provided in Exhibit 2.

The environment facing U.S. steel manufacturers is formidable. Exhibit 3 in this teaching note provides an analysis of the industry using Porter's 5 forces framework. Every aspect of the industry, with the possible exception of barriers to entry, suggests very low profitability.

This has been borne out by the industry's low profit margins over the past 2 decades, wide scale bankruptcies (particularly for large integrated producers) and massive elimination of jobs. Data on industry profitability is provided in Exhibits 4 and 5.

There are two qualifications to the Porter analysis. First, suppliers exert more power over minimill operators than over the integrated manufacturers. Whereas integrated mills have direct access to raw materials, minimills are dependent on supplies for an abundant supply of reasonably priced scrap.

Secondly, the profitability in the thin-rolled steel markets is higher than in the rest of the industry because substitute products have limited application in these markets and because barriers to entry (namely capital) have been traditionally higher than for the commodity end of the business. This distinction may not hold, however, with the advent of new technology.

In addition to being an industry with low potential for profitability, the steel industry involves high operating risks. The business is extremely capital intensive. (Property, plant and equipment comprises 72 percent of the assets on Nucor's balance sheet.) Steel output is tied closely to macroeconomic conditions. As a result, when the economy is soft, prices fall dramatically and output is rationalized. Most mills have breakeven production points of 80 percent capacity utilization. When lower demand persists for prolonged periods, higher cost steel manufacturers are forced into bankruptcy.

Key Success Factors in the Industry

Three characteristics stand out for as requisites for success in the steel industry:

Low cost provider position. Most steel markets are commodity products. Buying decisions are based on price with very limited product differentiation. All producers are expected to meet the same quality standards.

In a cyclical industry such as steel, the companies with the most competitive cost structures are the ones able to survive in the long-term. One useful metric for measuring cost effectiveness is the labor cost per ton.

Use of cutting edge technology. The decline of the American steel industry has been partially attributable to an uphill battle of competing against foreigners with more advanced technology.

Access to capital. The cyclically of the steel industry requires access to large pools of capital to survive industry downturns and to expand when market opportunities become available. The most successful companies are those which are able to generate large cash flows from operations during times when they are running at or near capacity utilization.

Nucor's Business Strategy

Nucor's business strategy follows closely along the lines of what is required for success in the steel industry. They have been one of the low cost providers in the steel industry since they entered this market 24 years ago. Their formula for success consists of several components:

Strategy:

Grow aggressively. Despite a contracting market, Nucor has always sought to capitalize on its low-cost provider position through expansion. This has meant successfully transitioning from a small regional producer to becoming the 7th largest steel maker in the U.S.

Avoid temptation to diversify. Nucor has grown exclusively within the steel industry rather than diversifying into other businesses. This strategy has entailed integrating both backwards and forwards within a period of 10 years.

Invest in technology. Nucor has used new technology several times to compete more effectively. Examples include using minimills (1968), developing a high-speed bolt factory (1986) and commercializing thin-slab casting technology (1988). A comparison of minimill vs. integrated mill is given in Exhibit 6.

Operations:

Minimize capital costa. Nucor could not afford to build integrated mills. The capital cost of building their minimills ($500 per ton) has been much lower than many of their larger integrated competitors ($3,000 per ton). Similarly, the capital costs for thin-slab casting are lower than conventional approaches which require repeated reheating.

Operate efficiently. Nucor's production costs per ton of steel have been the lowest in the industry—despite having the highest paid blue-collar workforce. The key is productivity; Nucor's productivity (as measured in tons of steel per man hour) was the second highest in the world in 1990. This lower labor expense can be seen in Exhibit 7, which provides an approximate comparison of Nucor's cost structure to an average for the industry.

Iverson recently commented "The way we look at it, this company does only two things well: it builds plants economically and runs them efficiently…. That is the whole company….

Finance:

Avoid using debt financing. Virtually all of Nucor's growth was generated from internal operations. Historically, Nucor's debt ratio (about 10 percent) has been significantly lower than that of its competitors (30–50 percent).

Critical Elements of Managerial Control System

The principal elements of Nucor's managerial control system are as follows:

Lean organizational structure. The case describes Iverson's aversion to bureaucracy. Nucor's corporate headquarters carried almost no overhead. Its managerial structure had only 4 levels—fewer than half of those used in other steel companies.

Highly decentralized environment. Nucor believed in letting divisions make their own operating decisions. Interference from corporate headquarters was extremely limited.

Uniform Performance Evaluations. All managers were judged by the financial results of their operations rather than subjective criteria. Every division was evaluated as a profit center using the same financial metric, Return on Assets, and the same target return.

Stringent Hiring Standards. Nucor's hiring practices were among the most selective in the industry. The high caliber of Nucor's workforce provided high productivity and allowed for minimum levels of supervisory involvement.

Pay-for-Performance Philosophy. Nucor's compensation philosophy was to pay well for high performance. Every worker in the company was on some type of incentive arrangement. Factory employees and top management had a considerable amount of their pay contingent on outstanding performance.

Strong Rapport Between Workers and Management. The larger steel companies historically suffered from poor relationships with their unions. Nucor's workforce, on the other hand, was nonunionized and accepted an agreement to work intensely in exchange for very competitive wages.

Investment in Training/Cross-Functionality. Nucor was not constrained by union regulations to employ workers in a particular job for a specified period of time. Nucor invested heavily in cross-training and expected all workers to be cross-functional. This flexibility provided the company with an edge over its competitors.

No Layoff/Share the Pain Program. Nucor had agreement with its workers that during periods of adverse business conditions, the work week would be reduced to 3 or 4 days. In exchange, management agreed not to lay off workers and to take a pay cut themselves.

Integration of Strategy and Control Systems

Nucor's strategy and managerial control systems complemented each other well. Nucor's basic strategy called for producing steel and steel products on a low cost basis. In order to successfully execute this strategy, Nucor sought to build marketshare and operate plants cheaply. Table 1 shows the relationship between this strategy and Nucor's control mechanisms.

Table 1
Relationship Between Strategy and Managerial Controls

Strategy	Managerial Control System
• Grow Aggressively	• Provide managers with maximum autonomy • Operate as profit centers and reward outstanding performance • Promote from within — encourages qualified managers to stay given ample career opportunities available
• Low Cost Provider	• Decentralized structure — eliminates the need for corporate O/H • Spartan headquarters/lack of exec perks — sets the tone for the rest of the company • Lean organizational structure — few meetings, memos
• Operate Plants Efficiently	• Pay-for-performance philosophy — piece rate pay system ensures high productivity • Investment in training so workers are cross-functional • Share the Pain Program — preserves flexibility to reduce costs during periods of slack demand • Utilize selective hiring process — minimizes need for supervisory staff

In summary, virtually every aspect of Nucor's control system—from its hiring policies to its compensation philosophy—supported its aim to be the low cost provider of steel and steel products.

Applicability of Organization and Control Systems in Other Companies

Nucor's managerial control systems have been well integrated into its environment given its culture, its strategy, and the nature of its business. A discussion of which particular organizational characteristics are appropriate for each major element of the control system is discussed in this section.

Lean organizational structure. Nucor practices a low-cost approach to organization; there are few "professional managers," assistants, etc. Every position in the organization carries significant responsibilities and employees must be willing to be stretched.

This approach is consistent with Nucor's no-frills culture and its low-cost business strategy. This approach works well in organizations with similar cultures and strategies. Wal-Marts and Texas Instruments represent examples from other industries.

Organizations with a culture which permits bureaucracy (General Motors) or a business strategy which pursues product differentiation (Hewlett-Packard) may find it more difficult to maintain lean organizational structures.

Highly decentralized environment. Nucor's highly decentralized structure eliminates the need for extensive corporate overhead. Each plant is its own division and profit center.

This approach is best suited to organizations where management is willing to confine its role to strategic planning. A second important characteristic is the divisibility of the business. At Nucor, each plant can be responsible for its own purchasing, manufacturing, and marketing without jeopardizing quality standards or incurring higher costs.

The extent of Nucor's decentralization would be difficult to achieve in organizations where certain functions need to be centralized in order to achieve operating economies or attain a critical mass. Pharmaceuticals, defense contractors, and high tech firms, for example, tend to rely on centralized R&D functions. Other organizations may need to use the same manufacturing plant for many different business lines.

Uniform Performance Evaluations. All of Nucor's divisions are measured using the same metric for evaluation (profit center) and using the same target ROA. This works at Nucor because all divisions are competing in the same business, with similar cost structures and employing similar strategies (low cost).

Using a standardized evaluation system obviously becomes more difficult when an organization competes across several different lines of business with different cost structures and success factors. For example, a diversified conglomerate might own a manufacturing plant which might be measured as a cost center while a marketing services firm which might be measured as a revenue center.

Stringent Hiring Standards/Investment in Training. Given the importance of productive labor to its business strategy, Nucor spends considerable time on the employee recruitment process and invests a significant amount of money training its workers.

Expanding this level of time and effort would not be appropriate in organizations where employee turnover is high (such as retail or fast food) or where labor productivity is more standardized (such as in an assembly plant environment).

Pay-for-Performance. All employees at Nucor earn some portion of their pay based on their own productivity.

One of the reasons a pay-for-performance approach to compensation works in Nucor's environment is that results and output can easily be measured. Managers understand that they are being held accountable for financial returns. Workers understand that the incentive piece of their pay is based on the productivity of their work team.

In other organizations, such as professional service firms, it may be more difficult to measure output. For example, should a commercial banker be rewarded for making a higher volume of loans? In other businesses, an evaluation may be made only after many years. This is often true in new business development (obtaining a new client in advertising may require 3 years worth of work) or in an R&D environment where productivity may be difficult to measure at all.

A final consideration is the willingness of an organization to put the pay of their employees at risk. Many organizations, such as hospitals, have been too paternalistic to use a pay-for-performance approach.

No Layoff Policy/Share the Pain program. Nucor is committed to providing job security in exchange for an agreement of its workers to reduce their work hours and of its executives to take a pay cut.

Many organizations with unions lack the flexibility to make the kind of deal Nucor has made with its workers. In other environments, the contempt held by executives for workers is so strong that they would never agree to a voluntary pay cut. It takes a very strong rapport and level of trust between management and its workforce to practice the type of agreement that Nucor has forged.

Note that the ability of any organization to maintain a no lay-off policy is becoming increasingly suspect. IBM, for example, which traditionally has had an unspoken agreement not to lay off workers, had to violate that policy.

Considerations for Nucor's Future Strategy

In 1992, Nucor found itself as one of the few profitable and growing companies in a very mature business. Iverson admitted, "You're not going to see any growth in the steel market, so the only way to make money is to reduce costs and have the technology to penetrate other companies' business."

The following are issues for Nucor to consider in shaping its future strategy.

Continue Investment in Technology. Steel is a mature product and the market has too much capacity. Prices will continue to fall. Nucor should continue to be the industry cost leader by pursuing new technology.

Focus on Higher Margin Markets. Nucor should replace production of commodity products in older facilities with thin-rolled products in new manufacturing facilities. If there is a future in the steel industry, it will be in the higher-margin thin-rolled markets where competition is more limited and where reasonable margins can still be maintained.

An article in the May 26, 1992 edition of *The Wall Street Journal* stated that Nucor had recently raised prices in the thin-rolled steel market. It reported,

It (Bethlehem Steel) is actually following a similar move by Nucor Corp. earlier this month. Suddenly, Nucor finds itself the pricing leader in the steel industry, even though its flat-rolled shipments are only a fraction of rivals'. "In some ways, Nucor is the new U.S. Steel," says John Jacobson, an analyst with AUS Consultants. "They're the cost leader and that gives them more leverage in terms of pricing."

Clearly, Nucor has a considerable amount invested in these markets and should continue to pursue them vigorously while it has a technological edge.

Establish Joint Ventures with International Partners. Given the maturity of the U.S. steel market, Nucor may need to expand abroad in order to continue growing. Given the advanced state of Nucor's technology, it would make an attractive partner for a local steel company in a region with a growing demand for steel products. AJV would require that Nucor revisit the applicability of its managerial control systems to a new operating environment.

Exhibit 1

Global and U.S. Output of Steel
(in millions of tons)

Year	U.S. Production Tons	% of World Total	Global Production
1974	144	18.0%	800
1975	122	17.2%	710
1976	128	17.5%	730
1977	127	17.0%	745
1978	140	17.8%	786
1979	120	14.8%	810
1980	119	15.0%	790
1981	112	15.9%	705
1982	81	11.5%	700
1983	86	12.0%	720
1984	87	11.8%	740
1985	86	11.0%	780
1986	82	10.5%	780
1987	87	11.0%	790
1988	99	11.8%	840
1989	95	11.0%	860
1990	100	11.8%	850

Exhibit 2

Operating Costs of Producing Cold-Rolled Coil in an Efficient Integrated Steel Firm, 1985			
	United States	West Germany	Japan
Operating costs			
Labor	$ 129	$ 70	$ 63
Iron ore	67	47	44
Scrap	18	11	—
Coal or coke	50	48	52
Other energy	24	22	15
Miscellaneous	115	126	112
Total costs (per ton)	$ 403	$ 324	$ 286

Exhibit 3

Porter Five Forces Analysis: The U.S. Steel Industry

Substitute Products: High

- Lots of substitutes readily available
  — Plastics, Aluminum
- Many are more attractive due to lighter weight and stronger tensile strength

Power Over Suppliers: Low

- Suppliers of scrap have power over electric arc furnaces
  — low threat of backwards integration, supply limited
- Low threat of backwards integration
- Integrated manufacturers using lime, coal have more power

Intensity of Existing Rivals: High

- Steel now a global industry
- Due to high labor costs, U.S. exports < 5% of production
- Foreign competitors more cost efficient; imports make up large percentage of U.S. market

Power Over Buyers: Low

- Very low power over buyers due to industry overcapacity and available substitutes
- Low threat of forward integration into markets, such as automotive, appliances, etc.

Barriers to Entry: Mixed

- High barriers because of capital intensity
- But technology for lower-end market is basic

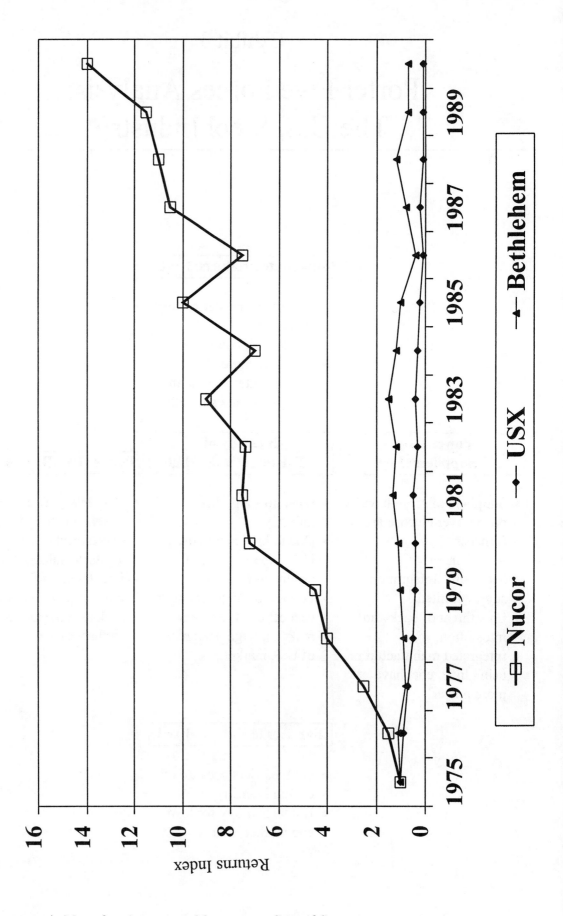

Exhibit 5

Comparison of Major U.S. Steel Companies: 1985–1990

Company	Profit Margins		Growth in Sales		Earnings Per Share				
	5-year Average %	Latest 12 mos %	5-year Average %	Latest 12 mos %	1986	1987	1988	1989	1990
Major Integrated Producers									
Armco	NM	NM	-14.2	-28.2	-5.42	1.67	1.4	2.28	-0.71
Bethlehem	NM	NM	-0.9	-6.7	-3.37	1.48	5.16	2.93	-6.45
Inland Steel	NM	NM	5.2	-6.7	0.95	3.09	6.99	3.15	-1.41
LTV Corp	NM	-73.2	-5.6	-3.5	-35.41	4.24	-8.97	2.06	0.38
USX Corp-Consolidated	21.2	-15.2	1.1	10.2	-6.53	0.49	2.62	3.53	3.14
Weirton Steel	NA	-98.9	NA	-10.4	NA	NA	-0.11	1.37	0.01
Wheeling Pittsburgh	NM	NM	10.1	-3.8	-50.75	8.43	33.1	23.26	NA
Minimills/Specialty Producers									
Allegheny Ludlum	NA	-49.5	NA	-8.1	NA	1.51	3.21	3.96	2.07
Birmingham Steel	NA	-58.3	NA	-0.1	0.89	1.07	2.31	3.16	1.33
Chaparral Steel	NA	-20.5	NA	3.5	NA	NA	1.57	0.74	0.63
Cyclops Industries	NA	NM	NA	-11.1	NA	2.81	4.15	5.04	-0.42
Lukens Inc.	NM	-6.4	10.1	6.1	1.15	2.58	3.91	4.73	5.07
NS Group	NM	2.1	28.9	13.9	-0.61	0.38	1.73	0.95	0.97
Timken	NM	-0.2	9.3	11	-3.35	0.39	2.34	1.88	1.85
Nucor Corp.	5.10%	29%	14.30%	16.80%	2.17	2.39	3.34	2.71	3.51

NM: Not meaningful
NA: Not available

Exhibit 6

Comparison of Steel Making Technologies: Integrated vs. Minimill

	Integrated	**Minimill**
<u>Production Process</u>		
Raw materials	Iron, ore,	Scrap
Fuel	Coal	Electricity
Process	Complex; uses ingot casting	Simple (3 steps); uses continuous casting
Size (tons per year)	As high as 6–7 million (avg. of 3.5 million)	150k to 1 million (avg. of 300,000)
Location	Concentrated in Indiana, Illinois, Ohio, Pennsylvania	Near market and scrap supply
<u>Markets</u>		
Market coverage	National	Regional
Product range	Broad; able to produce sophisticated sheet steel	Narrow; limited to commodity products
<u>Costs</u>		
Capital costs	$2,000 per ton	$500 per ton
Productivity (hours per labor ton)	4 to 8	2 to 4
Labor cost (per hour)	>$20	$10 to $12 less than integrated mill

Exhibit 7

1990 Cost Structure Comparison: Nucor vs. Avg. Steel Companies

	Nucor	Avg. Steel Industry
Revenues	100.0%	100.0%
Labor	16.9%	28.6%
Materials	72.5%	61.9%
Interest Expense	0.1%	1.7%
Earnings Before Taxes	10.5%	7.8%

Notes:

1. Nucor labor cost is an estimate based on avg. pay of $45,000 (5500 workers)
2. Source for Nucor data is 1991 annual report.
   Source for Industry data is American Steel and Iron Institute.

NUCOR CORPORATION
Linking Controls to Strategy

Vijay Govindarajan

Earl C. Daum 1924 Professor of International Business

The Amos Tuck School of Business

Dartmouth College

Hanover, NH 03755

Phone: (603) 646-2156

U.S. Steel Industry Context

Since 1950, the industry has been on a major decline

- Lower Demand

- Stronger Global Competitors

1960

Eight U.S. Companies

    U.S. Steel

    Bethlehem

    National   *Total Market*

    Republic   *Value $55 billion*

    Armco

    Jones & Laughin

    Youngstown Sheet & Tube

    Inland

1993

    Survivors (out of the 8)

        Market Value ≈ $13 billion

(000's in billions)

	1994 Revenues	1994 Market Value
Bethlehem	$4.3	$2.6
U.S. Steel	$5.7	$4.7
Nucor	$2.3	$5.1

Technological Shifts

		1965	1985
Pre WWII	Open Hearth Furnace	80%	9%
Pre WWII	Basic Oxygen Furnace	19%	60%
Late 1960s	Electric Arc Furnace (Minimill)	4%	31%
		100%	100%

Exhibit 1

Steel Production Processes

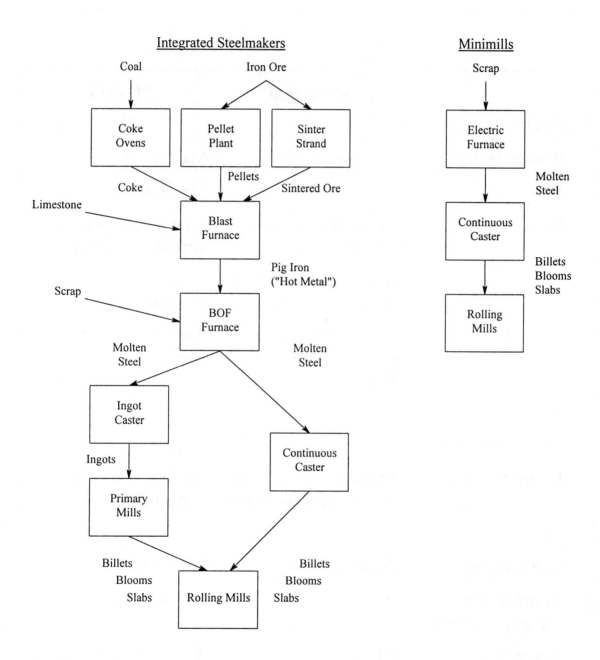

Integrated Steelmakers

Coal   Iron Ore

Coke Ovens   Pellet Plant   Sinter Strand

Coke   Pellets   Sintered Ore

Limestone

Blast Furnace

Pig Iron ("Hot Metal")

Scrap

BOF Furnace

Molten Steel   Molten Steel

Ingot Caster

Ingots

Primary Mills

Continuous Caster

Billets Blooms Slabs   Rolling Mills   Billets Blooms Slabs

Minimills

Scrap

Electric Furnace

Molten Steel

Continuous Caster

Billets Blooms Slabs

Rolling Mills

Source: Donald F. Barnett and Robert W. Crandall, *Up From the Ashes: The Rise of the Steel Minimill in the United States* (Washington, D.C.: The Brookings Institution, 1986): 4. © 1986 The Brookings Institution.

Exhibit 3

Comparison of Steel Making Technologies: Integrated vs. Minimill

	Integrated	Minimill
Production Process		
Raw materials	Iron, ore,	Scrap
Fuel	Coal	Electricity
Process	Complex; uses ingot casting	Simple (3 steps); uses continuous casting
Size	As high as 6–7 million (avg. of 3.5 million)	150k to 1 million (avg. of 300,000)
Location	Concentrated in Indiana, Illinois, Ohio, Pennsylvania	Near market and scrap supply
Markets		
Market coverage	National	Regional
Product range	Broad; able to produce sophisticated sheet steel	Narrow; limited to commodity products
Costs		
Capital costs	$2,000 per ton	$500 per ton
Productivity (hours per labor ton)	4 to 8	2 to 4
Labor cost (per hour)	>$20	$10 to $12 less than integrated mill

Operating Costs of Producing Cold-Rolled Coil in an Efficient Integrated Steel Firm, 1985			
	United States	West Germany	Japan
Operating costs			
Labor	$ 129	$ 70	$ 63
Iron ore	67	47	44
Scrap	18	11	—
Coal or coke	50	48	52
Other energy	24	22	15
Miscellaneous	115	126	112
Total costs (per ton)	$ 403	$ 324	$ 286

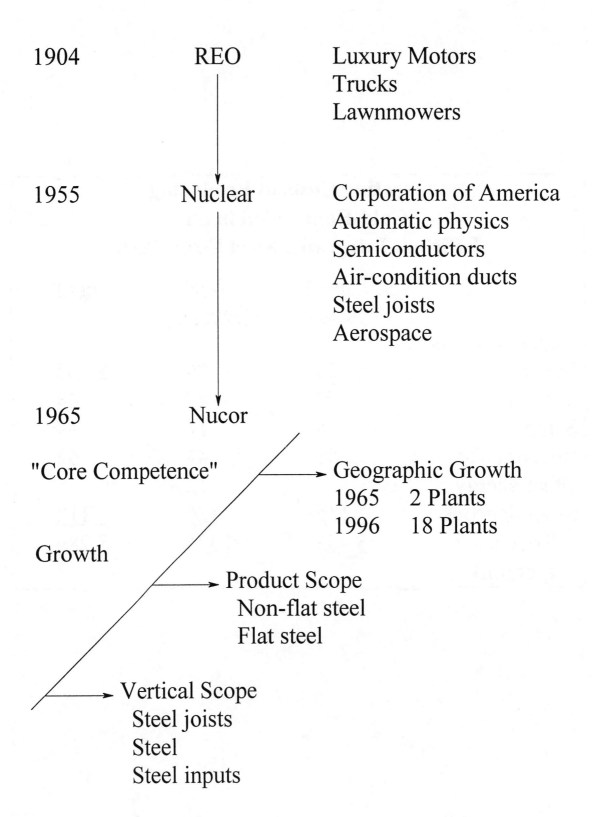

1904   REO   Luxury Motors
Trucks
Lawnmowers

1955   Nuclear   Corporation of America
Automatic physics
Semiconductors
Air-condition ducts
Steel joists
Aerospace

1965   Nucor

"Core Competence"   Geographic Growth
1965   2 Plants
1996 18 Plants

Growth

Product Scope
Non-flat steel
Flat steel

Vertical Scope
Steel joists
Steel
Steel inputs

Is Nucor a Successful Company

Stock Price   75/$2   90/$82

Sales Growth 1965–1995   18% p.a.

Capacity Growth 75–95 ≈ 25 times

1976–1985 Stock Price Increase ≈ 650%

1975–1985 Return on Equity ≈ 20%

Explanations for Nucor's Success

Industry Effect

Strategic Group (Minimill) Effect

Country Level (U.S. Home Base) Effect

Market Power (Scale Economics) Effect

Lock On Distribution Channels

Lock On Raw Materials (Scrap)

Lock On Technology

Lock on Location

Brand Name

Unique Strategy

Strategy Implementation

Steel Industry

Specialty Steel Companies

Integrated Steel Mills

Flats

Non-Flats

Minimills

Foreign Companies

BUYERS

Service Centers/Distributors

Automotive

Construction

Appliance

Exhibit 3

Incentive Compensation at Nucor

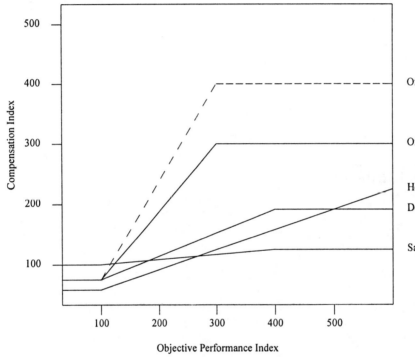

Source: Casewriter's estimates based on Nucor compensation schedules.

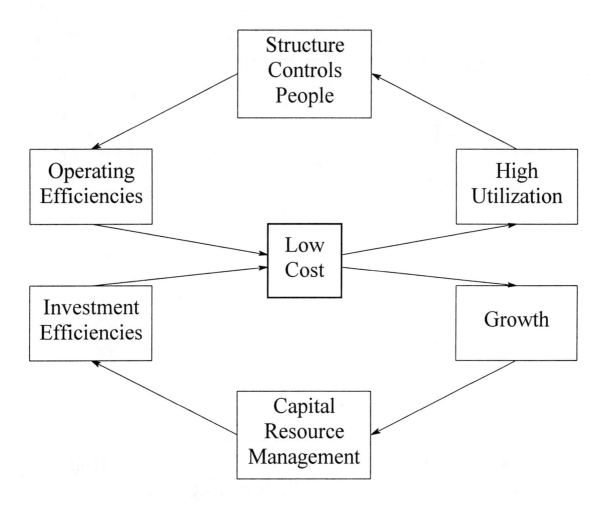

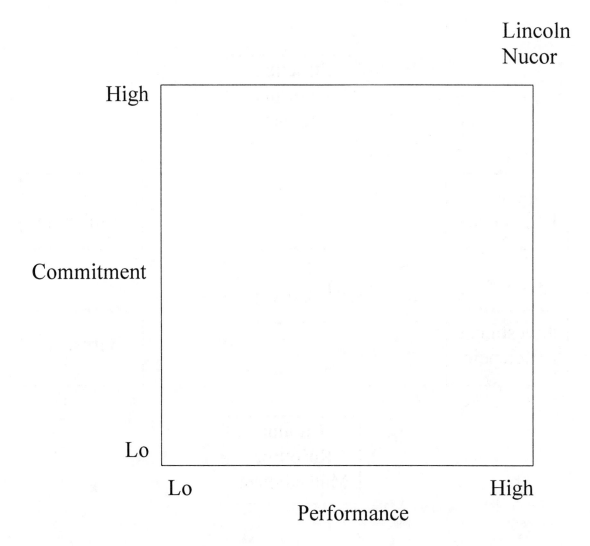

Why Difficult to Imitate

- Strategy Implementation $\rightarrow$ Core Competencies

- "Corporate Governance"

- Difficult to imitate piecemeal

- Pre-Commitments

Case 13-3

3M Company

Objective

To develop an understanding of how policies and philosophies can be used to implement a strategy of continuous innovation.

Synopsis

This short case looks at a company that is consistently considered to be one of the most innovative companies in the world. This case tries to give students some insight into what it is that 3M does in order to be so consistently successful at innovation. It does this through an exhibit that provides brief explanations of 14 different policies and philosophies that 3M uses to encourage innovation among employees.

Question

Evaluate the policies and philosophies of 3M from the standpoint of helping 3M implement its strategy rooted in innovation.

Step 1

Before jumping into the question, it might be worthwhile to probe the students on the idea of how would they visualize an environment that encourages innovation. What does this environment look like and feel like. What are the policies of such a company? The reason for this is that looking at 3M, we see 14 philosophies and policies, yet it is the interaction of these policies and philosophies that makes 3M successful. In addition, there is more to 3M's success than these 14 items. What about the long developed traditions and the selection of small towns for 3M factories.

Examining each piece separately does not allow us to see the power of all of the pieces together and what happens when one of the pieces is missing. In addition, it will help the student push the 3M situation into a more generalizable framework. Finally, after developing the class' view of what makes for an innovative company, compare it with 3M. What are the differences, what are the similarities. Because of the length of the case, this could be done real time beginning with the brainstorming, then handing out and reading the case and then comparing and contrasting the class' view of an innovative company with policies and philosophies of 3M.

This teaching note was written by Kirk Hendrickson, Tuck '97.

Step 2

The next step in evaluating the policies and philosophies is to look at each one separately and ask in what way does this item enable innovation within 3M.

Policy/Philosophy	Enables innovation by:
15 percent option	allowing engineers and scientists to experiment without deadlines or direction, allowing them to explore areas that normally would never get examined.
30 percent rule	setting goals for managers to ensure that they are constantly and consistently focused on new products.
Dual-ladder career path	allows individuals to select the path where they will be able to make the greatest contribution to 3M, rather than forcing high performers into management.
Genesis Grants	making money available internally for intrapreneurship. Keeps innovations within the company that many other companies let slip away.
Carlton Award	publicity recognizing technical achievement and innovation, providing a direct statement to other employees of the value 3M places on innovation and discovery.
Golden Step Program	supporting internal business development and risk-taking.
3-tiered research	having a continuous pipeline of products at different years out, so that there is neither an overemphasis on the long-term giving up the short-term, or sacrificing the long-term by focusing on the short-term.
Knowledge is for everyone	stimulating the exchange of ideas and inventions which helps cause ideas to incubate and increases exposure to the latest thinking in every organization. Prevents maximum leverage of ideas. Prevents "not-invented-here" syndrome.
Customer Contact	exposing scientists and engineers to new ways of thinking about the products that 3M is creating.
Intrapreneurs	creating opportunities for rapid advancement and reward as the result of being innovative. Encourages experimentation and risk-taking.
Tolerance for Failure	creating an atmosphere where failure is not punished, thus encouraging risk-taking and exploration of interesting, though maybe not obviously promising, areas.
Small Business Units	personalizing the atmosphere at 3M, making each SBU feel like a small company, increasing the commitment and loyalty to each SBU and thus 3M. Increases flexibility and quick response to industry opportunities.
Profit Sharing	allowing everyone to enjoy the fruits of innovation. Encourages lower level employees *within* a business unit to take a corporate focus since profit sharing is based on corporate profits.
R&D spending	putting 3M's money where its mouth is and make available the resources necessary to allow the experimentation and risk-taking.

Source: James C. Collins, Jerry I. Porras, *Built to Last: Successful Habits of Visionary Companies* (New York: Harper Business, 1995), p. 156–158;
Ronald A. Mitsch, "Three Roads to Innovation," *The Journal of Business Strategy*, September/October 1990, p. 18–21.

Step 3

Individually, each policy and philosophy contributes to innovation. Putting it all together, it is 3M's holistic approach to innovation that gives 3M its capability. The discovery of the Post-it note may have been accidental, but the systems that made it possible were very deliberate. These systems are designed to encourage employees to look for opportunity gaps, places where growth could occur that do not exist today. The result is that the scientists are engaging the future in a search for innovations, big and small that will move 3M one step closer to the future.

Examining how these policies and philosophies interact and support one another allows the students to look at how these different policies create a cooperative environment that is not undermined by counterproductive policies.

While 3M encourages open information sharing through conferences and discussion forums, it also has a profit sharing plan that rewards individuals for the overall company's success, encouraging cooperation. It allows small groups to pursue new ideas and create new business units out of nothing, encouraging people to work together and try new ideas, with no punishment for failure. In an environment like this, success comes from working together, not trying to hide your ideas from others. In addition, your financial well being is tied to the performance of the collective groups and not your individual effort in comparison to your peers.

An additional supporting policy is that 3M aggressively pursues patents and does not use trade secrets. Patents must be described in sufficient detail so that some one practiced in the art could reproduce the discovery. As a result, the information on 3M accomplishments becomes public record, so why not share this information, it is going to become public soon enough in any case.

By combining all of these policies, 3M is able to create an environment that encourages innovation at every turn.

3M's system has been described as a tree with new products branching off of its abrasive and adhesive core competencies. See Exhibit 1. With many branches and twigs, the tree continues to grow incrementally. Each of the new branches started as a little twig that was nurtured by 3M's systems. These systems nurture by providing a direction of where 3M wants to go, innovative new products, but does not specify how 3M is going to get there. As Bill Hewlett of HP so aptly described when discussing 3M, "You never know what they're going to come up with next. The beauty of it is that they probably don't know what they're going to come up with next either. But even though you can never predict what exactly the company will do, you know that it will continue to be successful."[1] 3M has indeed been very successful since its troubled beginnings. A success rooted in innovation.

---

[1] James C. Collins, Jerry I. Porras, *Built to Last: Successful Habits of Visionary Companies* (New York: Harper Business, 1995), p. 150.

Exhibit 1
3M: Technology Driven Strategy

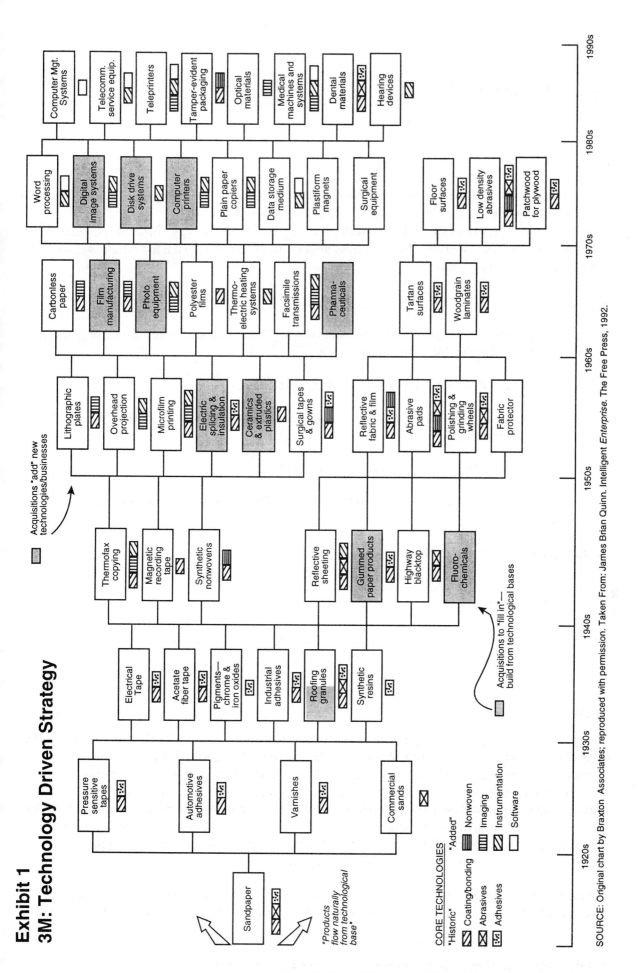

SOURCE: Original chart by Braxton Associates; reproduced with permission. Taken From: James Brian Quinn. Intelligent *Enterprise*. The Free Press, 1992.

Case 13-4 and 13-5

Texas Instruments Inc.

Note

Case 13-3 and 13-4 should be assigned for the same day. Case 13-3 compares and contrasts the strategy of Texas Instruments and Hewlett Packard. Case 13-4 describes the control systems at Texas Instruments. Students can evaluate TI's controls in the context of its strategy. Then, the students can make some predictions about how HP's controls might differ from TI's, given the differences in strategy between the two firms.

Prologue

I have had a very good success with this case with both MBA and executive audiences. I organize the class discussion around the following topics:

1. Texas Instruments' strategy and its management systems as of 1970.

2. Can you implement Texas Instruments' management systems in another company? What makes it work in Texas Instruments?

3. Why is OST system failing in Texas Instruments in the 80s?

4. Compare and contrast Texas Instruments' and Hewlett-Packard's strategy and management systems.

On the topic number 4, an excellent source is:

Steve Wheelright, "Strategy, Management, and Strategic Planning Approaches," *Interfaces*, January–February 1984, pp. 19-33.

The teaching notes by Dick Vancil and Brian Quinn cover topics 1, 2, and 3.

V.G.

Approach

This is my favorite case on strategic planning systems—for several reasons. First, TI's planning is the most effective that I have seen, primarily because the company has developed an explicit set of procedures to deal with the toughest management dilemma: the conflict between long-range objectives and short-range goals. Second, TI's system is unique, offering a sharp contrast to the more conventional systems studied earlier in Galvor. This forces the student to think through again the why and how of a strategic planning system. The greatest value of this case, however, is that it presents sufficient data that the student can examine the interrelationships among a company's entire well-designed set of carefully integrated management systems.

The case is also a very flexible classroom vehicle. For MBAs, I have used it both in a first-year required course and in a second-year elective on planning systems. With executive groups, I have used it in our Advanced Management Program and in a variety of single-company executive seminars. On occasion, in that last setting, I have used TI as the only planning case, and it still is fairly effective. No matter what the classroom setting, I always use TI as the last case on planning systems because, in my view, "it says it all."

Management Systems

Pedagogically, I like to start with question and allow the discussion to run in a fairly unstructured manner for awhile. If the students have not thought explicitly about "management systems" in earlier cases, they may have a little trouble broadening their scope to look beyond the planning system per se. But, because the data in the case are so explicit, it takes only a little prodding to start creating a real shopping list of TI's systems. As each new item is identified, I record it on the blackboard. Sometimes I organize the various items into sets, but other times it does not seem useful to do so. I always bring with me a set of the seven charts attached to this note (Exhibits TN-1–7), which I use as transparencies for summarizing the TI system. Knowing that I'm going to display a rather organized picture of the management systems, I think it's more important for the students to identify the items—and appraise them—than it is for me to impose too much structure on the discussion.

Let me comment at this point about the design of the seven charts. I don't hold any particular brief for the four peripheral boxes on Exhibit TN-1. Those four boxes are necessary simply to facilitate the graphic displays on the following four charts. More importantly, they also demonstrate that this is a set of highly interrelated management systems that collectively provide the context for TI's planning and control systems. Some of the items that appear in a particular box in Exhibits TN-2 through 5 could just as easily have been recorded in a different box, and I make no attempt to defend the particular four categories that I have selected.

I will not bother to comment here on each of the items that appears on Exhibits TN-2 through 5 because many of them are lifted directly from the case, and their relevance in the TI network is obvious. The charts do contain a couple of entries on which there is no data in the case, and I will comment briefly on those and on a couple of other items that I think are of particular interest.

Organization Structure. One of the most interesting things about TI is the design of its most basic management system: the organization structure of the firm itself. While there is nothing organizationally unusual about the lowest level building blocks (the product customer centers), they have been grouped in a rather unconventional way. Most companies with 77 profit centers tend to group them in some natural fashion such as the technology of the product, the character of the market, geographical proximity to each other, and so on. The advantage of such an approach is that the group vice presidents of the four major groups are then relatively independent of each other. TI has done it just the reverse, intentionally creating an organization structure with high interdependence and then, in my view, using a rather flimsy thread of logic to explain the result. Their structure is chronological: materials, components, systems, and services; it makes sense to me only because it achieves the intended result of helping to keep the company knit together rather than encouraging the fractionalization of it.

Cohesiveness. One result of this cohesiveness, and a great many other mechanisms that TI uses, is that managers in TI feel they "belong." This atmosphere comes through to some extent in the case, and it is clearly evident to anyone who knows much about the company. There is a strong sense of shared values among TIers. Two additional facts that are not in the case (but appear on Exhibit TN-3) are that TI has not made an acquisition since 1959 and that it follows a practice of not hiring executives into the company from outside. The following quote from a TI executive is insightful: "We're very opposed to acquisitions. How could we impose our culture on them? We can't accept the decentralized mode of operations of a financial conglomerator; we need our top-down goal setting."

Stock Options. Exhibit TN-5 mentions the stock option plan, but the case is too concise in describing how the options actually vest. Contrary to the inference that might be drawn from the case that the EPS targets must be met in *each* year, the vesting is more complex than that. The vesting is easiest to explain graphically, as shown in Figure A.

Figure A
Stock Option Vesting Provisions

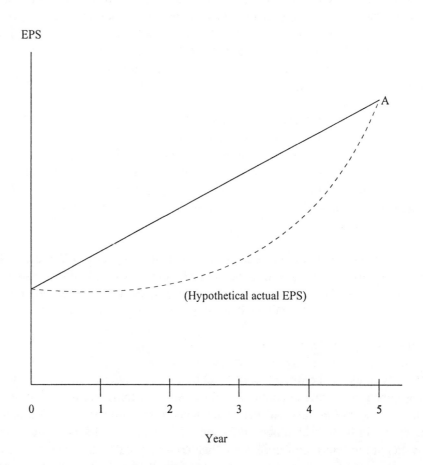

The EPS targets increase at a rate of 15 percent each year. An executive receiving an option on, say, 5,000 shares at the beginning of the first year will be allowed to exercise those options if earnings of the company in the fifth year are higher than A shown on the graph. One way to get to A would be to have actual earnings per share go up at 15 percent each year, in which case the executive would have a vested right in 1,000 shares each of those years. But he would still obtain all 5,000 shares even if the actual earnings turned out to be as shown by the hypothetical dashed line on the graph. Back in the early 1960s, TI's stock options were granted for periods of up to 12 years in this fashion; the time horizon was shortened to five years as a result of changes in IRS requirements for qualified options.

Once the students understand how the stock options system works, the question is: How does a system like this affect the behavior of TI's managers? Most students see quickly that the effect is to lengthen the manager's time horizon for corporate performance. Clearly, it would be easier to achieve the fifth year EPS target by depressing earnings in the first four years and using those funds to develop new products that will provide an important boost to profits in subsequent years. Some bias in this direction is clearly desirable in order to achieve long-term growth. On the other hand, too much bias of this sort is really not in the best interest of the stockholders. TI compensates for this, therefore, by tying its bonus incentive to annual profit performances—a creative tension, we hope, but at least an explicit tension between long-term and short-term which is quite different from the way most companies do this.

Executive Compensation. Another fact not brought out in the case is that these annual bonuses are relatively modest, running 10 percent to 20 percent of salary for most executives. According to one manager at TI, the bonuses are more important as a status symbol than as a financial reward. The real financial reward comes from advancement in TI, and promotions are given to persons who have demonstrated their understanding of how to strike a proper balance between current operations and strategic activities.

I find that it only takes 20 minutes or so to get most of the items shown in Exhibits TN-2 through 5 up on the blackboard. I then allow the discussion to evolve naturally toward an examination of TI's planning and reporting systems.

The OST System

The students will have little trouble identifying most of the characteristics of the planning and reporting systems shown on Exhibit TN-6. The systems are unusual, however, and some students may not understand Figure C in the case, which is the easiest place to demonstrate how the system actually works. A simple example such as the one shown in Table A can help to clear the air.

Table A

| | Original Budget | Sales Decline of $10 | | |
		Action #1	Action #2	Action #3
Sales	$120	110	110	110
Operating expense	70	70	60	70
Operating profit	50	40	50	40
OST expense	30	20	30	30
Organization profit	20	20	20	10

Suppose that after the original budget has been agreed upon, there is a mild recession such that sales fall by $10. What actions can a PCC manager take to cope with this development? It could be that no adjustment can or should be made—that is, that operating expenses would not be reduced. This result, shown as Action #3 in the table, would reduce the reported profit for the year by $10. But if an adjustment is to be made, Action #2 is clearly better than Action #1 because #2 protects the future by continuing to spend the budgeted $30 for OST. The important thing about the OST approach, however, is that it allows the higher level executives to ascertain whether this particular PCC manager has taken Action #1 or Action #2. A system which does not separate operating expenses from OST expenses does not permit such a distinction to be made.

Once the students understand how the system works, it's time to start pushing them for an appraisal of the effectiveness of the system and why it works. As a context for this discussion, it may be necessary to ask the class to specify the purposes that TI had in mind when it developed the OST system. Two broad purposes were defined by Mr. Harris early in the case: (1) to permit and encourage the company to undertake a large-scale innovation, and (2) to allow top management to have better control of the long-term vs. short-term trade-off involving corporate financial performance. Against those two purposes, the OST system earns high marks. Some students (particularly executive groups) may be skeptical, suggesting that the description in the case is some combination of an ego trip for TI's executives and a public relations campaign—they really doubt that any innovative company could manage itself in such a highly structured fashion. But most students will accept the case data as describing the reality of the situation, and are willing to try to probe the question of why the systems appear to be so effective.

Exhibit TN-7 summarizes my comments on this question rather cryptically so I will elaborate a bit here. As the first six charts show, a major reason why this set of management systems works is that the *structure* of the systems has been carefully designed so that they are consistent and mutually reinforcing. One example of this is in the "two-hat" concept. A dual mode of thinking (strategic/operating) is used consistently for setting specific goals, for reviewing performance, for establishing incentive compensation, and in structuring the involvement of top management by means of two separate high level committees. Another example is in the carefully designed proliferation of financial detail starting with a very few variables in modplan for up to 10 years, to more detail in a budget for up to 10 quarters, to very detailed forecasts for up to six months.

But structure, in my view, is only part of the reason for TI's success. The process elements of TI's management systems are probably more important. Here, I would include items such as the frequency of meetings of the two top management committees and the use of a confronting style for conflict resolution. Several of the organizational taboos also have a major impact on process: no staff planners, no executives hired from outside, no acquisitions, no "plan" to look back at, no "fancy methodology" for planning. But fundamentally, the OST system works because TI's top management uses it as the primary tool in making important decisions about the future of the company. OST funds are the strategic resource governing TI's future. The explicit availability of that pool of funds encourages innovation, presenting a "shocking challenge" to TI's managers. The fact that there is an open competition for OST funds facilitates the identification and funding of large-scale strategic "breakthrough" efforts. No formal comprehensive plans, and no staff planners, but it's a beautiful strategic planning system. Exhibit TN-8 presents a *Business Week* report on recent restructuring and decentralization of TI's management systems.[1]

Applicability to Other Companies

The third assignment question above works well with executive groups. In such a setting, I try to allow about a third of the class time for this question, and I discuss it before I present my summary of the seven charts.

Many executives conclude that TI's system is fine for TI but "it wouldn't work in my company." I've come to the conclusion that, in most cases, they are right. In my view, a critical requirement for a company, if it is to institutionalize the centralized management of development funds, is that there must be a homogeneity of orientation, style, culture, and shared values among its executives. The diversity of

---

[1] For a more detailed account, see Bro Uttal, "Texas Instruments Regroups," *Fortune*, August 9, 1982, pp. 40–45.

a company's businesses, per se, may be a major stumbling block. TI's businesses are fairly diverse, but they all come off an electronics base, and top management can believe that they understand the various businesses. Geographical dispersion can also be a stumbling block; some part of TI's success may be attributed to the fact that its headquarters in Dallas is the center of TI's world, and the majority of its managers are located there.

The evolution of TI's management systems is also important in understanding its success—and in constraining the sudden installation of an OST-type system in other companies. At TI, OST was initially established in 1963 with the purpose of managing only the few very big projects that would have a major impact on the future. A few years later, TI managers attempted to apply the concept to all development funds, but that didn't work very well until 1968, when they developed the "decision package," process and tied resource allocations to OST proposals, thus giving an OST manager a specific budget from the OST pool. Thus, by 1972, we see a mature planning system that is nearly 10 years old. For a top manager in another company, looking longingly at TI's systems, it is important to realize that it will take a long time to get from where he is to where TI is.

Finally, there are several key elements of a system for managing development funds which may be too much for many companies to swallow. Such a system does require that the division managers give up some of their autonomy over the future of their particular businesses. Top management must be willing to make a much larger commitment of time to the resource allocation process and to monitoring performance against preestablished goals. The reporting system must be changed to permit a financial separation between operating costs and discretionary expenses, requiring both separate budgets and reports and some form of project accounting. The reward system must also be modified so that both strategic and operating activities of a manager will be rewarded. That is a large number of changes from the conventional management systems found in most corporations. No wonder, then, that the TI systems are so unique.

Richard F. Vancil

Exhibit TN-1

Texas Instruments Management Systems

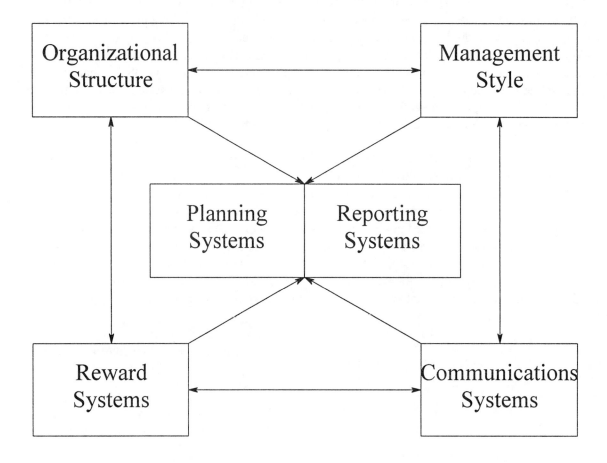

Texas Instruments

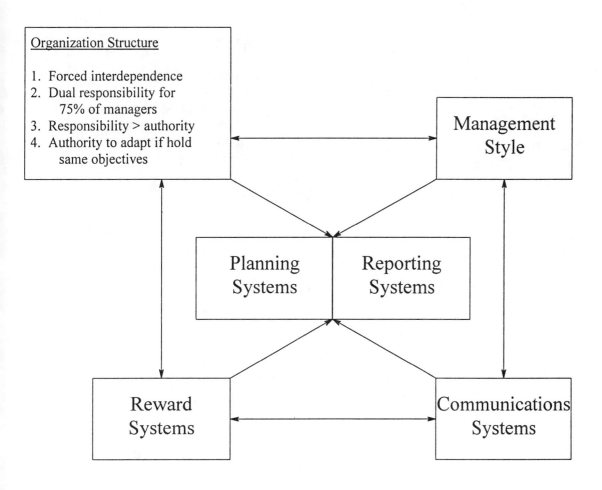

Organization Structure

1. Forced interdependence
2. Dual responsibility for
   75% of managers
3. Responsibility > authority
4. Authority to adapt if hold
   same objectives

Management
Style

Planning
Systems

Reporting
Systems

Reward
Systems

Communications
Systems

Exhibit TN-3

Texas Instruments

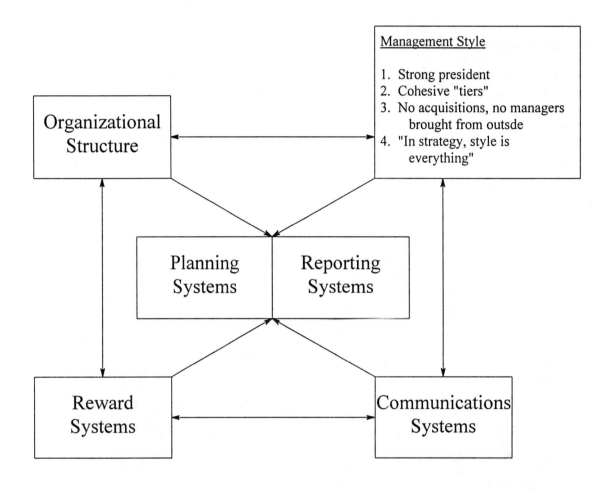

Management Style

1. Strong president
2. Cohesive "tiers"
3. No acquisitions, no managers
   brought from outsde
4. "In strategy, style is
   everything"

Organizational Structure

Planning Systems

Reporting Systems

Reward Systems

Communications Systems

Exhibit TN-4

Texas Instruments

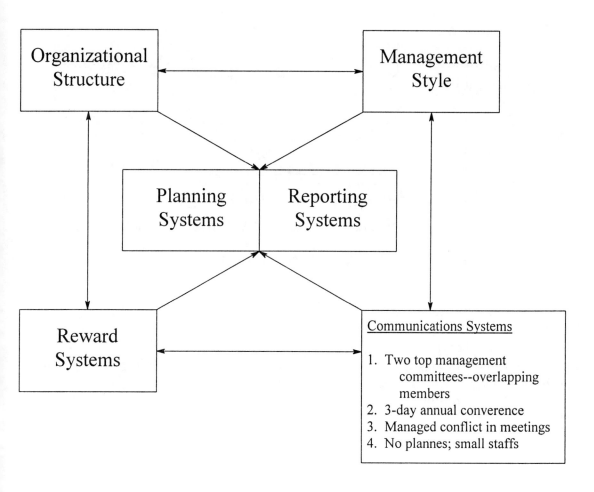

Exhibit TN-5

Texas Instruments

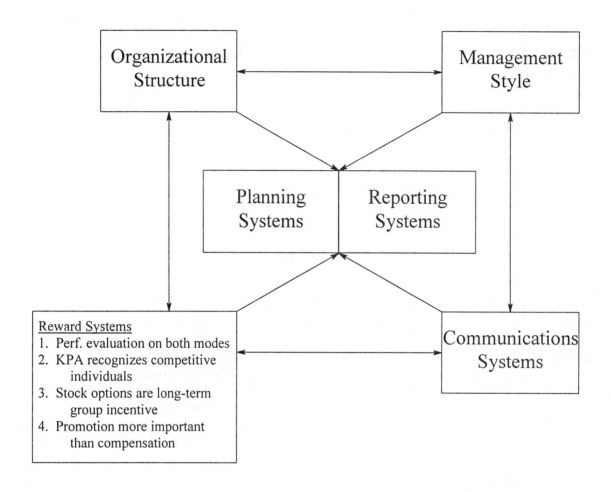

Texas Instruments

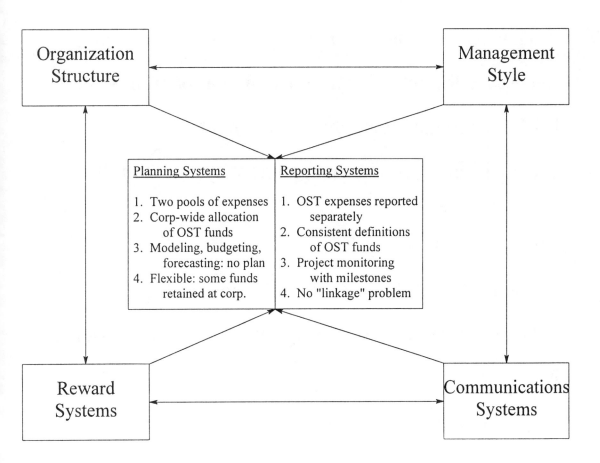

Organization Structure

Management Style

Planning Systems

1. Two pools of expenses
2. Corp-wide allocation of OST funds
3. Modeling, budgeting, forecasting: no plan
4. Flexible: some funds retained at corp.

Reporting Systems

1. OST expenses reported separately
2. Consistent definitions of OST funds
3. Project monitoring with milestones
4. No "linkage" problem

Reward Systems

Communications Systems

Exhibit TN-7

Texas Instruments Summary

Why OST works in this company:

A. Necessary for any effective resource allocation system

    1. Major top management involvement

    2. Consistency among management systems: mutually reinforcing

B. Attributes of OST

    1. Focused on critical resource for regrowth

    2. Decision-oriented planning; no extraneous nonsense

C. Attributes of TI

    1. Dynamic markets with good growth potential

    2. Homogeneity of personnel; shared values

    3. Conceptually explicit system appeals to "a bunch of engineers"

An about-face in TI's culture

For years, Texas Instruments Inc. managed innovation brilliantly with a corporate planning system that many observers considered one of the best—and most complex—in existence. But the Dallas electronics giant bean losing control. Now, after more than a year of soul-searching over whether to change its vaunted matrix management system, TI has uncorked a massive overhaul.

First TI created several new profit centers and delegated unprecedented responsibility to the managers of these businesses. This spring's stunning reorganization was capped in mid-June by the election of a new cadre of executive vice-presidents, setting up for the first time a clear mechanism to choose successors to Chairman Mark Shepherd Jr. and President J. Fred Bucy.

TI must reverse a record that of late has been spotted by delayed product introductions and missed opportunities—problems that highlighted the current economic crunch. Profits have declined for the past six quarters, and last year the Dallas company lost its longtime No. 1 spot in sales in the key U.S. semiconductor market to archrival Motorola, Inc.

Mistakes. "In essence, TI is doing nothing short of changing its corporate culture," says John J. Lazlo Jr., an analyst at San Francisco's Hambrecht & Quist. "It has no choice but to decentralize, to structure its businesses so they can play in the same ball park as their smaller competitors." But while TI may waste little time in reasserting itself, an heir apparent is unlikely to emerge soon. Shepherd, 59, has so far indicated no intention of relinquishing control of the $4 billion semiconductor giant. And it is clear that, before he steps aside, Shepherd wants to return TI to the preeminence it enjoyed in the early 1970s.

Even TI executives now admit that the company's problems are the result of a turgid management system that has be-come increasingly inept at coping with TI's 25% compound annual growth rate of the past decade. In an unprecedented recital of mistakes at the company's April shareholders' meeting, Bucy laid the blame squarely on TI's matrix struc-ture, a cumbersome overlapping of oper-ating and strategic managements. To correct the ills, TI is according new re-spect to marketing and making renewed efforts to decentralize—changes that strike at the heart of the company's life-long technology orientation and a plan-ning system that tended to push all deci-sions into the board room.

TI's restructuring actually began a year ago, when it started shedding such unprofitable product lines as digital watches and some electronic components. Further, TI began focusing development efforts more narrowly, killing a $50 million magnetic-bubble memory program, for example, that it figured would cost too much to bring to market.

The company continues to pare. It has essentially given up on multichip microprocessors—one of the most important and fastest-growing semiconductor product lines—redirecting its effort instead toward versions that pack all the elements of a computer into a single chip. And in the past year it has reduced its worldwide work force by more than 10,000, or 10%, mainly through layoffs.

Promotions. This most dramatic changes came this spring, when TI completely reorganized its two sickest operating groups, semiconductors and distributed computing. For both, TI redefined its basic profit-and-loss unit, the product customer center (PCC), to encompass a complete business. And it gave each PCC manager control of the resources—people, capital, and facilities—needed to run the business. Previously, PCC managers in the semiconductor group had been reduced to begging for those resources from huge central support entities, while the PCC structure in computers had fragmented into a series of individual product lines that were difficult to team together for a system sale.

The PCC management structure was also brought in line with TI's strategic planning organization, so that PCC managers will be responsible for making and marketing their products as well as for developing extensions to their product

> The reorganization stresses decentralization and a new respect for marketing

families. And an advanced-development activity was set up in the semiconductor group so that products and processes that leapfrog the state of the art do not get diffused among managers concerned with day-to-day operations.

The aftermath of that streamlining was a series of far-reaching changes in senior management and the election of the new executive vice-presidents. William N. Sick Jr., widely credited with turning around TI's consumer operations, added the semiconductor group to his responsibilities. He replaces James L. Fischer, who became chief financial officer. Also named to senior posts were Jerry R.

Junkins, who took over TI's computer business last fall, and Grant A. Dove, who runs the company's government, geophysical exploration, and materials and controls businesses.

The fifth executive vice-president is Stewart Carrel, a widely experienced TI manager who has the new job of coordinating technology, marketing, and planning. That move signals TI's new commitment to its customer. "The company has always developed products from a technology point of view, as opposed to what the market wanted," says Michael J. Krasko, a vice-president at Merrill Lynch, Pierce, Fenner & Smith Inc. "What we see happening now is a corporate determination to match technology prowess with what will sell."

Too early. Nowhere is that more apparent than in consumer businesses, where TI uncharacteristically named William J. Turner, a marketer with a scant two-year tenure at the company, as the group's new head. And the experience of Sick, the new semiconductor chief, "will bring that business a dimension of marketing awareness and strategies that we badly need," admits one TI officer.

It is still too early to tell whether TI's new attitude toward marketing will help it shed its reputation as an arrogant, middle-aged company. And some outsiders still question whether top management will ever really give up enough authority to let individual managers run their own businesses. "On paper, the moves are very positive," says James L. Barlage, vice-president for research at Smith, Barney, Harris Upham & Co. "But we'll be moving into a period of economic strength, and that will mask any improvements, just as the economy in the late 1970s masked the problems."◆

Additional Comments on Texas Instruments

In its early years, the Texas Instruments Company was an extraordinarily successful company, staying on the frontier of semiconductor technology and developing many leadership positions (both in cost and performance terms) in that complex industry. In the early 1970s, Mr. Haggerty, Chairman and CEO of Texas Instruments, sought to understand how Texas Instruments had managed itself in those sectors where it had been most successful. He began to set up the OST planning system to institutionalize those features of management which he felt had been most responsible for the company's success. In the late 1970s and early 80s the planning system of Texas Instruments was widely hailed as one of the most progressive such systems in the world. However, by the mid 1980s some of the problems and weaknesses of the system had begun to emerge. The case offers an interesting opportunity to look at a highly formalized planning system in contrast to Litton's more loosely structured planning system and to assess the costs and benefits of each.

TI's Planning System

This portion of the discussion can begin, "What do you see as the good features and weak features of the Texas Instruments planning system?" These are fairly readily apparent. The good features include:

1. A clear statement of the company's mission and concept,

2. The establishment of aggressive goals in its industry.

3. Business goals are made explicit.

4. The plan has a long term focus (5–10 years).

5. The planning process increases synergy (i.e. the sum is greater than its individual parts).

6. All plans are clearly anchored as individual responsibilities.

7. All stakeholders are carefully served.

8. The hierarchy among plans is clear, ensuring that all aspects of the company's goals will be served.

9. The corporate objectives or philosophies contain multiple goals. Each is anchored clearly in the organization for monitoring. Its business objectives provide performance measures which can be easily utilized to assess progress. The charter of each group is clearly delineated and focused on the basis of that group's strengths, weaknesses, opportunities, threats.

10. Concrete plans ensure that action will be taken in the high impact areas top management intends to emphasize or build.

11. Both long- and short-term objectives are supported. The plan has both permanent focal points and checkpoints for individual programs.

12. Cross divisional thrusts are clearly set forth, and interdivisional synergies are developed.

13. The plan is strategic, not just short-term-profit oriented. It is directed toward those things which create profits. It insures that non-quantitative areas as well as quantitative areas receive adequate support.

14. It is comprehensive, not allowing any important elements to "drop into cracks."

15. The plan does not just focus on crisis areas but areas needing future building. The IDEA system insures that innovation has a home in the organization.

16. The plan is flexible at the tactical level.

In short, the planning system of Texas Instruments insures that all aspects one would normally seek in a planning system are present and rationally arrived at. In terms of the critical factors for success in this industry, the planning system would seem to be well adapted. These critical factors for success include: innovation, early entry on the experience curve, obtaining scale economies, focus on efficiency of operations, focus on individual market areas, shared knowledge among different knowledge centers, leveraging the profits of each unit to insure that the company takes advantage of each level of value added. For a company producing a highly innovative product entering its maturity cycle, this kind of planning system would appear to be highly rational and helpful. However, it clearly has certain serious problems. These include:

1. Very great complexity.

2. Much accompanying paperwork, time commitment, and cost.

3. The probability of a bureaucratic structure developing to run the plan.

4. Much stress induced by the dual roles of individuals.

5. Inflexibility because of the rigidity of the planning process itself.

6. Open competition between people who must cooperate in a matrix structure.

7. The conflict between challenge and reality in goals. While normally very useful, challenging goals—if used for control purposes—can create frustration and confusion.

In summary, this planning system is superbly comprehensive. It looks like it would be very useful in a maturing product industry. However, it looks too complex and rigid to support the tumultuous nature of original innovation. It would seem to be costly and frustrating for the kinds of individuals who ordinarily do frontier research or innovation.

TI's Organization/Control System

The professor can next ask, "How well do you think TI's organization/control system supports its basic strategic concepts and its planning system? Again, there are a number of good and problem features in these areas. The most important are briefly summarized below. The good features include:

1. A clear marketing focus for all groups, divisions, PCCs and departments.

2. Interdivisional coordination and support toward defined goals.

3. The PCCs are small enough to provide innovation bases and flexibility in dealing with customers.

4. Activities supporting a single marketplace are clustered under one authority wherever possible to ensure close personal coordination.

5. The PCCs have a clear operations focus on their marketplaces.

6. There is a fast response venture capital system available.

7. The control system sees that resources are used as allocated.

8. The control system measures progress against the strategy's intentions.

9. The control system covers all important areas of strategic and management control.

10. The intended priorities are clear and milestones are developed for measurement.

11. Strategic and operations expenditures are separately controllable.

12. The IDEA and P&AE systems allow a certain flexibility for change.

13. The system maintains a clear productivity focus in a competitive industry.

14. If TI can develop its synergies while its competitors cannot, it could gain significant cost advantages.

However, the structure of Texas Instruments has certain significant problems that haunt management in it. Perhaps the most important among these are the following:

1. The complexity of the system insures that every person is working for many bosses.

2. Coordinating across so many interfaces must be time consuming and confusing.

3. How can an individual make choices when his various bosses are insisting on different modes of performance.

4. The peer review system puts people in highly conflicting situations.

5. The measurement and reward system implicitly ranks each individual against all others. This is directly contrary to the desired informal, voluntary coordination sought by this multi-level matrix system. This is probably the most critical single factor affecting organization and control. One can ask what kind of incentive system or performance measurement system would have been more appropriate than the KPA (Key Personnel Analysis) system used.

6. It is questionable whether the IDEA system was adequate to encourage innovation within TI. Getting an idea, once developed, introduced into the complex planning and control framework, would be extremely difficult.

Overall, Texas Instruments' experimentation with very complex matrix management was a frontier industrial experiment. It certainly should appeal to the rationality in any individual. However, it also points out how that rationality breaks down in a situation where markets are chaotic, technology is moving rapidly, and individual creativity and initiative are necessary to stay on the frontiers of the technology. The system may simply be more appropriate for a company or industry slightly further toward the maturity cycle than Texas Instruments was in the early 1980s.

Summary of Outcomes—Texas Instruments

The $145 million loss in 1983 resulted from a foray into home computers that eventually led to the resignation of TI's president, Fred Busy. A boom year in 1984 was followed by another hefty loss in 1985 when semiconductor sales slumped and fierce price competition raged in memory chips. Unlike most of its U.S. competitors, TI has elected to stay in this market believing that it is the key to developing new semiconductor design and processing techniques which it can exploit in new lines of custom and semi-custom chips. To demonstrate its commitment, TI has invested in two new $100 million chipmaking plants (one of which is in Japan) and pioneered a 4 megabit DRAM.

TI's new president, Mr. Jerry Junkins, has also been trimming the company's operations and focusing resources on semiconductors (especially high-profit vs. High-volume products), military equipment, and artificial intelligence technology. The new administration undertook a careful review of TI's planning practices, and informed reports indicated that the OST system was being deemphasized significantly within the company.

Summary

While the above outline brings out many of the most important discussion points, it is worthwhile to ask the students to evaluate each overall system's merits. Which one would they prefer to work under? Which one is most likely to be effective under what conditions? How can very bright and able people arrive at such diverse approaches to the problem of entrepreneurship and innovation management? How does this fit the way in which the history of technology suggests that innovations really come about? Would some conglomeration of the two systems be preferable? If so, how would they modify the planning and control systems in each company? One should try to diagram the nature of their changes in organization. It is interesting to note that students will tend toward a single solution for both companies that is quite comparable. This indicates that there is some real validity in the approach each company takes. The secret is to capture those aspects of these planning systems that are most appropriate for each individual company at a particular time in its innovation, product, market life cycle.

James Brian Quinn

CHAPTER 14
MODERN CONTROL METHODS

Changes from the Eighth Edition

This chapter describes just-in-time, total quality control, computer integrated manufacturing, and decision support systems, which are much-discussed techniques. Their implications on management control are described.

Cases

Iron River Paper Mill discusses total quality control.

Motorola, Inc. discusses just-in-time and computer integrated manufacturing

Responsibility Accounting vs. JIT describes two situations in which useful contrasts and comparison can be drawn between traditional systems and just in time, and between situations with different management responsibilities.

Case 14-1

Iron River Paper Mill

This case teaches well. This case enables students to:

a. Define quality, cost of quality (COQ), and the components of COQ;

b. Differentiate between prevention, appraisal, internal failure, and external failure costs;

c. Understand the difference between the traditional view of COQ and the Total Quality Control view;

d. Understand the methodology in developing COQ data;

e. Identify important issues in analyzing COQ data;

f. Understand the role of management control systems in measuring COQ.

I spend about 20 minutes at the beginning of class to highlight:

a. Why quality is critical for business success (Table 1);

b. How Total Quality Control differs from Traditional Views on Quality (Tables 2 and 3)

c. How controllers can use their expertise in "performance measurement" to convince companies to move from traditional views to Total Quality Control.

Then, I turn attention to Iron River Paper Mill. I put up Table 4 and ask the questions at the bottom of that Table.

This case gives details on the methodology of establishing COQ data. I make sure the students first understand the methodology (before turning attention to "so what?" questions). In this context, I raise the following issues:

1. Quality costs include: salaries and benefits, depreciation, insurance, taxes, etc. Will these costs "go away" if we undertake quality initiatives? If not, why include them?

2. Can goodwill and badwill be quantified?

   - Is "badwill" a valid concept?

   - What might the consequences of "goodwill" include?

     First price increase in upturn
     Last price decrease in downturn
     First to get the order in upturn
     Last to lose the order in downturn

   - How to quantify the cost of "badwill" (or the benefits of "goodwill")

When we turn to the interpretation of the COQ data, I make sure that students appreciate the following points:

1. "Quality cost" is a big number.

2. Many companies do not know where they are spending money—1, 2, 3, or 4.

3. Companies typically spend on quality in the wrong places—3 and 4 rather than 1 and 2.

4. Spending money "upstream" can save on "downstream."

5. Quality costing framework assumes a long-run view. Impact of investing "upstream" can yield benefits after several years ("elapsed time in impact").

6. As long as we use "consistent" bases to classify and collect quality costs, trends in quality costs yield useful insights.

7. Traditional cost systems are a great barrier to progress on quality initiatives.

Finally, I put up Table 5 and ask students to evaluate the three options.

— Joe Fisher

Table 1

Cost of Poor Quality
The Doom Loop

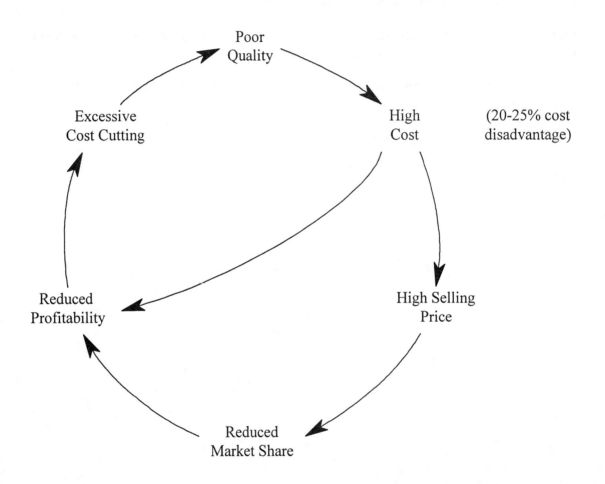

Table 2

Traditional View of
Quality-Cost Trade-Off

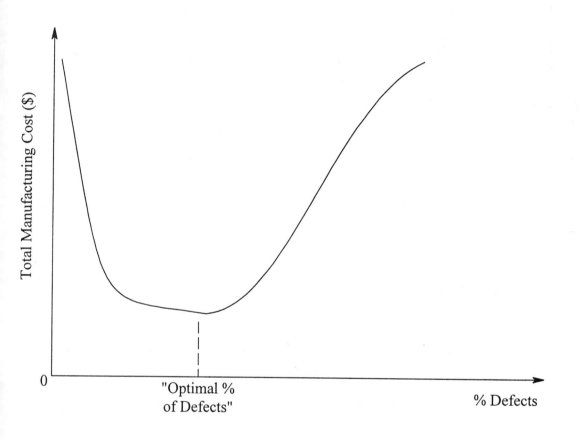

"Too much of a good thing isn't so good"

Table 3

Total Quality Control
View of Cost Trade-Off

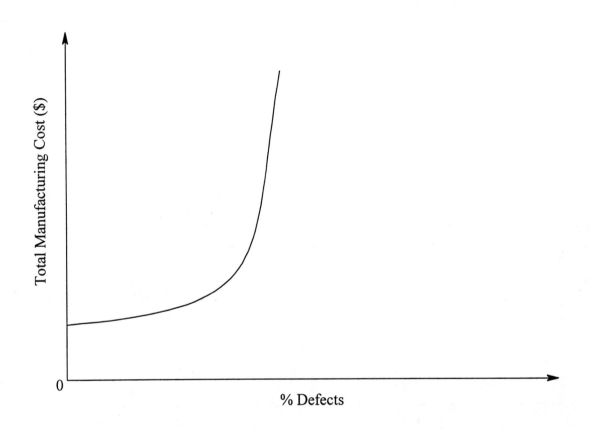

Table 4

Iron River Mill

	1987	1988	1989	1990
Prevention	$3.6 M			
Appraisal	$3.9 M			
Internal Failure	$24.7 M			
External Failure	$10.7 M			
Total COQ	$42.9 M			

(27% of Total Mill Cost)

- What does this say about Iron River's "Quality"?

- What are the profit improvement opportunities, if we can decrease COQ to 3% of total cost?

Table 5

Three Possible Approaches

Role for
Controllers

Low

1. Don't do quality-costing study. Just spend the money "upstream" to make the product "right."

2. Do a quality cost study as a "special" study (to assess the stage of quality management). Do not use this as a management tool on an ongoing basis, by preparing periodic QC reports.

3. Prepare quality-costing reports on a periodic basis (say, once a year) as a management control tool.

High

Motorola

The authors have spent time at several firms that are considered leaders in modern manufacturing and control systems. We found that most of these firms tried to simplify their accounting systems through the use of nonfinancial measures. This case deals with one of those firms, Motorola.

We start the discussion by giving an overview of the non-financial process." We observed the following taking place at the firms we interviewed:

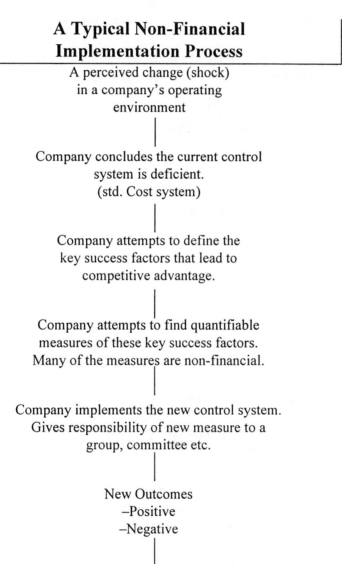

**A Typical Non-Financial
Implementation Process**

A perceived change (shock)
in a company's operating
environment

Company concludes the current control
system is deficient.
(std. Cost system)

Company attempts to define the
key success factors that lead to
competitive advantage.

Company attempts to find quantifiable
measures of these key success factors.
Many of the measures are non-financial.

Company implements the new control system.
Gives responsibility of new measure to a
group, committee etc.

New Outcomes
–Positive
–Negative

Define Market

Ask the students to define the market. It is interesting to note Motorola has targeted the slower growing bipolar market.

	1984	1990 (Est.)
Total High Performance Gates	$90 Mil.	$600 Mil.

	1984		**1990 (Est.)**	
	TOTAL	**%**	**TOTAL**	**%**
CMOS	$90 MIL	40% = 36M	$600 M	70% = 420M
BIPOLAR	$90 MIL	60% = 54M	$600M	**27%** = 162M

While market share of bipolar is decreasing, the overall growth of the total market swamps this effect. Market growth for the two segments are as follows:

BIPOLAR	**CMOS**
162/54 = 3 times	420/36 = 11.6 times

Define Motorola's position —

Why does Motorola stay in bipolar?   Dominant market leader
                                          Less competition then CMOS

Is it wise to invest in bipolar technology?

There is not enough information in the case to answer, but it looks good.

Organizational Structure

- Have participants state what each department does. Use exhibit 1 below and fill in as departments are described. It is important that the participants have a good understanding of what each department does. This understanding is critical when explaining Motorola's implementation process.

Division GM

| Product Engineering | Production Planning | New Products | Quality Assurance | Manufacturing | Marketing |

- This does not change with the move—Why? The case holds this constant—should this also change? Are there too many departments with different vested interests? There are no simple answers to these questions, but they may be worth addressing.

Key Success Factors (KSF)

Ask the students to identify KSF for Motorola.

Below are listed KSFs from previous participants

- Technology leader

- Fast turnaround (from agreed upon specifications to first delivery) (time from inquiry to agreed upon specification)

- Quick response to new customer specs

- Flexible fabrication facility

- High quality

- Moving down learning curve

- Protect proprietary nature of product

- Help customer create an efficient design

It appears that a *well-designed* circuit that *works* and can be *delivered in a minimal amount of time* is the goal. While *price* and *cost* are mentioned in the case, they seem to have secondary importance. The semi conductors are difficult to reverse engineer, so this results in minimal stealing of designs.

Our conclusion was that the following two aspects have overriding importance:

- Quality (has to work)

- Timeliness (need it quick)

Ask the students, is a standard cost system the correct way to control a plant with these characteristics? Consider taking a vote. A standard cost system is very good at motivating buying cheap inputs and maximizing utilization of machines in order to minimize cost. However, this has little to do with the problems facing Motorola. The students will (should) conclude that a standard cost is not the best way to control this plant. Exhibit 2 discusses some of the weaknesses we have noted in examining a standard cost system. Consider putting up exhibit 2 and discussing the characteristics of the Motorola plant prior to the plant layout changes. How does this match up with the KSF?

Ask the students, what are possible measures of the KSF?

Some of the measures mentioned by previous participants.

- % defects

- on-time delivery

- inventory levels

- customer returns

- new product cycle times (specs to delivery)

- order lead times (time from order to promised delivery)

- new product starts

- number of patents

- market share

- quantification of learning curve

Ask students, how do you control with these measures?

We don't have a clear-cut answer to this question. However, we can state what Motorola did. They gave the non-financial measures to the departments and told them they were responsible for the measures. The following gives the Motorola control system:

Product Engineering —
    Yields
    Manufacturing costs
        a)   Identify & eliminate non-value-added steps (i.e. inspections)

Product Planning — Client Billings
    Dollar amount product delinquent
        a)   Compare actual to promised
        b)   Compare actual to preferred
    On time percentage
    Dollar amount of inventory
    Cost of sales turns: cost of sales/finished goods inventory
    Also controls shipping and receiving
        Actual expenses to budgeted expenses

Marketing & Sales — Revenue Center
    Booking of new accounts
    Billings
        Compare to forecasted amounts
        (this is kind of strange since they do the forecast)

Quality Department — Cost of Non Conformance (Scrap)
    Avg outgoing quality (AOQ)
    Defective rate at final inspection station
    Number & dollar amount of returns

Manufacturing Departments
    Yields
    Cycle time
    Secondary importance cost

New Product Department
>   Explicit control of this department is not as rigorous as the other departments.
>   >   Two pieces are examined.
>   Actual to budget expenses
>   Cycle time (within this department) from Specs to prototype

Motorola then graphed performance on these measures over time. In essence, last week's performance became the goal to exceed for the current week.

Motorola then controlled with last week's (day, month) actual results being the "standard" for the current period. Motorola management wanted the graphics to show positive trends over time.

This control system can be contrasted with Analog Devices, where improvement is tracked and controlled by a committee. This committee is made up of persons from different functional departments.

Ask the students, what are possible problems (tensions) with the non-financial measures?

1. Tension between financial & non-financial measures what do you do when these conflict?

2. It is difficult to prove that optimizing the non-financial measures results in higher profit. This is especially a problem when senior management is controlled on a financial measure (i.e. ROI).

3. Tension between non-financial measures:

    scrap vs. customer rejections—Scrap is decreased by allowing the products to pass inspections. However, this may result in marginal products being delivered and consequent customer rejection.

    cycle times vs. on time delivery—If you just control cycle time, then wrong product or large lot size production may take place, which decreases on-time delivery.

4. Still can "game" the measure. Maximize non-financial measurement to overall detriment of firm.

Problems With Standard Cost Systems

Meeting the budget becomes the overriding goal

For example, under a standard cost system, a manager is motivated to avoid under-absorption of departmental costs by building up work-in-process inventory, even if that inventory is not needed.

Standards out-of-date

Given the dynamic environment facing Motorola, standards were quickly obsolete.

Unfavorable variance not actionable at operations level

A variance is made up of many activities and therefore a unique solution is difficult to determine. An operations manager states:

> "I receive stacks of variance reports every month, but they just aren't useful for me in trying to manage the plant operations. And it is not because these reports are slow in arriving on my desk. They would not be any more useful if I got them every day! The problem is that they don't help me understanding what is going wrong, or right, with my operations."

Even more telling was the following quote from two managers:

> "The first step in upgrading our manufacturing systems was to ignore any report coming out of accounting."

Timeliness of Reports (Accumulation and distribution)

The reports accumulated too much of a time period (monthly) and were distributed in an untimely fashion (two weeks after the close of the month).

Standards may not reinforce the concept of continual improvement

In a standard cost, there is the concept of "allowable waste," and the goal is to meet, not beat, the target. For Motorola, "kaizen" is the goal and no waste is "allowable," conceptually.

Additional Readings

"The Rival Japan Respects," *Business Week,* November 13, 1989.

"Life in the fast lane: Arrays shift into high gear," *Electronic Business,* July 15, 1985.

"Why gate arrays are slow getting out of the gate?" *Electronic Business,* April 15, 1985.

—Joe Fisher

Motorola, Inc.: Additional Comments

Approach

Quite apart from the issues, the case gives a description of one of the most exciting new technologies, gate arrays, and of computer products generally. It describes the changes in the cost accounting system that resulted from the change in the flow of products in which machines were grouped functionally to a flow in which operations were organized by "cells," each of which was operated by a production team. It describes the cost accounting system: standard costs, overhead allocated on the basis of direct labor (8 to 12 percent of employee's productive time was involved in recordkeeping), and late monthly reports of variances by functional activities. It leaves the student with the task of suggesting changes in the system that should be made in response to the change in the manufacturing process.

The question takes the student, step by step, through the thought processes that need to be considered in designing a new cost accounting system for the new environment.

Question 1.

The case suggests that the key success factors are accurate and rapid response to customer's needs; low production cost (but not much attention to low development cost because of the uncertainties involved); high quality, and on-time delivery; and accurate costs for pricing. Low in-process inventory contributed to costs, but may detract from on-time delivery.

Question 2.

(The question refers to "a" traditional system; the following relates to the current Motorola system. Many "traditional" systems do not allocate overhead on the basis of direct labor, nor do they have the poor and late reports that are mentioned here.) Overhead allocation based on direct labor becomes irrelevant in this situation. Also, monthly reports that were not timely, with variances that production people couldn't understand, did not help achieve the desired performance. The cost system probably didn't affect late delivery, but it might if productive time used to fill out reports could have been used to get out product. The existing system was not responsive to the change in the organization of the factory. It probably did not fix responsibility on the managers who were responsible (but we can't be sure of this, although it is implied in the comments about variances).

Question 3

For the preproduction operations, success is probably difficult to judge by quantitative measures. Customer satisfaction, as evidenced by repeat business and lack of complaints, is one important factor. Since each job is probably unique, standards may not be feasible. We don't know enough about this aspect to judge; it may be possible to set approximate standards of the time required for a given "gate" or arrays of similar gates.

For the production process, quality, timeliness, and cost are the factors. As the case indicates, unsatisfactory quality should be detected quickly, and the rule that the line is stopped as soon as a defect is detected is a good way of getting at this. This leads to a measure of the number and duration of such stoppages. Cost is a function of the number of defects, of the thruput per unit of time, and of the ability of the manager of each cell to have the optimum number of people and the optimum nonpersonnel costs (i.e. efficiency). Because the products seem to vary considerably, a satisfactory measure of the quantity of output may be difficult, but should be sought. Efficiency is also difficult to measure. Evidently, standards for the work of the cells won't be easy to come by, and the cells can't be compared with one another because each performs a quite different function. Dividing costs between the startup costs of a given job and the running costs of that job may be helpful. Even if standards can't be developed, a comparison of current costs with past costs of the same cell may serve the same purpose.

We don't know enough about the magnitude or nature of overhead costs to say much about them. They should be allocated to products in some way (unless they are trivial) in order to arrive at a basis for pricing. The basis should not be direct labor; perhaps it should be by job for overhead related to setup and by product for the remainder.

Question 4

The foregoing suggests a system based on cells and the products flowing through each cell. My first inclination would be to use a job cost system that collected overhead and running cost for each job in each of the nine cells, but this might involve more bookkeeping than is worthwhile. If so, the system might collect only the actual costs of each cell (not by jobs) and compare this with prior costs; this requires a reliable measure of the quantity of output, which, as indicated above, may be difficult. As a part of this system, the cost of defects should also be collected.

RNA

Case 14-3

Responsibility vs. JIT

Approach

This little case highlights a basic problem that JIT enthusiasts tend to overlook. Low inventories reduce carrying costs, (and the reduction is probably greater than had been recognized under conventional cost systems). However, it created its own management problems.

Students' attempt to wrestle with this dilemma should lead to greater recognition of the problem, even though there is no perfect way of solving it.

Although not apparent, the problems here have considerable similarity to those of Motorola (Case 14-2), and this case might be brought into the discussion.

Question 1

One solution to this problem is cooperation. If the sales manager cooperates fully with the plant manager, the optimum solution is arrived at. This assumes, however, that each has equal respect for the judgment of the other, which is unlikely to be the case in the real world. For example, the plant manager may not respect the sales manager's ability to judge the real opportunity cost of lost sales, and the sales manager may not respect the plant manager's ability to judge the real cost of rush orders. It assumes also that the problem is a management problem, whereas with hundreds of people involved, the actual problem arises daily or weekly with subordinates in each of the organizations.

Assuming that cooperation is not the solution, how can the system motivate each manager properly? An important part of the solution is to arrive at the actual inventory carrying costs. Since this optimum is influenced by the needs of both the sales manager and the plant manager, inventory costs should be apportioned between them in some way. One alternative is to transfer product from production to sales at a price that includes inventory costs, but this could involve considerable paperwork. Another solution is to divide the costs equally between them; this is arbitrary, but gets each of them interested in reducing these costs.

The other important aspect seems to be the cost of handling rush orders. A possible solution is to have the plant submit a quotation to the sales department for each rush order, which the sales department can either accept or reject. The plant manager is motivated to quote a reasonable price; otherwise the order won't be accepted, and the sales manager can judge whether customer satisfaction is worth this price. Again, this may be too complicated, considering the small dollar volume that probably is involved in each rush order. If so, the both parties should agree on a set of rules that will apply to costing all rush orders, and the sales department should accept all charges calculated in accordance with these rules.

Question 2

In this situation, the sales department seems to be the party primarily responsible for deciding whether development of a new or redesigned product should be undertaken. It should decide to do so only if its own cost, plus the manufacturing cost of prototypes and the later cost of production are lower than the estimated additional profits. For proposed new or redesigned products, therefore, the production department should submit an estimate of its costs, and should be held to these estimates (subject to unforeseen factors) if the sales department decides that the development should proceed. The manufacturing cost should of course be responsible for its engineering work in reducing the costs of existing products.

The learning curve effect could be handled by systematically reducing the standard manufacturing costs. This is the case in any operation in which a significant learning curve exists, although some companies do not recognize it adequately.

Question 3

The difference between the two situations in the above analysis stems partly from the fact that in the first, the two managers share responsibility in a way that is difficult to separate; whereas in the second, the responsibility of each party is easier to determine.

Another difference (pointed out by the author of the case) is that in the second situation manufacturing costs could be estimated from the cost standards with relative precision. Reliable cost standards (linked to formal planning models) provide a relatively good estimate of costs and consequently were accurate for bonus plans. As more is learned about the production process, consumer tastes, and demand patterns, standards become more useful for the control of operations and smaller cost centers are feasible.

RNA

Professor Mackey has the following concluding comment:

New strategies, like JIT, reduce inventories, increasing the opportunities for sales departments to influence manufacturing costs. If the costing system cannot measure the effects of the new influences, inefficiencies might result. To avoid this, changes in responsibility centers, such as the grouping of manufacturing and sales, can compensate by motivating individual managers to share information and coordinate their activities. If this is not done, investment in more detailed costing systems is required. Finally, if neither of these solutions is chosen, then cost accounting systems may lead to the failure of these new technologies because the new systems are vulnerable to data entry errors and other forms of sabotage. This may occur quite easily if managers perceive the new technologies to be the source of inequitable evaluations.

In conclusion, it should be clear that under the new technologies like JIT, management evaluation based solely upon function and controllability may no longer be a sufficient criterion for the establishment of responsibility accounting systems and their use as a basis for bonus plans. If interdependencies between departments are not explicitly considered, cost accounting-based bonus plans could be more of a liability than an asset. This would really give a department manager the jitters.

CHAPTER 15
SERVICE ORGANIZATIONS

Changes from the Eighth Edition

The materials on financial institutions have been moved to Chapter 16. The materials on nonprofit organizations have been moved to this Chapter 15. The section on human resource accounting has been deleted; the topic (as defined in the human resource accounting literature) is no longer much discussed and there are few, if any, applications.

Cases

Cookie Associates, Inc. is a straightforward description of management control in an advertising agency. This is a rewrite of Harley Associates, Inc.

Williamson and Oliver describes a proposed incentive compensation plan in a large public accounting firm.

Harlan Foundation raises Issues of pricing in a relatively small nonprofit organization.

Piedmont University describes issues arising from a proposed new management control system in a university.

Riverview examines management control issues in a retirement home.

Cookie, Inc.

Note

This case is a rewrite and update of an earlier case entitled Goodall Associates. However the issues remain unchanged.

Objectives

Several cases in the later chapters of the book can be used either to discuss the points made in the related text or as a basis for a broader review of the whole subject of management control. This is one such case. In the discussion below, the points are related to the specific problems of service organizations. Following this are two answers to a final examination in which this case provided a basis for summarizing the subject.

Discussion

The situation described here has all the characteristics of service organizations described in the text: absence of inventory and hence the importance of keeping the staff fully utilized, labor-intensive, difficulty of measuring output, and even a control system that is less well developed than that in the typical factory. It can be used to underline these points.

The greatest need, I believe, is for a better budgeting system and related system for scheduling work. This is a matrix organization, in which account supervisors must rely on services provided by the functional departments. Without a carefully prepared budget at the beginning of the year, it is difficult to decide on the proper size of these departments, and without a scheduling system it is difficult to see that the personnel of these departments are kept fully occupied.

It is possible that the creative personnel would resist attempts to install such a system, pointing out the unpredictability of some aspects of the work, but the facts probably are that much of the work that needs to be done can be foreseen reasonably far in advance.

The company does collect costs by account, and its procedures seem to be reasonable (provided that people do adhere to the rule that all direct costs, including the costs of administrative people who work on an account, must be assigned to the account). Having collected the cost data, however, there is no formal basis of comparing it with something. This is another reason for having a budget. In the absence of a budget, management may have a feel for the appropriate relationship between costs and revenue, but it is necessarily only a rough feel.

In Exhibit 1 we see an after-the-fact report on the profitability of an account. It would have been better if similar information were prepared on a budgeted basis for use during the year. The report permits discussion of two familiar questions: (1) the fact that the account does contribute to profitability, even though it shows a net loss, and (2) the fact that the account generates joint profit, that is, it is associated with other accounts of T&D Corporation. Discussion of these points will bring out the basic considerations involved in both of these matters.

With respect to the contribution margin, it is a fact that in the narrow sense the agency is better off to have the account than not to have it (assuming that direct expenses are properly recorded). However, many managers feel strongly that every account should pay its own way, and that the company should tolerate a loss account only under highly unusual conditions. Managers tend to feel more strongly about this, I believe, than the economics textbook discussion of contribution margin would imply.

It may be that the relationship of this account to other T&D Corporation accounts is relevant. We cannot tell this, of course, from the facts given. The account manager should be asked for his judgment as to whether abandoning this account will have an adverse reaction. It is quite possible that the unprofitability of the account as it now stands should be discussed frankly with the client.

In addition to abandoning the account, Mr. Brush would want to suggest other alternatives for discussion. Among these are: (1) shift to a fee basis, with the fee large enough to generate a profit; (2) explore whether 1990 costs will be reduced, in view of the large costs that have been generated to establish the account, which may be nonrecurring; (3) explore whether 1990 costs can be cut back by other actions, such as reducing the operating effort devoted to the account.

In order to have a basis for discussing these questions, a budget for 1990 would be much more useful than the history of 1989. Mr. Brush could develop a rough budget, probably, on the basis of conversations with the account supervisor. He probably could even develop alternative budgets showing the implications of possible changes in the way the account is handled.

This incident highlights one of the peculiar facts about the company's present system. Despite all the emphasis in previous cases about profit centers and profit as a motivator, this company tries to keep its middle management away from profit numbers. Probably, its reason is the fear that emphasis on profitability will lead to lessened quality of output. To me, this is a high price to pay for giving up all the benefits that a focus on profits can generate.

Examination Answer A

A management control system should serve certain basic information needs of Goodall Associates management; namely, to help budget and effectively use the company's resources; to properly assess those areas of new business the company is planning to enter and at the same time to reappraise existing business. Of equal importance is information concerning performance by personnel: are costs being controlled? are schedules being met? how good is the advertising message that is being produced? Moreover, information is required to appraise the workings of each functional area: are the personnel of the functional areas being effectively utilized? are the costs of operations of the divisions in line with budgeted costs? The management system also provides information for evaluation of the personnel of the business and as such acts as a means of motivating the personnel to act according to management wishes; it can be the basis of salary determinations and bonus allotments.

I will discuss each aspect of a management control system and in so doing will assess how the present system used by Goodall compares.

Budgeting

To be able to properly plan the growth of the company and to control the utilization rate of personnel in the company, Harley must collect data that estimates for the upcoming year, how much manpower, materials, and general administrative overhead costs will be needed to effectively service existing accounts and expected new accounts. From historical data, it can be determined in a general way what the costs and manpower requirements are. This process of budgeting total costs for the company, and also a breakdown of costs per department, will act as the basis for determining the staffing levels for each division, that is, whether additional staff should be added or whether the staff should be reduced. Moreover, the process of budgeting expected costs and personnel needs for the year provides the basis for determining how fast the company can grow because it determines the company's ability to take on new business. Furthermore, by setting particular budgeted levels for each department, management will be able to assess how well each department is doing in controlling its costs by measuring actual versus budgeted costs. At present, Goodall apparently does not do much formal budgeting or planning. Such a budgeting mechanism would ensure more effective utilization of personnel. It would also serve the purpose of making division management concerned about costs, since their performance against budgets will be evaluated.

In the area of strategic planning of new business, Goodall presently assess the quality of the client and likewise the quality of the product. Through a rather effective means of testing the market acceptance of a product and by determining the competitive environment, Goodall is able to ascertain the market share potential of a given product. This information forms the basis for assessing the advertising required for the product and consequently the advertising dollar amount required to support the product. With this information, expected advertising revenue per account can be obtained. In this aspect, Goodall has been effective.

On assessing the costs of not only new business, but also established business, the present system is adequate but could be improved. First, in estimating costs for new business, Goodall uses historical data gathered on comparable accounts and makes judgments about the costs of penetrating the market, but its present system of accumulating historical costs in that all direct labor and direct material costs on a project are collected, and these are used as a basis of allocating indirect costs. A better method of collecting the full costs of a particular account should be employed. This would entail recognizing the full amount of administrative and top management time that goes into servicing an account. It should be recognized that an account with a new client will take more time and money to establish than one with an on-going client. Consequently, the use of the 55 percent labor cost rule of thumb is not valid.

Having made a determination of the profitability of a new account, Goodall's next step is to plan for the actual processing and implementation of the account. With a pre-existing budget, management could determine the amount of time available in each department for handling the account and thus a schedule could be set up for the account. Thus, Goodall would be able to generate budgeted revenues and costs of an account, and also determine a schedule for implementing the account.

Apparently, Goodall does not have a formal scheduling system. Personnel submit each week a time sheet that records the amount of time spent on each account. Without some form of scheduling, account managers will compete with each other for the time of the functional personnel. Through a process of scheduling, and a method of setting priorities for accounts, management can assure that each account will receive adequate attention.

The setting of the schedule and budgeted costs and revenues, are the bases for monitoring how well each account is being handled. The nature of the task that is being performed by the advertising firm is such that profitability is determined by how well costs are controlled and how effective the advertising message is. The price of the service is set at 15 percent of total advertising dollars spent; thus actual profits derived from the excess of the 15 percent of revenue generated by the account over the total will cover the fixed costs of setting up the campaign. Of paramount interest to management is how effectively costs are controlled. By using the budgeted schedule of costs for a project, management can determine whether or not these costs are being controlled; and by having budgeted costs for each department, management can ascertain which departments are properly handling their costs and which areas need attention. Moreover, through the usage of a schedule, management can ascertain if a particular account is falling behind and thus needs more attention.

In terms of the actual quality of output, actual revenues generated vs. budgeted revenues will give an indication. However, this sort of quality control comes after the fact. Consequently, quality control steps must be undertaken during the process of building the campaign. Goodall presently uses an effective means of assessing quality, a research panel of several thousand citizens who are used to test the quality of the advertising. This information about the quality is timely and is pertinent to assessing the validity of the advertising method.

Thus, through the process of monitoring costs-schedule-and revenues generated, and by comparing these actual data to the budgeted figures, management can determine how well an individual account is being handled. Because of Goodall's responsibilities to its clients and its own needs of generating profits, each account must be periodically reviewed on an annual basis so that the budgeted costs and revenues can be realigned and the overall profitability of the account be determined for Goodall and for client. Goodall does a good job of reading the external environment and assessing what is happening in the present environment; thus Goodall is able to react quickly to changes in the environment and to give added support to accounts.

Assuming that top management makes decisions about retaining or adding new accounts, information about the profitability of accounts is necessary. However, evaluation of personnel by profitability would be an inadequate means of motivation. With data on budgeted vs. actual results by account, management would be able to assess the profitability of each client.

Moreover, operating personnel must also be concerned about the profitability of accounts. Presently, Goodall gives no feedback in terms of how profitable an account is. By using the budgeted figures on an account and using those figures as part of the evaluation of personnel, Goodall Associates should hold their personnel accountable to budgeted figures and assess performance relative to those figures.

With respect to performance evaluation, the major tasks that account managers have are (1) interfacing with the client to ensure proper flow of information between Goodall Associates and clients, and education of sales force of clients, (2) coordinating the efforts of Goodall personnel on an account and (3) the profitability of the account. Reviewing performance on the basis of actual vs. budgeted is a major component of this evaluation. However, it must be recognized that some accounts are more difficult than others. For instance, meeting budget on the introduction of a new product is harder than meeting budget on an established product. Thus, in terms of the individual's overall evaluation, different weights should be given to different types of accounts. In addition, client contact is important; thus on a quantitative basis the number of actual contacts with the clients should be recorded.

Furthermore, if at all possible, without upsetting the client/account manager relationship, some sort of feedback on the quality of the manager's responsiveness to the client should be obtained. While peer review must differ from similar sorts of reviews in accounting firms, other account manager's assessment of the strengths and weaknesses of each other can form the basis of an effective means of evaluating an account manager. Moreover, because he must draw on the talents of the functional departments, the functional heads should also report on the account manager's performance by examining and assessing his sensitivity and understanding of the particular functional tasks required in the campaign.

With these data, a weighted evaluation of the account managers and a ranking of their performance for evaluation can be made. The process of weighting is critical. The greatest weighting should be placed on the manager's ability to meet or exceed budgeted figures on accounts. This will reflect both the manager's ability to maintain costs and also to accomplish an effective campaign. The revenues generated reflect the quality of the relationship and the quality of the advertising to contribute to the overall morale and effectiveness of the company; peer review and review by functional heads can serve this purpose.

Examination Answer B

I think it is reasonable to suppose that Goodall's strategy is to remain one of the largest ad agencies providing the same type of services it now provides. It no doubt wishes to sell its services on the basis of its image, reputation, quality of work, success records, quality of its personnel and personal contacts, and wishes to maintain long-term relationships with its clients. Because these activities require the use of primarily human resources, the firm must attract, train, direct, motivate, and retain top people.

The management control system is a process by which top management directs the employees in the implementation of Goodall's strategy.

It seems to me that there are several things which the control system must attempt to assure:

1. The revenues to be derived from work performed are adequate.

2. Costs are controlled and minimized.

3. The quality of the work done is high.

4. New business is brought in.

Goodall is organized in a matrix system. This is because there are two general and important types of activities going on:

1. Activities related to a particular client (program structure).

2. Activities related to a particular expertise (creative management, info management, media management, production management) (responsibility structure).

Most of the firm's employees are engaged in both types of activities.

The key managers of the organization are the ones that head up the various activities—the account supervisors manage the programs, and the division supervisors manage the responsibility centers.

The responsibility centers should be thought of as cost centers, and the performance of their managers should be evaluated in terms of criteria #2 and #3 above, that is, they are responsible for the cost and the quality of the services they provide to the various programs.

The account supervisors are the key individuals in the firm; they direct the firm's activities on given programs and they maintain the relationships with the clients. I assume that they plan the client activities and are instrumental in decisions regarding new business. I also assume that they are responsible for new business brought into the firm, either directly through their selling efforts or indirectly through their performance and reputation. They should then be responsible for all four criteria listed above; revenues, costs, quality, and new sales.

Starting with the last criteria, new business, it should be possible to identify new clients with which individuals in the firm were responsible for bringing them in. This will be difficult at times, especially when a client comes to the firm because of its image, but whatever information can be accumulated here will be useful. I would assume that each account supervisor would be evaluated annually (which is reasonable and well accepted as an appropriate time frame) and that this and other information would be discussed then and used as an input into decisions regarding salary, promotions, increased responsibility, etc.

The primary area of management control of account supervisors would begin with the budgeting process. (The strategic planning and programming process would involve primarily top management and would include the account supervisors on a limited and casual basis.)

I propose that each account supervisor prepare an annual budget for each of his assigned programs. He might also estimate the time and cost to be devoted to selling and other nonprogram activities. This budget would start with an estimate of work to be done for each client and would be in terms of hours spent on account management, creative management, and media management. This would, of course, be a most difficult process. When new clients are added during the year, additional budgets will have to be made. Although this process would be difficult, it would be valuable for several reasons:

1. It would force account supervisors to think ahead. No doubt they would get better at this budgeting as years go by.

2. It would provide a basis for planning and coordinating the activities of the firm as a whole. It gives useful information for hiring, space requirements, capacity to take on new business, etc., and for possible strategic decisions.

3. It would provide a basis for evaluation and feedback at the year-end for the account supervisors, and it would provide a benchmark throughout the year.

This budget would be "blown up" into revenues, costs, and a work schedule.

Throughout the year, information is collected in the normal accounting system from time sheets, etc. which provide a comparison to budget for each client. The causes for differences should be explained by the account supervisor for each of his programs. (Each of the 150 products constitutes a program, and each of the 33 clients provide a means of grouping and summarizing the programs.) Budget vs. actual comparisons and explanations for variances should be included as part of the annual review of account supervisors. The evaluation of these differences must implicitly include an evaluation of the budgets themselves. Possible reasons for not meeting the budget include the following, for example:

- more (or less) time to do work than expected;

- more (or less) work requested by client than expected;

- unsuccessful test markets were redone;

- unsuccessful ad campaign cut short.

The above are examples of the type of things which may indicate the level of performance of account supervisors and may pinpoint areas of strength or weakness.

Information regarding quality of output is more difficult to quantify. It includes much more than meeting the work schedule; that is obvious. The success is generating profits is some measure of quality. The amount of new business generated is another. Another is the amount of business terminated or showing no growth. Another would be the subjective evaluation of the account supervisor's boss.

It is more difficult to measure the *output* of an account supervisor than the output of a widget factory. This means that more emphasis must be put on controlling the *input*. Since the input is directly controlled by the account supervisor himself, it seems to me that the firm must provide an atmosphere in which the account supervisor will give his best effort. This means that the firm must treat him with fairness and respect so that he will respond with a sense of responsibility toward and identification with the firm. (This seems like such a simple idea, but my experience indicates that it is often missed.)

I have described a management control system which is largely formal. It will be implemented, though, on a personal basis and be supplemented with an informal control system.

Once a year an account supervisor will sit down with his boss and discuss his budgets and actuals, new business and lost business, successful programs and unsuccessful programs, client complaints and client praises, and the informal evaluation of the boss. The salary, responsibility, and job changes will be based on such an evaluation.

The account supervisor will know that he is being evaluated on his performance in the following areas:

1. Planning and budgeting

2. Revenues

3. Costs

4. Schedule

5. Quality

6. New business

It is important that the account supervisor's boss be able to properly weigh the performance criteria in his mind and communicate them effectively to the account supervisor I think it is too difficult to try and put the results of such a subjective and complex evaluation into a number which will be meaningful. Some of the evaluation (especially as used in promotion decisions) will be based on potential as well as on performance.

He will have adequate feedback on a timely basis, once a year formally, and throughout the year informally. He should be getting budget reports frequently, say monthly, and he should be aware of other information being gathered in areas of campaign successes, client complaints, new business credits, etc. He will know that his performance in those areas determines his rewards and will be motivated accordingly. He will also be provided with information pointing out the causes of his performance, his strengths and weaknesses and can modify his efforts.

The firm will benefit by being able to coordinate and plan its activities better, and most important, it will be able to direct the performance of the account supervisors along the lines of the firm's objectives.

Case 15-2

Williamson and Oliver

This case deals with an evaluation of an incentive compensation system for partners in a large public accounting firm. It can easily sustain a 1 1/2 hour discussion. I try to organize the discussion around the following issues:

1. What is the strategy for Williamson and Oliver? A rough cut strategic analysis is presented in Table 1.

2. In light of the firm's strategy, is the new PIC incentive compensation system a positive or a negative force?

One can focus on several issues relating to the incentive compensation system:

a. What performance criteria to use?

b. Within each criterion, what indicators to use? Objective? Subjective?

c. What weights on each indicator? On each criterion?

d. Who sets the weights?

e. How big is the "bonus" in relation to salary?

Tables 2 and 3 contain some analysis on the performance measurement issues.

Some time during the class discussion, I try to get the class to come to grips with the following issues:

1. How to get PICs to act like general managers.

2. In that context, how to effectively balance long- and short-run concerns.

Short-Term	Long-Term
Chargeable hours (utilization)	Develop future managers
Revenue control (collection)	Develop new business
Profits	Enhance concept of Williamson and
Year-to-year volume	Oliver as one firm, especially since
	it has grown through acquisition

3. Management control implications of a very flat organization structure.

4. A CPA firm's profitability does not depend, to a significant degree, on a series of short-run, situationally specific, day-to-day decisions (like fashion merchandiser or commodities broker). It depends far more on factors that are long run in nature, factors such as:

- Client acquisition and retention

- Personnel turnover

- Hiring and development of top staff

- Marketing your reputation

In such a context are monthly financial reporting and variance analysis very much help?

5. Does tight financial control encourage PICs to think like general managers?

6. How to establish measurable yardsticks for long-term issues?

VG

Table 1

	Auditing		Taxation Med. & Small	Project Consulting	General Advisory Services
	Large	Medium			
Nature of Client Relationship	Adversarial and/or Conflicting Goals		Congruent Goals	Congruent Goals	Congruent Goals
Competition	Big Eight Accounting Firms	Medium/ Large Accounting Firms	Accounting Firms/ Financial Advisors	Big Eight/ Consulting Firms	Consulting/ Financial Advisors
Product Differentiation	Very Low	Medium	Very High	High	High
Price Sensitivity	Very High	High	Low	Low	Low
Growth	Low	Medium	Med./High	High	Potentially High
Barriers to Entry	High	Medium	Low	Low	Low
Staff/Partner Ratio	High		Medium	Medium/ Low	Low
Client Needs	Stamp of Approval		Expert Advice	Expert Advice/ Creative Solution	Expert Advice
Boston Consulting Group Positioning	Cow | Dog	Question Mark/Star	Star	Star	Question Mark

Table 2

Criterion	Pros	Cons

Net Income	Focuses on profits.
	Encourages managerial thinking.
	Encompasses many goals:
	    Client service
	    Human resource development
	    Chargeable hours growth
	    Cross-selling new services
	    Billable hours within budget
	    Maximum utilization rates
		Danger of short term orientation to meet net income goals
		Affected adversely by personnel transfers

Outstanding Days	Directs PICs attention to a critical resource — cash flow	Could be included in net income by using an interest charge for outstanding accounts receivable
Chargeable Hours Growth	Incents new business development because it is not affected by business mix Encourages developing junior people because it is not affected by their lower billing rates	Adversely affected by transfers
Versus Budget	Encourages careful planning Can compensate for differences in market potential Forces a commitment to goals	Success related to negotiation skills Does not have contingency provisions
Versus Last Year	Focuses on growth Can include a measure of differing market characteristics if they have not changed since last year	Does not consider market potential (which could have changed since last year, and/or might not have been exploited).
Versus Standard	Focuses on firm's desired performance level encouraging a firm outlook	Does not account for differences in market potential

Table 3

Potential Performance Measures

Client Service	**Human Resources**
Client surveys	Turnover
New client growth	Morale Survey
Number of new client proposals and/or bids	—Includes perceptions of professional development opportunities, quality of work, satisfaction with assignments and amount of client interaction, quality and timing of feedback, etc.
Client retention rate	
Average billings/client	

Case 15-3

Harlan Foundation

Approach

The two situations described in the case require different approaches to pricing decisions. This illustrates an important point about pricing and also about the measurement of costs: different purposes require different pricing principles and therefore different cost constructions. The Camp Harlan problem requires an estimate of full costs because the purpose was to set a price that would break even. The seminar requires an estimate of differential costs in order to obtain the breakeven number of participants, but the break even number is by no means the whole story; management had also to consider (a) the going rate for seminars and (b) the possibility of generating income.

Comments on Questions

Question 1 (Camp Harlan)

The direct differential costs of Camp Harlan are those in Exhibit 2: $151,300/400 person weeks = $378 per week. Round to $375 or $380.

However, it can be argued that the cost of 1/2 a staff person in the central office is a differential cost, for reasons given in the case. If the government, or other outside organization were reimbursing Harlan for the cost of the camp, the cost-reimbursement principles would probably include this overhead cost element. One-half a person @ $18,000 is $9,000 or $22.50 per person-week. The argument against including this cost is that the work would be done mostly in the slack season, and idle time might be available at no cost. The counter-argument is that idle time should not be permitted; if not enough work is required, staff members should take vacations, or even be laid off. Thus, the conclusion on this point is open to debate. (A vote might be taken on this, and the following points. With luck, the vote would not be too one-sided, and thus illustrate how legitimate differences of opinion affect the measurement of costs in this apparently straightforward situation.)

It could also be argued that a corresponding fraction of the 30 percent of central office costs that is not salary is a legitimate overhead cost item. Thirty percent of $9,000 is an additional cost of $2,700, or $6.75 per person week. Many grantor agencies would permit the inclusion of this type of overhead in a cost-reimbursement calculation. However, it can be argued that no additional costs will be incurred, so no reimbursement is justified.

The volunteers will donate their services, so there is no cost to Camp Harlan, except for meals, and these are already included in the food estimate.

It can be argued that the property did not cost Camp Harlan anything, so nothing should be included in the cost for this. Alternatively, it can be argued that if the Foundation sold the property, it would realize $500,000 so the forgone income on $500,000 is an opportunity cost. (This is not quite the same as depreciation, because most of the property would be land, which is not depreciated.)

Question 2 (Seminar)

Discussion of the price for the seminar should start with breakeven calculations so as to get a handle on the possible prices that might be charged. Probably there should be several breakeven calculations, with various prices. The question asks for one in which the price is very much on the low side. Assuming a fee of $100, the unit contribution margin is $100 less the $20 meal cost, or $80. The notebook is not a variable cost, since the copies will be printed in advance.

Fixed costs are:		
	Hotel rental	$ 200
	A/V rental	100
	Instructors	1,000
	Promotion	900
	Notebooks	600
	Unpaid meals	80
	Miscellaneous	200
	Total	$3,080

Breakeven is $3,080/$80 = 39 people. (No fractions of a person). At $180 contribution, breakeven is $3,080/$180 = 17+ people (so close to 17, that I would overlook the small loss at 17).

Except for the fact that the notebooks are a fixed cost (which may be difficult for some to accept), there is not much room for debate about these numbers. The contribution margin for this problem is less subject to debate than the full cost in the first problem, and this tends to be the case in problems of these two types.

A caution: the contribution margin accepts Coolidge's estimates; actually, one of the common problems in costing new ventures is that items of cost tend to be omitted or underestimated. Note that there is no "contingency" here as there was in the Camp Harlan cost estimate.

There can also be argument about the $900 of promotion expense; at the time the seminar is held, this is a sunk cost. However, in the decision to hold the seminar, this is a differential fixed cost.

This question can be raised: suppose the registration is so low that the seminar can't possibly make money; what then? Under these circumstances, the conference might be cancelled and all costs that can be avoided by cancellation will not be incurred. Sunk costs then become irrelevant, assuming that the other costs can be saved by cancellation. The relevant fixed costs Are then $3,080 – $1,500 = $1,580, and the breakeven depends on the contribution margin. At $80, and neglecting the damage to Harlan's reputation, the seminar should be cancelled if there are likely to be fewer than 20 participants. (The hotel and/or the rental agency might require a nonrefundable deposit, which would become a sunk cost.)

Discussing this, and possibly other, alternatives helps drive home the point that differential costs differ with each situation. Unlike full costs, there is no way of including differential costs, as such, in the accounting system.

Question 3

Since one purpose of the seminar is to generate income, the fee should be influenced by the market rate. Although the market rate is not necessarily governing, it is unlikely that participants would pay more than this rate (or if they did, they might complain that Harlan is gouging them), and there is little reason to charge less, except for the possible reason that a low rate might attract more participants and thus help the reputation of Harlan Foundation. Costs are irrelevant, except as a guide to the minimum fee.

Clearly, $100 is not prudent. It should be at least $150, the bottom of the typical rate range, and perhaps $200. In any event, despite what many texts say about how prices should be arrived at, the answer here depends on a quite uncertain judgment about how many people will attend at various prices. Problems in economics texts tend to assume this demand schedule; in the real world, no one knows it. Nevertheless, a price must be determined, and in advance of any knowledge about many people will come. A vote will drive home the point about the uncertainty of this type of problem (unless there is one unusually persuasive student who sways the whole class).

If students are asked to calculate full costs, the question arises as to whether Coolidge's earnings for one day should be included. One can calculate that the earnings of Coolidge + Harris are: $480,436 (total administration) * .7 (salary) = $336,300 − $180,000 (staff salary) = $156,300 (executive compensation). This might be split 60/40, so Coolidge would earn $60,000. The daily cost is $60,000/250 days = $240.

A similar calculation could be made for staff support.

RNA

Case 15-4

Piedmont University

Approach

The idea of profit centers in universities dates back many decades, probably to President A. Lawrence Lowell's dictum to the Harvard deans: "Every tub on its own bottom." Although he did not use the term "profit center" (and for selling purposes this term may create resentment on the part of faculty and deans), he clearly meant that each school's revenues should be adequate to pay for its operating costs. This idea continues to influence the management control system at Harvard.

The case provides an opportunity to discuss the principal problems that arise in implementing a profit-center structure, and the situations described range from those for which a strong case can be made to those for which the results would be clearly dysfunctional.

In discussing the several issues, two questions provide a central focus: (1) How would the recommended practice affect the motivation and attitude of the two parties: the party that receives the charge and the party that receives the revenue? (2) Are the benefits greater than the bookkeeping cost?

The case also permits a discussion of certain behavioral problems in management control: the danger that management runs in accepting an offer from a well-meaning, but perhaps not skilled, volunteer (and the difficulty of finding a graceful way of declining such help); the proper approach to gaining acceptance of ideas; the indication that a strong-minded president can "turn an organization around," especially during a honeymoon period when the seriousness of the situation is recognized.

Analysis

Question 1

General Administrative Costs. Charging these costs to individual schools would result in an operating statement that would report the extent to which the school's revenues were adequate to pay for its own costs plus a fair share of the central costs. The sum of the net incomes reported for each school would be the net income of the university. This charge might get the deans to recognize that the university necessarily incurs costs on their behalf, which must be met from some source. The practice might also cause the deans to question whether the central costs were too high, which would be one way of exercising control. Perhaps the central administration would be reluctant to tolerate such questions.

An alternative is not to charge these costs, or to charge only those that can be specifically identified with a given school (such as accounting, purchasing, personnel). This would reduce the technical and behavioral problems associated with the allocation of indirect costs.

Any basis of allocating indirect costs can be criticized because there is no "scientific" way of doing this, by definition. The criticism that the administration probably spends more than a proportional amount of time on the undergraduate school is probably justified, but there does not seem to be a feasible way of correcting this inequity.

If these costs are charged, the charge should probably be a budgeted amount, rather than the actual costs incurred. Allocating actual costs permits the central administration to pass costs to the individual schools costs that are greater than budgeted.

Gifts and Endowment. The deans quite naturally would not favor giving the president authority to distribute $5 million as he chooses. Actually, the process would require that the schools put in their requests and the president allocate the funds in a way that causes the minimum amount of dissatisfaction. The president could not allocate the funds in a way that is perceived to be grossly unfair; he would lose the support of the deans if he did this. Moreover, the "each tub on its own bottom" idea can't work perfectly. The theological school, for example, does not cover its costs by some $2.2 million (Exhibit 1), whereas the business school has a surplus of $3 million, reflecting the attractiveness of its program to donors, the ability of its students to pay tuition, the need for financial aid, the opportunity to obtain research grants and so on.

The business school surplus can lead to a discussion of the question of whether the president should have the authority to allocate such surpluses to other schools. Currently, this is a hot topic in many universities.

Also, if it is decided that the library should not generate its own revenue, the central administration must make up the shortfall.

This topic provides an opportunity to discuss the question: should each part of an educational institution pay its own way? Carried to the extreme, unpopular courses (Latin, Greek, advanced seminars) would be eliminated, even though they may make an important contribution to the university's total reason for being. Few would argue that each course should pay its own way, and by extension, the argument can be made that certain schools should be subsidized.

On the other hand, if a given school does not obtain resources sufficient to cover its costs, questions can be raised occasionally (not every year) about the desirability of continuing it.

Athletics. Overall, this is one of the less sensible of the consultant's proposal. A case can be made for charging a fee for scarce resources (such as tennis courts, golf courses, or ski lifts) as a way of rationing these resources (but the case is not particularly strong). Presumably, however, the university wants to encourage intramural athletics, and charging a fee would not indicate such encouragement. The rationing argument is not applicable to intramural athletics. Also, there is an indication that intramural and individual athletics should be asked to subsidize intercollegiate athletics, which does not make much sense.

Maintenance. Permission for schools to use outside contractors is an important aspect of this proposal. The maintenance department's concern about the decline in maintenance quality has some merit, but it should be possible to exercise adequate quality control. The maintenance department should be given the authority to do this.

If schools can use outside contractors, the maintenance department must compete with them, which tends to motivate it to be efficient. It must control its costs and obtain enough work so that it breaks even, or there is an indication of poor management or that the department is too large.

(There should be a proviso that if the maintenance department is willing to do the work at not more than the outside price, it should be given the job.)

Furthermore, if the schools are not permitted to go outside, they are at the mercy of the maintenance department with respect to the priority of meeting their requests and the amounts spent.

The pros and cons for maintenance are also applicable to other support departments: purchasing, accounting, and aspects of personnel department (but not university personnel policy).

Computers. A few years ago, many colleges and universities did not charge students and faculty members for the use of computers (except possibly for faculty members working on cost-reimbursable contracts). The primary reason was that they wanted to encourage the use of computers. The tendency now seems to be in the other direction with respect to mainframe computers, on the grounds that the usefulness of computers is now generally recognized; the practice of charging for computer usage is by no means universal, however. (It is somewhat ironic that many universities keep careful controls over the use of postage and long-distance telephone calls, which involve much less cost than computers.)

Probably most computer work within a school, especially work done on personal computers, is done without charge. The issue here, however, is charging for work done on the engineering school computers by faculty and students at other schools. Assuming that usefulness is adequately recognized, the arguments here are essentially the same as those for maintenance.

A special circumstance about computers is that they have software that can supply detailed information about usage at low cost, so recordkeeping cost is not as important a factor as is the case with some of the other services discussed in the case.

I doubt that time will permit the class to get into the details of how a charge should be calculated. There is much discussion about this in the literature: a low charge for off-peak usage; a charge for setup time and assistance from computer personnel that is separate from the charge-per-minute of running time; a charge for plotters and other peripheral equipment, and so on. There may be advantages in detailed, possibly elaborate, charring systems; the question often is whether they are worth the cost.

Library. This is the extreme case of a situation in which charging for services rendered is likely to be counterproductive (but an outside consultant may not appreciate this). The university wants to encourage library usage, and charging a fee would tend to have the opposite effect. As the case states, the recordkeeping involved would be considerable, with thousands of transactions, each involving only a few pennies of cost. (As is the case with computers, library costs might be charged to cost-reimbursable contracts, but the charge can be arrived at by approximations derived from sample tests or other methods that are less expensive than keeping detailed records.)

Cross Registration. On the one hand, it can be argued that if a course is offered, one or a few additional students does not cause any increase in costs. The argument against this is that the a fair share of the cost of the course should be charged to each student, more specifically to the school from which the student comes. Opinions will differ as to the relative weight to be given to each side of the argument. There is also the question of whether such a charge has a motivating influence on either the school from which the student comes or the school in which the class is located.

If a charge is made, the method suggested in the case seems reasonable, with the possible exception that tuition may be considerably lower than the real cost of education, with the difference being made up from gifts and endowment earnings.

Question 2

Probably the problems with profit centers will come up in the discussion of Question 1, and this question is intended merely as a means of catching gaps. In particular, the bad impression given by the term "profit center" should not be minimized; charging for services rendered is a more acceptable way of putting it.

The task of educating people when a new system is introduced should not be minimized. In particular, there tends to be friction and more arguments about how the charges are to be calculated than is warranted. Senior management should try to keep these arguments from becoming acrimonious. Otherwise, the deans and faculty will claim that the university is now being run for the benefit of accountants.

Question 3

One alternative to the profit-center approach is, of course, to keep the present system. The pros and cons of this should come out in the discussion of Question 1.

Students may propose other alternatives. It would be possible to charge certain expenses to the individual schools for information purposes, but not include them in the formal budgets nor make the corresponding credits to the departments that furnish the services. The idea would be to give the schools a better idea of the real cost of their operations without the work and possible friction that arises when these costs and revenues are included in the formal accounting system. This proposal, although similar to actual practice in some organizations (including the federal government), does not accomplish much in my opinion. Without the motivation provided by inclusion of these costs in their budgets and the requirement that they live within these budgets, deans are unlikely to pay much attention to these memorandum records.

Question 4

The discussion of this question can get bogged down because of differences in the recommended treatment of the issues in Question 1. It may be well to avoid it by asking for a resolution of each of these issues and then debating the question of whether this consensus—presumably the most desirable application of the profit-center idea—is better than the alternative.

As a strictly personal opinion (given here only as something to shoot at), I would definitely charge for maintenance work and similar support services (including the support functions of the central office). I would give the president authority to parcel out undesignated gifts and endowment earnings. I would probably charge for the use of the mainframe computers. I would probably not charge for tennis, golf, and skiing in order to ration scarce resources (on the grounds that a sign-up system is a better way of rationing). I would not charge for intramural athletics, or for the library. I would charge for cross registration only if there was a substantial amount of it; the recordkeeping cost would otherwise exceed the benefits.

And I would not ask the deans to approve the proposal, or any part of it, as it comes from an outside consultant. I would say that the consultant's proposal was submitted solely to stimulate discussion. (The weaknesses of certain aspects of the proposal are so apparent, that the whole idea may be rejected.) Having had the initial discussion, I would assign the job of developing a new proposal to someone in the administration (or possibly to a committee), so that the next version would be given to the deans as coming from within the institution and taking account of their concerns. If handled properly, I hope that the deans' reaction would be: we had an unrealistic proposal from a consultant which the president wisely rejected; we now have a practical one that is worth taking seriously.

Case 15-5

Riverview

Objective

The issue in this case is fairness. It is the central issue in many environments, both for-profit and nonprofit. The case raises questions about the treatment of past, current, and estimated future costs. It suggests techniques for assigning past and future costs to the current period: capitalization of costs, depreciation, funds or other provisions for costs that will be incurred in the future. These techniques can be analyzed in terms of how well they lead to fair amounts applicable to the current (or budget) period.

Approach

The Riverview deals with two aspects: fairness in arriving at annual fees, and fairness in presenting financial information on performance.

In the first aspect, an annual fee structure in a Continuing Care Retirement Community (CCRC) should be fair to the residents and to the Community itself. Residents should pay for (1) operating costs incurred in the current year, (2) their fair share of costs incurred in prior years, and (3) their fair share of costs that are estimated to be incurred in future years. The Community should receive sufficient funds to operate the community.

In the second aspect, financial accounting practices should be such that the operating statement "fairly presents" the results of operations.

The instructor may decide to focus primarily on only the first aspect, but some discussion of the accounting aspect may be helpful in showing the rationale for certain accounting practices.

The discussion of current operating costs is straightforward. It should help explain why the accrual idea is sound. Residents should pay only for the material that is consumed in the current period, not the material purchased in that period. They should pay for the costs of employees who work in the period, not the amount of wages paid; employee compensation includes pension costs related to the fact that the employee worked in the period, even though the pension is paid many years in the future.

The discussion of past costs in this case assumes that residents should pay all these costs (because there is no one else to pay for them). In other situations there may be a debate as to which costs are properly chargeable to students, clients, and other sources of revenue. There are two questions about applicable past costs: (1) Over how many years should they be amortized? and (2) What should be the pattern of the annual amortization amount? Both issues are partly subjective, but some objective considerations can be discussed. The case also should hammer home the point that depreciation is a recovery of historical costs; it does not provide for future replacements.

The discussion of future costs is the most difficult. It involves both the question of which costs are properly paid for by current residents and the question of how these costs are to be worked into the calculation.

Following is a memorandum that a consultant wrote for the management of a nonprofit organization that operates a number of CCRCS.

Arriving at Monthly Fees in a Continuing Care Retirement Community

Residents in a continuing care retirement community (CCRC) pay two fees: an entry fee and a monthly fee. These fees are the principal source of funds for the operation of the community. Currently, the fees in most CCRCs are arrived at annually by estimating the expenses of operating the community, calculated on the basis of generally accepted accounting principles less revenues from interest and other sources. I refer to such an estimate as the *accrual method (or current method)*. In this memorandum, I suggest an alternative approach and refer to it as the *modified accrual method*. It differs from the accrual method in the way it estimates the costs associated with land, buildings, and other capital assets.

The memorandum does not deal with the policy for arriving at entry fees (including how much, if any, of the entry fee is refundable upon the death of the resident), the division of the total monthly fee between health-care residents and apartment residents, or the division of total apartment fees among apartments of various types. These are separate policies that require separate analyses. For convenience I assume that the CCRC is a nonprofit organization; a for-profit organization has the same problem, with the additional complication that it should earn a reasonable return on its investment.

Principles of a Sound Fee Structure

Current residents should pay:

1. The operating expenses of the current year, after deducting the nonfee revenue in that year.

2. A fair share of the costs incurred in prior years for their benefit. These costs include the cost of the original plant, the interest on the funds borrowed to finance that plant, and the startup costs and losses incurred in the years before operations broke even.

3. A fair share of the costs that will be incurred in future years to replace assets that they now use and which will be worn out with the passage of time.

4. A reserve for contingencies, if such a reserve is needed.

5. A provision for working capital, it such a provision is needed.

Current residents should NOT pay anything for:

1. Additions to the property. Future residents who use an addition, such as a new swimming pool, should pay for it. The easiest way to implement this principle is to finance an addition with borrowed funds. Future residents should repay the principal and interest on these funds by amounts included in their fees.

2. Replacement of a building. If a building is destroyed, the insurance should provide for its replacement. Otherwise, it is assumed that the buildings will last indefinitely. This is consistent with what actually happens. Accounting charges the original cost of assets to expense; it does not provide for their replacement.

The fees should not change substantially from one year to the next.

To the extent feasible, the fee calculation should be compatible with generally accepted accounting principles (GAAP) so that the numbers are consistent with those reported in the audited financial statements. (This is not an absolutely essential criterion. Also, it is not necessary that the numbers be consistent with those reported on IRS Form 990.)

The fee should not decrease. If the budget shows that a decrease is technically feasible, the preferable course of action is to leave the fee unchanged and use the excess to build up contingency reserves. (The rationale is that residents are accustomed to the current fee and have adjusted their own spending patterns accordingly; they will understand the desirability of building reserves.)

These requirements are similar to those that usually govern the calculation of property taxes in a municipality.

With these principles, the CCRC's financial position should be sound for the indefinite future. Its revenues should at least equal both its expenses and its cash needs.

Elements of the Estimate

In this section I describe how the elements of the fee estimate are calculated in the modified accrual method and how these calculations differ from those made in the accrual (i.e., conventional) method.

Exhibit I is a balance sheet that will be used as an example in this discussion. It assumes the situation as of the end of Year 3, the third year after the CCRC accepted its first resident. At that time the CCRC was essentially at capacity. For simplicity, it assumes that all inflows and outflows except for the operating losses were incurred as of the balance sheet date. Actually, these transactions occurred prior to the balance sheet date, but this assumption greatly simplifies the calculation without affecting any of the points that will be discussed.

The balance sheet shows that the CCRC had acquired or constructed $1.2 million of land, $1.5 million of land improvements, and $40.3 million of buildings, furniture, and equipment. No depreciation had yet been taken on these assets. The assets were financed with a bond issue of $43 million, and no payments have yet been made on these bonds. The terms of the bond issue require that $26.4 million be held by a trustee as security for the bonds. The CCRC has received $33.6 million of entry fees. It has received $0.5 million of deposits from future entrants. The CCRC incurred $2.2 million of startup costs and $2.3 million of operating losses in the early years when it was not at approximate capacity. From now on, its fees must be adequate to provide for the requirements listed above.

Land, Buildings, and Equipment. The accrual method includes depreciation on the cost of buildings and equipment as an element of the fee. The modified accrual method includes in the fee calculation the principal payment on funds borrowed to acquire these assets.

A nonprofit CCRC necessarily obtains its funds by borrowing. As a nonprofit, it can't obtain equity capital. If it is sponsored by another organization, it may obtain some startup funds from that organization, but these are in the form of a loan that must be paid back. It follows that the total of the assets acquired to start the CCRC approximately equals the amount of debt incurred.

Following are the differences between the two methods:

- Depreciation is the same amount each year. Debt-service principal is an increasing amount each year. The difference is illustrated in Exhibit 2. In that illustration, debt-service principal is lower than depreciation through Year 10 and is higher than depreciation thereafter. However, interest payments on the debt have an opposite pattern from principal, and the total of principal plus interest is the same each year. Because the same amount of interest is added to depreciation each year, the total payments (depreciation plus interest) in the accrual method decrease each year. I know of no logical reasons why residents should pay more for these assets in the early years than in the later years.

- In the modified accrual method the cost of the land is included in the fee calculation. In the accrual method, land is not depreciated. (The difference is small, however; in the example, it is $1.2 million spread over 30 years, or $40,000 per year.

- Bonds usually have a shorter repayment period than the estimated life used in depreciation— 30 years vs. 50 years is a common comparison. The modified accrual method is therefore somewhat more conservative than the current method.

- The annual charge in the modified accrual method is the same as the amount of cash required to meet debt-service obligations. In the accrual method, the cash generated in the early years is more than enough to meet the debt-service obligations, and it is less than enough in the later years.

- Depreciation is merely a number; management can do nothing about it. Debt service is an actual outlay; it must be provided for. Including it in the calculation tends to focus attention on it and raise the question of whether refinancing is desirable.

Debt service principal, as such, is not recognized as an expense by GAAP. However, if the amount is subtracted from the cost of the asset, it becomes an acceptable method of depreciation. There will be two bookkeeping entries. One debits the Debt liability and credits Cash; the other debits Expense and credits the Allowance for Depreciation. As a minor qualification, this has the effect of depreciating land, which is not in accordance with GAAP.

Expensing Equipment Acquisitions. In the modified accrual method, annual expenditures for all but major equipment acquisitions are included in the fee calculation. In the conventional method, these amounts are capitalized and then depreciated over their useful life in the following years. Following are differences between the two methods:

- The amount used in the modified accrual method is the same amount that is used in planning and approving equipment expenditures in the budget process. The amount approved depends on current needs and what the organization can afford to spend. The depreciation number is merely a number, derived from past expenditures.

- The amount in the modified accrual method is the amount of cash that must be used in the current year. The depreciation number if unrelated to cash.

Expensing, rather than capitalizing, a normal amount for replacement of equipment and furnishings is not theoretically consistent with the treatment of fixed assets in business accounting; assets with a life of more than one year are supposed to be capitalized. However, many companies use a capitalization threshold that is high enough to approximate the proposed treatment of ordinary replacements at CCRCs. Despite the textbooks, the trend is toward expensing many assets that theoretically should be capitalized. Government accounting (both federal and state and local) does not capitalize these expenditures.

Fund for Renewal. The modified accrual method provides funds for major renewal projects by creating a fund for this purpose. Each year an amount is added to the fund. This amount, plus accumulated interest, will provide for the expenditures in the year in which they are estimated to be required. In estimating this amount, interest is assumed to be a low rate, say, four percent. The difference between this rate and the amount of interest actually earned provides for inflation of the cost of the expenditures and therefore permits expenditures to be included at amounts that are not inflation adjusted. The need for renewal is estimated annually, probably by the maintenance superintendent.

For example, the following is a hypothetical calculation for Year 4:

	Amount	Years Hence*	Charge
Paving	$113,000	12	$ 7,520
Fire alarm system	200,000	15	9,988
Lighting fixtures	258,000	11	19,130
Emergency generator	90,000	18	3,509
Roofing	200,000	19	7,228
Elevators	495,000	17	20,888
Total Year 4 charge			$68,268

For expenditures, such as roofing, that will be made over several years, this is the middle year.

This calculation would be revised annually.

Accounting for these expenses on a cash basis, as is recommended for routine items, would result in large charges in the years in which they are made. The fund for renewal smoothes out these charges. The modified accrual method had the same effect as those listed above for routine capital expenditures.

The annual addition to the renewal fund is not recognized as an expense by GAAP. This is why the proposed method is called the *modified* accrual method.

Some people argue that current residents did not cause the need for future replacements, and therefore current residents should not be charged for them. If this argument is accepted, these expenditures should be financed by borrowing in the year in which they are made. The future debt service on this borrowing spreads the cost over future periods.

Provision for Working Capital. Working capital is the difference between current assets and current liabilities. Current liabilities finance part of the current assets, and working capital makes up the difference. In the typical CCRC, the entry fees provide a permanent source of funds that should be adequate for this purpose. Although the amount of unamortized entry fees for each resident reaches zero, new residents add to the unamortized balance. At a certain time, the total amount will reach a steady state because the entry fees for new residents will offset the amortization of the entry fees of original residents. Indeed, the relationship suggests that the unamortized entry fees in a CCRC provide capital that is analogous to the paid-in capital in a business corporation. In the example, CCRC entry fees have provided $33.6 million in capital. Of this, $26.4 million of this is held by trustees to guarantee payments on bonds. Working capital is assumed to be $0.5 million, which easily can be financed by the remainder.

Provision for Contingencies. For the same reason, the $7.2 million of funds that are available after the $26.4 million earmarked for bondholders should be adequate for contingencies.

Summary

The modified accrual method of arriving at fees is more closely related to management decisions regarding the acquisition of capital assets than the conventional method. It also better reflects the current need for cash. It may not be entirely consistent with the treatment of depreciable assets in business accounting, but many businesses have capitalization policies that produce similar results. Moreover, generally accepted accounting principles permit the use of any depreciation method that is "systematic and rational"; the schedule of debt service principal payments meets these criteria.

I suggest that CCRCs test the modified accrual method with their own data. Exhibit 3 shows the results of such a test in one CCRC. It shows that the overall results are similar, even though the method of arriving at the amount needed for fees is different.

Exhibit 1

Example CCRC

Balance Sheet

As of September 30, Year 3
(Thousands of dollars)

ASSETS

Working capital	$ 500
Investments	2,700
Funds held by trustee	26,400
Land	1,200
Land improvements	1,500
Buildings and equipment	40,300
Startup costs	2,200
Provision for renewals	0
Total assets	74,800

LIABILITIES AND EQUITY

Deferred entry fee revenue	33,600
Refundable deposits	500
Bonds payable	43,000
Equity	(2,300)
Total liabilities and equity	$74,800

Exhibit 2

Annual Charges for
Plant with the Two Methods

(Thousands of dollars)

Assumed situation: The plant cost $50 million, and it was financed with a 30-year 7 percent bond issue, with equal annual payments for principal and interest. The plant is depreciated over 50 years. The sum of debt-service principal plus interest is $4,029 each year.

Year	Debt-Service Principal	Depreciation	Debt Service higher (lower)
1	$ 529	$ 1,000	$ (471)
2	566	1,000	(434)
3	606	1,000	(394)
4	648	1,000	(352)
5	694	1,000	(306)
6	742	1,000	(258)
7	794	1,000	(206)
8	850	1,000	(150)
9	909	1,000	(91)
10	973	1,000	(27)
11	1,041	1,000	41
•			
•			
15	1,365	1,000	365
•			
20	1,914	1,000	914
•			
25	2,685	1,000	1,685
•			
30	3,766	1,000	2,766
Total	50,000	30,000	20,000
50	0	1,000	(1,000)
Total	50,000	50,000	0

Exhibit 3

Example CCRC

Strategic Plan

	Year 4	Year 5	Year 6	Year 7	Year 8
A. As Currently Estimated					
Expenses, net of non fee revenue	$1,841	$2,695	$3,023	$3,610	$3,707
Interest expense	4,030	3,998	3,956	3,911	3,862
Depreciation	1,155	1,167	1,182	1,199	1,211
Needed from fees	7,026	7,860	8,161	8,720	8,780
B. As Proposed					
Expenses, net of non fee revenue	$1,841	$2,695	$3,023	$3,610	$3,707
Interest expense	4,030	3,998	3,956	3,911	3,862
Debt service principal	473	512	554	599	648
Minor capital expenditures	419	116	151	169	123
Provision for renewal	70	70	70	70	70
Needed from fees	6,833	7,391	7,754	8,359	8,410

CHAPTER 16
FINANCIAL SERVICE ORGANIZATIONS

Changes from the Eighth Edition

Materials on commercial banks and insurance companies have been taken from the former chapter on Service Organizations, the coverage of these industries has been considerably expanded. The insurance section now includes casualty insurance as well as life insurance companies. Management control in securities firms (investment banks, securities traders, securities brokers and dealers, investment funds) is another topic.

Management control in financial service organizations currently receives relatively little attention in the literature and in the classroom. These firms, although a relatively small fraction of the gross national product, are increasingly important in the economy. Shocking inadequacies in the management control systems of banks and thrift institutions have recently been uncovered; the resulting losses have a major impact on the federal budget and the national debt. We believe that much more attention will be given to this topic from now on.

Cases

Chemical Bank discusses management control issues in a commercial bank, with special attention to the control of branches. This case is set in the early 1960s.

Metropolitan Bank discusses these issues in a bank as of 1993.

Citibank Indonesia also is a commercial banking case, but in an international setting.

Case 16-1

Chemical Bank

Note

Chemical Bank is a classic case on management control in a commercial bank. One of the key issues is: should branches be set up as profit centers? The only problem with the case is that it is set in the early 1960s. A lot has happened to this industry since then! We still like this case and strongly encourage the instructors to use it.

In order to update the case, we conducted a field study in a large Bank (here called Metropolitan Bank) in 1993. Metropolitan Bank, like many large banks, now treats branches as expense centers with additional non-financial performance measures. A key reason for this change in the control system has to do with a change in strategy over the years. In the 60s, banks wanted their branches to generate deposits as well as loans. Metropolitan wants its branches to focus on deposit generation; loans are centralized. That is to say, its branches are more like production departments and marketing is centralized. In the context of the change in strategy, change in controls over branches makes sense.

We recommend using both cases in a single class session. Instructors can start with the Chemical case and get the students to appreciate why constituting branches as profit centers made sense in the 1960s. Then, instructors can move to the Metropolitan Bank case and explore with students why they changed their controls over branches as of 1993.

Objective

This case is drawn from the thesis of a doctoral candidate at Harvard Business School. It deals with the use of the profit center concept as a management control device for branch offices in a service industry. A particular problem in banking is how to set the transfer price for money.

Dr. Paik's thesis contains a great deal of additional information about Chemical Bank, and some particularly interesting set of data are excerpted in Appendix A.

I have also used this case as a final exam. The examination question, and two of the better student exam papers, are reproduced in Appendix B.

Discussion

The first specific question at the end of the case is a useful way to open up the discussion. Depending upon how much ground is covered under the guise of dealing with this question, the remaining questions may be then handled much more quickly. I like to use this opening question to set up the familiar analytical sequence of goals, organization, and key variables. This then permits an easy comparison between a bank and a manufacturing company, and also facilitates the remainder of the discussion.

Goals. Although the goals for a branch are described in paragraph 3 of the case, these are probably not a good statement of the goals for the bank as a whole. Although I am sure that the bank as a whole wants to earn satisfactory profits, and to grow in deposits and loans, both of these objectives are really a function of another factor which is an explicit goal of many banks: service to their community. The economic rationale of this high-sounding goal is straightforward: banks make a profit by loaning out the funds entrusted to them by depositors. An increase in loans requires a preceding increase in deposits. But in order to get an increase in deposits, the bank must perform a useful service to businessmen and residents of the community. One of the most important differences between a bank and a manufacturing company are the opportunities for product differentiation. Money is about the most homogeneous product imaginable and, in fact, money is not the bank's product at all. Its product is service to depositors and borrowers, and it must find imaginative and efficient ways to render better services than its competitors.

Organizational structure. Nominally at least, Chemical Bank is decentralized in the operation of its branch banks. Branch managers are told that they are responsible for the profits of their branch as though it were an independent bank. In fact, because each branch is a part of a much larger institution, the authority of the branch manager is severely limited. He cannot control the price that he pays for deposits, either in terms of the interest rate on savings accounts or the types of services to be offered on regular checking accounts. Given the risk preferences of bankers generally, plus whatever additional criteria Chemical Bank's top management has laid down, the branch manager operates within a very narrow range of discretion concerning the interest rate, that he can charge on loans. The most critical operating variable for his particular branch, its location, has already been determined. And the most important element of operating costs, payroll, cannot be altered substantially without careful justification at headquarters. What, then, can the branch manager do? Is he really profit responsible, or is the system described here merely an artificial control device for "motivating" him?

What does top management want an individual branch manager to do? My view of his role is to cultivate the banking potential of the geographical area in the vicinity of his office. This really means that he is the deliverer of the bank's services to depositors and borrowers; the branch manager's responsibility for efficient internal operations of his branch is of clearly secondary importance. Other than being a personable, intelligent representative of the institution, how can the branch manager go about performing his main job in an efficient and effective manner? What kinds of decisions does the branch manager have to make? I think that the most important, continuing decision is how to allocate the use of his main resource, his time and the time of other officers located in his branch. An aggressive (to the extent appropriate) bank is one in which the officers are continually attempting to develop new business (new depositors and/or new borrowers) through broadening their circle of contacts. To the extent that it is possible for a bank officer to direct his efforts either toward (1) the development of new depositors, or (2) the development of new borrowers, then an individual branch manager has an important job. Trade-off decisions must be made between the allocation of time to one activity or the other, and these decisions must be based on (1) the particular environment in which the branch is located, i.e., the relative difficulty of acquiring deposits versus acquiring loans, and (2) the overall balance of loans and deposits for the bank as a whole.

If this analysis is correct, then I think that the profit center system used by Chemical Bank is most appropriate. The transfer price on excess or borrowed funds tells the branch manager what the position of the total bank is regarding the relative value of loans and deposits. Against this transfer price, the branch manager can then decide for his specific location whether his resources may be better employed in trying to acquire deposits to earn the transfer rate, or whether he should be borrowing from the central bank and using his efforts to make loans at rates above the transfer rate. He is, implicitly, told to make these continuing resource allocation decisions against the objective of improving the overall profitability of his particular branch.

Developing this line of reasoning in a class discussion is never as straightforward as I have tried to set it forth above. Sometimes this rationale for the system does not come out until very late in the class, but I think it follows most directly from the discussion of what the branch manager's job is, and I try to develop it at this point in the discussion if it can be done without forcing the students too much.

Key variables. Given these objectives and the organizational structure for accomplishing them, what are the key variables to be used for control purposes both at the branch and at headquarters? For a particular branch, I think the answer to this question depends importantly on its size. A large branch, with several officer personnel, will need a more formal control system for the branch manager than a one-officer branch will require. Any branch manager, however, will be searching for measurements of (1) evidences of satisfaction or dissatisfaction with banking services among his existing customers, and (2) the extent and effectiveness of efforts to develop new business for his branch. At the headquarters level, however, I suspect that the problem is quite different. Although top management is also interested in both of the measurements just listed, they have the important additional problem of putting those measurements into a locational context in order to evaluate the performance of a particular branch manager. Branch profitability, therefore, may be a useful key variable at the headquarters level even though, as a general rule, profitability is not specific enough to serve as a useful key variable for operating management. At the headquarters level, the real control over branch performance lies in the selection of the branch manager. Profits, particularly in relation to a carefully prepared budget, reflect the branch manager's success in developing the potential of his location. Headquarters personnel should concentrate their efforts on those locations which seem to be falling short of their potential so that branch profitability really acts as a screen in helping to identify the branches that need help.

A great many other, not-so-key variables are reported in the branch earnings statement and the Branch Office Report and its supplement. The statistical data are not news to the branch manager, and I suspect that they are used primarily at headquarters to facilitate the beginning analysis of a branch that appears to be in trouble as identified by a variance in its earnings statement.

Question 2. This question is useful for two purposes: (1) if the discussion of Question 1 has not already raised the issue of whether a branch should be a profit center or a cost center, then the issue is easy to raise here because the earnings statement implies a profit center while the branch office report implies a cost center control system; and (2) even if the profit center concept for branches is validated, the publication of a statistical report, such as Exhibits 8 and 9, raises an interesting question because of the conflicting signals that it gives to the branch manager. On the one hand, he is told that he is responsible for the profits of his branch, yet at the same time, he knows that headquarters personnel are receiving a great deal of detailed data that are really encompassed in his branch earnings statement.

One of the important values of a management control system is as a device for defining the job responsibilities of the unit on which the report is prepared. It is difficult to tell a man exactly what his job is, particularly if there is much breadth to his responsibilities. Just how difficult this is in Chemical Bank, and the degree of success that they have had, is illustrated by the data collected by Dr. Paik and reproduced in Appendix A. Although it takes 15 minutes or more, I have had a great deal of fun in class by putting Dr. Paik's exhibits on the blackboard, line by line. Interpreting these data is not easy. The students' first reaction is that this is ironclad evidence of confusion, poor communication, and perhaps management. Obviously, branch managers and headquarters personnel would have a consistent ranking of goals in a well-run bank. Then, some student would usually point out that it might be very appropriate for an individual branch to have a different ordering of goals that reflect the characteristics of its particular location. About all that is accomplished by this little side discussion is to emphasize how difficult it must be for headquarters personnel to communicate the legitimacy of a shifting order of goals for different branch managers, but I think that that's an important point to make.

Question 3. Dealing with this question of the use of a return on investment yardstick for branch performance measurement really requires more knowledge of the banking business than the students are able to glean from the case. Theoretically, it seems to me that it would be possible to develop such a measurement by calculating the amount of capital, surplus and undivided profits (i.e., equity) that branch would need in order to support its level of deposits. Branch profits could then be computed as a percentage of the capital invested to arrive at the return on investment as it might be calculated for an independent bank.

The desirability of calculating such a measurement is less clear, however. Its main advantage would be that it would provide a more useful figure for comparing one branch to another than the figure that is now presented on the branch earnings statement, the "Net Earnings Ratio." This ratio, analogous to profits as a percentage of sales in a manufacturing company, is the ratio between net earnings before taxes and gross income for the branch. Obviously, this ratio varies significantly from one branch to another. A return on investment measurement would have much smaller variations but I'm still not sure whether the variations would mean anything. The branch managers has no responsibility for the overall bank's dividend policy nor for decisions to raise new equity capital. I believe that net earnings provides sufficient information for the branch manager to make his resource allocation decisions, and that he should not be provided with (and perhaps confused by) a return on investment figure.

Question 4. There are a great many noncontrollable and allocated costs that appear in the branch earnings statement. After the stage has been properly set by an earlier discussion of goals and organization, it is extremely worthwhile to discuss several of these cost items. The opening questions for each item is: How shall we handle this element of cost such that the branch manager will be motivated to act in a manner consistent with the overall goals of the bank?

The allocation of costs for check clearing and other clerical functions is probably the most dramatic one to discuss. Many students will argue that, since the branch manager can't control these activities, he should not be charged with the cost of them. What they really mean is that the branch manager cannot control the efficiency with which these activities are performed, but further thought leads to the discovery that he really *is* responsible for the incurrence of the activity. Or, at least, the branch manager is getting credit for the income that results from servicing a customer's checking account, even though he obviously cannot control the extent of the activity in the account. If the branch manager were not charged for the costs of servicing checking accounts, then the relative desirability of increasing the deposits in his branch would be higher; a new deposit would generate income for him at no cost. Failing to charge the branch manager with the costs of servicing accounts would, therefore, lead him to make erroneous decisions about the allocation of officer time in soliciting deposits rather than loans.

The counter-arguments on this item, as well as discussion of several other cost items, will be found in the student examination papers in Appendix B.

Question 5. My answer to the question as stated is "yes" because, as indicated earlier, I think a branch budget should be a careful attempt to predict the degree to which progress will be made in developing business in the branch's particular location, and I want to use budget variances as a measurement of the extent to which the branch manager is achieving the particular goals that have been agreed on in setting the budget. Therefore, noncontrollable rate variances on both interest costs and on allocated servicing costs should probably be broken out separately.

There is another fascinating question that can be raised at this point. Exhibit 5 is a little difficult for the students to understand, and once they do understand it, it comes as a revelation to many of them that the interest rate on excess or borrowed funds is really a transfer price between branches. The question then is: Should the transfer price be a "cost-based" price as calculated in Exhibit 5, or should some other price be used? First, we must recognize that the transfer price is cost-based in the sense of the opportunity cost of funds in the regular investment pool, not the explicit cost of servicing depositors' checking accounts. But we have seen that this transfer price is a key fact in the resource allocation decisions made by branch managers, and that increases or decreases in this price will have some effect on the way branch managers spend their time. The extent to which a small change in the rate will influence branch actions depends, appropriately, on the particular environment in which the branch is operating; a change of a given magnitude might have no effect at all in many branches but would probably have some effect on some branches. Thus, the ability of top management to establish and change the transfer price is a major tool for controlling the activities of the branch managers. For example, if for some reason the top management wanted to increase the deposits of the bank as a whole, it could raise the interest rate paid on excess funds and thereby encourage the branch managers to allocate more time to seeking deposits (and less time to seeking loans). Why top management might want to do this, and whether it would be a good policy or not, are difficult questions to answer, but it does seem to me that this control system provides top management with a useful tool for influencing the activities of branch officer personnel in a nicely subtle, decentralized manner.

Summary

As the above discussion indicates, this is an extremely "rich" case that can be used as a vehicle to discuss a variety of topics. Although it is easy to structure the discussion in almost any desired direction, I find that, if time permits, the most effective utilization of this case is just to let the discussion run while the students develop and improve their understanding of the situation. Used in this way, the instructor's main role is to keep signaling to the students that there may be additional levels of understanding for them to achieve in this case, and to occasionally take a few minutes to consolidate the gains that have been made.

—Richard F. Vancil

Appendix A

Chemical Bank (A)

Excerpts from *Use of Reports for Control of Branches* (an unpublished doctoral thesis), by Chei-Min Paik

(NOTE: Dr. Paik's brief summary report of his findings appears as the appendix, "Management Control in Branch Banks," pp. 169–183 in Hekimian, James S., *Management Control in Life Insurance Branch Offices* (Division of Research, Harvard Business School, 1965.)

Ranking of Branch Goals: A Questionnaire Study

In Chapter 1, the responsibility areas of the branch manager were identified and enumerated without ordering. But since the human and financial resources of the branch are limited, some weighting of the multiple goals in terms of importance is necessary for the resource allocation decisions by the branches. In the course of the field study it became apparent that, although the various responsibility areas were neither mutually exclusive nor independent of one another, both the branch managers and their supervisors emphasized certain areas more than others.

A questionnaire study as described below was conducted on the ranking of the values of the branch managership. Both the branch managers and headquarters supervisors were included in the study because it was hypothesized that the ranking would be different between the two groups as well as among the individuals. Eighteen branch managers and nine headquarters supervisors, picked "at random" out of total of 120 or so branch managers and some 15 headquarters supervisors at the Chemical Bank, participated. The exact format of the questionnaire is reproduced on the following page.

This case was prepared by Robert N. Anthony.

Copyright © 1972 by the President and Fellows of Harvard College. Harvard Business School case 172-228.

A Questionnaire

The following are some of the more important responsibility areas of the branch manager. Please rank them according to the degree of importance you would say you attach to each item as a guide for allocating your effort. Please use numeral 1 for the most important, 2 for the next important, 3 for the next..., and so on.

Development of personnel

Reduce operating costs

Increase deposits

Satisfaction of employees

Increase "profit"

Improvement in customer relations

Increase loans

Meet budget

Others _____

_____

Comments _____

Exhibit 6

Ranking of Branch Values

Values	Ranks	1		2		3		4		5		6		7		8		Total	
		No.	%	No.	%	No.	%	No.	%	No.	%	No.	%	No.	%	No.	%	No.	%
Development of Personnel	Branch Managers	3	18.8	4	25.0	1	6.3	3	18.8			1	6.3	2	12.5	2	12.5	16	100
	Headquarters Supervisors	2	33.3			2	33.3	2	33.3									6	100
Reduce operating costs	Branch Managers					1	6.3	2	12.5	5	31.3	4	25.0	4	25.0			16	100
	Headquarters Supervisors							1	16.7					3	50.0	2	33.3	6	100
Increase deposits	Branch Managers	6	37.6	2	12.5	4	25.0	3	18.8	1	6.3							16	100
	Headquarters Supervisors	3	50.0	1	16.7	1	16.7	1	16.7									6	100
Satisfaction of employees	Branch Managers	1	6.3	1	6.3	5	31.3	3	18.8	3	18.8	1	6.3	1	6.3	1	6.3	16	100
	Headquarters Supervisors					1	16.7	2	33.3			3	50.0					6	100
Increase profit	Branch Managers			3	20.0	1	6.7	1	6.7	2	13.3	4	26.7	3	20.3	1	6.7	15*	100
	Headquarters Supervisors	1	16.7	2	33.3					2	33.3			1	16.7			6	100
Improve customer relations	Branch Managers	5	31.3	5	31.3	3	18.8			3	18.8							16	100
	Headquarters Supervisors			2	33.3	2	33.3	1	16.7	1	16.7							6	100
Increase Loans	Branch Managers	1	6.3	1	6.3	1	6.3	4	25.0	2	12.5	5	31.3	2	12.5			16	100
	Headquarters Supervisors							1	16.7	1	16.7	2	33.3	1	16.7	1	16.7	6	100
Meet budgets	Branch Managers											1	6.3	4	25.0	11	68.8	16	100
	Headquarters Supervisors									1	16.7	1	16.7	1	16.7	3	50.0	6	100
Others	Branch Managers																	0	0
	Headquarters Supervisors																	0	0

Exhibit 7
Ranking of Four Selected Branch Values

Values	Rank 1 No.	Rank 1 %	Rank 2 No.	Rank 2 %	Rank 3 No.	Rank 3 %	Rank 4 No.	Rank 4 %	Total No.	Total %	
Reduce operating costs			7	38.9	10	55.6	1	5.6	18	100	Branch Managers
			1	16.7	3	50.0	2	33.3	6	100	Headquarters Supervisors
Increase deposits	16	88.9	2	11.1					18	100	Branch Managers
	6	100.0							6	100	Headquarters Supervisors
Increase loan	2	11.1	9	50.0	7	38.9			18	100	Branch Managers
			3	50.0	2	33.3	1	16.7	6	100	Headquarters Supervisors
Meet budget					1	5.6	17	94.4	18	100	Branch Managers
			2	33.3	1	16.7	3	50.0	6	100	Headquarters Supervisors

Tabulation

Answers to the questionnaire are tabulated in Exhibit 6 and Exhibit 7. Exhibit 6 summarizes answers from 18 branch managers, including the 16 managers represented in Exhibit 6, and the same six headquarters supervisors of Exhibit 6. Exhibit 7 is a mere abstraction of the ranking on four chosen branch values only. Suppose a particular respondent ranked the eight values listed in the questionnaire as below:

	Rank in Exhibit 6
Development of personnel	1
Reduce operating costs	2
Increase deposits	3
Satisfaction of employees	4
Increase profit	5
Improve customer relations	6
Increase loans	7
Meet budget	8

Then, for the purpose of inclusion in Exhibit 7 which deals only with four selected values, he would be counted in the frequency distribution on the following basis:

	Rank in Exhibit 7
Reduce operating costs	1
Increase deposits	2
Increase loans	3
Meet budget	4

In both exhibits, the upper line under each branch value is for answers from branch managers; the lower line for answers from headquarters supervisors. Under each rank, the left column is for the number of answers; the right column, for the percentage of the number of answers to the total number of answers. For example, in Exhibit 6, it is read that two branch managers, i.e., 12.5 percent of all answering branch managers, ranked "Reduce operating costs" as the fourth, while one headquarters supervisor, which represents 16.7 percent of all answering headquarters supervisors, ranked it as the fourth.

Detailed Analysis of Ranking. According to Exhibit 6, all who answered ranked "Meet budget" very low. Indeed, the clear majority ranked it at the bottom. This is interesting, particularly in light of the fact that the branch budget includes operating costs, deposits, loans, which rank high. Exhibit 7, which is the tabulation for only four branch values consisting of the above three and "Meet budget" confirms the unmistakably low ranking of "Meet budget" for the branch manager group; 94 percent of the total ranked it the lowest. However, for the headquarters supervisor group, only 50 percent of the total ranked it the lowest and the distribution spreads over a wider range, suggesting the possibility that the headquarters group in general is concerned with the value, "Meet budget," a little more than the branch manager group. Two headquarters supervisors ranked it second place.

The value, "Increase deposits," is given the highest ranking by both the branch and headquarters groups. "Increase loans," in contrast, is quite low in the rank order, with a distribution centering on the sixth for the headquarters group and around the fifth (or 4.75) for the branch group....

An "average" branch manager would rank "Reduce operating costs" somewhere between the fifth and sixth (5.5), while an "average" headquarters supervisor would rank it at around the seventh place (6.83). This discrepancy may be interpreted to reflect the fact that the branch managers are somewhat more microscopic than the headquarters supervisors. It seems natural that the branch managers are a little more "internal-operation oriented" and accordingly, a little more concerned with the operating costs than the headquarters supervisors.

"Development of personnel" and "Improvement of customer relations" compete for the second highest in the rank order. It could be said, from the examination of Exhibit 6, that for branch managers, "Improve customer relations" comes before "Development of personnel," while the order is the reverse for the headquarters supervisors. The conjecture is not so much that the headquarters supervisors belittle the importance of "Improving customer relations," as that the branch managers may be less farsighted than the headquarters supervisors. The wider scatter in the frequency distribution of the central management group for the value, "Development of personnel," may be interpreted to lend further support to the above tentative conclusion, or a related inference that the branch managers are confused as to the importance of "Development of personnel."

"Increase profit" displays a bimodal distribution both for the branch and central groups. The bimodality may be attributed either to confusion arising from the nebulousness of the term, "profit," or to the genuine existence of two different kinds of people in each group with two different sets of values. Granted that the term "profit" is nebulous and abused, yet it has some symbolic significance to most people. On this basis, the particular distributions may be interpreted to reflect more "profit orientation" of the central management group.

Appendix B

Student Examination Papers on Chemical Bank

This case was used as a four-hour exam in a first-year MBA course at Harvard Business School. The question assigned was as follows:

In light of our study of control systems as a means of motivating and evaluating responsibility centers within an organization, evaluate the system used by Chemical Bank and propose changes you believe would be suitable.

As identifiable sub-parts of your analysis, please discuss the adequacy of Chemical's system regarding:

a. *Cost allocation* of headquarters' expenses (pp. 3-8 of the case). Should these costs be allocated? Are these methods of allocation appropriate?

b. *Performance evaluation* of dissimilar branches. Does this reporting system provide enough information? Too much? Should Exhibits 8–9 be discontinued?

c. *Transfer prices.* If you believe the profit center system should be continued as a control device, please discuss the appropriateness of the data developed in Exhibit 5 for transfer pricing purposes.

Two of the best papers are reproduced below.

1. Examination Paper by Student #382

A management control system can only be evaluated within the context of the environment within which it operates and in light of the ends towards which it is designed to propel the organization. It is therefore necessary first to specify that environment.

We are dealing with the branch banking operations of the Chemical Bank (CB), and the goals for those branch banks were clearly set forth on page one of the case. Further, CB has already chosen to run its operations in an essentially decentralized manner. A branch manager is free to make whatever decisions he feels appropriate within the bounds set out by CB policy. For example, he can give raises to whichever employees he feels merit them, but he must be careful not to violate the range of pay for that employee's job classification. Further, CB has set up its operations in such a way that the branch banks are profit centers and the central banking services are cost centers. This last factor, however, is different from the fact of the goals and the organization in that it is a portion of the CB operations properly included in the control system: the former two are not.

In reading the case, it appears to me that there are two factors truly critical to the success of CB's branch operations. First, since a bank makes its money by loaning and reinvesting the money of its depositors, it is essential that the branches *maintain and expand* the volume of deposits, and, where profitable, the amount of their outstanding loans. Because interest rates on deposits are fixed centrally, the only real variable open to the branches for competitive exploitation is *service*.

Second, it is important that the branches forecast funds needs and availability closely so that the CB can keep as many of its assets invested as possible.

Given this environment and these two factors critical to CB's success, let me now turn to an evaluation of the control system as it now exists. I would like to analyze the control system in terms of three purposes which any effective control system must fulfill: Communication, Evaluation, and Motivation.

Communication

The control system must communicate in two directions. First, by its provisions and its demands, it must make clear to the branch managers those aspects of the banking operation which are most critical to CB. Second, it must indicate to CB not only what is being done, but what each of the branches *intends* to do.

The latter function is performed by the budget. At CB, each branch must submit a budget of its anticipated operations for the coming year. Unfortunately, we do not have a great deal of information about the system by which these budgets are created and okayed. They are set with the aid of standard forms and a set of CB policy statements, but we have little idea of how thoroughly they are examined or how inflexibly they are enforced. However, the absence of budgetary complaints in the comments of the branch managers and the absence of an analysis of budgetary variances suggests that the budget is indeed designed to indicate to the CB the magnitude of projected branch operations. This is as it should be, for CB is interested in overall profitability, not item-by-item costs. However the statements in Exhibits 2 and 3 are very valuable to the manager in keeping tabs of the operations of his own branch. The manager of Branch B should want to know why his employee benefits are up some $850 while his salaries are actually down $1,000.

Another area of communication is the portion of the control system dealing with allocated costs. it is through these costs that the branch manager is informed of the expenses inherent in the central bank operation and of the portion of those expenses attributable to his operation (because the branches are evaluated on the basis of earnings, these allocated costs are deducted from branch earnings).

There are two types of allocated costs, those for banking services and those for administrative services. Each of these classes has costs which are optional or required. Because the branch manager is judged (as I will later justify) on the basis of his performance against budget, it is essential that he be able to predict with some accuracy the magnitude of the costs he will incur. For this reason, I suggest that the CB system be changed so that allocated costs are charged, *by use whenever possible*, at a rate which has been predetermined. For the non-optional costs, this factor is not critically important, but serves to guarantee that any deviations from budgeted performance are indeed attributable to controllable management decisions. For example, rental, bookkeeping, and check clearance are not costs which the manager can elect to incur, but he may have some control over the composition of those costs. For example, if he knew that special statements were a very expensive bookkeeping function, he might be able to supply his customer with the information he needs in some other way. Or he might even speak to a customer who was requesting an inordinate number of special statements. If, however, he does know in advance what costs will be, he does not have this operational knowledge which CB would profit by his having.

Check clearance brings up another problem in cost allocation: the basis of allocation of cost. Again, the purpose of cost allocation is to distribute among the several branches the necessary costs of the CB. However, since each manager can have an influence on the magnitude of those accounts, he should be charged only for the portion of those costs attributable to him. At the same time, CB must be careful that the control system does not lead the manager to actions detrimental to the bank as a whole. In check clearance, it is obvious that the more checks a branch forwards to CB for processing, the greater the costs. Thus, an ideal customer would both write and deposit only a few large checks, and this fact of life is made clear by a charge on the basis of checks handled. However, one branch would therefore suffer if it cashed or accepted checks of the customer of another bank, yet this would be in the overall best interests of CB. Therefore, the basis of cost in such a system would better be the branch on which the check was written, or, if outside the CB system, the branch whose customer cashed or deposited the check. The important point, which is present in the CB system, is that any allocation can be challenged by a manager if it is felt to be unfair.

On optional services, the CB should be running on a straight fee basis. Installment loans, for example, can be services *or* can be turned over for central servicing. There should be a fixed charge for turning an account over, so that the manager could decide whether he could service the loan more profitably himself. Similarly, there should be a fixed scale for credit investigations so that a manager could decide whether to take a risk, investigate himself, or request a central investigation. The charges should be based on a projected break-even. Losses or gains could either be made up in later years or allocated to *all* branches with administrative costs. If one of these services cannot be supported on this basis, it should be dropped.

The final phase of communication involves the transfer price. By this mechanism, the manager is advised whether it is more profitable for him to loan out money himself (or even borrow money to loan out) or to deposit any excess in the central bank for them to invest. Furthermore, the two types of investments (with different interest rates) reflect the desirability of savings deposits over demand deposits. The former carry lower reserve requirements and, because they do not have to be paid out on demand, can more safely be invested in longer term (and higher yield, generally) and more speculative projects. In essence, the calculation in Ex. 5 computes the excess, or deficit, amounts which a branch has available for loaning. It then charges or pays for that deficit or at a rate of return computed by first charging the pro rata share of the special fund at its rate, and the balance at the regular rate (these on savings deposits only), and then charging the demand deposits at the regular pool rate. This is appropriate because it gives the manager a benchmark against which to judge whether he can more profitably loan or invest his deposited funds than can the central investment pool. This system automatically adjusts for the varying opportunities facing different branches in that the branch with no lending opportunity would deposit while the one with many opportunities would withdraw. The only change I would suggest is a minor one. As before, I feel the budgeted rates should be used in these calculations. Although it is unlikely that the budgeted and actual would ever be very different, the branch manager should know the rate he is facing.

Evaluation

Technically, evaluation is another form of communication, but a specialized one. I feel that much of the data provided in Ex. 8 and 9 is unnecessary in evaluation. The number of accounts opened or closed or the number of safety deposit boxes are unimportant. These may or may not have been profitable depending on the size of the accounts or the other benefits accrued by such services as personal money orders. What is important, however, is profitability, both absolutely and relatively. Absolute profitability should be measured by the ratio of earnings (I selected before taxes) to augment gross deposits. This ratio reflects the use to which deposited money has been put, and assuming the fairness of the transfer prices discussed earlier, measures the real substance of CB's vested interest. For 1959, these figures would have been:

	A	B
EBT	120	1,658
Aug. Gross Dep	13,707	75,853
Ratio	.87%	2.18%

Thus, for whatever the reason, Branch B is a much more profitable generator of deposits.

I also feel that a comparison of actual profits (or net earnings before taxes) to budget is important in that this figure can cover the environmental factors if the budgeted figures are carefully evaluated. In this case, B's EBT were more than 5.7 percent below budget, while A's were 16.5 percent over. If the budgeted figures accurately reflected the economic and environmental potential for growth, these measures are the key to measuring management effort. They cannot, however, be evaluated here because I do not know enough about the procedure for making budgets.

Motivation

There are two key aspects of the motivational role of a control system which I would like to discuss. First, the attitude toward the whole system . In reading some of the comments made by branch managers, I was dismayed that the manager of Branch A did not really know or understand the CB system, but assumed it was fair and accurate. This implies to me that he was not that vitally interested in the measures generated by the system, and that, not understanding how the costs were derived, he could not very well work to minimize those costs. I therefore feel that, for this manager at least, more stress needs to be placed on the control system measures of his performance. The B manager seemed better informed, so I can't generalize the previous statement, but I do urge that CB determine how well the control system is understood and followed.

The other area of motivation involves conflicts of interest. While CB has done a good job in the loan decisions (transfer prices) and in working on such things as check clearance, they still have no suitable provision for inter-branch competition. I feel that there should be an inter-bank transfer of profits or credit either for customers transferred from one branch to another or for business steered to another branch. I cannot be more specific, however, as I do not know the magnitude, type, or frequency of those transfers.

2. Examination Paper by Student #328

To evaluate the bank's control system, we need first to look at the company objectives and examine the role of the units being controlled; then we can see how well the system reinforces what management desires.

Translating growth and earnings generalities to the banking business implies that Chemical's management wants:

1. Deposit growth—deposits are the constraining factor on the loanable funds, hence control a bank's long term growth.

2. An appropriate earnings return on the bank's capital ("appropriate" could be definable in terms of industry or area average or in absolute "demanded rate" returns). This is a strategic decision, and regardless of the decision, management wants:

   (a) optimum use of funds as loans (or investments)

   (b) operating cost control.

Of the two types of units being controlled, branch offices and centralized service groups, the branches appear more significant. Let's examine their role first.

Bank management relates several things that are *not* the branch manager's job:

1. Branch location decisions.

2. Interest rates (the Banking Division VP says these are "uncontrollable," but Headquarters probably dictates the appropriate rate structures to use for deposits and loans).

3. Rent vs. own decisions on the branch offices.

4. The choice of which bookkeeping duties will be handled centrally.

By process of elimination we see the branch manager's job is to:

1. Acquire deposits and loans.

2. Decide on the relative emphasis he should give to each ("Branches are operated as if independent").

3. Staff and supervise the branch office proper according to the jobs assigned.

Management states that, under the present control system, they want three things from their branch managers:

1. Operation within his budgets.

2. Growth in deposits and loans.

3. Satisfactory profits.

I presume "his budgets" refer to his annual estimates on his controllable costs; if so, this goal reinforces the bank's desire to control operating costs. It appears that sufficient documentation will justify budget changes to take advantage of environmental changes.

Whether management really wants both deposit and loan growth from each branch is questionable. The banking division V.P. states that a comparison to the area potential is a more appropriate measure. Therefore, this goal should probably be altered to: meeting specific loan and deposit volume goals (budgets) which would be arrived at by weighing both the branches' and the bank's strategic position. The branches do, in fact, now have these goals shown on their earnings statement.

"Satisfactory profits" leaves a lot of room for a variety of profit calculations and any number of bases for the standard of satisfaction. Certainly, if a profit center concept is used, the goal would be to make the profit meet or exceed the standard. On the other hand, if a profit center is not used, management will desire satisfactory performance compared to some other standard.

So, goals 2 and 3 really say "we want satisfactory performance as measured by our system compared to subjective goals." Does the profit center concept reinforce management's desire for the branch manager to

> acquire deposits and loans,
> decide on the relative emphasis,
> staff and supervise his branch efficiently?

There appear to be five major interrelated variables which determine bank profitability:

1. Deposit *Volume*

2. Deposit Interest Payable (*rate*)

3. Loan and Investment *Volume*

4. Loan and Investment Interest Income (*rate*)

5. Operating Expenses

While the rate factors appear "uncontrollable" to the bank V.P., let alone to the branch manager, they do have a direct bearing on the relative emphasis he gives and the expenses he will incur to acquire loans and deposits. Since Chemical is giving its branch managers this emphasis decision, a profit center concept seems appropriate. If the cost allocations and transfer rates properly reflect the bank's position, profit measurement of the branches will encourage branch decisions in line with corporate objectives. Branch managers A and B seem to be aware of how they make "profits." Neither knows a whole lot about the allocations (though they believe these are fair) but each recognizes that both deposits and loans can make "him" money and each has a good idea of the relative emphasis his territory requires.

The profit center concept requires that the centralized services be allocated back to the branches (else income making deposits or loans would be worth any cost as long as it's someone else's cost). As far as I can see, the allocation methods are appropriate—they closely relate costs to the work done for each branch. Installment loans allocation could be distorted if some branches wrote typically longer term loans, but the controller feels the distortion is not great; at any rate it should wash out within the 2-3 year period of the loans. To me, the best indication of the appropriateness of the allocation is that the branch managers accept them, and feel they are fair.

The present system provides performance data which concentrates on the profit figure. Given that the branches are dissimilar, there is no way to compare these; although each can be compared to its own profit budget, which in turn was derived from loan, deposit, and operating cost elements. If there were a return on investment calculation, these would be more comparable and would tend to indicate which branches were using their funds most efficiently. Even though the budgeted profit probably bears some relationship to what management feels is adequate for each branch, given its position, this information should also be helpful to the branch manager as it would give him a better feeling for his growth objectives: whether he should be more aggressive or accept a slower growth. I propose that a return on investment calculation be shown on each branch earnings report. Management, from a strategic point of view, will have to establish the standards, but the desirable range should be fairly tight for established branches.

I believe evaluation emphasis should be placed on

> deposits vs. plan
> loans vs. plan
> return on investment vs. plan

The earnings figure will have to be calculated to arrive at the ROL. This implies management should change their present goals (2) and (3) to emphasize the deposit growth and loan and cost profitability of each branch. The profit center concept applies for the calculation of profit.

Since Exhibits 8 and 9 are statements which give details on two of the critical success factors, they should be continued. They give management and the branch manager a summary of volume mix and trends.

The investment division earnings allocation (transfer rate) appears appropriate; it reflects the bank's obtainable rate and hence properly influences each branch.

As far as I can tell, the short term portfolio rate does reflect the appropriate cost of borrowed funds (the rate foregone) and is a satisfactory return for the branches who cannot otherwise loan out the funds.

As for the centralized units, their job is to process, according to standard procedure, the volume put on them by the branches. They should be controlled by a variable cost budget which recognizes the volume effects that now show up in expense allocation.

In summary, I feel the present control system is appropriate but not entirely comprehensive enough to properly motivate the branch managers. Since Chemical gives its branches a good deal of authority on loan and deposit decisions, I feel a profit center concept is applicable. But, I feel performance emphasis should be shifted to

> deposit volume vs. goal
> loan volume vs. goal
> ROI vs. goal

The goals would be jointly set by the branch manager and top management and reflect explicitly what now must be "interpreted" into the system.

Case 16-2

Metropolitan Bank
Teaching Note

Retail Banking Strategy

Metropolitan Bank recognized that different customer segments use a different set of products and services offered by the bank and utilize a different mix of resources (e.g., branches, ATM, customer service phone numbers). RBG's strategy was to segment customers into five groups, and identify profitability and resource utilization for each. Over the next two to three years RBG will focus on the profitable groups and allow the others to either leave the bank or pay high enough prices to render them profitable.

Organization Structure

The organization structure in Metropolitan divides responsibility for different aspects of the retail banking group into distinct groups. The organization chart shows the eight areas that make up the retail banking group, all of which provide a distinct service. The case states the different functions that the groups perform.

The Bonus Incentive Plan

The case suggests the Bonus Incentive Plan (BIP) to evaluate branch managers' performance. Examining Exhibit 2, students can get a sense of the metrics that BMs are measured on. Asset growth constitutes 24% of the evaluation criteria, but branch managers are responsible for neither setting interest rates nor approving loans. Therefore students may question why BMs are responsible for growth in assets. Metropolitan Bank feels that the product and market groups will make these products competitive (in terms of pricing and approval standards) and the BMs have an influence on how well they are marketed, therefore effecting the generation of new assets.

Growth in deposits and revenue from non-bank investments (insurance, mutual funds, etc.) can be driven by branch personnel, to some extent. In the case of deposit growth, BMs cannot control rates on deposits, minimum required balances, or other criteria. They are able to provide fast and courteous service to existing customers by having some control over staffing. (District managers have flexibility in staffing over the branches in their respective district and they approve personnel training.) BMs can also waive certain fees related to deposit accounts such as overdraft charges.

Customer service is gauged by a quarterly survey which is administered by a third party to a random sample of current and past Bank customers. This information is used to compile the rating for the customer satisfaction metric of the BIP. This is perhaps the evaluation criteria for which they have the most control. The training and morale in the branch is directly influenced by their decisions. (Note: The bonus incentive plan sets forth the objectives that the branches must attain to receive a bonus. The actual distribution of the bonus dollars is the responsibility of regional managers, district managers, and branch managers.)

Transfer Pricing

The structure in Metropolitan tries to remove variability in branch profitability from BM evaluation through an elaborate transfer pricing mechanism for money. The central treasury group is basically a clearing house for funds generated and used within the bank. Transfer prices have also been set for nearly 75 services, most of which are provided by the sales and services group.

Case 16-3

Citibank Indonesia
Teaching Note

Purpose of Class

The Citibank Indonesia case (9-185-061) is intended to allow students to discuss some of the important issues related to the design and operation of planning and budgeting systems. The case also provides some opportunities for secondary learning about management of a multinational bank, the roles of a country manager, and problems faced by managers operating in third world countries.

The written case is enriched significantly by two videotapes:
> **Citibank Indonesia: Background Information** (5-186-061) (28 minutes)
> **Citibank Indonesia: Budget Issue** (5-186-062) (14 minutes)

The first videotape is intended for student viewing before class. The second is intended to be shown in class after students have had a chance to discuss the primary issue. Transcript of these tapes are available through case services.

Suggested Assignment

Watch 28 minute videotape before class.[*]

Question

What should Mehli Mistri do about the budget issue described on page 1 of the case?

Discussion

In the case, Mehli Mistri, Citibank's country manager for Indonesia, is faced with an issue related to his budget for 1984. He has prepared a bottom-up budget which he feels is very aggressive, but his superior is now asking him to raise the profit target by between $500,000 to $1,000,000.

This request (demand?) for a higher target comes from corporate headquarters. During the normal budget review process, the managers of the institutional bank came to the conclusion that

---

This case was prepared by Kenneth A. Merchant.

[*] See attached transcripts of video tapes.

the consolidated profit plan was inadequate. They raised the targets for the groups (geographical regions), and then managers of the groups and the divisions were faced with the task of allocating the higher targets down to the country level.

In preparing the case, the students are asked to put themselves in Mehli Mistri's position and to take one or more of the actions described on the bottom of the first page of the case. In class, some broader issues related to the roles of budgets in a decentralized company and budgeting system design will come out.

The videotapes are an important supplement to the written case. In the original version of the case, I included a full budget for Citibank Indonesia to show the significance of the amount by which Mehli is asked to increase his budget. I had to remove this information in the final version of the case, however, because information about the size and profitability of Citibank's operations in individual countries is very sensitive. Mehli makes the point several times in the videotape that the increase is significant. If students are still not comfortable with this vagueness, suggest that they assume the increase is somewhere around 10 percent of the total budget.

Pedagogy

The times I have used this case, I found it useful to start with some introductory comments on planning and budgeting systems. The need for such comments. of course, will vary depending on the students in the class and the material that precedes the use of the case.

Here is an outline of the lecture I gave:

1. Definition: A budgeting system is a combination of information flows and administrative processes and procedures that is usually an integral part of the short-range planning and control system of an organization.

2. Planning and budgeting processes are very important to most corporations of any significant size. HBS used to have a whole course on this topic.

3. There are three planning cycles in well-developed processes in large decentralized firms: strategic planning, programming and budgeting. These can be illustrated using the diagram in Vancil and Lorange (1975).[1] These three cycles need not be distinct. Many firms combine the cycles, and the processes need not be formal, but all the tasks must get done.

4. The planning and budgeting processes cut across all of the types of controls in my control framework.

    •   The links with *results control* are obvious, as budgeting involves setting targets which are often used later as standards against which to evaluate performance.

    •   Planning processes serve as *action controls*, in two important ways. First, the processes include actions that are felt to be good for managers to do, such as thinking about the future and communicating with other parts of the organization. Second, the often-formal

---

[1] R. F. Vancil and P. Lorange, "Strategic Planning in Diversified Companies," *Harvard Business Review* (January–February 1975), pp. 84–85.

reviews of plans are what I call "preaction reviews" which can help prevent inappropriate actions from occurring.

- Planning processes also serve as *personnel controls* as they provide training and serve to get information needed for decision making to the right managers.

5. Planning and budgeting processes serve both planning and control ends. Early in the process the emphasis is more on longer-term thinking—strategy formulation, if you will. Toward the end of the process, the emphasis is more on developing targets that are used for control purposes.

6. There are a whole range of variables that can be considered in designing planning and budgeting processes. One way to look at the choices is in terms of the following variables:

- Content—forms that need to be filled out. Many formats are standard, such as pro forma income statements and balance sheets, and cash flow forecasts, but many others are not.

- People—who is involved?

- Timing—for example, should long range planning be done before or after a consideration of what next year will look like?

- Format—for example, level of aggregation, use of graphics.

One of the important choices that must be made is how fast to narrow the span of strategic options being considered, as described in Lorange and Vancil (1976).[2] The choice that is made can be implemented by shaping combinations of the above four types of variables.

7. Planning and budgeting systems must differ depending on the company's situation; for example, technology, strategy, market environment, complexity of firm, resources available, type of people at the top and at the bottom. Since this is true, it is likely that a company's planning and budgeting system will have to change over time, as these factors change.

8. The design and operation of planning and budgeting systems is an art, not a science. I like to point out that my first job after my I received my MBA involved designing the annual planning process at Texas Instruments. Our little group reduced the size of the planning manual, which included forms and schedules, from 2.8" thick in 1970 to 1.21" thick in 1971.[3] To this day, I do not know if we improved or hurt the process, and I doubt if anyone else does either.

Early in the class I like to develop the diagram of Citibank's budgeting process shown in Figure TN-1. This makes several important points which can be discussed if desired. First, Citibank's process is relatively compact, as compared with some other processes that students may have seen (e.g., the ITT process described in Galvor). Second, it shows that the intent is bottom-up development of targets, except for the final top-down feedback that resulted from the review process in early November 1983. Finally, it shows that the sovereign risk review process

---

[2] P. Lorange and R.F. Vancil, "How to Design a Strategic Planning System," *Harvard Business Review* (September–October 1976), p. 80.
[3] This was the era of zero-based budgeting.

is taking place concurrently. That should lead to a discussion of what sovereign risk, is, why someone sitting in New York should be involved in setting sovereign risk limits in a decentralized company, and how an operating budget can be prepared before the sovereign risk limits have been set.

The concept of sovereign risk is new to many students. I like to view this process as just one of the key elements in Citibank's resource allocation process. They are asking the question: What markets do they want to be in? Within the confines of the charter of the institutional bank, a key decision is the weighting of the mix of markets (i.e., countries) to serve. The corporate people also look at scenarios (e.g. oil glut scenario) and try to ensure that the bank's portfolio will remain well diversified.

On the homework tape, Mehli Mistri explains that the centralized sovereign risk review process is not inconsistent with the philosophy of decentralization. Even from his perspective as a country manager, he says that the New York review is healthy because it adds objectivity and different perspectives from those of the managers in the field.

Here are some other issues that can be discussed:

1. Citibank has no long-term plan. As mentioned in the case (p. 3), the managers felt that the numbers looking out 3–5 years were too soft. That suggests the question as to when long-term plans are useful. Are they useless in situations of very high uncertainty? Or is that when they are most needed?

2. Citibank does have long-term goals. Are these helpful or harmful? Should they change over time, for example, with changes in products offered, markets served, or U.S. inflation rates?

3. Is there a danger that the last-minute, top-down goal-setting process described in the case will cause a loss of commitment to the goal? In the abstract, one would argue yes, but Mehli Mistri argues so strongly in favor of the budgeting system that we would have to guess that he will be committed to almost any goal given to him. But what about his subordinates?

4. Is there a danger of Mehli and other country managers taking actions to meet their short-run target at the expense of the long-term good of Citibank? Yes, clearly there is. Many critics have pointed out the management-myopia danger in industrial settings. Here is the same issue in a bank context. Here are some possibilities for short-term actions:

    -   Eliminate the low-earning loans (e.g., to the government). I pose the issue as follows, using the terminology we heard in Indonesia: Assume Mehli gets the following call from the lead bank manager organizing a loan syndication for the government. "At the express invitation of the Republic of Indonesia, I am delighted to invite you to join us in participating in this loan. The rate will be at 3/8 percent over LIBOR." What should Mehli's reaction be? His actual reaction, he said, was "Oh no!" But he also said that Citibank's record in such participations was very good. Citibank participated in most, but not all, of these syndications. The costs of not participating were relatively long-term, as the government, acting either as a regulator or a competitor, could make life very difficult for a "noncooperative" bank.

    -   Shift the lending to higher-risk (and higher return) customers.

- Make more loans, even if it means making loans with less complete analysis. In Indonesia there was a severe shortage of trained people.

5. Does the top-down goal-setting, which Mr. Mistri says on the homework videotape is relatively typical, create a culture of "sandbagging" when submitting budgets? Mehli Mistri says he did not pad his budget. Most MBA's and almost all executives with whom I have used this case do not believe him.

6. Only U.S. dollars are important to Citibank. Most of Citibank's shareholders are in the U.S., but this dollar focus can make life very difficult (or easy) for a country managers depending on the movements of the foreign currency vis-á-vis the dollar. But as Mehli points out on videotape, currency changes are a two-edged sword, as while revenues may fall in dollar terms as the rupiah devalues, expenses also fall. This issue could be the subject of a whole class, or more.

7. How should Mr. Gibson allocate the $4 million increase he has committed to? On basis of sales? Profits? Economies in country? Should be overallocate to protect himself? Does he have the basis to know if Mistri and his other managers were conservative in their original budgets?

Pedagogy

In a class of eighty minutes, I show the in-class videotape after about 45–50 minutes of class discussion. The first discussion should clarify case facts (e.g., sovereign risk), raise issues and get students to make the judgment Mehli Mistri had to make. He had four alternatives:

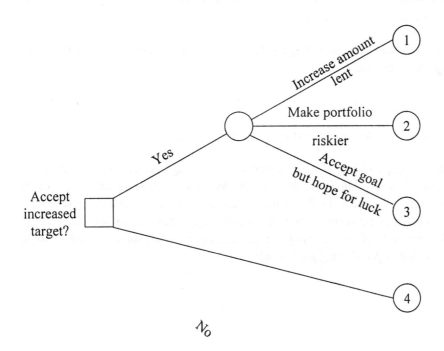

Just before showing the in-class videotape, have the students vote as to what they would do.

On the videotape, Mr. Mistri tells that he accepted a $1 million goal increase in large part due to the Citibank culture. He left in mid-year 1984, but his successor made the increased target.

An interesting question after the videotape is: If Mistri's budget had not been increased, would Citibank Indonesia have left $1 million unearned?

Wrap-up

At the end of class, I think at least the two following points should be made. The first is that budgeting systems are asked to play multiple roles, and no one system can do an optimal job at all of the roles. I develop this point on the blackboard using the format shown in Figure TN-2. Some of the ideas are adapted from Barrett and Fraser (1977),[4] and if desired this article can be used as part of the student assignment for this class. I suggest that firms use budgeting systems for five main purposes: motivation, planning, coordination, cost control and evaluation. Then I pick one important design variable—target difficulty—and list three levels of difficulty we could include in budgets: optimistic (aggressive), best guess as to what will occur, conservative. To illustrate the "no-one-system-is-beat" point, I ask students what type of budget target best serves what budget purpose. The answers are as follows, I think:

- Motivation—slightly challenging. Psychological studies have consistently shown that motivation is highest when goals are difficult but not impossible.

- Planning—best guess for cash planning. Conservative for coming up with estimates to give to financial analysts.

- Coordination—slightly conservative so that the various parts of the organization can depend on other parts to meet their targets.

- Cost control—conservative so managers don't staff up and otherwise anticipate revenues that might not be forthcoming.

- Evaluation—an after-the-fact assessment of what could have been accomplished.

To illustrate these choices, I draw the arrows shown in the figure.

The second concluding point is that while Citibank's planning process violates some of the textbook principles of budgeting, it seems to work. As Mehli says at the end of the classroom tape: the "proof of the pudding is in the eating." Despite his position of being the most likely not to like the budget process, he seems to feel that Citibank's process is a good one. The message is that we should be careful before we apply management principles, such as "goals should be established in a bottom-up fashion," universally.

---

[4] M. E. Barrett and L. B. Fraser, "Conflicting Roles in Budgeting for Operations," *Harvard Business Review* (July–August, 1977), pp. 137–146.

Figure TN-1

Budget Process

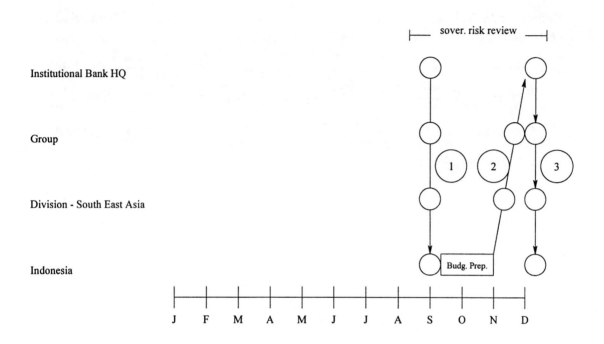

	1	timing and format instructions only
	2	budget reviews
	3	target change

Figure TN-2

Matching Budget Targets with Purposes

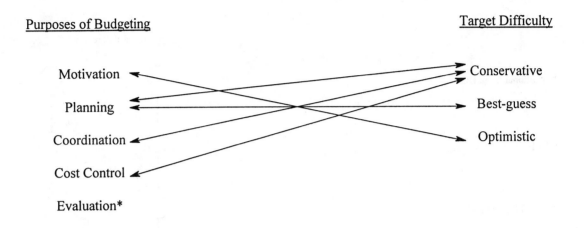

Purposes of Budgeting

Target Difficulty

Motivation

Planning

Coordination

Cost Control

Evaluation*

Conservative

Best-guess

Optimistic

---

* Target should be an after-the-fact assessment of what could have been accomplished, not any of the three choices listed.

CHAPTER 17
MULTINATIONAL ORGANIZATIONS

Changes from the Eighth Edition

The basic structure of this chapter remains unchanged from the eighth edition. The chapter covers two topics—transfer pricing and exchange rates—that are peculiar to control issues in multinationals.

Cases

AB Thorsten deals with problems that arose in a subsidiary located in another country.

Vick International Division deals with two issues: impact of management style on the control process and the need to fit controls to multinational strategic requirements.

Nestle (A) and (B) deal with difficulties involved in the management control of a subsidiary in an inflationary economy.

Xerox Corporation (B) deals with transfer pricing issues in their global operations.

Case 17-1

AB Thorsten

Prologue

This is an excellent case on management control in the multinational context. As part of the homework assignment, I divide the class into two groups—one group should advocate the Belgium perspective and the other Swedish perspective.

I structure the class discussion as follows:

1. I ask the class: What is the strategy of the Industrial Chemicals Division? Two possible options are: "commodity" chemicals and "specialty" chemicals. I do not force a consensus at this stage.

2. I then ask: What motivates Ekstrom?

3. I then invite the Swedish group to present their viewpoint on the capital investment proposal.

4. I then invite the Belgium group to present their viewpoint.

5. I allow the groups to "go at each other" for a while.

6. I disclose what happened (See the AB Thorsten (D) case attached for details on this).

7. I wrap-up with the following points:

   a. Need to link strategy with controls. Commodity versus specialty chemicals imply different controls.

   b. Capital allocations are not just driven by NPV calculations; it is a behavioral process, especially in a multi-country context.

   c. Need for management process.

Reproduced below is a detailed teaching note prepared by Peter Hendrick, along with AB Thorsten (D). Also enclosed is a teaching note prepared by Professor José de la Torre.

Teaching Note: AB Thorsten

Overview

The AB Thorsten case integrates many key concepts covered in the cost accounting and management control segments of the first year Control course. While an excellent review case, it's a little too complex for use as an introductory case. Specific concepts covered include:

- incremental cost analysis,

- discounted cash flow analysis,

- sensitivity analysis,

- transfer pricing,

- international operations,

- the interplay of organizational design and strategy,

- goal congruence in the management control system, and

- administration of an existing control system.

The following commentary falls into three segments dealing with (1) the investment decision, (2) the transfer pricing issue and (3) evaluating the management control system. To begin, some suggestions on teaching strategy.

Teaching Strategy

The AB Thorsten case demonstrates that you can't solve the tactical problems of plant investment, transfer pricing or organization structure until you have a clearly defined competitive strategy for the organization as a whole. On this premise, I would begin class by focusing on the specific problems and gradually expand the discussion to the strategic level. Properly executed, this should demonstrate that the only effective way to proceed is in reverse— e.g. from strategic to tactical. I propose structuring the class as follows:

Time	Issues
40 minutes	Discussion of the quantitative and administrative issues surrounding the plant investment decision.
15 minutes	Discussion of the alternative transfer price mechanisms and their behavioral effects assuming the additional XL-4 is produced in Belgium.
25 minutes	Discussion of the competitive environment and appropriate strategies for Roget S.A. Analysis of the fit between the existing management control system and the suggested strategies.

A list of teaching questions designed to provoke discussion of key issues is attached in Appendix VII. The key decision variables in the case turn out to be qualitative, behavioral or strategic. However, I would take pains to ensure that relevant quantitative analysis was performed even though, in this situation, it is not decisive. Handouts prepared from Appendix I and Appendix III should be used to ensure that the DCF analysis is understood by everyone.

Analytical Discussion

The following discussion mirrors the three sections of the teaching plan.

Where to build the plant?

Let's start with a discounted cash flow analysis. Ekstrom's proposal is summarized in Appendix I. Based on the corporate hurdle rate of 8 percent, the project is acceptable. However, the opportunity must be compared with the alternative Belgian proposal. Isolating the relevant costs is the crux of this comparison. Lavanchy's comments about spreading fixed costs in the (C) case are not relevant. These costs are sunk. The variable manufacturing cost calculation in Exhibit C1 is also misleading. As demonstrated in Appendix II, an average variable cost of Skr. 930 of Skr. per ton on the full 1,000 tons of production implies an incremental variable cost of Skr. 900/ton on the additional 400 tons for Swedish sales. This incremental variable cost is the relevant cost when comparing the two investment proposals. The comparable discounted cash flow analysis for the Belgian proposal is illustrated in Appendix III. The revised analysis favors the Belgian proposal.

	Swedish Proposal	Belgian Proposal
Net Present Value @ 8%	Skr. 246,000	Skr. 260,000
Internal Rate of Return	15%	58%

As illustrated in Appendix IV, the Swedish proposal would be favored at any hurdle rate less than 7½ percent. At any higher rate, the Belgian proposal is preferred. Given the corporate hurdle rate of 8 percent the Belgian proposal is preferred.

Because the Swedish proposal involves higher initial investments, it is less attractive the higher the discount rate. Yet the overriding criteria should be Net Present Value (NPV) of the differential cash flow at the applicable hurdle rate. How was the 8 percent hurdle rate determined? Should the high risk Swedish startup be compared with relatively riskless Belgian expansion using the same hurdle rate? My feeling is that the Swedish hurdle should be higher. This revision only makes the Belgian proposal even more attractive. The choice, however, is not that simple!

Asking why the IRRs differ so dramatically highlights the absence of fixed costs in the Belgian proposal. This is legitimate so long as Belgium has excess capacity for producing XL-4. In other words, the opportunity cost of the fixed plant is zero. A zero opportunity cost for seven years implies some very poor capacity planning in the past. It is also worth noting that the relatively short seven year time horizon favours the Belgian proposal with its lower fixed investment. The new fixed investment in Sweden is only partially recovered by including a salvage value. The longer the time horizon, the more the duty and shipping costs will tip the balance in favour of the Swedish proposal.

Discussing fixed costs leads to consideration of project risk and other qualitative issues. The higher fixed costs of the Swedish proposal entail greater risk particularly given the untried market for this new XL-4 application. Consideration of the "bail out" costs in the event the XL-4 market does not develop favours initial production in Belgium where experienced personnel are already in place. However when we look at the sensitivity of the Swedish proposal to changes in sales price, costs, volume and fixed costs we see that the impact of startup complications are not as significant as one would guess.

The NPV of the project will be reduced to zero if:

1. selling price declines *15 percent*, or

2. variable cost increases *27 percent*, or

3. volume is only *73 percent* of projected volume, or

4. plant costs escalate by *88 percent*, or

5. production is delayed *4 years*.

For detailed analysis, see Appendix V. One may conclude that the project is not really sensitive to startup problems but quite sensitive to changes in contribution. Additional issues include nationalism and perceived autonomy. Roget S.A. is committed to a philosophy of decentralization. Even if the Swedish proposal is sub-optimal, forcing production in Belgium will undermine the perceived decentralization in the company. Another consideration is the possible response of the Swedish government. The requirement of a majority of local directors for AB Thorsten's board suggests some nationalistic sentiments. The threatened resignation of Norgren confirms this line of thinking. One would have to anticipate an increase in the duty of XL-4 if Roget appeared to be exploiting the Swedish market from Belgium.

Finally, there is Ekstrom. He has a proven track record and his enthusiasm is crucial to the success of the new XL-4 application. Forget any future innovative ideas if he perceives all the benefits going to Belgium. The value of such innovation is great. Consider the potential sales and contribution resulting from Ekstrom's new application:

    Sweden: projected sales @ 400 tons
    Sweden has 5 percent of Industrial Product Sales
    Potential incremental volume of XL-4 for Roget = 16,000 tons
    Annual contribution at Skr. 320/ton

    Total potential contribution of Skr. *5.1 million (or $1.0 million)* per year

On the basis of his past performance, opportunities for Ekstrom to defect from Roget to a competitor are very real. Can Roget afford to lose him? Can Thorsten compete against him?

What should Gillot do now?

Any pragmatic discussion of the case incident will have highlighted the length of the approval process.

Critical Events	Cumulative Time
Ekstrom study approved	start
Study complete	26 weeks
Study approved in Sweden	27 weeks
Gillot questions sales forecast	28 weeks
Full day meeting in Belgium	29 weeks
Norgren threatens resignation	30 weeks
Gillot orders additional study	31 weeks
Study completed	35 weeks
	?
Present	104 weeks

Whatever options Gillot might have had to hedge his position (e.g. one year's production in Belgium until the market is proven) have been lost. Ekstrom is frustrated and tempers are high on the Swedish side. It is difficult to argue that Gillot has handled this situation well. I also question whether Gillot can stop the Swedish plant at this point—he has already approved the proposal at the Swedish board meeting! Having considered all the aspects, two rationales emerge:

1. The Swedish plant entails substantially more risk than producing, at least initially, in Belgium—so produce in Belgium.

2. The innovative application of XL-4 has tremendous potential when applied throughout the Industrial Products Division. This potential is unlikely to be realized without Ekstrom's full commitment to the trial application—so produce in Sweden.

What's the appropriate transfer price?

If Gillot decides to build the Swedish plant the analysis is complete. However, if initial Belgian production is selected, there is the problem of setting an appropriate transfer price.

Theoretically, there are four bases for transfer:

1. Transfer at a *market price* awarding most of the "profit" to the producer, in this case Belgium. Variations would include the deduction of promotion costs and the provision for some "standard" profit in Sweden.

2. Transfer at *cost* which would share the "profit" between Belgium and Sweden. This price could be set anywhere between incremental variable cost to average full cost plus a reasonable profit depending on how much of the "profit" was to be allocated to each company.

3. A *two step transfer* pricing system would involve the "lump sum" allocation of fixed overhead to Thorsten plus a variable cost charge per unit actually shipped. Given that there is

no incremental fixed investment for the additional 400 tons of XL-4, this method does not seem relevant. There might be some argument for charging 4/10 of the Skr. 180,000 fixed costs already in place but this contradicts the opportunity cost assumption implicit in the Belgian counterproposal. A capital charge might legitimately be made for the Skr. 74,000 incremental working capital required to produce for the Swedish market.

4. A *two book transfer pricing* system would transfer from Belgium at market price to Sweden at variable cost. This would lead to a double counting of profits and require some corporate offset account to eliminate the doubled profits.

All of these alternatives are complicated by the fact that the two proposals provide different Skr. values for the same cost definition. The impact of these different methods and values is summarized in Appendix V.

Each method allocates the Skr. 320 real contribution of the additional XL-4 in different ways between Sweden and Belgium.

Selling price per ton	Skr.1850
Average promotion costs	(180)
Shipping	(50)
Duty	(400)
Incremental variable cost	(900)
Real contribution per ton	Skr. 320

The two book system double counts the contribution so that Skr. 320 can be credited to both organizations. While this would be an ideal solution from a behavioral point of view, it requires additional bookkeeping—a significant undertaking if the practice became policy for all transfers within the Roget S.A. organization.

A *negotiated transfer price* might be a solution. In the Thorsten situation, however, the past delays and frictions have eliminated this alternative.

Behavioral implications of the alternative methods are readily apparent and endlessly debateable. These should be explored and developed as the key decision criteria. In effect, there is no "correct" solution to the transfer price question. Transfer prices are one way of shaping middle management actions along the strategic lines that top management chooses. A transfer price can only be termed correct in the context of a particular strategy. If centralized production is deemed the key strategic focus, then a transfer price giving more of the contribution to Belgium (the production base) will signal this emphasis to the organization and hence be "correct." If top management wants to focus on local market sensitivity and innovative applications, Sweden should get the lion's share of the contribution. A thoughtful analysis of the transfer pricing question will inevitably lead to the discussion of broader strategic questions and the appropriateness of the complete set of management control mechanisms now in place.

What is Roget's strategic focus? How is this reflected in the management control systems?

The case explains that Roget has increasingly decentralized over the last few years. Before discussing the management control systems, it's worth analyzing the strategic forces at work here. Several factors favour a centralized operation based in Belgium:

1. There are significant economies of scale available in chemical production.

2. Technically skilled personnel are critical to a successful operation. Such employees are most effectively trained and developed at a central manufacturing facility.

On the other hand, several factors suggest a decentralized organization would have significant competitive advantages:

1. International operations require the understanding of local governments and may require autonomous local managements or local directors.

2. Each national market requires product differentiation. This is best achieved with local operators sensitive to each peculiar market.

3. Opportunities for innovation are best exploited by independent and responsible local managers who are permitted to develop pride of authorship.

It all boils down to one simple question. What is the key success factor for Roget—identifying new applications or producing at low cost? While there is no clear answer, students must be aware that any concrete recommendations flow directly from an implicit choice one way or the other. Two conclusions apply regardless.

1. Whichever pattern is chosen, the management controls and systems must "fit" that pattern.

2. Given the basic strategic thrust at Roget, every attempt should be made to compensate for the vulnerabilities of that strategy.

To picture the strategic option, consider the following graph:

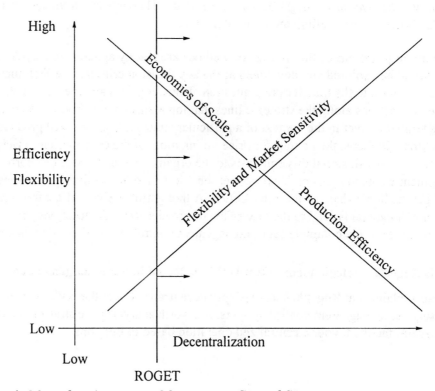

It is worthwhile to note the organizational evolution that is evidenced in the case. Some concept of the desired future organizational structure is critical to any effective action plan. Roget has demonstrated the typical evolutionary pattern of a growing multinational. A functional organization has been revised to one with a product focus (e.g. three product divisions). Now, foreign subsidiaries in the U.K. and Sweden show Roget moving toward a matrix structure with product/market overlap. Indeed, the friction we see in the case is typical of a matrix organization where country managers such as Ekstrom are often at odds with product managers such as Lavanchy. Gillot's role as integrator is typical and crucial in effective matrix organizations.

Given the decision on Roget's optimal strategy, one can select the optimal transfer price policy and evaluate the other management control systems.

We are told in the case that the two existing rules of the game are:

1. everybody's got profit responsibility, and

2. all interdivisional transfers are negotiated at arm's length.

The profit centre system now in place is somewhat of a compromise. Full decentralization would require local investment centres while subsidiaries might be reduced to revenue centres (sales offices) under a centralized scheme.

To recap, there seem to be two consistent approaches to the Roget situation.

	Strategy #1	Strategy #2
Key competitive factor	Low cost	New product applications
Key success factor	Economies of scale	Innovation
Key function	Production	Marketing
Organization	Centralized	Decentralized
Responsibility:		
Production	Investment centre	Cost centre
Marketing	Revenue centre	Profit/investment centre

With these alternative but consistent strategies outlined, other components of the management control system can be evaluated and modifications can be proposed.

The reward system includes a bonus based entirely on the local division results. This is consistent with the market-driven strategy (alternative #2). It clearly frustrates a production-driven strategy. However, It is tricky to link reward systems with strategic focus because the rewards can be used either to reinforce desired strategic focus or to compensate for competitive vulnerability of the chosen strategy. For example, a decentralized operation with autonomous investment centre managers might employ a bonus system based in part on company-wide profits to promote some beneficial cooperation between divisional managers. This would have helped in the Thorsten situation. On the other hand, the same company might use a bonus based strictly on divisional performance in order to reinforce the decentralized strategy. A special discretionary bonus, perhaps tied to an MBO system, would allow special focus on the longer term.

The areas of strategic planning, resource allocation, budgeting and daily operating control are barely touched on in the case. One reasonable recommendation would be to analyze and structure these functions more clearly in order to avoid the ambiguity and confusion demonstrated by the handling of Ekstrom's proposal. Also interesting and unexplored is the role of the corporate staffs. Ekstrom had the immediate assistance of five Belgian engineers in studying the plant proposal. This indicates very strong staff support more typical of a centralized organization. To stimulate innovation, this staff might be dispersed under the various local managers.

A final aspect of the case concerns Gillot's role as integrator. It is clearly his responsibility to smooth over the rough spots that will inevitably arise despite a consistent management control system. Only if he greases the machine with a healthy dose of sensitivity and flexibility will everything function as planned.

Overall, the AB Thotsten case presents a comprehensive and realistic problem in management control. Combining quantitative analysis with a rich behavioural environment, the case demonstrates the problems, techniques and organizational significance of corporate control.

— Peter Hendrick

Appendix I

Discounted Cash Flow Analysis
Swedish Proposal (in Skr.)

End of Year	Plant	Working Capital	Sales Price/Ton	Variable Cost/Ton	Contribution /Ton	Number of Tons Sold	Total Contribution	Promotion Costs	Taxes	Net Cash Flow
0	−700,000	−56,000								−756,000
1		−2,000	2,000	1,000	1,000	200	200,000	130,000	(35,000)	103,000
2		−7,000	1,850	1,000	850	300	255,000	75,000	20,000	153,000
3			1,850	1,000	850	400	340,000	50,000	75,000	215,000
4			1,850	1,000	850	400	340,000	50,000	75,000	215,000
5			1,850	1,000	850	400	340,000	50,000	75,000	215,000
6			1,850	1,000	850	400	340,000	50,000	145,000	145,000
7	+150,000*	+65,000*	1,850	1,000	850	400	340,000	50,000	145,000	360,000

*Sales value, net of appropriate taxes, assuming plant will be closed at end of seven years.

Internal Rate of Return = 15%
Net Present Value at 8% = Skr. 246,000

Appendix II

Relevant Cost Analysis

Calculation of incremental variable cost of Swedish volume

Projected average variable cost in Belgium
at 1000 tons per annum   Skr.   930

Projected total variable cost
at 1000 tons per annum   Skr. 930,000

Projected average variable cost in Belgium
at 600 tons per annum   Skr.   950

Projected total variable cost
at 600 tons per annum   Skr. 570,000

Additional variable cost to produce
400 tons per annum for Sweden   Skr. 360,000

Incremental variable cost per ton   Skr.   900

Appendix III

Discounted Cash Flow Analysis
Belgian Proposal (in Skr.)

End of Year	Plant	Working Capital	Sales Price/Ton	Incremental Cost/Ton*	Contribution /Ton	Number of Tons Sold	Total Contribution	Promotion Costs	Taxes (50%)	Net Cash Flow
0	0	−54,000								−54,000
1		−10,000	2,000	1,350	650	200	130,000	130,000	NIL	−10,000
2		−10,000	1,850	1,350	500	300	150,000	75,000	37,500	27,500
3			1,850	1,350	5000	400	200,000	50,000	75,000	75,000
4			1,850	1,350	500	400	200,000	50,000	75,000	75,000
5			1,850	1,350	500	400	200,000	50,000	75,000	75,000
6			1,850	1,350	500	400	200,000	50,000	75,000	75,000
7		+74,000	1,850	1,350	500	400	200,000	50,000	75,000	149,000

*Incremental manufacturing cost   Skr.   900
Shipping from Belgium to Sweden   50
Swedish import duty   400
Total incremental cost   Skr.   1,350

Internal Rate of Return = 58.16%
Net Present Value at 8% = Skr. 260,228

Appendix IV

Comparative Analysis of Net Cash Flows

(Skr. '000)

Year	Swedish Proposal	Belgian Proposal	Differential Cash Flow if Swedish Proposal Accepted
0	(756)	(54)	(702)
1	103	(10)	113
2	153	27.5	125.5
3	215	75	140
4	215	75	140
5	215	75	140
6	145	75	70
7	360	149	211

Discount Rate	NPV of Incremental Cash Flow
5%	67.4
6	39.0
7	12.2
7.47	NIL
8	(13.2)
9	(37.3)
10	(60.0)

Appendix V

Sensitivity Analysis on Price and Variable Cost

Impact of a Skr. 1 change in contribution:

Year	ΔContribution/ Ton		Tons	ΔContribution	Tax	Net Cash Flow
1	Skr.	1	200	Skr. 200	Skr. 100	Skr. 100
2		1	300	300	150	150
3		1	400	400	200	200
4		1	400	400	200	200
5		1	400	400	200	200
6		1	400	400	200	200
7		1	400	400	200	200

NPV of Skr. 1 change @ 8% Skr. 906

NPV of Project Skr. 246,000

Break Even Selling Price = 1850 – 2460,000/906 = Skr. 1578.5

∴ Break Even with 15% price decline

Break Even Cost = 1000 + 246,000/906 = Skr. 1271.5

∴ Break Even with 27% variable cost increase

Appendix V (continued)

Sensitivity to Volume

Calculate NPV of one ton lost sales per year.

Year	Contribution/Ton	Taxes	Net
1	1000	500	500
2	850	425	425
3	850	425	425
4	850	425	425
5	850	425	425
6	850	425	425
7	850	425	425
8	850	425	425

NPV @ 8% = Skr. 2282

Break Even = 246,000/2282 = 108 less tons/year

= (400 – 108)/400 = <u>73% of projected volume</u>

Appendix V (continued)

Sensitivity Analysis on Plant Cost Overruns

Calculate NPV of Skr. 100 plant cost overrun.

Year	Investment	Tax Shield	Net Cash Flow
0	(100)		(100)
1		10	10
2		10	10
3		10	10
4		10	10
5		10	10
6			—
7	150/7		21

NPV @ 8% = Skr. –48

Break Even cost overrun on plant = 296,000/.48 = Skr. 617,000

= Skr. 617,000/700,000 = 88%

Break Even with an 88% cost overrun

Appendix V (concluded)

Sensitivity to Start-Up Delays

(Skr. '000)

Year	As Projected	1 Year Delay	4 Year Delay
0	(756)	(700)	(700)
1	103	(56)	
2	153	103	
3	215	153	
4	215	215	(56)
5	215	215	103
6	145	215	153
7	360	145	215
8		360	215
9			215
10			145
11			360
NPV @ 8%	+246	+177	−4

Appendix VI

Analysis of Transfer Pricing Alternatives

	Transfer Price (Skr.)	Swedish Contribution[1]	Belgian Contribution[2]	Total Contribution
1. Market price	1850	(180)	500	320
Market price — promotion costs	1670	NIL	320	320
2. Thorsten variable cost	1000	670	(350)	320
Roget incremental cost	1350	320	NIL	320
Roget variable cost	1380	290	30	320
Roget full cost	1560	110	210	320
Roget full cost plus (8%(74,000 W/C))/400	1575	95	225	320
3. Two step 1380 + (8%(74,000))/400	1390	275	45	320
4. Two book				
Roget variable cost	1350	320	320	640
Thorsten variable cost	1000	670	320	990

[1] Based on a Swedish selling price of Skr. 1850/ton less promotional expenses of Skr. 180/ton or Skr. 1670/ton.

[2] Based on an incremental variable cost of Skr. 900, plus Skr. 50 shipping and Skr. 400 duty or Skr. 1350 in total. This assumes that shipments are C.I.F.

AB Thorsten

Suggested Teaching/Assignment Questions

1. From the point of view of the parent company, Roget S.A., which of the two proposals is more attractive?

2. Should Gillot let Ekstrom build the plant in Sweden?

3. As Ekstrom, what would you do if the project is not approved?

4. What role does the Swedish government play in your decision regarding the Swedish proposal?

5. In the long run, how can you ever justify paying Skr. 400 duty per ton for no added value?

6. How would you evaluate Gillot's handling of the proposal so far? What could he have done differently?

7. Why has the process of evaluating the proposal taken two years?

8. Suppose the new application for XL-4 fails to win market acceptance. How does this possibility affect your analysis?

9. If initial production is in Belgium, what would be an appropriate transfer price? How would you implement this decision.

10. Existing company policy requires division managers to negotiate an arm's length price for internal transfers. How well do you think this will work between Ekstrom and Gachoud?

11. What are the competitive advantages of Roget S.A.? Are the management control systems designed to support these advantages?

12. How has the organization structure of Roget been changing over the last five years? Why? How does this affect your decision in the Thorsten situation?

13. What possible advantage is there to the ambiguity of the Thorsten situation?

14. How does your proposed transfer price between Belgium and Sweden fit with your overall analysis of the management control systems?

15. What changes in the management control systems would you recommend to Gillot?

AB Thorsten (D)

Anders Ekstrom, Managing Director of Sweden's AB Thorsten, is apprehensive about the profit position of XL-4, an industrial adhesive product.[1] He is now selling XL-4 at a price of Skr. 1,850 a ton, which is Skr. 300 less than its delivered cost. At the same time M. Gillot, Senior Vice President of Roget S.A., and Ekstrom's immediate superior in Belgium, is wondering what decision he should take regarding Ekstrom's request that he lower the price at which the Belgian company sells XL-4 to the Swedish company.

AB Thorsten is a wholly owned subsidiary of Roget S.A., one of the largest chemical companies in Belgium. Thorsten buys XL-4 from Roget's Industrial Chemical Products Division, at a transfer price of Skr. 1,700 a ton (Skr. 2,150 with transport costs and import duties). This case describes the problems faced by management as it tries to resolve a conflict arising from this transfer price. It covers a 14-month period, during which the following events took place:

1. Fourteen months ago, Ekstrom introduced XL-4 to Swedish customers at a price of Skr. 2,500.

2. Six months ago, after his request for a lower transfer price was turned down, he lowered the price to a more competitive Skr. 2,200.

3. Two months ago, his request for a lower transfer price again denied, he reduced his selling price a second time, to Skr. 1,850.

Ekstrom now says that he may withdraw XL-4 from the Swedish market if he cannot find a way to make it show a profit.

Organization Structure: Roget S.A.[2]

Roget S.A. began operations 40 years ago, manufacturing and selling chemicals in the domestic Belgian market. It has grown steadily, partly through growth and partly through purchase of companies such as Thorsten, so that it now produces 208 products in 21 factories. Its organization structure is shown In Exhibit Al. (See AB Thorsten (A), ICH 14H35.)

According to M. Juvet, Roget's Managing Director, "we are organized on a divisional basis. For example, take the Industrial Chemicals Division, headed by M. Gillot. This is set up as a separate company, and Gillot is responsible for profits. This concept of decentralization is extended down to the departments under him—except that they are responsible for profits on a geographic basis instead of product basis.

"One of these is the Domestic Department, under M. Lambert. This department sells industrial chemicals throughout Belgium and exports its products to countries in which we do not manufacture. It has its own factories to supply both of these markets, and its own sales force in Belgium. The Domestic Department, like our other Brussels-based departments, markets most of its export volume through our foreign subsidiaries and uses independent selling agents only in countries where we don't have our own personnel.

---

[1] The letters "AB" and "S.A." are the equivalent designations in Sweden and Belgium of "Corp." or "Inc." in the United States and "Ltd." In the United Kingdom. The title of "Managing Director" in Sweden and in Britain is approximately the same as that of "President" in the United States.
[2] Note: Those who have studied previous cases in this series should skip the next three sections of this case and jump ahead to the section headed, "Rejection of the Swedish Proposal."

"M. Lambert runs this department on his own. He is responsible for its profits just as he would be if it were an independent company. In much the same way, Ekstrom is responsible for the profits made by AB Thorsten.

"A big company like Roget benefits from this kind of organization. We must divide the work of management. No man can do it all. Placing responsibility for profits enables us to measure the result of operations, and is an important means of attracting and motivating top quality executives. Each head of a product division will have more initiative and will work harder if he is in effect head of his own company. Our bonus system, based on division profits, adds to this kind of motivation."

Company Background: AB Thorsten

AB Thorsten was purchased by Roget eight years ago. After a period of low profits and shrinking sales in Sweden, Roget employed Mr. Anders Ekstrom as Managing Director. A 38-year-old graduate of Royal Institute of Technology, with sixteen years' experience in production and marketing, Ekstrom appears to be an executive with a good deal of ambition and a wide acquaintance with modern financial and planning techniques.

When he joined the company, Ekstrom decided that the best way to restore Thorsten's profitability was to introduce new products, promote them aggressively, and back them up with a first-class technical services staff. In the four years since he became Managing Director, Thorsten's sales have increased from Skr. 7 million to Skr. 20 million, and profits have increased in even higher ratio.

Early History of the XL-4 Project

XL-4 is an adhesive product used in the paper-converting industry, and one which Ekstrom and his management are sure will enjoy a large market in Sweden. Although total production in Roget's Belgian plant for all other markets is 600 tons a year, Ekstrom's market studies have convinced him that 400 tons a year can be sold to paper companies in Sweden, provided that his customer engineering staff helps customers to modify their own equipment, and that the price can be lowered. He has conclusive evidence that large paper companies can reap significant cost savings due to lower materials handling costs and faster drying times.

Ekstrom and his top manufacturing and sales executives spent six months preparing a feasibility study which proposed building a plant in Sweden to manufacture XL-4, and presented this at a Thorsten Board meeting one month later. He states, "We did a complete market study, engineering study and financial study, using discounted cash flows, which showed that we should build a factory in Sweden with a payback period of 4 years and a rate of return of 15% on invested capital. This was presented at a Thorsten Board meeting in Stockholm and approved unanimously.[3]

"During the next two months, several things happened. First M. Gillot informed me that there were objections from Lambert [Vice President, Domestic and Export Department], Lavanchy

---

[3] Swedish law requires that all corporations have two Swedish Directors for every foreign Director. Thorsten's Board is composed of a Swedish banker, a Stockholm industrialist, Mr. Ekstrom and M. Gillot, a Senior Vice President of Roget S.A. Details of this proposal are reported in AB Thorsten (A), ICH 14H35.

[Director of Manufacturing in the Industrial Chemical Products Division] and Gachoud [Director of Sales in the same division]. I convinced him that we should hold a meeting with all these men in Brussels, but that meeting ended in chaos, with me arguing over and over for the plant in Sweden and the others saying over and over that we would have too many problems in manufacturing, and that we did not have the capabilities and experience in the adhesives industry that they possessed in Belgium. They also had no confidence in my market projection, saying that they didn't think that we could sell 400 tons a year.[4] Finally, M. Gillot asked the Belgian executives to study the matter further and give him a formal report on whether the plant should be built."[5]

Rejection of the Swedish Proposal

After studying all of the reports on the XL-4 project, Gillot decided not to approve the proposal for a Swedish plant. "I am sorry to inform you," he wrote to Ekstrom, "that your proposal to manufacture XL-4 in Sweden has been rejected. I know that you and your management have done an outstanding job of market research, engineering planning, and profit estimation, but two other factors worked against you. First, it seems more profitable for our Belgian plant to manufacture XL-4 and export it to Sweden. Second, executives in our Domestic Division here are convinced that the product should be made in Belgium where we have the experience and know how. They are also not sure that you can sell 400 tons a year in Sweden.

"I want you to know, however, that we in Headquarters are most appreciative of the kind of work you are doing in Sweden. This adverse decision in no way reflects a lack of confidence in you or a failure on our part to recognize your outstanding performance as the Managing Director of one of our most important daughter companies."

Introduction of XL-4 into Sweden

Immediately after this decision Ekstrom decided to order XL-4 from Roget Domestic and Export Division. "At this point I decided to prove to them that the market is here. They quoted me a delivered price of Skr. 2,150 a ton (head office billing price of Skr. 1,700, plus Skr. 50 transportation and Skr. 400 import duty).[6] Because of heavy promotion and customer engineering costs (my engineers helping paper companies adapt their machinery), I had to have a gross margin of Skr. 350 a ton. This meant I had to sell it for Skr. 2,500." He penciled the following table:

Head office billing price	Skr. 1,700
Shipping cost	50
Import duty	400
Delivered Cost	Skr. 2,150
Allowance for promotion and engineering costs	350
Swedish selling price	Skr. 2,500

[4] Events during these two months are reported in AB Thorsten (B), ICH 14H36.
[5] The reports of these executives are presented in AB Thorsten (C), ICH 14H37.
[6] Some of these figures are actually expressed in Belgian francs. To avoid possible confusion, all figures have been expressed at their Swedish kroner equivalents.

"I knew I could never achieve sales of 400 tons a year at this price. It was higher than the prices of other adhesives suitable for this market, and Swedish paper companies are very cost-conscious. I knew that we could do some business at this price, however, and this would give our engineers some practical experience in converting customers' equipment to take XL-4. Later on, we could reduce the price and try for the main market.

"I wrote to M. Gachoud, Director of Sales for the Domestic and Export Department in Brussels, showing him the figures, saying that we could eventually reach 400 tons a year in sales, and asking him to reduce the head office billing price. He declined.

"For the next eight months sales were disappointing. At the end of this period, still having faith in our research over the last two years, I decided to lower the price to Skr. 2,200. I hoped that this would induce paper companies to try XL-4 and prove to themselves that it would lower their costs significantly. Of course, this was only Skr. 50 more than my cost, and I could hardly continue permanently on that basis. With me and my company being judged on profits, it is not worth our while to spend all of this time and resources on XL-4 for such a small mark-up.

"Sales did increase during the next four months, to 150 tons, and I knew I could sell about 200 tons regularly at this price. But I was still intent on proving the market at 400 tons.

"This time I went personally to see M. Gachoud in Brussels, and practically demanded that he lower the price of XL-4 exported from Belgium to Sweden. He explained that with a sales volume of 150-200 tons a year in Sweden, sold at an export transfer price of Skr. 1,700, and with strong doubts in his mind that we could ever reach 400 tons a year, he could not agree to the reduction.

"At this point I decided to prove that I was right by executing a bold move, backed up by the use of modern financial planning methods. I lowered the price to Skr. 1,850 a ton. I figured that someone in Brussels had to understand my reasoning, if I explained it well enough and backed it up with forceful direct action.

"Please don't get the idea that this was simply a political trick. I wouldn't have done it if I hadn't believed that it would bring in added profits for the group as a whole. I felt sure that volume would go up to 400 tons, and at that rate we would produce a profit contribution of at least Skr. 113,000 a year for the Roget group. This is Skr. 24,000 more than I could hope for at the old price and a volume of 200 tons.

"I showed my calculations to M. Gillot after I had decided to go ahead. Here is a little table of figures that I sent to him then (all figures are in Swedish kroner):

	At 200 tons		At 400 tons	
	per ton	Total	per ton	Total
Selling Price	2,200	440,000	1,850	740,000
Variable Costs:				
Manufacturing (Belgium).......	930		930	
Shipping (Belgium-Sweden) ..	50		50	
Import Duty (Sweden)............	400		400	
Total Variable Costs	1,380	276,000	1,380	552,000
Factory Margin..............................		164,000		188,000
Promotional Costs		75,000		75,000
Profit Contribution to Roget Group...........................		89,000		113,000

"Let me explain this table. I knew that the Belgian cost accountants used a figure equivalent to Skr. 1,250 a ton as the full cost of manufacturing XL-4. The production people told me, however, that the Belgian plant had enough capacity to supply me with 400 tons of XL-4 a year without additional investment for expansion, and that they could manufacture the additional 400 tons at a variable cost of Skr. 930 a ton. This meant that the fixed costs were sunk costs and I could ignore them. This is why the manufacturing cost figure in the table is Skr. 930.

"Adding in the transportation costs and import duties brings the total variable costs to Skr. 1,380 a ton. My own promotional and engineering costs amounted to about Skr. 130,000 during the first year, but we were already over that hump. They are budgeted for this year at Skr. 75,000 and will go down to Skr. 50,000 a year from now on, mostly for technical services to customers. To avoid an argument, though, I used Skr. 75,000 in the table I sent to M. Gillot.

"This gives me the profit contribution of Skr. 113,000 a year that you see at the bottom of the table. This is Skr. 24,000 more than I could have expected at the old price. To me that's conclusive.

"I tell you all this to emphasize that my main motive was to improve our group's profit performance. Even so, I must admit that I still hope to persuade M. Gillot to let me build an XL-4 factory in Sweden. That plant will be profitable at a volume of 400 tons and a price of Skr. 1,850, and I suppose that this may have been at the back of my mind, too. If I can show him that the 400 tons is not a Swedish dream, I think he'll go along. It's ridiculous to pay import duties that amount to more than 20 percent of the selling price if you don't have to, and if I could have convinced him on the size of the market fourteen months ago, I think that I would have had my plant."

In the two months since this last price reduction, sales of XL-4 have increased to a rate of 270 tons a year. Ekstrom feels certain that within another 12 months he will reach the 400-ton level. He also says, however, that he finds himself in a quandary. "The Swedish company is losing Skr. 300 on every ton we sell, Plus a great deal of selling and engineering time that could be switched to other products. This is bound to affect the profits of my company when I give my annual report to M. Gillot. This is why I quit trying to deal with Gachoud. Last week I wrote to M. Gillot, asking him to direct Gachoud to sell me the product at Skr. 1,100. I'm hoping for a reply this week."

The Parent Company's Transfer Pricing Policy

Gillot has not yet decided what to do with this request. As he says, "Transfer pricing in this company is pretty unsystematic. Each of us division managers is expected to price his own products, and the top management executive committee doesn't interfere. I have the same kind of authority over transfer prices as I have over the prices we charge our independent agents. We've never thought of them as separate problems. I've never been in a situation like this, though, and I want to think it through carefully before I act.

"Our attitude toward transfer pricing is probably the result of the way we operated in foreign markets in the beginning. We developed our export trade for many years by selling our products to independent agents around the world. We still do a lot of business that way. These agents estimated the prices at which they could sell the product and then negotiated with the export sales manager in Brussels for the best price they could get.

"When we began setting up our own daughter companies in our bigger markets, we just continued the same practice. Of course, daughter companies like Thorsten cannot shift to a competing supplier, but they have great freedom otherwise. For example, they can try to negotiate prices with us here at headquarters. This healthy competition within the company keeps us all alert. If they think Belgium is too rigid, they can refuse to market that particular product in their home country. Or, if they can justify building their own manufacturing plants, they can make the product themselves and not deal with the Belgian export department at all."

A Norwegian Example

Head office practices have resulted in head office billing prices that vary widely from market to market. In some cases, outside agents are able to obtain products at lower prices than Roget charges to its own subsidiaries. Ekstrom particularly wanted to tell the casewriters about a Norwegian example. XL-4 is sold in Norway through an independent agent. This agent sells XL-4 to his customers at the equivalent of Skr. 1,290 plus Norwegian import duty. He persuaded Gachoud to sell him XL-4 at a price of Skr. 1,225, thus in effect giving him an agent's commission of Skr. 65 a ton. Roget also agreed to pay the shipping costs to Norway, amounting to Skr. 52 a ton. This meant that Roget received only Skr. 1,173 a ton to cover manufacturing and administrative costs and provide a profit margin. This was less than the average full cost of production in Belgium (Skr. 1,250) and Skr. 527 less than the Skr. 1,700 price at which Roget billed AB Thorsten.

"At one point," Ekstrom says, "I even thought of buying my XL-4 through the Norwegian agent.

But then I realized that this would be destructive warfare against Belgium. The total profits of the Roget group of companies would be less by the amount of the Norwegian agent's commission. I would be blamed for this when Lambert or Gillot reported it to the Executive Committee."

Other Factors to Consider

Division managers' performance in Roget S.A. was judged largely on the basis of the amount of profit they were able to generate on product sales, including both sales to agents and sales to subsidiary companies. The managing board relied on this to induce the division manager to work for greater company profits.

The performance of the daughter company managers was appraised in much the same way. Ekstrom, for example, knew that group management in Brussels judged his performance on the basis of the amount of profit reported on AB Thorsten's income statement. Because of his success in the past four years, Roget's managing board gave him a good deal more freedom than the managers of any of the other subsidiaries enjoyed, but this happy state of affairs would come to an end if Thorsten's reported profits began to slide.

Gillot says that he must also consider three other factors before reaching a decision. First, Ekstrom's profit analysis must be evaluated. Second, Ekstrom's feelings of responsibility as head of the Swedish company must not be destroyed. Finally, he must review the points made by Lambert and Gachoud. Gillot says that Lambert told him, "If Ekstrom decides to take advantage of company rules and discontinues selling XL-4 in Sweden, we can certainly find an independent agent in Sweden to handle it. That's one bridge we'll never have to cross, though. Ekstrom will never push it that far. He believes in introducing new products as the key to his success. If we stand fast, he will simply raise the price back to a level that is profitable for both of us."

Taxes and foreign exchange regulations had no bearing on M. Gillot's decision. Income tax rates in Belgium were about the same as in Sweden, and no restrictions were placed on Thorsten's ability to obtain foreign exchange to pay for imported goods or pay dividends. In fact, Roget's top management insisted that each daughter company play the role of good citizen in its own country, by measuring taxable income on the same basis as that used by management in the evaluation of the subsidiary's pre-tax profit performance. No attempt was to be made to divert taxable income from one country to another.

As this case is written, both Ekstrom on the one hand, and Lambert and Gachoud on the other, are waiting for M. Gillot to settle the transfer pricing question and let them know his decision.

Teaching Note: AB THORSTEN (1)

Case Synopsis

The management of AB Thorsten, a Swedish subsidiary of Roget Industries Ltd. of Canada, wishes to invest in a local production facility to manufacture one of its chemical products. While the product itself is not a new compound, Thorsten's engineers have devised an innovative way to use it that would allow customers in the paper processing industry to realize significant operating cost reductions, provided they make specific investments in their own production technology in order to adapt it to Thorsten's design. Anders Ekstrom, Thorsten's General Manager, submits a proposal to the Thorsten Board of Directors, and receives initial encouragement from top management at headquarters. However, the proposal is soon contested by Roget's Canadian operating management and a difficult conflict emerges between subsidiary and home office management

Pedagogy and Teaching Objectives

'This case should be positioned at the beginning of that section of the course dealing with organizational issues and, particularly, subsidiary-headquarters relations. The case is written in such a way that it invites a discussion of the relative merits of either position, and of the appropriateness of different capital budgeting techniques when applied to international investment proposals But the real issue is camouflaged by this discussion. In fact, the absolute amount of the monetary implications is relatively insignificant

What really matters is that Roget is rapidly growing out of its traditional organizational structure and administrative systems. An organization that suited the company well when it was essentially a domestic (North American) corporation with occasional export sales abroad, is no longer able to cope with the complexity of numerous foreign subsidiaries operating at arms' length. But the diversity of Roget's businesses suggests that no one approach will be able to satisfy the tradeoffs required between central control and operating autonomy across business units.

Therefore, what appears to be an inconsequential argument between two units of the corporation, in fact represents the harbinger of serious problems in the future. While the case does not allow a complete discussion of these complex issues, it does serve as an excellent vehicle to examine the dimensions of the problem in a relatively simple environment. Later cases can develop these insights further by tackling more complex situations.

The major discussion themes are thus:

1. Appropriate capital budgeting techniques for international investments.

2. How to incorporate risks in international capital appropriations.

3. Trade-offs between global optimization and local responsibility.

This teaching note was prepared by Professor José de la Torre, Anderson Graduate School of Management, UCLA, 1989. The valuable inputs of Professors Gordon Shillinglaw, Columbia University, and Deigan Morris, INSEAD, and of Robert Piret, UCLA, are gratefully acknowledged.

4. Organizational evolution in multinational enterprises; going from an international to a multinational structure.

5. Aligning structure, systems and people with an evolving need to address global concerns while maintaining initiative and entrepreneurship at the local level.

Assignment and Study Questions

Depending on how much emphasis the instructor wants to give to different aspects of the case, you may want to omit some of the following questions. I prefer to assign them all, and then allocate time in class according to my objectives for the day. The reason for this is that a good understanding of the issues and a healthy argumentative class discussion leads to a better appreciation of the organizational issues at the crux of the case.

1. What are the most important elements of Thorsten's proposed investment as presented by Ekstrom? ...as presented by the Canadian management team? What are the key arguments for and against the alternatives presented by the contending parties from Canada and Sweden?

2. Is everything that is being expressed by Ekstrom and the Canadian management above board? What are the respective hidden agendas that can be anticipated for each party and in what way do they coincide? In what way can they be expected to diverge?

3. If you were in Gillot's shoes, would you support the Swedish or the Canadian proposal? Why? Is there a third alternative that you may prefer, and how would you introduce it?

4. Mr. Juvet is concerned that the issues in the case may spread to other divisions and subsidiaries. What lessons can we derive from this incident that might help him in thinking through these issues? What recommendations might you make to him as to how to begin to deal with the problems his various divisions face?

Case Analysis and Teaching Plan

In teaching the Thorsten case, the instructor should begin by polarizing the class into a "Swedish" and a "Canadian" camp by taking a poll among the students. I record the results on the board, and I single out those that are reticent to take a definitive position. This third group might be set aside as a "neutral" set of observers that can be called upon later on to mediate and advise Juvet on a final outcome.

Next, I proceed with a detailed discussion of the Ekstrom proposal and the basis for his argumentation in favor of the Swedish direct investment plan. This can be followed by an equally detailed discussion of the Canadian counter-proposal, with special attention paid to the "tools" that the Canadian analysis relies upon and how these financial methods can be used or misused.

The discussion can then re-focus on the chronology of events that have led up to the conflict situation, the results from the Board of Directors meeting and subsequent events. The instructor may then ask the general question of why did events turn out the way they did: is the issue really one of financial investment with a serious money issue at hand, or is it really a problem of agendas, communication, organization, and leadership? Whose interests are in play with respect to each proposal, what are the expected hidden agendas of each party, and how does the organizational and cultural changes that Roget Industries has been experiencing influence the latter? The case can be closed by a brief discussion of agency theory in the context of organizational evolution in multinational companies.

1.   Background

Roget Industries Ltd, is a large industrial firm which produces 208 chemical products in 21 factories worldwide, though primarily concentrated. in North America. Thorsten is a recent acquisition whose first four years of operational performance was poor. Roget hired Ekstrom to turn the company around, a task at which he has, up until now, been rather successful. Thorsten's sales now represent five percent of total divisional sales.

Thorsten's innovation with XL-4 represents significant cost savings for those firms that choose to convert their production facilities in order to accommodate the process change. This implies a difficult marketing job which, if successful, could bring about significant growth in the potential market for XL-4 worldwide. Whether or not competitors can or will respond to this competitive threat is yet unknown.

Roget Industries is said to encourage multinational operations and local autonomy, including bottoms-up product development. The stated purpose is to develop a strong human asset base, while maintaining expertise in technology and management. According to its President, Mr. Juvet, Roget aims to maintain its growth of the last five years, encourage individual profit responsibility, and focus on corporate efficiency. Bonus systems are based on local profit performance and provide liberal rewards.

The case centers on the pros and cons of the proposed XL-4 production facility that Ekstrom would like to see built in Sweden and that Canadian operating management opposes. The conflict centers on a broad range of results from different analytical methods and on other intangible arguments. The Swedish position emphasizes the rules of the game; the Canadian position is focused on financial rationality and the advantages of a marginal or comparative investment perspective versus the risks associated with the Swedish investment.

Gillot, the divisional manager, appears indecisive and reluctant to take sides in an increasingly bitter dispute. Juvet is concerned with the corporate impact of these type of problems which raise doubts about the validity of the current organization and systems. Since these are the same to which he attributes his firm's past successes he is understandably reticent to change matters dramatically.

2.   Ekstrom's position

There are a number of arguments that can be invoked to support the Swedish position:

- The project is a Swedish initiative, within the rules set by the corporation, and following all standard procedures.

- The Thorsten Board of Directors approved the project with Gillot in attendance. How he turn back on his decision now?

- The difference between the Swedish and Canadian net present values is insignificant. The Swedish project has an IRR of 15 percent (greater than the eight percent corporate hurdle rate) and a 4-year payback period. The Canadian counter-proposal has an IRR of 60 percent and a 2.5 year payback period. However, is IRR a relevant measure?[1]

- The sales estimates provided by the Swedish subsidiary are proven by extensive application trials, and give confidence in the outlook for the project. Besides, the Swedish team is close to the market and will bear the brunt of any optimistic forecast. Also, we have not counted export sales to other Scandinavian countries in the sales estimates. These would be easy to obtain if necessary to balance Swedish sales.

- The plant is necessary to indicate commitment to the market. We are asking paper converters to rely on a new process. They would be reluctant to do so if they must rely on imports from across the Atlantic. (See the Copperweld case for a similar argument.)

- The losses due to tariffs and duties are dead-weight losses. Better to suffer those additional costs ourselves and invest in market share.

- There are considerable exchange and tariff risks related with an export strategy.[2] In general non-contractual foreign exchange risks over long-term periods can only be effectively hedged by matching costs and revenues in different currency areas.

- Gillot is running a large risk that he will lose Ekstrom. The fellow has an excellent track record, and he has proven to be a resourceful manager. Furthermore, we are alienating our Swedish directors, and this could have negative political consequences in the long run.

- A Swedish plant would allow for double sourcing around the globe and increase flexibility to everyone's advantage. Customers would love it. And if, as we believe, our method proves right, the world market for XL-4 would boom.[3]

---

[1] Ekstrom may argue that it is totally irrelevant in this case. For example, if one takes the total investment figure of Skr. 7.65 million and place it at 15.7 percent (the Swedish IRR figure) it yields annual returns of Skr. 1.20 million. On the other hand, the Canadian 60 percent rate applies only to the first Skr. 740,000, yielding an annual return of Skr. 444,000. If the balance, that is, the funds not invested in the Canadian model, or Skr. 6.91 million, are invested in Eurobonds at the 8 to 9 percent suggested by Mr. Bols, they would yield an additional Skr. 590,000 a year. The total return of following the Canadian plan (assuming no better alternative for the excess funds), would be Skr. 1.03 million a year, Skr. 170,000 a year *less* than the return from the Swedish investment. Of course, the analysis would also be only partially right, since it ignores alternative investment projects throughout the corporation, or the option of returning the balance to the stockholders.

[2] This argument could cut both ways. If we assume the 1980/81 exchange rate to be close to PPP (purchasing power parity), the current 1986 (Q2) rate should be around Skr. 4.07 per C$ (see Exhibit 13). Instead, it is at Skr. 5.20/C$. An expectation of a return to PPP would strengthen the argument in favor of Canadian sourcing. But if the true PPP figure is that prevailing in the 1983/84 period, the reverse would be true and the Swedish plan becomes the better alternative.

[3] At 400 tons per year, a market that represents only 12 percent of the world market (see Exhibit 6), successful introduction of the Swedish formula to other countries could represent a worldwide potential of more than 3,000 tons per year. This is three times the current manufacturing capacity!

- The absolute money figures are small: the incremental investment of Skr. 7 million represents only 3.5% of Thorsten's annual sales, and less than 0.2% of divisional sales. The issue is more concerned with the tradeoff between autonomy and economies of scale. Canada's position smacks of bad faith on the part of headquarters. What will be the impact on corporate entrepreneurship if the rules of the game only benefit the firm at the corporate level?

- Company morale requires that initiative be rewarded. Roget's policy of promoting from within will not be quite so appealing to the more competent members of the subsidiaries' management team if it is felt that Canada calls all the shots in the firm.

3.   The Canadian postion

On the other hand, there are a number of compelling arguments that serve to support the contentions of the Canadian management group:

- How likely is it that the market will indeed increase from 12 tons per year (current sales level) to 400 tons per year? Shouldn't Ekstrom be required to confirm the result of his trials with real sales before the investment is made?

- Ekstrom underestimates the production problems that such a scale-up implies. If the technology is not that easy to transfer, if problems occur, or if there is a long learning period in breaking in the Swedish plant, this will represent significant costs that need to be taken into account in the investment decision.

- Thorsten already has a strong presence in Sweden, its credibility as a firm is high, and it is conceivable that it would be just as easy to try to sell 200 tons per year out of Canada before attempting to produce XL-4 in Sweden. It this innovation is so good, a local plant will convince only those customers who would be marginally affected by it anyway. It is better to keep manufacturing technology at home where people understand it and can develop it fully, and then disseminate it throughout the worldwide operations of Roget Industries.

- The timing of the cash flows favor the Canadian proposal. Exhibits TN-1 through TN-3 illustrate this. First of all, most of the cash flow coming from the Swedish proposal comes in the form of a balloon payment late in the project's lifetime. This is a considerable risk issue, since the Swedish proposal seems to exhibit symptoms of a J-curve effect. For roughly the same Net Present Value, the Canadian project's cash flow profile is fairly smooth over time, whereas the Swedish project's costs are front-loaded and its revenues back-loaded.

- At discount rates over 7.4 percent the Swedish proposal drops in NPV relatively to the Canadian option, and turns negative at 16 percent; simply another reflection of the higher risk associated with the Swedish plan.

- Analysis shows that Ekstrom has not made a very reliable estimate of the salvage value of the Swedish plant after 7 years. In fact, Ekstrom has not really carried out much risk or sensitivity analysis on his own project's figures. For example, a 10 percent drop in sales... a 10 percent increase in costs ... both together....[4]

- Roget already has excess capacity for XL-4 in Canada and any opportunity to take advantage of economies of scale in production would be diluted by investing in another facility in Sweden. Such optimization strategy is particularly important in a global industry as this one appears to be.

4.   The real issues

When one considers the arguments that can be advanced by the contending parties, it appears evident that a number of less tangible issues need to be analyzed and brought into the case discussion. A good place to start is to ask the class to help prepare a chronological analysis of all major events and decisions. This is presented in Exhibit TN-4. A few questions might be prompted by the chronology:

- Why, during the six months that the market research studies and the engineering estimates were being made by a joint team of Swedish and headquarters personnel, did no one indicate that excess capacity existed in Canada?

- Why did Gillot not share with Lambert's team the results of the study sent to him by Ekstrom for discussion at the board meeting prior to his arrival in Stockholm?

- Why did the Canadian objections surface only after the investment proposal has been approved?

The first of these questions may cast some doubts as to whether Ekstrom is acting on good faith in these proceedings. He must have known that excess capacity existed in Canada and, yet, he insisted on pushing through the investment proposal without offering to test the market beforehand with Canadian imports. Could the incentive systems and transfer pricing policies of Roget have anything to do with this behavior? Or is the problem one of lack of communications and information flow? In fact, one might argue that Ekstrom comes across as being a bit too self-confident and high-minded, almost to the point of arrogance. Is he trying to show off?

Concerning Gillot's change of heart after the board meeting, it may be worthwhile to remind the class that the size of the investment is minuscule relative to Gillot's total business portfolio. He probably read the proposal on the plane on his way to Stockholm, and approved it on the basis of its own merits, without knowing of the situation back at home. Once back in Montreal, his local management, particularly Lavanchy, learned of his decision and reacted in a defensive manner. They obviously resented the way in which, in their view, Ekstrom pulled this trick on them. Why does the divisional manager undertake such a responsibility without staff support? Does he have to attend all subsidiary board meetings on this basis?

The XL-4 process innovation may represent a breakthrough in technology. If accurate, it should be transferred back to Canada and applied worldwide. In the eyes of the Canadian team, they

---

[4] The Lotus spreadsheet distributed with this case permits the instructor to carry out these and other calculations on the figures submitted by both parties.

may fear being shown-up by the Swedes, and the financial analysis may well just be a way for them to cover for being less than aggressive in the past.

There may be limits to economies of scale, and the technical and market experience gained by producing in Sweden may not be fully reflected in the financial analysis. Furthermore, this situation may not be a good guide for other similar decisions in the future. Manufacturing location may or may not be related to the market, nor equally sensitive to centralization. In each case, it may be worthwhile to analyze what is the best way to break up the value-added chain (manufacturing, sales, service, etc.) in order to maximize the advantages of globalization/ fragmentation for each activity.

Exhibit TN-5 summarizes this analysis of the overt and hidden agendas that characterize each of the major players, and speculates on what may be their justification, the constraints they face, and their ultimate objectives. It also suggests some contributory factors determining these positions. Clearly these are all highly speculative, but they may offer some insights into possible solutions to the problem.

Summary and Conclusions

Overall, Roget Industries and its subsidiary Thorsten are suffering from three key problems that relate to the growing internalization of the organization:

1. **Strategic Issues.** The company has not spelled out clearly its objectives as a multinational enterprise, and the top management of the firm does not itself seem to have a clear idea of where they see the firm going in the future. The apparent indecisiveness of Gillot may be evidence of this lack of direction concerning international operations at Roget. Simple goals on such issues as level of international diversification, geographic market presence, profitability, growth, and so forth, by product division are elementary.

2. **Structural Problems.** The company has undergone a major evolution from a functional to a divisionalized form. But international operations are currently too small to claim any attention by top management under the current structure. Lambert and Ekstrom are supposedly at the same level in the hierarchy, but they clearly represent different magnitudes of business and wield different power. To the extent that the subsidiaries are dependent on the "home" company for technology, finance and other resources, and if conflicts result, the current structure forces resolution at the level of the division senior vice-president. This is clearly not desirable. Stress between corporate headquarters and subsidiaries is to be expected: it therefore needs to be managed and dealt with through appropriate mechanisms, and not left to drift in ambiguities too long.

3. **Administrative System.** The incentive systems and reward measures are clearly ambiguous with respect to corporate level objectives, to the extent that these exist. The decentralized and focused responsibilities of subsidiary management pushes everyone to sub-optimize operations at a micro or local level at the expense of any corporate-wide interests. Also, whereas the capital budgeting system involves project identification at a decentralized level, approvals to proceed with test marketing, analysis, and finally investment are made at headquarters, and this latter task is performed in a manner that is less than systematic. Finally, communication systems seem to be lacking. The relationship between Ekstrom and headquarters staff is one of mutual mistrust and suspicion. Some of this might be attributed

to the ill behavior of various people, but the lack of integrating mechanisms (e.g., transnational committees, personnel rotation policies, etc.) and the erroneous incentive systems have contributed greatly to these non-cooperative attitudes.

In adjudicating this conflict, Juvet and Gillot must be careful that any short-term response does not compromise long-term solutions. I would ask Ekstrom to wait one year for his new plant, and guarantee him that if a certain level of sales is achieved (say, 200 tons) he will be authorized to construct the plant. Canada would ship him all the XL-4 needed at an appropriate transfer price (e.g., full costs plus 10 percent). While this goes on, I would get top management to agree on and articulate a series of strategic principles for the firm and the divisions. These would include clear statements on the issues raised in point 1) above.

Next should begin a more complex exercise, one for which we have insufficient data. Management must come to grips with the question of whether each division should operate on a centralized, manufacturing and technology-oriented basis, as a decentralized market-oriented organization, or to what degree it mix the two in some form of matrix. The answer, and the optimal balance, is probably different for each of the divisions. But in any event, management must move quickly to review all incentive systems, corporate decision rules, personnel and compensation systems, transfer pricing rules, etc. in light of its growing internationalization.

Subsequent Events

As the AB Thorsten (2) case, reproduced following these notes, attests, the corporate response was anything but that suggested above. After much conflict and wasted opportunities, Gachoud left the company, branded the scapegoat, and Ekstrom got his plant. Subsequently, Gillot moved up to Juvet's position as President of Roget Industries, and Ekstrom, who by now had demonstrated the wisdom of his proposal and had expanded business to the rest of Northern Europe, was offered Gillot's position as divisional head and senior vice-president. He declined and left Thorsten to assume the presidency of a larger Swedish company.

References

On the capital budgeting issues:

1. Eiteman, David K and Arthur I. Stonehill, *Multinational Business Finance*, 4th edition, Reading, Mass.: Addison Wesley, 1989, chapter 10.

2. Flood, Eugene Jr., and Donald R. Lessard, "Deviations From Purchasing Power Parity and the Implications for the Multinational Business," Harvard Business School, 1982.

3. Shillinglaw, Gordon, *Managerial Cost Accounting*, 5th edition,, Homewood, Ill.: Richard D. Irwin, Inc, 1982 chapter 18.

On the managerial issues:

1. Bartlett, Christopher A., "How Multinational Organizations Evolve," Journal of Business Strategy, Summer 1982.

2. Doz, Yves, and C. K. Prahalad, "Patterns of Strategic Control Within Multinational Corporations," <u>Journal of International Business Studies</u>, Fall 1984.

3. Hill, Roy, "Overseas and Overlooked?", <u>International Management</u>, August 1979.

4. Stopford, John, and Louis T. Wells, Jr., *Managing the Multinational Enterprise*. New York: Basic Books, 1972.

Exhibit TN-1

Comparative Cash Flow
and Present Value Analysis
Swedish vs. Canadian Investment Proposals
(in thousand Swedish kroner, NPV at 8% discount)

Category/year	Swedish Proposal[1] Cash Flow	NPV	Canadian Proposal[2] Cash Flow	NPV	Incremental[3] Cash Flow	NPV
Investment:						
Year 0	−7,560	−7,560	−540	−540	−7,020	−7,020
Year 1	−20	−18	−100	−93	80	74
Year 2	−70	−60	−100	−86	30	26
	−7,650	−7,638	−740	−718	−6,910	−6,920
Operations:						
Year 1	1,050	972	30	28	1,020	944
Year 2	1,600	1,372	390	334	1,210	1,038
Year 3	2,150	1,707	750	595	1,400	1,112
Year 4	2,150	1,580	750	551	1,400	1,029
Year 5	2,150	1,463	750	510	1,400	953
Year 6	1,450	914	750	473	700	441
Year 7	1,450	846	750	438	700	408
	12,000	8,854	4,170	2,929	7,830	5,925
Salvage values:						
Year 7	2,150	1,254	740	432	1,410	823
TOTALS	6,500	2,470	4,170	2,643	2,330	−173

---

[1] Derived from Exhibit 2 in the case.

[2] Derived from Exhibit 9 in the case.

[3] The incremental cash flows associated with undertaking the Swedish investment over the Canadian production requirements.

Exhibit TN-2

Cumulative Net Cash Flows,
Discounted at 8%

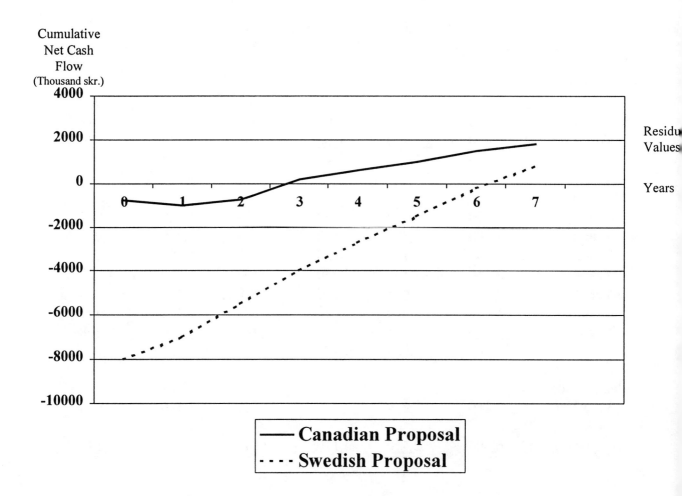

Exhibit TN-3

Net Present Value Profiles
as a Function of Discount Rates

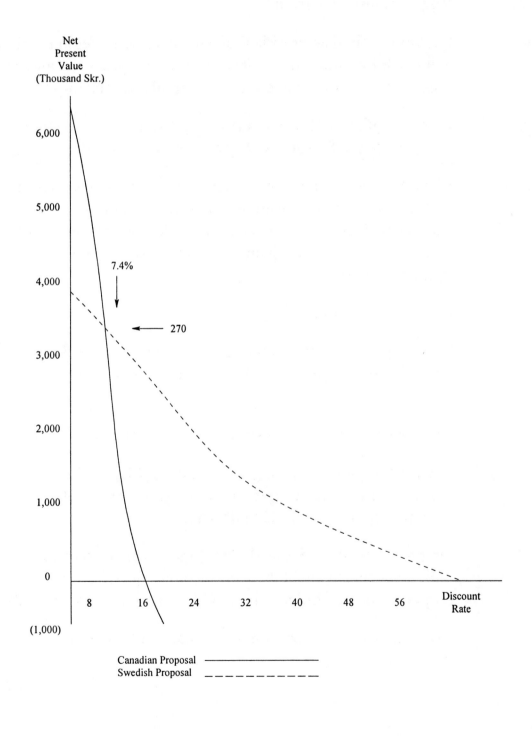

Net
Present
Value
(Thousand Skr.)

6,000

5,000

7.4%

4,000

270

3,000

2,000

1,000

0

8   16   24   32   40   48   56   Discount
Rate

(1,000)

Canadian Proposal ————————
Swedish Proposal — — — — — —

Chronology of Major Events

Time	Event
1978	Roget acquires Tborsten
1982	Ekstrom is hired as President of Thorsten. Sales begin to climb and reach four times their 1981 level in four years (by end of 1985). Profits are considered to be "highly satisfactory."
9/85	Ekstrom informs Thorsten's Board of his intention to study the XL-4 market in Sweden. Gillot approves.
6 months	Market research team confirms that cost savings are possible and conducts trials at customer facilities. A joint Sweden-Canada engineering team carries out a feasibility study for the construction of the new plant and makes estimates of investment costs.
4/86	Report sent to Gillot. No reaction. Three weeks later, Board meeting takes place in Stockholm. Project is approved by Swedish directors and Gillot.
5/86	One week later, doubts surface in Canada and Gillot communicates these to Ekstrom. Ekstrom demands a hearing. Later that month, a meeting takes place in Montreal with all domestic and Swedish staff attending. After much debate, the meeting concludes without a decision.
6/86	Norgren, one of the Swedish directors, threatens to resign. Gillot, concemed about the possible consequences for corporate morale, orders a new study from his Canadian staff. Juvet expresses concern that issues are similar in other divisions.

Exhibit TN-5

Main Actors in the Conflict: Real and Hidden Agendas

| ACTORS | PRIVATE AGENDAS: | | JUSTIFICATIONS |
	Overt	Hidden	
Gillot	Make the right decision Be fair	Maintain good relations with Canadian colleagues N. America is 86 percent of the division	Canadian are experts Maximize divisional profits
Lavanchy	Use spare capacity	Maintain control over manufacturing decisions	Technical complexity Better resource use
Gachoud	Avoid making a costly error	Avoid looking like a fool Stop Ekstrom from demonstrating new processes	Uncertainty and risk Need to prove concept before commitment
Ekstrom	Increase sales and profits	Build up his own empire and reputation	Rules of the game Track record Market trials

ACTORS	CONSTRAINTS	ULTIMATE OBJECTIVES	CONTRIBUTING FACTORS
Gillot	Out of his depth Setting precedent	None evident Don't rock the boat	Unclear international strategy, if any New situation
Lavanchy	Limited managerial skills Narrow experience	Montreal as center for technology and manufacturing	Incentive system Lack of knowledge of Swedish reality
Gachoud	Little imagination	Kill the project and stop Ekstrom	Incentive system No interest in other markets
Ekstrom	Removed from seat of power Foreigner; new boy on the block	Get plant at all cost Prove that he is right Get a top job with a local company?	Incentive system Lack of knowledge of headquarters people and culture

AB Thorsten (2)

After studying all the reports on the XL-4 project, Mr. Gillot decided not to approve the proposal for a Swedish plant. He wrote to Ekstrom:

> I am sorry to inform you that your proposal to manufacture XL-4 in Sweden has been rejected. I know that you and your management have done an outstanding job of market research, engineering planning, and profit estimation, but two other factors worked against you. First, it seems more profitable for our Canadian plant to manufacture XL-4 and export it to Sweden. Second, executives in our Domestic Division here are convinced that the product should be made in Canada where we have the experience and knowhow. They are also not sure that you can sell four hundred tons a year in Sweden.
>
> I want you to know, however, that we in headquarters are most appreciative of the kind of work you are doing in Sweden. This adverse decision in no way reflects a lack of confidence in you or a failure on our part to recognize your outstanding performance as the managing director of one of our most important daughter companies.

Introduction of XL-4 into Sweden

Immediately after this decision, Ekstrom decided to order XL-4 from Roget's Domestic and Export Division.

> "At this point I decided to prove to them that the market is here. They quoted me a delivered price of Skr. 21,500 per ton [this was based on a head office billing price of Skr. 17,000, plus Skr. 2,500 transportation and Skr. 2.000 import duty]. Because of heavy promotion and customer engineering costs (my engineers must help paper companies adapt their machinery to XL-4), I had to have a gross margin of Skr. 3,500 a ton. This meant I needed a selling price of at least Skr. 25.00 per kilo."

Mr. Ekstrom penciled the following figures:

	Per kilogr.	
Head office billing price	Skr.	17.00
Shipping cost		2.50
Import duty		2.00
Delivered cost	Skr.	21.50
Allowance for promotion and engineering costs		3.50
Swedish selling price	Skr.	25.00

> "I knew I could never achieve sales of four hundred tons a year at this price. It was higher than the prices of other adhesives suitable for this market, and Swedish paper companies are very cost conscious. I knew that we could do some business at this price, however, and this would give our engineers some practical experience in converting customers' equipment to take XL-4. Later on, we could reduce the price, and try for the main market.

This case was prepared by Professors Gordon Shilliglaw and Charles Summer at the International Management Development Institute (IMEDE), Lausanne, Switzerland. Copyright IMEDE, revised with permission, 1988.

"I wrote to Mr. Gachoud, Director of Sales for the Domestic and Export Department in Montreal, showing him the figures, saying that we could eventually reach four hundred tons a year in sales, and asking him to reduce the head office billing price. He declined.

"For the next eight months sales were disappointing. At the end of this period, still having faith in our research over the last two years, I decided to lower the price to Skr. 22.00 per kg. I hoped that this would induce paper companies to try XL-4 and prove to themselves that it would lower their costs significantly. Of course, this was only Skr. 5.00 more than my cost, and I could hardly continue permanently on that basis. With me and my company being judged on profits, it is not worth our while to spend all of this time and resources on XL-4 for such a small mark-up.

"Sales did increase during the next four months, to a rate of about 150 tons a year, and I knew I could sell about two hundred tons regularly at this price. But I was still intent on proving the market at four hundred tons.

"This time I went personally to see M. Gachoud in Montreal and practically demanded that he lower the price of XL-4 exported from Canada to Sweden. He explained that with a sales volume of 150–200 tons a year in Sweden, sold at an export transfer price of Skr. 17.00 per kg., and with strong doubts in his mind that we could ever reach four hundred tons a year, he could not agree to the reduction.

"At this point I decided to prove that I was right by executing a bold move, backed up by the use of modern financial planning methods. I lowered the price to Skr. 18.50 a kg. I figured that someone in Montreal had to understand my reasoning, if I explained it well enough and backed it up with forceful direct action.

"Please don't get the idea that this was simply a political trick. I wouldn't have done it if I hadn't believed that it would bring in added profits for the group as a whole. I felt sure that volume would go up to four hundred tons, and at that rate we would produce a profit contribution of at least Skr. 1.1 million a year for the Roget group. This is Skr. 240,000 more than I could hope for at the old price and a volume of two hundred tons.

"I showed my calculations to M. Gillot (see Exhibit 1) after I had decided to go ahead. Let me explain this table. I knew that the Canadian cost accountants used a figure equivalent to Skr. 12,500 a ton as the full cost of manufacturing XL-4. The production people told me, however, that the Canadian plant had enough capacity to supply me with four hundred tons of XL-4 a year without additional investment for expansion and that they could manufacture the additional four hundred tons at a variable cost of Skr. 9,300 a ton. This meant that the fixed costs were sunk costs and I could ignore them. This is why the manufacturing cost figure in the table is only Skr. 9,300 per ton.

"Adding in the transportation costs and import duties brings the total variable costs to Skr. 13,800 a ton. My own promotional and engineering costs amounted to about Skr. 1,300,000 during the first year, but we were already over that hump. They are budgeted for this year at Skr. 750,000, and will go down to Skr. 500,000 a year from now on, mostly for technical services to customers. To avoid an argument, though, I used Skr. 750,000 in the figures that I sent to Mr. Gillot.

"This gives me the profit contribution of Skr. 1,130,000 a year that you see at the bottom of the table. This is Skr. 240,000 more than I could have expected at the old price. To me that's conclusive.

"I tell you all this to emphasize that my main motive was to improve our group's profit performance. Even so, I must admit that I still hope to persuade Mr. Gillot to let me build an XL-4 factory in Sweden. That plant will be profitable at a volume of four hundred tons and a price of Skr., 18.50 per kg., and I suppose that this may have been at the back of my mind, too. If I can show him that the four hundred tons is not a Swedish dream, I think he'll go along. It's ridiculous to pay shipping costs and import duties that amount to more than 20 percent of the selling price if you don't have to. If I could have convinced him on the size of the market fourteen months I think that I would have had my plant."

In the two months since this last price reduction, sales of XL-4 increased to a rate of 270 tons a year. Ekstrom felt certain that within another twelve months he would reach the 400-ton level. He also said, however, that he found himself in a quandary.

"The Swedish company is losing Skr. 3,000 on every ton we sell, plus a great deal of selling and engineering time that could be switched to other products. This is bound to affect the profits of my company when I give my annual report to Mr. Gillot This is why I quit trying to deal with Gachoud. Last week I wrote to Mr. Gillot, asking him to direct Gachoud to sell me the product at Skr. 11,000 per ton. I'm hoping for a reply this week."

The Parent Company's Transfer Pricing Policy

Mr. Gillot had not yet decided what to do with Ekstrom's request. As he put it:

"Transfer pricing in this company is pretty unsystematic. Each of us division managers is expected to price our own products, and top management doesn't interfere. I have the same kind of authority over transfer prices as I have over the prices we charge our independent agents. We've never thought of them as separate problems. I've never been in a situation like this, though, and I want to think it through carefully before I act.

"Our attitude toward transfer pricing is probably the result of the way we operated in foreign markets in the beginning. We developed our export trade for many years by selling our products to independent agents around the world. We still do a lot of business that way. These agents estimated the prices at which they could sell the product and then negotiated with the export sales manager in Montreal for the best price they could get.

"When we began setting up our own daughter companies in our bigger markets, we just continued the same practice. Of course, daughter companies like Thorsten cannot shift to a competing supplier, but they have great freedom otherwise. For example, they can try to negotiate prices with us here at headquarters. This healthy competition within the company keeps us all alert. If they think Canada is too rigid, they can refuse to market that particular product in their home country. Or, if they can justify building their own manufacturing plants, they can make the product themselves and not deal with the Canadian export department at all."

A Norwegian Example

Head office practices had resulted in head office billing prices that vary widely from market to market. In some cases, outside agents were able to obtain products at lower prices than Roget charged its own subsidiaries. Ekstrom told the case writers about a Norwegian example. XL-4 was sold in Norway through an independent agent. This agent sold XL-4 to his customers at the equivalent of Skr. 12.90 per kilo, plus net shipping costs and Norwegian import duty. He persuaded Gachoud to sell him XL-4 at a price of Skr. 12.25, thus in effect giving him an agent's commission of Skr. 650 a ton. Roget also agreed to pay a portion of the shipping costs to Norway, amounting to Skr. 520 a ton, in order to reduce the local selling price. This meant that Roget received only Skr. 11.73 per kilo to cover manufacturing and administrative costs and provide a profit margin. This was less than the average full cost of production in Canada (Skr. 12.50) and Skr 5.27 less than the Skr. 17.00 price at which Roget billed AB Thorsten.

"At one point," Ekstrom said, "I even thought of buying my XL-4 through the Norwegian agent [Norwegian import duties would be refunded on re-export sales to Sweden, but Swedish duties would then apply]. But then I realized that this would be destructive warfare against Canada. The total profits of the Roget group of companies would be less by the amount of the Norwegian agent's commission. I would be blamed for this when Lambert or Gillot reported it to the Executive Committee."

Other Factors to Consider

Division managers' performance in Roget Industries Ltd. was judged largely on the basis of the amount of profit they were able to generate on product sales, including both sales to agents and sales to subsidiary companies. The managing board relied on this to induce the division managers to work for greater company profits.

The performance of the daughter company managers was appraised in much the same way. Ekstrom, for example, knew that group management in Montreal judged his performance on the basis of the amount of profit reported on AB Thorsten's income statement. Because of his success in the past four years, Roget's managing board gave him a good deal more freedom than the managers of any of the other subsidiaries enjoyed, but this happy state of affairs would come to an end if Thorsten's reported profits began to slide.

Mr. Gillot indicated that he must consider three factors before reaching a decision on the transfer price request. First, Ekstrom's profit analysis must be evaluated. Second, Ekstrom's feelings of responsibility as head of the Swedish company must not be destroyed. Finally, he must review the points made by Lambert and Gachoud. Gillot reported that Lambert told him. "If Ekstrom decides to take advantage of company rules and discontinues selling XL-4 in Sweden, we can certainly find an independent agent in Sweden to handle it. That's one bridge we'll never have to cross, though. Ekstrom will never push it that far. He believes in introducing new products as the key to his success. If we stand fast, he will simply raise the price back to a level that is profitable for both of us."

Taxes and foreign exchange regulations had little bearing on Mr. Gillot's decision. Corporate income tax rates in Canada were about the same as in Sweden, and no restrictions were placed on Thorsten's ability to obtain foreign exchange to pay for imported goods or pay dividends. In fact, Roget's top management insisted that each daughter company play the role of good citizen in its own country, by measuring taxable income on the same basis as that used by management in the evaluation of the subsidiary's pretax profit performance. Not attempt was made to divert taxable income from one country to another.

Exhibit 1

Profit Contribution to Roget Group
from Swedish Sales of XL-4
(in thousand Skr.)

	At 200 tons		At 400 tons	
	Per ton	Total	Per ton	Total
Selling price..	22,000	4,400,000	18,500	7,400,000
Variable costs:				
Manufacturing (Canada)	9,300		9,300	
Shipping (Canada-Sweden)......	2,500		2,500	
Import duty (Sweden)	2,000		2,000	
Total variable costs	13,800	2,760,000	13,800	5,520,000
Factory margin		1,640,000		1,880,000
Promotional costs		750,000		750,000
Profit contribution to Roget group..		890,000		890,000

Teaching Note: AB THORSTEN (2)

Case Synopsis

This case continues the issues raised in AB Thorsten (1). After considering the evidence before him, Gillot decided not to approve the proposal for building an XL-4 plant in Sweden and asked Ekstrom to first demonstrate the viability of the project by importing materials from Canada. Gachoud then proceeded to charge a very high transfer price which, in effect, made it impossible for Ekstrom to sell XL-4 profitably in Sweden. By the end of 1986, losses were accumulating and Ekstrom faced the decision as to whether give up and discontinue imports, or try once again to get through headquarters' obstinacy and convince them of the potential for the product.

Pedagogy and Teaching Objectives

Transfer pricing policy is a critical issue in international business, and this case allows for a discussion of the variables that might enter into the design of such a policy. Although extreme by most standards, and complicated by the simmering antagonism between the Swedish and Canadian management, the conflict over prices is clear cut and the data permit an estimation of the opportunity losses that poorly designed transfer prices can signify for an international company.

In addition, the case lends itself to re-emphasize the organizational discussion that began in the previous case. It is now clearly obvious that people are playing dirty and that personal agendas are getting in the way of corporate performance. Drastic surgery is needed, and it now includes the dismissal of one or more key divisional executives who are systematically sabotaging operations.

Assignment and Study Questions

1. Is the transfer price being charged to Sweden reasonable and appropriate?

2. How should an appropriate transfer price be determined? What criteria should be employed?

3. Should transfer prices be made uniform to all destinations? ...standard for all products? ...based on a standard formula? ...or adjusted to each circumstance? What are the advantages and disadvantages of any such formulation?

This teaching note was prepared by Professor José de la Torre, Anderson Graduate School of Management, UCLA, 1989. The valuable inputs of Professors Gordon Shillinglaw, Columbia University, and Deigan Morris, INSEAD are gratefully acknowledged.

Case Analysis and Teaching Plan

I generally start the discussion by asking if anyone thinks that the price being charged Sweden (17,000 Skr. per ton plus transportation and duty) is "right." Generally, no one person agrees. I then ask why is it not fair or appropriate. The discussion tends to focus on the students' views as to what should be a "good" transfer price. I let this go on for a while, generating a lot of discussion, and then try to organize the points being raised around a series of follow-up questions.

1. What are the cost-volume-profit relationships?

From Canada's point of view the situation is as follows (on a per ton basis):

		At 600 tons/year	At 1,000 tons/year
Variable costs	=	Skr. 9,500	Skr. 9,300
Fixed costs	=	3,000	1,800
Total		Skr. 12,500	Skr. 11,100
Transfer price	=	17,000	17,000
Marginal contribution	=	7,500	7,700
Accounting profit	=	4,500	5,900

From Sweden's point of view, only at the high price of Skr. 25,000 are profits more attractive than under the local manufacturing alternative, and sales have stalled at that level. A comparison of margins realized on imports from Canada at the current transfer price with those in their original plan (Exhibit 3 in the first case) can be seen in the table below.

Original Plan		Year 1	Year 2	Year 3+
Marginal contribution	=	2,000	2,550	3,400
Fixed costs[1]	=	1,000	1,000	1,000
Promotion	=	1,300	750	500
Gross margin	=	(300)	800	1,900
Imports at:		Price = 25,000	Price = 22,000	Price = 18,500
Gross margins on				
imports	=	3,500	500	(3,000)
Promotion[2]	=	850	850	850
Gross margin	=	2,650	(350)	(3,850)

2. How is aggregate demand affected by prices?

The data permit us to estimate the demand curve for XL-4 from three points. At a price of Skr. 25,000 per ton, demand was "disappointing," or close to zero. At Skr. 22,000, demand was running at a yearly rate of 150 tons (or 200 t/yr over time?), and at Skr. 18,500 it had climbed to

---

[1] Assumes straight-line depreciation as the economic cost of the fixed assets employed, with no salvage value.

[2] Average of first three years, or Skr 850 per ton. This ignores Ekstrom's claim that he has incurred high engineering costs since that would have occurred under any circumstances.

270 tons/year (or 400 t/yr over time?). A graphic representation of this relationship allows for a crude approximation of the (joint) profit maximizing price and volume, which is close to Skr. 19,500 per ton and 340 tons, given that marginal costs are Skr. 13,800 (variable costs plus shipping and duty).

3. What is the right transfer price and how should the profits be split?

The options for determining the right transfer price, and the factors entering the decision are many. For example:

- Is it a short-term transaction, one-of-a-kind, or are there prospects for long-term sales?

- Are there measurable equivalent prices determined in arms' length transactions? ...alternative sources of production?

- Is excess capacity available or is expansion eventually required?

- Are there alternative uses for fixed resources employed?

- What are the competitive implications?

- What are the tax implications?

In general, transfer pricing at marginal rates will be employed only in short-term situations, where alternative uses are nil, and where competitive conditions require it. Otherwise, full-cost-based transfer prices will provide a more accurate and neutral set of incentives. But when competitive conditions call for it, there is no reason why a dual (or triple) pricing structure cannot be instituted. One set of prices may be used to judge resource allocation issues in the home country, a second for evaluating and rewarding management in the selling country, and a third for official tax or reporting purposes.

Yet, the application of standard transfer pricing rules avoids the expenditure of considerable corporate energy on sub-optimizing behavior. The use of negotiated internal prices, in the absence of a market reference price or freedom to source outside, increases the sources of conflict in what are by definition conflictual situations. Best to assign transfer prices on a basis that truly reflects the long-term opportunity cost of employed resources (except, perhaps, when opportunistic situations arise), and adjust the incentive system ad-hoc by providing exceptions as required for competitive or strategic reasons.

For a summary of subsequent events see the Teaching Note to the previous case in the series.

References

A selection of works on transfer pricing, both in divisional and multinational settings, may include:

1. Abdel-Khalik, A. Rashad and Edward J. Lusk, "Transfer Pricing — A Synthesis," The Accounting Review, January 1974.

2. Eccles, Robert G., "Analyzing your Company's Transfer Pricing Practices," <u>Journal of Cost Management</u>, Summer 1987, pp. 21–33.

3. Hirshleifer, Jack, "On the Economics of Transfer Pricing," <u>Journal of Business</u>. July 1956, pp. 172–184.

4. Melville, Larry J. and J. William Petty, "Transfer Pricing for the Multinational Firm," <u>The Accounting Review</u>, October 1978, pp. 935–951.

5. Menssen, Merle D., "A Contract Price Policy for Multinationah," <u>Management Accounting</u>, October 1988, pp. 27–31.

6. Shillinglaw, Gordon, *Managerial Cost Accounting*, 5th edition, Homewood, Ill.: R.D. Irwin, 1982, Chapter 18.

AB THORSTEN
Managing Corporate-Subsidiary Relations Within the Multinational Firm

Vijay Govindarajan

Professor of Strategy and Control

The Amos Tuck School of Business Administration

Dartmouth College

Hanover, NH 03755

Phone: (603) 646-2156

Chemicals Industry

5-year Return on Equity =   12%

All Industry Average   =   15%

  DuPont
  Dow Chemical
  Union Carbide
  Monsanto
  AB Thorsten
        •
        •
        •

Industry Structure

  Suppliers
  Buyers
  Substitutes
  New Entrants
  | Direct Rivalry |

Direct Rivalry Among Existing Competitors

High. Why?

1. Significant number of large competitors

2. Slow industry growth, mature

   - Acquisition

   - Take market share from competitors

   - New applications of existing products

3. Low product differentiation

   - Commodity chemicals

   - Specialty chemicals

4. Most companies have product breadth or have flexibility to produce the variety of products

5. High fixed costs $\rightarrow$ need for volume $\rightarrow$ undifferentiated product $\rightarrow$ price competition

   - Tend towards large size mills, due to scale economies

   - Environmental requirements

6. Tendency to overbuild capacity → excess capacity

- Need for large, cost-effective plants, long runs

- Cyclical demand

- Capacity added in large increments

- Many firms have resources to add large capacity

7. Foreign competition

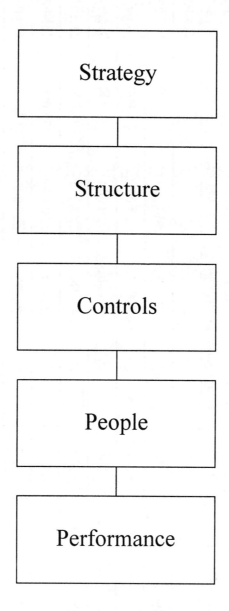

Discounted Cash Flow Analysis
Swedish Proposal (in Skr.)

End of Year	Plant	Working Capital	Sales Price/Ton	Variable Cost/Ton	Contribution /Ton	Number of Tons Sold	Total Contribution	Promotion Costs	Taxes	Net Cash Flow
0	−700,000	−56,000								−756,000
1		−2,000	2,000	1,000	1,000	200	200,000	130,000	(35,000)	103,000
2		−7,000	1,850	1,000	850	300	255,000	75,000	20,000	153,000
3			1,850	1,000	850	400	340,000	50,000	75,000	215,000
4			1,850	1,000	850	400	340,000	50,000	75,000	215,000
5			1,850	1,000	850	400	340,000	50,000	75,000	215,000
6			1,850	1,000	850	400	340,000	50,000	145,000	145,000
7	+150,000*	+65,000*	1,850	1,000	850	400	340,000	50,000	145,000	360,000

*Sales value, net of appropriate taxes, assuming plant will be closed at end of seven years.

Internal Rate of Return = 15%
Net Present Value at 8% = Skr. 246,000

Relevant Cost Analysis

Calculation of incremental variable cost of Swedish volume

Projected average variable cost in Belgium at 1000 tons per annum	Skr.	930
Projected total variable cost at 1000 tons per annum	Skr.	930,000
Projected average variable cost in Belgium at 600 tons per annum	Skr.	950
Projected total variable cost at 600 tons per annum	Skr.	570,000
Additional variable cost to produce 400 tons per annum for Sweden	Skr.	360,000
Incremental variable cost per ton	Skr.	900

Discounted Cash Flow Analysis
Belgian Proposal (in Skr.)

End of Year	Plant	Working Capital	Sales Price/Ton	Incremental Cost/Ton*	Contribution/Ton	Number of Tons Sold	Total Contribution	Promotion Costs	Taxes (50%)	Net Cash Flow
0	0	−54,000								−54,000
1		−10,000	2,000	1,350	650	200	130,000	130,000	NIL	−10,000
2		−10,000	1,850	1,350	500	300	150,000	75,000	37,500	27,500
3			1,850	1,350	5000	400	200,000	50,000	75,000	75,000
4			1,850	1,350	500	400	200,000	50,000	75,000	75,000
5			1,850	1,350	500	400	200,000	50,000	75,000	75,000
6			1,850	1,350	500	400	200,000	50,000	75,000	75,000
7		+74,000	1,850	1,350	500	400	200,000	50,000	75,000	149,000

*Incremental manufacturing cost   Skr.   900
Shipping from Belgium to Sweden   50
Swedish import duty   400
Total incremental cost   Skr.   1,350

Internal Rate of Return = 58.16%
Net Present Value at 8% = Skr. 260,228

1. TP = 1700 + 450 = 2150   Volume = 50T
    SP = 2500

2. *Write* to Gachoud, asking for   *No*
    price cut

3. SP = 2200   Volume = 150T

4. *Visit* Gachoud, ask for price   *No*
    cut

5. Cut price to 1850   Volume = 270T
    Confident can get it to 400T in a year   (in 2 months)

6. Send analysis to Gillot showing higher corporate
    profit at 1850, though Sweden must show losses. Ask
    for a price cut.

WHAT SHOULD GILLOT DO NOW?

Selling Price/ton	2200	1850
Variable costs:		
Mfg.	900	
Duty	400	
Shipping	50	
	1350	1350
Contribution/ton	850	500
# of tons sold	× 150	× 400
Total Contribution	127,500	200,000
(−) Promotion Costs	75,000	75,000
Incremental Contribution	52,500	125,000

Swedish Proposal

PROS		CONS	
1.	Nationalism (board will resign)	1.	Better economics in Belgium option
2.	Might increase duty otherwise	2.	Untried market
3.	Preserve autonomy	3.	Why sink a new capital investment?
4.	Implications for Ekstrom	4.	Less experienced in production
		5.	Can "bail out" in Belgian proposal
		6.	No "risk" in Belgian proposal
		7.	Both production and marketing involve "risk" in Swedish proposal

WHAT TO DO? DEPENDS UPON STRATEGY!

Transfer Pricing Alternatives

1. Transfer at a *market price* awarding most of the "profit" to the producer, in this case Belgium. Variations would include the deducation of promotion costs and the provision for some "standard" profit in Sweden.

2. Transfer at *cost* which would share the "profit" between Belgium and Sweden. This price could be set anywhere between incremental variable cost to avergage full cost plus a reasonable profit depending on how much of the "profit" was to be allocated to each company.

3. A *two-step transfer* pricing system would involve the "lump sum" allocation of fixed overhead to Thorsten plus a variable cost charge per unit actually shipped. Given that there is no incremental fixed investment for the additional 400 tons of XL-4, this method does not seem relevant. There might be some argument for charging 4/10 of the Skr. 180,000 fixed costs already in place but this contradicts the opportunity cost assumption implicit in the Belgian counterproposal. A capital charge might legitimately be made for the Skr. 74,000 incremental working capital required to produce for the Swedish market.

4. A *two-book transfer pricing* system would transfer from Belgium at market price to Sweden at variable cost. This would lead to a double counting of profits and require some corporate offset account to eliminate the doubled profits.

WHICH ALTERNATIVE TO CHOOSE?
DEPENDS ON STRATEGY!

	Strategy #1	Strategy #2
	"Global" Strategy	"Country-Based"
Competitive Advantage:	• Economies of Scale • Low Cost	• Innovation • Differentiation
Key Function:	• Production	• Marketing
Organization Structure:	• Centralized production	• Decentralized production and marketing
Staff:	• Centralized	• Decentralized
Responsibility Structure:	• Production: Cost center • Marketing: Revenue center	• Countries: Profit centers
Transfer Pricing:	• Standard cost	• Market price
	Bonus based more on corporate performance	Bonus based more on country performance

Strategy	Strategy
Commodity Chemicals	Specialty Chemicals
↓	↓
Centralized Manufacturing	Decentralize Manufacturing & Marketing
Production: Cost Center	
Countries: Revenue Center	Countries: Investment Centers
Transfer Price: At standard cost	Transfer Pricing: Arm's length, negotiated, market price
Bonus: Big % based on corporate profits	Bonus: Big % based on country results; some % based on corporate results
People like Ekstrom not key	People like Ekstrom are key

Wrap-Up Comments

1. Capital Expenditure Evaluation System pretty good—DCF, IRR.... *But* still does not guarantee that good decisions will be made.

2. Strategy implementation is a balancing act among three, often conflicting, rationalities:

   - Economic Rationality (Value Maximizing)

   - Political Rationality (Power Enhancing)

   - Social Rationality (Emotional Need Satisfying)

   - What is "rational" depends upon where you "sit"

3. Multinational context. Has to manage:

   Strong Local Identity

   vs.

   Need for Corporate Identity

4. Has to balance:

   Cost of decentralization → Potential "sub-optimal" decisions

   Benefits of decentralization → Ideas which won't occur at the central level

   ALL THESE ARGUE FOR GOOD MANAGEMENT PROCESS

Case 17-2

Vick International Division

Prologue

This is an excellent case on management control over foreign subsidiaries which are tailored to the subsidiaries strategic context.

I ask the students to view the following videotape before class:

Videotape 9-880-005: McGuire and Kyle on "Management Philosophy, Executive Style, and the C-P-R System"

I follow Dick Vancil's teaching outline. The video tapes can be ordered from Harvard Case Services (Phone (617) 495-6117).

VG

Overview: Objective for the Class

This is a good case to kick off a module on the role of top management in implementing strategy. The size of Tom McGuire's division is small, compared to the larger companies that follow. The product technology is simple, leaving only the international scope of the activities as the primary source of complexity. The value of videotapes is also nicely demonstrated in this case: having videotapes of both McGuire and Fred Kyle gives the students a good introduction to the importance of executive style because of the sharp contrast between these two gentlemen on that dimension.

More important, even this simple situation allows the students to gain their first insight into one of the primary themes of this module. Top managers, or even a division manager like Tom McGuire, operate with (at least) a dual agenda: developing the business, and developing the people who manage the business. In the Vick case it is clear that Tom McGuire is attempting to implement two strategies simultaneously. The product/market strategy for his division requires the development and introduction of new products that can be sold in several countries. His managerial strategy focuses on the education and professionalization of his farflung management team, which he sees as a more serious potential constraint on the growth of his division than the development of product-market technology. The MBA students don't really recognize the conflict between these two strategies until the end of the class when Kyle makes the point vividly on the videotape. It is a sobering experience for them, which the instructor must then reinforce briefly in his closing comment.

Classroom Pedagogy

As the comment above suggests, I'm not wedded to any particular sequence in touching all the bases that must be covered prior to showing the in-class tape. The comments below follow the sequence of the proposed assignment questions.

Business Strategy. McGuire inherited a diverse, moribund collection of foreign subsidiaries headed by salesmen who were trying to push Vick products into their local markets. I'm not burdened with any expertise in marketing, but I have no trouble accepting McGuire's strategy as being both coherent and effective—if he can pull it off. One way of describing his strategy (although students rarely state it this way) is that he is trying to gain economies of scale as he attempts to penetrate the local markets in his part of the world. The opportunities for scale economies in manufacturing and selling are slim; the products are simple enough that they must be produced and sold locally. That leaves product development and marketing as the primary candidates for making the whole greater than the sum of the parts. In order to achieve that, McGuire must focus his resources, and that leads him to the strategy of reducing the breadth of his product line and selling the remaining products in many markets.

One key success factor in this strategy is the quality (safety, reliability) and effectiveness of the product line. The technology of the health and beauty-aids business does not seem awe inspiring to me, but having the "right" product clearly makes a big difference. The other success factor has to do with marketing. With a limited range of products, McGuire must seek to own the consumers in each local market, appealing directly to them so that they will pull a large volume of products through a distribution network that is served merely by order-takers rather than salesmen.

Managerially, the critical task for McGuire is marketing. Product development expenditures are probably controlled mainly by Vick's domestic division, if the NyQuil/MediNite adaptation is typical. Marketing, on the other hand, must be particularly sensitive to the local idiosyncrasies of consumers in each country. At the same time, good marketing talent is always scarce, and it would be a pity to have to reinvent the wheel completely in each of McGuire's countries. In the case, the essence of McGuire's strategy is personalized by Olson's role in the introduction of MediNite to Australia. McGuire knows that if Olson is used properly, his marketing skills can serve many markets.

Resource allocation is not really an issue for McGuire in the same sense that it is in later cases in this module. McGuire is growing his business by investing funds for the modification and launching of new products in his various markets. He does this by deciding how many resources to have in each market that can be used for that purpose (such as Das in Mexico). Given that, his main resource allocation task is to prioritize the sequencing of new product introductions. One way of looking at McGuire's resource allocation problem is to see that his critical resource is *time* in the marketplace. There is a quite explicit cost in delaying the introduction of a new product that turns out to be successful; the lost consumption can never be recovered. McGuire, in effect, is allocating resources when he delays the introduction of Alpha in Mexico.

Olson's Role. Another thread that runs through each of the cases in this module concerns the role of line and staff in implementing strategy. The potential conflict between these two roles is not discussed in those terms by McGuire, but it may be useful for the instructor to put that label on the issue. It is also probably useful to point out that, in conventional terms, Olson is "staff" while the managing director of each of the countries is "line," and is responsible for the operations and profitable performance of his subsidiary.

McGuire has dealt with the potential conflict between line and staff in an unusually explicit way, by defining formal roles and permitting an individual to play different roles in different situations. It is useful to ask the students to evaluate Olson's role in the MediNite introduction in

Australia, thus reinforcing (or perhaps introducing) the strategic importance of his role. My own opinion is that Olson did play an effective role in Australia and, more important, his effectiveness was no greater than that which I have observed in other organizations where formally defined roles are not used. Put another way, there are lots of ways for staff personnel to work effectively with line managers, and we see that happening in McGuire's division. The question that falls out from that is: why are formally defined roles necessary? That leads us into the broader question of the entire set of management systems that McGuire has established.

Management Systems. This is the first core issue in the case, because it is McGuire's management systems that have triggered the incident involving Product Alpha. I like to open up the discussion by simply asking the students to give me their evaluation of McGuire's systems. The assignment question is structured logically in three parts (what has he done? why has he done it? how good is it?), but starting with the bottom line seems to create a more lively discussion—and more thinking on the part of the students.

Invariably, at least in the six or eight times I've taught this case, the initial reaction from the class is that McGuire's systems are rigid, overly elaborate, and bordering on the bureaucratic. I keep soliciting such comments, and recording them on the blackboard, until eventually one student decides to take the contrary view and to defend McGuire. This then moves the discussion back a notch to the question of why McGuire has set up the systems, and a more useful discussion can then proceed. In the event that a contrary view is never raised by the class, my ace in the hole would be to ask, "Why are the systems that McGuire has installed so different from those that are used by Vick domestically and in Europe?" A question like this forces the students to make a careful differentiating assessment of McGuire's situation, and leads to the realization that his systems have something to do with his attempting to cope with the quality and diversity of the managers running his various markets. (If this question is not needed at this point in the discussion, I use it a bit later as a way of reinforcing the students" discussion of McGuire's situation.)

It is fairly clear from the case, and even more so from McGuire's comments on the homework tape, that McGuire views the development of his country managers as his most important task. He has designed his management systems, and particularly the Product Marketing Guides (PMGs), as a way of educating these managers in the field of marketing and developing a common language about marketing that they all can use. If we accept his assessment of the situation, then it is hard to fault his objective. That brings us back to the question of how good a job he has done in achieving his objective. Once we have reentered the discussion, I try to enrich it by asking two questions (in either order) at some appropriate point:

1. *What are the costs and benefits of this system when viewed from the perspective of a country manager like Kyle?* The latent issue here concerns the uniformity or symmetry of management systems applied across a diverse set of organizational units. Some of McGuire's managers need more education than others, but all of them have been made to toe the same disciplined line. Kyle recognizes this point, and comments on it effectively on the homework tape. It is useful to have a brief discussion of it in class because it adds bite to the disciplinary question that emerges from the in-class tape.

2. *Are McGuire's systems designed to meet the strategic needs of his divisions, or are they simply an expression of his own personality?* I have never had to take the initiative in asking this question because the students identify it fairly early on. When the issue is raised, I

frequently recast it as, "If McGuire got hit by a truck, how much of his managerial apparatus would be retained by his successor?" Again, Kyle comments on this in the homework tape, inferentially making the point that he might not change the structure of the system very much but that he would operate within the system in his own style and that the process of management would be somewhat different. One virtue of a brief discussion of this question is that it leads rather naturally into a discussion of the contrasting styles of the two executives, discussed below.

Unless a student has voluntarily offered the information, I do not ask the students to identify the elements of McGuire's systems. Instead, I try to facilitate the PMG-focused discussion described above, and then move on to style. In my closing comments, I then close that loop by listing the important elements and commenting on them briefly.

Elements of McGuire's Management Systems

1. **Continuous Planning and Review (CP/R) .** This is a fairly conventional planning, budgeting, and performance monitoring system.

2. **Product Categories.** This simple device of setting up three types of products within the division can be a useful way of clearing the air even though it didn't work very well for Alpha. (We'll see categories used again in the Corning and GE cases.

3. **Manager's Guides.** It's hard to differentiate this from the conventional type of job description.

4. **Work Plans.** Just another form of project scheduling and control.

5. **Product Marketing Guides.** As discussed above, these are formal and detailed, but the content is probably conventional.

6. **Formal Role Assignments.** This is the most unique piece; the intent is good, but Alpha makes it clear that the approach is not infallible.

Contrasting Styles. The first time that a student uses the word *style*, I stop the class and ask them to spend two or three minutes playing a new game with me. "Style is one of the topics we're interested in, and we have two managers here who come across quite differently in the homework tape. What do we mean by style? Let's not try to define it in some dictionary sense; let's just see if we can describe it. Even describing it for a single individual is hard, but we may be able to make some progress if we can differentiate between McGuire and Kyle in terms of our perceptions of their styles. Can you do that?"

I then put two column headings on the blackboard, one labeled *McGuire* and the other *Kyle*, and listen carefully to the students trying to pick out a single word to enter in parallel fashion under each column. Whenever possible, I try to sharpen the contrast that is implicit in the student's comment. Typical word pairs for McGuire/Kyle are: analytical vs. intuitive, task-oriented vs. people-oriented, aloof vs. friendly, and so on. After six or eight pairs, or three or four minutes, I do close off the game, saying that that's enough of this for today. I don't try to deliver a conclusion from that brief exercise, but I point out that I want them to think about the style of each executive that we'll be viewing in the cases that follow, and that we'll try to make progressive sense out of those perceptions as our data base enlarges.

I believe that this very brief discussion of style does have an immediate payoff for students. After they have viewed the in-class tape, it seems to me that the students are able to deal with McGuire's situation with much more sensitivity and perception, based on their earlier attempts to characterize the individual.

Who Is the Villain?

Up to this point in the discussion, any time a student has made a comment about Product Alpha, I have suggested that we defer discussing that until a bit later. When the time finally arrives, I then legitimize discussing it with an unstructured question such as, What happened with Product Alpha? Unless the discussion gets heated in a hurry, I then try to energize it as follows: Did something go wrong with Product Alpha? Yes? Why? Who caused it to happen? Who is the villain in this piece?

I then put that last question on the blackboard: Who is the Villain?, underline it as though it were a column heading, and implicitly ask for the students to give me their candidate.

Almost like a whodunit, it's possible to cast suspicion on almost every character in the case. Das is the one. A young, ambitious manager in a hurry, he is trying to end-run the system and simply got caught. No, it's Kyle. He is Das's boss, and he gave Das too much rope; Kyle should have intervened sooner. But Olson, in any event, should have stepped in and prevented the fiasco. Olson knew that Alpha was a development product, and he failed to assert himself in the role that he was supposed to play. Or was it, after all, McGuire's own behavior that converted a minor bureaucratic error into a major brouhaha? McKinley, shown as assistant general manager of the division in Exhibit 3, is not mentioned in the case. If he is proposed as a candidate, I reject the nomination, explaining that, although it's not stated in the case, he is sitting there in a shelf job until he finds new employment elsewhere.

The candidates will not be proposed in the order given above, and when McGuire is mentioned, I intervene to offer another piece of important information which is not contained in the case. I explain that for reasons of modesty McGuire would not release the case if it were disclosed that he is uniformly viewed by everyone in his division as a certified marketing genius. McGuire is the "old man" with a lot of experience and a proven record of performance. I suggest that one reason for his intervention might be simply that he felt he could make a *contribution to Das by helping him position the new product.* (It's also important to introduce this "fact" about McGuire prior to showing the in-class tape because one of the students' questions relates to that.)

As each candidate for villain is introduced, I don't permit much discussion, and as soon as the list is complete I suggest that we focus our analysis on McGuire. Das's motivations for the crime are fairly clear and understandable, if misguided. Neither Kyle nor Olson has a very clear motive for causing the incident. But McGuire *did* cause it. Let's focus on his motives.

Why Punish Das?

At this point we're now only three or four minutes from being ready to show the in-class tape. My objective is to polarize the class to the extent possible and then, in effect, let McGuire and

Kyle comment on their discussion. I set it up by trying to get the students to agree that McGuire did not have to meet directly with Das in this situation. He had many other options, working either through Olson, Kyle, or in some other manner. I also ask the students to be generous enough to assume that McGuire knew that a direct meeting might be painful for Das. Why did McGuire intervene?

The two primary motives will emerge from the class fairly quickly. The first is substantive: *McGuire was trying to protect Das from making a mistake.* The students will cite the sentence in the case that says that an Approver is supposed to protect an inexperienced Prime Mover from a serious mistake which might damage the division or the subordinate's career. McGuire, knowledgeably, must have felt that a serious mistake was impending. If the mistake were not serious, McGuire might have left Das alone and allowed him to learn a lesson from a relatively minor error. With that avenue foreclosed, in McGuire's opinion, he chose to educate Das directly by trying to help him on the substantive issue of positioning the product.

The alternate motive is that McGuire felt that Das had already made a serious error by failing to adhere to the procedures laid down in the PMG system. If Das's behavior were tolerated without punishment, others in the division would begin to view the PMG discipline as a discretionary set of forms to be filled out when they got around to it. In particular, punishing Das would be highly visible throughout the division because he is apparently viewed as a very capable manager doing well in one of the largest countries in the division. Some student is also likely to point out that overt punishment of Das may cause him to leave the company.

Just prior to showing the tape, I try to bring the discussion to a head by commenting that it's likely that McGuire had mixed motives behind his intervention, but ask the students which one they believe was paramount. My MBA students tend to be generous, and McGuire is usually credited with the substantive rather than a disciplinary motive by a margin of 3-to-1.

The Closing Discussion

After the in-class tape, the MBA students seem almost stunned. Another quick vote on what McGuire's motive really was reveals a major shift in the position of perhaps half the class. McGuire may believe that he was acting in good faith and for substantive reasons, but Kyle clearly feels that McGuire's primary motive was to discipline the system.

If my timing is working right, there are only five to ten minutes of class time left after showing the in-class tape. I use a couple of minutes of that for an epilogue, disclosing that Das left Richardson-Merrell shortly after the incident, took a better job with another package goods company in Spain, and after 18 months returned to Richardson-Merrell and is now a managing director for Vick International in India. Kyle also left Richardson-Merrell at the end of 1980, taking a job with Smith Kline & French International that is almost identical to the job that Tom McGuire still holds with Richardson-Merrell.

My final comments include both those given earlier about the elements of McGuire's system, and the main objective for the case as described in the second paragraph of this teaching note.

Homework and Classroom Tapes

Vick International Division

Videotape 9-880-005 (40 minutes): Tom McGuire, president; Fred Kyle, managing director, Mexico and Central America; "Management Philosophy, Executive Style, and the CP-R System"

Videotape 9-880-006 (15 minutes): Tom McGuire; Fred Kyle; "Project Alpha"

VICK INTERNATIONAL
Managing Head Office-Subsidiary Relations Within Multinationals

Professor Vijay Govindarajan

The Amos Tuck School of Business Administration

Dartmouth College

Hanover, NH 03755

Phone: (603) 646-2156

Fax: (603) 646-1308

Discussion Questions

- What's your evaluation of the CP-R system and related elements?

- Why did McGuire implement this system? How effective is it in implementing his strategy for the LA/FE division?

- What's your appraisal of Olson's role in the MediNite Case?

- What went wrong with Project Alpha? Who's the villain?

- What lessons for Das? Kyle? McGuire?

Tom McGuire's Strategy for LA/FE

- Shift from:

  Sales volume $\rightarrow$ Profitability
  Selling $\rightarrow$ Marketing
  Existing products $\rightarrow$ New products
  Push $\rightarrow$ Pull

- Shift from "Salesmen Pushing Vick Products in Local Markets" to "An Integrated Marketing Approach"

- The key is: "We become proficient in the transfer of strategy and marketing expertise across countries."

- Economies of scale in marketing function; very little in manufacturing and selling (R&D—is it centralized in Vick's domestic operation?)

- Do not reinvent the wheel in marketing in each country

- Emphasize fewer products with high volume/high profit potential; can be cross-sold in many countries, tailored to the country needs ("Global Efficiency *and* Local Responsiveness")

- Avoid "one-market products" or "one-product markets"

- Resource allocation issue: "Time" in the marketplace; prioritize sequencing of new product introductions

Analysis of Vick International's Competitive Environment

Buyer Strength	Supplier Strength	Threat of Substitutes	Threat of Entrants	Internal Rivalry
• Price regulations • Many buyers • Strict legal environment	• In-house development • Probably not dependent on a few suppliers	• Many varieties on market • Marketing driven rather than value driven competition • Many local competitors	• Low capital requirements • Easy to transfer successful products among countries	• Many big, international firms • Global business segments • Economies of scale and scope
• Low Buyer Power	• Low Supplier Power	• Big Risk from Substitutes	• Big Risk from New Entrants	• High Degree of Internal Rivalry • Possibilities for Differentiating Strategies

- *Highly Competitive Industry*
- *Significant First-Mover Advantages*
- *Importance of Scale and Scope Economies*

Elements of McGuire's Management System

- "My analysis of the situation was that the division had an inadequate budgeting system, ineffective tracking and control mechanisms"

- Continuous Planning & Review (CP-R):

  - Quarterly review and update on last year, this year, and next three years

- Product Categories:

  - Developmental
  - Commercial
  - Nondivisional

- Formal Role Assignments:

  - Approver
  - Prime Mover
  - Concurrer
  - Contributer

- Managers Guides: Job Description

- Work Program: Project Planning and Control

- Product Marketing Guides (PMG 1-8, MC-1, MC-2...)

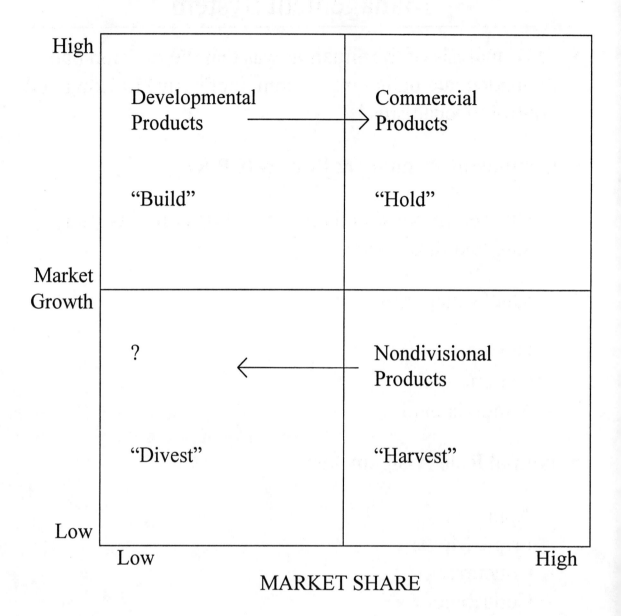

Types of Multinational Strategy

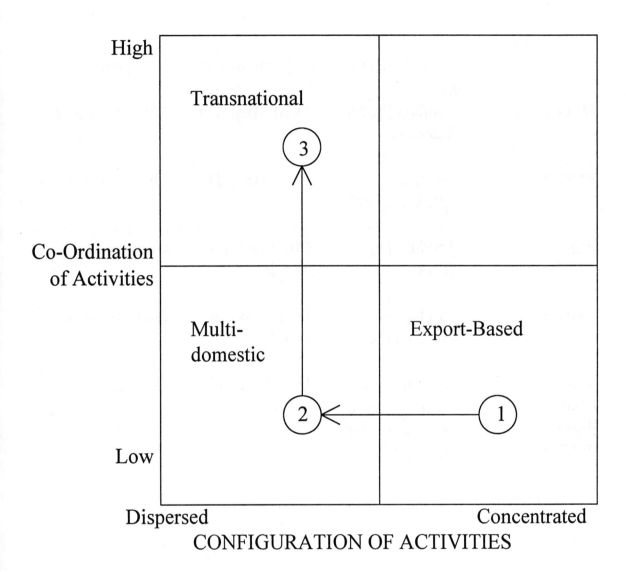

Product Marketing Guides

	Document	Prime Mover	Approver
PMG-1	Product Profile Statement	Divn Mktg. Dir.	Divn. President
PMG-2	Product Marketing Policy	Divn Mktg. Dir.	Divn. President
PMG-3	Product Data Book	Country-level people	Country Mgr
PMG-4	Product Mktg. Assessment	Country-level people	Divn. President
PMG-5 PMG-6 PMG-7 PMG-8	Specific aspects of mktg, advtg, promotion, and sales/distbn	Country-level people	Division

Selected Financial Data

	Year ending June 30					
	1973	1974	1975	1976	1977	1978
Net Sales ($ millions)	57.0	63.0	86.0	106.0	112.0	136.0
Controllable Mktg. Exp. % of sales	15.7%	16.1%	13.1%	14.9%	15.5%	17.6%
Operating Profit as % of sales	9.4%	10.5%	12.1%	14.6%	16.7%	15.1%
ROAE	13.5%	15.4%	18.5%	24.2%	28.5%	27.3%
Marketing Expense $	8.9	10.1	11.3	15.8	17.4	23.9
Operating Profit $	5.4	6.6	10.4	15.5	18.7	20.5

Adapted from Exhibit 2 in case, "Selected Financial Data."

1978 Vick International LA/FE

Highest-Ever Marketing Costs Lower LA/FE Profitability

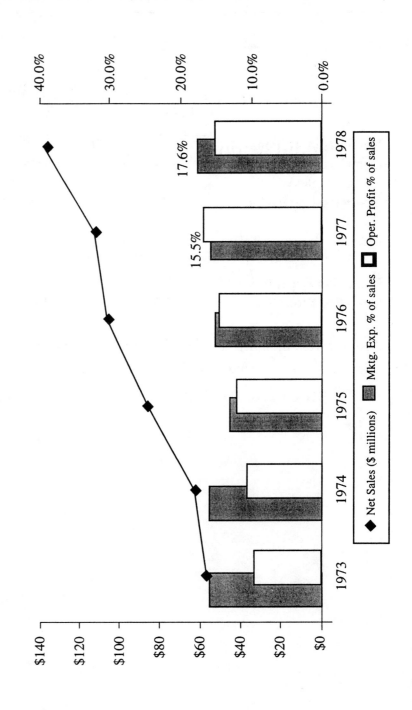

Issues Discussed on Day 1

1. What systems did McGuire put in place?

2. Why did he do it?

3. How good is it?

4. Why have uniform systems across all countries?

5. Are McGuire's systems designed to meet the strategic needs of his divisions or are they simply an expression of his own personality? If McGuire got hit by a truck, how much of the managerial apparatus would be retained by his successor?

Analysis of Vick International's Organizational Environment

	CHAOS	ORDER	GROWTH
Time	• "Pre-McGuire"	• 1976–now	• Future
Characteristics	• Little Information Sharing • Random Business Practices • Unused Potential for Product Transfer	• Much Information Sharing • Structured Business Practices • Potential Being Utilized	• Much Information Sharing • Combination of Both • Little Potential Left
Profit Drivers	• Technical Competence	• Establishment of Practices • Transfer of Products	• New Product Introductions

- **Big Need for "Clean-up" when McGuire Took Over**
- **Present Environment Demands More Flexible Approach**

Management Styles
Must Evolve with the Division

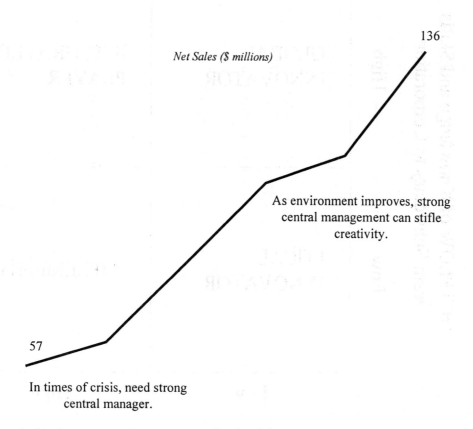

136

Net Sales ($ millions)

As environment improves, strong
central management can stifle
creativity.

57

In times of crisis, need strong
central manager.

| 1973 | 1974 | 1975 | 1976 | 1977 | 1978 |

Subsidiary Roles
Within the Corporate Network

OUTFLOW of Knowledge and Skills from Subsidiary to Corporation

	Low	High
High	GLOBAL INNOVATOR	INTEGRATED PLAYER
Low	LOCAL INNOVATOR	IMPLEMENTOR

INFLOW of Knowledge and Skills from Corporation to Subsidiary

Source: Gupta & Govindarajan (1991)

Did something go wrong with Product Alpha? If so, who caused it to happen? Who is the villain in this piece?

Two Possible Motives

"Substantive" Motive

1. McGuire intervened to protect Das from making a mistake. He chose to educate Das directly by trying to help him on the substantive issue of positioning the product. Strategic positioning of Product Alpha would be better as a result of McGuire's intervention.

"Disciplinary" Motive

2. McGuire felt that Das has already made a serious error by failing to adhere to the procedures laid down in the PMG system. If Das' behavior were tolerated without punishment, others in the division would begin to view PMG as a set of discretionary forms to be filled out when they got around to it.

Kyle's viewpoint on the issue

"Here is the whole program, not just Alpha but the whole program of nutritional new product, at stake because of the way Das was handled."

McGuire's viewpoint on the issue

"It is desperately important that we get this management system, CPR, installed in this division and right now, even if we have to sacrifice a new product."

McGuire's observations

"People are going to test the system, they want to find out whether you do mean it, and the way they are going to test it is that they are going to be prepared to run the risk of violating the rules.... Frankly I was seeing a testing of this system for the very first time.... Under these circumstances, you do have to come down like a ton of bricks.... If you mean that you want the system or the process to last and you really believe in it, then you are going to have to pull people to heel and make it stick."

Lessons

For Das:

- Don't operate in a vacuum.

- Follow the "Grandfather Principle"—know the agenda of your boss and your boss's boss.

For Kyle:

- You may not believe fully in the system but it's your responsibility to protect your people.

For McGuire:

- The system is thorough and the objectives are sound but need to reassess:

    - Implications for "time to market"
    - Implications for "ownership" of ideas by product champions
    - Implications for "new product development" vs. "product extensions"

Summary Thoughts

1. The value of videotapes in understanding management style. Management style affects the way control systems get operated.

2. Historically, McGuire's strategy was to diffuse product and marketing know-how developed in head office to different subsidiaries (e.g., NyQuil). The CPR planning and control system proved effective for implementing this strategy. However, McGuire now wants new product development to come from subsidiaries but these should not be one-market products. This poses a basic dilemma:

   > Need for new product development →
   > Need for autonomy for the units
   >
   > But not one-market products →
   > Need for divisional co-ordination and control to diffuse innovation to other units

   CPR is not effective for the latter. What planning and control approach might work here?

3. Top managers operate with dual agenda: developing the business and developing the people who manage the business. McGuire is attempting to implement these two agenda items simultaneously:

A. The product/market strategy for his division requires the development and introduction of new products that can be sold in several countries.

B. His managerial strategy focuses on the education and professionalization of his far flung management team.

4. There are two generic approaches to developing people:

A. Let them act, make mistakes, and learn from the mistakes:
   – Promotes greater innovation
   – Riskier approach
   – Could be disastrous if (i) people are allowed to repeat mistakes, and (ii) if there are no systematic mechanisms to dissect and learn from mistakes

B. Create a system so that people are prevented from making mistakes and develop the necessary good habits:
   – Low risk, low innovation
   – Might people remain dependent on the system?

McGuire prefers approach "B" over "A." However, in an increasingly turbulent market environment, I would generally prefer "A" over "B."

5. In McGuire's case, his two agenda items—business development and people development—are in conflict. He also sees his management development agenda as a more serious potential contraint on growth of his division than the development of the product/market strategy. (Note, that this perspective is widely shared by most companies today. Managerial capability is far more important than current business success.)

McGuire is willing to sacrifice Project Alpha (the product/market strategy) in order to protect and foster his CPR system (the people development strategy).

Case 17-3

Nestle S.A. (A)

Note:

The teaching note for the (A) case is attached. The case (B) is reproduced in its entirety. Instructors could either distribute the (B) case or summarize the key points from the (B) case in class.

Approach

Students may become frustrated with these cases. As one said, "Nestle is a huge, well managed company with 100 years of experience, and they dropped the ball. Why do you expect us to do better?" It the student comes away with an appreciation of the difficulties involved in the management control of a subsidiary that is operating in a highly inflationary economy, that is valuable information, and it is probably enough to expect.

These cases describe, month by month, the information that became available to headquarters in more depth and with greater frankness than anything I know of in the literature. The fact that there were serious problems was evident early in the history, but the reports don't provide information that is a reliable basis for acting to solve these problems. Informal visits and contacts seem to have been more important than the formal reports. The central questions are: (1) Could the information have been better? and (2) What role can headquarters play in the affairs of a division in another country?

My own opinion on the second question is that headquarters cannot do much in the management of a foreign division (perhaps, this also applies to any division, but that is not the issue here). Headquarters can provide some guidance, and it must have a way of determining whether the division management is competent. In short, headquarters can direct, but it cannot manage. If it decides that management is not performing properly, the best solution, in most cases, is to replace division management, and do it quickly.

The questions are structured so as to help the student answer the above question, but the following analysis discusses the overall problem, rather than the answers to specific questions.

There are two cases, so as to permit two class meetings. They can be assigned for one class; this increases, but does not double, the effort required.

Although the cases do describe some issues relating to differences in foreign exchange rates, I do not discuss these, simply because the other issues are important and complicated enough to consume all the available time. Thus, policies regarding when to import and when to export, and when to borrow in foreign currencies rather than local currencies, could be added to the following list of policies, but I have not done so.

Analysis

With a little reflection, students can list the policies that a manufacturing company should follow in an inflationary economy. They all relate to the fact that money and other financial instruments are becoming less valuable, per unit, whereas physical goods are becoming more valuable. To get the discussion started, following are some possible policies (they are debatable):

1. Acquire more materials than are needed for current consumption, and produce more goods than are needed for current sales, provided you are reasonably certain that these goods can be sold, and provided that the inventories can be financed as in the next policy. (Some students disagree strongly with this policy. They argue that increases in inventory increase working capital requirements and mask a decline in productivity because they spread overhead costs over more units.)

2. Delay payment for these materials and other production costs for as long as possible. Finance as much of the inventory as possible with borrowing denominated in local currencies, provided that the interest rates were well below the anticipated rate of inflation.

3. Set selling prices so as to produce an adequate gross margin above current cost of sales, that is, the costs at the time goods are delivered to customers. Include an allowance for interest cost in these prices. Don't invoice at today's prices unless the goods are to be delivered today. Use special off-price deals only in unusual circumstances.

4. Reduce the terms of receivables to as short a period as is feasible, and try especially hard to collect overdue accounts and stop shipments to customers who are seriously delinquent.

Note that different policies are appropriate for inventory than for receivables. These are the two important components of working capital, and they should be viewed separately.

Vendors and customers have opposite policies to those listed above, so the above principles cannot be followed exactly; purchase and sales contracts are a matter of compromise between these conflicting points of view.

Reports

How should reports be structured so that management knows the extent to which these policies are being followed? This is difficult. If the preceding list of policies (or some alternative list) is accepted, the reports should focus on measures that show whether these policies have been put into practice. This is the "key variable" principle discussed earlier in the text. For example, accounts receivable is clearly a key variable, and more detailed information (e.g. aging of receivables, bad debts written off) may have been provided for this item.

Part of the solution is to provide good information on physical quantities of purchases, production, inventory, personnel, and sales; these will show the actual flows which may be obscured by monetary amounts.

For the monetary amounts, one possibility is to state them in constant units of currency (which is approximately the same as saying that they will reflect physical flows). (Nestle did not do as much of this as it could have.) To do so could obscure whether the policies outlined above are in fact being followed because these policies involve recognizing the importance of monetary amounts.

An alternative is to express both budget amounts in terms that will permit the variances caused by inflation to be separated from the variances caused by differences in physical volumes. This is more feasible now, with appropriate computer programs, than it was as of the time of the cases. The (B) case does indicate that price variances were separated from volume variances, but this is not the same as identifying inflation as a separate causal factor.

Another useful approach is to establish ratios ("key variables") that should be watched carefully. An obvious one is the ratios of receivables to sales (i.e. days sales in receivables.) An increase in the ratio indicates that customers are taking advantage of the inflationary situation (just as the company is trying to do with purchases).

In addition to developing the most useful numbers, it is essential that the reports flow to headquarters quickly. The reporting lags indicated in the cases for the early 1980s would be intolerable today, not only because of the development of practically instantaneous means of communication but also because computers permit the raw data to be assembled and summarized more quickly. (Even so, in both the 1980s and today, prompt action must be taken on the basis of the reports; the cases report several occasions on which the response to the reports was slow.)

Summary of Events

The story begins in 1979, although there were turbulent times in earlier years. Budget amounts in 1979 represented huge increases over 1978, and reports showed erratic swings in actuals (see especially receivables, "Debtors" in Exhibit 1, and sales, Exhibit 3). The reports may have been viewed as defective meters, that is the wild fluctuations indicated that there was something wrong with the reports, rather than with the situation being reported. The principal reported serious criticism was the increase in receivables in the letter of October 2 (repeated on November 28). Reported performance for the October and November 1979 were so good that they overshadowed earlier indications of problems. By hindsight, we learn that the high sales volume may have reflected the situation described in the next paragraph.

There was mention of a case in which goods were shipped in December had been invoiced in December, and there was some follow-up on this. This was an obvious violation of company policies, and the action may not have been strong enough. The erroneous accounts receivable amount for October (Exhibit 1), and the negative sales number for December are clues that something was wrong with the system.

The principal concern at the Centre with the 1980 budget was with the receivables (85 days sales, compared with a long-term objective of 40 days). There was mention of a 10 percent increase in personnel, but no questions appear to have been raised about this.

By hindsight, it appears that the action taken on accounts receivable was not strong enough. Even though responses to the letters were not convincing, there was no further action.

At this point, students are asked whether further action should have been taken in February 1980. Opinions can differ. Clearly, control over accounts receivable had been lost, and there does not appear to have been action about the personnel increase, but these are only two of the perplexing problems that the manager of the market had to deal with, and in other respects performance in 1979 and the budget for 1980 may have been regarded as satisfactory in view of the very difficult environment.

At the beginning of the (B) case, we learn that the zone director was "disappointed" with performance in 1979. However, there is no indication that he did anything about it. It is quite possible that managers at the Centre didn't know what should be done in this confusing environment, and they relied on exhortations to the head of market to do the best he could.

In the early months of 1980 the Centre did continue its criticisms of accounts receivable (but without enforcing specific actions). Apparently, there was inadequate recognition of the seriousness of the whole situation until Mr. Huber, the chief financial officer of the Argentine market, was summoned to the Centre and gave his personal views. It is interesting that this personal visit seems to be more important than the formal reports.

From then on, the Centre began to act strongly. The action was heavily influenced by Centre people who visited the market, another indication that the formal reports were inadequate. The actual reports made by these people seemed to contain essentially the same information that was provided by the regular reporting system, but more attention was given to the reports of visitors than to the formal reports. This is often the case. It indicates that the reporting system was an inadequate way of finding out what the problems actually were.

In August, the head of market was finally galvanized into taking corrective action. By that time the situation had deteriorated so badly that a huge loss was inevitable. The remainder of the case describes actions taken to stem the losses. Basically, the objective seems to have been to reduce SANPA's structure to the dimensions it had in 1975. They were drastic, specific decisions that were implemented promptly. They involved changes in policies, new organization arrangements, replacement of certain managers, and bringing in assistance from other parts of the Nestle organization.

Question 2 of the (B) case asks the student to think about organizational arrangements. It does seem to me that the Centre relied too much on the reports prepared under the direction of the head of market. The problems might have been detected earlier, and corrective action instituted earlier, if (a) there were more frequent visits to the market by Zone people who worked at the Centre, and (b) the chief financial officer was given more authority to report the situation as he saw it. The latter possibility raises the problem of the relationship between the division controller (in this case, the chief financial officer), and the division manager that was discussed way back in the Rendell case [Case 2-1]).

RNA

Subsequent Developments

Based on information by the Finance Director in a visit to bankers in New York, the Chief Executive Officer decided that a Swiss franc loan in September 1980 was too risky, and that a decision should be delayed until early 1981.

The Zone Director decided that SANPA's internal audit department should report directly to the Managing Director of SANPA, rather than to the head of the administrative division.

The Zone Director replaced SANPA's external auditors.

In early October, the Chief Executive Officer announced that an experienced manager and a finance-control specialist would be temporarily assigned to Buenos Aires to "implement the various corrective measures" and to replace Messrs. Gonzalez and Huber.

After visiting Argentina in October, a member of senior technical management recommended that fresh milk intake be reduced substantially and that the existing surplus of milk powder be sold on the world market. All milk factories would be kept open, but at reduced volume.

On October 10, 1980, a senior management meeting decided to permit SANPA to borrow the equivalent of SFr. 80 million in foreign currency.

In October, the new external auditors reported that the market had too much autonomy. Overly optimistic reports from the head of market were not adequately questioned, nor was there an adequate follow-up and implementation. Also production reports were submitted and analyzed separately from sales reports; consequently, the Centre had not noticed that production programs were based on overly optimistic sales forecasts.

October was another disastrous month. The Zone Controller suggested at that time that perhaps all Argentina production facilities should be closed until the situation improved and that the Argentina market would be served by goods imported from other markets. This suggestion was not adopted.

As of 1990, Argentina still had not solved its inflation problem.

Comments by a Senior Manager

Late in 1984, a member of senior management, who was not directly involved in the 1979-80 Argentine matter, gave the case writer his analysis of the situation. It is summarized below.

In my opinion, the unhappy situation was the result of several accidents and events, all in the same adverse direction.

High inflation started to slow down, while interest rates continued to rise, becoming higher than the inflation rate. SANPA was therefore no longer able to maintain adequate inventories. This change was not perceived by local management who tried to reach budgeted sales volumes through aggressive promotions. The resulting receivables were of lower quality and became more difficult to collect. At the same time, the manufacturing and purchasing programs were not adapted to the new situation. These factors caused a huge increase in working capital, at a very high cost.

Latin America was still in a state of euphoria. It was on top of the world. Growth rates, fantastic projects, everyone willing to lend them money—everything was impressive. And our people at the Centre who were dealing with Latin America felt the same way. There was one big euphoria.

The Head of the market lost control. He had a few terrible salesmen who sold the stuff and said: "We will deliver it in six months." When you are in an economy with 170 percent inflation, and you tell people that you will invoice now because you want the sales to count in your turnover [i.e. sales] numbers and you will deliver in six months, but the market may not get paid for another six months, you have a very bad situation. The sales people were also giving money to their customers in the form of unjustified rebates, gifts, etc., in order to get sales volume.

Also, in this period we had a few problems at the Centre. We had one senior manager who frequently pointed out that there was trouble, but without specifying what exactly was wrong or what should be done. So, eventually, although he cried and shouted, nobody believed him. Actually, few people believed that the situation was as serious as it actually turned out to be.

The Head of the market in Argentina had many years of service and a good track record, it is true, but in more normal times. The Centre therefore tended to rely on him and to follow the Argentina market less closely than they followed other markets. Also, several major projects were underway in Latin America, limiting somewhat the zone manager's time for following all current affairs. Finally, the Head of market was close to retirement and for obvious reasons wanted to show continued growth and positive results in his last year of service.

Sales were high on paper, but effective sales were decreasing. Customers were not paying on time. Stocks were very high, debts were also high, but cash flow was low in relation to the reported sales.

I could add many other causes. In combination, it is to be expected that we acted three or four months too late. In an inflation period, when you have already issued invoices and have not been paid, you can lose a lot of money in three or four months.

At that time, our then Chief Executive Officer jumped in. He went himself a few times to Argentina, he shut down factories, he reduced stocks, he solved the problems himself with the help of a few people. He acted in a fantastically quick, short, and simple way. He solved many problems in a few months. He brought in some help from the head of another market. He did everything right.

We lost millions in Argentina, but we would have lost much more if he had not intervened. And even with perfect foresight, we would have lost much money anyway in that terrible environment.

I would have done the same as he did. Maybe we closed too much of the business to solve the problem; that is the only thing that I might have done differently. But it is always easy to be more clever than the man on the spot when you are talking after the event. One could in no way avoid the loss; one could only act quickly to avoid further losses and to resolve the situation.

When you have such high inflation that you don't see what figures expressed in Liras, Pesos, etc., really mean, when you get numbers that are in the millions and billions, you lose track of what is actually going on.

Part of the trouble was indeed our reporting system. We had elaborate, long reports, with everything classified in detail. At the same time, the Centre was too much departmentalized by function; there was perhaps not enough co-ordination. It seemed that everyone at the Centre relied on someone else; nobody was fully responsible. I think we have learned that no one should be appointed to a Zone or market oriented key position at the Centre who has never worked in a market.

Nestle S.A. (B)

Mr. Smith, zone director of Nestle S.A., was disappointed with the performance of the Argentine market in 1979. As the months of 1980 went by, his concern increased.

Developments in Early 1980

In the first months of 1980, inflation continued to fall and by April, the annualized rate had dropped to 90 percent.

Total imports were up by 40.9 percent the first half of 1980, making local producers suffer and leading to an increased number of bankruptcies. Gross domestic product (GDP) grew by only 0.2 percent, with the industrial sector down by 2.3 percent and agriculture 6.4 percent below the same period of 1979. For the whole of 1980, a negative growth of at least 3 percent was forecasted. Financing costs remained high, and this led to a slowdown in investment expenditures and a liquidation of inventories, even in industries not directly threatened by the import boom.

Several factors prevented inflation from falling as fast and far as government had hoped, and two of them had a particularly strong impact on the economy and, thus, also on the performance of companies.

First, because people lacked confidence in the economic and political outlook, they diverted cash to foreign financial markets or to speculative investments instead of reinvesting them for productive purposes. Certain distributors started to import Nestle products manufactured in neighboring countries and to offer them at prices considerably below comparable products manufactured by SANPA (S.A. Nestle de Productos Alimenticios).

Second, many industrial companies went bankrupt, and this led to a serious banking crisis. The Central Bank, which had guaranteed deposits up to a certain limit, was forced to come to the rescue, paying out more than US$ 2 billion to depositors in April and early May of 1980. Such a large outflow of funds, financed largely through printing new money, led to increased inflation.

As shown in Exhibit 1, actual sales for SANPA were far below the budgeted amounts. Outstanding receivables rose to an unprecedented 121 days by the end of March. Excess working capital tied up in debtors was pesos 61.6 billion at the end of March. Collections were only 73 percent of budget. The sales result for February and March were explained with the same reasons given in January (i.e., low stock rotation in the trade, vacation period, and, for certain products, selling prices above those of the competition).

Hope was expressed that sales would increase because of "massive media or point of sales promotion activity currently under study." In March, when selling prices were increased by 6 or 7 percent, it was argued that demand had been hurt by "increased schooling fees and unusually high temperatures, which led to a shift in consumer preference toward the refreshment drinks market segment." To stimulate demand, special discounts were introduced. For example,

---

This case was prepared by F. Voegtli. This condensed version was prepared by Professor Robert N. Anthony, Harvard Business School. Names of most persons are fictitious. Copyright © 1990 by Nestec S.A., Vevey, Switzerland.

Nescafe customers could get up to 16 percent reductions for a large quantity purchased on a cash payment basis.

Exhibit 1 Budgeted and Actual SANPA Sales for January to June 1980 (in pesos millions)

Month	Original Budget	March Revision	Actual	Difference vs. Latest Budget
January	26,656	26,657	10,765	(15,892)
February	32,319	32,320	14,883	(17,437)
March	47,450	47,450	23,789	(23,661)
April	61,631	48,371	29,406	(18,965)
May	79,695	63,286	45,832	(17,454)
June	84,297	82,473	65,071	(17,402)
Total	332,048	300,557	189,746	(110,811)

Exhibit 2 SANPA Accounts Receivalbe Collections and Excess Working Capital January to June (in pesos millions)

Month (1980)	Planned Collections	Actual Collections	Performance (%)
January	39,600	23,876	60
February	55,104	36,289	66
March	60,291	44,193	73
April	64,800	44,541	69
May	72,816	37,523	52
June	58,980	33,047	56

Month (1980)	Value of Excess Finished Goods Stocks	Value of Excess Debtors Outstanding	Impact on Working Capital
January	21,367	111,066	132,433
February	27,257	94,701	121,958
March	32,603	61,581	94,184
April	37,214	38,876*	76,090
May	31,306	23,915*	55,221
June	30,614	9,691	40,305

*Reduction partially due to a modification of the standard from 40 days to 45 days in April/May and 60 days in June.

Working capital increased, as shown in Exhibit 2. Most excess stocks were due to milk products, where it was not easy to reduce production on short notice, because the fresh milk of contracted suppliers usually could not be refused or resold.

From pesos 232 billion at end March, indebtedness was expected to stabilize at a level of around pesos 220 billion over the following three months. Besides taking additional peso financing, SANPA increased its foreign borrowings by US$ 2 million in February and US$ 5 million in March.

Instead of a budgeted operating profit in the first quarter, the market reported a net loss, plaining it with low sales "due to a temporary softening of demand." Sales volume was only 45 percent of budget and 50 percent of the corresponding period of 1979.

Developments in April, May, and Tune

The March budget revision (key numbers received in late April; details on May 27) showed the following estimates for the year; sales, pesos 821.5 billion; net operating profit, 9.47 billion; net profit, 20.93 billion; expected inflation, 70 percent for 1980; marginal contribution, minus pesos 30.8 billion due to sales shortfall and plus pesos 48.3 billion due to higher selling prices and lower variable selling and distribution costs; overhead, plus pesos 47.7 billion (of which pesos 34.6 billion was interest, which thus increased to the equivalent of 21.7 percent of sales, with borrowings forecasted to reach pesos 335 billion by year end). The revision contained such comments as "... the normalization of demand allows us to foresee normal stock levels..." and "debtors should stand at 75 days credit by year end."

On April 28, the zone controller sent another letter, the fourth within seven months, to Mr. Gonzalez to remind him of the worsening debtors situation and to express strong doubts about the goal of 60 days' outstanding credit by end April, promised in a letter two months earlier. Mr. Gonzalez was asked to comment as quickly as possible on the corrective measures already taken or planned. No reply was ever received at the Centre in Vevey, Switzerland, the headquarters of Nestle.

In mid-May, Mr. Gonzalez came to the Centre to participate in the annual conference for Nestle's major market heads. Following discussions on financial policies, Mr. Gonzalez was asked not to take out any more new foreign currency loans, even if the latter would appear to be more advantageous on a short-term basis.

On May 21, the monthly report for April arrived. It noted that the worst flood of the century had been experienced by the province of Buenos Aires. Sales and debtors collections were once more far below budget. Although sales of chocolate were far below budget, the report stated that most production programmes, including the one for chocolates, had been fully executed.

On May 23, P. Huber, SANPA's administrative manager, sent a telex to the Centre with some new forecasts for outstanding debtors, a projected financial position, as well as with a schedule of the due dates for the various foreign currency loans/debts. It was apparent that these debts could not be paid without additional financing from the Centre.

On May 29, the zone director sent a letter to Mr. Gonzalez, confirming an earlier message according to which SANPA was not to contract any new borrowings in foreign currencies. The market was reminded that such foreign currency loans always required prior approval by the Centre.

In early June, the finance director of the Centre informed the vice president controller of his concern about the financial situation of the Argentine operations. His note concluded that the debtors situation should be improving since Mr. Gonzalez had reported the receipt of some large payments during the month of May. The monthly treasury report received on June 9 did not confirm the improvement in the debtors situation promised by Mr. Gonzalez (see Exhibit 2), and the zone controller immediately sent a note on this subject to the zone director, qualifying the debtors situation as "disastrous" and urging the zone director to make the market take some drastic corrective action. A copy of the note was sent to the finance director, who in turn sent it to the chief executive officer.

On June 11, the zone controller completed his analysis of the long-term plan (LTP) for the period 1981 to 1985 on the proposal received from the market a few days earlier. The LTP projected a favorable growth of both volume (plus 6 percent on average) and profitability (slight increase); some major new investments were requested for 1981, requiring a capital increase or a long-term loan from the Centre.

Since the LTP proposal contained few details on the profitability assumptions, P. Huber, who was in charge of the financial aspects of the Argentine companies, was summoned to the Centre to participate in the LTP discussions. Asked in a private meeting with the finance director why he had not informed the Centre of the seriousness of the situation in Argentina, Mr. Huber said that he had warned the market head from the beginning, even years back, of the negative financial impact of uncollected overdue accounts receivable; as proof he showed internal notes on this subject sent by his treasurer to all parties concerned with SANPA in 1977 and 1978. Mr. Huber further said that Mr. Gonzalez had never listened to him and had even prevented him from writing to the Centre. Finally, he said that he suspected that fraud had taken place in the marketing and sales are in recent months.

The finance director thereupon decided to send a team of internal auditors to Argentina. He asked the manager of the department to personally head the team. The last internal audit of SANPA by the Centre had taken place in the first half of 1977. On June 18, the finance director informed the CEO of his audit decision.

On June 18, Messrs. Gonzalez and Huber discussed the debtors situation with the zone director. They argued that the pesos 71 billion outstanding at end-May corresponded to only 79 days credit outstanding, which was an improvement over the 122 days one month earlier. However, a more detailed analysis showed that pesos 12 billion related to invoices of 1979 (equal to over 150 days outstanding) and that pesos 5 billion had been paid' by the customers in the form of postdated checks (which thus could not immediately be cashed). Gonzalez and Huber promised to reduce the outstanding credit to 60 days by end-August using, if necessary, professional debt collectors. The zone controller insisted that Huber should send a monthly report of overdue debtors by age group (1-30 days, 30-60 days, etc).

On June 24, the zone director summed up the outcome of the LTP discussion with Messrs. Gonzalez and Huber in a note to the CEO:

> The proposed LTP was not accepted. Although the planned volume increase for the years 1981 to 1985 looks achievable, the figures of 1980 are far too optimistic. 1980 results will be around SFr 700 million [one Swiss franc (SFr) equals roughly US$ 1.40] of sales and a net loss of SFr 2 million, according to Mr. Gonzalez. This looks too high, and I have asked the market to make another budget revision. Sales were very depressed up to April (they are recovering now). The high financing costs due to debt collection difficulties and the increasing stock level for finished goods increase interest costs. In order to reduce the financial pressure, I have asked the market to install a strict austerity programme and to freeze all expenses on the level already spent or contracted as per June 15 (around 60 billion).

The audit in Argentina started on June 27. Within two weeks the audit manager was able to come up with a conclusion, which he communicated to the zone controller by phone on July 9 and to the finance director at the Centre by phone and letter on July 13 and 18, respectively:

> Major customers are still overstocked with goods, and demand is thus still weak; debtors collections continue to be difficult and the situation is serious (pesos 118.4 billion outstanding at end-June, of which pesos 15.9 billion are above 90 days); general overheads cannot be cut easily, although the organizational structure is too heavy in view of the reduced sales volumes; production programmes were based on overoptimistic sales budget, which has led to excessive stock levels requiring additional bank borrowings (six months' stock coverage for milk powders, the chocolate stocks on hand are sufficient to cover the forecasted sales up to the end of 1980!); interest charges are increasing at a horrid pace, and SANPA's financial situation has become so desperate that urgent financial assistance by the Centre might be required; in the distribution area goods invoiced in May are still in the warehouse two months later, as customers do not want them; cancellation in 1980 of large quantities of goods invoiced and shown as sales in 1979.

Exhibit 3   SANPA Cumulative Production and Sales, January to August 1980 (in tons/000s liters)

Product Category	Cumulative Production Year-to-Date			Cumulative Sales Year-to-Date						
	Feb.	April	June	Feb.	March	April	May	June	July	August
Milks	5,804	9,868	11,620	558	1,020	2,538	4,021	5,999	8,780	11,123
Dietetics	345	843	1,523	305	478	633	804	944	1,135	1,312
Instant drinks	942	1,941	3,105	272	552	993	1,511	2,231	2,693	3,088
Chocolates	801	1,530	1,962	118	306	508	638	842	931	1,066
Culinary	604	1,240	1,922	92	278	526	1,368	1,821	1,921	2,207
Ice-creams	2,324	2,951	3,268	1,725	2,515	2,618	2,698	2,733	2,766	3,875

Developments in August and September

Having heard what was going on in Argentina, the zone director immediately called Mr. Gonzalez, who was on leave in Europe, and asked him to return at once to Buenos Aires to work out an emergency plan through which sales volume could be increased and the overheads drastically reduced. Less than a week later, Mr. Gonzalez called the Centre. He stated that local bank credits had become extremely expensive and that he, therefore, needed a loan from the Centre of as much as 100 million Swiss francs. He described the major measures introduced or planned in an effort to restore profitability and bring the financial degradation to a halt; a general hiring freeze, a reduction of personnel at three factories and in the sales force, additional selling price increases for most products, a reduction in travelling and training expenses, and the cancellation of the 50-year jubilee celebration (for which there was a budget of pesos 2 billion).

The zone director asked Mr. Keller, the zone controller, to make a trip to Argentina. Upon his return, the latter described in an August 15 note to the CEO, the finance director, and the zone director his impressions:

> Turnover now estimated by market at pesos 740 billion, net loss at pesos 96 billion as a result of low sales and enormous financing costs. However, unfavorable sales prospects for chocolates and culinary products make these forecasts still too optimistic,

and actual results might come out closer to sales of pesos 700 billion and a net loss exceeding pesos 100 billion. If no corrective measures are taken now, 1981 will be similarly disastrous. The control set-up needs to be strengthened.

From discussions with local banks, Mr. Keller concluded that some were still willing to lend money to SANPA if they had some free capacity left. Interest expenses were now estimated at 27 percent of turnover for 1980, and total bank borrowings were the equivalent of pesos 295 billion as at July 31, 1980 (pesos 245 billion, US$ 18.4 million, Swiss francs 13 million); SANPA feared that by year end this figure would go up by another pesos 100 billion due to the financing of excess debtors and finished goods. Keller recommended that SANPA convert some peso borrowings into US$ loans; by taking a US$ 20 million loan, SANPA would save US$ 500,000 in interest each month, given the large interest rate differential of some 4 percent per month.

The vice president finance approved a loan of US$ 10 million only, arguing that SANPA's foreign exchange exposure was already large and that he did not like the existing devaluation risk. Total US$ loans thus went up to 28.4 million.

According to SANPA's monthly report for June, which got to the Centre in late July, inflation seemed to have stabilized in the range of 5 to 6 percent per month; but local interest rates were still moving upwards, an international decision by the banking sector to prevent foreign capital from leaving the country. Demand for capital goods was down further, and labor disputes in the country as a result of the recession were increasing.

SANPA reported low levels of sales and collections. A shift in the consumer spending pattern was partially held responsible for the sales shortfall, as Argentines seemed to prefer cheap imported capital goods (e.g., color TV sets) and making cheap trips abroad to buying local food products. Cumulative tonnage sold in the first six months of 1980 was down 56 percent over 1979 for chocolates, 45 percent for milk powders, and 23 percent for instant drinks. Only ice-creams and Fruticon volumes were ahead for the same comparative periods. On finished goods stocks and debtors, the report showed high values of more than pesos 100 billion each, with another pesos 50 billion tied up in raw and packing material.

The bimonthly operations report for May/June, received on August 5, mentioned for the first time a "strong reduction of production programmes," permitting the complete elimination of overtime. The largest programme cut was for chocolates, with only 114 tons being produced in June, compared to 322 tons in June 1979. The report also stated that the cumulative milk purchase and usage figures for the first six months of 1980 were some 25 to 30 percent above the amount for 1979. This had a positive effect on milk prices, which had increased at a rate less than half of the inflation rate.

On August 15, the zone director reported to the chief executive officer his impressions formed during his visit to Argentina from August 4 to 9, 1980:

> Strong recession in certain sectors of the economy; the government team gives the impression of being very united, which makes a continuation of the economic policy more than likely. The country's total foreign debt will soon reach US$ 25 billion, which points to a maxi-devaluation, though probably not before October. Local interest rates have stayed positive in real terms for several months, which attracted speculative foreign

money and made local people invest their money short term. An economic recovery should begin in late 1981 or early 1982.

For SANPA, the situation looks really bad. When recession started in late 1979, they tried to offset the declining demand by a "sell in" policy up to the end of the year. Certain products, such as chocolate and coffee, faced strong competition from cheap imports sold at prices up to 50 percent below SANPA'S. The situation worsened when local competitors, facing the same problems, began to liquidate their surplus stocks at ridiculously low prices and when customers started to return goods they could not sell, forcing SANPA to offer even more attractive terms to finally get rid of these products. During all this time the production programmes were not modified immediately. In addition, distributors and retailers reduced their stock levels and used their suppliers as credit source in light of the recession and the trend to positive real interest rates. The debt collection performance has improved over the last six months; but on the marketing side, people believed for too long in a forth-coming upswing of consumer demand. Although for milk products the situation is not too bad, coffee and particularly chocolates have really been hurt; and some wrong decisions were taken in an attempt to liquidate chocolate stock in 1979. The regular selling price adjustments carried out by SANPA helped to maintain marginal contribution rates above 60 percent but led to astronomical price differences compared to the competition.

The note then summarized the corrective actions that the zone director had already initiated or planned to introduce. They included staff reduction of 250 persons at head office and sales/distribution; a reduction of fresh milk intake by 50,000 tons; limit chocolate product to four varieties and import the rest from Brazil; replace key managers "who had contributed to the current situation"; study feasibility of closing one factory; have two experienced managers from other markets sent to Buenos Aires to assist Messrs. Gonzalez and Huber.

The zone director also stated that the financial pressure of SANPA could be relieved by granting it a loan from the Centre in the amount of some SFr 80 million, at an interest rate of 7–8 percent per year.

Around the same time Mr. Keller, the zone controller, tried to put some figures to the problem of excessive stocks. While for chocolates and green coffee there was no possibility of selling the excess quantities, for milk powder a decision had to be taken. The financing cost was pesos 1.1 billion (Swiss francs 1 million) per month using full cost and S percent interest; the variable costs of production had been pesos 21 billion (SFr 18.5 million), and the powder could be sold on the world market for a total of some US$5.7 million (SFr 9.5 million). Should the excess milk powder, equivalent to two months domestic sales, be offered abroad or kept for local sale?

In a preliminary report of the mission to Argentina (which had lasted from June 27 to August 19, 1980), the manager of the corporate internal audits department highlighted key findings: The financing cost (8.5 percent per month) was far above the cost increase incurred by SANPA for raw and packing materials (4.7 percent per month) and the replacement cost ex factory of finished goods (4.5 percent), which makes compulsory a policy of minimum stock levels. In the debtors area, there was a complete absence of systematic credit limits as from the middle of 1979, and, to push sales, payment conditions granted to the trade became increasingly generous. Only on August 13, 1980, was the responsibility for the trade credit policy given back to the Administrative Division. The monthly debtors statements were and partly still are completely unreliable. Production programs were based on overoptimistic sales forecasts, which had constantly to be revised downward. Large quantities of finished goods were invoiced in late 1979 but were delivered in the first months of 1980 (pesos 13 billion in Buenos Aires distribution centre alone), or were never delivered at all and had to be credited back to the customers in 1980. The profit implication of this, together with free goods and commissions given to customers in 1980 on those 1979 sales (no provisions had been made at year end as the promotion had been hidden from the manager of the Administration Division) was more than pesos 18 billion negative, which means that 179 results for SANPA and Fruticon had actually been strongly in red instead of yielding a small profit as reported. For chocolates, certain customers were given discounts of up to 46 percent of the invoice amount in 1979, at a time when the marginal contribution was barely above 50 percent and interest rates were 6 percent per month; the full responsibility for promotions was with the sales administration department. At the distribution centres (DC), large stock differences existed and could not be explained (pesos 13 billion at Buenos Aires DC). There was no directive clearly defining the authority granted to the various managers (e.g., approval of free goods promotions, approval of credit notes). There was weak administrative assistance from head office to the DCs for their difficult tasks, such as debt collection, accounting, and the updating of debtors and stocks positions.

The end-June budget revision arrived in early September. It forecasted sales of pesos 728 billion; net operating loss, pesos 107 billion; net loss, pesos 96 billion; expected total year end debt, pesos 425 billion.

The treasurer of the Centre submitted a recommendation to the finance director on August 18 after having contacted some banks on the outlook for the peso. If the Centre made a loan of US$ 50 million to SANPA, the latter could save US$ 11 million in interest by year-end 1980 (given interest rates of 5.5 percent per month for peso loans and 1.0 percent for US$ loans) while facing a devaluation risk equivalent to some US$ 20 million.

On August 19, the chief executive officer wrote to the zone manager that he was in principle willing to give his approval for a Swiss franc 80 million loan from the Centre to SANPA at some 7–8 percent per year. He had come to the conclusion that it did not make much sense to pay 60–66 percent interests to finance the mounting losses; the interest rate differential was so large that it would offset a devaluation of up to 50 percent. However, given the devaluation risk, he wanted to postpone a final decision until the return from a trip to New York and Buenos Aires that the finance director was going to make to obtain first-hand information from banking circles and SANPA in light of this pending financing decision. The decision should not be delayed beyond October.

In early September, the finance director informed the CEO of his opinion on the general situation in Argentina, the specific problems of SANPA, and on the peso devaluation risk:

> Peso was devalued only 87 percent against the US$ since December 1978, whilst consumer prices jumped by 250 percent during the same period. Government economic policy is hurting internal trade and the key industries, such as meat, milk, chemicals, etc.; if this policy is maintained for much longer, it will ruin the country. Argentine's foreign reserves are very artificial, as they are mainly composed of short-term debt, half of which becomes due before year-end 1980. US$ 2 billion will leave the country by end-September, and American banks have covered their peso exposure in view of the potential devaluation risk. Local interest rates are now at 4.5 percent per month, but some people expect them to rise to 8 percent again before year end. SANPA management was not able to explain to me how they had arrived at the figure of Swiss francs 80 million

used in the request for a Centre loan. Debtors and stocks still seem to be too high, and more effort could be done in those areas. Instead of sending money from the Centre, we should ask the market to cash in as much money as possible, maybe even through the sale of excess fixed assets, and to drastically reduce the production programmes, as there will be no economic recovery before 1982! Since there is a high devaluation risk—probably 30 percent and most likely between November and January—and since the market has not yet presented a detailed restructuring plan, I recommend that no loan be sent to SANPA at this stage.

Exhibit 4   SANPA's Estimates of Bank Borrowings

| | Forecast (billions pesos) | | | | |
	4 Months Previously	3 Months Previously	2 Months Previously	1 Month Previously	Actual
1979:					
July	50	53	64	76	83
August	53	66	78	90	93
September	65	79	86	93	109
October	79	86	79	111	128
November	86	68	108	125	147
December	52	95	128	162	180
1980:					
January	84	125	169	197	223
February	123	169	193	230	211
March	158	185	221	203	232
April	178	215	198	218	248
May	219	207	218	243	264
June	214	221	237	262	291

Questions

1. Looking back (including events described in the (A) case), do you think the Centre should have acted more quickly and more vigorously than it did? If so, what action should it have taken, and when?

2. Did organizational arrangements within the Centre and between the Centre and the markets impede the process of making and implementing sound decisions? If so, what changes do you recommend?

3. Did the reporting system contribute to the problem? If so, what changes do you recommend?

Case 17-4

Xerox (B)

1. This question offers the instructor the opportunity to explore the more direct issue of domestic transfer pricing and discuss the mechanism Xerox uses to resolve conflict. In this situation, transfer pricing adjustments from the factory are not going to solve the problem. Rather, it is the mechanism which reflects the business decision of the company. Two profit centers, customer operations and manufacturing must jointly find a way to satisfy the customer. The business decision has a range of options from not making a response to matching prices. This, in turn, will reflect in the economic performance of the units. Transfer pricing adjustments will reflect the degree of sharing.

    The factory uses a Full Standard Cost transfer price. As a profit center they match expenses with revenue with a minimal profit. Adjustments on their part will result in recording a loss The situation does force factory management to review their cost systems in light of the significant price difference.

    The transfer pricing system is designed to allow the customer operations to make the profit on the product in the market place. They are responsible for responding to economic and competitive pressures and opportunities. If they are unable to be successful they must seek assistance from the corporation.

    The Xerox culture of placing the customer first and cooperative communication allow the proper dialogue to take place. The student should note the emphasis on open discussions and a willingness to share business problems. In the past, the strictly manage-by-the-numbers culture would result in self interest profit center talks where often the transfer pricing is blamed for the problem. Now, with the FEC and the open controller network, managers are able to discuss the problems and come to a shared agreement. The transfer pricing system allow negotiation if factors in the competitive area change The culture makes the transfer pricing system work to support the overall Xerox strategic intent. The student has the opportunity to apply the messages from the A case.

2. This question looks at the multinational transfer pricing system for Xerox and their rules for currency valuation.

    Because the Venray plant added more than 1/3 of the product value, the market-based transfer price to the US was valued in US dollars. Venray management was responsible for managing the transaction currency as well as the translation exposure. Managers referenced the PDR to determine the economic effect on the Venray unit performance.

    a. US dollars

    b. The Venray facility

    c. The local currency is Dutch Guilders and the transaction currency is US dollars. The Venray controller has to manage the exposure with hedging being one of the possible techniques. From the A case we know Venray is part of the Rank Xerox organization.

They report their results in US dollars. Thus, Venray may well not hedge on the transfer to the US but use the dollar accounts receivable as part of the overall currency management system.

d. The effect of currency on the performance measures is the difference between the actual currency rates and the PDR (the plan development rate) for the current budget cycle. The PDR is the reference point for performance measurement. At Xerox the Venray management is responsible for any swing below 3–5%. If greater than this difference, corporate will make adjustments in the performance targets.

e. This is an open question permitting the integration of the corporate and finance department culture with the transfer pricing policy. The culture and openness of the finance group is key to making the transfer pricing policy work. The key concept to convey is that transfer pricing is a mechanism not a goal. The instructor should focus on the process. Most students will find the system quite workable and fair.

— Larry Carr

Venray Plant Reporting Organization

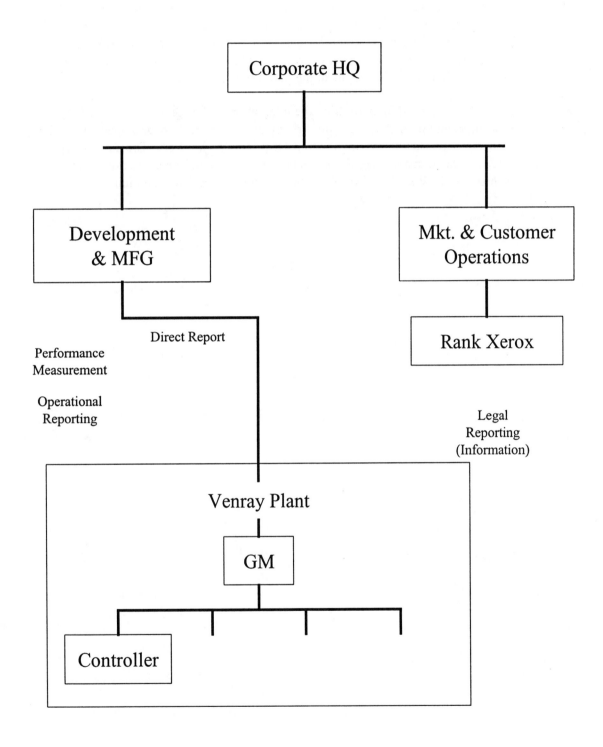

CHAPTER 18
MANAGEMENT CONTROL OF PROJECTS

Changes from the Eighth Edition

This chapter retains the basic structure from the eighth edition.

Cases

Northeast Research Laboratory describes control of an unsuccessful project in a large non-profit research organization.

Modern Aircraft Company asks the student to use the critical path method in planning the development of a small aircraft.

Northeast Research Laboratory

Objectives

This case raises issues about management control in (1) a matrix organization, (2) a project-oriented organization, (3) a professional organization, and (4) a research/development organization. Although NRL is also a nonprofit organization, this fact has no bearing on the analysis; exactly the same analysis would be applicable in a profit-oriented organization. The focus is on a specific project, but the experience with that project can be used to generalize about management control in all the circumstances listed above.

Discussion

There can be no question but that a mistake was made. A project which was important, and which was generating substantial revenue, was suddenly and unexpectedly terminated. The fact that it was in difficulty was not known to management. Our task is to analyze why the unfortunate result occurred and what, if anything, to do so that a similar situation is less likely to happen in the future.

Cause of the Failure

The individuals involved in the case were technically competent, and the technical quality of the work was high. The failure is clearly not due to technical incompetence. It is therefore a failure for which the management control system must take responsibility.

We can identify the following specific weaknesses (which are mostly those implied in Exhibits 3 and 4):

1. The project changed direction at the request of the client. This change was not documented, nor was it called to the attention of management. The change was contrary to the project leader's judgment as to what should be done, and this implied that serious trouble might arise, but possibility of such trouble was not called to management's attention. (In fact, the weekly status report of the project, Exhibit 2, contains no hint of difficulty.)

2. There was a lack of coordination among the organization units involved, particularly Physical Sciences and Electronics.

---

3. There was inadequate management involvement in the project. Higher management did not know what was going on and did not take steps to find out what was going on.

Suggested Corrective Action

As pointed out in the text, there are three aspects of project control: (1) time, (2) cost, and (3) quality of the work done. They are interrelated, and the system must see that all three aspects are controlled simultaneously.

Different types of control are appropriate for different types of projects. In this organization, several hundred projects are being worked on at one time. Many of these projects, probably the large majority, are proceeding smoothly, and there is no need for much management involvement in them. There should be some way of separating out the small fraction of "problem projects" that require close watch, and paying special attention to these projects.

With respect to the cost and time dimensions, it is relatively easy to identify problem projects by comparing actual costs with budgeted costs (as is well done on Exhibit 2) and comparing actual progress with budgeted milestones. NRL does not seem to have a formal system for measuring actual progress against predetermined milestones. It would perhaps be desirable to make a plan at the inception of the project, and compare progress against this plan. This plan would presumably show manpower requirements of the various organization units involved, and therefore would help to improve workload planning in these units and also improve coordination and communication between the project leader and the functional units. (It is possible that such a mechanism existed although not mentioned in the case.)

These devices, however, say nothing about the quality of the work. There is no objective way of measuring quality and therefore no way of comparing actual against planned, as was the case with cost and time. Nevertheless, significant information must be communicated to higher management in some way. The following elements seem relevant:

1. Above all else, the atmosphere in the laboratory must be such that project leaders are encouraged to report incipient problems to their superiors. If there is a negative response to such reports, project leaders will be motivated to cover up problems, hoping that they will go away with the passage of time. It does not matter whether these reports are oral or written. Any good project leader can write a progress report that hides problems for a long time.

2. There should be a way of separating high-risk projects from the others at the inception of the project, and of revising the list of high-risk or problem projects as events require. There should be no stigma attached to the project leader of a high-risk project. For high-risk projects, there should be more frequent and more detailed reports on work done than for other projects. (There should be a brief report on all projects.) The reports themselves are less important than meetings with higher management on high-risk projects, at which problems are discussed frankly and then resolved. At management meetings, little time should be devoted to reports on low-risk projects, although all projects should be reviewed occasionally so that possible additions to the problem list will be identified. As a guess, not more than 10 percent of the projects, measured by magnitude, should be classified as high risk, perhaps less than 10 percent.

3. Despite the professional person's abhorrence of paperwork, there should be full documentation of important events that occur during the project. This will provide a record that will show more clearly what went wrong. The existence of such a record, if known to Denby, might have caused him to act differently than he did, and most likely would have changed the nature of his critical letter. It would also have been of great use in discussions with Mr. Kenny, who is presumably alienated from NRL and unlikely to give it future business.

4. It is possible that the control system for responsibility centers (as distinguished from projects) is also inadequate, but we have little information on this. Responsibility centers need a basis for planning how their personnel are to be used, and of course they need a mechanism for controlling their costs.

In a research/development organization, the control of costs is not as crucial as the control of quality. There is no need, however, to assess the relative importance. The system can control all three aspects--cost, time, and quality. Even the best system will not uncover all problems in a research/development organization because of the nature of the work. The appraisal of quality is very much a matter of professional judgment, which is the reason why face-to-face meetings are more important than written reports.

RNA

Case 18-2

Modern Aircraft Company

1. CPM Network

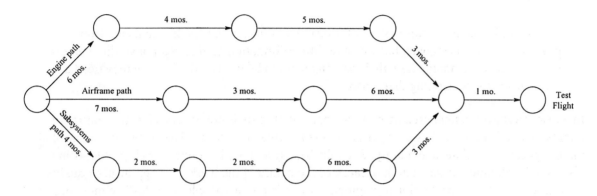

2. Time in months for the fully assembled prototype:

Paths		Slack Time
Engine	6 + 4 + 5 + 3 = 18 months	0 mos
Airframe	7 + 3 + 6 = 16 months	2 mos
subsystems	4 + 2 + 2 + 6 + 3 = 17 months	1 mo

   Therefore, it will be *18 months* until the F-69 is fully assembled, i.e., engine, airframe, and subsystems.

3. Time in months for the first test flight:
   18 months plus 1 month for the series of powered checks, taxi tests, etc. Therefore, it will be *19 months* from the start of this project until the first test flight.

4. What is the critical path?
   The engine path (18 mos) is the critical path, by definition, since there is 0 slack in that path.

5. A one-month delay in obtaining bomb bay rods will not affect the final assembly date because that activity is in the *Airframe Path* where there is 2 months slack time. Therefore the use of overtime should *not* be authorized.

6. A two-week delay for the engine alignment jig will cause the project to slip two weeks because that activity is on the *Engine Path,* the critical path with *0* slack. Therefore the use of overtime is justified and should be authorized.

7. A two-month delay in delivery of the UHF radio will cause the project to slip 1 month because that activity is on the *Subsystems Path* which only has 1 month of slack time. Therefore the use of overtime should be authorized.

— Prof. John E. Setnicky

Harvard Business School Publishing

Customer Service Dept., 230-5, 60 Harvard Way, Boston, MA 02163-1001

Customer #:_____

Internet Inquiries: Custserv @ cchbspub.Harvard.edu

Ordered By (fill in the blanks or attach your business card or label here)

( )   ( )
Tel. #   Fax #

Ordered for   Email address

Institution

Dept./Title

Street

City   State/Prov.   Zip/Postal Code

Country

To purchase teaching notes include the telephone number of the Personnel Department so we may verify the teaching status of the "ordered for" customer.

Billing Address (if different from "ordered by")

Name

Institution

Dept./Title

Street

City   State/Prov.   Zip/Postal Code

Country

This is my: ☐ Home Address   ☐ Organization Address

Shipping Address   ☐ same as "billing address"   ☐ same as "ordered by"

Name

Institution

Dept./Title

Street

City   State/Prov.   Zip/Postal Code

Country

PAYMENT METHOD

☐ Check Enclosed. (Payable to Harvard Business School Publishing in U.S. funds drawn on a U.S. bank.)
☐ AmEx   ☐ VISA   ☐ MasterCard/Eurocard

_____
Signature

Cardholder Name (if different from "ordered by") please print clearly

Card #

| | | | | | | | | | | | | | | | | | |

Exp. Date____ /____

☐ Authorized purchase order enclosed.   P.O.#_____
No int'l. purchase orders accepted.   Terms: Net 30 Days from invoice date.

Item No.	Qty.	Title	x Price ea.	Total Price

Special Instructions (please print clearly):

Subtotal

Minimum order $10.00
Canadian customers add 7% GST #12473845
Massachusetts customers add 5% for videos

7% GST

5% Video Tax

Shipping & Handling (See chart below.)
• No shipping & handling charges for videos shipped within the U.S.
• Videos shipped internationally - $50.00
• Catalogs shipped within the U.S. - FREE

Shipping & Handling

• Prices subject to change without notice.

TOTAL

ORDER TOLL FREE
1-800-545-7685
or (617) 495-6117 ext. 423A
FAX: (617) 495-6985

SHIPPING & HANDLING   1. Choose product type and quantity.   2. Circle shipping method selected.   3. Add totals. Write total in box.

CASES/REPRINTS	Standard Delivery U.S., 48 States	2-Day Delivery U.S., 48 States	2-Day Delivery AK, HI, PR	Delivery to Canada	International Delivery
1 to 15	4.00	6.00	10.00	14.00	18.00
16 to 49	5.00	10.00	14.00	16.00	28.00
50 to 99	6.00	15.00	22.00	20.00	35.00
100 to 199	10.00	30.00	40.00	30.00	55.00
BOOKS					
First Book	4.00	8.00	12.00	14.00	20.00
Each Additional	1.00	2.00	3.00	2.00	5.00

Catalogs and videos shipped internationally-use book rates. International customers are responsible for all taxes and duties.
Overnight or bulk orders-please call for information.

423A